MATTHEW,
A Commentary,
Volume 1

BY THE AUTHOR

A Theology of the Holy Spirit
The Holy Spirit: Shy Member of the Trinity (co-author)
The Christbook

MATTHEW

A Commentary By Frederick Dale Bruner

VOLUME 1 THE CHRISTBOOK MATTHEW 1-12

WORD PUBLISHING
Dallas·London·Vancouver·Melbourne

For
Katherine Booth Bruner
Mr. and Mrs. Fred S. Bruner
Dee and Hal Eads

MATTHEW A COMMENTARY
VOLUME 1

Library of Congress Cataloging-in-Publication Data

Bruner, Frederick Dale.
    The Christbook: a historical/theological
commentary.

    Bibliography: p.
    1. Bible. N.T. Matthew—Commentaries.
2. Jesus Christ—Person and offices—Biblical
teaching.   3. Reformed Church—Doctrines.   I. Title.
BS2575.3.B79 1987   226'.2077   87-6270
ISBN 0-8499-0526-5

Printed in the United States of America
12349 RRD 9 8 7 6 5 4 3 2

Contents

Preface
The Why, How, and Who of the Commentary

I. WHY? MISSION

This commentary was born in the world of mission. My wife and I had been called through the United Presbyterian Church (USA) by the United Church of Christ in the Philippines to teach at Union Theological Seminary, Philippines. My assignment was to teach Christian doctrine. Our students were mainly Filipinos, most of them from rural homes and schools. The seminary also had a modest complement of students from other Asian countries—India, Indonesia, Thailand, Malaysia, and Korea. How does a Westerner teach theology to Third World students?

Badly, to begin with, in my case. I remember trying at one point to teach Romans, chapters 1 to 5, thinking the universality of Paul's Fifth Gospel with its profound doctrines of anthropology and sin (Rom 1–3) and of Christ and salvation (Rom 3–5) might lift the class above my Western parochialism and give these classic doctrines an authority I wasn't delivering. (Moreover, Paul was at least part Asian, teaching Western Christians at Rome—a nice serendipity.) But Paul's theology, probably the deepest of all theologies, is pervasively propositional, somewhat abstract, and venerably old. And, finally, in any case, the teaching of the contents of biblical books belonged to another department in the seminary.

Later I tried Karl Barth's engaging *Dogmatics in Outline.* This theology was at least closer to our time (1946/47), and it taught my subject, Christian doctrine. But though I think Barth is our finest twentieth-century theologian, his theology is even more abstract and rarefied than Paul's, and it is very Western. The class was still not alive.

I got Luther's *Large Catechism,* the finest one-volume Christian doctrine I have ever read. Happily, Luther's earthy, colorful, and unabstract language spoke more immediately to the students than had even twentieth-century Barth. Luther's Roman Catholic provenance helped and it didn't help: it helped in its closeness to our students' experience in the largely Roman Catholic Philippines; but it also hindered in that, though Luther is richly catholic and wholesomely sacramental, his anti-Roman animus could make some students unecumenical, and the thrillingly ecumenical era was just then dawning in the Roman Catholic Church (the Second Vatican Council ended the year my teaching began, 1965). And there were twentieth-century Asian issues to which responsible Christian doctrine should address itself. A sixteenth-century European theology, even the profoundest, was still not the answer.

After several years of struggling to find the right text for teaching Christian doctrine in Asia, something good happened in the Sunday School class at our barrio church, *Ang Simbahan sa Nayon,* where some of the seminary students attended. I was teaching the parables of Matthew 13 where Jesus explains the meaning of the kingdom of God. The same students whose eyes glazed over when I taught the doctrine of God in the seminary's Christian doctrine class seemed alive with interest when they heard Jesus teach the kingdom of God in parables. This made me think.

Could I teach the church's great doctrines of God through the medium of Matthew 13's picture-stories of the kingdom of God? I would begin with an attempt at a faithful exegesis of the biblical text; I would continue by directing Jesus' teaching to the church's great creedal and dogmatic statements in the past; and I would end by addressing the church's major doctrinal and social questions and positions in the present. Perhaps the biblical *content* would give my doctrinal material a wonted authority with my students, and perhaps the biblical *form* (parables, Jesus' penetratingly earthy and unearthly élan) would give the doctrines a needed access to our part of the world in our time.

The project started.

II. HOW? THEOLOGICAL EXEGESIS

I began to teach the Gospel of Matthew doctrinally. Providentially, Matthew turned out to be the most systematic and didactic of all the Gospels. With a little imagination, for example, it is possible to see catechetical Matthew emphasizing particular doctrines in his Gospel chapter by chapter, as I will try to show now in rough outline. (I will underline the sermons that characteristically punctuate and doctrinalize Matthew's Gospel.)

A. An Outline

Matthew chapter 1 teaches God—present in concrete particular in Jesus Emmanuel ("God with us"). Matthew 2 teaches "Man"—present in the two classic responses to God's visit: the responses of the magi (human nature under the power of grace) and of Herod (human nature under the power of sin). Matthew 3 teaches repentance in baptism, the saving meeting place of God and human beings. Matthew 4 teaches ministry as Jesus learns how (and so teaches his church to learn how) to resist temptation and to enter public service. These first four chapters, then, the Christmas Stories, teach the church the doctrine of the *coming* of Christ.

Matthew chapters 5–7, the Sermon on the Mount, teach discipleship to the *Word* of Christ through mercy, faith, and justice. Matthew 8 and 9, the Ten Miracles, teach salvation through the *work* of Christ—that is, salvation by grace and into freedom. Matthew 10, the Sermon on Mission, teaches evangelism in the *mission* of Christ. Matthew 11 and 12, the Six Portraits, teach the *person* of Christ: he is both Savior and Judge. So in the first twelve chapters of the Gospel we have a little christology in which we learn the introductory facts about the coming, Word, work, mission, and person of Jesus.

In Matthew chapters 13–28 Jesus turns his attention in a visible way to the formation of a church. Everything becomes more corporate. The word "church" appears in no other Gospel, but Matthew's Jesus now speaks emphatically of building "my church" (16:18), and twice he talks of a disciplinary church (18:17a, 17b). Where in Matthew 1–12 Jesus had addressed disciples and Israel, in chapters 13–28

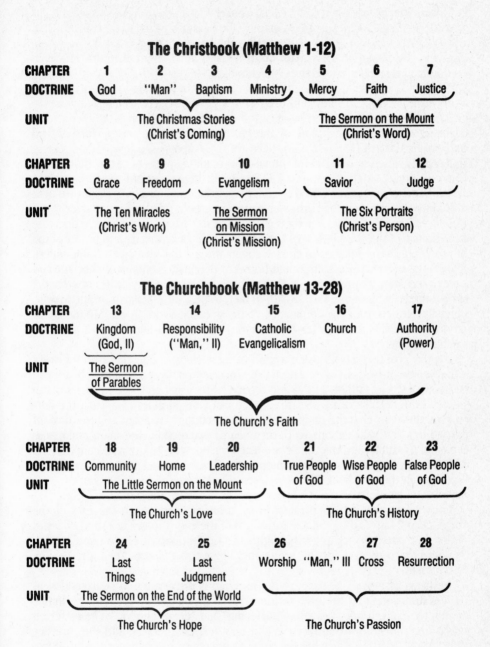

The Christbook (Matthew 1-12)

CHAPTER	1	2	3	4	5	6	7
DOCTRINE	God	"Man"	Baptism	Ministry	Mercy	Faith	Justice
UNIT		The Christmas Stories (Christ's Coming)			The Sermon on the Mount (Christ's Word)		

CHAPTER	8	9	10	11	12
DOCTRINE	Grace	Freedom	Evangelism	Savior	Judge
UNIT	The Ten Miracles (Christ's Work)		The Sermon on Mission (Christ's Mission)	The Six Portraits (Christ's Person)	

The Churchbook (Matthew 13-28)

CHAPTER	13	14	15	16	17
DOCTRINE	Kingdom (God, II)	Responsibility ("Man," II)	Catholic Evangelicalism	Church	Authority (Power)
UNIT	The Sermon of Parables				

The Church's Faith

CHAPTER	18	19	20	21	22	23
DOCTRINE	Community	Home	Leadership	True People of God	Wise People of God	False People of God
UNIT	The Little Sermon on the Mount					

The Church's Love   The Church's History

CHAPTER	24	25	26	27	28
DOCTRINE	Last Things	Last Judgment	Worship	"Man," III Cross	Resurrection
UNIT	The Sermon on the End of the World				

The Church's Hope   The Church's Passion

An Outline of Matthew's Gospel

he addresses Israel also, but now in clear concentration he addresses especially his disciples. In Matt 1–12 Jesus taught mainly who he is and began to form his church; in Matt 13–28 Jesus teaches mainly what his church is while never ceasing to reveal who he is. By virtue of their main audience and aims, then, chapters 13–28 in Matthew can rightly be called the Churchbook.

The church, according to Matt 13, is the place where Jesus sows the Word of God in the world of God, forming and preparing a people for the coming kingdom of God. Matthew 13, then, is a reprise of the doctrine of God (cf. Matt 1), but now especially we learn the doctrine of the Word of God in the seven Word-of-God parables. In Matt 14 (13:53–14:36) there are five responses to Jesus' Word, teaching a second time the doctrine of human nature and its ways of responding to the visits of God (cf. Matt 2). Matt 15 (15:1–16:12 in my outline) teaches, as in a summary, the catholic-evangelical church principles, respectively, of Scripture over tradition (*sola scriptura*), of faith over experience (*sola fides*), of grace over merit (*sola gratia*), and of Christ over signs (*solus Christus*). Matt 16 teaches the doctrine of the nature of the church, Matt 17 the doctrine of the authority and power of the church, Matt 18 the doctrine of church community (in the Sermon on Community), Matt 19 the doctrine of the church at home, or domestic economics (marriage and money), and Matt 20 the doctrine of church leadership and service. (I consider the highly ethical chapters of Matt 18–20, in fact, to be a little Sermon on the Mount, filling in the details of the commands of the great Sermon on the Mount. More comprehensively, Matt chaps 13–17 teach the church's faith, and chaps 18–20 teach the church's love.)

Matthew chapters 21–23 teach a kind of Israelology, a doctrine of the history of the people of God. In Matt 21, first by focusing on a representative history of the people's Christ (20:29–21:27) and second by focusing on three histories of the people's faith (21:28–22:14, the three people-of-God parables), we learn the doctrine of the true church. In Matt 22, by presenting "The Four Questions" of the people's critical relations to government, resurrection, the main commandment(s) in the Bible, and the Christ, we learn the doctrine of the wise church. And in Matt 23, in Jesus' excoriating Sermon of the Seven Woes—against false religious leadership in the people of God—we learn the doctrine of the false church. Matt chaps 21–23, then, teach church history, or the history of the people of God.

Matthew chapters 24–25 present Jesus' dramatic Sermon on the End of the World: chap 24 gives the signs (or anti-signs) of the end (the *eschaton*) and of Jesus' coming (the *parousia*); chap 25 highlights the final judgment of God and teaches disciples how to prepare for this judgment. These two chapters, then, present the church's hope.

The heart of every Christian gospel message is the death and resurrection of Jesus. Matt chapters 26–28 teach the doctrine of the church's passion in the double sense of the English word *passion*—"suffering" and "deep concern." The suffering and triumph of Jesus are in fact the church's deepest concern, and they are her major gospel. Matt 26 A teaches the church's doctrine of worship (centered appropriately in the Lord's Supper); Matt 26 B and 27 A, the trial stories, teach for a third time in a sustained way the church's doctrine of human nature (total undependability); Matt 27 B, the cross, teaches the doctrine of the atonement (total dependability); and Matt 28 teaches the doctrines of the resurrection and of the church's world mission.

That is how I have outlined and taught Matthew's Gospel. The outline gives a much oversimplified picture, but it helps the memory, and that is no little service. It is, in fact, one of Matthew's catechetical aims to teach Jesus in a more systematic and ordered way than Mark's Gospel had done.

B. Characterizations

"Matthew," the traditional name given both to our author and his document, wrote his Gospel, most New Testament scholars believe, in the eighties of the first century of the Christian era in Antioch, using Mark's Gospel, a Sayings Source (called Q), and his own considerable systematic resources to teach Jesus in a fresh, new way—in a *doctrinal* (or, ethically doctrinal) way.

Matthew's distinctive flavor and style can be characterized by some comparisons with the other three Gospels (comparisons that are deliberately and provocatively overstated in order to bring out each Gospel's salient or promontory). Matthew took Mark's rough technicolor stories and "catechized" them in Matthew's distinctively black and white, rounded, christologically focused, doctrinally stylized, and easily memorized narratives and discourses. Matthew is Revised Standard Version Mark and the church's Iron Catechism. Mark is the Gospel for evangelists, Matthew for teachers, Luke for deacons or social workers, and John for elders or spiritual leaders.

Mark sees Jesus from beneath, historically, in all his rich humanity, transparent to the mystery of deity. Matthew sees Jesus in profile, doctrinally, highlighting Jesus' head (as Rembrandt does with Paul) so that we especially see Jesus' powerful thinking and teaching. Luke is a study of Jesus' hands and, behind the hands, a study of the heart that moved the hands into a ministry to all kinds of people but especially to outsiders, the marginal, and the disdained (the poor, Samaritans, women, bourgeois collaborator-tax-collectors, the physically, mentally, and spiritually ill, and the like). John is a portrait of Jesus from above, from the eagle's eye, revealing Jesus to us in all his majestic preexistent deity, visible now palpably in human flesh. In ancient church tradition, with a true perception, Mark is pictured as a man, Matthew as a lion, Luke as an ox, and John as an eagle (e.g., Aug., *Tract. in Jn.*, 36:5:210). Still another way to see the Gospels comparatively is to say that in theological form Mark is Luther, Matthew is Calvin or Thomas, Luke is Wesley or Xavier or Chrysostom, and John is Augustine or Barth.

C. Method

I wrestled first with the texts themselves in Matthew in order to find their real meanings. I confess that my regular Sunday School teaching has predisposed me to find what the texts *say* and not just what they *said*. To be sure, we can only dependably know what texts say when we learn what they said, and a too eager attempt to "say" before having been "said to" can fill pastors' and teachers' libraries with books more comparable to cotton candy than to theological meat, with what Karl Barth disdainfully called "paperback theology."

Historical-*critical* commentary at its best does the indispensable spadework of uncovering ancient philological and cultural parallels and meanings. All other commentary worthy of the name builds on the discoveries made in historical-critical studies. But historical-*theological* commentary has another concern. Commentaries on texts believed to be the Word of *God* and not just the words of Matthew and Mark (though the texts are also the words of Matthew and Mark) cannot be satisfied with knowing what texts *meant then* unless they translate these ancient meanings into modern language and dare to say what they believe the texts *mean now*. For the genius of Holy Scripture is its perennial ability to keep saying the most important things of all, Scripture's seminal gift of being, by the power of the Word of God that came then, the Word of God that comes now. "Word of God" (*theou logos*) commentary is *theological* commentary.

Historical-theological commentary builds upon the work of historical-critical commentary but tries, in consultation with the faithful fathers and mothers, brothers and sisters of the whole catholic church, to say today the *theou logos* that crackled inside the human words of Matthew and Mark yesterday.

A church that is not nourished yesterday, today, and tomorrow by the wholesome food of the Word of God in Scripture—a church not ruled and dominated by exegesis—is a church on her way to death. For too long the mainline churches in Christendom have illustrated this death march by teaching and preaching a Bible that has been only marginally appropriated (witness the death of the biblical language requirement in many seminaries and denominations) because, it is said, there are in fact so many other imperative issues. (What is Hebrew in a hungry world?) We have become churches without doctrinal passion (for doctrinal passion would be "fundamentalism," the kiss of death) and a result has been people leaving our churches in droves and flocking to what are called independent or Bible churches where, at least, they are given doctrines served with fire. A return by the mainline churches to a responsible christocentric biblical passion will be a return to apostolic-catholic-Reformation Christianity with all of this Christianity's perennial sources of spiritual and social renewal.

The great peril of theological commentary, let me say right here at the beginning, is the peril of allegorical exegesis, treating Scripture like a wax nose, making it say whatever the theological commentator already believes it should say, and so "using" Scripture rather than being used *by* Scripture to say only what it says. I am aware of this peril, and I am not sure that I have always escaped the sin of the manipulation of texts to teach my own convictions, the sin, that is, of not allowing Scripture everywhere to correct and re-form my own and my interpreters' dearly held doctrinal convictions. The *historical*-theological study of the texts (by a constant reference to the church's long commentary and creedal traditions) can protect one from private interpretation and from privatizing, parochial readings. I have aimed everywhere to be a catholic interpreter of texts by calling in the major interpreters in the history of the church to help me find the meanings of every verse in the Gospel. But I am sure at points, perhaps at many points, even after I have cited a whole family of witnesses, pro and con, that I have still been eccentric and aberrant in my conclusions. I look forward now to the critique of the church.

In this century the major instance of theological commentary is Karl Barth's powerful, prophetic, and idiosyncratic *The Epistle to the Romans* (1919; 1922; and often). Barth's several Prefaces to successive editions of his commentary make an attractive case for theological exegesis. The opening two sentences of "The Preface to the First Edition" (1918) make the case all at once: "Paul, as a child of his age, addressed his contemporaries. It is, however, far more important that, as Prophet and Apostle of the Kingdom of God, he veritably speaks to all men of every age" (p. 1). In "The Preface to the Second Edition" (1921) Barth took on the critics of his first edition: "I have been accused of being an 'enemy of historical criticism.'" After defending himself against this accusation Barth admits, nevertheless, a certain resentment:

"My complaint is that recent commentators confine themselves to an interpretation of the text which seems to me to be no commentary at all, but merely the first step towards a commentary. . . . Now, [real commentary] involves more than a mere repetition in Greek or in German of what Paul says; it involves the reconsideration of what is set out in the Epistle, until the actual meaning of it is disclosed. . . . By genuine understanding and interpretation I mean that creative energy which Luther exercised with intuitive certainty in his exegesis; which underlies the systematic interpretation of Calvin; and which is at least attempted by such modern writers as Hofmann, J. T. Beck, Godet, and Schlatter. For example, place the work of [the historical-critical] Jülicher side by side with that of Calvin: how energetically Calvin, having first established what stands in the text, sets himself to re-think the whole material and to wrestle with it, till the walls which separate the sixteenth century from the first become transparent! Paul speaks, and the man of the sixteenth century hears" (pp. 6–7).

The major problem with Barth's theological commentary, in my opinion, is that one can come away from it more impressed with Barth's prophetic interpretations than with Paul's apostolic words. Nevertheless, one cannot escape the conviction that the God of Karl Barth is the God of the Bible. Barth's theological passions were so strong that he really belonged in dogmatic theology where, after his *Romans*, he instinctively moved, to the service of the whole church.

In my experience, the most compelling treatment of the special problems and possibilities of theological exegesis is Hans Windisch's essay "The Meaning of Theological Exegesis" in his book *The Meaning of the Sermon on the Mount: A Contribution to the Historical Understanding of the Gospels and to the Problem of Their True Exegesis* (tr. S. MacLean Gilmour. Philadelphia: The Westminster Press, 1951 [from the revised German edition of 1937], pp. 154–67). I will summarize the main arguments of the essay and then comment.

Windisch distinguishes between the two legitimate but necessarily separate disciplines of historical and theological exegesis. The concern of historical exegesis is "the message in its original setting, while theological exegesis has to do with the message itself" (pp. 154–55). But since theological exegesis's "message itself" is always embedded in a historical text, and since only an unprejudiced historical science can decipher this text, it is not just desirable, it is essential that theological exegesis work very closely with historical exegesis. Historians, for their part, must not let any theology or point of view affect their research; they must restrict themselves "to the source in its historical setting . . . [and] view it only as a historical datum and be governed by a rigid respect for it" (p. 155), otherwise we will never be able to trust the historians' discoveries. If they overlay their discoveries with interpretation and do not distinguish discovery from interpretation, the original text is lost in the subjectivity of the interpreter. Thus historical exegesis does us the greatest service when it is *not* theological.

The situation with theological interpretation is quite different and requires different restrictions and commitments. "Theological exegesis accepts the NT and every part of it as a testimony and a gift of the Church. It looks for the authoritative Word of God in this literature . . . [and] finally, it closes the gap between past and present and endeavors to interpret the NT, its statements, admonitions, warnings, threats, and promises, as directed to us in our own situation" (p. 157). But God's Word for the present situation does not come magically (*deus ex machina*) to the theologian, it comes (as a fruit of faith and prayer, one may add) from the theologian's closest collaboration with the faithful, scientific, and rigorously objective historian. The historian uncovers and translates the text in all the glory of its original meaning. The theologian re-covers the text in the contemporary idiom and thus re-translates the ancient text into modern life, trusting that this recovery and retranslation will assist the church today to hear the *same* Word of God spoken yesterday. "Thus it is that theological exegesis, though it goes beyond historical exegesis, nevertheless presupposes it and builds upon it" (p. 157).

But both disciplines must remain, for the sake of their integrity, antiseptically separate and distinct. For though they work with the same subject matter—Scripture—historical exegesis works with Scripture according to the norms of the sciences of religion and history, while theological exegesis works with Scripture according to the norms of the sciences of theology and dogmatics. The science of religion and historical interpretation approach the text phenomenologically; theological interpretation, on the other hand, "takes a definite creed or system of faith as its point of departure . . . [and] proceeds from the assumption that the Bible is not an ordinary product of the history of religion and not an ordinary religious message, but a book that God has inspired and a message he has given" (pp. 157–58).

Theological exegesis will always begin with the original meaning of the biblical text (and so will in the beginning always be in the company of historical exegesis), "but it will not stop there." Theological exegesis will try to grasp the text's meaning "in all its depth, to free it as a whole from its antiquated accouterments, and to fashion out of it a witness of God and of his revelation that will be intelligible to the man of our own time who is in search of God." Thus theological interpretation is by definition theological and dogmatic, but it is modern, too, "in the sense that its chief concern is to make the Biblical passage transparently clear to the present generation and to the particular faith that it professes" (p. 160).

Thus after the rediscovery of the ancient text's meaning, theological interpreters have the special responsibility, not just the luxury, of relating the text to the present situation. That is their calling. They must employ the text "to criticize the contemporary social and ecclesiastical scene. In a word, the historian criticizes the Bible, while the theologian with the help of the Bible criticizes himself [and, may I add, "his church"], and his times" (p. 165). Historians must *abstract* themselves as much as possible from the present in order to be fair to the past; theologians must *penetrate* the present as often as possible in order to be fair to the past in a different way, namely, by retranslating the past's essential message into the present. When this past is the Word of God, theologians feel pressure to translate with peculiar urgency, because *this* past is never merely past.

Windisch's argument suggests that to dare to translate venerable ancient texts as Word of God into the present requires not only a certain *chutzpah*, or charisma, but also a definite *subjective* approach to texts. (Objectivity is the required charisma of historical exegesis, subjectivity of theological exegesis.) And this necessarily subjective element "represents both the strength and the weakness of all theological exegesis" (p. 166). The strength of subjectivity is its sympathetic affinity with past and present; its weakness is its unavoidable selectivity and its dangerous tendency to read what it wants to read out of the texts. Congenitally, theological exegesis will always "be inclined to make the passage conform to a particular point of view that has been determined by doctrinal, philosophical, critical, and personal factors. In all this there is the danger of twisting the meaning of the passage, misinterpreting it, or actually doing violence to it" (p. 155).

Thus two attitudes converge in theological exegesis: *struggle*, the struggle rightly, fairly, accurately to interpret texts, and *modesty*, the modesty to admit predilections, biases, subjectivities, and as often as possible to be willing therefore to let texts, historians, and other theologies and interpretations challenge the interpreter and the interpreter's theology. "All theological exegesis," Windisch concludes, "is a struggle for the true understanding of Biblical passages. In fact, struggle is its very lifeblood. . . . [And] true exegesis, . . . despite all the determination with which it will seek to make its particular attitude prevail [since theological exegesis is necessarily polemical and corrective], will always be characterized by a certain modesty" (pp. 166–67). Windisch believes that *historical* exegesis, by and large, has been more modest and circumspect in acknowledging its limits than has a *theological* exegesis that, precisely because theological exegesis must be dogmatic, sometimes forgets its humanity and so its fallibility.

I find Windisch's program of theological exegesis exhilarating and ennobling. For some reason, theological exegesis has not flourished in our century. Can it be done? Should it? Is the compartmentalization of academic disciplines partly responsible for the infrequent attempt by doctrinal theologians to do biblical exegesis? Whatever the reason or reasons, the frequent complaint that commentaries are boring, or that they are useful only for other academicians, may be a criticism more of theologians for their sin of omission in not writing commentary at all than it is of historical-critics for their sin of commission in writing technical commentary. After all, historical-critical commentaries are supposed to be scientific, not entertaining.

We who teach and love Christian doctrine and who want to go deeper into both doctrine and Scripture are provided a banquet of resources by professional biblical studies. It is the responsibility of some of us who teach Christian doctrine to use these biblical resources to do theological exegesis. One reason for contemporary doctrinal poverty in the church is Christian doctrine's general loss of contact with the fructifying biblical fonts. Throughout her history the church's main doctrinal teachers have also been exegetes (Augustine, Thomas, Luther, Calvin). College and university religion teachers, with their wider range of courses, outside strict disciplinary constraints, have an opportunity to do theological exegesis. I seek to take that opportunity in this commentary.

III. WHO? PERSONAL DEBTS

Readers of a theological commentary deserve, then, to know their author's theology, presuppositions, and sources. I come at the texts with a doctrine that is consciously, gratefully, and in some respects penitently evangelical, and that is confessionally a Reformation theology. I was raised, nurtured, and confirmed in my late mother's St. Francis Episcopal Church in Los Angeles, California. (*The Book of Common Prayer* remains a most treasured resource.) I experienced Jesus Christ evangelically in my Occidental College freshman year at the Forest Home Christian Conference Center in connection with college friends from the First Presbyterian Church of Hollywood, California. In this living Hollywood congregation, in the heart of American paganism, I learned the gospel afresh. I met there and was deeply influenced by Dr. Henrietta C. Mears, the finest Bible teacher I have ever heard. (Dr. Mears's background, theology, and associations were mainly Baptist, though she insisted on sending her "boys" to the Presbyterian Seminary in Princeton.) Dr. Mears's College Department, which she herself taught for thirty-five years, showed me and thousands of other college students the excitement of being Christian. (The Department's motto was "To Know Christ and to Make Him Known.")

I received my major evangelical impressions and convictions there, particularly the elixir of Christ-centeredness, the power and authority of the Bible, the uniqueness of warmhearted evangelical fellowship, and the imperative of Christian mission.

Princeton Theological Seminary gave me the biblical languages, for which I will always be deeply grateful, and it introduced me to the rich Reformed heritage. (Dr. Edward Dowey, in his first year at Princeton Seminary, my last, opened up to me Calvin's prodigious *Institutes.*) The University of Hamburg, Germany, gave me the historical-theological languages, love of research, and the Reformation of Martin Luther. Union Theological Seminary, Philippines, gave me the Third World, social-justice Methodism, the Vatican II Roman Catholic Church (particularly at the Divine Word Seminary and at Ateneo de Manila), and the challenge of teaching in a revolutionary setting; it was in immediate contact with these Philippine realities that the commentary was conceived and much of this first volume written. Finally, Whitworth College brought me the Adult Class of Spokane's First Presbyterian Church every Sunday, freed me from most other extracurricular assignments, and gave me the precious gift of teaching and the time to do it, making possible the completion of "Theological Matthew," my working title for the whole project.

These are my doctrinal debts, and I acknowledge them gladly. They form my theological optic. The lens in the theological glasses with which I read Holy Scripture were ground, then, in Canterbury, Hollywood, Princeton, Hamburg, Manila, and Spokane, by Episcopalians, Baptists, Presbyterians, Lutherans, Methodists, Catholics, and no doubt by plenty of pagans too (with my own paganism in the fore). The catholic and Reformation creeds of the church and the evangelical teachings (in roughly this order) of Henrietta Mears, John Calvin, Martin Luther, Adolf Schlatter, and then increasingly what I can only call the church's commentary tradition (in my opinion the most dependable apostolic succession of all)—these have shaped my historical-theological interpretation of Matthew's Gospel.

I want also to thank in print the following persons: Floyd Thatcher of Word Books for his confidence in me and in this commentary and for his seeking me out; Carey Moore, academic editor of Word Books and my personal editor, for Christian, gentle, and yet firm direction and counsel at every stage in the final drafts of the manuscript; to five academic deans at Whitworth College for graciously allowing a teacher time to write: Drs. David Winter, Duncan Ferguson, Shirley Richner, Richard Ferrin, and Darrell Guder; to Whitworth College colleagues for those unselfish attentions to college life that make a community distinctively Christian (such as an active commitment to spending time with students), for committee fidelities, and for patience with reclusive teachers who seem only to want to read and write; to my colleagues in the Religion and Philosophy Department of the college who have thoughtfully criticized chapters in this book over the course of several colloquia and who have become valued friends: Drs. Forrest Baird, Howard Redmond, and in particular our chairman and New Testament specialist, Dr. Roger Mohrlang, who has given me both withering critique and the best regular theological conversations I have ever had; to our sons, Frederick Carlton Booth Bruner (University of Chicago, history) and Michael Mears Bruner (University of Washington, literature) for close friendship and many long Sunday afternoon conversations; to Dr. and Mrs. F. Carlton Booth, my wife's parents, for their camaraderie with our family at every stage of our life; to the Adult Sunday School Class at First Presbyterian Church, Spokane, for a spiritual home; and to our own dear pastor for special friendship, the Rev. Dr. Richard Leon, Carolyn, their children, and their congregations in Hamburg, New York, the Union Church of Manila, and the First Presbyterian Churches of Spokane and (just now) of Bellevue, Washington.

In the Philippines (1964–1975) several churches and institutions let me try my newborn Matthew on them, and I want to thank them for their patience and grace: our home church where it all started, *Ang Simbahan sa Nayon*, the pastors Hermenio Clemente and Sol Toquero, the people, the council, the Sammy Guerreros and Juan Flaviers, and the Pala Pala Basketball Boys; our congregation for fifty-two challenging Sundays of Tagalog Matthew and Christian koinonia, the Calamba (Laguna) United Church of Christ, the Emilio Capulongs, the Chipecos, Romaldezes, and the Valuenzuelas; our neighbor and ecumenical friend, the Roman Catholic Divine Word Seminary (S.V.D.), and the privilege of a semester teaching Matthew's Gospel there, the class, Miguel Cinches, Edicio dela Torre, and Kim Suela; the Philippine Protestant mother congregation and so, appropriately, the place of our sons' baptisms, the Ellinwood-Malate Church, and its bishop and pastors, Estanislao Abainza, Dario Alampay, and Cirilo Rigos; the especially fraternal Loyola House of Studies (S.J.) at Ateneo de Manila, Catalino Arévalo, and Pedro de Achútegui; our friendly conservative-evangelical neighbor, the Philippine Missionary Institute, the Arsenio Dominguezes, David Felicianos, and Ben Dayrits; the different and dramatic world of the Subic Bay Naval Chapel and its chaplain Alex Aronis and his family; the exciting Summer Institute of Linguistics (Wycliffe Bible Translators) Nasuli Biennial Conference and the Dan Weavers; the international Union Church of Manila and the Earl Palmers, Dick Leons, and Sofie Asa; and our home and place of professional incubation for ten years, Union Theological Seminary, Philippines, its three presidents, Ben Guansing, Jacob Quiambao, Emerito Nacpil, our neighbors Gil and Rosalina Abesamis, and our faculty colleagues and their families, Gerald Anderson, Daniel and Ruth Arichea, Enrique Cainglet, Ermie Camba, Idelia Candelaria, Noel Canlas, Alex Christie, Nael Cortez, Richard and Jan Deats, Dick Fagan, Joe Gamboa, and Gene Hessel.

Finally, may I thank an extended family of (primarily) pastors and churches in the United States (mainly 1975–1987) who on more than one occasion have befriended

Kathy and me with teaching missions in Matthew's Gospel and with corrections, questions, and affirmations that are reflected on almost every page of the commentary. (For convenience, I will list the senior pastors' or equivalents' names in alphabetical order, and [F]PC will represent [First] Presbyterian Church.) Will Ackles, FPC Clarkston, WA, and now Calvin PC, Seattle, WA; Tom Arbogast, Ross Point (American Baptist) Bible Conference, Post Falls, ID; Dick Avery, Shadle Park PC, Spokane, WA; Hap Brahams and Peg Cantwell, La Jolla PC, CA; LaVern Brassard and John Day, Columbia PC, Vancouver, WA; Howard Butt and his colleagues Howard and Carole Hovde, Eddie and Gail Sears, Sam Fore, Dwight Lacy, Dorothy and Henry Parish, Robbie and Joan Robinson, Ila Burnett, and Frances Worley, of Laity Lodge, Kerrville, TX; Carnegie Calian and Pittsburgh Theological Seminary; Glen Carlson, Immanuel Lutheran Church of Rosenthal, Stony Plain, Alberta, [Canada]; Howard Childers and Jeff Yergler, Westminster PC, Amarillo, TX; Bill Craig, FPC Burbank, CA; Joel Crosby, Knox PC, Spokane, WA; Stuart and Cathy Cummings-Bond, St. Peter's By The Sea PC, Palos Verdes, CA; Gary Demarest, La Canada PC, CA; Gary Dennis, Westlake Hills PC, Austin, TX; Mark Dowdy, Sunnyside PC, WA; Howard Edington, Tino Ballesteros, and John Tolson, FPC Orlando, FL; Louis H. Evans, Jr., while at the Bel Air PC, CA, now at the National PC, Washington D.C.; Ben Fairchild, FPC Kennewick, WA; Ron Frase and his colleagues in the Whitworth College Chapel and the Whitworth Institute of Ministry, Doug Clegg, Dick Cole, Carol Cook, Quinn and Nancy Fox, Lori Nelson, and Lorraine Robertson; Cragg and Barb Gilbert, Jo Bennett Mitchell, The Campbell Farm, Wapato, WA; Dick Gronhovd, Whitworth Community PC; Larry Hall, St. John the Divine Episcopal Church, Houston, TX; Bill Hansen, Church of the Valley PC, Apple Valley, CA; Jack Hansen and Mark Frey, Valley Community United PC, Portland, OR; Ken Harrower, Mt. Hermon (CA) Christian Conference Center; Ed Hart and Rick Irish, FPC Coeur d'Alene, ID; Bruce Heiple, Sierra PC, Nevada City, CA; Les Hyder, FPC Waitsburg, WA; Andy Jarvis, FPC Walla Walla, WA; Buzz Kahn, Cross of Christ Lutheran Church, Bellevue, WA; Jack Lancaster, FPC Houston, TX; Bruce Larson and Marti Aiken, University PC, Seattle, WA; Paul Leggett and Alex Samson, Grace PC, Montclair, NJ; Ernie Lewis, Presbyterian Congress on Renewal; Jim Little and Jan Willette, Lafayette-Orinda PC, CA; Murray Marshall, FPC Seattle, WA; Bill McCullough, Solana Beach PC, CA; John McCullough and his colleagues Dana Wright, Bruce Howell, and John Mason, at Bethany Community Church, Seattle, WA; Don Meekhof, FPC Ellensburg, WA; Roger Meriwether, Emmanuel PC, Thousand Oaks, CA; Donn Moomaw, Bel Air PC, CA; Bob Munger while at FPC Berkeley; George Munzing and Tim Fearer, Trinity United PC, Santa Ana, CA; Ted Nissen, Colonial PC, Kansas City, MO; Earl Palmer, FPC Berkeley, CA; Vic Pentz and Steve Barker, FPC Yakima, WA; Claude Ponting, Opportunity PC, Spokane, WA; Errol Rohr and Gary Burge, King College, Bristol, TN; Erv Roorda and Jim Rettig, Manito PC, Spokane, WA; Bob Sanders, University PC, Fresno, CA; Jim Scott and Mary Robinson, FPC Sandpoint, ID; Evelyn Smith, Millwood PC, WA; Randy Smith, St. Luke's Methodist Church, Houston, TX; Nathan Stone, Manor Baptist Church, San Antonio, TX; Leigh Taylor, FPC Vancouver, WA; John Thomas, FPC Reardan, WA; Henry Wells, Chuck Shillito, and Mark Nazarian, Fair Oaks PC, CA; Ron White and Suzanne Rudiselle, Princeton Theological Seminary Institute of Theology and Center of Continuing Education; Ken Working, Longview (WA) Community Church; Randy

Young, Mountain View PC, Marysville, WA; Louis Zbinden and Jim Singleton, FPC San Antonio, TX.

My sons wondered if this long list of names might seem to be seeking to impress. Perhaps, indeed; who knows one's motives? But I want to believe that my main desire for this permanent record is to thank from the heart the congregations, pastors, teachers, and faithful who have so decisively shaped my life and, so, this commentary. I think I now understand why Paul put so many names in his letters— each name represents a dear and valued fellow-believer or fellowship of believers.. And they add up.

I want to dedicate this volume to my dearest and closest friend, my wife Kathy, for, in Milton's words, "those thousand decencies that daily flow / From all her words and actions, mixt with Love," who read and reread my manuscripts with her characteristic life-ebullience and whose joining me a year ago in full-time theological work and writing made it possible not only to finish Matthew but to have fun finishing it; to my good and affectionate father and mother, Mr. and Mrs. Fred S. Bruner, for a disciplined home, faithful Lutheran Christianity, and for the vastly underrated gift of parents to children—playing catch in the backyard while growing up; and to my dear, saintly, and courageous sister, Dee Bruner Eads, and her solid husband Hal, who together fight the good fight of dialysis, day after day and year after year, with true Christian faith, in the Methodist obedience, and who remain the most sensitive listeners in conversation that we know. I am very thankful to God for this family of love.

*　　*　　*

My chief desire in this commentary is to help pastors, teachers, and students, young and old, hear the Word of God that is present so richly in Matthew's Gospel, with all of Matthew's peculiar and powerful emphases—especially his emphases on the commanding Jesus and the obedient church. May Matthew's *Christbook* and *Churchbook* be a first installment in paying the long overdue debt I incurred to the people of God in the Philippines when I first tried there, with so much difficulty, to find a text for teaching Christian doctrine.

—F. DALE BRUNER
Department of Religious Studies
Whitworth College
Spokane, Washington

Commentary Key, I
Major Abbreviations, Authors, and Titles

References are put in the briefest possible way in the commentary (e.g., Allen, 117; Bult., 260), and they refer in most cases to a commentary or study, usually in Matthew. The key below identifies the references. The bibliography at the end of the second volume of the commentary gives full publication data. (The standard abbreviations in the biblical field are collected in the *Journal of Biblical Literature* 95 [1976], 330–46.)

A supplementary Commentary Key, including information especially appropriate to the second volume, will be found in the front matter of that volume, *The Churchbook*.

A	*Codex Alexandrinus* (fifth century)
Abbott	Walter M. Abbott, S. J., ed., *The Documents of Vatican II* (1966)
ACW	Ancient Christian Writers (1946–1986)
Albright-Mann	W. F. Albright and C. S. Mann, *Matthew* (1971)
Allen	Willoughby C. Allen, *Matthew* (3rd ed., 1912)
ANF	The Ante-Nicene Fathers (1951–1953)
Aug.	Augustine of Hippo (d. 430)
Ep.	*Epistles*, NPNF 1
Harm.	*Harmony of the Gospels* (ca. 400), NPNF 6
LSM	*The Lord's Sermon on the Mount* (ca. 394), ACW 5
Serm.	*Sermons*, NPNF 6
Tract. in Jn.	*Tractates on the Gospel of John* (ca. 416), NPNF 7
AV	*Authorized Version* (King James) (1611)
B	*Codex Vaticanus* (fourth century)
Bacon	Benjamin W. Bacon, *Studies in Matthew* (1930)
Bainton	Roland H. Bainton, *Here I Stand: A Life of Martin Luther* (1950)
Barc.	William Barclay, *Matthew* (rev. ed., 1975 [1958])
Barr.	C. K. Barrett, *John* (2nd ed., 1978)
G. Barth	Gerhard Barth, "Matthew's Understanding of the Law" in Born.(kamm-Barth-Held), *TIM* (1963)
Barth, *CD* (*KD*)	Karl Barth (d. 1968), *Church Dogmatics* (*Kirchliche Dogmatik*) (1932ff)
Bauer, *WB*	Walter Bauer, *Wörterbuch zum Neuen Testament* (1958)
BDB	F. Brown, S. R. Driver, and C. A. Briggs, *Hebrew and English Lexicon of the Old Testament* (1972)
BDF	F. Blass, A. Debrunner, and R. W. Funk, *A Greek Grammar of the New Testament* (1961)
Beare	Francis Wright Beare, *Matthew* (1981)

Bengel	John Albrecht Bengel (d. 1752), *Gnomon of the New Testament* (3rd ed., 1773; ET ed.; 1862)
V.G.	German Version of the New Testament (1753)
Berner	Ursula Berner, *Die Bergpredigt* (1979)
BJ	*La Bible de Jérusalem* (rev. ed., 1973)
Bonn.	Pierre Bonnard, *Matthieu* (2nd ed., 1970)
Born.	Günther Bornkamm
"End"	"End-Expectation and Church in Matthew," *TIM*
Jesus	*Jesus of Nazareth* (1960)
"Storm"	"The Stilling of the Storm in Matthew," *TIM*
TIM	Bornkamm-Barth-Held, *Tradition and Interpretation in Matthew* (1963)
Brown	Raymond E. Brown, *The Birth of the Messiah* (1977)
Bult.	Rudolf Bultmann, *The History of the Synoptic Tradition* (1963)
C	*Codex Ephraemi Rescriptus* (fifth century)
Caird	G. B. Caird, *Luke* (1963)
Cal.	John Calvin (d. 1564), *A Harmony of the Gospels* (1555, ed. 1972)
Inst.	*Institutes of the Christian Religion* (1559/1560; LCC 20–21, ed. 1960)
Institution	*Institution of the Christian Religion* (1536, ed. 1975)
Chrys.	John Chrysostom (d. 407), *Homilies on the Gospel of Matthew* (386–388), NPNF 10
Conz.	Hans Conzelmann, *Jesus* (1973 [1959])
D	*Codex Bezae Cantabrigiensis* (fifth, sixth century)
Davies	W. D. Davies, *The Setting of the Sermon on the Mount* (1964)
SM	*The Sermon on the Mount* (1966)
Derrett	J. Duncan M. Derrett, *Law in the New Testament* (1970)
Dupont	J. Dupont, *Les Béatitudes* (1958–1969)
EKL	*Evangelisches Kirchenlexikon* (1956)
ELC	*Encyclopedia of the Lutheran Church*
ET	English Translation
Eus., *H.E.*	Eusebius of Caesarea (fourth century), *Ecclesiastical History*
FC	Fathers of the Church (1947–1984)
Fent.	J. C. Fenton, *Matthew* (1963)
Fitz.	Joseph Fitzmyer, *Luke* (1981, 1985)
Frank.	Hubert Frankemölle, *Jahwebund und Kirche Christi [in Matt]* (1974)
Goulder	M. D. Goulder, *Midrash and Lection in Matthew* (1974)
Green	H. Benedict Green, *Matthew* (1975)
Grund.	Walter Grundmann, *Matthäus* (1968)
Guelich	Robert A. Guelich, *The Sermon on the Mount* (1982)
Gundry	Robert H. Gundry, *Matthew* (1982)
Gut.	Gustavo Gutiérrez, *A Theology of Liberation* (1973)
Haen.	Ernst Haenchen, *Der Weg Jesu* (1968)
Hare	Douglas R. A. Hare, *The Theme of Jewish Persecution of Christians in the Gospel according to St. Matthew* (1967)

Held	Heinz Joachim Held, "Matthew as Interpreter of the Miracle Stories," in Born.(kamm-Barth-Held), *TIM* (1963)
Hill	David Hill, *Matthew* (1972)
Humm.	Reinhart Hummel, *Die Auseinandersetzung zwischen Kirche und Judentum im Matthäusevangelium* (1966)
Hunter	A. M. Hunter, *Design for Life* (The Sermon on the Mount) (1965)
IB	*The Interpreter's Bible* (1951)
IDB	*Interpreter's Dictionary of the Bible* (1962)
J	Yahwist (tenth-century B. C. writer)
JB	*Jerusalem Bible* (1966)
JBC	R. E. Brown *et al.* (eds.), *The Jerome Biblical Commentary* (1968)
Jeremias	Joachim Jeremias
Euch.	*The Eucharistic Words of Jesus* (1966)
Par.	*The Parables of Jesus* (1971)
Prom.	*Jesus' Promise to the Nations* (1958)
Jero.	Jerome (d. 419), *Commentaire sur S. Matthieu* (ca. 398), ("Sources Chrétiennes," No. 242)
Johnson	Sherman E. Johnson, "Matthew," *IB* (1951)
Jos.	Flavius Josephus (d. ca. 100)
Ant.	*Antiquities of the Jews*
Ap.	*Against Apion*
J.W.	*The Jewish War*
Kilpatrick	G. D. Kilpatrick, *The Origins of the Gospel acc. to St. Matthew* (1946)
Kings.,	Jack Dean Kingsbury, *Matthew* (1977)
Par.	*The Parables of Jesus in Matthew 13* (1969)
Story	*Matthew as Story* (1986)
Struc.	*Matthew: Structure, Christology, Kingdom* (1975)
Kissinger	Warren S. Kissinger, *The Sermon on the Mount* (1975)
Kl.	E. Klostermann, *Matthäus* (4th ed., 1971 [1938])
Kümmel	W. G. Kümmel, *Promise and Fulfillment* (1961)
Küng	Hans Küng, *On Being a Christian* (1976)
Lagrange	M.-J. Lagrange, *Matthieu* (1923)
LCC	The Library of Christian Classics (1953–1966)
LCL	The Loeb Classical Library (1912ff)
Lohm.	Ernst Lohmeyer, *Matthäus* (3rd ed., 1962 [1946])
Lu.	Martin Luther (d. 1546)
BW	*The Bondage of the Will* (1524/25)
Cl.	Otto Clemen's *Luthers Werke in Auswahl* (1912–1933; 1955/56)
LW	*Luther's Works* (American Edition) (1955–1976)
SM	"The Sermon on the Mount (Sermons)," *LW 21* (1530–1532)
W²	Joh. Georg Walch, *Dr. Martin Luthers sämmtliche Schriften* 2nd. ed.; St. Louis [Edition] (1880–1910)

WA	*D. Martin Luthers Werke,* Weimar [Edition] (1883ff)
LXX	The Septuagint (Greek translation of the Hebrew Scriptures, third century B.C.)
Marsh.	I. Howard Marshall, *Luke* (1978)
McArthur	Harvey K. McArthur, *Understanding the Sermon on the Mount* (1960)
McK.	John L. McKenzie, "Matthew," *JBC* (1968)
McN.	Alan Hugh McNeile, *Matthew* (1952 [1915])
Meier	John P. Meier, *Matthew* (1980)
Vis.	*The Vision of Matthew* (1979)
Metz.	Bruce M. Metzger, *A Textual Commentary on the Greek New Testament* (1971)
Mey.	H. A. W. Meyer, *Matthäus* (3rd. ed., 1853)
Mg.	Margin
Minear	Paul S. Minear, *Matthew: The Teacher's Gospel* (1982)
Mohrlang	*Matthew and Paul* (Oxford Doctoral Dissertation, 1979)
Mounce	Robert H. Mounce, *Matthew* (1985)
NEB	*The New English Bible* (1961, 1970)
Nineham	D. E. Nineham, *Mark* (1963)
NPNF	A Select Library of the Nicene and Post-Nicene Fathers (1886–1900; 1952–1956)
NT	The New Testament
NAEL	Norris Anthology of English Literature
ODEP	*The Oxford Dictionary of English Proverbs*
Orig.	Origen (d. ca. 254), "Matthew," ANF 10
OT	The Old Testament
p	Papyrus (a Greek text, from the second to the fourth century B.C.)
P	The Priestly Writer(s) in the Old Testament (sixth century)
Patte	Daniel Patte, *Matthew* (1987)
PCB	M. Black and H. H. Rowley (eds.), *Peake's Commentary on the Bible* (1962)
Pelikan	Jaroslav Pelikan, *The Christian Tradition* (1971ff)
Pl.	Alfred Plummer, *Matthew* (5th ed., 1922)
PssSol	The Psalms of Solomon (first century)
RGG	*Religion in Geschichte und Gegenwart* (3rd ed., 1957)
RSV	*The Revised Standard Version* (1946, 1952)
RV	*The Revised Version* (1885)
S	*Codex Sinaiticus* (fourth century)
Schaff	Philip Schaff (ed.), *The Creeds of Christendom* (1931)
Schl.	Adolf Schlatter (d. 1938)
Das	*Das Evangelium nach Matthäus* (1961 [1895–1903; 1928–1936])
Der	*Der Evangelist Matthäus* (1929)
Die	*Die Evangelien nach Markus und Lukas* (1961 [1895–1903; 1928–1936])
Schn.	Julius Schniewind, *Matthäus* (10th ed., 1962 [1937])

Schw.	Eduard Schweizer, *Matthew* (1975)
Stend.	Krister Stendahl, "Matthew," *PCB* (1962)
Str.-B.	H. Strack and Paul Billerbeck, *Kommentar zum Neven Testament aus Talmud und Midrasch*, I: *Matthäus*, (1961 [1926])
Streck.	Georg Strecker, *Der Weg der Gerechtigkeit* (3rd. ed., 1971)
Swete	Henry Barclay Swete, *Mark* (3rd ed., 1919)
Tay.	Vincent Taylor, *Mark* (2nd ed., 1966)
TDNT	G. Kittel and G. Friedrich (eds.), *Theological Dictionary of the New Testament* (1964–1976 [1932ff])
TEV	*The Today's English Version* (The Good News Bible) (1976)
Thompson	W. G. Thompson, *Matthew's Advice to a Divided Community* (1970)
Trill.	Wolfgang Trilling, *Das wahre Israel* (1964)
TWNT	G. Kittel and G. Friedrich (eds.), *Theologisches Wörterbuch zum Neuen Testament* (1932–1979)
Waetjen	Herman C. Waetjen, *Matthew* (1976)
Walker	Rolf Walker, *Die Heilsgeschichte im ersten Evangelium* (1967)
Wind.	Hans Windisch, *The Meaning of the Sermon on the Mount* (1951 [1937])

Chapter One
Introduction to the Doctrine of God

MATTHEW CHAPTER 1 HAS TWO MAIN PARTS: a genealogy and a birth or naming story. Matthew writes neither of these stories from merely historical interests or for purely objective reasons (though he intends to be historical and to make objective observations). He turns dull genealogy into evangelism and a birth story into a lexicon for the names of the Son of God. First, in the genealogy Matthew lays out how the Christ-promising God shaped Israel's history to keep the divine promise. As we will see, we can learn a great deal about God the Father from Matthew's genealogy and its ordinarily uninteresting names of fathers (and a few interesting mothers). Second, in the birth or naming story in the second half of the chapter, Matthew twice refers to the Holy Spirit and twice gives Jesus special names. We will draw from Matthew's double reference to the Holy Spirit an introductory doctrine of the Holy Spirit, and from the two names given Jesus we may gather fundamental material for Matthew's understanding of the Son of God. Thus Matthew chapter 1 introduces us to the person and work of God—the Father, the Son, and the Holy Spirit—an introduction that is repeatedly enriched in every successive chapter till we learn what the Gospel's final sentence means in commanding baptism in the "name of the Father and of the Son and of the Holy Spirit," Matthew's God.

1:1 "The Book of Genesis [*Biblos geneseōs*] of Jesus Messiah, Son of David, Son of Abraham." The first two words of Matthew's Gospel in Greek, *Biblos geneseōs,* can be understood in three main ways: (1) as a *short* title for the genealogy that follows in 1:2–17—"The book of the genealogy," RSV; comparably, NEB, TEV; also Allen, 2; Bacon, 265 ("the pedigree"); Lohm., 4; Schrenk, *Biblos,* TWNT, 1:615; Stend., 770; Streck., 53 n. 1; Brown, 49, 57; Kingsb., 25; or, (2) as a *medium* title for the stories of Jesus' birth or beginnings that follow in chaps 1–2, 3–4 thus, e.g., Schw., 21; or, (3) as a *long* title for the entire Gospel, using the Greek name for the first book of the Hebrew Scriptures (from the third century B.C. translators of the so-called Septuagint or LXX, Speiser, *Gen.,* xvii)—*Biblos geneseōs,* "The Book of Genesis," specifically, the genesis, as the following words tell us, "of Jesus Messiah," thus, e.g., Schniewind, 9, who translates *Biblos geneseōs* as "History of Jesus Christ"; Davies, 67ff—"The Book of the Genesis of Jesus Christ"; Hill, 75; cf. Brown, 66 n. 7, 69—"Genesis," 231 n. 1. Historical-critical exegesis usually prefers the short title, theological exegesis the long.

In Matthew's conviction no less than John's (Rev 21:6; 22:13), Jesus is *Alpha* as well as Omega, *Genesis* as well as Telos. Jesus is not only the end and the goal, he is the beginning and origin of God's purposes with the world. Matthew never tires of showing that the real meaning of major texts of the Hebrew Scriptures was and is Jesus and his career (e.g., 1:23; 2:6, 18; 3:3; 4:15–16, and passim).

In Matthew, Jesus is not only new on the scene; he is also the meaning of the old texts. The real Genesis is Jesus. Would the evangelist who ends his Gospel majestically with the Great Commission and its "Look! I am with you all the days, right into the consummation of the age" (28:20), begin his Gospel prosaically with an antiseptic "birth record"? Perhaps indeed! But some will find it easier to believe that the first two words say what they sound—*Biblos geneseōs*, "Book of Genesis"—and that Matthew intends with these opening words to suggest that the deep Genesis in history was not the birth of the world but the birth of the world's Savior, that at the center of history is an even greater Genesis than at the beginning, and that this New Genesis, this Re-generation, this Jesus, is even more important than creation itself. The Book of Genesis title promises something: All who heed the Gospel's theme that follows—discipleship to Jesus—will themselves experience the new genesis or re-generation that makes persons new creations.

Biblos geneseōs may even be "telescopic" (Fent., 35–36), serving as three titles at once: "The Book of Genesis" (Matt 1–28), "The Book of the Birth Stories" (Matt 1–2), and "The Book of the Genealogy" (Matt 1:1–17). (Cf. also along this line, Bonn., 13; Gründ., 61.)

The word *geneseōs*, applied to Jesus Messiah, would remind cultivated readers in the Roman Empire of the new "beginnings" promised to the world by the Roman emperors, particularly Caesar Augustus. His birthday in 7 B.C. was celebrated in a famous inscription (cited, with emphases added, in R. M. Grant, "Augustus," *IDB*, 1:319):

"It is hard to say whether the birthday of the divine Caesar is more joyful or more advantageous; we may rightly regard it as like *the beginning of all things,* if not in the world of nature, yet in advantage; everything was deteriorating and changing into misfortune, but he set it right and gave the whole world another appearance. . . . *The birthday of the god* [Augustus] *was the beginning of the good news* [cf. Mark 1:1!] to the world on his account."

Who really brought this new beginning to the world—who is really divine—Caesar Augustus or Jesus Messiah?

"Jesus Messiah." "Jesus" is the Greek translation of the common Hebrew name *Joshua*, the name of a man. "Jesus" is first of all the name of a human being. (For the deep reason for the name *Jesus* in Matthew, see 1:21.) "Messiah" means "Anointed," or "Christ," and is a royal title; it is not Jesus' last name. Jesus Christ or Jesus Messiah means "Jesus King" or "King Jesus" in the language of gentiles. The Messiah is the great hope of the Jewish people, and it is Matthew's bold claim that the Jewish Messiah has arrived and has already released saving benefits into world history—in his teaching, his miracles, his person, and supremely in his sacrificial atoning death and in his death-defeating and mission-giving resurrection—and that he will come again to consummate history.

"Son of David, Son of Abraham." The two great baskets of saving promise in the Hebrew Scriptures are the promise to David of a son who would be a Forever King and the promise to Abraham of a seed who would be an All Nations Blessing—a temporal promise (forever) and a spatial promise (all nations), a promise meeting Israel's deepest longings for Another David, and a promise meeting the gentiles' deepest longings for a universal savior. The name "Son of David" says "Israel, behold your Messiah!"; and the name "Son of Abraham" says, "Nations, behold your hope!" Jesus is both in one. According to Jerome, 72, Matthew omits all other fathers in this his Gospel title and mentions only Abraham and David "because to them alone was the promise of the Messiah made."

"Son of David." The word of the Lord said to David through Nathan, portentously:

"When your days are fulfilled to go to be with your fathers, I will raise up your offspring after you, one of your own sons, and I will establish his kingdom. He shall build a house for me, and I will establish his throne *for ever*. I will be his father, and he shall be my son; I will not take my steadfast love from him, as I took it from him who was before you, but I will confirm him in my house and in my kingdom *for ever* and his throne shall be established *for ever*" (1 Chr 17:11–14 RSV, italics added; cf. 2 Sam 7). Also valuable for appreciating the Son of David promise, in addition to the important seventeenth chapter of the Pharisees' Psalms of Solomon, are the canonical Isa 9:1–7; 11:1–9; Jer 23:5f; 33:15f.

Later in the fourth and climactic question in The Four Questions of Matthew 22 (vv 41–46), Jesus will challenge a one-sided understanding of the Messiah as only the (human) *Son* of David and not as also David's (divine) *Lord*. But while Jesus is much more than Son of David, he is nothing less. Jesus, in Christian faith, is God's own Jewish self-address to the Jewish people as their Son of David; and through or around the Jewish people, Jesus is King of the gentile world that also longs for a Forever King.

> I have made a covenant with my chosen,
> I have sworn to David my servant:
> Thy seed will I establish *forever*,
> And build up thy throne to *all* generations (Ps 89:3–4).

"Son of Abraham." "And in your descendants [seed, *zeraka*, singular] shall all the nations of the earth bless themselves" (Gen 22:18 RSV). Compare the apostle Paul's commentary on this verse: "Now the promises were made to Abraham and to his offspring. It does not say 'And to [your] offsprings [plural],' referring to many; but, referring to one, 'And to your offspring [singular],' which is Christ" (Gal 3:16 RSV). This is Christian faith speaking, in theological exegesis. The first appearance in Hebrew Scripture of this universal promise was at the very end of the great Call of Abram, where Abram was challenged to leave his past and follow the Lord into the future and into greatness and blessing, becoming the divine medium of blessing to all who blessed him and of cursing to all who cursed him, "and [thus] in you all the families of the earth shall be blessed" (Gen 12:1–3 RSV, mg.). This faith plan of salvation, rooted in one person but focused on the whole earth of nations and families, now receives its classical form in the seed of Abraham, Jesus. All this is contained in Matthew's cryptic designation of Jesus Messiah as "Son of Abraham."

I. THE GENEALOGY: GOD THE FATHER, THE OVER-US GOD, BRINGING DEITY TO THE WORLD (1:1–17)

"I believe in God the Father Almighty, Maker of heaven and earth." (*The Apostles' Creed*)

In the first half of the first chapter we see a long list of names—a genealogy, stretching from Abraham to Jesus. Matthew is fascinated by the "three times four-teen" shape of this genealogy where important knots in Israel's history are tied three times, every fourteen generations (1:17). We will understand this three-times-fourteen formation best if we picture a kind of leaning capital N, an *N* in which the first fourteen generations head upward from Father Abraham to King David like this (/), the second fourteen generations plummet downward from King Solomon to the Babylonian Exile (\), and then finally the last fourteen generations move up-ward again from exile to the Christ (/).

(/) *The birth record of Jesus Christ, son of David, son of Abraham:*
Abraham was the father of Isaac;
Isaac was the father of Jacob;
Jacob was the father of Judah and his brothers;
Judah was the father of Perez and Zerah by Tamar;
Perez was the father of Hezron;
Hezron was the father of Aram;
Aram was the father of Amminadab;
Amminadab was the father of Nahshon;
Nahshon was the father of Salmon;
Salmon was the father of Boaz by Rahab;
Boaz was the father of Obed by Ruth;
Obed was the father of Jesse;
Jesse was the father of David the king.

(\) *David was the father of Solomon* by Uriah's wife;
Solomon was the father of Rehoboam;
Rehoboam was the father of Abijah;
Abijah was the father of Asaph;
Asaph was the father of Jehoshaphat;
Jehoshaphat was the father of Joram;
Joram was the father of . . . *Uzziah;*
Uzziah was the father of Jotham;
Jotham was the father of Ahaz;
Ahaz was the father of Hezekiah;
Hezekiah was the father of Manasseh;
Manasseh was the father of Amos;
Amos was the father of Josiah;
Josiah was the father of . . . *Jechoniah and his brothers*
at the time of the Babylonian Exile.

(/) *After the Babylonian Exile,*
Jechoniah was the father of Shealtiel;
Shealtiel was the father of Zerubbabel;
Zerubbabel was the father of Abiud;
Abiud was the father of Eliakim;
Eliakim was the father of Azor;
Azor was the father of Zadok;
Zadok was the father of Achim;

Achim was the father of Eliud;
Eliud was the father of Eleazar;
Eleazar was the father of Matthan;
Matthan was the father of Jacob;
Jacob was the father of Joseph, the husband of Mary;
of her was begotten Jesus, called the Christ.

Thus the total generations from Abraham to David were fourteen
generations; and from David to the Babylonian Exile fourteen more
generations; and finally from the Babylonian Exile to the Christ
fourteen more generations. (Matt 1:1–17)

The translation, with the emphasized women's names, is Raymond Brown's, 57. (B. W. Bacon emphasized the women's names in his translation as well, 265.) In addition, I have emphasized the two notorious omissions (the dots), and the two alterations in the David-to-Exile line (Asaph, Amos) and the fifth woman, "Mary," in the final line.

Each of these three movements or lines teaches a distinct doctrine of God and makes for pleasurable brooding. And when we see all three movements together we see a picture of the creative way that God the Father shaped history for the coming of his Son. (We have in the genealogy, in fact, both a little doctrine of God and a systematic mini-theology of the Old Testament.)

A. Line One: From Abraham to David: The Four Women and the Doctrine of Divine Mercy (1:2–6)

On close examination, the first fourteen generations (counting David's paternity of Solomon) include four peculiar names. Four of the fathers listed here, and only four, are connected with named women. And all four of the women are, in one way or another, irregular.

The four women are Tamar, Rahab, Ruth, and Bathsheba. Tamar, we recall, was the woman obliged to play the harlot in order to trick her father-in-law, Judah, into keeping his promises to her (Gen 38). The fruit of this tricky union is one of the great-grandfathers of our Lord. Rahab "the harlot" is best known for her assisting the spies in Israel (Josh 2) and so winning a better name for herself; in the New Testament she even becomes a model of faith (Heb 11) and of works (Jas 2). Rahab the believing harlot was one of the great-grandmothers of our Lord.

Ruth is morally the least questionable of the four women, but she was a Moabite, a descendant of the incestuous Lot (Gen 19), and thus low on the social and spiritual register of some of the racially proud and protective people of God. Nevertheless, this *gentile* became the literal great-grandmother of David and so a distant great-grandmother of our Lord (see the Book of Ruth). The fourth woman even Matthew blushes to name directly. He calls her, circumspectly, "the wife of Uriah," indicating incidentally that she was not the lawful wife of David. We know this woman as Bathsheba—more the victim than the agent in the Old Testament's most scandalous case of seduction (2 Sam 11). Bathsheba, too, is a great-grandmother of our Lord.

Several things about these four women arrest the reader's attention. First, the simple fact that women are mentioned at all is noteworthy. Usually the names of men suffice in biblical genealogies, and women's names are added only if they will ensure the purity of the line or enhance its dignity. Three of these four women do not immediately serve either of these purposes. And this leads us to the second major surprise: all four women are non-Jews. We have already noticed this in the case of the well-known Ruth the Moabitess. But a closer reading of the other texts discovers that Tamar was a Canaanite, Rahab a Jerichoite, and Bathsheba, through her husband, a Hittite.

Most genealogies in the late Old Testament period have the purpose of showing that a line has been kept pure *from* gentile contamination. But this first genealogy in the New Testament has the surprising office of teaching us that the line that led from Abraham to Jesus, the Son of David, was intersected again and again by gentile blood. King David himself had a Canaanite great-great-great-grandmother, a Jerichoite great-great-grandmother, a Moabite great-grandmother, and a Hittite "wife." Matthew wants the church to know that from the start, and not just from the Council of Jerusalem (Acts 15), God's work has been interracial, and that God is no narrow nationalist or racist.

Hominum confusione Dei providentia. The bloodline of the Messiah—from Abraham himself, who of course was originally gentile (Rom 4)—has been extended through history by gentile as well as by Jewish parents. And all this by the overruling providence of God, not by human caprice. God is catholic and unprovincial in his work, as the genealogy shows, and so the people of God should be catholic and unprovincial too (that is, interracial, intercultural, and international).

And this leads us to the third and perhaps most important observation: all four of the women are anomalous. In three of the four cases they are sexually-morally anomalous. Except for the case of Ruth (and she was a little aggressive), few parents use the stories of Tamar, Rahab, or Bathsheba as positive moral instruction for their sons and daughters. One gets the impression that Matthew pored over his Old Testament records until he could find the most questionable ancestors of Jesus available in order, in turn, to insert them into his record and so, it seems, to preach the gospel—the gospel, that is, that God can overcome and forgive sin, and can use soiled but repentant persons for his great purposes in history (for Judah's repentance, cf. Gen 38:26; for David's, 2 Sam 12:13 and, traditionally, Ps 51).

These four scandals in their way preach the gospel of divine mercy, which is Matthew's whole mission to proclaim. Matthew will later teach us that Jesus came "not for the righteous, but *for sinners*" (Matt 9:13); but already in his genealogy Matthew is teaching us that Jesus came not only *for,* but *through,* sinners. God did not begin to stoop into our sordid human story at Christmas only; he was stooping all the way through the Old Testament. The mercy of God is the deepest fact Matthew finds in his Hebrew Scriptures and in Jesus (cf. 9:13; 12:7), and so through the four women he highlights this mercy in the first line of his genealogy.

The four model matriarchs of Jewish history were Sarah, Rebekah, Rachel, and Leah, the wives, respectively, of Abraham, Isaac, and Jacob. These four women are conspicuous by their absence here. Their husbands are all here, and so there was opportunity for Matthew to include the good wives. But Matthew gives the church four new matriarchs, and all of them preach the gospel of the deep and wide mercy of God.

And so the genealogy already teaches us something about Matthew's style. Matthew is not interested in passing on to us mere history, uninterpreted facts, or, in this case, a dry list of the names of the Messiah's ancestors. Matthew is always preaching gospel.

1:3–6 On the unusual inclusion of women in the genealogy at all, see Str.-B., 1:15; Kittel, *Thamar*, TWNT, 3:1; Hill, 74; Brown, 71, in a fascinating section entitled "Why Bring on the Ladies?" 71–74. On the proof of purity as a major purpose of genealogies, Str.-B., 1:2; Lohm., 1–2. Von Rad notes that the purity of God's people was not thought of as compromised by racial intermarriage in *early* Israel's history. "That changed only after the exile, especially because of Ezra and Nehemiah" (*Genesis*, rev. ed., 378). But the Jewish commentator Speiser believes that even in the earliest documents in Genesis (Gen 12:10–20, [J]) "the ultimate purpose of biblical genealogies was to establish the superior strain of the line through which the biblical way of life was transmitted from generation to generation. In other words, the integrity of the mission was to be safeguarded in transmission, the purity of the content protected by the quality of the container" (*Genesis*, 93–94). Later, for example, "Isaac must not take a wife from among the Canaanites, for that would affect the purity of the line through which God's covenant was to be implemented" (ibid., 183).

Matthew, by emphasizing early racial intermarriages, is, among other things, returning the people of God to their original racial universality. Contrast current rabbinical law in the political state of Israel where a child's religion is determined exclusively by its mother. The child of a Jewish man and a gentile woman is not considered a Jew. But by this law the historical son of David, King Solomon himself, would not be Jewish (not to mention Obed, the grandfather of David).

By his insertion of the four foreign women into his genealogy it is clearly one of Matthew's purposes to attack racial and national chauvinisms in the people of God and to warn the new people of God, the church, against any return to national or racial enthusiasms. Jesus' own racial heritage is mixed, not just at insignificant points in Israel's history, but with persons as significant in that history as Judah and David. Racial prejudice is condemned on the opening page of the New Testament.

It is important to note, moreover, that it was not the foreign women, but the believing males—Judah and David in particular—who were the villains in the stories. Cf. Lohm., 5; Grund., 62. This needs to be said not only to avoid sexism, but also to avoid a subtle racism that would suggest it was the reputed racial impurity of the women that caused the moral impurities of the men.

All four women were non-Israelites, even (as we have seen) Bathsheba through marriage, cf. Schn., 11; Lohm., 5; Bonn., 16; McK., 66; Schw., 25; Green, 53; Brown, 72. Brown, 72–73, argues against the foreign thesis for the women's inclusion in the genealogy, but not strongly, in my opinion, and on p. 74 he even speaks for the thesis.

There is some exegetical debate about calling the women "sinners" (pro: Cal., 1:59; Schn., 11; contra: Grund., 62; Stend., 771; Brown, 71, but see 72). Agreement comes in seeing in these four women at least God's "holy irregularity" (Stend., 771; Hill, 74). The introduction of the women into the genealogy is Matthew's creative work, Brown, 70, 74; contra Streck., 89.

On the four matriarchs praised in rabbinic literature—Sarah, Rebekah, Rachel, and Leah—with whom Matthew deliberately contrasts his four new Gospel matriarchs—Tamar, Rahab, Ruth, and Bathsheba—see Str.-B., 1:29; Lohm., 5, 8; and especially Kittel, *Thamar*, TDNT, 3:1. Cf. also the contemporary Passover Haggadah song: "Who knows four? I know four. Four are the matriarchs; three are the patriarchs; two are the tablets of the covenant; one is our God . . ." (N. Goldberg, *Passover Haggadah*, New York: Ktav, 1949, 1966, p. 45).

Jerome, 1:72, the fourth-century church father, believes "it should be noted that in the genealogy of the Savior the mention of no holy women is included, but, rather, those whom Scripture blames (*reprehendit*) in order to show that He who came for sinners would efface the sins of all." The problem with an exclusively "sinners" thesis, I should point out, is that it can be used as racist grist. Good Ruth (and, properly understood, victimized Tamar, converted Rahab, and used Bathsheba) protect us from an unintentionally racist or exclusively "sinners" interpretation.

Chrysostom, 3:3:16, Jerome's fourth-century contemporary, believes the four women and their husbands are brought forward "to show that all are under sin," even Israel's forefathers. "If by the great ones [such as Judah and David] the law was not fulfilled, much more by the less. And if it was not fulfilled, all have sinned, and Christ's coming is become necessary." The strength of this interpretation is its placing the sin where it belongs: on the "racially pure" *men*.

Luther, as might be expected, sees in the four Gospel matriarchs God's desire to "show how much love He has for sinners." It is, writes Luther, as though God intended for the hearer of this genealogy to say, "Oh, Christ is the kind of person who is not ashamed of sinners—in fact, He even puts them in His family tree!" Then Luther gives this point a fine ethical twist: "Now if the Lord does that here, so ought we to despise no one . . . but put ourselves right in the middle of the fight for sinners and help them" ("Sermon on the Day of Mary's Birth," 8 Sept. 1522, W^2 11:2371). Calvin makes a similar point, 1:59; also Schl., *Das*, 7; Schn., 11.

The other major interpretation of the four women's inclusion is their serving as illustrations of the sovereignty of God in overruling human sin or weakness: Allen, 2, 5; McN., 5; Schl., *Der*, 2–3; Lohm., 5; Grund., 62; Schw., 25; Green, 53. A satisfying, simple discussion of this matter is found in Kittel's article on Tamar and the other three women in TDNT, 3:1–3.

B. Line Two: From Solomon to Exile: The Four Alterations and the Doctrine of Divine Judgment (1:7–11)

The second line plunges into judgment. From the height of Israel's political and spiritual glory under King David, Israel declines until it falls into the pit of exile, losing its land, temple, kings, and so, seemingly, almost all of God's promises. As Matthew recounts this story in his genealogy he makes four significant alterations— all of which again, I think, intend to make a point. First, he changes the fourth king, Asa, into the psalmist Asaph by simply suffixing the single Greek letter *phi*. Then, after Joram, he omits three kings (Ahaziah, Joash, and Amaziah) and so skips three physical generations and sixty years (842–783) of Israel's history. Third, by altering a single letter he changes the king Amon into the prophet Amos (see the RSV for a faithful record of the textual situation with Asaph and Amos). And finally, he omits Jehoiakim just before Jehoiakin (or Jechoniah).

It is easiest to see why Matthew changed King Asa into the prophetic psalmist Asa*ph* and King Amon into the prophet Amo*s*: Matthew wanted in this second line to teach a second, *prophetic* truth about God—*judgment*. (The first or patriarchal truth is mercy.) Just as some patriotic Americans know the list of American presidents by heart, so some of the devout members of the old people of God knew their Judaean kings by heart. Clearly, Matthew was not trying to put anything over on his readers when he made his alterations. (It was well-known that Asa was Abijah's son, and Amon the son of Manasseh.) Is it possible (or is it only fanciful) to think that Matthew wanted to convey the message of judgment by his four alterations in the second line as he had conveyed the message of mercy by his insertion of four women into the first? Of this much I am sure: Matthew wanted to write evangelical genealogy, that is to say, interesting genealogy, theological genealogy!

Asaph is the author of Psalms 50 and 73–83; Amos is the well-known eighth-century prophet. Thus "Asaph and Amos" say "psalmist and prophet." Psalmists and prophets had well-defined and highly regarded offices in Israel. They were, respectively, the singers of God's praise and the warners of God's judgment. "And King Hezekiah and his officers commanded the Levites *to praise the Lord* in the words of *David and Asaph the seer.* So they praised him most joyfully and bowed down and prostrated themselves" (2 Chr 29:30 NEB; cf. Pss 50 and 81 for Asaph's message of judgment).

Amos is the prophet of social justice *par excellence* in Scripture. Economically insensitive worship appalls the God of Amos:

> Spare me the sound of your songs;
> I cannot endure the music of your [choirs].
> Let *justice* roll [down] like a river
> and righteousness like an ever-flowing stream (Amos 5:23–24 NEB).

The prophets warned Israel toward the Lord and justice in order to save her from herself and judgment. "The Lord sent prophets *to bring them back to himself,* prophets who denounced them and were not heeded" (2 Chr 24:19 italics added, NEB).

So Asaph and Amos spell "social justice," and together they stand for all seers and prophets sent by God to snatch God's people from the catastrophes of exile and judgment (cf. 2 Chr 36:15–17 for a summary). The message of God's mercy must always be enriched by the prophetic message of God's justice, or divine mercy is trivialized. "Where there is no prophecy the people cast off restraint . . ." (Prov 29:18 RSV).

I believe, then, that Matthew changed Asa to Asaph, and Amon to Amos, among other reasons and at least, to teach that the true God not only forgives, he also demands. The second thesis of *The Theological Declaration of Barmen* (1934) puts the theological truth involved here perfectly: "As Jesus Christ is God's assurance of the forgiveness of all our sins [the first line of the genealogy], so in the same way and with the same seriousness he is also God's mighty claim upon our whole life [the second line]." In Matthew, in fact, God's mighty *claim* in Jesus is almost as important—it is certainly as emphasized—as God's massive mercy in Jesus. Matthew is the most demanding of all the Gospels, with the possible exception of Luke.

The two sets of omissions in this second line (three kings omitted in v 8, one king in v 11) are less easy to understand. Are they due to inaccuracies in the Greek Bible from which Matthew took his lists? Are they because the omitted kings were wicked, accursed, or assassinated? Was there simple eye-error (Matthew skipped a line inadvertently or misread a name)? Or a copyist's error? Is the confusion pre-Matthean? All these interpretations have been suggested.

In reading the stories of the omitted kings one is primarily struck by how very nearly the entire messianic line of David was snuffed out. The royal house of David (and with it, God's messianic promise) came close in the times of these kings to being extinguished from history. At times only one breathing man perpetuated God's promise of a son to David. The history of the house of David from Joram on moves like a Hitchcock thriller, where the tenuousness of the house's existence and the fidelity of Yahweh to the promise of a Davidic descendant are balanced against each other in story after story. (The reading of a series of texts will deepen this impression: 2 Chr 21:4–7, 12–17; 22:10–11.)

It is possible that Matthew erased Kings Ahaziah, Joash, and Amaziah from his genealogy in order to teach his church how near the promise of Yahweh to David's house came to being erased by the people's sin and to teach us how faithfully, nevertheless, Yahweh keeps his promise. This is not the only possible interpretation of the omissions (see another approach below, 14–15), but it does have the strength of accenting the theme of the second line, which is judgment. "'The Lord is slow to anger, and abounding in steadfast love, forgiving iniquity and transgression, but he will by no means clear the guilty . . .'" (Num 14:18 RSV).

1:7 The idea of prophetic *judgment* is more likely the cause for Matthew's changing King Asa to the psalmist-prophet Asaph (thus Grund., 63; Schw., 24; Streck., 71; Gund., 16) than is a copyist's error (thus BJ; Bonn., 16; Brown, 60–61). Not only the law and the prophets were fulfilled in Christ, but the Psalms (i.e., Asaph) as well, and thus the whole of the Hebrew Scriptures (Schn., 10; Meier, *Vis.*, 53 n. 15; cf. Luke 24:44 for the three-fold division of old Scripture). Green, 53, correctly points out that Septuagint manuscripts vary between Amon and Amos wherever King Amon is mentioned, cf. 1 Chr 3:14; 2 Kgs 21:18; 2 Chr 33:20 in the LXX. But the best texts in Matthew uniformly have Amos and Asaph (*S, B, C* from the fourth and fifth centuries); one fifth-century manuscript—*W*—has Amon and Asa; the other manuscripts with the Asa and Amon readings are from the eight- and ninth-centuries (*K, L*). Cf. Metzger, 1–2; Brown, 61, suggests that "the desire to spare Matthew an error here may stem from a theory of inerrancy or from an overestimation of Matthew's knowledge of Scripture." True, but I am convinced that Matthew here is creative, not mistaken.

1:8 ". . . and Joram the father of Uzziah." But Joram was *not* the father of Uzziah; he was the father of Ahaziah (1 Chr 3:11); Joram was the great-great-grandfather of Uzziah (also called Azariah, 1 Chr 3:12). Matthew has skipped three physical generations. The easiest explanation for this is simple *error*. Even in English, Ahaziah and Azariah look alike to a copier. (In Greek orthography, in LXX variants, we even have *ozias* and *ozias*, i.e., Uzziah and Uzziah in 1 Chr 3:11–12. A copyist's eye skipped from the first to the second Uzziah and thus three kings were missed, according to Schweizer, 22f; cf. a slightly different account of the orthography in the omissions in Allen, 4; Brown, 82.)

In the history of exegesis there are explanations other than error for the omissions. The most frequent is *sin*. Jerome, 1:74, e.g., believes that "because the evangelist proposed to establish three series of fourteen names, corresponding to three distinct periods, and, the race of the impious Jezebel being mixed with that of Joram, he therefore deleted her remembrance to the third generation in order that she might have no place in the holy nativity." Similarly in modern exegesis, Grund., 63; cf. Brown, 82 n. 45; Gund., 16; Hill, 76, faults the infamous Athaliah.

Chrysostom, 1:14:6, with his typical candor, is not satisfied with sin as an explanation and prefers simple *agnosticism* here. "For if, because [these kings] were exceeding ungodly, he therefore passed by their names in silence, neither should he have mentioned the others, that were like them," such as Ahaz and Manasseh. Thus here is Chrysostom's delightful conclusion to this knotty problem: Why "hath he in the middle portion passed over three kings . . . ? [This question] I leave for you to examine."

Calvin, 1:59–60, dismisses the thesis of error, and feels Chrysostom's kind of discomfort with Jerome's thesis of sin, and for similar reasons, but suggests as his explanation what we can call the thesis of evangelical *freedom*. "We should pay no heed to those who say this was done through forgetfulness, nor is the argument very probable that these were unworthy of inclusion in the genealogy of Christ. The same would apply to many others whom Matthew mixes indiscriminately with the godly and the holy. It is more true that as he wished to compile a list of fourteen kings, he was not over-particular in making his selection."

Matthew, Calvin (1:55) concludes, simply "allows himself to cut some [kings] out of the series . . . to aid the reader's memory." Similarly, McN., 2; BJ (1953) to 1:17; Green, 53; Bonn., 15; Gund., 16. The "begat" at the end of 1:8, therefore, "must be understood *mediately*, like the word *Son* [of David and of Abraham] in the first verse" (Beng.).

1:10 ". . . and Manasseh the father of Amos, and Amos the father of Josiah." Amon was king; Amos was prophet. Our best Greek texts (*S*, *B*, *C*) have Amos (*K*, *L*, *W* have Amon). It is possible to call the middle line of Matthew's genealogy, in fact, the *prophetic* line (following the first, patriarchal line) because of the character of Israel's history along this line between 1000 and 600 B.C. Matthew's gratuitous insertion of Amos the prophet into the genealogical line of kings simply highlights this prophetic fact in Israel's history (cf. Gund., 16). The same sovereign freedom that allowed Matthew to put women in his patriarchal line encourages him to put prophets in his prophetic line. (Asaph, as we saw at Matt 1:7, cf. esp. 13:35, is also a *prophet*.)

Brown, 61, has little patience with this thesis of prophets and suggests that the source of Matthew's Asaph-Amos is simple error; he points to Matt 23:35 and 27:9 for other examples of Matthew's errancy. Green, 53, notes that Asa and Asaph "are only variant forms of the same name" and holds that while it is possible that Matthew intends to include prophets in Jesus' genealogy this way, "not very much can be built on this." Sober historical exegesis talks like this. Theological exegesis, without abandoning the cautions of historical science, looks for patterns and meanings. The meaning of judgment in the second line is suggested not only by the context of impending judgment in this period but by the presence in our best texts of the prophet of judgment himself, Amos. The fact that Matthew's Amos is removed about a hundred years from his correct location in history makes no difference at all to an evangelist who is writing not only history but, supremely, gospel, and educational, theological gospel at that.

C. Line Three: From Exile to the Christ: The Long March and the Doctrine of Divine Good Faith (1:12–16)

The third and final series of names leads *up* again—this time to Jesus the Christ. This line teaches the good faith or faithfulness of God. God's middle word is judgment; but judgment is never intended to be (though to unbelief it is) God's last word. God's last word to faith is divine *good faith*.

God had promised Abraham a universally blessed Seed (Gen 12:1–3; 22:18)—and Israel waited; and God had promised David a Son forever upon his throne (2 Sam 7:12ff; 1 Chr 17:11ff)—and Israel looked. And en route God brought Israel *up* in mercy, *down* in judgment, and finally *in* by faith—in to the Seed of Abraham and the Son of David, the Messiah himself.

Around 1000 B.C. under King David, God's promises had seemed imminent—an era of unprecedented prosperity and possibility, a kind of millennium seemed to dawn ahead (as at the beginning of our twentieth century, incidentally). But the 500s of the first millennium before Christ were years of hell for Israel—out of the land, away from the temple, by the waters of Babylon, under judgment, Israel wept. Yet it was precisely when God seemed most distant and his promises most unreal that God was, in fact, shaping his third and climactic series of messianic ancestors.

When Israel thought everything had fallen apart, God started to put it all together again. He brought Jesus the Christ.

I believe that the most important single fact for Matthew in the composition of his genealogy was what the genealogy chronicled as a whole: that God keeps his Word (though outwardly, and for some time, it does not look this way). God had promised Abraham and David something big, and though it took a long time, God delivered. "The mills of God grind exceeding slow, but they grind." This is the meaning for Matthew of the whole history of Israel, of the entire Old Testament, and of this little thumbnail summary of the Old Testament called Matthew's genealogy. "Look," he says, "God promised a Christ and he brought him." And between the promise and its delivery God used the ups and downs of Israel beneficently to shape a little theology of divine mercy, judgment, and good faith. All God's works begin in mercy, proceed through judgment, and issue in good faith. God is love, but *holy* love, and, finally, *faithful* love (*ḥesed*). This is Matthew's reading of the Old Testament. Matthew took the spectacles of the Christ and with them he read his Old Testament. With these spectacles, and only with them, a person can make sense of Old Testament (and world) history and their outward hopelessness. Jesus is the fulfillment of everything the Old Testament is trying to say. Jesus is the Word that makes the words make sense. Jesus is the Christ.

"The Church believes that . . . in her most benign Lord and Master can be found the key [*clavem*], the focal point [*centrum*], and the goal [*finem*] of all human history." ("The Pastoral Constitution on the Church in the Modern World," 10; *The Second Vatican Council*, 1965)

It is a common complaint that the church's preaching tends historically either to be too sentimental or too scolding. That is, it tends to preach either a saccharine mercy without justice or it scolds judgmentally with too little love. Love without justice is insipid, and justice without love is harsh. The thesis of mercy and its (seeming) antithesis of justice need a synthesis, and this synthesis is supplied by God in good faith in bringing Jesus as the Christ, the whole point of the genealogy.

God's deep and wide mercy must always be in the forefront of our preaching (Matthew's four women), but never without the note of the judgment of God (Matthew's four alterations), or else mercy gets maudlin. God's holy justice and his severe judgment against social injustice (by the people of God especially) must always be near the center of our preaching and sound more profoundly from our churches (Asaph and Amos), but never, even in the most prophetic preaching, without proceeding finally to God's own last Word—to Christ, God's good faith in human form.

1:16a "and Jacob the father of Joseph the husband of Mary, of whom Jesus was born, who is called Christ." Matthew says the father of Joseph was Jacob; Luke says the father of Joseph was Heli (Luke 3:23). "Who was Jesus' grandfather?" (This is the title of a full discussion in Brown, 86–90.) The almost unanimous exegetical answer to this question is that it is best not to try to harmonize Matthew's and Luke's genealogies.

Why did Matthew go to all the trouble of tracing Jesus' Abrahamic-Davidic family tree down to Jesus' father Joseph, only at the last moment to deny Joseph biological paternity? The non-Semitic reader is a little put off by this last minute switch. It is apparently not as disconcerting to the people of the Bible. For "by Palestinian law, the head of a family was no less the father of his adopted children than of those children that he had procreated" (Bonn., 17). Joseph's fatherhood was no less God-given than ours: ours comes through the mystery of nature; Joseph's came through God's miraculous creative power (Schl., *Das*, 8). Jesus is a bona fide son of David by virtue of God's giving him Joseph (who *is* a biological son of David) to be his legal father, as the next paragraph will explain in some detail. Jesus *is* an actual, legal son of David. Beare, 67, shows that if a *virgin* birth of a son of David is to be recorded, Jesus will *have* to be adopted, not generated, by a male descendant of David. "The genealogy and the story of the miraculous conception [in the next paragraph], accordingly, are not incompatible with one another," Beare concludes, "but complementary."

It is not necessary to put Mary in David's line: "I must admit that it cannot be certainly established" (Cal., 1:54). Furthermore, it is Matthew's design to give Joseph's genealogy, not Mary's. Even if Mary were of the line of David, in Israel "descent was not traced in the female line" (Beare, 67).

Summary One: The Kingdom of God: Introduction to the Doctrine of the Sovereignty of God

In his summary at the end of the genealogy (1:17), Matthew writes almost exultantly, "Therefore, all the generations from Abraham to David were fourteen, and from David to the Babylonian Captivity fourteen, and from Babylonian Captivity to the coming of Christ fourteen." For Matthew this three times fourteen said order, harmony, and meaning. When Matthew looks back over the history of the old people of God and sees fourteen generations between key periods in the people's history—between Abraham, David, Exile, and the Christ—he is impressed, in a word, with the *sovereignty* of God. Behind, under, above, and through all the chaos, sin, and rebellion of Israel's up-and-down history, God was working his purpose out as year succeeds to year. To the human participants in this history, things didn't look too orderly. But when one looks back on Old Testament history through the lens that the history of Jesus Christ offers, one sees that God's hand was steady and sure, that the historical "N-shape" had a draftsman, that God was in control. Three times fourteen means the sovereignty of God.

In his genealogy Matthew shows that Jesus not only (as in his miracles) exorcizes present evil, but that he exorcizes past and future evil too, by casting out of history the demon of meaninglessness.

It is well known that Matthew loves to show how Jesus fulfilled the Old Testament; Matthew often writes: "this happened so that what the Lord said through the prophet might be fulfilled" (see especially chapters 1 and 2 of the Gospel). In his genealogy, however, Matthew shows fulfillment not only of particular passages in the Old Testament but of *the Old Testament as a whole*. Jesus is the fulfillment of the whole Old Testament story and of all its events taken together in their totality.

Summary Two: Biblical Freedom: Introduction to the Doctrine of Holy Scripture

Matthew's several liberties in his genealogy, particularly the "four alterations" in his second series of fourteen, have something introductory to teach us about the doctrine of Holy Scripture. First, as we have seen, between Joram and Uzziah in 1:8, Matthew skips four whole chapters in 2 Chronicles and drops three historical persons: Ahaziah (2 Chr 22), Joash (2 Chr 23–24), and Amaziah (2 Chr 25). Ahaziah is a minor figure, but Joash and Amaziah are important; together they occupy over half a century of Israel's most fateful history (837–783 B.C.). And at the end of the second line, Matthew omits still another person—Jehoiakim (2 Chr 36:1–8; 609-598 B.C.). Only by omitting these four figures is Matthew able to get his magic fourteen.

Various reasons have been advanced for Matthew's omissions, as we have seen: for example, at least three of these persons were placed under an explicit curse of God and that therefore the evangelist hesitated, not wishing to have cursed persons in the genealogy of the Christ; that Matthew had access to other lists of kings than those we have in our canonical Old Testament; or a third theory, that Matthew unintentionally missed four figures. I confess to skepticism toward all three theories. (a) About the cursed kings, Matthew did not hesitate to place the four dubious women (or, more precisely, their dubious husbands) in his first series, since it was exactly such who focused the great facts of the gospel incomparably: the free mercy of God and the catholicity of the church. (b) About Matthew's other lists, I believe that Matthew's texts of the kings were more or less those available to us in our Hebrew and Greek Bibles and their translations. (c) And about Matthew's simply missing these kings: perhaps, but I doubt it.

I respectfully submit the hypothesis that Matthew intentionally dropped these four persons in order more clearly to make his three-times-fourteen point—that God works in sovereign order. Matthew knew that his readers could read, that they could check his list of kings with the Old Testament's lists any time they wanted. Matthew was not trying to put something over on us; he was, with the sovereign freedom appropriate to an evangelist of Jesus Christ, letting history preach gospel. Matthew dropped about four chapters and four kings from his Old Testament genealogy in order to have a smoother, more memorable chronology—in order to get fourteen. (This is also John Calvin's interpretation, 1:55–60, see above, p. 11.)

Matthew did not falsify, he simplified—Uzziah *was* the son of Jothan according to the rabbinic rule that "the sons of sons are also sons." In obedience to the *point* of Scripture and of this genealogy—Jesus the Christ—Matthew sharpened the *pointers* to him—the Old Testament witnesses—because he believed that this best "made the point."

Can we imitate Matthew? Can we follow in Matthew's footsteps in the matter of biblical usage, as Matthew followed in Christ's (see Jesus' freedom with Scripture, for example, in chapters 5, 15, and 19 of this Gospel)? Every Christian sermon does. Every sermon or Christian message is a rereading and a reshaping of the biblical witness for particular hearers. The question is this: Is this shaping true to the point of the text? Or does it miss the point?

There is a final textual curiosity in the genealogy, which will also illumine the doctrine of Scripture in Matthew's Gospel. The third series, if counted carefully, has only thirteen members, not Matthew's beloved fourteen. Two of the traditional solutions for this seeming discrepancy are these: (1) that number thirteen is "Jesus" and number fourteen is "who is called the Christ," referring to the return of Christ in glory (as distinguished from the historical Jesus), or (2) that number thirteen in the series is *Mary* and number fourteen is Jesus who is called the Christ. The argument for both these seemingly desperate measures, an argument not to be altogether despised, is that Matthew could count.

But I find these solutions unsatisfying. I prefer for theological reasons to live with the possibility that Matthew made a mistake. (In the Notes, below, I will offer other interpretations.) I can count, too, but that does not mean that I cannot miscount. Is an inspired author given an even mathematical inspiration? I do not think so. If we pursue this question far enough we are driven to Jesus himself. We solemnly and rightly confess that Jesus is both God and man. If we take his humanity seriously and do not divinize it by confusing the natures and so rob him of a whole dimension of his reality, then we allow him to make mistakes, too. I do not believe that as a child or young man Jesus got one hundred on *all* his papers, that he never stumbled in the dark, or that he made every basket (or whatever he played) that he shot in the backyard. True humanity means mistakes; being human means errors. Jesus shared our human nature entirely, excepting only *sin*, as the author of the Epistle to the Hebrews assures us; the author does not say "and excepting errors, too." (Heb 4:15; cf. Chalcedon, A.D. 451: "in *all* things like unto us, without *sin*"). "A disciple is not above his Lord," not even a canonical evangelist. Matthew made mistakes. Let us rejoice in this. It is precisely the wonder of the gospel that it is passed on in earthen, not golden vessels in order, as Paul once said of his own ministry, that the exceeding greatness of the treasure of the gospel might by contrast be all the more impressive (2 Cor 4:7).

I *like* Matthew's thirteen. I like it precisely because it "de-magics" Scripture, humanizes, and normalizes it. I find it enhances that to which it points: a Christ who both then *and* today, in Scripture then and in disciples now, uses fallible witnesses to make an infallible point.

I prefer to speak in this way of Matthew's work rather than to speak too dismissively of the nonhistoricity of his genealogy or biblical citations (as in, e.g., Bult., 354; Conz., 27f). Brown, 562, especially, shows that finding even large parts of Matthew's infancy narratives technically unhistorical is not the same as finding them untrue or finding Scripture uninspired. "The acceptability of this approach [to Scripture] involves a recognition that there are ways other than history by which a people can be instructed. I have little hope that those for whom history is the only biblical genre will be open to such an approach" (cf. also Brown, 26, 31–37; similarly, Green, 50–51; Fitz., 17–18).

This free, evangelical approach to Scripture is as old in church history as is the witness to the Gospel of Mark by Papias in the early second century: "When Mark became Peter's interpreter, he wrote down accurately though by no means in order [!], as much as he remembered of the words and deeds of the Lord; for he [Mark] had neither heard the Lord nor been in his company, but subsequently joined Peter, as I said. Now Peter did not intend to give a complete exposition of the Lord's ministry but delivered his instructions to meet the needs of the moment. It follows, then, that Mark was guilty of no blunder if he wrote, simply to the best of his recollections, an incomplete account" (Eusebius, *Ecclesiastical History*, 3:39:15). Conservative Christians should consult now the "Theological Postscript" of Gundry's Matthew commentary, 623–40, to see the intellectual freedom possible for evangelical Bible students, precisely because of the freedom exemplified by the evangelist Matthew himself.

We want to read Holy Scripture as Matthew's Christ did. And *he* said, "I did not come to destroy the law and the prophets [that is, the Scriptures], I came to fulfil them" (Matt 5:17). I believe that it is demonstrable from the Gospel texts that (in the evangelist's opinion) Jesus read Holy Scripture as the words of God. The temptations story is the most impressive evidence of this fact (Matt 4:1–11, where all three times Satan is routed by Jesus' peremptory, "It is written"). And here again, "a disciple is not above his or her Lord." If Jesus read Scripture as his way of listening to God, who am I not to listen this way or to listen less reverently? If he needed Scripture, how much more so do we? Our problem everywhere in the church—and not least in the evangelical churches—is not too much attentiveness to Scripture, it is too little. And we need, most of all, to be attentive to that *to which* Scripture gives its central attention: the point. "You search the scriptures, because you think that in *them* you have eternal life; and it *is* they that bear witness to me; yet you refuse to come *to me* that you may have life" (John 5:39–40 RSV, italics added). The Scripture's *Christ*—not just the Scripture—gives life (cf. also 2 Tim 3:15). It bears repeating: The Bible is not about the Bible. In the final analysis Holy Scripture, like the Holy Spirit, "does not bear witness to itself." It exists to point to Jesus Christ and to encourage confidence in him.

Matthew's gratuitous three times fourteen and particularly his fallible thirteen do not diminish this point; they enhance it. Even with Matthew's mathematics, Jesus Christ is preached. The four royal subtractions are permissible because they allow a clearer pointing to the kingdom or sovereignty of God; the error of thirteen is covered because, after all, the gospel is not about the infallibility of Matthew. The gospel is about the Lord Jesus Christ and his miraculous ability to use errant witnesses to make his inerrant case. (And it can be added, parenthetically, that many errors of Holy Scripture are about as consequential as Matthew's thirteen here—rather inconsequential.) John the Baptist's Christ-pointing finger ("Behold the lamb of God!"), like his fiery message, is crooked and craggy, but it points the right way (a lesson that Karl Barth liked to make from Grünewald's painting of the crucifixion). The prophets and apostles did not always count right, but by a divine condescension their *sums* were almost always perfect.

It is these *sums, affirmations,* and *teachings* of Scripture (and not Scripture's incidentals) that are covered by divine inspiration; the humanity (and so the fallibility) of the authors is left intact and untouched. Affirmation and utterance are two different things. This dual witness, this divinity and humanity of Scripture, is spelled out admirably in several contemporary church confessions. "Therefore, since everything asserted [*asserunt*] by the inspired authors or sacred writers must be held to be asserted by the Holy Spirit, it follows that the books of Scripture must be acknowledged as teaching firmly, faithfully, and without error *that truth which God wanted put into the sacred writings for the sake of our salvation.* . . . However, since God speaks in sacred Scripture through men *in human fashion,* the interpreter of sacred Scripture, in order to see clearly what God wanted to communicate to us, should carefully investigate what meaning the sacred writers *really intended,* and what God wanted to manifest by means of their words." ("Dogmatic Constitution on Divine Revelation [*Dei Verbum*]," 11–12; *The Second Vatican Council,* 1964).

Another beautiful remark in this same Constitution on this subject follows: "The sacred authors wrote the four Gospels, selecting some things from the many which had been handed on by word of mouth or in writing, reducing some of them to a synthesis [theological Matthew!], explicating some things in view of the situation of their churches and preserving the form of proclamation *but always in such fashion that they told us the honest truth about Jesus*" (19).

A recent United Presbyterian confession, in the Reformation tradition, puts it this way: "The one sufficient revelation of God is Jesus Christ, the Word of God incarnate, to whom the Holy Spirit bears unique and authoritative witness through the Holy Scriptures, which are received and obeyed as the word of God written. The Scriptures are not a witness among others, but the witness without parallel. . . . The Scriptures, given under the guidance of the Holy Spirit, are nevertheless the words of men, conditioned by . . . the places and times at which they were written. They reflect views of life, history, and the cosmos which were then current." *The Confession of 1967*, 27, 29. Finally, from the conservative-evangelical churches: "We affirm the divine inspiration, truthfulness, and authority of both Old and New Testament Scriptures in their entirety as the only written word of God, without error *in all that it affirms* [*N.B.*], and the only infallible rule of faith and practice." *The Lausanne Covenant* (1974), article 2. Cf. Donald Bloesch, *Essentials of Evangelical Theology* (San Francisco: Harper and Row, 1978), vol. 1, chap 4.

On Matthew's apparently erroneous thirteen generations (cf. 1:17 and 1:12–16), Jerome, 1:74, explains that the error is the fault of copyists who confounded the names Jechoniah and Jehoiakim in orthography, and, consequently, "the fourteenth generation will be counted as that of Christ himself" (*quarta decima uero generatio in ipsum Christum reputabitur;* 1:76). Does Jerome mean that the fourteenth generation is Christ's church? Chrysostom, 4:1:21, believes the fourteenth generation includes "both the time of the captivity, and Christ Himself, by every means connecting Him with us." By "the time of the captivity," Chrysostom appears to count the fifty plus years of captivity (589/88–538 B.C.) as a fourteenth generation; an unusual interpretation. By "Christ Himself" I take it that Chrysostom means, like Jerome who uses the same words (above), that the fourteenth generation is Christ's generation of, or presence with, the church, another unusual interpretation and not something Matthew speaks of in this language. (But see Matt 19:28 where Jesus speaks of the "*regeneration*"—*palinggenesia*—when the Son of Man sits in judgment.)

Calvin's interpretation, 1:61, is typically careful: "That we only read of thirteen has probably happened through the fault or error of copyists." (Calvin's commentaries make clear that Calvin was not, as his *Institutes* can occasionally make one think, a biblical inerrantist. He speaks frequently of errors, even of the Gospel writers themselves, as, e.g., 3:211; cf. 3:2–3, 66, 71, 177, etc.).

Is it possible that the fourteenth generation in line three is the unnamed but major "generation" in the entire series—the *divine* "generation" of Jesus in the womb of Mary? This is possible, but it stretches language to the breaking point, since "generation," then, is given two meanings. (Gundry, 19, believes, indeed, that "the one chronological generation carries two other kinds of generation within it, a legal [Joseph's] and a physical [Mary's].") A recent Matthew commentary brings us full circle to the view of Jerome with which we began this survey: "There is no fully satisfactory explanation of the fact that the last section actually contains only thirteen generations. Possibly Matthew thought of a further genealogy elapsing between the birth of Jesus and his effective assumption of Messiahship (. . . 26:64; 28:18) [observing] the frequent deprecating references [in Matthew's Gospel] to 'this generation' (11:16; 12:39ff; 23:36, etc.)," Green, 54 (this is also similar to Stendahl's eschatological view cited above).

Putting aside the baffling thirteen, the *meaning* of Matthew's mathematically curious but theologically wonderful third genealogical line, good faith, is best caught by the prophet Amos (9:11): "In that day I will raise up the booth of David that is fallen," or by the second verse of the Bible, "Darkness was upon the face of the deep; and the Spirit of God was moving over the face of the waters."

Summary Three: The Genealogy as a Whole and Its Little Theology of God

Matthew has taken a list of some forty names and transformed it into a little theology of God. What in the hands of a less gifted writer would have been dry as the Sahara—a genealogy—turns, in Matthew's hands, into a collection of gems. For the genealogy reveals what theology calls *God's nature*. God's mercy, justice, and faithfulness—these are the elements of Matthew's little theology of God in his three-pronged, *N*-shaped genealogy.

When seen from above, these three threads in God's tapestry called Israel weave the pattern of *the sovereignty of God* (Summary 1, above). When seen from below, in the humanity of Matthew's handling of these threads, the tapestry spells a doctrine of *the Scriptures of God*—the humanity of the divine Word (Summary 2, above). Just as when a rug is turned over and we see the knots and joinings its maker has put there, so when we look at Matthew's genealogy from beneath, we see something of his artistry and occasionally, from one point of view, his fallibility (thirteen). A modern university might not like its historians to do history with Matthew's freedom of addition, subtraction, alteration, and proofreading. On the other hand, a little history taught with Matthew's panache, a few lists of kings with the flair of Matthew's freedom, might not be a bad idea.

God's mercy, justice, and good faith (seen from the twin angles of God's ordering-sovereignty and scriptural-humanity) are the gifts of the genealogy to theology. Later, Matthew's Jesus will ask *us* for these three good gifts: "justice and mercy and good faith; these things you ought to have done . . ." (Matt 23:23). But Matthew's God gives them to us before he asks them of us.

Matthew's achievement in this opening, seventeen-verse prelude has been to teach a remarkably deep doctrine of God—without ever using God's name. It is characteristic of Matthew to use the divine name sparingly (e.g., his preference for "kingdom of heaven" over "kingdom of God"). Matthew tries hard not to take the divine name in vain. Matthew talks about God mainly by talking about Jesus. Matthew would have this be the church's main method of talking about God, too.

I suggest that this is one way out of the current embarrassment with God-talk. It has been rightly felt that there is a promiscuous use of the divine name abroad, that there is much talk of God with little reliable content. Matthew's method provides a solution. We let God define God, as he has done in the Old and New Testament witnesses to Christ. Careful expository teaching of Scripture is the way to talk of God reliably; other references to deity, no matter how earnest or even eloquent, are in danger of irresponsibility because they are not said in immediate response to God's own self-revelation in the biblical Christ. But when Jesus' story is told, God unveils himself. It is possible to move quite sparingly with the divine name and yet say a great deal about it. God's name does not ordinarily have to appear for God to be present—but Jesus' name does. For Jesus, as we see with clarity in the next section in the Gospel, is the way God is *with* us.

For church-historical references to God's attributes of mercy, judgment, and good faith, see the whole fifth chapter of *The Scots Confession* (1560) and Calvin, *Inst.* (1560), I. x.2.

Matt 1:1–16: The Genealogy The overriding concern of the genealogy is to show that Jesus really was in and of the line of David—that he was the Son of David (Lohse, *huios David*, TWNT, 8:489). The oldest assertions about Jesus' descent in the New Testament are assertions that Jesus was the promised Son of David; but some historical-critical exegesis believes that the genealogies of Matthew and Luke were created artificially to verify this assertion historically (e.g., Conz., 27f).

Why did Matthew begin his Gospel with, of all things, a (normally uninteresting) genealogy? First, a genealogy is not uninteresting to serious Jews, particularly to rabbis who, especially in Matthew's time, took a lively interest in them (Büchsel, *genealogia*, TWNT, 1:661–62). Second, a genealogy that summarizes Old Testament history as succinctly as Matthew's serves as an ideal bridge between the Old and New Testaments. Third, a genealogy establishes a person's real humanity. Matthew's genealogy, like Luke's, packed with real human beings, assures us that Jesus "is no demigod from pagan mythology but a real man with a family tree" (Caird, 77). Fourth, of more theological significance, in Jerome's words (1:72), Matthew "begins with the realities of Jesus' fleshly nature in order that through the man we might begin to learn God." The human genealogy teaches the divine nature.

Matthew's personalized genealogy reminds readers of the genealogies of the Yahwist (J) document in Genesis; see Gen 4:17, 20–22, 26; 5:29, and Skinner, *Genesis*, 2. (Ordinarily, Matthew's more formal style puts one in mind of the Priestly document [P], and it is Mark's freer, earthier manner that recalls the J document.)

1:17 "So all the generations from Abraham to David were fourteen generations, and from David to the deportation to Babylon fourteen generations, and from the deportation to Babylon to the Christ fourteen generations" (RSV). The three-times-fourteen pattern honors the Messiah's coming as nonaccidental and as the fruit of the sovereignty of God, Str.-B., 1:43; Schl., *Das*, 6; Schl., *Der*, 6; Grund., 62; Davies, 73; Hill, 74; Schw., 24, 26; Streck., 89; Brown, 68f. Bultmann, 357, does not believe that the three-times-fourteen scheme originates with Matthew; Brown, 70, shows how it can.

Matthew's and Luke's genealogies of Jesus cannot be reconciled. We have seen Calvin's freedom in this connection already (at 1:12–16 above); he writes here that Matthew, because of his three fourteens, "felt free to overlook some names which [the historical] Luke had no right to omit, as [Matthew] did not tie himself to that [historical] rule" (1:58). The frequently heard opinion that Matthew's infancy narratives come from Joseph and his family and that Luke's come from Mary and her family (e.g., by Bengel) is nothing more than pious deduction (Brown, 35). Matthew's and Luke's infancy narratives are not only different, they are, as Brown, 36, shows with documentation, "contradictory to each other in a number of details."

We may say, then, quite openly, that Matthew's genealogy is a work of theological craftsmanship more than it is a simple historical list. It is not only a genealogy; it is a theology. It is not only history; it is sermon. If it is called artificial (Davies, 62; Brown, 74), as historical interpretation must call it, it is not the artificiality of myth-making, but the artifact of a theological architect.

Matthew is seeking with historical names to say that history has come to its point, that the history of the people of God since Christ is *continuous* with the history of the people of God before Christ, and that this long history has simply received its term or final stage in the coming of the long-expected Seed of Abraham, Son of David, the Christ (Davies, 72; Meier, *Vis.*, 53). On the other hand, Jesus is *discontinuous* with holy history, for he is a whole new departure in history, a new creation of the Spirit of God, an event as momentous as creation itself. The apostle Paul does a great deal with both facts (continuity and discontinuity) theologically. Meier, *Vis.*, 53, best summarizes Matthew's theological statement in the mathematical seventeenth verse: "Matthew shows the believer that, when you 'add up' the meaning of history, the 'bottom line' is Jesus Christ, the son of David."

While there are fourteen names (not including the nongenerating twin, Zerah) and thirteen historical generations between Abraham and David (Matthew, Luke, and 1 Chronicles agree here), there are, historically, considerably more than fourteen generations between David and Exile (about eighteen; Luke has twenty-one) and between Exile and Jesus (there are about twenty-one, as Luke 3:23 -27 and other contemporary accounts indicate). But Matthew's *list*, which may have been handed down to him as sacred tradition, can be computed in such a way that, counting David twice and counting Josiah twice just before the Babylonian Exile (and Matt 1:17 itself counts both David and Exile twice, it should be noted), one can, with a little imagination, get three times fourteen (when, for example, one inserts or understands the words "by God" after the theological passive "was born" in 1:16). And if the thirteen generations between Exile and Jesus bother one unduly, then, as we have seen, the *divine* generation of Jesus (in Mary, and between the names Joseph and Jesus) can be counted as a fourteenth "generation." But I still find this double use of generation contrived.

One can derive pleasure but not much benefit from the several other attempts to understand the three times fourteen: Gematria, where the letter values of David's Hebrew name equal fourteen—D equals 4; V equals 6; D equals 4; the lunar month, with fourteen days of a waxing moon (Abraham to David), fourteen days of a waning moon (David to Exile), and a final fourteen to the full moon of the Christ; three times fourteen equals forty-two, and in Revelation 13:5 forty-two months are allotted to evil before God's final intervention; three times fourteen equals six times seven, equals six weeks of waiting and the seventh salvation week (Bonn., 15).

Excessive attention to numbers or to strange details—i.e., tricky theology—has never been a healthy exercise in the church and has contributed to theological aberrations (e.g., theological Dispensationalism); such provide a basis for the apostolic warning to charge persons *not* "to occupy themselves with . . . endless genealogies which promote speculations rather than the divine training that is in faith" (1 Tim 1:3–4).

II. THE BIRTH OF THE MESSIAH: GOD THE SPIRIT, THE IN-US GOD, BRINGING DEITY INTO THE WORLD (1:18–20)

"I believe in Jesus Christ, . . . who was conceived by the Holy Spirit, born of the Virgin Mary." (*The Apostles' Creed*)

According to Matthew's Gospel, God's definitive revelation of God does not occur in impersonal nature or in random social history, but in the particular nature and in the social history of Jesus of Nazareth and His–Story—in Old Testament preparation and New Testament presentation. Nature and history by themselves are equivocal and ambiguous. Only the Messiah Jesus finally and fully unveils the true God personally, savingly, and responsibly in history. The church holds this exclusive first principle tenaciously, however narrow it may seem to others to be. This New Testament, Christ-centered exclusivity, the equivalent and continuation of the Old Testament war against idols, is an important part of the necessary offense of the gospel and its "scandal of particularity."

The church's second principle, the one to which we now proceed in Matthew's story, is that *only the Holy Spirit* can bring Christ inside persons.

"Now the birth [literally, the genesis*] of Jesus Christ was like this. When his mother Mary had been legally engaged to Joseph, before they came together, it was discovered that she was expecting a baby—by the Holy Spirit. Joseph, her fiancé, was a righteous man, but he did not want to shame Mary. So he decided to divorce her quietly. When he had given serious thought to all these things, look, an angel of the Lord appeared to him in a dream, and this is what he said: 'Joseph, son of David, don't be afraid to take Mary as your wife, because what has been brought to life in her happened by the Holy Spirit'" (1:18–20).*

The Holy Spirit is mentioned twice in these three verses and both times, in the same words, the Spirit is explicitly called the source of Jesus in Mary—*ek pneumatos hagiou*. The Holy Spirit is the one who brings Jesus to birth in persons, the one who makes Jesus alive in human life, who makes Jesus historical and real.

The genesis of Jesus inside human life is the exclusive work of the Holy Spirit, the *Creator Spiritus,* who began the world's *creation* (Gen 1:2) and who now generates the world's *salvation.* The permanent value of the creedal doctrine of the Spirit's conception of Jesus in the virgin Mary is this: it is the Holy Spirit *and not human initiative* that brings Jesus into historical and personal life (then of Mary's, now of ours). When Jesus Christ comes to anyone in history, even in his first coming to Mary, it is always the result of the work of the Holy Spirit, not of human preparation or enterprise. Every conversion is a virgin birth. Divine initiative does not demean the human work of Christian ministry any more than it diminishes Joseph's prior engagement to Mary; it simply protects the sole source of the miracle of New Life (cf. 1 Cor 3:6–7).

"With human beings this [New Life] is impossible; but with God absolutely everything is possible" (Matt 19:26). Only God can reveal God; only God the Holy Spirit can enable human beings to receive God. The Holy Spirit is the miraculous How of New Life. Mary's virginal conception, by the power of the Holy Spirit alone, teaches this thrilling doctrine of the Holy Spirit *pictorially.*

A. The Gospel of the Story: God's Ways Are Not Ours

When the Holy Spirit brings Jesus into history, much that good people think proper is contradicted. In Galilee, the provenance of this story, an engaged man and woman were not to come together as husband and wife until their marriage. Consequently, Mary's pregnancy before marriage was humiliating for Joseph. Why should the Gospel story begin on such a scandalous note?

The old people of God had been prepared by the stories of the patriarchs and the birth accounts of Isaac and Jacob in particular to know that at the great turning points in sacred history God intervened miraculously in conceptions. But apparently the old people of God never anticipated a messianic virgin birth. What we have before us is quite unique, not to surrounding cultures—many of which had stories of the virgin-conceptions of heroes—but unique to Jewish messianic expectation. If it was God's intention to introduce the Messiah to Israel by means of a virgin birth it is difficult to see how this virgin birth could have occurred without embarrassment to someone. It would have been possible to reduce embarrassment, however, by involving only one person—Mary *prior to any engagement*—rather than by involving two persons, betrothed Mary and Joseph, as in our story.

Seen in the context of the entire Gospel, the initially embarrassing pregnancy of Mary may have served Matthew's purpose by showing at the very beginning of the story of Jesus Christ that God's ways are not our ways and that God's righteousness is not our righteousness.

Joseph, Matthew says pointedly, was "a righteous man." And Joseph found what was happening offensive. But Joseph was overcome by a divine intervention, and he made a new decision—the decision to marry Mary. Joseph now dared to believe the Word that Mary's child was *God*-given and so decided to go this initially embarrassing and lonely route of marrying a pregnant fiancée. From the instant that Jesus appeared on the world scene, even at his conception, he caused righteous people *to rethink what was righteous.* In Jesus a revaluation of all values commences in history, a revaluation that has never ceased wherever the gospel of Jesus appears.

1:19 "and her husband Joseph, being a just man and [*kai*] unwilling to put her to shame, resolved to divorce her quietly" (RSV). Whether Joseph's righteousness is (a) *merciful* righteousness (translating the *kai* in the middle of the sentence as "and," thus RSV; Schw., 30–31) or (b) *strict* righteousness (translating the *kai* as "but," thus TEV; cf. the NEB with the equivalent "and at the same time," which creates the tension of "but"; Cal., 1:61–62; Brown, 122–27, convincingly), or (c) both (Bonn., 20), Joseph, in any case, *acted* mercifully, thus going beyond the requirements of the law—the earliest example in the Gospel of the "*exceeding* righteousness" required by Jesus of his disciples (Matt 5:20).

Surprising here is that Joseph's acted righteousness of mercy ("unwilling to put her to shame") led him to decide for a *divorce*. Legal engagement—betrothal—was as binding as marriage and could only be dissolved by divorce. (The word *apolusai* here, even in the Catholic exegete Brown, 128, has to mean divorce because of the word's usage in the rest of the Gospel, Matt 5:31–32; 19:3, 7–9.) This nativity text is not often enough drawn into discussions of divorce in Matt 5 and 19. The text teaches us that divorce *can* be considered an act of righteousness even in a Gospel that so stalwartly protects marriage against divorce. A certain Joseph-like righteousness may be later solicited in the expression, unique to Matthew's Jesus, in which Jesus forbids divorce "*except* on the ground of unchastity," 5:32; cf. 19:9–10 RSV, meaning that in certain cases of unchastity the disciple should divorce. It is remarkable that we find the problem of divorce as early as the opening narrative of the Gospel.

We must notice next that even the qualified righteousness of divorce—the very limit of the humanly possible—is *overcome* in our text by the intervening and superior saving righteousness of God, which commands and moves Joseph *not* to divorce, even though everything Joseph previously understood as righteousness told him that a quiet divorce was the only honorable solution. God's ways are not always our ways. For further discussion of this idea, see Schl., *Das*, 9; Schl., *Der*, 9–10; Lohm., 14.

By the decision to give Mary a letter of divorce "quietly," unguilty Joseph was prepared to take some of the social shame and personal guilt of the failed betrothal upon himself, without complaint (Grund., 68), and precisely that kind of decision is Christian righteousness, too, according to Matthew's Gospel. Christian righteousness, therefore, is not so much or only the determination to be personally impeccable (a frequent misunderstanding) as it is the determination, if necessary at one's own expense, to bear the guilt of others. (Bonhoeffer's *Ethics* and life speak often of this.) Substitutionary atonement is not only doctrinal truth, done by Christ, though it is that supremely; it is also ethical truth, done by Christ's people for other people.

B. The Doctrine of the Story: The Christocentricity of the Spirit

What is of greatest systematic importance in this text is the truth that the office of the Holy Spirit, from the very beginning of the Christian story, is to bring Jesus Christ into human life. The work of the Spirit is Christ-centeredness. We can learn from Matthew's first two references to the Spirit that the Spirit's main work is the earthly, historical work of making Jesus a living person in the inner life of another historical person. The Spirit's work is surprisingly human, even fleshly, *sakrōthenta*.

In *The Nicene Creed* (381) we confess with the universal church that we believe "in one Lord Jesus Christ, the only-begotten Son of God, . . . who for us men, and for our salvation, came down from heaven, and was incarnate [*sakrōthenta*, literally, "flesh-made"] by the Holy Spirit [*ek pneumatos hagiou*] of the Virgin Mary, and was made man."

Where the *Holy* Spirit is at work we find Jesus Christ being made *human.* Where other, sometimes seemingly holier spirits are at work we find Jesus Christ being made excessively spiritual and without much contact with the flesh at all. The apostle John said that the acid test of the spirits is whether they confess that Jesus Christ has come "*in the flesh*" [*en sarki*], "as a *human* being" (TEV), or whether they "loose" Christ's deity from his humanity and so allow him, like a loosed balloon, to fly mainly above us, spiritually, without any serious earthly contacts or problems at all (see 1 John 4:1–2).

Practically speaking this means that one test of a responsible doctrine of the Holy Spirit in our churches is this: Is Jesus Christ allowed to be a human being? Or is he too ghostly, yes, *too* divine? "This is how you will be able to know whether it is *God's* Spirit: anyone who acknowledges that Jesus Christ came as a *human* being has the Spirit who comes from God" (1 John 4:2 TEV). As we will see in this Gospel, there is a place for witness to Jesus as Very God of Very God, without the slightest diminution. But in our time, even in churches where Scripture and orthodox doctrine are thought to be taken with great seriousness, one of the most neglected doctrines of all has been the doctrine of the *true* humanity of Jesus Christ (and of his Scriptures, church, and Christians). Where Christ's humanity is not taken seriously, neither is the world's. (Here we have a fundamental reason for a spiritual Christianity's frequent failure in social ethics.)

It is my impression from a study of the doctrine of the Holy Spirit in the New Testament that the true humanity of Jesus Christ is one of the two major "lectures" of the Holy Spirit. (The other lecture is, in Paul's words, the Spirit's teaching us to say that "Jesus is *Lord,*" i.e., God.) To put this in another way, the Holy Spirit has two major works: first, to bring Christ *down* to earth and make him real and human to us (as here and in 1 John 4), and second, to lift him *up* as our divine Lord (as at the passion-resurrection and 1 Cor 12). In other words, the Holy Spirit is a good theologian and gives two main courses: The True Humanity of Jesus Christ the first semester and, the second semester, The True Divinity of Jesus Christ. (Sometimes, perhaps even frequently, we get these courses from the Spirit in the opposite order. I did.) It is the work of the Holy Spirit, by whatever course, to bring Jesus Christ *into* human lives. "Into" is the key preposition in the work of the Spirit.

The christocentricity of the Spirit's work is especially visible in the Johannine Paraclete doctrine of the Holy Spirit, where John's Jesus says the Spirit "will bear witness to *me*" (John 15:26), "will glorify *me*, . . . will take what is *mine* and declare it to you" (John 16:14). Similarly, Luke's Jesus tells the apostles that when the Holy Spirit of power comes "you shall be *my* witnesses" (Acts 1:8). In the whole New Testament, *Jesus* is the Spirit's point.

In fact, Matthew's Jesus comes to us literally "out of" (*ek*) the Holy Spirit. This word means that Jesus' entry into the life of Mary (and thus of the world) is the work of the Holy Spirit and not of any human being. *Ek* ("out of" or "by") is used seven times in the first chapter: four times of the four preceding mothers, a fifth time of Mary herself, and now twice of the Holy Spirit. By pointing to the *ek*-centric births of the four irregular women, Matthew was preparing the way for the great eccentricity of the Spirit-conception of Jesus in the virgin Mary. God's work is often, to human eyes, eccentric, off-center, odd, indeed even foolish and weak, as the cross most dramatically revealed (1 Cor 1), but as now Christmas reveals, too.

In summary, wherever there is the spirited preaching of Jesus Christ with the intention of making Jesus Christ alive in persons—the genesis of a new life for them, getting Jesus *into* them—there we are in the presence of the work of the Holy Spirit. For the mission of the Spirit is bringing Jesus into people's lives.

1:18c ". . . she was found to be with child of the Holy Spirit" (RSV). On the parallel consciously drawn by Matthew (and expected in rabbinic thought) between the Spirit at work in creation at the beginning of time (Gen 1:2) and the Spirit at work in messianic salvation now at the end of time, see Davies, 71. As the Spirit was active at the foundation of the world, so it was expected that the Spirit would be active at the world's renewal, Hill, 78. As the preposition most descriptive of the Spirit is *into,* so the adjective most descriptive of the Spirit is *creative,* Str.-B., 1:48; Schw., *pneuma,* TWNT, 6:399–400; Lohm., 18. Only God can give children, as the patriarchal narratives in Genesis, with their exciting stories of overcome barrenness, most prominently teach, Schw., 30. In both the Old and New Testaments "the Spirit is the power of God that enables . . . doing what human ability cannot achieve," Schw., *pneuma,* TWNT, 6:401.

Because of a legitimate concern for nonsexist language in the church, it is appropriate to point out that the word for "Spirit" in Scripture is not usually masculine. The Hebrew word for "Spirit" in the Old Testament, *ruah,* is feminine—"she"; the Greek word, *pneuma,* is neuter—"it" (cf. Brown, 124). In speaking and writing English we must make a choice of pronouns when referring to the Spirit—shall it be "he," "she," or "it"? The personal "she" is surely preferable to the impersonal "it" for the Spirit, and is probably preferable to a gratuitous "he"—why should male language get all the divine names? Without trying to be theologically cute or fashionable, I will use the feminine gender in referring to the Spirit. I will be glad when this usage does not attract attention to itself (or to my partial or token liberation). The Father and the Son already have masculine designations; theological equal opportunity and grammatical sensitivity permit us to refer to the Spirit (and to the church), in good conscience, with feminine pronouns. Though we cannot assume that Matthew thought yet of the Spirit in personal terms (as modern thought considers the personal), yet Matthew 10:20; 12:31–32; and 28:19 all suggest that the Spirit is more than impersonal. John's Paraclete texts (in John 14–16) are the first in the New Testament to move quite explicitly in the personal direction. See Brown, 125; BDF, 257.2. Unfortunately for the consistency of my thesis, John's Paraclete is masculine in gender. The synoptic Gospels' major symbolic term for the Spirit, however, *peristera,* "dove," is feminine. A biblically responsible and yet culturally sensitive language of divinity is difficult to fashion without offending some brothers and sisters. C. K. Barrett, *The Holy Spirit and the Gospel Tradition* (London: S.P.C.K., 1958), 35–38, discusses some older mischievous feminizations of the Spirit. For an antifeminist position from a doctrinally sensitive theologian, see Donald Bloesch, *The Battle for the Trinity: The Debate over Inclusive God-language* (Ann Arbor, Mich.: Vine Books, 1985); for a culturally sensitive "third way" that, nevertheless, sees the problems, culturally *and* theologically, with the feminization of the Spirit, cf. Randy Q. Maddox, "Toward an Inclusive Theology: The Systematic Implications of the Feminist Critique," *CSR 16*:1 (Sept. 1986), 7–23, esp. 16–17.

III. THE NAMING OF JESUS: GOD THE SON, THE WITH-US GOD, BEARING DEITY IN THE WORLD (1:21–23)

"I believe in Jesus Christ his only Son our Lord" (*The Apostles' Creed*).

Matthew now gives us two of the coming Messiah's names. In these we learn the essentials of the person and work of their bearer. They serve as an introduction to the doctrine of the person of Christ. After having taught Joseph that Mary's child was "of the Holy Spirit," the angelic message concluded by saying this:

"'She will have a baby boy, and you will give him the name "Ya-Sus" [Yah(weh)-Saves], because he himself will save his people from their sins.' Now this all happened so that the Word spoken by the Lord through the prophet would be fulfilled, which says, 'Look! The virgin will be expecting a baby, and she will give birth to a son, and people will give him the name "Emmanu-El,"' which, when translated, means 'God is with us!'" (1:21–23).

A. The First Name: "God-Saves" (Ya-Sus)

The Greek name *Iēsous* is the Hellenizing of the Hebrew *"Yeshua"* (familiar to us as "Joshua"), a shortening of *"Ye-ho-shuah,"* and means *"Yah(weh)* is the one who saves," or in simpler language, "God-Saves." The simplest meaning of the name given by the angel to Joseph, "Jesus," is that the man Jesus will be the agent of God's definitive salvation. But historical Christian theology has seen more here. In the two words of Jesus' name, "God-Saves," the church has believed we possess the two deepest definitions, in order, of the two major christological truths (1) of who Jesus finally *is* and (2) of what Jesus really *does*. (Cf. Fitz., 1:347, for Jesus' name.)

Matthew's way of putting it accents the mystery. "You will give him the name 'Ya-Sus' because he himself [*autos*] will save. . . ." Who is this who is emphasized as "he himself"? God or Jesus? Matthew, I believe, intends the fusion and confusion (or mystery). It is a first principle of all good theology that only God can save; "salvation is the *Lord's*" (Ps 3:8), "deliverance belongs to *the Lord*" (Jonah 2:9), "and *he* will redeem Israel from all his iniquities" (Ps 130:8) italics added.

Matthew's "he himself" grammatically can only mean Jesus. One possible conclusion—a conclusion that I admit I *want* to believe Matthew intends for his readers to draw in this particular text—is that Jesus is really, somehow, God—with us. And this is precisely what Matthew in 1:23 goes on to say that Jesus is.

Jesus is to be that rare person whose name means exactly what it says. "God-Saves" is not only Jesus' name, it is his perfect definition; if both words—God, saves—are taken with full seriousness, Jesus is known with full responsibility. If either word is diminished, so that Jesus is but an exalted representative or instrument of God or even a kind of son of God, but not Very God of Very God Himself, in person; or, on the other hand, if Jesus is indeed very helpful with our problems, or generally assists us, but does not utterly rescue us, liberate us, really *save* us— deeply and dramatically—then, in either case, the word *Jesus* is so diluted that he is only *homoi-ousios* (*like* God), he is not *homo-ousios* (sharing the very same divine substance with God, *Very* God). The name *Jesus* is to be invested with its full and literal signification: Jesus is the God himself who saves us himself.

At the same time, the name *Jesus* (or Joshua) was a common man's name, and Jesus is an entirely human being. How Jesus is both entirely human *and* entirely divine and how he is both without either "entirety" cancelling or diluting the other, is the great mystery of Christendom. But Christians have no difficulty in believing that God is capable of the combination.

Jesus will not be a god—or even God—*disguised* as a human being and walking around Palestine. To say that Matthew intends Jesus to be seen that way ruins the gospel, is heterodox (Docetism), and destroys Jesus' true humanity. At the same time, I do not think that a single story of the really human Jesus is understood in the evangelist's spirit without the *conclusion* that Jesus is no one less than the really saving Lord (Ya-Sus) who is

God with us (Emmanu-El). The texture of every Gospel paragraph is entirely human; the depth or meaning of every paragraph is thrillingly divine. Jesus is a human Jew— "Joshua"; Jesus is also divine Lord—"God-Saves," "Emmanuel." Only when seen through this dual optic does the gospel of Jesus make sense. And Matthew, perhaps quite unintentionally, begins to grind the lens of this dual optic here in the initial chapter of his Gospel, a lens that will be polished still more in John's Gospel.

Jesus' work is to save. Save whom? And from what? "Save his people from their sins" (1:21). The God-Saving work of Jesus is to rescue a whole social unit, a people (*laos*). Jesus does save individuals, but his purpose is to save them into a society, to make them citizens of a people.

The Gospel will later hear Jesus describe the people whom he will save, in words unique among the Gospels, as my "church" (*ekklēsia*, 16:18) or later, even more provocatively, as "a nation" (*ethnos*, 21:43). The singular in each instance (*laos, ekklēsia, ethnos*) is striking. We will watch the Jesus of the Gospel of Matthew form *a community*, a community that is well-grounded ethically (the Sermon on the Mount, 5–7), missionary (the Sermon on Mission, 10), Word-centered (the Sermon on the Kingdom, 13), disciplined and forgiving (the Sermon on the Congregation, 18–20), and adventist (the Sermon on Hope, 23–25). The purpose of this man named God-Saves is to salvage a people.

Who are "his people" in 1:21? The old or the new people of God? Jews or Christians? Israel or the church? (a) Israel: Schl., *Der*, 19; Schw., 31. (b) Church: Lohm., 11; Bonn., 421; Grund., 70; Meier, *Vis.*, 54 n. 17, pointing ahead to Matt 16:18. (c) Both Israel and the church: Chrys., 4:13:26: "To him that listens with understanding, [Matthew] darkly signifies the Gentiles too. For 'His people' are not the Jews only, but also all that draw nigh and receive the knowledge that is from [Jesus]." Also in this double sense, Streck., 99 n. 1; Brown, 131: "Israel, for Matthew, included both Jews and Gentiles." The idea of the people of God is beautifully developed in Vatican II's "Dogmatic Constitution on the Church (*Lumen Gentium*)."

This people is the "third race" of those who, whether Jew or gentile, are called into the community of Jesus the king. Christians are Christ's *ethnic group* (*ethnos*, 21:43), his people, his church, his nation, his own "fourth world." But more of this later. The important thing to see now is that the "whom" of the God-Saves is "his people" and to appreciate the communal, social, churchly dimension of the person and work of Christ.

The problem *from* which Jesus saves his people is also worth attention. "From their sins." The expression is so familiar to us by now that we must see how contrary it was and is to popular messianic expectation. The first Moses had given his people an (at least) *political* salvation from their oppressors—this is one of the most important meanings of the Exodus from Egypt. The second Moses—the coming Messiah—was expected to do the same. It was a well-worn rabbinic principle that "as the first Deliverer, so shall the second be." Therefore, the fact that we are *not* told here that Jesus "shall save his people *from their enemies*" (Luke will say this, but it is not what Matthew says), still comes as a disappointment to many.

There had been three great bondages in Israel's history: the Egyptian, the Babylonian, and now the Roman. A Messiah who came now and did not at least deliver the people politically could hardly be considered a serious or full-blooded Messiah.

A Liberator who came only to save from sins and not to save from sinners seemed piddly. A Messiah who did not save his people politically and economically must have struck a serious Jew as an excessively spiritual, insufficiently earthy, or (in the words of later Christian theology) as a docetic Messiah.

"He . . . will save his people from *their* sins." Jesus' central mission is to save his people not from *other* people's sins but from *their own*. "From *their* sins." Judgment begins with the household of God (cf. 1 Pet 4:17). The unmistakable focus of Jesus' work in this Gospel is first to liberate his people from their *own* imperialisms, colonialisms, structures, and sins. Matthew's Jesus will not rivet his people's attention on an external enemy, as most liberators and liberation movements do; he will not forge a burning hatred by which to ignite a revolutionary movement to action, as most revolutionaries, from Mattathias the Maccabean to the most recent Marxist-Leninists have found necessary. Rather, Jesus concentrates all his fire on *his* people, *his* church, and on *their* sins.

This was one of the most interesting discoveries in the study of the Gospel of Matthew. Hell, for example, is not a place with which the external enemies of the people of God are threatened; hell is always, in Jesus' teaching, the existential threat for precisely those who think they are *in* the people of God. This Gospel teaches profound self-criticism; it rarely permits God's people to descend to the cheaper, easier, and more immediately impressive envenoming of external enemies.

Has Jesus been co-opted? Did he compromise with the establishment by refusing to let his people fight their enemies? I believe that what makes Jesus truly nonconformist and radical is his Great Refusal of hatred. The only thing to be hated is sin—and our own sin in particular. What will *really* reach the establishment? Our hatred of it or our rigor with ourselves? "He will save his people from *their* sins." Jesus in Matthew is not God-Saves-Us-From-Them. He is God-Saves-Us-From-Ourselves. Perhaps this is the way he saves us, in the long run, from them, too.

While the Christian must avoid the contemporary perversion of the gospel from the right—the pious perversion—which says "just preach the gospel," which may be translated, "don't touch my wallet," one must as alertly ward off the enemy from the left—the Marxist perversion—which preaches class warfare as the means of social salvation.

The traditional church, it must be added, has often let working people down by letting herself be co-opted by conservative political authority and monied interests. The traditional church is too frequently a vehicle more of carnal religious nationalism than of divine prophetic critique. Religious patriotism, which the biblical prophets hated, is too often sanctified by the church. There should be no flag in Christian sanctuaries. The Old Testament prophets' social witness—and the prophet of prophets, the teaching of the synoptic Jesus—are, surprisingly, not often heard in many conservative-evangelical churches, for both these sources are felt to be liberal and unevangelical. Theological Dispensationalism is responsible for much of conservative Christianity's neglect of the social prophets and the teaching Jesus.

How will Jesus save us? An important question, and the entire Gospel is written to answer it. We can anticipate that answer already by looking out over the content of the Gospel and saying in a preliminary way that Jesus intends to save us by convicting us through the demand of the holy law that convinces us of our need to change, and by the gift of baptism that equips us with God's Dove-Spirit, who is the power to change and who gives us the assurance of our adoption in Christ (chap 3). Jesus calls us, then, enlisting the decision of discipleship, and promises to make us fishers of people (chap 4)—which means effective with people in his way. Jesus then magnifi-cently shows us what this Way is in the countercultural nonviolence of the Sermon on the Mount (5–7), and he lives this Way in a compassion for individuals and groups that (literally) touches—in modern language, that comes to grips with—the con-crete needs of real people in the world around them (the Ten Miracles, 8–9).

The remainder of the Gospel will spell out this Way in richer colors, but we may say in preliminary prospect that Jesus intends to be our God-Who-Saves by law and gospel, by teaching and touching, by preaching and social engagement, by talking seriously about God and by taking seriously the other person and the social situa-tions with which the other person presents us. Finally and supremely, in the Lord's Supper, Jesus touches us himself ("this is my body"), giving us the cleansing and empowering benefits of his cataclysmic passion ("this is my blood . . . and it brings the forgiveness of sins," 26:28). It is the Risen Jesus who does all this "with," and so through, his church (28:20).

I do not believe that this Gospel Way of teaching and touching (of Word and sacrament, of prayer and fellowship, Acts 2:42) will ever strike many people as very dramatic, impressive, or even effective—any more than did Jesus' own passion. We remember the doubts of John the Baptist himself (11:2–3).

Jesus' Way may seem inadequate; but when he is followed, his Way may at least give a warranty no violent movement for change can: it will never intentionally violate anyone. Such small promises may be ultimately more profound than all grand promises of world upheaval.

How does Jesus save his people from their sins? Luke's Christmas story makes more explicit than Matthew's that forgiveness is the first way that Jesus' salvation affects his people: "Because you, child, will . . . grant to his people knowledge of salvation in the forgiveness of their sins" (Luke 1:76–77; cf. Brown, 159 n. 75). But Matthew does not say in Matt 1:21 *how* Jesus will save his people, and there is no explicit allusion to the cross here either (Bonn., 21). The how must be read from the context of the whole Gospel. Matthew's Gospel clearly makes obedience to Jesus' commands a means of grace—with all the theological difficulties this involves. Yet the commands of Matthew's Jesus are so often embedded in contexts of promise and grace (e.g., the great commands of the Sermon on the Mount are preceded by the Beatitudes and followed by the Lord's Prayer) that legalism is avoided. Finally, "the connection of salvation with the person of Jesus lies simply in the fact that *he* offers this salvation as present, final possibility, that he now comforts the poor, and calls sinners to himself" (Conz., 51–52).

It is touch and go whether demand or mercy dominates Matthew's Gospel. In relation to the other New Testament writings it is clear that demand is the main contribution of Matthew (see esp. Mohrlang's *Matthew and Paul*). I believe that the cross-resurrection of Jesus is the deepest source of Jesus' saving power in the comprehensive New Testament gospel, but if this source is stressed one-sidedly, Jesus' moral emphasis in Matthew's Gospel is short-circuited. Following Jesus' teachings (e.g., on anger, violence, money, marriage, or ambition) saves people from real sins just as effectively as believing Jesus' death and resurrection saves people from deep sin. There are many realities to be saved from, and the whole Christ of Matthew's whole Gospel saves human beings from all of them.

B. The Second Name: "The With-Us God" (Emmanu-El)

"Now this all happened so that the Word spoken by the Lord through the prophet would be full-filled, which says 'Look! The virgin will be expecting a baby, and she will give birth to a son, and people will give him the name "Emmanu-El,"' which, when translated, means 'God is with us!'" (1:22–23).

It is important to notice that Matthew does not ordinarily say that "this happened *as* it is written," but rather, "this happened *so that* [*hina*] what is written might be fulfilled." This "so that" means that the Old Testament words preceding the events of Jesus' life were seen as *powers,* as forces that were pregnant with life, life that burst into fulfillment in the history of Jesus. Holy Scripture did not coincidentally fulfill itself in the life of Jesus; it inevitably, ineluctably fulfilled itself in him because the same Spirit who had conceived those words of promise then, conceives this act of fulfillment now. Holy Scripture (like the Holy Spirit) is full of Jesus Christ. All Scripture "longs" to be filled with Christ and to be interpreted in his light. It was made for him.

1:22 "This all happened so that the Word spoken by the Lord through the prophet would be fulfilled." As we saw the duality of the divine-human savior in the preceding verse (where Jesus is both God-Saves and a man named Joshua), so we see the duality of the authorship of the divine-human Scriptures in this verse, for the Word is spoken, we are told explicitly, "by the *Lord* through the *prophet.* " Scripture comes from two sources: the Lord and the prophet. If we divinize Scripture we lose its humanity; if we humanize it we lose its divinity. The same balance—of "both fully divine *and* fully human"—must be kept in our treatment of Scripture as in our treatment of Jesus. Historical-critical exegesis honors the humanity of Scripture; theological exegesis honors its divinity. Historical exegesis keeps us honest; theological exegesis keeps us relevant. Karl Barth's doctrine of the Word of God at the beginning of his *Church Dogmatics* (I/1, paragraphs 3–7) honors the three forms of the Word of God—revealed (Jesus Christ), written (the prophetic-apostolic Scriptures), and spoken (the indispensability of preaching) in a now classic way. Cf. also Barth's excellent doctrine of Holy Scripture itself, *CD,* I/2, chap 3, paragraphs 19–21.

Matthew's nearly dozen formula citations—"this happened so that the Word . . . might be fulfilled" (half of which, interestingly, are in the opening four chapters of the Gospel, and as many as eight of which are from Isaiah alone, the Old Testament "gospel" par excellence, cf. Brown, 97)—come to more than all the formula citations in the other three Gospels combined (McK., 67). Matthew loves the idea that *Jesus* is what the whole Old Testament is about and that God's entire plan of salvation is nothing else than Jesus the Messiah and discipleship to him. The simplicity of God's one plan of salvation according to Matthew militates mightily against the complicated many ways in theological Dispensationalism with sundry ages and the different plan of salvation in each age. The clinching argument against theological Dispensationalism is the discovery that the Bible is not a puzzle but a gospel, that it is not about ages but about Jesus. Paul's understanding of the unity of salvation history through faith in God's promise is spelled out with all necessary clarity in Galatians, especially chaps 3 and 4. Matthew and Paul are one in this simplicity and christocentricity. Augustine's *Anti-Pelagian Treatises,* Luther's *Large Catechism,* Calvin's *Institutes,* and Barth's *Church Dogmatics* are recommended as commentary on Scripture's unity in Christ.

The emphasis in the famous virgin birth passage (1:23) is more upon Jesus' miraculous name, Emmanu-El, than it is upon his miraculous birth from a virgin. Yet it should be admitted that the believer who has (in becoming a believer) experienced a veritable "virgin birth" through the miracle of faith has little difficulty in believing that there was an actual virginal conception of Jesus in the womb of Mary. The personal miracle makes the historical miracle credible. (One is reminded of the incident of the converted miner in the Wesleyan evangelical revival in eighteenth-century England. Asked by his mocking co-workers if he really believed that Jesus had changed water into wine he replied, "I don't know if Jesus really changed water into wine; but I know that in my house he changed beer into furniture." The miner's personal miracle disposed him, of course, to believe in the biblical miracle. This is the case with most believers who read of the virgin birth.)

At the same time, one feels squeamish when some make so much of the virgin birth that the impression is left that *unless* Jesus had been born of a virgin our salvation could not have occurred. To say this is surely to overdo a good thing. God is capable of having himself brought to birth in human history through the normal channels of marital intercourse. The virgin birth is not necessary for God or for us; but it is a beautiful doctrine, enshrining the important evangelical truth that God comes to human life without the initiatives of human nature.

I believe that one may be a Christian and have questions about the historicity of the virgin birth. The silence of the weighty theological literature of Paul and John on this doctrine is not insignificant. But "the ancients were also wise," and the early church's careful attempt to protect this doctrine in its creedal formulations deserves our respect. When one has done the requisite exegesis and has studied the christological controversies, one may make an honest decision one way or another. Meanwhile, I believe it is good form to be traditional and creedal in this doctrine, not least because the virgin birth has evangelical contours.

"Emmanu-El" means, literally, "with us El(ohim)," "with us God." And since Matthew in his own translation of the expression inserts the definite article *the* before the word *God* (*ho theos*), literally, "with us the God," I will often translate Emmanuel in the following intentionally provocative way in order to bring out *the later church's* understanding of the name (for "people will give him the name") in the sharpest possible manner—"The With-Us-God." There is a minimal way and there is a maximal way of understanding Matthew's "Emmanuel": minimally, the name means that the man Jesus is God's agent of divine saving presence in human history (God *in* Jesus); maximally, the name means incarnation—that God assumes human nature personally (God *is* Jesus). Matthew probably meant the minimal meaning; the later church ("*people* will give him the name") correctly came to understand Matthew's "Emmanuel" maximally, because though Matthew's christology is not yet John's or Nicea's, it is en route, and if it matters that the church teach in unity the full truth of the coming of Jesus Christ (and it does matter, profoundly), then the church not only may but must teach both the minimal (human) and the maximal (divine) Jesus.

In the Old Testament, God was supremely The Above-Us-God (though he often visited here "below," most prominently in the Angel of the Lord, see Genesis, *passim*). And in Islam, Allah is, by definition, *always* The Above-Us-God. However, the glory of the New Testament revelation is that the great Above-Us-God *came down and became one of us*. In Islam, as Kenneth Cragg has helped us to see, Allah *sends*—angels, prophets, books—but he is too holy to *come*. For God to touch earth is, in Islam, called *shirk*, and anyone who claims that God has a Son or became a human being or anything like a human being commits *shirk*, makes God gross, blasphemes God's glory.

But in the gospel we have learned to think of God in another way. The gospel's God is precisely so great that he *can* come down. He is not trapped in heaven above us. And this God's love is so immense that he *wants* to come down. And he has proven his love by the fact that he *did* come down and touch our ground. Indeed, he even allowed himself to be "shirked" by men, condemned, and nailed to wood. The greatness of the gospel's God is that God not only sends, he comes. Christmas is the story of God becoming one of us. God literally "be-littled" himself in order to accommodate himself to us. In the words of the *Te Deum,* "he *humbled* himself to be born of a virgin," and he became a regular human being right here with us. The pulse of the gospel is in that great condescension. And that condescension, that great stoop we call Christmas, or in theology, the incarnation, is the fulfillment of every Old Testament promise of God's coming. Christmas is God's own self-shirking.

The moment God became one of us the salvation of the world began to be fulfilled—*and* (of theological interest) the problem of the Trinity began to be posed. It may have been intellectually easier on us for the Great God to have remained above us as One (to be sure, One in Three). But the moment God touched earth, *in person* (not by proxy), the problem of our understanding how God can be both here and there at the same time began. How can God be both Above-Us and With-Us at the same time and still be *one* God? God can! "I believe in God the Father *All-Mighty.*" The church's doctrine of the Trinity is the careful attempt to show how "God can," for God is "one in substance and yet distinct in three persons, the Father, the Son, and the Holy Ghost" (*The Scots Confession,* 1). It is no great problem for the tri-une God to come to earth, to "be his own double" (in Barth's phrase). *God* is not stymied by historicity. It is probably not possible for us mentally to grasp God's being fully with us as a human being and, at the same time, God's being fully above us as God. But God was willing to cause us this temporary intellectual confusion in order to bring us a permanent existential salvation.

As with the miracle of the virgin birth, when one has tasted the grace of God's "withing" through evangelical faith in Jesus, one instinctively believes the divinity and truth of the church's doctrine of the Trinity. For Christians believe the divinity of the *object* of their faith, who is Jesus, and the divinity of the internal *source* of their faith, who is the Spirit, and the divinity of the *sender* of Son and Spirit, who is God the Father. Thus to become a Christian is instinctively to be trinitarian. And though the understanding of the Trinity involves intellectual problems, the deep personal satisfactions compensate for the mental difficulties. The satisfaction, essentially, is the assurance that in Jesus we have to do with no one less than God.

The Trinity question is, finally, the Christ question. Who is Jesus, really? Hans Küng's very helpful modern theology, *On Being a Christian,* 129–33, esp. 130, is correct in its critique of a too simplistic equation of Jesus with God, if this equation means that God is *all* that Jesus is. For it is heterodox to deny that Jesus is, at the same time that he is fully God, also fully human. Some protestors against the gnostic-Docetic-spiritualistic-heresy that teaches "Jesus is God" (and therefore is not really human) fall, however, into the opposite Ebionitic-humanistic-heresy of saying "Jesus is a man" (and therefore not really God). Küng, in my opinion, comes dangerously close to this latter error. Only the full-blooded Jesus of Matt 1:21–23, who is both Joshua the man and God-Saves in truth, a human baby and Emmanuel, can do justice to the rich variety of all the New Testament texts and to the depth of human need.

Historically, the christology of the New Testament found the "christological moment" (the spiritual equivalent of "The Big Bang") occurring at progressively earlier and earlier periods. In Jesus' own preaching ministry the christological moment coincided with the soon coming of (the Son of Man with) the kingdom of God (in an excitingly tense relation with Jesus' own appearance in his historical ministry); the earliest apostolic preaching, recorded, e.g., in Acts, found the christological moment in Jesus' own resurrection; Mark, our earliest written Gospel, found it occurring already, proleptically, in Jesus' baptism and classically in Jesus' passion (without diminishing its later Great Coming in the parousia or return of Jesus as the Son of Man with the kingdom); Matthew and Luke, still later, found the christological moment at least commencing even earlier (as in our text) in Jesus' conception; and, perhaps most deeply of all, John (later than all) and Paul (earlier than all) understood the christological reality to have occurred, to be sure, in Jesus' coming, passion, and resurrection, but to have mysteriously preexisted in the divine life of the Son with the Father. This "Backward Christology" is discussed learnedly in Bacon, 148–50 (who calls this process "the recession of the Epiphany"), and brilliantly in Brown, 26–32, 134–35, 181, who adds the important concluding note, 134 n. 6, that "orthodox Christians need have no conflict with such a thesis of a growing retrospective evaluation of Jesus, provided it is understood that the evaluation involves an appreciation of a reality that was already there—Jesus was who he was during his lifetime, even if it took his followers centuries to develop a partially adequate theological vocabulary in which to articulate his greatness."

Though Nicea's "Very God of Very God" definition of Jesus may not, therefore, be read *into* Matthew's texts by careful historical exegesis, it can be read *out of* them by Nicene Christians and by responsible theological exegesis. Brown, 31, 140–42, argues strongly for a careful distinction between Matthew's and Luke's conception christologies, on the one hand, and Paul's and John's preexistence christologies, on the other, and he presents the thesis that in Matthew and Luke we do not have a literal incarnation of a preexistent deity but the beginning of the career of the Son of God on earth. Nevertheless, Brown, 529, must take seriously the meaning of the word he himself uses—"eternal"—when he writes, "For ordinary Christians the virginal conception [of Jesus] has proved an effective interpretative sign of that eternal divine sonship." If "eternal" is to be more than poetic (and "ordinary Christians" nonpejorative), then we cannot get around this fact: Jesus Christ is not only the one *in* whom God is with us (in which case Jesus would be, as in all Arian interpretations, finally, someone other than the true essential God); Jesus *is* God with us—and this must be confessed with less embarrassment than it frequently is by modern exegetes and theologians.

Everything depends in the last analysis on whether one prefers the preposition *in* (cf., e.g., 2 Cor 5:19) or the copula *is* when relating God to Jesus. Both are true—God was *in* Jesus and God *is* Jesus—but the first is subordinate to the second, the "in" serves the "is," and it is the "is" that saves. It is true, of course, that Jesus' Jewish name, Joshua, was a common name, setting Jesus among, not apart from, his contemporaries, and that thus Jesus was truly a man and not a demigod (Schw., 31). But this is not Matt 1:21–23's emphasis. Gundry, 34, puts it well: "Matthew does not portray Jesus as God's Son merely in the sense that Jesus acted in God's behalf and submitted perfectly to God's authority. His emphasis on the virgin birth, on [the risen] Jesus as being always with his people, on the worship of Jesus and the bringing of offerings to him, and on the title *kyrios* ('Lord') and his putting Jesus as the Son alongside the Father and Holy Spirit in a baptismal formula (28:19) all point to essential [*is*] as well as functional [*in*] deity. That Matthew does not use Greek philosophical terms to describe this deity hardly spoils the point."

1:23 "'Behold, a virgin shall conceive and bear a son, and his name shall be called Emmanuel' (which means, God with us)" (RSV). It is not entirely accurate to say that the supernatural element in Jesus' birth is not stressed or glorified, Stend., 771. Although the only explicit reference in Matthew to the virgin is here in our text and is a quotation from Isaiah, I am not convinced this means we can come to the conclusion that "in fine, even in Matthew the Virgin Birth is quite peripheral," Schw., 34. This is the opening narrative in Matthew and as such it is intended to condition our reading of the rest of the Gospel. But we do not need to go so far as Goulder, 156, who says that "the virginal conception gives a physical basis to the divine sonship, which is stressed in the Temptations."

Bonnard, 18f, reviews the three standard objections to the virgin birth: (a) rationalistic and positivistic—God doesn't intervene thus; but, Bonnard replies, one could argue thus against the entire evangelical witness; (b) historical- or comparative-religion objection points out that the virgin birth plays a limited role in apostolic preaching, appearing only in Matthew and Luke—a weightier argument; and (c) theological or christological objection finds the virgin birth in conflict with the preexistent Son of God and the doctrine of the heavenly Son of Man.

In this last connection, Raymond Brown (as we saw) argues that the virginal conception does *not* mean the Incarnation of the preexistent Word. For Matthew to say that Jesus is "begotten by the Holy Spirit" means that Jesus became *then,* in the begetting, the Son of God, not that he was the Son of God before the begetting. The later church will harmonize this christology with Paul and John's christologies; "that [harmonized product] became orthodox Christian doctrine" (Brown, 141f).

As I mentioned above, I learn from this that historical exegesis may not gratuitously read *into* Matthew's distinctive christology the church's later harmonization; theological exegesis may read this harmonization *out of* the text if it presents the historical case. But theological exegesis must go a step farther—to the truth question. Was the Son of God whose career Matthew believed began at conception, *in fact,* though not yet (perhaps) in Matthew's mind or texts, the *eternal* Son of God to whom Paul, John, and the later orthodox church bore witness? If we believe that the correct answer to this question is more than an academic game, that it is ultimate—and the church's first four centuries show just how ultimately this question was taken—then we will find it not only permissible, but essential to read Matthew with the Nicene optic: the eternal Son of God assumed the temporal humanity of Jesus in the virginal conception of Mary. Not to believe this is to endanger the foundation of the Christian faith.

Pauline and Johannine preexistence christology full-fills Matthean and Lukan conception christology, just as Christ full-fills the OT. In the legitimate contemporary quest for the truly human Jesus, churches should not believe that pastors or teachers who deny Jesus Christ's eternal deity are harmless to the church's truth and that they may, in any case, have at least part of the truth or one of the NT's several possible christologies. This will not do. Only God saves. Therefore it is of final, not ephemeral, importance that Jesus be confessed and worshiped as true God. If he is not so confessed and worshiped then we belong to an idolatrous community that pays inordinate attention to a man or a demigod, when the First Commandment explicitly warns us that "You shall have no other gods before me." It is all or nothing at all.

See Brown's thorough "Appendix IV: Virginal Conception, Was Jesus Conceived Without A Human Father?," 517–33, for the problem of the historical truth of our text, and his conclusion "that the scientifically controllable biblical evidence leaves the question of the historicity of the Virginal Conception unresolved. . . . I think it is easier to explain the NT evidence by positing historical basis [*sic*] than by positing pure theological creation" (527f). At another place, Brown puts his conclusion this way: "In my judgment, both Matthew and Luke think that Jesus was conceived without a human father, but are more interested in theological import than in historicity" (140 n. 22). Virginal conception and birth, moreover, do not deny Jesus' true humanity—Matthew's and Luke's accounts tell us the story of a suffering *man.* Indeed, it was the earliest *opponents* of the virginal conception in church history who denied Jesus' true humanity, Brown, 529.

Put simply but theologically, if the first Adam was without human parents and yet was truly human, why cannot the last Adam be without a human parent and be truly human? "Is anything too hard for the Lord?" (Gen 18:14) "With human beings, to be sure, this is impossible, but with God absolutely everything is possible" (Matt 19:26). Brown, 531, summarizes this point: The virginal conception "was an extraordinary action of God's creative power, as unique as the initial creation itself (and that is why all natural scientific objections to it are irrelevant, e.g., that not having a human father, Jesus' genetic structure would be abnormal)."

The nearest OT parallels to the virgin birth of Jesus are the miraculous births of significant persons, especially of Isaac and Jacob in the patriarchal stories of Genesis (Gen 12–50). If those stories are not exactly records of virgin births, yet in their miraculously occurring beyond the possibilities of natural birth they are very similar; they all stress the creative initiative of God, Str.-B., 1:49; Stend., 771. The OT stories concern, however, the *ability* to conceive, whereas the NT story concerns the gift of conception itself, Delling, *parthenos*, TWNT, 5:834.

The virgin birth shares with the Genesis stories the beautiful truth that God gives what history cannot; in the birth of the Messiah, Matthew expected something beyond history and nature, Schl., *Der*, 5; all human possibilities of sanctifying life are at an end where God's possibilities begin. In this sense, Matthew's account is like Jewish apocalyptic, except that it is quiet apocalyptic, happening in obscure insignificance, Lohm., 18.

On the absence of references to the virgin birth in Paul and John, see Schw., 34, and an excellent discussion in Brown, 518–21. The moral and spiritual modesty of the biblical accounts is admired in Schl., *Das*, 8–9, Schl., *Der*, 12 (no "how" of the virgin birth, only "that"), Stend., 771; Brown, 523. The virgin birth presents Jesus as both the historical Son of David *and* as the divine Son of God at once. Indeed, the virgin birth with its corollary of Jesus' two natures (human and divine) is close to being an exact fulfillment of the great promise of an everlasting king to David in Nathan's prophecy: "Thus says the Lord of hosts, . . . I will raise up *your son* after you [= the Son of David] . . . , and he shall be *my son* [= Son of God]" (2 Sam 7).

On the uniqueness of a virginal conception in the Jewish setting, but not in the gentile, see Bultmann, 291 ("unheard of in a Jewish environment," and therefore the OT texts come from Hellenistic sources, ibid., 291f, 304). According to Schweizer, 33, the virgin birth did not so much set Jesus apart from the Greek world as it "placed him in the company of all the great men of the age," from Plato to Alexander. Bacon, 151, and 151 n. 3, believes that for Hellenized, sophisticated Jews and gentiles, a virgin birth "could be ascribed to Emmanuel with no more offense than to a Christian of today"; e.g., the Roman writer Plutarch, a contemporary of Matthew and Luke, writes, "'The Egyptians believe, *not implausibly,* that it is not impossible for the Spirit of God to approach a woman and produce in her certain beginnings of parturition,'" *Vita Numae,* 4 (emphasis added). Virginal conception in pagan or world religions often involved immoral sexual conduct, but the chaste character of the event in our texts is impressive; we are not witnesses of a "sacred marriage" (*hieros gamos*), Brown, 522. Bonnard, 21, like Schweizer, 34, is convinced that the idea of a savior born of a virgin was not strange to the ancient world, and he cites Isa 9:5(6), 11:1, and Mic 5:1(2) as documentation. But is there a *virgin* birth in these texts?

1:23b "And people will call his name 'Emmanu-El,' which means, 'God with us.'" The Hebrew text of Isa 7:14 says that "*she* will call his name Emmanu-El"; the Greek LXX hears a command, "*you* shall call his name Emmanu-El." Matthew differs from both and says "people" or "they" will call him by this name (third person plural *kalesousin*).

There is some point in Matthew's plural rendering because we never hear Jesus called Emmanu-El by his mother or by any particular person in the Gospels or Epistles. But if one were to ask the faithful through the centuries what they believe Jesus *means* to them, and thus in this sense what they *call* him, "God with us" is as good an answer as it is possible to give in three words. Cf. Chrys., 5:3:32; Cal., 1:69; Schl., *Der,* 23; Lohm., 17. All the classic and related Emmanu-El texts in the Old Testament (Isa 7:10–16; 8:8, 10; 9:5–6; 11:1ff; Mic 5:1–2) seem, as Gunkel pointed out long ago, to indicate that in fact the coming Messiah *will* be of more than human origin; thus Jesus is himself, in person, the presence of God for us human beings (Schn., 15). This wonderful *"God* is present" fact is so stressed in our text that it is not an exaggeration to say that Emmanu-El, not the virgin (or the virgin birth) is the *focus* of the verse (McK., 67). Matthew consistently "raises the status of Jesus into the divinity by using the appropriate expressions" (Bult., 358).

Emmanu-El is probably, after the name Jesus, the most appropriate expression of who Jesus really is. Meier, *Vis.,* 54 n. 18, correctly sees what is involved in Matthew's calling Jesus Emmanu-El, i.e., the crucial theological grammar of *in* or *is*: "We must not weaken Emmanuel so that it simply says that in Jesus God draws near to His people. Contrary to his usual style, Matthew takes pains to translate Emmanuel so as to stress its force: Jesus *is* God with us" (emphasis Meier's). Similarly, Kingsb., 37, 80–81; Gund., *passim* (who, in my opinion, overdoes deity).

How do we understand and why do we believe in the Trinity? *The Athanasian Creed* (about A.D. 500), one of the three ancient creeds received and used by the worldwide Evangelical Lutheran Church and honored by the Roman, Reformed, and Anglican churches, puts it best: "Just as we are compelled by Christian truth to acknowledge each person [Father, Son, and Holy Spirit] by himself to be God and Lord, so we are forbidden by the Christian religion to say that there are three Gods or three Lords."

How do we understand the incarnation of Jesus Christ? The heart of *The Nicene Creed,* 381, puts it best. We have been won to faith in the "Very God, . . . who for us men [*tous anthropous,* for us human beings], and for our salvation, came down from heaven, and was incarnate by the Holy Spirit of the Virgin Mary, and was made man [*enanthrōpēsanta,* made human]." This Nicene sentence summarizes the theological teaching of the first chapter of Matthew. Cf. *The Augsburg Confession,* 1530, art. 3; *The Scots Confession,* 1560, chap. 6; *The Heidelberg Catechism,* 1563, Q. 35; *The Second Helvetic Confession,* 1566, chap. 11; and *The Thirty-Nine Articles* of the Church of England, 1562, chap. 2. Even the doctrinally timid United Presbyterian *Confession of 1967,* after its preface, has these words (the emphases are mine): "THE CONFESSION. *In* Jesus Christ God was reconciling the world to himself. Jesus Christ *is* God with man. [See both *in* and *is.*] He is the *eternal* Son of the Father, who became *man* and lived among us to fulfill the work of reconciliation. *He is present in the church* by the power of the Holy Spirit to continue and complete his mission." Nevertheless, there is a certain doctrinal weakness, almost a felt reluctance in the christological confessing of *The Confession of 1967* which I find unimpressive and symptomatic of the malaise of the church. Only where confessing Christ is a joyous privilege rather than a hastily reviewed presupposition will the church be well.

Quiet Joseph: An Early Model of Matthew's Understanding of Righteousness. An Introduction to Christian Ethics (1:24–25)

The first chapter ends with a glimpse at the decisions of "righteous Joseph," and gives us an opportunity to say a preliminary word about the meaning of righteousness in Matthew.

"And when Joseph got up from his sleep, he did what the angel of the Lord had instructed him to do, and he took Mary as his wife; and Joseph did not have personal intimacy with Mary until she had her baby boy; and Joseph gave the boy the name—'Jesus'" (1:24–25).

Bonnard, 22, points out that throughout these opening chapters the divine initiative that finds man strictly *in*active—here even asleep—is followed in every case by immediate, concrete, and humble human *action*. Thus divine initiating grace does not cancel human responsibility, it enables it; it does not render believers comatose, it makes them obedient. Grace enables obedience as sleep enables action. Jesus' blessings precede his commands in the Sermon on the Mount, Matt 5; God's initiative precedes Joseph's obedience in the opening narrative of the Gospel. Classical Protestantism has been strong on initiating grace; Catholicism has been strong on responsive obedience. We need each other, and scriptural study and faith are drawing us closer together.

Joseph never speaks in the New Testament. In Matthew's Gospel, where Joseph appears more than anywhere else, Joseph does a number of important things. He overcomes his initial hesitation and obeys the divine summons to marry the questionable Mary; later he is commanded to flee to Egypt with the child and his mother; still later, counseled by a dream again, he is instructed to return with the family to the land of Israel and then to settle with them in the north in Galilee. In every scene Joseph simply acts without speaking. His speech is to do the will of God.

We may call him "Quiet Joseph." His hallmark is obedience—prompt, simple, and unspectacular obedience. And in this sense Joseph prefigures the Gospel of Matthew's understanding of righteousness: to be righteous is simply to obey the Word of God; righteousness is, simply, to *do*—a favorite word in this Gospel—what God has said. The unostentatiousness of Joseph's obedience prefigures Jesus' description (in the heart of the Sermon on the Mount) of righteousness's way of not seeking to be noticed by people. Righteousness, in Matthew, is to obey simply. The "more" that Jesus requires for entrance into the kingdom (5:20) turns out, on longer exposure to the Gospel, to involve also a simple "less" of pretentiousness or show. In Jesus' teaching it was the devout separatists who were "too much"; what God wants, the entire Gospel teaches us somewhat surprisingly, is a little *less*. Less is more. Thus Joseph, the divinely chosen adopting father of Jesus, lives out for us in his noiseless way a preliminary definition of righteousness in this Gospel. Righteousness is doing the will of God promptly and simply.

An additional feature in Joseph's career completes his portrait and this brief introduction to Christian ethics in Matthew. "Joseph, her fiancé, was a righteous man (*dikaios*), but he did not want to shame Mary. So he decided to divorce her quietly (*lathra*)" (1:19). In this verse it is the phrase between the two principal words ("righteous" and "quietly") which defines Joseph's character most subtly and so deserves special attention: "he did not want to shame Mary." Righteousness, Matthew's Jesus will show again and again, is not wanting to shame people, a sensitivity to persons. We might say that the *vertical* dimension of Gospel righteousness is sensitivity to the Word and will of God; the *horizontal* expression of this righteousness is sensitivity to other human beings. Righteousness in personal relations is "not wanting to shame" another—it is an exquisite sensitivity to the honor of the other person.

Mother Mary: An Introduction to the Sexual Ethics of the Gospel (1:25)

The final teaching to discuss in the first chapter is the relation of the final verse to the doctrine of the perpetual virginity of Mary. "And Joseph did not have personal intimacy with Mary until she had her baby boy; and Joseph gave the boy the name—'Jesus'" (1:25).

Of most importance to Matthew in this text is Joseph's obeying the instruction to give the child the name "God-Saves," "Jesus." As was Joseph's habit, Joseph obeyed—simply and quietly—"he named him 'Jesus,'" thus as a biological and legal son of David himself, Joseph incorporated Jesus into the line of David. But of almost equal interest to the reader is the unself-conscious way in which the evangelist writes that *prior to*, or literally "until" (*heōs*) the child's birth, Joseph did not "know" Mary. We are conditioned by a certain tradition to think that Joseph would *never* "know," that is, would never have sexual relations with Mary. But this scruple is not present in the evangelist's mind; Matthew's "until" suggests, without any impropriety or embarrassment, that *after* Jesus' birth Joseph and Mary would live together completely as husband and wife. The burden of proof rests on those who would contest the simple meaning of the word *until*.

1:25 The imperfect tense of the verb *know* (*eginōsken*) teaches continuous action or, as in this case, continuous inaction, and I have tried to bring out the force of this by translating "did not have personal intimacy with Mary." "To know" in biblical language means "to have intimate relations with," and is a body and soul knowing, not merely an intellectual knowing. (This fact has implications, incidentally, even for learning. We learn when we enter a subject with all that we are.) "The imperfect *eginōsken* is against the tradition of perpetual virginity," Allen, 10; so also Grund., 71; Schw., 35; in this direction but cautious, Green, 56; Hill, 80. Bonnard, 22, and Calvin, 1:70, are reserved: Bonnard believes Matthew 1:25 does not sustain perpetual virginity, nor does it deny it absolutely; Calvin, "Let one thing suffice for us, that it is falsely and foolishly inferred from these words of the Evangelist, what happened after the birth of Christ." Against Mary's ever having sexual relations: Jerome, 1:78; Chrys., 5:5:33; cf. ZG ad loc. It would seem to the unprejudiced reader of these verses that the full marital relationship is honored, not banned, by the special ways the marriage is mentioned.

It is a fact worth mentioning that the major Protestant church fathers, from Luther to Wesley, believed in Mary's perpetual virginity. Thus this particular topic does not usually appear on the agenda of Catholic-Protestant talks.

Let me say immediately that I doubt that Mary was perpetually virgin. This text in Matthew and the references in the New Testament to Jesus' brothers and sisters are fair causes for doubt (Matt 12:46ff; 13:55). I am aware that it is said that these brothers and sisters can be called cousins, or children of Joseph's by another marriage, but I find this explanation forced.

Let me ask the prior question. What does Mary lose if she relates intimately to Joseph? Her virginity, to be sure, but does she then lose her purity, her worthiness, her dignity? Something close to affirming this question lies behind the traditional defense of Mary's perpetual virginity. We are given the strong impression in some teaching that should Mary have become a wife to Joseph physically she would have lost something spiritually. I believe that this persuasion is dangerous, doctrinally and morally, and that it is allied to other errors in the field of sexual ethics—from the subjects of priestly celibacy and women's ordination to scientific contraception and annulment.

I believe that this Matthean text in particular refers naturally to Mary's later physical relations with her husband, and that other New Testament texts refer quite naturally to Mary being the mother of other children. Her physical relations with Joseph and her natural motherhood of subsequent children (without any prejudice to her real virgin birth of Jesus that preceded) were not considered sinful or degrading by the evangelist Matthew. After Jesus, Mary became a complete wife to Joseph; she lost her virginity but gained God's normal will for the wife of a husband—intimate knowledge of her husband, the gift of other children, and a means of the mutual expression of tenderness and love. Shouldn't the holy family be a real family? Mary is not degraded by her relations to Joseph; on the contrary, it seems to me that Mary is degraded, and the institution of marriage is unintentionally disparaged, if the principal mother in history is left physically isolated from her husband in an unnecessary act of heroism or ascetics—and, particularly, if this isolation is celebrated.

The theological intention of wanting Mary to be a perpetual virgin not only does damage to the doctrine of marriage; just as seriously, it has contributed at times to a near deification of Mary. The most serious traditional Protestant argument against the Roman dogma of the virgin Mary is that Mary became, not only in popular piety, but in formal definition, an invoked intercessor, a semidivine figure, and so a near idol. The titles *mediatrix, auxiliarix,* and the like, all placed Mary dangerously close to the Godhead. Devotions were addressed to her. Prayers were at least mediated through her. And although Marian minimalists won the important contest at Vatican II, I do not believe that the most recent definitions have been fortunate—though they do seem less fulsome and exuberant than earlier formulations.

Mary has tended to replace the tender, compassionate side of Jesus in some popular Catholic piety: Jesus has been Judge, Mary the mediator. But Protestants have not found anything approximating the Roman dignifying of Mary in the apostolic accounts. We believe that the Marian honors are dubious at best and pernicious at worst. We believe that a thorough demythologizing of Mary is required if church teaching is to be wholesome, not least in the ethical field. And we believe that this is required for three reasons: (1) textually: the biblical texts will not bear the weight of the Marian dogma; (2) morally: the dignity of sexual relations is undermined by the veneration of Mary's perpetual virginity; and (3) theologically: the integrity of the sole mediation of Jesus Christ has been threatened by Marian devotion.

Christians must be willing to give Mary her deserved place in the church. She *is,* properly understood, "the mother of God" in that she is the mother of Jesus Christ who is not only a man with us—he is that—but he is also God's great personal act of condescension. Jesus is God himself with us, and this not merely symbolically or analogically, but God really, essentially, and substantially. Jesus really is God and man with us. And Jesus' mother Mary really bore him into history (*not* into eternity!), and this historical task gives her the right to bear the names the early church gave her, not for her own sake but for the sake of protecting the full deity of her son—*theotokos, Mater Dei,* "The Mother of God," and *Notre Dame,* "Our Lady." Mary is the mother of God into history—this we must boldly confess if we wish to hold to the total deity of Jesus Christ, "Very God."

"Mother" is, in fact, the name most frequently used by Matthew to dignify Mary (1:18; 2:11, 13, 14, 20, 21; 12:46; 13:55). Matthew only uses the word *virgin* once—and then only in his quotation from Isaiah. The rest of the time the name Matthew gives Mary is, simply, "his [Jesus'] mother." I suggest that it is when we, too, keep to this apostolic simplicity in our references to Mary that we most honor her. She, like John the Baptist, wishes to decrease that Jesus may increase. I believe that we give the greatest honor to Mary—and to the institution of marriage and to the exclusive deity of the triune God—if we begin to subtract from the plethora of titles that have accumulated around Mary's head. She may, of course, be called the blessed virgin, and even at times, cautiously, the mother of God. But to go beyond these titles seems dangerous.

I wish to point to one other important fact. Had Matthew's God wished to give signal honor to the state of *virginity* he would have called a young woman who had made a decision to enter that state. But that is not the case. Mary was visited "when she was legally engaged to Joseph" (1:18). The divine visitation awaited an engagement, not a vow of virginity. A frequent depiction of Mary is that of a maiden resolutely determined to have no sexual relations with men. But in this paragraph Matthew introduces us to the story of a young woman who planned, *and who entered,* marriage. We meet Mary at the beginning of the paragraph as a fiancée, and we leave her at the end of the paragraph, by the divine command, as a completely married woman. Perpetual virginity—either as a decision *prior* to Joseph or *after* her delivery of Jesus—is far from the mind of the evangelist. Mary is not only "the blessed virgin" in the sense we usually think she is; she is also "the blessed fiancée." Mary's decision to be married was not an obstacle to the divine call; it seems to have even been an advantage, for in the second chapter Joseph is a real protector of his family.

Nor are we told that Joseph was warned never to touch Mary. Quite the contrary: "Joseph, . . . don't be afraid to take Mary to be your wife"; and "he did not know her until. . . ." What has been done by the devout to protect Mary's perpetual virginity—before, in her attitude toward marriage, and afterwards in her husband's relation to her—has been countered by the biblical texts. We are not taught that Mary rejected men or that Joseph rejected marriage; we are told things quite different by the simpler and, I think, nobler nativity stories. Mary's full marriage may seem to some to make her less godlike. But in my opinion this normalization of Mary dignifies her: she becomes a real woman rather than a plaster saint, a true and therefore a model mother. (A human Mary like a human Scripture actually dignifies both. Both bear the divine into the world, but both remain entirely human in the process.) By Mary's normal marriage the sexual relation receives a deep and divine salute (a salute that would have been missing in the Christmas story if we had known *only* of Mary's virginal conception of Jesus). Matthew's strong *heōs* ("until"), his later unself-conscious reference to Jesus' brothers and sisters, and Luke's "she gave birth to her *first-born* son" (Luke 2:7) all deliver this salute. It is an important tribute in the midst of the current confusion about sexual ethics. If men and women are to be allowed to be full men and women in the church, then we must begin by letting Mary become a full human being in Scripture. If God is to be treated as God—and God alone—then Mary must be treated as a human being. Both theologically and ethically, therefore, it is of importance that we allow Mary to be what she is in Matthew: the virgin mother of Jesus and subsequently the full wife of Joseph.

1:25 Delling, *parthenos*, TWNT, 5:833 and n. 56 summarizes at this point: "That Mary lived in chastity even after the birth of Jesus is only accepted in the Western church since A.D. 350. The idea of the virginal origin of Jesus does not intend to demean the marital relationship; its concern is not Mary but Jesus. It does not intend to exclude the male in order to give a ground for the sinlessness of Jesus," for, in the first instance the sinfulness of human beings is traced by Judaism (and, may I add, even sometimes by the NT, as e.g. at 1 Tim 2:14), interestingly (and probably sexistly), to woman.

For the brothers and sisters of Jesus, who appear also in Matthew (12:46–50; 13:55 f), see von Soden, *adelphos*, TWNT, 1:144, 16ff. McKenzie, 67, overstates: "The NT knows nothing of any children of Mary and Joseph." According to Chrysostom, 5:5:33, Jesus' brothers and sisters are spoken of in the NT only in the way that Joseph is spoken of as Jesus' father, i.e., technically but not biologically. Joseph should be spoken of as the legal father, not as the adoptive or foster father of Jesus, Brown, 139 and 139 n. 18. Some less weighty texts (C, D) have "until she gave birth to her *first-born* son," but this is manifestly a borrowing from Luke 2:7.

The Lukan word "first-born" does, however, support Matthew's indications of the couple's later full and fruitful marital relationship (contrast Jerome, 1:80, 82). Schlatter, *Das,* 12, is correct: Joseph's obedience in the Matthean verse consists not only in his honoring Mary's vocation of virginity prior to Jesus' birth, but in his living with her as his wife after the birth. Luther's 1522 Sermon on the Feast of the Birthday of Mary (W^2 11:2364) points to the damages done to Christ and people by an excessive attention to Mary.

In fairness, the Roman Catholic Brown, 530, should be heard on what is involved in the area of sexuality here: "All Christians should be wary of any implication that the conception of Jesus in wedlock would detract from his nobility or Mary's sanctity. In its origins, the virginal conception shows no traces whatsoever of an anti-sexual bias and should not be made to support one. . . . in no way did that [divine] intervention make ordinary conception in marriage less holy."

"And he called his name Jesus." The "he" here is Joseph. The virgin birth honors the mother; the name-giving honors the father, hence the unity of the paragraph's references to the two human figures, Joseph and Mary; Lohm., 14.

For traditional definitions of Mary in the Roman Catholic Church, see the English translations of Denzinger, e.g., *The Church Teaches: Documents of the Church in English Translation,* translated and prepared for publication by Clarkson, Edwards, Kelly, and Welch (St. Louis, Missouri: B. Herder Book Co., 1955), the section "The Mother of God," pp. 203–13. For Vatican II, see the "Dogmatic Constitution on the Church," chap. 8: "The Role of the Blessed Virgin Mary, Mother of God, in the Mystery of Christ and the Church," e.g., in *The Documents of Vatican II,* ed. Walter M. Abbott, S.J. (New York: Guild Press, 1966), pp. 85–96.

The revelation of *God* has been the theme of the first chapter of Matthew. The knowledge of God is the knowledge we need most. "Today all sorts of subjects are eagerly pursued; but the knowledge of God is neglected. . . . Yet to know God is man's chief end, and justifies his existence. Even if a hundred lives were ours, this one aim would be sufficient for them all" (John Calvin in John McNeill's Introduction to Calvin's *Institutes,* lxxi).

Chapter Two
Introduction to the Doctrine of Human Nature

"Who for us men, and for our salvation, came down from heaven, . . . and was made man." *(The Nicene Creed)*

The Situation

It has been argued that the religious question today is not so much "Who is God?" as it is "What is man?" We continue to wonder, "Is there a God in heaven?" Yet almost as persistently we are asking ourselves today, "Is there humanity on earth?" As someone has put it, the question is not so much "Is there life after death?" as "Is there life before death?" It is frequently (and too confidently) said in theological circles that Luther's sixteenth-century question "How can I find a gracious God?" has been replaced in our time by another question, "What is the meaning of life?" The question is, in the words of Mary Magdalene's love song, "What's it all about?" The modern reality-question has replaced, or is another name for, the ancient God-question. The search for the meaning of things is the current idiom of the religious question.

Appropriately, the World Council of Churches, founded on serious christological and christocentric commitments ("Christ the Hope of the World," "Christ the Light of the World"), turned its attention not long ago to *Humanum* studies. It may be an index of the same concern that Vatican Council II's agenda document in the Catholic Third World and beyond—*Gaudium et Spes* ("The Pastoral Constitution on the Church in the Modern World") focuses on a fresh redrafting of a doctrine of the human person (the first half of the document) and on some of the human person's major modern problems (the second half). Ever since the Son of God became a human being, Christians *can* say, as Karl Barth has argued on this basis, that man *is* the measure of all things (*Church Dogmatics*, III; cf. Plato, *Cratylus*, 4).

Conveniently, the special theme of Matthew chapter 2 is the dual response of human beings to a third human being, to God's self-revelation in Christ—the good response of the magi and the bad response of Herod to the Christ Child. Holy Scripture is not interested in the doctrine of man per se, for in Scripture's opinion there is no such thing as man or woman *per se*. Human beings are creatures, and they were created in the image of God, and thus they were made to image, face, and relate responsibly to God their Creator and to God's Anointed. Scripture considers human nature in the only way human nature can be considered if it really is created—that is, what is its relation to God, is it in a facing or defacing relationship with its Creator? Thus by studying the two great responses of the magi and Herod to God's coming in his "third man," the Christ, we are in fact studying the biblical doctrine of human nature in the most concrete and pictorial way possible. We learned God in chapter 1; in the responses to God's Christ in chapter 2 we learn human nature.

41

An Outline of Chapter 2

In chapter 2, human nature reveals itself dialectically in three sittings—as the magi from the East coming in worship, as King Herod and his entourage coming in rejection, and finally as the child Jesus himself, representing at once ideal Israel and Emmanuel, God with us. In these three profiles, artfully drafted by the evangelist Matthew, we find a clue to that many-sided mystery called "Man."

All three of the main characters of the chapter are introduced in the opening verse. "Now when *Jesus* was born in Bethlehem of Judea in the days of *Herod* the king, look, *magi* from the East arrived in Jerusalem." (1) The coming of *Jesus* has already been used by Matthew in chapter 1 to teach us the coming of God—Jesus is Emmanu-El, "The With-Us-God." In the present chapter Jesus continues to be Emmanu-El and begins also to be, as it were, Emmanu-Ādām, "The With-Us-Man." (2) *Herod* will reveal to us that side of human nature which is most problematic, what in classical theology is called original sin. And (3) the *magi* will reveal what man the sinner may become through God the Visitor; the magi introduce to us what theology has traditionally called (prevenient, "preceding") grace.

The big initial themes of Matthew chapter 2, then, are people coming to the Christ Child with *worship* in their hearts (the magi, vv 2, 11) and people coming to the Christ Child with *murder* on their minds (Herod and his group, vv 13, 16). In the language of Christian doctrine, Matthew chapter 2 shows us people coming to Christ either "in faith" (magi) or "in rebellion" (Herod), and so coming, respectively, under either God's mercy or judgment. The quiet subtheme of the entire chapter is the Representative Child, the New Israel, representing (especially in his outward weakness) the presence of God's grace under the suffering of human sin, and, so, illustrating in his life what we can call God's good faith.

We will look at each of the three representative persons (introduced in the first verse) in the order in which they appear in Matthew's development: first, the magi—humanity under the power of grace (vv 1–12); then, King Herod—humanity under the power of sin (vv 3–5, 7–8, 16–18); and third, the Child—the New Israel and representative humanity (vv 6, 11, 13–15, 19–23).

Matt 2 teaches in personal form the two great responses to divine revelation: faith-seeking-magi and faith-rejecting-Herod (Brown, 177–78; 213–14). Thus understood, chap 2 is the necessary completion of or reaction to chap 1's revelation. Matt 1 and 2's revelation-response teaching gives the infancy narratives their status as a Gospel in miniature (Brown, 183). The magi's faith dominates the first half of chap 2; Herod's unfaith dominates the second half of the chapter. The irony of the chapter is that gentiles seek, find, and worship the Messiah-King of the Jews, and that Israel in the person of her usurper-king Herod seeks to murder her true king (Lohm., 26; McK., 67; Schw., 37; Davies, 327). Thus the first are last, and the last first—a frequent theme in Matt (cf. 19:30; 20:16, 26–27; 23:12, etc.). Indeed, the heathen preach Christ to Israel (v 2), and it is precisely "star-crossed" magi(cians) who do the preaching, persons considered the very antonym of the Spirit-inspired prophets of Israel (Schl., *Das*, 13; cf. McN., 22). Thus the magi are the NT antitype of the OT Balaam, the pagan magician who knew God (Num 24:4, 16, LXX), came from the mountains of the East (Num 23:7; 22:5), preached salvation to Israel, and spoke of a star that will proceed from Jacob (Num 24:17) (Lohm., 25; Schw., 37).

There is also a double or (high-low) christology present in this chapter: one born *king* is worshiped in great stillness only by *strangers;* the king is only a *small child,* but the child is *worshiped* (Lohm., 26). There is no great demonstration; there is just the turning to Jesus of a few heathen (Schn., 18). There is also a twofold revelation. In their own country, the gentile-magi are initially led by a *star* to Jerusalem; then in Jerusalem they are decisively led by the Jewish *Scriptures* to the Christ (Brown, 178, 182). Nature begins, Scripture completes. One is reminded of the beautiful juxtaposition of natural and biblical revelation in Psalm 19 A and B.

In his adulthood, Jesus was known as Jesus of *Nazareth.* Why, then, all this emphasis on his birth in *Bethlehem?* The usual answer to the question is this: Bethlehem is stressed in order to overcome the hostile questions of the old people of God about the obscure and Galilean provenance of Jesus. How can a *Galilean* fulfill Israel's messianic Scriptures? See John 1:45–46 and 7:41–42, 45 for just such questions (Brown, 179–80). Are the stories of Matt 2 historical? See Allen, 14, who answers yes for everything except the wandering star. But McNeile, 23, believes the stories are a Christian midrash [i.e., "the popular and imaginative exposition of the Scriptures for faith and piety," Brown, 198]; similarly, in recent interpretation, the stories are a combination of history and story (Bonn., 23–24; Brown, 561 n.9).

I. THE MAGI: HUMANITY UNDER THE POWER OF GRACE (2:1–12)

"Now when Jesus was born in Bethlehem of Judea in the days of Herod the king, look, magi from the East arrived in Jerusalem saying, 'Where is the one who was born king of the Jews? We're asking because we saw his star at its rising and we have come to worship him.' When King Herod heard this he was deeply troubled—and all Jerusalem with him. So he gathered together all the senior pastors and the Bible teachers of the people of God, and he pushed them with this question: 'Where is the Christ supposed to be born?' And their answer was, 'In Bethlehem of Judea, because that is exactly what was written by the prophet:

"And you, Bethlehem, in the land of Judah,

    are by no means the least important among the rulers of Judah;

    because out of you is going to come a Ruler

    who will shepherd my people Israel."'

"Then Herod secretly summoned the magi and interrogated them about the time of the star's appearance. Then he sent them to Bethlehem with these instructions: 'Go and look hard for the Child; and when you find him, come back and tell me so that I too may come and worship him.' So when they had finished their audience with the king, they left, and look!, there was the star that they had seen before at its rising, and now it was moving on ahead of them until it came and stood shining right over the place where the Child was. When they saw this star they felt the deepest, most profound joy. And when they came into the house and saw the Child with Mary his mother, they fell down and worshiped him, and they opened up their resources and brought him gifts—gold and frankincense and myrrh. And when they had been warned in a dream not to go back to Herod, they departed for their country by another way" (Matt 2:1–12).

2:1–12 Are the magi good men or bad? Commentators, as we will see, have said both, in a way strikingly comparable to the doctrinal question: Is human nature basically good or basically evil? We may pursue the doctrinal question first to illustrate the relevance of the exegetical question.

As early as the Creation and Fall stories in Genesis we are confronted with a dual answer to the question of human nature. (1) Human beings were created good and placed in a good relation with God (the deepest meaning of the mysterious expression "the image of God," Gen 1–2). But (2) by a horrible rebellion, human beings chose to distrust God's Word and its goodness, chose to strike out on their own to live independently of God's Word, and so became very bad (the meaning of the biblical word "sin," defined by the stories of Gen 3–11). "The Lord saw that the wickedness of man was great in the earth, and that *every* imagination of the thoughts of his heart was *only* evil *continually*" (Gen 6:5 RSV). God thus proceeded to deal with the human race in a twofold way to lead it back to himself: in judgment (the Flood) and in mercy (the Call of Abraham). And God has been dealing with us in the same way ever since—indeed, decisively, in his Son, in the center of history, God assumed for the whole world the judgment that falls on sin and offered to the whole world a free amnesty of mercy. Meanwhile, in summary, human beings are both good essentially and bad existentially, both creatures in God's image and so good, and rebels against God and so bad.

It is possible to interpret the magi story in the two doctrinally classic ways reviewed above and be true to its central teachings. First, the magi appear as mainly *good men* in Matthew's telling (McN., 14; McK., 67; Brown, 168). Second, the magi represent the *evil gentiles* disdained by devout Israel and so play a role somewhat comparable to that of the gentile women in the genealogy. The magi were outsiders both in race (gentiles) and in profession (astrology). Yet *they* were invited to the party. Whatever one thinks of the magi—whether one interprets them as sincere men literally "following their lights" or as idolatrous men captive to superstition—one thing is clear: God in his kindness led them by a sure route to his Son.

Matthew wishes to say by the inclusion of the magi in the heart of his Christmas story, as he had by the inclusion of the women in the heart of his genealogy, that God surmounts racial or moral barriers to his saving work and makes the church interracial and merciful by calling to the Son precisely those persons whom many of the people of God consider unworthy. The magi are walking illustrations of God's catholicity and grace.

There is a little doctrine of revelation in the magi's story, too. The star ("natural revelation") leads the magi to Israel's Scripture in Jerusalem ("scriptural revelation"), which in turn leads them to the Child in Bethlehem ("saving revelation"). It is interesting that the star (or nature) does *not* lead the magi directly to Christ. There is an intermediate stop in Jerusalem in the Israelite church where the Word is opened; then and only then is focus finally given to the star and to the magi's search. The star brings us to Jerusalem; but only Scripture brings us to Bethlehem. Nature can be used to bring us into the church; the church's Bible brings us to the church's Christ. To be sure, the star *re*appears, but only *after* the Scriptures said "Bethlehem" (2:4–9). God uses the natural world and our experience in it to convict us of our need, to awaken longings, and, where God's grace supports, to bring us to the Word in the church. This Word directs us, finally, to our destination: to the Christ. God's revelation in nature raises the question and begins the quest; God's revelation in Scripture gives the answer and directs the quest to the goal. God's revelation in Christ-the-goal satisfies the quest. Natural revelation can only bring human beings halfway; scriptural revelation has the power to bring us home. God in his goodness is the author of both revelations and uses both.

Chrysostom, 6:1:36ff, and Calvin, 1:83, are convinced that even the "natural" revelation of the star was a supernatural gift of the Spirit. On the twofold star and Scripture revelation, cf. esp. Brown, 168, 178, 182, 199f and Meier, *Vis.*, 54f. Bengel, 1:76, admires the way that in revelation God adapts to those he calls: "The magi are led to Christ by a star; the fishermen by fish [Matt 4:19]." Augustine counsels: "Behold what He has made, and love Him who made it" (Serm.18 [68]:2:314). In the words of the hymn, "All nature's works His praise declare, To whom they all belong; There is a voice in every star, In every breeze a song." Psalm 19 says it best of all. And the psalm ends, appropriately, not with the praise of creation, but of Scripture, Ps 19:7–11.

We can penetrate more deeply into the *grace* of God's invitation of the magi if we appreciate that magi were not only understood as good or wise men. The *magoi* (the plural of the Greek *magos*) to whom Matthew refers were, first of all, to be sure, wise men, scholars of the stars in (probably) Persia and the land of the two rivers. At the root of the ancient study of the stars was the conviction that the microcosm of humanity is in a magnetic-symbiotic relationship with the macrocosm of the heavenly bodies. Astro*nomy* ("astral *nomos* or law") was the study of the *laws* or movements of the stars; astro*logy* ("astral *logos* or word") was the study of the *message* or meaning of the stars' movements for earthly life (cf. Grund., 80). The two disciplines, now rightly separated, were combined in the same persons in the ancient world. Because of their skill in deciphering the meanings or messages of the stars, the magi were widely considered "wise men."

But in the religion of Israel the opinion was very different. In Israel's conviction the magi were idolaters, short and simple. This conviction is carried over into the New Testament where every other reference to a *magos* is unfavorable (see, e.g., Acts 8:9–24 for Simon the *magos*, and Acts 13:6–11 for Elymas or Bar-Jesus, the *magos* and false prophet). The magi were held to be people who looked, and who taught others to look, to beggarly creatures rather than to the Creator for guidance; they looked to their own calculations, "wisdom," and mental creations (to zodiacs, for example), for delivering the meaning of things. Israel cordially despised the magicians and astrologers of the gentile world and felt that God had decisively rescued his people from the tyranny of the stars and from those who claimed to know their secrets.

For official Israel's view of magi see Str.-B., 1:76; Schl., *Das,* 12–14; Schl., *Der,* 23–29; Green, 57; Davies, 79; and for full discussion, Delling, *magos,* TWNT, 4:360–63.

Yahweh's miraculous intervention in the Exodus from Egypt had delivered Israel from the house not only of physical slavery but from spiritual and mental thraldom to the constellations as well. To Israel and to the early church, then, astrologers would be the least deserving guests at the birthday party of the Christ.

This is why Matthew—the evangelist!—is delighted to see exactly such persons invited. The invitation of the astrologers to the coming-out party of Christ indicates the deep and wide mercy of God that Matthew had already either found or inserted in his Old Testament genealogical studies. The God and Father of our Lord Jesus Christ is *for all* people—the genealogy showed this in the four women; and now the invitation of the astrologers (as we say, "of *all* people!") proves this "for-all-ness" of God in another dramatic way. The Gospel that ends with the Great Commission *to* the nations (28:19) begins here at Christmas with a surprising invitation *of* the nations, and, indeed, of what many considered the nations' worst elements.

When we read "magi," therefore, we may think, as the serious readers of the people of God did, not only of wise men and astronomers, but also and equally of magicians and astrologers. (The English word *magician* comes from the Greek word *magos*, and the word *magician* might in fact be the best translation of the New Testament word *magos*.) To be sure, the magicians *became* wise men by their following God's beckoning revelation; but what they *were*, from the point of view of God's people instructed by God's Word, was the dregs of un-wisdom, of *hubris*, and of deception. "For the king of Babylon stands . . . at the head of the two ways, to use divination; he shakes the arrows, he consults the teraphim, he looks at the liver" (Ezek 21:21 RSV; Isa 47 is one long and stinging indictment of Babylon's enchanters and sorcerers: "let *them* stand forth and save you, those who divide the heavens, who gaze at the stars, who at the new moons predict what shall befall you," Isa 47:13 RSV).

But God in Jesus comes precisely to and for *magos*-man-and-woman, touches our planet, is born in Bethlehem, and dies a few years later just outside Jerusalem "for us." *Magos*-man is sought-after-man, loved-man, divinely-loved-man. The most degraded kinds of people—those who fancied themselves wise but were actually fools—were God's first guests at the historical unveiling of his Son. This is one meaning of the magi for the church's doctrine of the human person. The human person per se is in trouble; the human person *per Christum* (through Christ) has been deeply helped. This is one way Christians are taught to look at people and at themselves—as troubled people who have been helped. And it is the special contribution of the magi in our story that they focus this evangelical looking.

"And you [gentiles] he made alive, when you were dead through the trespasses and sins in which you once walked, following the course of this world, following the prince of the power of the air, the spirit that is now at work in the sons of disobedience" (Eph 2:1f RSV).

There is another consideration. It has always been a little embarrassing to theology that God's initial means of revelation to the magicians was *their idol*—the stars. And yet we must look closely at exactly what happened. This chapter shows the sovereign control of the God and Father of Jesus Christ over *nature* and its stars just as the opening chapter of the Gospel had shown that sovereignty over *history* and its genealogies. God takes the unusual in both history (chapter 1, the four women) and nature (chapter 2, the star) and uses them for his glory. The God of Jesus Christ is the Creator both of heaven with its stars and of earth with its genealogies, and he moves and uses both as he will.

Matthew certainly does not intend to encourage his readers to look to the heavens for saving revelations. As Ignatius of Antioch wrote shortly after Matthew, Jesus Christ was celebrated not least because he brought the world a decisive liberation from bondage to the stars (*Eph.* 19; similarly in other church parents: Justin, *Dial.*, 78; Tert., *Idol.*, 78; Origen, *Cels.*, 1:60). Matthew had not by any means intended to deliver people over again to the ambiguous messages of stars. Matthew does not want Christians to consult astrologers.

Astrology "was always a pseudo-science, for it depended upon the theory that the earth is the centre of the universe, and that the planets are living powers, mighty spirit-beings which have the moral characteristics of the gods of the old mythology whose names they bear" (Beare, 74).

Ever since the coming of Jesus Christ, then, we are not referred to any other source of saving revelation than one: the ministry of the biblical Word of Jesus Christ. *The Theological Declaration of Barmen* (1934), thesis 1, puts this persuasion perfectly:

Jesus Christ, as he is attested for us in Holy Scripture, is the *one* Word of God which we have to hear and which we have to trust and obey in life and in death. We reject the false doctrine [which suggests that] the church could and would have to acknowledge as a source of its [preaching], apart from and besides this *one* Word of God, still other events and powers, figures and truths, as God's revelation.

The uncertain stars have been superceded by the sure Word, the heavenly bodies by the luminous gospel. Wherever this gospel is preached in purity and the sacraments of this gospel are administered in accordance with a pure understanding of God's Word, fresh light falls on the face of Jesus Christ, and people find him and their own gifts and go home in a new way. From now on, the work of the *ministry* is to do the work of the star. What was said of the star then should be said of the church's teaching since then: "it came and stood shining *right over* the place where the Child lay" (2:9). Church teaching, like the ancient star, is to be utterly christocentric.

The sixteenth-century Reformation and twentieth-century New Reformation theologies have taught this christocentricity with charismatic energy. Karl Barth, for example, illustrates the importance of christocentric preaching in Luther's theology in several telling citations from Luther. "'The oral and public sermon . . . the voice or word cried forth by the mouth' is now for [Luther] the light. . . . The star of Bethlehem, the star of the wise men, should be in every case 'the lively preaching . . . of Christ as the same is hid and promised in Scripture; . . . for the Gospel teacheth nought but Christ, and Scripture likewise hath nought but Christ. . . . To have Scripture without the knowledge of Christ is to have no Scripture'" (WA 10^I, pp. 625–28). Again: "'Christ is completely wrapped in Scripture as the body in the swaddling clothes. Preaching is the crib in which he lies and is set, and from it [preaching!] we get food and provender' (Sermon on Luke 2; 1523, WA 12:418, 24)"—Karl Barth, *Church Dogmatics*, I/1, paragraph 4.4, pp. 122–23. Barth's "Doctrine of the Word of God" in *Church Dogmatics* I/1, paragraphs 1–10, and I/2, paragraphs 19–24, is evangelicalism at its best.

The theological meaning of Matthew's star, which beckons the magi, is that "*every* expectation is fulfilled in Jesus, not only that of the Old Testament, but also the expectation of the whole [natural] world: here is the world-king whom all await" (Schn., 18). "Jesu, Joy of Man's Desiring" is the meaning of Matthew's star.

But it is now that the irony intended by Matthew occurs. The despised and pagan astrologers who have nothing but their natural idols are led to Israel who has the written Word, and, when this Word is heard (by both groups!), it is *the pagans* who eagerly follow it, while the leadership of the people of God sits complacently (or conspiratorially) at home. The despised believe the Word, the devout ignore it. This was exactly the situation Matthew found in the late first century, too. The people of God, to whom the Word had originally been given, heard the Word, but many did not believe it; the gentiles outside the Word heard the Word and believed it. The people to whom the promises were especially given do not now believe these promises enough to walk the ten kilometers to receive the promises that lay present and breathing in the Child.

This theological paradox is stressed in Schl., *Das*, 12–14; Schn., 18; Davies, 327; Bonn., 24; Schw., 37. For the historical-theological meaning, cf. McN., 22. The biblical-theological significance of the magi passage is summed up well at Eph 2:12–13.

The call of the magi is the doctrine of grace. *The doctrine of grace* in the history of the early church can be studied in the following resources: the theology of Augustine, especially his anti-Pelagian writings (conveniently summarized in *On the Grace of Christ*, 418, chap 24, and *On the Spirit and the Letter*, 412, chap 40); The Sixteenth Council of Carthage, 418; The Indiculus, ca. 435–442, esp. chaps 1, 6, and 9; The Second Council of Orange, 529; and now Jaroslav Pelikan, *The Emergence of the Catholic Tradition (100–600)* ("The Christian Tradition," 1; Chicago: The University of Chicago Press, 1971), chap 6.

The scholastic theology of the late medieval church taught, in Bonaventura's famous formula, "If a man does all within his power *[facit quod in se est]*, God gives him grace." According to scholastic theology, God called only the sincere—only *good* magi! This false doctrine persists in all cultures: "God helps those who help themselves"; *"Wer immer strebend sich bemüht, den können wir erlösen"* ("Whoever really strives and tries,. that person we can save." Goethe's *Faust*); *"Nasa Dios ang awa, nasa tao ang gawa"* ("It is up to God to give the grace, but it is up to man to do the work." Tagalog proverb).

However, the church's teaching on grace, following the biblical teaching on revelation, insists that all persons come to God in another way: If the magi seek God's Christ, it is because God's grace, using external means, first seeks the magi. Pre-scholastic Augustinian Catholicism and magisterial Reformation Protestantism taught this fundamental truth very clearly.

The pellucid biblical source of this teaching, of course, is the grace theology of the apostle Paul, which can be summarized in the following string of remarks: "So [getting] God's grace depends not on human will or effort, but on the merciful God" (Rom 9:16); "If God's choice [of people] is by grace, then it is no longer on the basis of works [i.e., doings, strivings, even sincerity, etc.]; otherwise grace would no longer be grace" (Rom 11:6); "Now to one who works [e.g., "does all within his power," or "his best"], his wages are not reckoned as a *gift*, but as his due; but to one who does *not* work but *trusts* him who justifies the *ungodly* [!] his faith is reckoned as righteousness" (Rom 4:4–5); "We are justified *gratis* by his *gratia* through the liberation which is in Christ Jesus" (Rom 3:24).

The Reformed branch of the church teaches the doctrine of divine grace with the most flair. *The Scots Confession* (1560) is the boldest: "This our Faith and the assurance of the same, proceeds not from flesh and blood, that is to say, from any natural powers within us . . . ; for by nature we are so dead, so blind, and so perverse, that neither can we feel when we are pricked, see the light when it shines [!], nor assent to the will of God when it is revealed, unless the Spirit of the Lord Jesus quicken that which is dead, remove the darkness from our minds, and bow our stubborn hearts to the obedience of his blessed will. . . . without all respect of any merit proceeding from us, be it before, or be it after our Regeneration. To speak this one thing yet in more plain words: As we willingly spoil ourselves of all honour and glory of our own Creation and Redemption, so do we also of our Regeneration and Sanctification, for of ourselves we are not sufficient to think one good thought, but he that has begun the work in us, is only he that continues us in the same, to the praise and glory of his undeserved grace" (Chap XII, "Of Faith in the Holy Ghost").

For Anglican Christianity, articles ten and thirteen of *The Thirty-Nine Articles of the Church of England*, are instructive and in the Augustinian tradition. John Wesley's twenty-five *Methodist Articles of Religion* (1784), an abridgment of the Thirty-Nine Articles, ominously drops the Anglican thirteenth article "Of Works before Justification," signaling the gradual departure of a part of Protestantism from the Augustinianism that was present at its creation.

Luther's deservedly famous answer in *The Small Catechism* (1529) to the question of the meaning of the third article of the Creed ("I believe in the Holy Spirit," etc.) wraps this matter of prevenient grace up best: "I believe that by my own reason or strength I cannot believe in Jesus Christ my Lord, or come to him. But the Holy Spirit has called me through the Gospel [and] enlightened me with his gifts. . . ."

Matthew clearly teaches that the star, the people of God in Jerusalem, and their Holy Scriptures are the external means of grace used by God in bringing the magi to Christ. The point of both Matthew's teaching in particular and of the church's official understanding of the whole of biblical teaching in general is this: if anyone comes to Christ it is at God's bidding and by God's power.

2:11–12 What then happens to people when they come into *contact* with the living Jesus Christ? Matthew indicates the fundamental changes when he writes at the very first encounter: "And when they came into the house they saw the Child with Mary his mother, and they fell down and worshiped him, and they opened their resources *[thēsauros]* and brought him gifts—gold and frankincense and myrrh. And having been warned in a dream not to go back to Herod, they went home to their country another way" (2:11–12).

The simplicity of the account—the first reported encounter between "the world" and the actual Christ—is noteworthy. The baby does not, as in the apocryphal Gospels and even in the Koran, speak precocious wisdom or do miracles from the crib. He is a baby. No halos are in evidence, no great glory. And reverence is given exclusively to the child (*autō*, singular, not Mary).

The two most striking features in the account are (1) the worship and (2) the going home another way.

1. *Worship* (2:11): In his temptations Jesus will reply that worship belongs only to God: "You shall worship *[proskynēseis]* the Lord your God and him only *[monō]* shall you serve" (Matt 4:10). In the light of this fundamental Jewish and Christian conviction, it is surprising that here at the beginning of the Gospel—and then again at the end of the Gospel too—*Jesus* is "worshiped" (*prosekunēsan*, 2:11; cf. 28:9, 17). I believe that Matthew intends to say here, indirectly but unambiguously, that Jesus is divine.

Proskynēseis can mean either showing royal honor in human fashion—thus Cal., 1:84, 88; Lohm., 22 n. 1; Schl., *Der*, 31; or it can mean literal worship of the divine—thus, with particular attention to Matthew's usage, *TDNT*, 6:763–74, and esp., Bultmann, 358 (who writes that Matthew "raises the stature of Jesus into the divine by using the appropriate expressions"; e.g., Jesus is "worshiped" in Mark's Gospel only once, but in Matthew ten times); Grund., 77; Green, 59. In the NT, both Peter and an angel emphatically rejected *proskynēseis*-worship: Peter, "I too am a man" [Acts 10:25f; Rev 19:10; 22:9]. Chrysostom,

7:5:47, in commenting on the magi's worship of the child in Matt 2:11, sees *both* the humanity and divinity involved: "Let Marcion [denier of Jesus' true humanity] be ashamed, beholding God worshiped *in the flesh*. Let Paul [of Samosata, denier of Jesus' full deity] be ashamed, beholding him *worshiped* as not being merely a man."

The church's history confirms this first great reaction of people to Christ: the nations do proceed to worship Jesus. Meeting him, people *are* moved to worship. He has what God is; he draws from us what only God can rightly draw—worship. Jesus Christ is Lord of the whole world. ("Nations shall come to your light, and kings to the brightness of your rising," Isa 60:3. "May all kings fall down before him, all nations serve him," Ps 72:11.)

Worship opens people up so that they give gifts (2:11; cf. Acts 2:44!). In worshiping Christ, people find themselves opening their resources and giving what they have to him. The meaning of life begins to be the giving of oneself to the honor of Jesus Christ. To worship Christ is to wish to give him goods and services.

2. *The Other Way Home* (2:12): The magi were then, finally, directed to return home another way. One is tempted to capitalize Matthew's word "way" here because Matthew will use the word elsewhere with theological overtones (7:13–14: the "narrow way"; 21:32: John the Baptist bringing "the way of righteousness"; cf. also Mark 10:52; Acts 9:2, 9, 23; 22:4; 24:14, 22). Matthew may wish to indicate—or more accurately, I like to see Matthew indicating—the truth that encounter with Christ means not only a new metaphysical relationship (worship) but also new moral, material or social relationships: it means "going another Way" (cf. Gund., 158 and Hill, 82, who see this intention in Matthew).

II. KING HEROD: HUMANITY UNDER THE POWER OF SIN (2:3–5, 7–8, 16–19)

The second major figure in Matthew's cast of characters in this chapter is the person Matthew consistently calls "King" Herod *until* significantly, the magi worship Christ. For immediately after their worship, Herod is symbolically dethroned and is never again called king. The magi's worship is Jesus' coronation. In the words of the Christmas folk song, "a new king's born today."

2:1–3 Matthew intentionally contrasts the two claimants to kingship in this chapter's opening verses when he tells us that "when Jesus had been born in Bethlehem of Judea in the days of Herod *the king*, look, magi from the East arrived in Jerusalem and said, 'Where is the one who has been born *the king* of the Jews?' . . . When Herod *the king* heard this he was troubled and all Jerusalem with him" (2:1–3). Who is king?! Jerusalem had good reason to be troubled whenever Herod was troubled because Herod's troubles usually meant the people's. Herod had killed three of his own sons in his mad drive to keep his crown. Caesar Augustus had said only partly in jest that "it is better to be Herod's pig than his son" (Grund., 84; a pun in Greek—*hys* means pig; *huios* means son, as Beare, 82, shows). Thus when the innocents from the East naively asked King Herod where the newborn *king* was, they unintentionally kindled a fury that was only partly sated by the slaughter of the innocents. "Christ is the peace of the righteous, the trouble of the wicked" (Quesnel).

In Herod we see even more clearly what theology calls original sin—depth sin, deep sin. The human person is infected with a diseased self-centeredness, and

Herod serves as simply a more graphic representation of what *all* of us are, more subtly, within. The human person fights passionately for self-sovereignty and will go to almost any length to retain one's own crown, one's own self-rule, one's own power. "The man whose one desire is to do what he likes has never any use for Jesus Christ" (Barc., 1:30).

Herod therefore teaches us that one of the first reactions of raw human nature to the kingship of Jesus is rebellion. If Jesus is Lord then we are not. If Jesus *is* king then what we thought was our sovereignty is over.

It is of theological importance that we realize that Herod is not merely the Gospel villain; he is Everyman. Herod's reaction to a center of the universe other than himself is ours generally and specifically: dis-ease. Paul put this most clearly when he began his great section on the doctrine of human nature by writing, "For the wrath of God is revealed from heaven against all ungodliness and unrighteousness of persons *who suppress the truth*" of the God-given knowledge of God in creation (Rom 1:18–20). And these persons who suppress the truth, Paul goes on to show, are not just a group within the human race, or a minority or even a majority of the human race: they are *all* of us, and therefore Paul concludes his section on the human situation by quoting a psalm that says "'there is not *one* person who is righteous, no, not one; there is no one who understands, there is not *one* who seeks God'" (Rom 3:10–11; cf. Ps 14:1–3; 53:1–3).

Consequently, it is important for our understanding of the Christian teaching of the *Humanum* to see that Herod here, though an extreme case, is not an isolated one. Herod is what I am deep down inside. As the gentile magi, before they were led to Christ, represent what we are in an external sense—aliens, "alienated from the commonwealth of Israel, and strangers to the covenants of promise, having no hope and without God in the world" (Eph 2:12 RSV), so Herod represents what we are in an internal sense—rebels, "following the desires of body and mind, and so . . . by nature children of wrath" (Eph 2:3 RSV). It is only as we learn to see ourselves in the problematic persons of the Gospel—from the four questionable couples in the genealogy, through Herod here, the Pharisees later, and, Romans at the passion— that we will be reading the Gospel texts existentially. Herod is original sin, and this sin lives on, according to Reformation teaching, even in baptized Christians. Though original sin is covered and pardoned by God's grace in baptism, and wrestled with and conquered by God's Spirit in the Christian life, it is still there inside us, and it constantly tempts. Herod lives, and he lives in us, tempting us ever and anew to doubt, hate, and resist the real king. "For our flesh in itself is corrupt and inclined to evil, *even after* we accept and believe God's Word" (Luther, *Large Catechism*, 110, emphasis added; cf. the present tense verbs in *The Heidelberg Catechism*, Q. 60).

On the importance—indeed, the necessity, of seeing past biblical figures ourselves (of seeing Herod in us, for example, in this chapter), readers are reminded of Huck Finn's irrelevant learning of the Old Testament from Widow Douglas: "After supper she got out her book and learned me about Moses and the Bulrushers, and I was in a sweat to find out all about him; but by and by she let it out that Moses had been dead a considerable long time; so then I didn't care no more about him, because I don't take no stock in dead people." Nor do we.

In the church's history it was the Protestant Reformation, reappropriating Augustine, that came down hardest on what we will call the Herod-nature of the human person, on what classical theology calls original sin. In one of his early disputations, Luther vehemently rejected scholastic optimism about human nature and insisted in a ringing counterthesis, "Man is *not* 'able by nature to want God to be God'; indeed, he wants himself to be God and he does not want God to be God" (*The Heidelberg Disputation,* 1518, thesis 17). Luther, the theologian whose great cry was "Let God be God!," was also the theologian who through his study of Scripture came to the conviction that human nature is not at all godly, unless out of pretense; rather, our basic inclination is self-deification, that *incurvatus in se,* that "bent toward self," which, by definition, bends us away from the living God.

Calvin, too, insisted that if we are ever tempted to look for any good in ourselves apart from God, we should be warned that we are taking advice from our enemy, the one who tempted our first parents to independent living ("you will be like gods," Gen 3). "If it is the devil's word that exalts man in himself, let us give no place to it unless we want to take advice from our enemy. . . . 'Cursed is the man who trusts in man and makes flesh his arm'" (*Inst.* II.ii.10).

Herod, the big king who resisted the coming of the little king, is what about half our own heart is. Paul calls this heart in us "flesh," meaning not just our so-called lower nature, but also and especially all those things we think are our higher nature—our reason, conscience, soul, pride, and dignity.

The whole doctrine of original sin—of Herod—is intended to teach us *our need.* We are in a bad way. Later, Jesus will tell a Peter puffed up with his own dedication but failing in particulars that "the Spirit is willing and able, but human nature is *sick*" (26:36–41, where the exposition will explain this translation). We need a savior—even (or especially) we who think we are strong Christians.

2:4–6 It is important to see that Herod had a chance. When he heard the magi's strange question he summoned all the clergy and theologians he could muster and inquired of them just where "the Christ" (the Jewish way of saying "the last-time king") was to be born. Their answer was quick because it was common dogma, based on a clear Micah text: Bethlehem. "And you, Bethlehem, land of Judah, you are not at all the least important of the leaders of Judah, because out of you is going to come a Ruler who will shepherd my people Israel" (Matt 2:6, from Mic 5:2, with additions from 2 Sam 5:2).

Matthew typically alters his Old Testament citation from its original "You, O Bethlehem . . . , who *are* little," to "You, O Bethlehem, . . . *are by no means* the littlest," reminding us of his alterations in the genealogy, and revealing his theology: "From the moment that Jesus is born, Bethlehem is no longer the little town without importance that she was a short while ago" (Bonn., 26). "Matthew intended, by this alteration, to praise God for His grace" (Cal., 1:86). Cf. Schl., *Der,* 35; Lohm., 23; Green, 58. The continuation of Micah 5:2 points mysteriously to the Messiah's preexistence, "whose origin is from of old, from ancient days" (on which cf. Chrys., 7:1:44). The Messiah as "shepherd-leader," imported into Mic 5:2/Matt 2:6 from 2 Sam 5:2, reveals Matthew's appreciation of the gentleness of the Messiah (Brown, 118; cf. Ps 28:9; Ezek 34:23–24).

Herod, too, heard this Scripture. This was Herod's chance. When "Bethlehem" was read in his hearing it was God's oral invitation to Herod to come, too. Herod and magi—both sinners, both aliens from God—both heard God's gracious Word in clarity and so received engraved invitations to the party. But Herod—and even more surprisingly, the whole synod and its theological faculty—heard this Word and did not pursue it. The Word "came to his own home, and his own people received him not" (John 1:11 RSV). This is one of the great theological mysteries: Israel rejected her Messiah while the gentiles accepted him.

Herod was original sin, depth sin. Yet his sin was not so deep that God's grace did not reach down to it, too, and give Herod the freeing Word. Herod got the Word. Herod had a chance. Herod heard the gospel in its most embryonic form— "Bethlehem"—and he did not (or would not) heed it. But it was not the gospel's fault; the gospel came to Herod, too, and he did not want it, except to murder it.

2:7–8 Herod's last public act in the presence of the magi was to find out when they had seen the star. We may surmise that the magi's answer was in the neighborhood of one to two years before because Herod later has all children in Bethlehem under two years killed. Herod then sent the magi on their way with the royal command to "Go and look real hard for that child, and when you find him come and tell me so that I, too, can come and worship him" (2:8). (Herod says "look for the child"; he could not bring himself to say "look for the *king*," Chrys., 7:3:46.)

The hypocrisy of Herod's commission reeks; his sloth, too. If he had had the most elemental religious yearnings, awakened by the Word, he would have made the two- or three-hour trip south to Bethlehem and taken a look. But neither his superstitious respect for the magi's calculations nor a remnant of religious respect for Micah's Word moved him. (Cf. Chrys., 7:3:45; Beng., 1:79.)

2:16 Herod's final active scene in the Gospel is his slaughtering of the innocents. The magi had gone home another way, Herod had heard about it, and he was livid.

"Then when Herod saw that he had been tricked by the magi he was furious, and he sent to have all the infants annihilated in Bethlehem and in the whole surrounding region who were two years old and under (according to the date he had gotten from the magi)" (2:16).

The theological lesson is this: Those who begin by hating the Child will end by hurting children. Hating revelation leads to hurting people. If people will be ungodly they will be inhumane. Herod is the Gospel's earliest evidence of this fact. (See the same truth and sequence in Gen 3 and 4.)

Paul's great doctrine of human nature says the same thing. "Since they thought it best not to have God in their minds [theological Fall], God handed them over to thoughtless minds [anthropological Fall] to do vicious things: filled with all kinds of rottenness, greed, wickedness; full of murder, envy, jealousy, guile, crudity, gossip, bad-talk, God-hating, arrogant, self-important, . . . creative only in doing evil, disrespectful to parents, without understanding, without fidelity, without heart, without mercy" (Rom 1:28–31).

This Romans paragraph is an almost perfect description of Herod's history in Matthew chapter 2. The Romans paragraph and the Matthean story are deep examinations of the pathology of history. What Paul describes systematically, Matthew describes biographically. If we let our Herod-nature get the upper hand, if we will not even take half-seriously the Word when it comes to us, the game is over. And the result is not going to be just a missed *individual* opportunity—sin is more social than that; the result is going to be a number of hurt people. The truth that Matthew pictures and Paul describes is that wherever God is resisted humanity is attacked.

Therefore in this locus of the doctrine of human nature just as the magi serve as an *encouragement* to us—as examples of how God's grace can summon us, no matter how unworthy we are—so Herod is a *warning* to us, an example of what can happen to us if we despise grace. If, like the magi, we heed the holy ministry and listen to its Word and go to Bethlehem, there will be worship and another Way. But if, like Herod, who also was given the Word, we will listen only enough to find ways of resisting, then it is not only we who will be hurt but innocents around us; for sin, like righteousness, is social.

The Confession of 1967, in its section entitled "The Sin of Man," defines sin like this (and like Herod): "In sin men claim mastery of their own lives, turn against God and their fellow men, and become exploiters and despoilers of the world. They lose their humanity in futile striving and are left in rebellion, despair, and isolation."

2:17–18 Matthew's own commentary on the slaughter of the innocents is worth noting:

"Then was fulfilled the word spoken through Jeremiah the prophet when he said, 'A voice can be heard in Rama, weeping and much bitterness; Rachel is crying for her children, and she refuses to be comforted, because they are gone'" (2:17–18).

History cannot overwhelm the evangelist, not even the most evil history. In everything tragic that happens—including most particularly the cross, where the evangelists notoriously avoid sentimentality—Matthew sees the sovereignty of God. The people of God is a single great community stretching over the centuries, and as the long-deceased matriarch Rachel wept at the later exile of her children to Assyria and Babylon (in 722–721 and 597–587 B.C.), so now she weeps again at the murder of the innocents (in about 5 B.C.). In Matthew's opinion, what Jeremiah had written poetically about Rachel's *exile*-weeping, really reached its *ful*fillment in the history of Jesus. The *full*-filling of all Scripture in *Christ's* history is the deep meaning behind Matthew's constant citing of Old Testament sources.

Calvin, 1:103, as often, catches the sense of the text: "That [Jeremiah] attributes the grief to the dead Rachel is a personification to increase the sensation of emotion." Matthew does not mean that Jeremiah contained a prediction of what a much later Herod would do, "but that at Christ's coming the grief which the Benjamites had suffered many centuries before was renewed" (ibid.). The text means what it means, not what it says Matthew's use of the Old Testament is more catechetical than documentary (Bonn., 29), more theological than historical (though it is sometimes historical), and more christological than chronological. Matthew's approach to Scripture invalidates many historical corrections he receives from unimaginative commentators.

While we may no longer be able to interpret Scripture as naively or wide-rangingly as Matthew did, we can appreciate that Jesus was *so* real to Matthew that Matthew was persuaded that all Old Testament verses found their dimension of depth only in Jesus' history. Everyone who has felt the "expulsive power of the new affection" brought by Christ also knows how one looks at *everything* differently after Him—and not least, how one looks differently at God's Word in the Old Testament. "When anyone is united to Christ, there is a new world" (2 Cor 5:17, NEB), and part of this new world is a new Bible.

But what is even more to the point is this: history's savageries do not throw Matthew. Matthew finds in his own Book of Signs—the Hebrew Scriptures—a sign of the meaning of the recent tragedy in Bethlehem—not a sign that solves, but a sign that sympathizes. Matthew's Jeremiah sign sympathizes with the tragedy of the innocents not by saying, cheaply, "It's not so bad," but by saying, "Rachel, too, weeps."

Just as the Egyptian exile stands near the beginning of Israel's history, and the Babylonian exile in the middle, and now the Roman "exile" at "the end," so in the *decisive* history of Israel—the history of Israel's Messiah—a slaughter of the innocents stands at the beginning of the Gospel (chap 2), a slaughter of the innocent Baptist in the middle (chap 11), and a slaughter of the innocent one himself at the end (chap 27). The history of the people of God is the history of the mystery of iniquity, but underneath the iniquity, sympathizing with its victims and judging its agents, stand God's prophets and evangelists giving perspective.

For Jesus to live now, innocents must die; for all to live hereafter, the innocent Jesus must die (Grund., 84). The number of children killed, if any, ranges in the commentaries from a plausible twelve or so to, in one accommodation to Rev 14:1–5, even 144,000, "equaling the number of 'those who have not defiled themselves with women,'" to which Brown, 204–05, tartly adds, "a safely attributed virtue at the age of two."

Then Herod dies. "And when Herod had died, look an angel . . ." (2:19). The terseness of this reference to the death of the old ogre is in good taste. Matthew gives not one hint of a fact that fascinated all other historians of Herod's death— that the death was awful and agonizing. (See James Michener's chapter on Herod in *The Source* for a popular depiction of the event.) Matthew will not use Herod's macabre death to prove the wrath or justice of God or to vindicate his own evangelical history. Matthew knows, as Schlatter, *Der,* 45, comments, that pointing to the fall of one's enemies can be self-serving and, when done to justify the ways of God, can be perverse. Matthew simply records that Herod died, without any histrionics or pointing of morals.

"Put not your trust in princes, nor in a son of man, in whom there is no help. When his breath departs, he returns to the earth; on that very day his plans perish" (Ps 146:3–4).

But the point of Herod for the doctrine of human nature is this: Herod is *not* dead; Herod lives on, in us. Original sin continues—in us, the people of God (and not just in the enemies of God). The exaggerated ambitions, pretensions, self-centeredness, greed for position, grudge against God, guile, and finally human cruelty and insensitivity, which are all the fruit of our war with God—all these live still in us and must be contended with until the last judgment. Human nature is still the battleground between two great kings—Herod and the Child. We know who overcomes, but meanwhile the battle rages and Herod is here as a warning to the Christian reader of who he or she, in no little measure, still is.

THE DOCTRINE OF ORIGINAL SIN. From the teaching of the early church on human nature we have this definition, "No one, not even he who has been renewed by the grace of Baptism, has sufficient strength to overcome the snares of the devil, and to vanquish the concupiscence of the flesh, unless he obtains help from God each day to persevere in a good life" (The *Indiculus, ca.* 435–442, chap 3).

From the teaching of the Reformation church we have this discussion by Melanchthon: "So we teach nothing about original sin that is contrary to the Scripture or the church catholic, but we have cleansed and brought to light important teachings of the Scriptures and the Fathers that had been obscured by the sophistic arguments of modern theologians. . . . Recognition of original sin is a necessity, *nor can we know the magnitude of the grace of Christ unless we acknowledge our faults.* . . .

"[Luther] has said that the Holy Spirit, given in Baptism, begins to mortify lust and to create new impulses in man. Augustine speaks the same way when he says, 'Sin is forgiven in Baptism, not that it no longer is, but it is not imputed.' . . . Human nature is enslaved and held prisoner by the devil, who deludes it with wicked opinions and errors and incites it to all kinds of sins. . . . Christ was given to us to bear both sin and penalty and to destroy the rule of the devil, sin, and death; *so we cannot know his blessings unless we recognize our evil*" (*Apology of the Augsburg Confession,* 1531, 2:32–50, emphasis added).

The single deepest remark on the mystery of original sin that I have encountered is Luther's: "This hereditary sin is so deep a corruption of nature that reason cannot understand it. It must be *believed* because of the revelation in the Scriptures (Ps 51:5; Rom 5:12ff; Exod 33:20; Gen 3:6ff)" (*The Smalcald Articles,* 1537, 3:1:3). Bainton, 228, summarizes Luther's thought here well: "The very recognition that we are sinners is an act of faith. 'By faith alone [Luther wrote] it must be believed that we are sinners, and indeed more often than not we seem to know nothing against ourselves. Wherefore we must stand by God's judgment and believe his words by which he calls us unrighteous.'" Luther means that we habitually underestimate the seriousness of sin. (We remember Anselm's trenchant "You have not considered the gravity of sin.") Almost every time I look at newborn babies in a nursery I think, "original sin can't be true." But almost every time I attend a good movie and have to sit through previews of coming attractions to see it, I think, "original sin is true." Human experience is a teacher with a forked tongue. But Scripture tells us the hard truth about ourselves. Scripture shocks us again and again with its pictures of God's wrath against sin, from the Flood and the exiles to the cross and the last judgment.

If it were not for Scripture's teaching of the viciousness of sin we would have a hard time believing or feeling, much of the time, that we are all *that* bad. But sin runs deeper than feelings or appearances—the church's doctrine of original sin does us the service of drilling this depth perception of the human problem into our consciousness and conviction. Finally—"the smoking pistol"—we see ourselves most clearly in our execution of God's Son (Matt 26–27). Original sin must, indeed, "be believed because of the revelation in the Scriptures." John Calvin's *Institutes,* Book 2, the opening chapters, gives the church the classic representation of the human problem in the doctrine of sinful human nature.

Karl Barth's commentary, *The Epistle to the Romans* (sixth edition, 1928, pp. 85f), has a powerful paragraph on the doctrine of original sin which deserves to close this consideration of the doctrine of original sin in the person of Herod. "'We have before charged that . . . all are under sin. As it is written' [Rom 3:9–10]. Is there in all this [teaching of universal human sinfulness] something new and surprising? Is it resignation following upon disillusionment, or enthusiasm born of pessimism? Is it violence offered to the riches of human life, a revolt against history, or the arrogance of some form of Gnostic radicalism? No, the indictment of which we disapprove so strongly—'it is written'; it has been 'proclaimed long ago' ([Rom] 1:2). The whole course of history pronounces this indictment against itself. How can a man be called 'historically minded', if he persistently overlooks it? If all the great outstanding figures in history, whose judgements are worthy of serious consideration, if all the prophets, Psalmists, philosophers, Fathers of the Church, Reformers, poets, artists, were asked their opinion, would one of them assert that men were good, or even capable of good? Is the doctrine of original sin merely one doctrine among many? Is it not rather, according to its fundamental meaning (see, however, v. 12), *THE* Doctrine which emerges from all honest study of history? Is it not the doctrine which, in the last resort, underlies the whole teaching of history? Is it possible for us to adopt a 'different point of view' from that of the Bible, Augustine, and the Reformers?" (Emphasis in the original.)

III. THE CHILD: REPRESENTATIVE HUMANITY
(2:6, 11, 13–15, 19–23)

The third part of this chapter, revolving around the Christ Child, is more difficult to characterize without being artificial than are the first two parts, revolving around the magi and Herod. It is clear that for Matthew the magi mean God's calling outsiders, and that Herod means the obstinacy of insiders. But what, clearly, does this chapter's story of the Christ Child mean?

The Child is, of course, Emmanu-El, God with us (chap 1). But he is also a human child (chap 2), and one has the feeling that Matthew is indeed trying to tell us something human about Jesus in this chapter. Jesus is too young to act yet; in this chapter he is always acted upon. In the latter part of the chapter where he (and not the magi or Herod) is the focus, he is mainly a refugee child, a fugitive, a most wanted person. The key facts that emerge around him are mainly geographical (Stendahl). It is the route Jesus travels that fascinates Matthew and that Matthew emphasizes.

On closer investigation, interpreters have discovered that Jesus' career in chapter 2 retraces the career of Old Israel almost exactly. Jesus goes from the promised land in Israel to the classic land of escape, Egypt, just as all the patriarchs (from Abraham to Joseph) had done in the beginning. Then, like a second Moses in a kind of second Exodus, Jesus is called up out of Egypt to return to the land of promise again ("Out of Egypt I have called my son"). By means of his itinerary Matthew is saying: "Look, the New Israel!"

Thus Jesus represents human nature in a third way—not just as outsiders who are mercied like the magi, nor just as an insider who is judged like Herod, but as a New Israel, as human salvation wrapped up in the life of a single Jewish Child.

In chapter 2's cast of three characters (the mercied one, the judged one, the faithful one), we are reminded of the genealogy in Matthew 1 where in three great historical lines we saw the three theological themes of God's mercy, God's justice, and God's good faith. Now the magi display God's mercy; Herod, God's justice; and the Child, God's good faith. All the Old Testament promises that God made to Israel about her being a blessed and a blessing people (Gen 12:1–3 or Gen 22:18, for example) come true in one Israelite who is, as it were, Israel *Redivivus*, substitute-Israel. In Matthew chapter 1 Jesus was the Representative God, in Matthew chapter 2 Jesus is the Representative People of God.

The full story about human nature is not told when all we know about humanity is that God can have mercy on it, as with the magi, or that God can exercise judgment on it, as with Herod. The Old Testament tells us these two great truths tirelessly. The great new fact about human nature, which becomes finally clear in Jesus, is that humanity has a representative before God who does what Israel was supposed to do, who is "the true human being," the *verus homo*, the Messiah for whom all history has been waiting, and who in his own person, representatively and substitutionally, "fulfills all righteousness" (3:15) for all humanity.

The final meaning of Matthew chapter 2 is *Ecce homo!*, "Behold the Man!"

It is Karl Barth in our century who has most insistently taught us that our knowledge of not only God but of ourselves is given real substance and placed on dependable foundations only when drawn from the study of Jesus Christ, *verus homo, verus Deus*. We learn important data about human persons from the social sciences. But this learning is always, in the nature of the case, tentative, growing, and open to revision and refinement. We need this sophisticated scientific information in order to live intelligently. But meanwhile we need more basic, raw information about human nature in order to live Christianly. This existentially important anthropological information about ourselves and others is given where we should always have expected to find it: in God's great revelation in the man Jesus. Christian theology in our century has been moving back to its sources in Scripture and Scripture's focus, the Christ, to obtain its knowledge not only of the divine will but of the human person as well. For in Christ have been placed "*all* the treasures of wisdom and knowledge" (Col 2:3).

The comic flap over Margaret Mead's and Derek Freeman's Samoa gave social science a needed humility. Melvin Maddocks concluded his essay on this affair by writing, "And this, finally, may be what needs to be revised—the naive notion that the ambitiously named 'social sciences' . . . are precise, methodologically proven avenues to truth rather than hypotheses compounded of some information, some imagination, and some prejudice by admirably ingenious and self-contradictory human beings." ("Will the Real Samoa Stand Up?," *Christian Science Monitor*, Feb. 14, 1983, p. 22).

Appropriately, the third main figure explaining human nature in this chapter's trilogy of figures is Jesus. As Jesus was the climactic figure in chapter 1, explaining God, so now Jesus is the last fully developed figure in chapter 2, explaining Man. He is called "Jesus" only in the first verse of the chapter. Then one name for Jesus dominates all the others in this chapter and is used more than twice as often as the rest of the titles put together: nine times Jesus is called *the Child* (2:8, 9, 11, 13, 14, 20, 21). The frequent use of exactly this title "Child" indicates Matthew's desire here to underline the Christ's fragility, humanity, and sonship to God (Schw., 41).

2:13–14 This Child and his hounded early history remind us also of the child who was Israel's first deliverer—Moses (cf. Exod 1:15—2:10).

"And when [the magi] had withdrawn, look, an angel of the Lord appeared in a dream to Joseph and said, 'Get up and take the child and his mother and flee to Egypt and stay there until I tell you, because Herod is preparing to seek the child and put it to death" (2:13).

Patriarchal history had *ended* in withdrawal to Egypt (Gen 46–50); evangelical history *begins* there (Matt 2). As a wicked king once sought the lives of newborn

Hebrew boys in Egypt (Exod 1), so now another wicked king seeks the life of the newborn Child in Bethlehem. As the old deliverer suffered a hunted life, so the new deliverer suffers a hunted life, too.

The vulnerability of the one just honored as King-Messiah is bound to impress readers. "In spite of the wonder of His birth, the human Infant must be rescued not by miracle but by flight" (McN., 18). Jesus' flight can encourage believers who wonder about their troubles (Chrys., 8:3:51; Calvin, 1:99–100: "This flight is part of the foolishness of the cross, and one that overcame the entire wisdom of this world."). Chrysostom, 8:4:52, adds a nice comment at this point: "Joseph, when he had heard [these orders to flee], was not offended, neither did he say, 'The thing is hard to understand: Didst thou not say just now, that He should 'save His people'? and now He saves not even Himself: but we must fly, and go far from home, and be a long time away: the facts are contrary to the promise.' . . . [But] if from his earliest infancy [Jesus] had shown forth wonders, He would not have been accounted a Man."

2:15 Then, just as Old Israel had been brought out of the land of Egypt, so now is Israel's refugee-deliverer.

"And the family stayed there in Egypt until the death of Herod in order that the Word spoken by the Lord through the prophet would be fulfilled, that which said, 'Out of Egypt I called my son'" (2:15).

When Hosea wrote the line (speaking for God) "Out of Egypt I called my son," Hosea meant Israel; when Matthew read and then reproduced that line he thought Jesus. Hosea's "out of Egypt I called my son," Matthew believes, applies in its deepest sense to God's *real* Son in Egypt. Thus the verse takes a meaning that Hosea never imagined but that evangelists have the license to find.

Alford (in Beng., 1:81) believed this text showed "the almost universal application in the New Testament of [Old Testament] *prophecy* to *Christ;* the Holy Spirit thus sanctioning the view that *He* [the Christ] was the subject of all allusions and dark sayings [in Scripture]." This is an important hermeneutical principle. Matthew, like the rabbis, believed that the prophets spoke not only to *their* "then," but also to the definitive "Then" of the messianic time (Schl., *Der,* 41–42). "Matthew sees that the filial relationship of God's people is now summed up in Jesus who relives in his own life the history of that people" (Brown, 215).

Jesus goes down into Egypt land (in a kind of prefigured crucifixion) and is brought up out again (in a kind of geographical resurrection) in order to inaugurate the New Exodus of the people of God, the definitive exodus, the exodus that will count this time for everyone. As Matthew 1 taught the New Genesis given history by the birth of the promised Son of Abraham, Son of David, so Matthew 2 teaches the New Exodus in the migration in and out of Egypt of Jesus the New Moses (cf. Brown). Jesus fulfills the accepted scriptural requirements for messiahship: Matthew chapter 1 shows this in the persons from whom Jesus descended (Abraham and David); Matthew chapter 2 shows this in the places Jesus touches (Bethlehem, Egypt, Israel) (Green, 51; cf. Stendahl's seminal article, *Quis et Unde* [1964], pp. 94–105).

Another way to explain Matthew's "theological geography"—of Bethlehem (Davidid)—Egypt (Bondage)—Ramah (Exile)—Israel (Kingdom)—Nazareth

(Messianic Ministry)—is this: Jesus takes up into himself the whole of Israel's (and so, representatively, the whole of humanity's) experience, drinks it to the dregs, and "fulfills" it. "What Israel was has now been absorbed into the person of Jesus" (Meier, *Vis.*, 55, n. 19). In the singular career of the New Israel who is Jesus, Israel finally does everything predicted of her in Scripture. All of Isaiah's promises come true in Jesus. Israel comes through in one Israelite. It is the biblical principle of what Oscar Cullmann called "progressive reduction." When all humanity failed (Gen 1–11), Israel was recruited to be the way of salvation for all humanity (Gen 12ff). When Israel failed, Jesus of Nazareth, the Israelite, succeeded in the name and for the sake of Israel (Matt 1ff). Then in "progressive expansion" Jesus forms his church, the new people of God, to be the salt, light, and discipler of all nations (Matt 5:13–16; 28:18–20) until his return for the consummation of the ages. Jesus recapitulates in his person and reinaugurates in his church Israel's history of salvation in the world.

Jesus makes the theological anthropology of Matthew chapter 2 complete. The magi and Herod represent humanity's need; the Child represents humanity's provision. There are two themes in the gospel of the New Testament, and they combine to make one gospel: the grace of our Lord Jesus Christ and humanity's deep need for that grace; sin and grace, need and salvation, the human problem and the divine solution. When either of these is insufficiently appreciated the respect for the other diminishes. One of the reasons for the Reformation stress upon the deep depravity and fearful lostness of persons apart from Christ, beyond the fact that this is the pervasive witness of Scripture, was the desire to magnify the wonder of God's grace in Christ. "We cannot know his blessings unless we recognize our evil" (*The Apology of the Augsburg Confession*). We need to appreciate the magi and Herod in us if we are to appreciate the Christ for us.

To summarize: the major truth we learn about ourselves here is that in Jesus the human problem has been carried, *the human race has been represented.* We are covered. The prophet said it best: "We have all strayed like sheep [the magi-cians], each of us has gone his own way [Herod], but the Lord has laid on *him* [the Child] the iniquity of us *all*" (Isa 53:6). Almost the moment Jesus is born he becomes a refugee—hunted and hated. All his life, even in infancy, he experiences in himself that single verb used in the Apostles' Creed to summarize his career between conception and crucifixion—he "suffered." We may even say that his suffering began prenatally in the public shame experienced by his parents (1:18–19). Now in the second chapter he appears in his own country only to be immediately hounded from it.

The suffering of Jesus, which culminated at the cross, began at birth. But this suffering, our confessions are eager to point out, did not occur in a vacuum or meaninglessly. It was "for us." "Who *for us* men and *for our* salvation came down from heaven . . . ; he was crucified also *for us,*" as the Nicene Faith sings three times for emphasis. "We despised and rejected him; . . . But he endured the suffering that should have been *ours.* He felt the pain that *we* should have borne" (Isa 53:3–4).

Calvin, 1:104, correctly sees why Jesus' childhood was one of suffering: "We must still remember God's purposes, to keep His Son, from the beginning, under the elements of the cross, as this was to be His means of redeeming the Church."

The final providence of God in the theological history of Matthew chapter 2 is the Child's becoming a "Nazorean."

"And when he got to Galilee, Joseph made his permanent residence in a city called Nazareth —so that the Word spoken through the prophets might be fulfilled, namely, that he would be called a 'Nazorean'" (2:23).

A child's home was important in Israel because the child received its name from its place. Since so many Jewish children bore biblical names it was often necessary to attach to the name the town from which the child came. Joseph's first devout instinct on being permitted to return to "the land of Israel" was to bring his providence-laden son either to Bethlehem (a town heavy with Davidic promise) or to Jerusalem (a city full of special promise in Scripture). But the ruler in these places was dangerous, and so Joseph was led north to the most obscure and insignificant of places—to a town in Galilee called Nazareth.

Nazareth was so obscure that when the first-century Jewish historian Josephus listed the towns of Galilee he did not even mention it. It may have been what in the Philippines is called a *"poók"* or a barrio, a settlement too obscure to be called even a village or town. Nazareth was Nowheresville. This obscurity, I like to think, is at least one of the reasons for Matthew's curious plural and unspecified scriptural reference to "the Word spoken through the *prophets.*" What Word? Which prophets? Interpreters of Holy Scripture have been rummaging through Scripture ever since Matthew's citation to locate his sources. They have not been able to find any un-equivocal reference to Nazareth or a Nazorean in the prophets. The two main candidates for sources are, *first,* the promise to the family of David, "then a root shall grow from the stock of Jesse, and a branch [*nēṣer*] from his roots" (Isa 11:1); and *second,* Judges 13:5, 7, and 16:17 that speak of a boy who was to be a *nezîr,* that is, a "Nazarite," or as in some texts, a "holy one," "consecrated to God from birth to the day of his death." There are reasons for believing that these Isaiah and Judges texts are the most likely candidates for Matthew's "prophets" here. There is an attractive third view that harmonizes with the function of Jesus in this chapter: in both Isa 42:6 and 49:6 Yahweh addresses his Servant, using the verb *naṣar* in each text as the One specially "kept" for the messianic vocation of being and creating a remnant "light for the nations" (B. Gärtner, summarized in R. Brown, *John,* 2:810).

Jerome, 1:88, is helpful here: "If the evangelist makes a precise citation he never writes 'which the *prophets* [plural] said,' but simply, 'which the *prophet* said.' But speaking now of 'the prophets' plural, he shows that he has taken not the letter of the Scriptures but the sense." (In the Jewish canon the Book of Judges was one of "the former prophets.")

Jerome's interpretation is shared by other commentators (e.g., Allen, 17–18; Gund., 40), in particular in agreeing that by "prophets" Matthew is "referring to all passages which speak of the Messiah as despised" (Olshausen in Beng., 1:84). Cumulatively, (a) the lowliness and obscurity of the Branch (or "twig") of Isa 11:1 (cf. Isa 4:2; 14:19 [Heb]; Jer 23:5; 33:15; Zech 3:8; 6:12 for other messianic-plant references), (b) the plural "prophets," and (c) the fact that these Righteous-Branch texts are the only texts "to which there is a multiple prophetic witness," all lead Green, 61, and Gundry, 40, following Zahn, to opt for the *lowliness* interpretation of our difficult text. (Both the ancient rabbis and Qumran interpreted the OT Branch texts as witnesses to messianic obscurity, Gund., 40.) Calvin, 1:105, likes Bucer's advocacy of Judges 13:5: "all that Scripture tells [in

Judges 13:5] to Samson's credit must be transferred to Christ by right. . . . Christ is the primary example, Samson is the subsidiary antitype." Strecker, 59–62, in exegetical exhaustion or despair, dismisses the Isa 11:1 and Judges 13:5 options and believes that Matthew just pulled his Nazorean citation "out of the air."

For theological reasons I like to consider the (Jerome-Zahn-Allen-Green-Gundry) possibility, and it is no more than a possibility, that for Matthew a person from Nazareth, a Nazorean, was considered a nobody and that this, too, is what prophets had often predicted the Christ would at first be considered and become for us. For example, Matthew will later cite the prophetic text that says, "See, your king is coming to you, . . . *humble* and mounted on a donkey" (Zech 9:9 at Matt 21:5). And we will discover that the Matthean Beatitudes, especially the inaugural ones, are the flowering of two prophetic promises in particular: "But this is the man to whom I will look, he that is *humble* and contrite in spirit and who trembles at my word" (Isa 66:2); "for thus says the high and lofty one who inhabits eternity, whose name is Holy: 'I dwell in the high and holy place, and also with him who is of a contrite and *humble* spirit, to revive the spirit of the *humble*, and to revive the heart of the contrite'" (Isa 57:15; and cf. especially Matt 11:29 where Jesus says of himself, "I am gentle and lowly in heart"; the other main beatitude source is Isa 66:1–3, with Ps 37:11, "the meek shall possess the land"). Supremely, one thinks of Isaiah 53, cited in part a little while ago, as, for example, "He [the servant of the Lord] grew up before him [the Lord] like a young plant, and like a root out of dry ground [Nazareth?!]; he had no beauty, no majesty to draw our eyes, . . . He was despised, he shrank from the sight of men" (Isa 53:2–3).

One likes to think that the Nazorean divinely promised through the prophets was the suffering Messiah, the Servant of God whose roots were transplanted first from Bethlehem to Egypt, and then from Egypt into the parched ground of Nazareth. He came to take a low place in history with us and for us. Even the town where he would grow up, the town that became half his name, indicates half the truth about him, the truth later nailed over his head on the wood, "Jesus of Nazareth [his lowliness], the King of the Jews [his majesty]" (John 19:19).

"He shall be called a Nazorean," then, may mean at least this: "he shall be considered a nobody." It is the Great God's way to work exactly with nobodies in order, in Paul's words, "to bring to naught the somebodies" (1 Cor 1; cf. Judg 6–7 and Gideon).

He who will be majestically called "The With-Us-God" and "God-Saves" (Matt 1) will also be modestly called "The Child" and "Jesus of Nazareth" (Matt 2). We have descended from Jesus' absolute deity in Matt 1:23 (from Isa 7:14) to his absolute humanity in Matt 2:23 (from Isa 11:1), from the God-with-us to the Branch-for-us. Jesus is not only from God and "our God" he is for man and our man. God is able to become a complete human being, even a nobody, for our sake. This is possible for God. And given the character of God, it is likely that if God did visit us on earth the visit would be like this—in great modesty. Luke underlined this modesty by speaking of a manger; Matthew, by speaking of a barrio.

Thus the last word in the church's doctrine of human nature is not the magi and their miraculous conversion, nor Herod and his perverse resistance to conversion; the last word in the doctrine of man is God's own naming of Jesus: "He shall be called a Nazorean." What does this mean for our doctrine of human nature? It means that we should not only emphasize that humans are lost by nature (like magi) or sinners by choice (like Herod); we should also say that they have been represented by Jesus. Jesus is The Man-For-Us. Jesus is as essential to the full doctrine of human nature as he is to the full doctrine of God.

The Christmas stories of Matt 1 and 2 are both simple history and deep theology. There are kernels of historical fact in the middle of each story: Jesus was in fact born of a Mary and adopted by a Joseph and so legally inserted into David's line; and the response to Jesus was in fact a divided one, with many gentiles accepting him and many Jews, increasingly, rejecting him. Around this historical core a rich mantle of evangelical theology was wrapped, forming little mini-gospels of Christ. Matt 1 (Birth) and Matt 2 (Response) preach Christ almost as effectively as Matt 27 (Cross) and Matt 28 (Resurrection). They are, like all the other Gospel stories, confessions of faith and sermons (Davies, 66–67; Green, 50–51); together they form "a proleptic passion narrative" (Meier, *Vis.*, 53), a gospel before the Gospel, an overture with main themes. "The first chapters [in Matthew] . . . determine the 'dimension' in which the reader must see Jesus" (Schw., 45).

Rudolf Bultmann, 354, in his usual hard-nosed way, says that Matthew's infancy narratives present us with "the motifs of dogmatics and legends about Christ," and he means to be complimentary. But why put it this way? Why not say that historical events of consequence are celebrated with the only material available to a faith that writes: stories that spell out the significance of the events? These are *inspired* stories, the church believes, and therefore authoritative and credible stories. But inspiration is not always the same thing as historicity; inspiration can also tell stories, parables, and poems (Brown, 33–34, 562; Fitz., 17–18). We are bound to these stories as God's way of describing Christmas; but nowhere are we bound to the historicity of each incident in the stories. Did a real honest-to-goodness star start, stop, and shine down like a spotlight on the Christ Child? Possibly, but even deeply conservative Chrysostom doubted it (6:3:37; also the quite conservative Gundry, 28: the star is "simply literary and theological"). The imagination understands. The text is authoritative; literalist interpreters are not.

The text means what it means. If "unhistorical" meant "untrue" then every parable would be untrue. (Parables are stories—in modern language, fiction.) There is sometimes a difference between story and (hi)story; but both can be divinely inspired.

The four Matthean Christmas paragraphs (Genealogy, Naming, Magi, Flight) preach the gospel in an incomparable way. They are little masterpieces (Brown, 38). At least every Christmas they give their teachers the opportunity to say the deepest and most helpful things to people about God and Jesus. The stuff of early first-century Palestinian life is able, it seems miraculously, to become the stuff of our own late twentieth-century lives.

The Doctrine of Human Nature in the *Pastoral Constitution on the Church in the Modern World*

For special reasons the Second Vatican Council's "Pastoral Constitution on the Church in the Modern World" *(Gaudium et Spes)* (1965) is of unusual interest to the Reformation churches. In this Constitution, particularly in its opening twenty-two articles, Roman Catholicism presents us with its most recent drafting of a doctrine of the human person. But not only that. Here the Council has also given us its freshest official explanations of human salvation. As is well known, the question of salvation was the burning question of the sixteenth-century Protestant Reformation. Wherever Reformation theology is true to itself, salvation will continue to be its great concern. It is here as nowhere else (unless at the doctrine of revelation) that Reformation theology is most alert in any theological discussion.

The Council identifies appealingly with the human problem throughout the Pastoral Constitution. Again and again it faithfully points to Jesus Christ as God's self-identification with and answer to humanity's deepest questions and most perplexing riddles. If this Constitution is characterized, rightly, as anthropocentric (human-centered), it must also be called, fairly, christotelic (Christ-pointed). For it points unfailingly to "the God with a face," to Jesus Christ as our true end and goal, the fulfiller of our history and of our deepest needs. "Jesus Christ is the goal of human history, the focal point of the longings of history and of civilization, the center of the human race, the joy of every heart, and the answer to all its longings" (45).

The drafters of the Constitution were determined that the optimism and hope of Christ's already accomplished salvation would dominate the spirit and the formulations of the document. The Constitution, they agreed, should not be allowed to fall under the shadow of any seemingly hopeless human lostness in sin. Consequently, at the very outset we read that "the Council focuses its attention on . . . that world which the Christian sees as created and sustained by its Maker's love, *fallen indeed* into the bondage of sin, *yet emancipated now* by Christ (*sub peccati quidem servitute positum, sed a Christo . . . liberatum*)." (2; The "now" is in the official translation and in the sense, but not the Latin, of the sentence.)

It is the expression "fallen indeed . . . , yet emancipated now" that most troubles classic Protestant conviction. For example, in its definition of original sin, the *Augsburg Confession* emphatically stated that original sin "is truly sin, which *even now* (*nunc quoque*) damns and brings eternal death on those who are not born again through Baptism and the Holy Spirit" (art. 2). The point of this original Protestant "even now" is that even after the finished work of Christ the world is in urgent need of gospel proclamation if it is to benefit from Christ's work savingly. The "even now" of the Reformation, therefore, stresses the importance of preaching, not because it undervalues the cosmic success of Christ's work, but because it values this work of Christ so much it wishes to see persons receive it in the Word and so come into the church.

Reformation thought likes the logic connecting Paul's two great sentences: "God was in Christ reconciling the world to himself, not counting their trespasses against them, and entrusting to us the message of reconciliation. *So* [*oun*, "therefore"] we are ambassadors for Christ, God making his appeal through us: We beseech you on behalf of Christ, be reconciled to God" (2 Cor 5:19–20). God *has* successfully reconciled the world to himself through Christ, but people need to *receive* this reconciliation in order to be truly (and not just potentially) *emancipated now*. The Constitution's "yet emancipated now" works, it seems to me, with a somewhat different logic. The human person has *already been* emancipated from bondage and needs only to know it in order to become in that significant phrase, "more human."

Reformation Protestants value Christ's reconciling work. But we believe that the human situation prior to reception of the *message* of Christ's reconciling work by faith and baptism is a *dangerous* situation. Nevertheless, we have confidence in the power of Christ's Word, wherever it is preached, to change that situation. Without that Word we are not at all certain that persons are emancipated from their several bondages.

Furthermore, the Vatican Council in this Constitution places an undue confidence in the objectively emancipated person and, particularly, in that person's ability, subjectively, to emancipate himself or herself from sin. "Man achieves such dignity when, emancipating himself from all captivity to passion [*sese ab omni passionum captivitate liberans*], he pursues his goal in a spontaneous choice of what is good, and procures for himself, through effective and skillful action, apt means to that end. Since man's freedom has been damaged by sin, only by the help of God's grace [*gratia Dei adiuvante*] can he bring such a relationship with God into full flower [*plene actuosam*]"(17). But this crucial formulation strikes Protestants, and some Catholics, too, as an at least semi-Pelagian description of human salvation (see Father [now Cardinal] Joseph Ratzinger's trenchant critique in *Commentary on the Documents of Vatican II* [1969], 5:138). "Man" is the subject of both sentences. And grace appears as but a help in bringing an already apparently planted, growing, and flowering relationship with God into "*full* flower." Was it not the function of Augustine's controversy with Pelagius to end the writing and even the thinking of such sentences?

The Constitution also teaches that man—undifferentiated man—may look forward ultimately to a complete deriddling of death for all at the end. In the otherwise moving existential paragraph on the mystery of death we read "that man has been created by God for a blissful purpose beyond the reach of earthly misery" and that bodily death "will be vanquished, according to Christian faith, when man who was ruined by his own doing is restored to wholeness by an almighty and merciful Savior." The paragraph concludes with a cosmic extension of the answer to the death question when it asserts of our loved ones who have died that "faith arouses the hope that they have found true life with God" (18).

But where in this document, one must ask in the light of the New Testament witnesses, is death seen not only as an anxiety that receives a comforting answer (the document is faithful here), but also as a guilt that requires a grave solution and that obliges an urgent life-or-death decision? Where in the whole discussion of human nature are there treatments of the future judgment of God, the separation of the quick and the dead, the awesomeness of moral life before the judgment, and the danger of failure?

Everything seems too smooth in the Constitution's doctrine of the human person and human salvation. Already emancipated, able with help fully to emancipate ourselves, we walk, one senses, toward a glorious dawn accompanied by the background music of the Pastoral Constitution on the Church in the Modern World. The Constitutional Quartet, I am afraid, ends on too high a note; the bass and cello have been wholly removed, the violins sing sweetly, and the viola plays only in the major key.

Both Catholic and Protestant theologies today, it seems to me, are threatened at their vitals by the intrusion of a new Origenistic universal-salvation dogma that almost wholly neglects the left-hand, bass notes of sin and judgment. But both these notes are integral parts of the gospel. Without taking seriously human sin and divine judgment the gospel pales into platitudes or becomes politics with religious pretensions.

There is an instructive parallel here in recent Protestant theology. The *Church Dogmatics* of Karl Barth, the major modern Protestant doctrinal body of work, has corrected Protestant liberalism at the doctrine of revelation but has succumbed to liberalism's congenital defusings of sin and judgment at the doctrine of salvation. Similarly, it seems to me, Vatican II in the Revelation Constitution has proceeded far beyond the subjectivism of early twentieth-century Catholic modernism by rooting the church's doctrine of revelation in the soil of a firm and faithful Scripture. But has contemporary Catholicism in its Constitution on the Church in the Modern World been able to avoid a rather large-scale forfeiture of the determinative doctrines of depth or original sin on the one side and of God's real future judgment on the other? It seems to me that Barth's universalism threatens his beautiful doctrine of revelation; it also seems to me that the analgesic optimisms of The Pastoral Constitution on the Church in the Modern World threaten the majesty of The Dogmatic Constitution on Divine Revelation.

Thus what I at first greet in this Constitution—the humble service of the world— I must at last question: Is the new Roman church's servant role in the world due in part to a certain loss of nerve, to a loss of the sense of the gravity of the human situation and of God's justice in judgment? Doesn't this Constitution *flatter* human nature, almost as if it is afraid to offend it? What is there to do in an already emancipated world, after all, *except* to serve it, to be more or less at its disposal, to help it along?

Yet one who values the Augustinian-Reformation tradition of the seriousness of sin must be careful in questioning service to the world. For very often in the Gospels, service *is* evangelism ("He who receives one such little one receives me"), and in the modern world a service-less evangelism is an illegitimate scandal. Therefore, when Protestantism laments the Vatican Council's approach to world service, it cannot and must not mean that it laments the Council's desire to serve the world. The great burning question, of course, is, *What best serves the world?* I submit that the greatest service the church does the world is to tell the world its true condition. And this condition, Reformation theology believes, is not as good or as innocent as the Pastoral Constitution makes it appear.

Evangelical eschatology is grim not rosy, sober not sanguine. But Teilhard seems to have weighed more heavily than the Gospels in the final drafting of the Constitution's eschatological statements. The strong Catholic insistence on the preeminence of the Gospels should have been visible in the Constitution's eschatology, too, where it seems, on the contrary, the Prison Epistles (Colossians and Ephesians) with their cosmic inclusiveness eclipsed the synoptic Gospels with their eschatologies of danger (Mark 13; Matt 24–25; Luke 12, 17, 21).

Summary and Conclusion

The major objection I anticipate to the doctrine of the human person that I develop from Matthew chapter 2 is this: it is too pessimistic. It stresses the problematic magi and Herod too much. Is the Reformation doctrine of human nature— with which I have operated in my exegesis—*this* bleak? Does the Reformation give the human person sufficient credit for the obvious good that is in him or her? Does it believe that God can only be great if man is miserable (L. Bouyer)? Does it, in its obsession with the Fall (Gen 3–4), overlook God's good Creation and the image of God (Gen 1–2)? These are serious questions and deserve serious answers.

The human person was created good. And even after the Fall the human person remains God's creature. We have not turned into only sin. The human person *is* a sinner and, deeply understood, is profoundly depraved. But *what* is depraved is God's good gift of creation. Humans are still made in the image of God. But according to Reformation teaching this image has been so badly distorted, so abused, that the image no longer "re-presents" or reflects what a mirror image is supposed to represent faithfully and reflect purely. We no longer willingly face God, which is the original meaning of creation in God's image. The only true image of God since the Fall is Jesus Christ himself (Col 1 and 2). *He* faces God willingly and joyfully. *He* is the *eikōn*, the image, the visible expression, of the invisible God. All who have been joined to him by baptism are in the repair shop of the Holy Spirit (according to Paul) or discipleship (according to Matthew), being gradually conformed to that image. But until the general resurrection we will not be completely restored to that image except—a glorious "except"!—in the eyes of God who considers us, by grace, completely righteous, completely Family (Paul's theology of justification, seen most clearly in Romans 4).

The big point in the Reformation doctrine of the human person is this: left to ourselves we are worse off than we think, we are in more trouble than we suppose, we flatter ourselves too much. Our great need is Jesus Christ and attachment to him. And we will hardly feel this need for as long as we preen ourselves on ourselves. Consequently, Reformation theology feels that it is of the first importance that we be disabused of our *hubris* and be restored to genuine humility. Finding clues everywhere in Scripture to our tragic situation apart from faith, I concur with Reformation theology's conviction that it belongs to the first responsibilities of serious doctrine to tell us that, *per se*, we are magi and Herod, but that *per Christum* we have been objectively made well and will begin to be subjectively made well, personally, when we believe the gospel and follow Jesus. When God invited the magi first to the birthday party of his Son, he showed his deep and wide grace. But grace, by definition, is not given to the deserving. ("Amazing grace, how sweet the sound, that saved a *wretch* like me. . . .") Hence unless we come to feel our "magi"-cal character, our own alienation from, and our own rebellion against, the reality of God, how will we ever feel wonder for grace? Magi will follow no star unless given the gift of need. We *need* a sense of our sin. It is a great gift to be given it. It is the church's responsibility to mediate it in the expository preaching of Scripture's law.

But good doctrine of the human person will *not* concentrate exclusively on the magi and the Herod in us, or put us down from a sadistic satisfaction in seeing people low. Responsible doctrine of persons will teach the magi and Herod only in order to teach the Child. *The saving Christ* is not only the alpha (the doctrine of God), he is also the omega (the doctrine of persons).

The most important fact for Matthew about the life of Jesus in this chapter is that Jesus, even before he could himself consciously act, was led by divine providence to a retracing of the steps of failed Israel to take up into himself the abortive call of his people, to be the final Moses-Deliverer, the authentic Joshua-Savior, the real Davidic-King—the Man. Jesus is what Israel was meant to be. Jesus tastes our entire human experience, takes our journey, goes our way, shares our problem, and feels our sin—for us.

Matthew's final purpose in this chapter, it seems to me in summary, is to tell us: "Look how good God was to invite magi; and see how ominously Herod responded; and, especially, note what the Child went through for us all." In this chapter, I think, the magi are to teach us God's prevenient grace, Herod our depth-sin, and Jesus our representation. The human person, we may say in summary, is (1) like magi, graced; (2) like Herod, an endangered species, in peril of the dis-grace of damnation if there is not a turning around; and (3) in Jesus, "an assumed person," in the original sense of the word assumed: a person whose life has been taken up into another's, fully borne and represented by another, and brought to its intended destiny by that other, a destiny entered (the rest of the Gospel teaches us) by the faith of discipleship.

More important than *the Christian* (whose "becoming" is seen in the magi), and more important than *the anti-Christian* (whose moves are seen in Herod), is *the Christ* himself. Therefore we do not teach a good doctrine of human persons when we point only to the rebellious (the Herods) or to the converted (the magi) and then stop. We teach good doctrine of human persons when we proceed to tell the story of the man who lived for us all, for the rebellious and for the converted, for Herods and for magi, for the good and for the bad. The finally best way to teach the doctrine of the human person is to tell the story of Jesus.

We are in constant, almost innate, danger of overvaluing human nature's ability and goodness and so, inevitably, of undervaluing the world's need for the salvation of the gospel. It is the refreshing contribution of Reformation theology constantly to challenge this anodyne tendency by the blunt restatement of awkward apostolic truths, as, for example, in the answer to the eighth question of *The Heidelberg Catechism* (1563):

"Q. But are we so perverted that we are altogether unable to do good and prone to do evil?

"A. Yes, unless we are born again through the Spirit of God."

People need the Lord.

Chapter Three
The Law of Repentance and the Gospel of Baptism
The Doctrine of Initiation

"We acknowledge one baptism for the remission of sins" (The Nicene Creed).

Where do we find God *today*? Perhaps magi were led by a star to a baby two thousand years ago and there found God. But there seem to be few such stars today. Where, then, do we meet God today? The third chapter of Matthew's Gospel serves as an answer to this question. We meet God in repentance and baptism, in the confluence of law and gospel, and this chapter will spell out the meaning of these great theological terms in the stories of the early careers of two men: John the Baptist and Jesus of Nazareth.

I. JOHN THE BAPTIST: THE REPENTANCE-LAW OF GOD AND THE DEMANDS OF BAPTISM (3:1–12)

"And we believe in the Holy Spirit, . . . who spoke by the prophets" (The Nicene Creed).

"Now in those days John the Baptist makes his appearance, preaching away in the desert of Judea, and saying, 'Turn your lives around! Because here comes the kingdom of heaven!' This is the very person spoken of by Isaiah the prophet when he said,

> *'A voice is howling out in the desert,*
> *"Prepare the way of the Lord,*
> *Make straight his paths!"'*

"Now this John had clothes made of camel's hair; he wore a leather belt round his waist, and his diet was locusts and wild honey. Then Jerusalem started pouring out towards him, and all of Judea, and persons from all over the country near the Jordan River. And the people were being baptized by John in the Jordan River, openly admitting their sins" (Matt 3:1–6).

3:1–2 Twice Matthew will use the same present tense verb (*paraginetai*, "appears," or "makes his appearance") to introduce the two main characters of this chapter. "In those days John the Baptist makes his appearance . . ." (3:1); "Then Jesus from Galilee makes his appearance . . ." (3:13). The historic present tense verbs mean that the offices of these men still live today wherever their stories are told (Lohm., 34–35). John constantly "appears" wherever his history is read. His ministry lives on in its telling. John's ministry is a present tense ministry and is never to be relegated to a place of mere historical or antiquarian interest.

Wherever the story of Jesus Christ is told in fulness it begins with the story of John the Baptist. Wherever the gospel is heard in its depths it is preceded by the law

69

in its seriousness. Without law there is no gospel (without Old Testament, no New), and without John the Baptist preceding we do not rightly hear Jesus following. Thus it is no accident that in all four Gospels John the Baptist's ministry does indeed precede Jesus' own. John belongs to the substance of the story of Jesus and is not a mere introduction to it. In John, in fact, "holy history starts all over again" (Bonn., 31) after a long quiescence. John comes on like the last great prophet of the Hebrew Scriptures and like a walking, breathing law of God, full of doom and holiness and ultimacy. John the Baptist is in the front of our New Testament four times (once in each of the four Gospels) in order to put the law of God in front of us four times just before Jesus comes to us four times with gospel. John is the law of God in person; Jesus is the gospel of God in person.

John appears "preaching away in the desert of Judea and saying, 'Turn your lives around! Because here comes the kingdom of heaven'" (3:1b–2). John's great task was preaching—Matthew emphasizes John's preaching more than John's baptizing (Lohm., 36, 45; Grund., 90). Indeed, Matthew for special reasons leaves out what both Mark and Luke include, the expression: John was "preaching *a baptism of repentance into forgiveness of sins*" (Mark 1:4; Luke 3:3). The emphasized words are not in Matthew's Gospel. Matthew, of course, will record that John the Baptist baptizes (3:6, 13). But John's baptism, Matthew believes, cannot grant forgiveness of sins.

Matthew is eager to see all forgiveness of sins located only in the gift of *Jesus* to his people. Matthew is so christocentric that he does not like seeing God's great gifts distributed apart from Jesus. Jesus' Word and sacrament will give what even the great John the Baptist's Word and sacrament cannot: the Holy Spirit (as John himself will admit in a moment, 3:11) and the forgiveness of sins (which Matthew's Jesus explicitly places in the Lord's Supper at 26:28).

John can do much according to Matthew: he can preach God's law of repentance, he can prepare the way, he can baptize, he can receive *confession* of sins, and he can, most of all, point to the Christ, the fulfillment of the law. But John cannot, and his ministry of the law cannot, *forgive* sins or *give* Spirit. That is to say, even John's magnificent ministry of the law cannot supply the power that removes our main problem (sin) or that installs our main resource (Spirit).

John the Baptist's message, as summarized here by Matthew, is simple: "Turn your lives around! Because here comes the kingdom of heaven!" The first thing we must notice is the message's mood: it is urgent. John believed that if we did not turn around we would be sorry. John's view of life was serious. Like the prophets of the Hebrew Scriptures whom he personally brings to a pitch and climax, John believed that the great thing persons need to *do* is change, or else.

In secular Greek usage, *metanoeite* "repent," meant a (mental) change of mind or an (emotional) regret; it did not mean the biblical *change of the whole direction of life* (TDNT, 4:972–76; see for John the Baptist's urgent, return-to-God usage, *loc. cit.*, 995–96. Germans usually translate the word repent with *umkehren*, "turn around," and Bonn., 31, argues for the French word *retour*).

The old English word *repent* translates the Greek word for the Hebrew root *šûv (shuv)*. The term means, literally, "come back," "turn around," or in today's vernacular, "shape up," or "move!" In John the Baptist, God does us the honor of taking us seriously, personally grabbing us by the lapel and telling us that we must turn around if we are to meet God from the right direction. We are going the wrong way.

The imperative to turn is backed by a reason. "Because (*gar*) here comes the kingdom of heaven!" John was convinced that the Great Visitation was about to take place and so people needed to be warned to abandon all that was despicable and to come to baptism as God's way of cleansing people for the visit and as the people's way of showing that they wanted to come back and meant to live appropriately. As we know, John's premonition was correct: God did make his Great Visit. We also know that the visit of God was, in its way and at first, gentler than John thought or taught. Yet we may doubt that a gentler John, a prophet with a less urgent message, would have brought any change to the people of God at all. God wanted John—and the people through John—to be exercised about their need for change and about the kingdom's imminent coming. We need the message of John the Baptist; we need all the urgency we can get about the things of God.

Matthew's John does not tell us, specifically, *how* to change (apart from baptism and, later, fruitbearing) or what exactly to turn *from* (sin is understood, but the word, interestingly, is not used by Matthew's John the Baptist). John leaves the discerning of the despicable to the conscience, which knows (Schl., *Der,* 56; Schl. *Die,* 196). (However, Matthew will presently nuance the Baptist's message, as originally found in Mark and Q, in the direction of religious people, Matt 3:7–12, while Luke will nuance the Baptist's message in the direction of secular people, Luke 3:10–14.)

The important expression "the kingdom of heaven" (Matthew ordinarily uses the plural "of the heavens"; Luke normally calls it "the kingdom of God") is the Baptist's way of talking, and later Jesus', about God's great coming visit. Kingdom is a social word first of all. It tells us and all hearers that God is about to do a big world thing, not just a big individual thing—a cosmic thing, not just a heart thing. What is going to happen when God comes is not going to be grapeshot or shotgun; it is going to be a cataclysmic-cosmic explosion, reshaping the face of the earth. A *kingdom* is coming when God comes, and not just a few words here, a few acts there. (The *basileia* article in TDNT, especially K. L. Schmidt's contribution, 1:479–90, is fundamental for understanding the kingdom's original meanings.)

What is important to appreciate is that the human responsibility—repentance, turning around, changing—is not urged *in order that* the government of God may come but, explicitly, "because" God's government is coming, whether we change or not. That is to say, we do not bring in the kingdom by our changes; we "suffer" the kingdom's coming, either blessedly by going to our knees or banefully by turning our backs. "Here comes God's government: Move!" Indeed, the divine coming and its message *enables* the human moving and its change. "Because God turns toward man, the new turn of man toward God is possible" (Schn., 24). Because God draws near, we receive the power from this nearness to turn toward God.

3:3 All four Gospels unite in seeing John the Baptist as the direct fulfillment of Second Isaiah's opening vision,

> "'A voice is howling out in the desert,
> "Prepare the way of the Lord,
> Make straight his paths!'"" (Matt 3:3, adaptation of Isa 40:3; Mark 1:3; Luke
>   3:4; John 1:23).

All Israel expected a Next-to-Last-Man: Malachi told Israel he would be an Elijah (Mal 4); Isaiah told Israel he would be a howling Preparer; so all Israel looked for this penultimate person. Matthew (with the other evangelists) says, "Here he is!" John the Baptist is the Next-to-Last-Man.

The theologically most interesting fact about the synoptics' Isaiah verse is this: Isaiah wrote "make straight . . . a highway for our *God*," meaning Yahweh; Matthew, Mark, and Luke all altered this to read "make straight *his* paths," meaning Jesus. Beare, 90 (like, e.g., Bacon, 137), is put out by the evangelists' free use of the Old Testament: "They were persuaded that the Old Testament in all its parts was written with Christ and the gospel in view," Beare writes, "and they applied its words in ways that seem strange, arbitrary, and even perverse to us." To us? For Christendom, as for Matthew, the coming of *God* occurred through the coming of *Jesus* (Schl., *Der,* 59; cf. McN., 25; Bonn., 33; Gund., 45). The first *act* in "The Gospel of Isaiah" (Isa 40–66), after the gracious *title* "Comfort, comfort my people" (40:1–2 RSV), is the announcement of the stirring voice; here he now is. Isaiah's Gospel begins like the New Testament's.

3:4 As if to reinforce this basic evangelical conviction, in the next verse John the Baptist is even given the preparer Elijah's prophetic wardrobe: "John's clothing was a rough coat of camel's hair, with a leather belt round his waist, and his food was locusts and wild honey" (3:4; cf. Zech 13:4 and, especially, 2 Kgs 1:8 where Elijah is expressly described as "a hairy man. . . . with a leather belt round his waist." Chrysostom, Jerome, and Bengel all draw ascetic or simple-lifestyle conclusions for believers).

As we will later see in this Gospel (chapters 11 and 17), one of the major first-century rabbinic arguments against Jesus being the Christ (after the chief argument of Jesus' ignominious crucifixion) was the contention that Elijah had not come before Jesus, as the prophets had predicted Elijah must. In order to forestall this argument temporarily, Matthew and Mark say in effect, both by their quoting from Isaiah and by their sartorial descriptions, that "here he is, here is that Next-to-Last-Man, that Elijah-like man whom the prophets predicted."

Both in appearance and in message (as we will shortly examine), John the Baptist was rough. He appears to us all as a little crude, a little fundamentalist, a little fanatical. And yet he was (and is) God's instrument. John, in contrast to Jesus, as the evangelists will later show, was something of an ascetic and abstained from the softer stuff of civilization in clothes, food, drink, and places of residence and work. John exercised a certain independence from this world and a certain disregard for the amenities of life. ("It is not possible at once both to do [or preach] penance and to live in luxury," Chrys., 10:6:8.) Later, Jesus will be confronted with the rigor of John the Baptist in an unflattering comparison: "John's disciples fast but yours don't" (Matt 9:14). But while Jesus could not recommend John's radically ascetic way to his own followers (for reasons he will indicate, 9:15–17), Jesus nevertheless always stood foursquare behind the legitimacy of the Baptist's ministry in the history of God's salvation (see, for example, Jesus' Sermon on John in Matt 11:4–19). We must therefore allow John to look a little like Tarzan, to shout a little too loudly for our ears, to be a little crude. Perhaps God sometimes works like this. God's law *is* tough.

3:5–6 John ministered to people from all over Judea, and the people came flocking to him (3:5). Apparently a revival set in (even the secular historian Josephus confirms this), and many people were impressed that this man was not only in dead earnest but that what he said represented the real state of the union in Israel. And so "they were being baptized in the Jordan River by John, openly admitting their sins" (3:6). (*Exomologoumenoi* is a compound: *homologeō* literally means "agree," "admit," and then "confess"; the prefixed *ek* [*ex*] adds the force of "out," "outloud," or "openly.")

The stern, serious message of John the Baptist has as its major effect a deep sense of sin and unworthiness. But John did not allow this malaise to remain a mere emotion in the heart; he offered something to it—baptism. Along with his challenge in words, John offered his hearers a way to take their "turn," a place to show they accepted his words—he offered a public bath or baptism. Baptism is a kind of drowning and cleansing at once, which says in so many words, "die, sin!" As we have seen, *Mark and Luke* believed that the waters of John's baptism supplied what John's hearers most wanted: repentance *with* forgiveness. Matthew, for christocentric reasons of his own, preferred to avoid this charged claim. But in context, Matthew says almost as much: when people get baptized, confessing their sins, they get *some* kind of saving help from God. The important thing to see here at verse 6 is that the remedy for sin is not denying sin's presence or explaining it away or exculpating it; it is admitting it. We are free from sin only when we face it; we disown sin by owning up to it. The first way to repent is to admit our sins openly. Repentance is not first of all a good work; it is freely admitting our bad work, our sins. God forgives only *sinners.* The law is the threshold to the gospel. "He who conceals his transgressions will not prosper, but he who confesses and forsakes them will obtain mercy" (Prov 28:13; cf. esp. Ps 32).

John the Baptist's baptism was like Qumran's except that he did not require people to leave their homes and join a separated community, nor did he require, as Qumran did, intensive Torah study (Grund., 92–93). John the Baptist's preaching and baptism were for *all* Israel, not for an elite within it, and John did not join the converts to himself and form a "party of John" (Bonn., 34). John the Baptist also had no *Heiligungsmethode* or techniques of sanctification (Schl., *Der,* 62). There is a primitive simplicity about John's ministry that is impressive.

3:7–12 *"When John saw many of the (separatist) Pharisees and (sophisticated) Sadducees coming to his baptism, he said to them, 'You bunch of snakes! Who warned you to run from the coming wrath of God? Then you had better live the kind of life that shows you really mean to repent. And don't you dare tell yourselves, "We have Father Abraham on our side," because I tell you that God can make children for Abraham out of these stones here. Already the ax is laid at the root of the trees; every tree not bearing good fruit will be chopped down and thrown into the fire.*

"'Now I just baptize you with water to bring you into repentance. But the one who is coming after me is so much stronger than I. I am not even worthy to carry his sandals. He will baptize you with Holy Spirit and fire. He has his winnowing fork in his hand, and he will make his threshing floor clean; he will gather his wheat into his barn, but the chaff he will burn with unquenchable fire.'"

In these six verses Matthew gives us the burden of John the Baptist's ministry in the form of John's famous "Fire Sermon." Three times in the sermon the word "fire" appears and each time ominously and warningly. The anatomy of this sermon will disclose as in a summary the character of God's law.

3:7 "When John saw many of the (separatist) Pharisees and (sophisticated) Sadducees coming to his baptism, he said to them, 'You bunch of snakes! Who warned you to run from the coming wrath of God?'"

The law-message is especially directed to those who stand under it—the religious. The law is addressed especially to those who claim it especially (cf. Rom 3:19). In Jesus' time these were the Pharisees and the Sadducees; in our time it is we ourselves. The message of the law must be heard most seriously by those of us who claim to take God most seriously. John's message tells us that the major problem of the church is—the church. As we see later in the teaching of Jesus, too, the chief problems of the people of God were not the Roman occupation or other external (political, economical, or social) factors. The chief problems of the people of God were the most visible representatives of the people of God themselves. These were in two groups. First, there was the lay group of the Serious or Dedicated (as we might call them)—the Separatists or "Pharisaim"; and second, there were the leading clergy—the sophisticated Sadducees. These two groups were, respectively, (as we might call them) the Laymen United for a Biblical Confession and their bitter enemies, the Clergy United for a Relevant Ministry—these two groups, each believing itself the major bearer of God's saving will in history—were, John now forewarns us, God's major opponents.

We must allow these facts to sink in. I who write and most all of us who read belong to one of these two groups: we are either serious lay Bible students or we are ordained church leaders. In either case we cannot escape being members of one of the two major problem groups, perennially, in the people of God. We must begin to read the words "Pharisees and Sadducees" and see *ourselves* or we will miss half the message of Matthew. In my exposition I will often call the lay Pharisees either the Separatists or the Serious, and the ordained Sadducees the Sophisticated or the Clergy in order for the texts to come home to us.

The Pharisees placed all of national life under the law of the Bible; for the Sadducees, natural needs and desires determined behavior (Schl., *Der,* 67–68). The Pharisees were the pious, Pietistic lay movement, the earnest separatists within the old people of God; the Sadducees were in large part made up of the proud, priestly nobility (Schn., 22). When John the Baptist attacked these groups he was attacking in God's name the *pride* of those who made so much of the law of the Bible, and the *security* of those grasping for power, possessions, and honor in religious ladder-climbing (Schl., *Der,* 69). John the Baptist's message "applies to those in Israel who practiced religion as their special concern and privilege" (Schl., *Die,* 197). Bornkamm, "End," 15–16, maintains that John's sermon contains, in fact, Matthew's basic critique of the Christian church of Matthew's time in the late first century. Bonnard, too, 423 note, wonders if John the Baptist's invective may not include *Matthew's* warning to overconfident baptized Christians whose absence of fruit concerned Matthew. Schweizer, 47, entitles Matthew 3:7–10 (the first half of John's sermon) "Against Smugness." See Bultmann, 117, for interesting views on the origins of John's sermon.

We should begin our assessment of John's sermon by admiring John's audacity. Ordinarily when lay and clerical dignitaries grace our meetings we give them particular attention and show them certain offices of respect. When John the

Baptist sees them approaching he addresses them directly: "you bunch of snakes!" This is not an address calculated to win friends or (favorably) influence people.

The ministry of the law must be restored to our preaching—not as a saving institution but, first of all, as a damning institution. There is too much "accept ourselves" preaching that ignores the tough notes of John's law and of even Jesus' gospel. We need John; we need the law of God. "For through *the law,*" writes the great preacher of the gospel to the gentiles, "comes the knowledge of sin" (Rom 3:20). Consequently, if we are continually to experience salvation from sin—yes, even we Christians who have already in certain important senses been saved from the guilt and power of sin by a confrontation with Christ—then we must again and again allow ourselves to be addressed by the stinging indictment of the law of God. The law has the cheek to tell us that *we* are the enemy, that the enemy is not primarily other evil people. The law warns *us;* it condemns both the spiritually serious and the socially sophisticated in the people of God, the religious right and the religious left.

3:7c "Who warned you to run from the coming wrath of God?" The kingdom of God is much more than the wrath of God, of course, but it is nothing less. The coming of God in Scripture (as here in John, later in Jesus) is always also the coming of burning justice. A coming of the kingdom without judgment for evildoers does not exist except in the imagination of the sentimental. The wrath of God has been largely lost in preaching from all but the fundamental churches on the right and from the liberation churches on the left; and in both cases, unfortunately, it is present often in irresponsible and self-righteous (i.e., *other*-condemning) forms. One fruit of the mainline churches' craven skipping of the judgment of God texts that are on every other page of Scripture is a dull gospel. After all, what urgent need for a gospel is there when Christians' lives are in no ultimate danger, when— as we hear constantly—"God is love, and we are accepted as we are"? Teaching the John the Baptist texts honestly will restore the needed message of God's judgment to our churches.

The wrath of God is not the intemperance or irritability of God; it is the love of God in its friction with the injustice and hatefulness of persons. It is the warm, steady, patient, but absolutely fair grace of God in collision with the manifest selfishness and unfairness of human beings. "Where grace *[gratia]* manifests itself, wrath is also shown to the ungrateful" (Beng., 1:88). God's wrath does not contradict God's love; it proves it. A love that pampered injustice would not be lovable.

Why did these leaders come to John's baptism at all? This was exactly John's question, in effect: "Why are you coming to my baptism when you have never before been conspicuous for feeling yourselves in the wrong or for confessing your own sins? Since when *your* fear of a coming wrath?" I believe John suspects that the Serious and Sophisticated had come only to look. Or if they had joined the others in baptism it was only because so many other people had—or for show—but not because they felt that they themselves really needed baptism (cf. Bonn., 35; Hill, 92).

3:8–9 The moment he saw them, John unleashed his Fire Sermon, a sermon that has stood ever since as one of the most blazing indictments of self-secure religion in the literature of spirituality. "You bunch of snakes! Who warned *you* to run from the coming wrath of God? Do fruit [an expression meaning "live a life"] worthy of repentance. And don't you dare tell yourselves, 'We have Father Abraham on our side' [meaning, "We will be all right because we have the right heritage"], because I tell you, God can make children for Abraham out of these stones here" (3:8–9).

Apparently the spiritual leadership of Israel—whether lay-Pharisee or clerical-Sadducee—took special comfort from a covenanted relationship to Abraham, the guaranteed biblical locus of many of the divine promises. Connected with this Abrahamic pedigree, then, was a deep sense of being eternally secure. But John's baptism was offered only to the honestly *insecure*. Baptism was not really necessary for persons standing in a theological heritage guaranteeing them exemption from the wrath of God. But if John's baptism meant at the very least *a confession of sins*, then what kinds of sins could persons confess who were aware of no final break between themselves and God? How can the secure confess?

On Abraham's atoning substitutionally for all of Israel's sins see Str.-B., 1:116–20. When an Israelite felt his personal insufficiency he was taught to flee to the substitutionary righteousness of Abraham and the other patriarchs. One of the most dramatic (and effective) examples of this is Exod 32:13–14. But John the Baptist said that the unconscionable use of substitution maimed repentance because it released people from the responsibility of performing the righteous deed (Schl., *Der*, 73–74). Cf. Justin Martyr, *Dialogue with Trypho*, 140. These religious among the old people of God "thought they *could not* fall away" (Beng., 1:88), "that in God's economy there was a favoured nation clause" (Barc., *Luke*, 33).

John was more aware than the people's leadership that by offering his baptism to Israel he was being profoundly subversive. Israel had hitherto initiated with baptism only gentile proselytes who joined the people of God; *outsiders* were unclean, needing the washing of baptism. But with John the Baptist an initiating baptism is announced which asserts that *all insiders*, too, the people of God themselves, are in need of an urgent baptism and a complete change if anyone is to face the coming kingdom of heaven.

This first sermon in the Gospel of Matthew is revolutionary teaching, and it throws a searchlight of accusation upon all the customary claims of the heirs of Abraham (and, as we will see, on the claims of the heirs of Jesus). If being children of Abraham saves, then John's baptism is superfluous; but if John's baptism is necessary for salvation, then simply being children of Abraham does not save. This and nothing less is what John the Baptist's ministry means.

John's baptism meant that Jews, too, were heathen (Schn., 24); it meant, in contrast to the apocalyptic faith of the time, that the coming world-fire of judgment was not aimed at only the despised gentile *goyim*, but at—especially—the religious leaders of the people of God; it meant nothing less than a fundamental denial of the special privileges of the people of God (Lohm., 39, 45–46). John's sentence—"God can make children for Abraham out of these stones"—unites Israel with the whole pagan world and ends her specialness (Lohm., 41). "Think not," said John to Israel's leadership, "that if you should perish, you would make the patriarch childless" (Chrys., 11:3:69).

Whenever I encounter this verse and the sense of privilege that Israel felt in belonging to Abraham, I think of my own relationship to the Reformation and my heritage in the theologies and Confessions of the Lutheran and Reformed churches. And I must do some serious rethinking. I tend to believe that I stand in an advanced relationship with God because I stand in this heritage. John the Baptist wants to disabuse me of this conviction for a moment. My relationship with God ought not, ultimately or intimately, depend on the heritage to which I belong, but on something else. I believe that it is a deep privilege to be an heir of Luther, Calvin, and of the Protestant Reformation. I believe that to imbibe Luther is to imbibe catholic theology at its best. And yet if I advance my Lutheran, Calvinist, or Reformation heritage before God as a kind of shield behind which to hide the reality (or unreality) of my faith in Christ, then John the Baptist points his long bony finger in my face and says, "Shape up! God can make evangelicals out of rocks."

I do not know if John the Baptist would even like Christians to plead their Mediator-Substitute, Jesus Christ, in whose name we Christians pray, behind whose merits we dare face God, and who we believe is the exclusive means of our relation with God. (John would not like this pleading if it meant avoiding personal responsibility.) If John the Baptist, however, should go so far as to deny the Christian *any* mediation or substitution—and the text in front of us can mean just that—then many Christians will feel obliged to say with Jesus later in this Gospel that while John was the greatest man born of woman, yet "he or she who is least in the [newly inaugurated] kingdom of heaven is greater than [John]." (11:11) This means that as necessary as John the Baptist's message of the law is for us to hear, the gospel (and with special clarity, the gospel of Christ according to Paul), which tells us that we *do* have substitution before God in the righteousness of Jesus Christ, is superior. The gospel is over the law.

The law, however, strips us of all defenses. It presents us nude before God. It will not allow us any substitutes, any holy heritage, any cover-up—it is just we and God standing there all alone. This is the office of the law: to strip us of all substitutes, to show us ourselves by ourselves, our need, our helplessness, and our sin. Without the law of God to tell us this, we would be easily over-confident, self-secure, smug. God uses the law—God uses John the Baptist—to accuse us, to humble us, to bring us to our senses and to reality. This reality will be greater than John the Baptist, as John will admit in a moment; it will supply what John can only demand, and it will forgive the sin that (Matthew believes) John can only condemn. Nevertheless, we must not demean John or the law because they are not Jesus or the gospel.

It has been the frequent temptation of the church to become antinomian (i.e., antilaw) when she discovers the wonder, freedom, and joy of the gospel. When Christians learn that the real way to stand before God is by faith in the grace of Jesus Christ and not by faith in one's own works of the law, Christians are tempted to hate the law for its having seemed to teach them to find their salvation in it or in themselves or in their obedience to the law. But the Reformation taught us most clearly that we must let the law *continually* do its stripping, condemning, accusing work on us so that we might *continually* flee to the gospel, seek its resources, and walk in its powers. Without the law we would feel little need for the gospel; without knowing our sickness we would not seek the Physician. John the Baptist with his withering message belongs in the Christian canon and church, not as Savior, but as the one who prepares for the Savior.

Yet one must hasten to add that God *does* want the personal reality that "John the Law" insists upon. John is right: God wants fruit worthy of a life that has changed its direction. It will be the claim of the Gospel of Jesus Christ according to Matthew that the source of *power* for the fruit demanded by John will be found in the sermons and sacraments of the One to whom John pointed.

3:10 "Already the ax is laid at the root of the trees; every tree not bearing good fruit will be chopped down and thrown into the fire" (3:10). This sentence summarizes John the Baptist's message of the holy law of God (3:7–10) before John turns to his even superior message of the gospel of the One who comes after him (vv 11–12). John believes that God is a God who judges evil living. All persons are like trees: those bearing good fruit are spared; those not bearing good fruit are "thrown into the fire." (Jesus uses exactly the same sentence in 7:19; cf. also 12:34a; the singular "fruit" indicates not multifarious good works, plural, but "the global comportment of a sincerely repentant person," Bonn., 36; cf. Gal 5:22f.) When it has become almost axiomatic in our churches to say that "God is love and will not condemn anyone," John stands in contradiction. We are in danger of losing half the biblical freight: the justice, holiness, and moral seriousness of Yahweh. Where this holy justice dimension of the character of God (and so, of God's people) is lost, the gospel sinks, and the "love of God" turns insipid and the people of God saltless.

As the law-and-judgment-message of the destroying Flood precedes the gospel-and-salvation-message of the Call of Abraham in the opening stories of the Hebrew Scriptures (Gen 6–12) in order permanently to secure the fundamental fact of the holiness of God and to retain God's saving grace in its character as "amazing" (cf. von Rad, *Gen.*, rev. ed., 129), so in the opening pages of the New Testament the message and baptism of John precede the message and work of Jesus Christ in order to keep Christ's saving grace from being understood as indulgence and his free pardon *of* sin from being understood as free license *to* sin. Everything God does in and for us in Christ is done so that we might be personally righteous. God the Judge is a God our time needs.

John warns in this verse, for the first of three times in this brief sermon, of the "fire" next time. The biblical God is no less passionate for justice than the most committed revolutionaries. God is certainly not recommended to those rightly concerned for social justice if God is spelled only l-o-v-e. For the love of the biblical God is *holy* love. It is fire, and it is the warning of the final judgment of fire. The measure of this fire's reincorporation into our preaching will be the measure of the church's recommitment to social justice. There is a correlation between the disappearance of the church's preaching of hell and the shrinkage in the church's passion for justice. And if some tell us that "God does not frighten us into heaven" or that hellfire is not a legitimate motive in true Christian preaching, let us ask them to study the sermons of this Gospel and see if they can sustain these theses. The biblical God, through the prophets and apostles and above all through Jesus himself in Matthew, *does* frighten, does threaten, does talk straight, and we must accustom ourselves again to hearing God talk this way. The biblical love of God is tough love; it is also gentle love, but it is never unjust love or a love that winks at injustice.

3:11 But probably John the Baptist's greatest contribution to the gospel was his utter christocentricity. John knew that his message was not the Last Word, and he knew that his baptism was not the One Baptism. Therefore, like every good prophet before him he turned finally from his serious message of the law of God to point— as the last of the Old Testament prophets—to the sum of the promises of God. "Now I baptize you with water to bring you into repentance [*eis metanoian*]. But the one who is coming after me is so much stronger than I. I am not even worthy to carry his sandals. *He* will baptize you with Holy Spirit and fire" (3:11).

Legalism preaches *only* law. Even when legalism uses gospel words and phrases, it is constantly throwing us upon our own resources, even our resources of decision. But the responsible evangelical ministry of the law points away finally from all that we do for God (as important as, in its right place, this is) and points to all that *God* will do for us in his Christ (and that is more important). John preached a Coming One who would bring a baptism that would have in it not only water (as John's had) and not only the challenge to change, but (what John's did not have) the gift of the change-agent in person, the Holy Spirit. John believed that the Christ would bring not only a new willing (a change) but, in the words of the psalmist (Psalm 51), "a willing Spirit" (the changer), to will and to work the decisive changes continually. John the Baptist's message of repentance awakened *desire* for righteousness; Christ's "Baptism with the Holy Spirit conveys this righteousness" (Allen, 25) by giving the Holy Spirit (Stend., 773).

"I am not even worthy to carry his sandals." We may be sure that we are hearing the preaching of the divine law and not moralism when we hear the law talking modestly about what it can do and pointing to Jesus as the real giver of change. Whenever church preaching or teaching begin to imply that our unaided obedience can accomplish something final before God, then the law has pointed to itself as at least the gospel's sandal-bearer and has thus disqualified itself as evangelical law.

The law—that is, plainly spoken, any message telling *us* what to do, telling us to change, telling us to live a good life and to love—can only tell us these things; it cannot give them. The law—moral exhortation—can only show us our need; it cannot liberate us from it. *Lex semper accusat,* "the law always accuses" us, the Reformers insisted, and they were right. The law or moral exhortation has a place in the church, John the Baptist's place: important but preliminary, warning but not liberating, preparing but not providing. And where the law is divine and authentic (and here it can be tested), it will admit these limitations.

3:11c "*He* himself [*autos*] will baptize you with Holy Spirit and fire." The last time we met this emphatic "he himself" [*autos*] was in the great introduction to Jesus' name: "You shall call his name 'God-Saves' because he himself [*autos*] will save his people from their sins" (1:21). This twofold "he himself" reserves to Jesus exclusively the work of salvation. Here the Baptist calls Christ's salvation a "baptism." The word *baptism* was not merely figurative. It was difficult for John the Baptist to imagine a Messiah who would not use baptism, so sure was John of this medium in God's saving work. John was proven right by the church's later baptism (28:19). (Jesus' church baptism differed in spiritual *effect* from John's, but not in physical *means*—both physically baptize with water, Lohm., 43.)

The phrase "baptize with Holy Spirit and fire" is notoriously one of the most difficult to interpret in the New Testament. Both Luke and John emphatically placed Jesus' great gift of the Spirit *after* Jesus' death and resurrection (Luke 24:49; Acts 1–2; John 7:39; 20:22). It is not so clear that Matthew and Mark postponed the Spirit's work. For the first two evangelists the meaning of this fiery spiritual baptism may have originally been the coming *eschatological* kingdom with its Great Divorce of salvation and judgment. It is also possible that these evangelists understood Jesus' *whole ministry* as a giving of Spirit and fire. Every time Jesus spoke he either washed or burned. Whoever received his Word was washed; whoever refused his Word was burned. Jesus' Word was full of Spirit, and wherever his Word went (like Mary and the little lamb) his Spirit was sure to go. I believe it is legitimate to understand Jesus' entire ministry in this Gospel as a perpetual baptizing with either the Holy Spirit (blessing us) or with fire (burning us). The final blessing and burning occur at judgment day.

But I believe the church has meanwhile correctly applied this great messianic baptism to her sacramental life, to the baptism that Jesus himself gave his church at the end of this Gospel as part of her equipment in mission: "baptizing them in the name of the Father and of the Son and of *the Holy Spirit*" (28:19). When the church in obedience to her Lord gives baptism, she gives baptism's special gift: the person (in biblical language, "the name") of the triune God, which means the church is God's instrument for baptizing us *with the Holy Spirit*, too. (The Pentecostals and charismatics are wrong in offering a baptism in the Spirit independent of and even superior to the baptism "into [*eis*] the name of the Father and of the Son and of the Holy Spirit." There is only "one baptism" [Eph 4:5], and with the Nicene Faith the whole Christian church solemnly insists: "we acknowledge *one* baptism.")

It is not merely symbolic, therefore, when John calls the Christ's work a *baptizing* with Holy Spirit. The word *baptize* literally means that Jesus will actually baptize people in the full sense of the word—wash with water. But where John's water was *only* water, Jesus' water will wash with the cleansing power of the Holy Spirit. Jesus' baptism will be much more than baptism in water, but nothing less. (See John 3:5; Titus 3:5, and all of Acts' conversions, especially Acts 2:38 and 8:36, 38, for clear confirmations of the intimate connection between real water and the Spirit. "For [Christian baptism] the gift of the Spirit is characteristic," Bult., 247 n. 1, also 250.)

What does it actually mean when John the Baptist says, "He will baptize you with Holy Spirit and fire"? The evangelists Mark and John only heard John the Baptist promise a baptism with Holy Spirit; fire is not mentioned in their Gospels. Matthew and Luke, on the other hand, heard the Baptist promise a baptism with Holy Spirit *and* fire. What did John the Baptist actually say, and what did he mean by what he said?

See Dunn, 11–12, for a review of the literature on this subject. Some interpreters believe (1) that originally, historically, John's message was that the Messiah was coming with a single baptism in *fire*, that is to say, with a baptism of judgment, but that Christians edited grace into John's message later by inserting the words "Holy Spirit" (e.g., Bult., 111; Davies, 369; Caird, 74; Schw., 51). Other interpreters believe (2) that John preached only a baptism with the *Holy Spirit* and that the two additional words "and fire" are really adjectival, in the construction called hendiadys ("one through two"), so that what John the Baptist was really saying was this: "He will baptize you with the fiery Holy Spirit" (e.g., Chrys., 11:6–7:73; Beng., 1:89; Bonn., 38; Hill, 94), an attractive opinion.

The third major interpretation is (3) that the Coming One will baptize people *either* with the Holy Spirit *or* with fire, that is, that he will baptize the truly penitent in the grace of the Holy Spirit, and that he will baptize the impenitent in the fire of judgment (e.g., McN., 29; Schl., *Der*, 80–81; Lohm., 44; with a twist in Gund., 49). I personally find this last view the most satisfactory in the light of the use of the word *fire* as judgment in the surrounding sermon, verses 10 and 12. This view's dual baptism with the Holy Spirit and fire, with grace and judgment, has the advantage of context and is exactly the way the next verse describes the coming Messiah's work: "He will gather his wheat into his barn [the baptism with the Spirit], and burn the chaff with a fire that never goes out [the baptism with fire]." The Messiah's gathering of his people is his baptism with Spirit; the Messiah's burning of the chaff, or of the unreal among his people, is his baptism with fire.

3:12 "He has his winnowing fork in his hand, and he will make his threshing floor clean; he will gather his wheat into his barn, but the chaff he will burn with unquenchable *fire*." (Interestingly, as Bengel, 1:89, noticed here, "John's whole discourse, and therefore the commencement of the Gospel, agrees entirely with the last clause of Old Testament prophecy, Malachi [4:1–6].") John's fire sermon ends with its major word—"fire"—a word of warning and of the deepest seriousness. "Fire" means that baptism's blessings are not automatic or perpetual fire insurance independent of good faith. John preaches the Great Divorce that comes with the Messiah, the Great Division of history that commences with the Messiah's First Coming and ends with his Second. (We missed this division—the judgment of God—in the Second Vatican Council's doctrine, discussed in the last chapter.) It is characteristic of the sermons in Matthew's Gospel to end not on a joyful, triumphant note as (homiletically) sermons are usually supposed to end, but on solemn, fearful notes of judgment. This is true of the Sermon on the Mount (5–7), as well as of the Sermons on the Kingdom (13), on the Community (18), and on the End (24–25). It is also true of John's fire sermon here. The John and Jesus of Matthew are antieudaemonistic, we might even say antiecstatic, and extremely sober. Rather than exult in heaven, the sermons of Matthew's Gospel prefer to warn of hell, finding warning more profitable for the church.

Chrysostom, 11:7:72: "'Think not at all,' saith [John the Baptist], 'that your Baptism suffices, if ye become ordinary [*phauloi*, worthless] persons hereafter.'" Bengel, 1:90: "Everyone is either baptized with Spirit, or burned with fire: there is no third lot." As one matures, one becomes either wheat or chaff (Lohm., 45); a decision is urgent (Chrys., 11:8:73). The baptized must live lives of repentance or else.

It will be one of Matthew's major purposes to show that the Messiah who came, however, did *not* come in all the fiery colors of John's pictures. John, like most of us and like most of John's contemporaries, expected the Messiah to be a sensation. Jesus did shake things up in Galilee and Jerusalem, but not with overt fire, and not too spectacularly. The absence of the spectacular will be perpetually offensive in the Gospel. "Blessed is he," Jesus later tells the wavering John, "who is not offended by me" (11:6). But it is not John's fault that the Coming One proves himself strong precisely by refusing to be strong the way people expect strength. The ax, shovel, and fire are still in the Messiah's hands, to be sure, but they move more deliberately and less dramatically than John anticipated. In whatever way they work, an ax finally severs, a shovel finally deposits, a fire finally burns, and thus every word of John is finally true. "God comes with leaden feet, but strikes with iron hands."

I submit that John's ministry, the ministry of the law of God, the ministry of moral exhortation and seriousness, belongs as an integral part of all faithful preaching. The art in our time as in every time is how to preach the law without turning it into gospel; how to keep moral exhortation from degenerating into moralism, how to keep moral seriousness from pretensions of self-salvation; how to make fire without an excess of smoke. The law is not the gospel. And yet the gospel is not lawless. And there is no immoral road to salvation.

Contemporary church teachers walk a narrow path between the yawning chasm of legalism on one side and the abyss of antinomianism (antilawism) on the other. The law must be preached, but in such a way that finally (like John) it points away from itself to Christ.

The Repentance-Law of God in the Reformation Confessions

We may introduce this section and its importance by remembering that the Protestant Reformation was born in a battle for the right understanding of the biblical word "repentance." The *Ninety-Five Theses* of Martin Luther are an extended commentary on the true way of repentance and on false substitutes for repentance (such as indulgences). Luther's famous first thesis says it all: "When our Lord and Master Jesus Christ said, 'Repent, etc.,' he wanted the *whole life* [*omnen vitam*] of believers to be a life of repentance."

It is important to notice that the *first* of the three realities that *The Heidelberg Catechism* (1563) believes it necessary for believers to know for salvation is "the greatness of my sin and wretchedness" (Q. 2) and that this knowledge comes, explicitly, "from the Law of God" (Q.3). But if knowledge of sin, *not* power for righteousness, is why the law is preached, another question occurs: Why, then, is the law preached *at all? The Heidelberg Catechism* (Q. 115) asks this question:

"Why . . . does God have the Ten Commandments [of the law] preached so strictly since no one can keep them in this life? Answer: First, that all our life long we may become increasingly aware of our sinfulness, and therefore more eagerly seek forgiveness of sins and righteousness in Christ. Second, that we may constantly and diligently pray to God for the grace of the Holy Spirit so that more and more we may be renewed in the image of God, until we attain the goal of full perfection after this life." This answer gives an almost perfect rationale for John's stern sermon of law.

(Note here also that the Decalogue or law is to be preached to *Christians* "all our life long," for the ends mentioned in the answer, and also that full perfection, in Reformed teaching, comes only after this life.)

The Westminster Confession of Faith (1647) then lifts what it calls "Repentance unto Life" to such a pitch that I am afraid it obscures the gospel—something I find this Confession doing rather often. But there is one fine sentence worth preserving in the Westminster's chapter on repentance: "As there is no sin so small but it deserves damnation; so there is no sin so great that it can bring damnation upon those who truly repent" (chapter 15:4).

The important question of substitution, raised in John the Baptist's reference to Abraham, is addressed by *The Scots Confession* (1560) in its fifteenth chapter "The Perfection of the Law and the Imperfection of Man." One sentence in this chapter captures the essential Reformation conviction (with both its glory and peril). "As God the Father beholds us in the body of his Son Christ Jesus, he accepts our imperfect obedience as if it were perfect, and covers our works, which are defiled with many stains, with the righteousness of his Son."

When the Lutheran Confessions speak of repentance, the reference is most frequently to Christians. Lutheran theology strongly affirms that Christians *can* fall from grace and salvation. Cf. *The Augsburg Confession,* art. 12; The *Apology of the Augsburg Confession,* art. 12: 46, 50–51, 53. But finally and summarily:

"John, who preceded Christ, is called a preacher of repentance—but *for* [*doch zur; sed ad;* but only toward] the remission of sins. That is, John was to *accuse* them all and convince them that they were sinners in order that they might know how they stood before God and recognize themselves as lost men. In this way they were to be prepared to receive grace from the Lord and to expect and accept from *him* the forgiveness of sins. Christ himself says this in Luke 24:47, 'Repentance and the forgiveness of sins should be preached in *his* name to all nations'" (Luther, *The Smalcald Articles* [1537], Part III, art. 3. Repentance, 5–6, emphases added).

II. JESUS' BAPTISM: THE GOSPEL OF GOD AND THE SUPPLIES OF BAPTISM (3:13–17)

"And we believe in the Holy Spirit, the Lord and Giver of life." (The Nicene Creed)

3:13–15 *"Then Jesus makes his appearance at the Jordan River. He came all the way from Galilee to John so that he could be baptized by him. But John tried hard to dissuade Jesus, saying, 'I am the one who needs to be baptized by you, and yet you are coming to me?!' But Jesus' response was, 'Let me do it now, for in precisely this way it is thoughtful for us to fulfill all righteousness.' So John let him."*

Like John in the first verse of this chapter, Jesus is now introduced with an arresting historic present tense verb, suggesting perpetuity: "Then Jesus makes his appearance." From John we perpetually learn the law. From Jesus we perpetually learn the law and the gospel. Few can excel John in urging the holy law of God; Jesus is peerless in gospel. The gospel of Jesus will not cancel the law of John (which is the law of God). The gospel will fulfil the law and place us in a relation with God that transcends the law and yet makes us want to be law-abiding.

Let us first of all simply be surprised that Jesus got baptized at all. John had predicted the Christ as a baptizer (with Spirit and fire), not as a *recipient* of baptism. It is as if one were to announce the coming of a great preacher at a series of evangelistic meetings, and one night this preacher arrives—not at the platform but at the altar, not at the podium but at the penitents' bench, not to preach but to kneel.

This is Jesus' first adult act in the Gospel. Until now in Matthew, Jesus has been a child. The first surprise in Jesus' adult ministry, then, is in fact the first deed of his ministry: his seeking baptism at all. I like to consider this Jesus' first miracle: the miracle of his humility. The first thing Jesus does for us is *go down with us*. His whole life will be like this. It is well known that Jesus ended his career on a cross between thieves; it deserves to be as well known that he began his ministry in a river among penitent sinners. From his baptism to his execution Jesus stays low, at our level, identifying with us at every point, becoming as completely one with us in our humanity in history as, in the church's teaching, he was completely one with God in eternity. Jesus' "at-one-ment" with the human race, visible already at baptism, is as impressive and as important for human salvation as Jesus' at-one-ment with the heavenly Father, most visible at the Transfiguration and most potent at the cross.

In what we can call Jesus' *identification-baptism* there is a whole theology of the relation of minister to people, and of disciples to others. (On Jesus' identification with us, cf. Caird,

77.) "Jesus loves me, this I know, for his baptism tells me so./Sinful ones to him belong;/ we are weak, but he is strong." This adaptation of an old Sunday School song is one meaning of Jesus' baptism. Almost every phrase in the second verse of the hymn "We Gather Together" is also a commentary on Jesus' decision to be baptized with us: "Beside us to guide us, our God with us joining,/Ordaining, maintaining His Kingdom divine;/ So from the beginning the fight we were winning;/Thou, Lord, wast at our side; all glory be Thine!"

3:14 "But John tried to dissuade him, saying, 'Look, I am the one who needs to be baptized by *you*, and yet you are coming to *me?!*'" Only Matthew has this story of John's disbelief and challenge. Matthew inserts it in order to deflect the misunderstanding that Jesus needed forgiveness of sins. If John's baptism meant confessing sins and repentance, as John the Baptist said it did, then what is Jesus doing in baptism? Is Jesus, then, really divine?

3:15 Jesus' reply does not answer these questions directly, but it does reveal the self-consciousness and the sense of mission of the One who will speak so often in this Gospel, as Matthew understood that consciousness and mission. "Let me do it now, for in precisely this way it is thoughtful for us to fulfill all righteousness" (3:15). Jesus' answer does not reveal a sense of sin.

Why does Jesus speak so expansively of his baptism as an act "to fulfil *all* righteousness"? Wouldn't these words be more appropriate before his cross or after his resurrection? Is mere baptism a fulfilling of *all* righteousness? I believe that Matthew liked this expression—it is, in fact, Jesus' opening remark in this Gospel—because it honored what Jesus is about to inaugurate, Christian baptism. Jesus' final remarks in this Gospel will honor baptism, too, by commanding the discipling of the nations, "*baptizing* them into the name of the Father and of the Son and of the Holy Spirit" (28:19). Matthew shares the faith of the church that God placed in little Christian baptism the whole saving name of God with *all* its righteousness.

Thus Jesus' words "to fulfill all righteousness" are not fulsome or excessive. For as we will see, in the baptism that Jesus now personally transforms—from being a merely Johannine baptism with water to being a Christian baptism with water and Spirit—God will grant the cosmic signs of a right relation with himself—an open heaven, the Dove-Spirit, and a supernatural declaration of divine love (3:16–17). These boons were first given to *Jesus* in order to declare his Messiahship to him and to the world; then, by explicit mandate, these ineffable gifts will also be given to *us* in our baptisms (28:19: in the gift of the name of the heavenly Father, the well-loved Son, and the Holy Spirit). Jesus' baptism does indeed fulfill all righteousness because it is both a microcosm of the gifts Jesus' ministry brings and because it will later become the dominically instituted medium for delivering to disciples saving fellowship with the Father, the Son, and the Holy Spirit. Christian baptism is the God-instituted initiation service into, and the delivery system of, the work of Christ and the name of God, that is, of all righteousness. Thus when Jesus says that his baptism will "fulfill all righteousness" he is not exaggerating, because after his death on the cross (Matt 27) the Risen Jesus will institute baptism as the initiation—and initiating—ceremony into the divine Name (28:19) where we do indeed receive all the privileges and responsibilities described in this Gospel. Even most Christians underestimate baptism. Jesus' opening words in this Gospel "estimate" baptism considerably.

Jesus' decision for baptism, says Luther (W^2 12:1137), is "as if Christ wanted to say, 'Although I am not myself a sinner, yet nevertheless I now bring with me the sin of the whole world, so that I am now only a sinner and the greatest sinner of the whole world.'" Again: "This is 'all righteousness': to consider yourself unrighteous" (Lu., W^2 11:2139). Jesus is baptized not *because* he shares our need but *in order* to share our need (Schl., *Der*, 85, 89). "Righteousness" in Matthew usually means right behavior (Lohm., 50 n. 1; Streck., 179), covenant loyalty even when the partner fails (Grund., 97), and here especially it means willingness to be identified humbly with sinners (Aug., *Serm.*, 2 (52):1:259; Davies, 96). Cf. Joseph's righteousness in 1:19.

In response to the first question about Jesus' baptism we may say that Jesus sought baptism not from a consciousness of personal sin but from an unusual concern for public righteousness. And what was right for him in this particular situation was to seek out and submit to a rite that to all outward appearances seems to be the altar-call of an eccentric country evangelist. What is righteous is sometimes strange and common. "If God received baptism from a man, no one should consider himself unworthy to receive it from a fellow slave" (Jerome).

The Church and the Para-Church

We may learn from Jesus' choice to be baptized by John not to be *too* particular about our associations in God's work. Wouldn't Jesus have done better to start his own ministry, *de novo*, without identifying himself so closely with John's almost revivalist preaching, style, and baptism? But Jesus receives John's baptism, and in a moment he will repeat John's core message word for word in his own first sermon (cf. Matt 4:17 with 3:2). Jesus is not eager to be novel or zealous to be unique. What Jesus did by submitting to John's baptism and later by continuing John's message of repentance is simply another example of the humility of divinity. Jesus took everything John had to give and made it his own. Jesus was open to God's gifts in others.

There is a lesson here for the churches and for the para-church (or independent) ministries, which are often in rivalrous tension. John's location *outside* the temple in the desert, outside the holy city in the barren wilderness, and away from the traditional means of grace, all mark him as a type of the independent. Jesus' habitual use of synagogues and Scriptures, his identification with the institutions of Israel's life from his circumcision on the eighth day to his passover supper the night before his death, all mark Jesus as a type of the institutional. Yet Jesus chose John's baptism. The church reaches out to the para-church, the conservative to the radical, the traditional to the nontraditional. At their best, the para-church organizations—and here I am thinking only of those I have personally experienced, such as Young Life, Inter-Varsity, World Vision, Fellowship of Reconciliation, Sojourners—have the gift of keeping the church honest, and they exercise certain prophetic and vanguard roles in evangelism, discipleship, peace-work, and social action. The church should be as undefensive as her Lord in her willingness gratefully to receive the ministrations of these sometimes awkward para-church ministries. God has a way of using irregular John the Baptists. Jesus knew this. The church needs to know this, too. It is a sign of the church's sickness when she is *too* churchly and when she professes indiscriminate scorn for ministries outside official church channels. We need tranquilly to know that "he who is not against us is for us" (Mark 9:40).

But it is just here that the para-churches experience their litmus test. If they are in principle antiecclesiastical or believe themselves even slightly superior to God's institutional church—superior to, yes, God's organized church, God's vulnerable, cumbersome, awkward, too formal, too conservative (or too liberal), too slow, and utterly fallible church—then such para-church ministries are illegitimate and their days are numbered. At the beginning of the divine plan of world salvation in Scripture the Lord solemnly told Abraham that those who cursed Abraham and his seed and descendants—i.e., the church of God—God would curse (cf. Gen 12:1–3 and the patriarchal promise throughout Genesis). Para-church groups that are anti-institutional-church are doomed. Only where para-church leaders and members sincerely and faithfully attend, encourage, support, and correct (from within!) the institutional church, and do not seek to show her up or to compete with her often slower (but surer) way do para-church groups exercise *authentic* Christian ministries, however splendid their Christian vocabulary, experiences, and results may for the time being be. Jesus needs John the Baptist. But John the Baptist needs Jesus, too.

*   *   *

It is noteworthy that Jesus explicitly includes John the Baptist in his first public act: "it is thoughtful for *us* to fulfill all righteousness." As far as possible, Jesus' ministry is social and inclusive and not merely individual. Jesus wants to do his work *with others* (cf., e.g., the poignant use of "with" in Matt 26:36, 38, 40). Even at the beginning of his ministry, Jesus does not intend to be a loner. In a moment he will begin recruiting disciples (4:18–22). Right now Jesus wants John the Baptist to be a part of his initial obedience in ministry. It is significant, therefore, that Jesus' opening sentence in the Gospel includes "us" in his work.

McNeile, 31, believes the "us" with whom Jesus wants to associate in baptism is the Jewish people who are now going down into baptism, referring to Heb 2:17. Strecker, 180–81, believes the "us" is Matthew's editorial reference to the Christian community, indicating that Christians, like their Lord, are obliged by baptism to erect righteousness in the world.

"Then John let him" *(tote aphiēsin auton)* (3:15c). This is the first time that an effect to the Word of Jesus is recorded in Matthew. And it is the standard effect: Jesus' Word causes what it commands; it effects what it asks. When Jesus speaks, people listen, and realities change. In the next chapter, for example, at the end of his temptations, Jesus commands Satan to go, and we read the result, "then [Satan] left him" *(tote aphiēsin auton,* 4:11), exactly the Greek words used of John here. Again, in the middle of the fourth chapter, Jesus will call the disciples, and Matthew will record that "immediately they left *(aphentes)* the boat and their father and followed him" (4:22; cf. 4:20). In all these cases the same verbal root—*aphiēmi*—is used, the verb used also to translate "forgive" and meaning, as we see in the examples above, "allow, yield, remove, go away." It will be one of the great purposes of the Gospel to tell us that Jesus' Word is strong, that it not only says things to do, it causes the doing of the things it says. It is a causative Word. Present in an extremely modest way in a strikingly gentle-man, the Word does everything. There is a whole doctrine of the church in this network of facts about Jesus' Word.

3:16–17 We are brought finally to the great scene in this baptism chapter—the baptism of Jesus himself. It will be well for us to study this scene carefully since it inaugurates the meaning of Christian baptism in the person of no one less than Jesus himself.

"And when Jesus had been baptized, immediately he came up from the water; and look, the heavens were opened to him, and he saw the Spirit of God coming down like a dove right toward him. And look, a voice speaking from the heavens, saying, 'This is my priceless Son; I am deeply pleased with him.'" (3:16–17)

Three great realities occur over Jesus (open heaven, Dove-Spirit, Voice), two of them singled out by Matthew's punctuating word "look!": (1) "look," the Dove-Spirit descends from the newly opened heavens and comes right to Jesus, and (2) "look," the Father's Voice announces Jesus as his priceless Son. These two "look marked" gifts tell us the two main facts we need to know about *Jesus* (that he is the Servant and the Son of God), and they also tell the future *church* the two main gifts she is given in her Christian baptism (divine favor and the Holy Spirit, cf. Acts 2:38). Let us look first at Jesus and then at his church.

1. First, the Dove and the Voice tell us in two different ways, visually and audibly, that Jesus is the Servant-Son of God. Jesus is the long-awaited *Servant* of the Lord, promised especially in Isaiah, the Servant upon whom the Spirit was promised as coming in a special way (Isa 11; 42; 61; cf. Matt 12:18–21). Jesus is also the long-expected *Son* of God, anointed here into the office of Messiah (Ps 2:7; cf. also 2 Sam 7:12ff and parallels). This little aerial show at Jesus' baptism is meant to tell the whole watching world (in Matthew) that Jesus is everything promised and expected in the Old Testament, that Jesus is It. The first and most important meaning of Jesus' baptism is that Jesus is publicly installed into the office of the Christ, and in Matthew's Gospel especially this installation is proclaimed by the divine Voice to the world. Jesus' baptism was God's visual and aural way of saying to history, "Dear world, this is it, here he is." Luther says in his sermon on this text that everything promised in the Old Testament points in some way to Jesus' baptism, where the career of the Liberator of the earth is inaugurated by a crowning with the divine Spirit.

"In the New Testament and Old Testament practically all the Scriptures point to the baptism of Christ; the Scriptures do not make much ado about the birth or childhood of Christ" (Lu., W² 11:2129). In his baptism, Jesus "becomes another man, not in his person but in his office" (ibid., 2140). "The Father wanted to make the world sure, here, that it ought not have any doubt about Christ, and that is why the Father confirmed Christ Himself [from heaven]" (ibid., 2128).

Jesus is the one through whom the whole divine world opens up, and thus *to him* [*autō*, in some texts] "the heavens were opened."

"Lord," cried the prophet for his people, "look upon us from heaven, where you live in your holiness and glory. Where is your great concern for us? Where is your power? Where are your love and compassion? Do not ignore us. . . . *Why don't you tear the skies open and come down?*" (Isa 63:15; 64:1 TEV). "And look! The heavens were opened" (Matt. 3:16; in Mark 1:10 the heavens were vividly "torn open," *schizomenous*, as if in answer to the prophet's cry). Jesus is the One long promised, to whom the heavens open, toward whom the great Spirit of God comes pointing down, and upon whom, definitively, the Spirit settles. "Then a shoot shall grow from the stock of Jesse," the prophet had promised, "and a branch shall spring from [Jesse's] roots [i.e., from the promised Son of David, son of Jesse]. The Spirit of the Lord shall rest upon *him*" (Isa 11:1–2 NEB).

Above all, Jesus is the person bearing the Father's own personalized Word of recommendation and his declaration of authenticity here in baptism: "This is my priceless Son; I am deeply pleased with him." Jesus is the absolutely unique *(ho agapētos)* Son of God, and so, especially precious to his Father. Jesus is not only the promised Son of David (though, as the whole first chapter established, he is that). He is also the very pleasing Son of God, as the second chapter first clearly told us (2:15: "Out of Egypt I have called *my Son*"), and as now the Father's Voice in the final verse of the third chapter confirms. The Nathan oracle had promised both sonships:

When your life ends [David] and you go to join your forefathers, I will set up one of your family, *one of your own sons*, to succeed you, and I will establish his kingdom. It is he shall build me a house [the church!, cf. Matt 16:18], and I will establish his throne for all time. I will be his father, and he shall be *my son*. I will never withdraw my love from him. (1 Chr 17:11–13 NEB)

By surrounding Jesus' baptism with so many of the crucial Old Testament associations—Servant of the Lord, Son of God, Son of David, Spirit-Bearer, Christ, etc.—Matthew is trying to say that in Jesus God has given us all his promises. In Paul's accolade, "*all* the promises of God find their Yes in him," they are all fulfilled in Jesus (2 Cor 1:20). In Jesus we have everything we need: an open heaven, the presence of the Spirit of God, and the closely identifying life of the Son of God himself.

To solemnize this central truth, the whole Trinity is visible or audible here at the baptism: the Father in the Voice, the Spirit in the Dove, and the Son in the water (Aug., *Serm.*, 2(52):1:259; Jero., *ad loc.*). The Trinity has a special affinity for baptism, for the Trinity's next explicit appearance is at the end of the Gospel, again in a baptism text, where Jesus commands that baptism be given to the discipled nations in "the name of the Father and of the Son and of the Holy Spirit" (28:19).

"This all happened [at Jesus' baptism] so that we might know that this is not a minor matter, but that a lot rests on this, and thus He [God] insured this through holy people [*durch heilige Leute*], through Himself namely, and his Spirit, so that all creatures might confess that [Jesus] is the Christ, and so that we would hang on Christ and not think anything of anyone else" (Lu., W[2] 11:2132). Schweizer, 41: "Even in the first formulation of our section the statement is made that [1] heaven, which has been closed for a long time, is open once more; that [2] the Holy Spirit is working again; and that [3] God's voice is again sounding forth. Everything was viewed as the ultimate fulfillment of all that was only provisional and symbolic in the Old Testament."

2. The connection between Jesus' baptism here at the head of the Gospel (3:16–17) and the church's baptism at the end (28:19) is intimate and real. The story of Jesus' baptism exists not only to teach what happened to *Jesus* at the beginning of his

ministry just as the story of Jesus' Last Supper with his disciples (26:26–30) exists not only to teach what Jesus ate in his final evening. Jesus inaugurated Christian baptism by his ministry-opening baptism in the same way that he inaugurated Holy Communion by his ministry-ending meal. The practical purpose of the story of the baptism of Jesus is to teach the church what happens to her in Christian baptism. Everything Jesus did on earth he did in service—"The Son of Man did not come to be served but to serve" (Matt 20: 28), and his service begins as early as his baptism. Jesus' baptism serves us by, among other things, teaching us exactly what happens to us in our baptisms.

"The dove itself at that time . . . appeared, that as in the place of a finger (so to say) it might point out to them that were present . . . the Son of God. *Not however merely on that account, but to teach thee also, that upon thee* no less at thy baptism the Spirit comes" (Chrys., 12:3:77; similarly Jero., *ad loc.:* "to show by the descent of the dove the coming of the Holy Spirit in the baptism of believers"). Again: "For He was not washed and cleansed from His own sins (since He had none), but from my sins and the sins of the whole world. When I believe that, I am freed from my sins and don't know of any more sin" (Lu., W² 13:1138). "A most glorious manifestation of the Holy Trinity [occurred at Jesus' baptism], and a proof of what occurs when *we* are baptized, since Christ was not baptized for Himself" (Beng., 1:91). Jesus' baptism, in short, is "the model for Christian baptism" (Gund., 41), "the prototype of Christian baptism" (Beare, 99), the fulfillment not only of *his* righteousness but "of *all* righteousness" (3:15).

A. The Open Heaven of Justification

Practically put, baptism means that people can now pray. The heavens are no longer brass. The windows of heaven have been opened up right over Jesus the Christ. And all who submit to *him*, over whom alone these heavens are open, do indeed find a right relation with God (justification), an unusual freedom to pray, and a sense that their prayers go somewhere. It is not the least of the gifts of baptism that it enables prayer. Paul teaches that one of the major gifts of baptism, and of the conversion to Christ it seals, is the gift of the Spirit who enables believers to pray, "Abba, dear heavenly Father" (cf. "the baptismal [point-in-time] aorists" in the texts where this prayer occurs, Rom 8:15; Gal 4:6; see also Acts 19:3–6).

The reading in several of the manuscripts (*C, K, L, P, W,* and in Irenaeus, Hippolytus, Eusebius, Chrys., and Aug.) which says that the heavens were opened "to him" (*autō*), i.e., over Jesus Christ, teaches the church that, in and under Christ and only in and under Christ, persons have "every spiritual blessing in the heavenlies" (Eph 1:3). We should beware of alternate routes to the heavenly world or to the supernatural. "Wherefore were the heavens opened? To inform thee that at *thy* baptism also this is done" (Chrys., 12:3:77).

B. The Dove-Spirit of Sanctification

The second main gift of baptism is the Spirit of sanctification. The Spirit comes down like a dove. But *what* the Spirit does in Jesus' baptism and *how* the Spirit comes in Jesus' baptism are also important. What does the Dove-Spirit do? According to this story, she is seen "coming down upon Jesus." God's Spirit, like

God's Son in ministry, first goes *down*. The whole Gospel will teach us to reverse the directions of the spiritual. One of the main reasons for the lowliness of Jesus throughout the Gospel is the influence upon him of the downward Dove-Spirit. To stand under the influence of the Holy Spirit is to be led, like the Spirit, downward into the service of persons and into the common ministries of life. As the next chapter with Jesus' temptations will teach us more clearly, to be under the influence of a false spirit is to be led increasingly *up* into experiences of the remarkable, the extraordinary, and the glorious. The evil one leads up—"ye shall be like gods!" (Gen 3:5). The holy one leads down. The whole ministry of Jesus proves this. (Paul's ministry proves this too, as 2 Cor 12 in its context shows.)

And when the Dove-Spirit comes down, she does not come in a form that might have been suggested by John's just preceding portraiture—like a lion or a tiger, but she comes down like a gentle dove. Jesus is, to be sure, "the Lion of Judah," as John the Baptist had in effect pictured him. The Word of Jesus has strength. And yet the remarkable office of the Spirit of Jesus is to nuance strength, to modulate power, and to deliver what is deeply needed in common and public life—the way of gentleness. (We need a new birth of gentleness in our time. A world holocaust will only be humanly averted when enough people and nations learn that gentleness is the real strength, that justice is the best national defense, and that peacemaking really is stronger than warmaking.) That the Christian Spirit should be identified with a dove has world-historical significance. When the church grasps even a portion of the gospel's downward and dovelike message—theologically (the humility of God, grace) and ethically (gentleness, nonviolence)—the church will be in a stronger position than she now is under a frequently nationalistic and so inevitably militaristic spirit.

The dove-form means that things spiritual must be tested ever since Jesus' baptism not by their external power and effects, but by their manner and method. "There is no way to peace; peace is the way." Peace is not only the end we seek, it is the means we use. The gently strong or sensational, not the outward, becomes the acid test of the *Christian* Spirit ever since the descent of the dove. (The Book of Acts, read in its entirety, confirms this gospel truth.)

Jesus was surely given power by the descent of the Spirit at his baptism—but not the kind of power for which John the Baptist's preaching prepared us. If we reread John's Fire Sermon, we expect a spirit or symbol of outward power to be given Jesus. But he gets a dove. There is a theology of the Holy Spirit in this investiture. Christians, too, are given power by the gift of the Spirit in baptism. But it is dove-power. And the power that the Dove-Spirit activates in believers is, as in the Messiah before, a gentle and quiet power—a unique and novel kind of power in culture. "'He will not shout or scream'" (Matt 12:19).

Just as Jesus completely redefined what the Messiah is by his humble baptism with sinners, so the Holy Spirit completely redefines what spiritual power is by coming down like a dove. The dove is the biblical symbol of creation and recreation ever since Genesis 1:2 (in the Spirit's "moving" verb in the Hebrew), of peace and new life ever since Noah (Gen 8:8–11), and of gentleness and innocence ever since Jesus' Sermon on Mission ("Be as cautious as snakes and as gentle as doves," Matt 10:16 TEV).

It is not necessary to believe that Jesus lacked power prior to his baptism, and it is definitely wrong to think that baptism was Jesus' "second spiritual experience," a kind of Wesleyan entire sanctification or a modern-day charismatic filling of the Spirit. Matthew had carefully told us that Jesus had been conceived by the Spirit (1:18, 20), and so the church has always held that it is consistent with the nature of God to believe that the divine Spirit remained with Jesus from conception. What the baptismal descent of the Spirit teaches is not that a partially inspired man at last experiences the fullness of the Spirit. The words and behavior of Jesus immediately prior to his baptism reveal an already present maturity and betray no internal lack (3:13–15). Rather, if I may put it this way, the Spirit who until baptism had lived with Jesus (let us say) in street clothes, gets dressed up today like a dove as if to say, "from now on we have something special to do." Today at baptism Jesus is inaugurated into his royal work. And the Dove-Spirit wishes to play a part in this inauguration and does so, for once rather dramatically, by a little sky show intended to impress her Friend with his big day.

The major gift to *Christians* in their baptism, after the fundamental gift of the open heaven (justification), is the enabling gift of the Spirit. "Repent and be baptized," the very first group of church converts was urged, "in the name of Jesus for the forgiveness of your sins [justification], *and you shall receive the gift of the Holy Spirit* [sanctification]" (Acts 2:38).

Jesus' baptism—in *water*—was Spirit-baptism; Christian baptism in water is Spirit-baptism in fact. The stories of Acts, carefully studied, prove this (cf. Acts 8:36; 10:47; 19:5–6). There is only *"one* baptism" (Eph 4:5), not two (not a so-called water-baptism as one thing and a Spirit-baptism as another). When people are joined to Christ they are, at the same time, joined to the Spirit (1 Cor 12:13, classically). To turn to the Lord and to be Spirit-filled are not two things but one (cf. Acts 4:31), just as the Lord and the Spirit are one (2 Cor 3:17). To have Christ in the heart is, by definition, to have the Spirit in the heart, and vice versa (Rom 8:9–11). "What God has joined together, let no human being tear asunder."

"In God's work of salvation, the paschal mystery of Christ's death and resurrection *is inseparably linked* with the pentecostal gift of the Holy Spirit. Similarly, participation in Christ's death and resurrection *is inseparably linked* with the receiving of the Spirit. *Baptism* in its full meaning signifies and effects *both* [participation in Christ's work and reception of Christ's Spirit]." *Baptism, Eucharist, and Ministry* (1982), Baptism, 14, emphases added.

In Matthew's carefully crafted formula at the end of the Gospel, Christian baptism is baptism "into the name [singular "name," not plural "names"—there is only one God] of the Father [above us in the open heavens], of the Son [with us in the water], and of the [dove] Holy Spirit [in our hearts in sanctification]." Paul celebrated the Spirit-giving *one*-baptism for *all* members of the church without distinction in unforgettable words: "For indeed we were *all* brought into *one* body by baptism in the *one* Spirit, whether we are Jews or Greeks, whether slaves or free men, and that *one* Holy Spirit was poured out for *all* of us to drink" (1 Cor 12:13 NEB). The moment baptism is stripped of the Spirit, or gives the Spirit only to *some*, not all, we have a split church and everything is ruined. 1 Cor 12:13 deserves serious study by charismatics.

Baptism is not understood if its central fact—the descent of the Spirit in it—is not appreciated. In baptism the Christian is not only given access to the Father in heaven in prayer, the Christian is also given God himself in the Son and God herself in the Dove-Spirit. Not only are the doors of heaven opened above, the presence of heaven is delivered within. In theological language, not only is the baptized one given justifying access to the Father above in prayer, he or she is also given the Father's sanctifying Spirit within in power. A right relation with God above is indicated in our baptism story by the open heaven over Jesus. This is justification (the gift of prayer). Then an intimate internal relation with God is pictured in our baptism story by the gift of the *Spiritus Sanctus*. This is sanctification (the gift of power). Above us and within us we have good friends.

C. The Voice of Adoption

The final words in Jesus' baptism are the most important words of all and are at the end for emphasis. The Voice from heaven identifies in tones of unexampled affection with the man undergoing this baptismal experience: "This is my priceless Son; I am deeply pleased with him." Only twice in the synoptic Gospels does God the Father speak *immediately* to us from heaven: at baptism and at the Transfiguration. (All other times God speaks to us *mediately* through his Son, who in his humanity is God's authorized Word to us.) The only two times that the Father speaks to us immediately he says the same thing: "This is my priceless Son; I am deeply pleased with him" (3:17; 17:5). If we hear the Father's twice-repeated Voice at baptism and Transfiguration correctly, the *one* fact that God the Father wants believers to know, above absolutely all other facts in life, is *how much we have in Jesus.* "My priceless Son, deeply pleased." If we know this, we know the most important fact in the world. "Here," God is saying in so many words, "in this man, is everything I want to say, reveal, and do, and everything I want people to hear, see, and believe. If you want to know anything about me, if you want to hear anything from me, if you want to please me, get together with him" (or, in the three words added emphatically by the Voice at the Transfiguration: "Listen to *him!*" Matt 17:5). This is the first and major meaning of the Voice.

The second meaning is like the first. All the kindness heard in the Father's Voice for his only true Son is *conveyed to us in baptism,* in adoption, the third great gift of baptism after justification and sanctification. (For baptism as adoption, see Chrys., 12:3:77 and Cal., 1:132.) The church believes that the most *surprising* gift of God is that human beings can have the favor with God that Jesus himself enjoyed as God's unique Son. The church calls this favor adoption or grace. (Jesus' baptism was not *his* adoption; he is Son of God from the beginning, cf. 2:15; Jesus' baptism was his ordination; our baptism, however, is our birth or adoption into Jesus' family as well as our ordination into his service. In our baptism we are allowed to hear the words spoken at his: "You are my priceless child; I am deeply pleased with you." God might let us pray to an open heaven; he might even let us have something of his Spirit; but does he have to *like* us—this much? Does he actually want us in his family? "Yes," Christian baptism answers. The simplest meaning of baptism is—"God likes us!" (Edw. Schroeder).

In baptism the whole Christian blessing is delivered to us without diminution. And the deepest blessing of baptism is that we become as pleasing and as dear to the Father as the Father's very own Son, which is very dear indeed. In the simple little baptismal service in our churches when (after the first generation) usually as little children we were placed under and within the triune Name, we received more than a wet forehead. We became especially adopted children of God. Heaven is opened above us, the Spirit is placed within us, the Son stands by us, and the creature is home at last in the family of God.

The gospel in all this (beyond the history of all this) is that what was given to Jesus then is given also to us now in Christian baptism. It is not so miraculous that Jesus should be honored with gifts at baptism; it is that we should be.

"This is an absolutely perfect, powerful, mighty saying, 'This is my dear Son,' because everything is inside it, and it summarizes what is in the whole of Scripture. . . . For the words sound, yes, as if He looked all around and yet found no one except this One, and says, 'This is it!'; as if to say, 'Here is finally one person who pleases me and is my dear Son; the others are altogether out.' . . . Now we must see that this glorious praise and honor is said of Christ for *our* sake. . . . *He* doesn't need it. . . . So it applies to *us*, not Christ." (Lu., W^2 11:2141–42; cf. 2144)

Many of us were baptized as infants. Over the long haul of church history the church has in the main believed that our infancy is no hindrance to God's giving us saving gifts (see the Gospels' Reception of Children stories—and the disciples' initial objections—e.g., at Matt 19:13–15). Indeed, much of the church has regularly believed that the grace of the whole affair is, if anything, enhanced by the normal recipients of baptism—little children. Over the years the gospel with its central message of faith will be spoken also to these children as they grow up, urgently inviting them to continue to believe what they have been given—given in the passion *for* them in A.D. 30 and applied in baptism *to* them in their own personal A.D. Where faith is not sustained in the hearts of baptized children, the gifts really given by God in baptism are left unused in an unopened section of the human heart. The gifts can even be rejected and, apparently, by most they are (see the very important discussion of this fact of most or many in 1 Cor 10 A), and then there is only judgment, as John's Fire Sermon made blazingly clear. But when the faith given in baptism is maintained and confirmed, when baptized persons turn to Christ in fresh decisions of faith, they find that Christ had earlier turned to them. This turning of Christ *toward* us was first seen at Christmas, then at his baptism *with* us, but most momentously at his passion *for* us; then, afterward, this divine turning toward us was existentially seen or felt *by* us in the evangelical delivery system called the sacraments (and in this case, in the initiation sacrament of baptism); finally, it all becomes alive *in* us, again and again, by personal faith, which by God's grace can begin very early in a child's life, as early as baptism.

Our faith *receives* the gifts of God. But our faith does not *deliver* the gifts to us; God does through his means of grace. The delivery of the passion to us occurs ordinarily in baptism. And for all we know (and Luther liked this view, LW: 36:300–01; cf. Cal., *Inst.*, IV.xvi, 19–20) a divinely given *infant faith* can receive the gifts given then and there in baptism. No one should laugh (Gen 17–18). "Is anything too hard for the Lord?" (Gen 18:14 RSV). The invitation to re-receive the gifts *previously* given to the people of God then happens again and again in the preached Word and the supper sacrament with their gospel messages of faith and repentance.

Infant initiation honors a parental God, a God who bestows gifts on us (like all good parents) even before the children can adequately respond. Infant baptism is gospelform; it is something God does for us before we do anything for God. (Cf. circumcision in the Old Testament. The New Testament's initiation sacrament, with its wider grace, is for both sexes, and it is no less inclusive of the very tiny child.) One reason the church has come to love infant baptism over the years (and I may say this myself as a convert to infant baptism) is the fact that few things in the church celebrate the Father's unmerited grace quite as much as the sacrament of baptism given to the little children of repentant believers. "Repent . . . the promise [of baptismal grace, Acts 2:38] is for *you* [the repentant] and for your *children*" (Acts 2:39).

One senses that some resistance to infant baptism comes from a Pelagian emphasis upon what believers must *do* first, from a too anthropocentric emphasis on our decision as the decisive fact in salvation. But why did the Reformers, and especially Luther and Calvin, the great champions of justification *by faith alone*, so stubbornly fight for the retention of infant baptism? The Reformers knew that infant baptism celebrated *and communicated* the one reality that is more important than anything we do—the prevenient grace of God, of a God who does saving things for people even when they are very young. Happily, infant baptism cannot be spoiled by the presumption of "my decision" or by any inward or outward good work done or good motive engendered by the recipient of grace. No infant can take credit for its prior commitment. If appearances in this case do not deceive, we seem as infants to be rather bewildered by what is going on when we are baptized. But God is superior to all appearances; inwardly God infuses faith. This ambience in infant baptism is so much like the rest of the gospel that it helps us to believe that this seemingly common event is God's way in the church of arriving in human lives. Infant baptism looks very much like the feed-bin (or manger) in which Jesus arrived. Infant baptism has been cherished in the historic church, I suspect, because it is shaped like the gospel.

If I were to put in two words, then, what I think the baptism of Jesus teaches us, it would be this: (1) Jesus is *everything* to God the Father, without exception; and (2) *Everything* that Jesus receives from the Father in baptism is given freely to us, without exception. I wish to stress the "everything" in both theses. If we leave out anything, we do injury to either Jesus as Christ or to baptism as Christian. Jesus has everything the Father has to give, and he gives us this everything in the unlikely place called baptism in the church. This is a great mystery, but it is worthy of God and God's gospel.

A Discussion of the Case for Believers' Baptism

The most recent consensus on baptism, the important "Lima Text," *Baptism, Eucharist, and Ministry* ("Faith and Order Paper No. 111"; Geneva: World Council of Churches, 1982), begins its discussion of baptismal practice with these words: "While the possibility that infant baptism was also practised in the apostolic age cannot be excluded, baptism upon personal profession of faith is the most clearly attested pattern in the New Testament documents" (11; p. 4). The many persons whom we explicitly see in baptisms in the New Testament, from Jesus to the apostle Paul, were adults and believers when they entered baptism. (The baptized "households" in Acts, while possibly containing infants, are not sufficiently in focus for us to make an apodictic exception to the norm of adult baptisms in the New Testament witnesses.) Baptists ask the rest of the churches to take this New Testament presentation seriously.

The sequence in the initiations in the accounts of conversions in the Book of Acts is the sequence of Word—repentance (faith)—baptism. Why don't we retain this sequence, ask Baptists. Evangelical Christians in non-Baptist churches, who have had conversions that are deeply experienced, often ask their teachers why their denominations' official teachings mandate infant baptism. In my experience as a teacher, this question about believers' and infant baptism ranks with the question of predestination (and free will) and the question of the salvation of the many (in its honest, usual form, "If Christ is the only way of salvation, what about those who haven't heard?") as one of the three most vexing doctrinal questions in Christian education. Like most teachers in the catholic tradition of the church, I make my arguments for infant baptism along the lines developed in outline above—God's household-wide work of salvation (from Noah's ark to Acts' households), the analogy of circumcision, the initiative-taking love of God for persons before they are even able fully or maturely to love God in return or in advance, and the Catholic and Reformation precedents. But the deep personal conviction that infant baptism is gospelform and best honors the shape of God's saving work in the world, as witnessed to in Scripture and church history, should not blind the interpreter to the power of the witness of believers' baptism as it is presented to us in the Baptist and independent churches.

The baptizing of *any child,* independent of the faith or churchmanship of the parents, or independent even of a serious and intact commitment of church and parents to a full-throttle Christian education program of children, from infancy through youth into adulthood, is so scandalously prevalent in the churches that the Baptist protest is difficult to refute on practical grounds. Indiscriminate infant baptism is the Achilles heel of the Orthodox-Catholic-Reformation churches' initiation practice. Parents not loyally devoted to the life of the church should not ask for their children to be baptized, and churches should decline such baptisms when sought. Faith is that important. But parents only casually related to the church are constantly defying good faith and are bringing children to baptism for social or superstitious reasons, and so they are taking God's name in vain. And the consenting churches are co-conspirators. The baptism itself is not in vain—"let God be true though every man be false" (Rom 3:4); God acts savingly in his sacraments. But how can infant faith (I believe in this phenomenon with Luther) be sustained, challenged, and discipled where, after baptism, there is virtually no contact with the Word of promise and command? God must find very unreal and even insulting our use of the divine sacraments without a commitment to the continuing ministry of the divine Word from which and toward which we baptize and communicate.

It is difficult to know which offends God more, the works-righteousness, Pelagian decisionism that threatens believers' baptism, or the antinomian secularism that threatens the sacramental churches. Perhaps an ecumenical council of all the churches will be necessary for the resolution of this critical initiation question. A council may be necessary since Scripture can be argued persuasively by each side—by the covenantal side (see circumcision, and Calvin's arguments, *Inst.* IV. xvi) and by the Baptist side (see, recently, the conversion of the Reformed theologian Karl Barth to this position, *CD* IV/4). The Lima text, *Baptism, Eucharist, and Ministry,* makes this commentary, reasonably and temperately, I believe, after its even-handed presentation of believers' and infant baptism:

"In some churches which unite both infant-baptist and believer-baptist traditions, it has been possible to regard as equivalent alternatives for entry into the Church both a pattern whereby baptism in infancy is followed by later profession of faith and a pattern whereby believers' baptism follows upon a presentation and blessing in infancy. This example invites other churches to decide whether they, too, could not recognize equivalent alternatives in their reciprocal relationships and in church union negotiations" (Commentary [12]; p. 5).

If the Orthodox, Catholic, and Reformation churches should make this concession of a *dual* practice of baptism, the Baptist churches can be asked with greater force to recognize the Bible's *one* baptism, for in the careful words of *Baptism, Eucharist, and Ministry,* "Baptism is an unrepeatable act. Any practice which might be interpreted as 'rebaptism' must be avoided" (13; p. 4). For there *is* only "one baptism" (Eph 4:5), and every Christian baptism is performed by Christ through his ministers and is therefore valid wherever it is performed in a Christian church in the triune name (cf. Aug., *Tract. in Jn.,* 4–6:31–48). It is not right for any church to say that her baptisms "take" while baptisms in other churches do not.

Worse things could happen to the church than for there to be an ecumenical declaration of the universal practice of believers' baptism. The dedication of infants to God in prayer can be trusted to cover the little ones with saving grace. The desecrations of indiscriminate infant baptisms will have been removed from the face of the earth and from the practice of the churches. The full drama of the conscious, spiritual, and physical joining of one's personal decision for Christ with God's prior personal decision for the believer, sealed in the waters of baptism, preferably by full immersion, will restore to the Catholic, Orthodox, and Reformation churches the thrill of Christian initiation in a way that present practice cannot match. The evangelistic impact of believers' baptisms is documented by the missionary vitality of many Baptist churches.

But one haunting doubt persists. In believer-baptism churches the question must be asked: "When does a young person believe enough to be baptized?" Is the little eight-year-old believer believing "enough"? Or should we wait until he or she is eighteen and can make a more intelligent decision? But if these questions are recognized as being (as they are) too rationalistic, intellectualistic, and legalistic, why could not a believing five- or six-year-old child be baptized? The "enough" in the question "when does a child believe enough?" is fraught with works-righteousness and betrays the point of greatest weakness in Baptist initiation practice. Where has *grace* gone when we ask (as we must in believers' baptism) if a child's faith is "enough"? The soft underbelly in Baptist initiation practice is the temptation so to center on an individual's faith quantitatively that the free grace of God is effectively made marginal. For this and other reasons, biblical and church-historical, I opt for the baptism of the infants of loyal church parents in churches with evangelical Christian education programs. Nevertheless, the baptism of only those who can personally confess their faith is a baptism that cannot be cheaply dismissed by us who are catholic Christians. And if confessed-faith-baptism is a baptism secured against the incursions of Pelagian decisionism ("does one believe enough?") and Donatist exclusivism ("other baptisms than ours do not work")—that is, if it is a baptism confessing that it is the *Lord* who really baptizes in all Christian baptisms (John 1:33, and Augustine's comments), and that this lordly baptism is effective in all Christian baptisms, independent of the purity of the human ministers of baptism—then catholic Christians will be able to break bread with Baptist Christians in ecumenical brother- and sisterhood in the fundamental question of Christian initiation.

Christian baptism is a place where Christians vigorously differ. This sacrament of the unity of the church (1 Cor 12:13) is frequently, in fact, the sacrament of our greatest disunity. Let Christians on both sides of the aisle pray for unity in teaching here, for the sake of God's honor, for the churches' deeper fellowship, and for the world's discipleship.

A Closing Word to Matthew Chapter 3

We are now in a position to answer the question posed at the beginning of this chapter: Where does God meet us now? I believe that Matthew has answered this question in giving us the present tense "appearances" of John the Baptist and of the adult Jesus of Nazareth. Matthew's answer is this: God meets us in the preaching of his searing law and in the gracious gift of empowering baptism in the gospel. God meets us, this chapter has taught us, in righteous Demand and in merciful Supply. He requires the good of us, and then in baptism he gives us all the "goods" to do good (or, the grace to be accepted as good). God rightly asks the righteous life of us and then gives us the gifts for living the righteous life: access to the Father in prayer, the dove-power of the Holy Spirit, and gratuitous adoption through the Son into the family of God. In Paul's language, God asks righteousness of us (Rom 1–2) and then freely gives us his own (Rom 3–4).

John the Baptist warns us of the dangers of a life that is not righteous, and so whets our appetite for the means to righteousness. Jesus comes giving us these means: and the first of these for most of us is the gift of the triune God in baptism (3:16–17; cf. 28:19). (God's other means of grace—the fellowship of the church herself, the preached Word, the supper, prayer—are all then enjoyed by the faith of discipleship begun and given at baptism.)

The Christian has learned from Jesus that the admonitions of culture, conscience, and even the law in the church are not God's last Word. They are his next-to-last. God's Last Word is Jesus Christ himself, coming down in amazing grace and deep humility, identifying himself with us, taking our place, representing our humanity before God and receiving gifts from God representatively for us, and now standing beside us.

Baptism is part of the gospel. Baptism is tactile gospel.

The clearest distinction between law and gospel that I have found in the church's confessions is that which occurs in the nine questions and answers of *Craig's Catechism*, 1581.

THE DIFFERENCE BETWEEN THE LAW AND THE GOSPEL

Q. Where does this difference come from?
A. From the Spirit who is joined with the Gospel, and not with the Law.
Q. What follows from this?
A. The Law commands, but it gives no strength.
Q. What does the Gospel do?
A. It gives freely all that it requires of us.

Q. What other difference is there between them?
A. The Law has no compassion on sinners.
Q. What about the Gospel?
A. It offers mercy only to sinners.
Q. What other difference is there?
A. In the manner of our justification.
Q. What does the Law demand in our justification?
A. Our own perfect obedience.
Q. What does the Gospel demand?
A. Faith only in the obedience of Christ Jesus.
Q. Does the Gospel favour the transgression of the Law?
A. No it gives strength to obey the Law.

Texts to study for the appreciation of God's salvation-initiation of whole families (including their children) into the people of God, and now of baptism, include the following: Gen 6:8, 18; 7:1; (cf. Heb 11:7; and 1 Pet 3:20–22); Gen 17:11–14; 19:12, 15–16; Matt 19:13–15; Mark 10:13–16; Luke 18:15–17; Acts 2:28–39; 11:14–15; 16:14–15, 31–33; 1 Cor 7:12–16; cf. John 3:5; Acts 19:3–6; Rom 6; Tit 3:5. Luther, LW 35–38 (Word and Sacrament); *Large Catechism*, Baptism; *Augsburg Confession*, art. 9; *Apology of the Augsburg Confession*, art. 24; John Calvin, *Geneva Catechism*, QQ. 333,337; *Inst.*, IV.xv-xvi; *The United Presbyterian Book of Confessions: The Nicene Creed*, art. 3; *The Scots Confession of Faith*, 21:3:21; *The Second Helvetic Confession*, 19:5:178–79; 20:5:187; (contrast *The Westminster Confession of Faith*, 28:5); *The Heidelberg Catechism*, QQ. 65–74; *The Confession of 1967*, 51. See also *The Anglican [Thirty-Nine] Articles of Religion*, art. 27; the *Methodist Articles of Religion*, art. 17; at Vatican II, representatively, the *Dogmatic Constitution on the Church (Lumen Gentium)*, particularly 7, 11, 14, and the *Constitution on the Sacred Liturgy (Sacrosanctum Concilium)*, passim; and now the ecumenical *Baptism, Eucharist, and Ministry* (Lima Document), Baptism.

Chapter Four
The Doctrine of Ministry

"I believe in the holy catholic church, the communion of saints." (The Apostles' Creed)

In chapter 4, Jesus begins to minister. (He had ministered to us already, of course, in being baptized with and for us.) This chapter finds its unity by showing us in several ways *how* the baptized Jesus decided to minister. Then it also shows baptized disciples how they too, by following Jesus, may minister ("Follow me, and I will make *you* fishers," 4:19). Ministry is what this chapter is mainly about.

Matthew's first core christology—his first systematic teaching about Christ—lies ahead of us in the five chapters that follow this chapter: in the Sermon on the Mount (5–7) and in the Ten Miracles (8–9). There in Jesus' Word and works is Matthew's ministering Jesus. Interestingly, both chapters 4 and 10 (right before and right after the sermon and miracles of chapters 5 through 9) are devoted to the same subject—to Christian ministry. It is as though Matthew is trying to say to us, fore and aft, "I not only want you to see Jesus as an historical figure of the past; I want you to learn how to follow him in the present. I not only want to show you *his* ministry, I want to show you *yours* in his name."

The meaning of life for the Christian disciple is to find some sort of *ministry* in life under Christ's leading. This chapter will teach us how to minister by introducing us to Jesus' ways of ministry.

With the noun *ministry* and verb *minister* in this chapter and elsewhere I intend to indicate a reality and activity as wide as the whole people of God; *ministry*, in fact, is that for which *every* baptized Christian's unique gift of the Spirit exists. "As *each* [of you] has received a gift [literally, a *charisma!*], employ it [*diakonountes*, literally "be ministering" or "be table-waiting" it] *for one another* as good stewards of God's varied grace" (1 Pet 4:10; see the exciting "each" [Christian] in 1 Cor 12:7, 11, 18, 27 ["individually"]; cf. *Baptism, Eucharist, and Ministry* [1982], Ministry, 5). "Communion of saints" *means* "Christians' sharing of gifts"—ministry.

In Matthew chapter 4 we have the privilege of seeing firsthand how Jesus warded off spurious ministries in the *temptations* of the first half of the chapter, and how he entered true ministries in the *services* of the second half of the chapter.

There are, in outline, two sets of ministry stories in chapter 4: (1) the temptations of Jesus (vv 1–11) and (2) the services of Jesus (vv 12–25). In the temptations, Jesus proves himself to be what he was assured of being at his baptism—the Son and Servant of *God* (see 4:3, 6). In the services, Jesus proves himself to be what he displayed by seeking baptism at all—the Son and Servant of Others or "the Son of *Man*."

The title "Son of Man" is one of the most difficult of all of Jesus' titles to understand. It first appears in this Gospel at 8:20, and is discussed in an introductory way there. In

99

relation to the title "Son of God" the words "Son of Man" are symbiotic. As Son of God and Son of Man, "from two sides Jesus is what he is: from his fellowship with God and from his fellowship with men. Through these two fellowships Jesus' life receives its form and his work receives its goal" (Schl., *Der*, 286; cf. Grund., 282). Interestingly, NT scholarship has learned that the title Son of Man is an even more divine title than Son of God (see esp. Colpe, TDNT, 8:400–77).

I. THE THREE TEMPTATIONS: THE MINISTRY OF THE SON AND SERVANT OF GOD (4:1–11)

A. The First Temptation. Sensationalism (The Stomach Test)

4:1–4 *"Then Jesus was led out into the wilderness by the Spirit to be tempted by the devil. And when he had fasted for forty days and forty nights, he was hungry. And the Tempter came up to him and said to him, 'If you really are the Son of God, then tell these stones here to become bread.' Then Jesus responded by saying, 'It is in writing, "A human being will not live by bread alone, but by every single Word that comes pouring out of God's mouth."'"*

Here, as in the first sentence of chapter 2, we are given the chapter's cast of characters in the opening line: Jesus, the Spirit, and the devil. Two questions immediately arise for the modern reader: (1) Does the divine Spirit lead anyone, and particularly the newly anointed Messiah, into temptation? And (2) Is there really a devil? To the first question we may say quite confidently with the text that yes, the Spirit of God does lead Jesus, not specifically "into temptation," but "into the wilderness," and there specifically "*to be* tempted by the devil" *(peirasthēnai)*. The Spirit is free; free to lead us not only into good things, but into confrontation with bad things. This truth Matthew quite ingenuously believes and teaches.

There is no dominically instituted rite of confirmation in the Gospels except temptation. Temptation (trouble) is the sacrament of confirmation brought to every baptized person, and this not accidentally but by divine arrangement. Precisely because God loves his people he strengthens them by testing (cf. Exod 15:22–17:16). So the first question, Would the Spirit lead Jesus into the wilderness to be tempted? may be answered quite simply by yes, indeed.

It may seem a bit subtle to say that "the Spirit leads into the wilderness but not into temptation"; perhaps we should simply say that "the Spirit leads into temptation." But we should recognize the not-so-subtle distinction made in the text: it is not the Spirit who introduces the doubts, ambitions, and enthusiasms of the temptations. God does not do the tempting in these stories, and so it is thoughtful not to say that God or the Spirit led Jesus *into* temptation. But God's Spirit does lead Jesus to a place where Jesus can *be* tempted.

The Greek word *peirazō* can be translated "test" "when God stands in the forefront," or as "tempt" wherever "the Devil stands in the forefront," concludes Gundry. Thus in our complex text "the leading of the Spirit and the enticements of the Devil give the verb *[peirazō]* a double connotation here" (Gund., 55): both test and tempt. Cf. Gen 22:1ff and Abraham's test/temptation.

It is theologically important that God be treated respectfully, and this means that God must not be held responsible for vicious evil in history. (It is one purpose of the parable of the weeds in chapter 13:24–30, 36–43, esp. vv 28, 39, to teach this important truth; for God's judicial "evil" of judgment cf., e.g., Deut 32:39; Amos 3:6.) But this caveat should not breed a timidity that removes God from history. This timidity occurs when we do not allow God the freedom to bring us places where we can be tempted or tested.

The second preliminary question concerns the reality of the devil. Does such a being exist? It is important to notice that our text nowhere pictures the devil. He is not physically described. We are permitted by the text to believe that the devil operated mainly with words, thus by suggestion and argument, by introducing ideas, thoughts, and possibilities to the mind. The focus of all three temptations is words, that is, thoughts (which are quiet words).

Nowhere in the New Testament, or in the Old Testament for that matter, is there an etiology of the devil, describing whence he came (Milton knows; the Bible is allusive). In the New Testament there is simply the conviction that an anti-God force, most often conceived personally, exists and works in history especially against the purposes and people of God, with the special aim of *splitting*. ("To split" is the root meaning of the verb *diaballein,* the root, in turn, of the noun *diabolos,* the main New Testament word for devil. Cf. Luther, *Large Catechism,* 119: the devil's "main object is to lead us to ignore and utterly cast away both God's Word and works," i.e., to split human beings from God.)

The conviction that there is a supernatural enemy of God and persons is as old as our oldest Creation and Fall account (Gen 2–3, from about the tenth century before Christ) and is not to be traced only to Israel's postexilic experience or to the influence of Persian dualism. Jesus shared his people's and his period's conviction of an enemy, and his evangelists and apostles passed this conviction on.

There *is* a mystery of iniquity in history, and all peoples have attempted to explain it in various ways. In Western intellectual history in the one- to two-hundred year period between rationalism and romanticism (roughly, from the seventeenth through the nineteenth centuries), the reality of this malevolent being was put in serious question or transmuted, romantically-idealistically, into metaphors for the riddle of existence or the abysmal depths of being.

In our time even progressive theologies ascribe what they call systemic evil to quasi-demonic institutions, and they trace structural violence to oppressive social, economical, and political "principalities" in history. These descriptions are meant to point to supra-personal or supra-individual powers that work history's main maladies. By speaking in this way of systems and structures, progressive Christians seek to escape the personalistic-individualistic descriptions of evil current in conservative Christian circles. Sin, it is said, is not primarily individual or perhaps even moral (in the narrow sense); it is primarily social, economical, and political; and the roots of sin are not present so much in the hearts and consciences of individual persons, or, they are present there only insofar as they exist primarily in malevolently structured interrelationships of oppression and injustice. These Christians cite with approval biblical texts that tell us "we are not contending against flesh and blood [i.e., merely human individual realities], but against principalities, against the powers, against the world rulers of this present darkness" (Eph 6:12), texts that until recently were considered strange or fundamentalistic by the progressive.

In the final analysis, the church teaches the existence of the devil because the biblical writers (who are normative for us) taught such an existence and instructed us that Jesus reckoned with such an existence, too. And "a disciple is not above his Lord."

The various theories of demonic influence in the New Testament do not have to be accepted *in toto* by modern Christians. But acceptance of the existence of the (defeated but defiant) devil seems requisite for a Christian theology that takes its lead from Scripture and the Christian tradition. It seems historically true that when belief in the existence of the devil is banished from the front door, some evil power or theology of evil, by whatever name, reappears with a vengeance at the back door. A progressive national theology in Germany dismissed the demonic as myth and then experienced the hyper-demonic forces of Nazism with Nazism's own perverse demonology of the devilish Jew. I believe it is theologically sensible to hold that the evil we face is at least supernatural in inspiration. But progressive Christians are correct (and consonant with Scripture) in asking the church to take much more seriously our own human culpability in social evil, especially our too easy acquiescence in that great system of evil known as the status quo. The devil is not to act as a surrogate for human responsibility.

Nevertheless, according to the clear witness of the whole New Testament, the devil exists. It is, in fact, a preliminary relief for struggling Christians to know of this existence; otherwise they feel attacked by utterly uncanny or unconquerable forces. But the whole gospel teaches us that Jesus conquers the devil and the demonic, and gives believers the strength to conquer, too.

The fullest contemporary historical-theological study of the concept of the devil is the Cornell University Press trilogy by Jeffrey Burton Russell, *The Devil: Perceptions of Evil from Antiquity to Primitive Christianity* (1977); *Satan: The Early Christian Tradition* (1981); and *Lucifer: The Devil in the Middle Ages* (1984), from which the most relevant conclusions are these: "The central message of the New Testament is salvation: Christ saves us. What he saves us from is the power of the Devil. If the power of the Devil is dismissed, then Christ's saving mission becomes meaningless" (*The Devil*, 229; cf. 249, 257–60; see Russell's review of the seven major objections to belief in the devil today in his second volume, *Satan*, 220ff).

In his latest volume, Russell's own personal conclusions are these: "A real force is actively present in the cosmos urging to evil. This evil force has a purposive center that actively hates good, the cosmos, and every individual in the cosmos. It urges us too to hate good, the cosmos, other individuals, and ourselves. It has terrible and immense effects, but it is ultimately futile; every individual can defeat it in himself or herself by drawing upon the loving power of God. For Christians, then, the person of the Devil may be a metaphor, but it is a metaphor for something that is real, that really brings horror to the world every day and threatens to lay the entire earth waste" (*Lucifer*, 305–06; cf. the review by Norman Cohn, *The New York Review of Books*, April 25, 1985, 13–14).

Some modern biblical and theological commentators take different positions. Beare, 107–08, for example, writes, "There is no doubt that the early Christians, like most of the Jews of the time, believed that there was such a mighty spirit of evil; nor can we question the fact that Jesus himself shared these beliefs. None the less, we must recognize that this is a mythical conception that has lost appeal to the minds of men; we cannot ourselves accept it without falling victims to superstition." Contrast Caird, 79.

Bainton's classic study of Luther, *Here I Stand*, 66–67, expresses what is involved here, in my opinion, best of all: "But what of the conflict between God and the Devil? Is God lord of all, or is he himself impeded by demonic hordes? Such questions a few years ago would have seemed to modern man but relics of medievalism, and fear of demons was dispelled simply by denying their existence. Today so much of the sinister has engulfed us that we are prone to wonder whether perhaps there may not be malignant forces in the heavenly places. All those who have known the torments of mental disorder well understand the imagery of satanic hands clutching to pull them to their doom. Luther's answer was not scientific but religious. He did not dissipate the demons by turning on an electric light, because for him they had long ago been routed when the veil of the temple was rent and the earth quaked and darkness descended upon the face of the land. Christ in his utter anguish had fused the wrath and the mercy of God, and put to flight all the legions of Satan. In Luther's hymns one hears [this] . . . :

> In devil's dungeon chained I lay
> The pangs of death swept o'er me.
> My sin devoured me night and day
> In which my mother bore me.
> My anguish ever grew more rife,
> I took no pleasure in my life
> And sin had made me crazy. . . .
> Thus spoke the Son, 'Hold thou to me,
> From now on thou wilt make it.
> I gave my very life for thee
> And for thee I will stake it.
> For I am thine and thou art mine,
> And where I am our lives entwine,
> The Old Fiend cannot shake it.'"

Almost the whole of Luther's hymn "A Mighty Fortress" is a commentary on the devil and on Christ's and Christians' victory over the devil.

4:2 "And when Jesus had fasted for forty days and for forty nights, he was hungry." Moses had fasted for forty days and forty nights prior to his reception of the law (Exod 24:18). Jesus now fasts for forty days and forty nights before unveiling the gospel. Israel had wandered behind Moses in the wilderness for forty years living only by the supernatural provision of God. Jesus "the prophet like Moses" (Deut 18:15, 18; Acts 3:22), the New Israel (Matt 2; Exod 2), now undergoes similar rigors and is tested in similar ways. Israel's "baptism in the waters of the Red Sea" (1 Cor 10:1–2) was followed by Israel's confirmation of testings in the wilderness of Sin; similarly, Jesus' baptism in the waters of the Jordan is followed by his confirmation of testings in the wilderness of Judea.

We should probably also see the Second Adam in Jesus' temptation experiences (though Mark stresses this more than Matthew). Where the First Adam had been tested and found wanting (Gen 3), the Second Adam is now tested and found faithful. Where one man's disobedience under temptation had made all sinners, now another man's obedience under temptation works for the righteousness of all (cf. Rom 5 B).

Chrysostom, 13:1; 80, learns from the setting for this temptation that the devil especially attacks the lonely (like Eve in the Garden, Gen 3), and that when we are with others in Christian fellowship the devil is not as apt to attack: "Wherefore [let us] be flocking together continually"! Luther had similar counsel (Bainton, 363), as did Milton's Adam (*P.L.*, Book ix). Chrysostom also sees fasting as a shield against temptation, whereas

Luther had never seen a right fasting or a fasting that did not encourage trust in good works; right fasting is to accept God-sent hardships (W^2 12:1278). Calvin, 1:134–35, points out that neither Jesus nor Moses fasted every year, but only once in their lives according to the biblical records.

4:3 "And the Tempter came up to Jesus and said to him, 'If you really are the Son of God, then tell these stones here to become bread.'" The devil's major office, we learn here by his name "the Tempter," is to tempt, seduce, and split relationships—especially those of and with Christ, his baptism, and his Word. "Fouling up Christ" is the devil's favorite activity; no other temptation (even today, even for believers) compares in seriousness.

Jesus' fasting left him hungry. We learn in this verse that the Tempter first approaches Jesus' point of weakness (Lu., W^2 12:1274). This is the devil's most obvious tactic; to hit the human at its weak spots first. It is when the human is hungry that it is most tired, depressed, and discouraged, and thus that it is most easily tempted (Brecht). Jesus' stomach is empty; so it is to Jesus' stomach that the first temptation is directed.

"*If* you are the Son of God . . . ," the temptation begins. Doubt is the classic lever of temptation. If God's Word is doubtful (cf. Gen 3:1 and Matt 3:17), if God's gifts in baptism are uncertain (maybe baptism doesn't really mean sonship, or the gift of the Spirit), then there are other options for finding out how we stand with God. By means of doubt the Tempter would move Jesus to use God. (The tempting phrase can also be translated "*Since* you are the Son of God, tell these stones, etc.," and thus be a temptation for Jesus not to doubt but to rely on his Sonship "in self-serving ways," Gund., 55; similarly, Bonn., 44.)

It is said that we live in an age of doubt, in an age of the death of God. We must be careful how we say this. We ought not imply that human nature has normally liked the truth of God and that only recently, in our time, have people found God unreal. As the *Apology of the Augsburg Confession* (1531), 167, 170, 303, reminds us, ever since the Fall, human nature has universally resisted the true God, hid from God, doubted, and distrusted God. Adam and Eve hid from God immediately after their rejection of God's command (Gen 3:8). And the apostle Paul has taught us that we are not naturally seekers after God's truth, but that we are suppressers of it (Rom 1:18–3:20). Human nature doubts God; it lives in doubt of God's reality because it *wants* to. The last three centuries have simply succeeded in making this fact explicit and praiseworthy. Care needs to be taken lest we glorify doubt and make doubt seem more mature, advanced, and thoughtful than faith. Doubt of God is not a virtue to preen. The praise of doubt is sometimes fulsome, especially in college settings, and it is often boorish. Let us doubt a great deal, but not God. Let us especially doubt what the world exalts, "for what is exalted among men is an abomination in the sight of God" (Luke 16:15). And one of the things the world exalts is doubt of God.

"The Tempter said to him, 'If you are the Son of God. . . .'" The pressure of this temptation is to move Jesus to doubt—or what is the same thing, to move him to prove—his baptism. Baptism had given Jesus the clear assurance that he was God's priceless Son and that the Father was deeply pleased with him (3:16–17). Is Jesus really God's unique Son, and is he really deeply pleasing to the Father? Transformed rocks will instantly dispel uncertainty. Why not test the truth of baptism's Voice? The assurance of faith is of utmost importance. This assurance is delivered satisfactorily, adequately, classically in the gift of baptism. Where baptism becomes questionable other signs are inevitable. (See the sign of speaking in tongues sought by those who question the gift of the Spirit in what they call water-baptism.) Where there is doubt if baptism works, where it is suggested that maybe baptism doesn't *do* anything (except symbolize), then the search will be on for deeper assurances, better baptisms, and clearer experiences, where, finally, we can be *really* sure that we truly are the sons and daughters of God in the power of the Spirit.

Jesus is given this opportunity for a second experience beyond baptism in the possibility of a specifically miraculous transformation, appealing to the senses—a literal sensation. "If you are the Son of God, tell these stones to become bread." Baptism is not externally miraculous: there are no visible transformations necessarily involved. There are only water and the accompanying promises of heaven, Spirit, and Father. But the devil now offers the opportunity of the supraverbal, the super-promissory—a transformation that the eyes can finally see and prove.

We must recall, first, that this was a real temptation, that Jesus was *tempted* to do it. He was hungry. Second, all Jesus had to show from his baptismal experience was his memory of and belief in baptism's gifts. But memory can play tricks and faith can ebb. Doesn't baptism mean an open heaven (then why not ask help of heaven?), the Dove-Spirit (surely the Spirit makes miracles possible?), and the assurance of Sonship (and if a Son, then "will your heavenly Father give you a stone when you ask him for bread?" Matt 7:9)? Jesus was tempted to go beyond baptism to a remarkable experience of confirmation, to a more visible proof of the things baptism merely showed and talked about but did not prove in any immediately or visibly transforming way. Baptism assured inwardly but it did not transform outwardly. These are the dynamics of Jesus' first temptation.

The form this satanic voice assumes in addressing disciples is, "How can you be the child of God you say you are when you still have so many problems? Get rid of your problems [turn your stones into bread], and then we can believe your relation to God." The devil will let Christians be satisfied with Christ, his church, other Christians, and themselves only when all these are transforming and transformed realities, miraculous with success, radiant with power, obviously making it (men and women aglow). The issue is sharp and clear: either we believe the Voice of baptism—"You *are* the son of God"—or we believe the other voice: "You are the son of God when you prove it sensationally."

Beware all arguments from transformation. It is not the transformed that proves the truth; it is simple trust in the Word of the truth—a trust that may have to be lived out untransformed (though trust itself is the great transformation). It is this focus upon the Word that Jesus provides in his reply.

4:4 And he responded and said, "It is in writing, 'A human being will not live by bread alone, but by every single Word that comes pouring out of God's mouth'" (4:4, from Deut 8:3).

In all three of his answers Jesus begins by saying, "It is in writing" ("It is written"). He means, "Scripture says." Jesus was a man of Scripture. The temptations intend to drill this important truth into the church's mind. Ministry is Christian in the measure that it is ruled by Scripture. We learn from Jesus' opening phrase that Jesus obeyed the Spirit specially given him in baptism not by obeying immediately accessible spiritual voices or by getting special spiritual guidance from the air or in his mind. Jesus obeyed the Spirit and overcame Satan by recalling Scripture and believing baptism. The Spirit of *God* leads to confidence in Scripture and sacrament: false spirits lead everywhere else.

This incident teaches that in times of emergency the church is not to seek special experiential revelations or signs and wonders. In the temptations Jesus is not recorded as having recourse to immediate, direct conversation with the Father; he too went through the mediate, indirect, lowly course of Bible knowledge and obedience. There is no higher way, no less (as they say) literalistic way to God than through the written Word. Theological mystics, ancient and modern, have attempted to get the church out from under the "obscuring umbrella" (Nels Ferré) of written words into the immediate sunlight of the direct presence of God. It cannot be done and should not be tried. The Son and his church have dependable commerce with God the Father only through God's chosen media of writings and sacraments; all more spiritual and seemingly more direct routes are in fact detours. (Even Christian prayer is re-sponse and re-quest, and when it is most responsible prayer seeks, answers, and follows the lines laid out by God's preceding Word, especially the model Lord's Prayer.)

Christian faith and ethics are only trustworthy faith and ethics when they are not ashamed to be the much maligned "book religion." (Karl Barth made this especially clear against Paul Tillich and others in *Church Dogmatics,* I/1, 54f, 183f.) When Jesus confronted the devil he put him down by means of a Book, "It is in writing." If Jesus found his way into ministry and around temptation through the faithful remembering of Scripture and sacrament, the church should not think that she can find better ways.

"A human being will not live by bread alone." The text does not say "The *Messiah* will not live by bread alone." Even here (as in baptism earlier), Jesus completely identifies himself with human beings and treats himself as one of them (cf. Bonn., *ad loc.*). The Son of God is Son of Man. "The Savior's answer . . . show[s] that he who was tempted is a human being" (Jerome).

"Not by bread alone." Both Jesus and the Scripture he cites are too realistic to say "not by bread at all." Man lives by bread at least. We must have bread to live. Jesus teaches us to pray for it (6:11), says the Father knows we must have it (6:32), and even promises that where God's kingdom is sought first, bread, too, will be brought us (6:33b). Jesus gives bread where it is lacking (chapters 14 and 15). He will confront us at the last day with our reality or unreality in faith by asking us if we have given bread to others or not (25:31–46). *Human beings live by bread.* It is because of this inescapable fact that the devil is able to turn Jesus' hunger into a real temptation.

Jesus, newly aware through baptism of his historic vocation, is God's Servant-Son, which means he is God's Messiah, which means in turn that he has important work to do. He has to live to work; he has to eat to live. No bread, no Messiah. Thus Jesus' temptation is like Abraham's (Gen 22). Abraham was called to be the father of many nations, but then he was asked to sacrifice his only (legitimate) son. How can the promise be fulfilled when one kills the only form in which it exists? If Isaac goes, the promise goes with him; if Jesus dies of hunger, the Messiah dies with him. Only faith in the reality of the promising God sustains a person in such situations. Jesus, like Abraham, hangs on to God's promising Word.

"A human being will not live by bread *alone.*" Humanity lives by bread, but not just by bread. In our time, overfed societies are learning the truth of this saying.

Glutted with bread, their sons and daughters have sought (what they called) grass in order to *live*. Affluent society has learned that human beings do not in fact live by bread alone. When people seek the meaning of life in the accumulation of bread and things they find their health and homes in premature dissolution. *Human beings do not live by bread alone.* The human person has hidden hungers, deep cravings, a psychic yearning for more. What is this more?

"But by every single Word that comes pouring out of God's mouth" (4:4c). The compound present participle—"pouring out" (*ekporeuomenō*)—is exciting: it pictures a God in constant present conversation with his world through his Word. ("God *spoke* to the fathers, prophets, and apostles; He *still speaks* [*adhuc loquitur*] to us through Holy Scripture," CHPo., 1.) The deep famine of the world is a famine, known or unknown, for the Word of God. Since, on the authority of Jesus, human beings only *live* by the Word of God, there are more hungry people in the world than we think. Jesus was able to find God's Word literally nourishing him. Somehow this Word is not only spiritual, it is also able to be physical: it is so deep it can even reach the stomach. (We can remember this in time of economic crisis.) "God's Word can feed me," this temptation teaches. Real life is a trusting obedience under God's Word; real (and not just spiritual) food is believing God's Word. There is even biological nourishment in confidence in Scripture. Man really *lives* by every Word that comes pouring out of God's mouth. "Therefore if anyone is not feeding on the Word of God, that person is not living" (Jerome).

We tire of hearing the superspiritual tell us that spiritual things are more important than material things, because this truism is often used as a dodge from hard material ministries. But the church will overreact in her rightful disdain for the superspiritual if she lets herself be dislodged from the priority of the Word of God. (Compare the apostolic conviction and the priorities, but also the social sense, in Acts 6:2–4; similarly, Jethro's counsel, Exod 18:19–21.) If we lose a spiritual sense for the royalty of the Word, we soon lose a social sense for the urgency of bread. The merely (or, I think I can say, even the mainly) social-justice church will soon lose even her social-justice energies if she is not continually nourished by the only pure source of energy in the world—the biblical Word of God.

Thus in his first major temptation Jesus learned to make his ministry a continual feeding on the Word of God. From this feeding, through his ears as it were, Jesus is determined to find the main food he needs. He rejects the temptation to repeat the manna miracle—a miracle expected, incidentally, of the Second Moses (Schn., 29). The rabbinic rule had been, "As with the first Moses, so with the second (the Messiah)." In Matthew 2 we saw Jesus depicted as a kind of Second Moses. Yet now Jesus rejects a temptation that was tempting precisely because it came so near to being right: "As Moses and the people of Israel got the food they needed in their wilderness by miraculous bread from heaven, so now you—if you really are the Son of God—have the same right, perhaps even the same responsibility, to get the same provision. After all, even Messiahs have to eat." (Cf. Cal., 1:137.) "Take charge of your life, and don't be too religious" (cf. Bonn., 44). But Jesus may have been in the synagogue with the Book of Deuteronomy lately (all three of Jesus' answers to the Tempter are taken from Deuteronomy 6–8), and his exposure to Scripture there or elsewhere had convinced him that his road as Messiah was to be less sensational than expected. Before Jesus performs any miracles, he learns here for the rest of his life to reject the selfish use of the miraculous (Schl., *Der*, 103–04). Jesus did not assume for himself as Son the right to demand special, exempting privileges from his Father—not *although* but *because* he was a good Son. A son is most fully a son when he obeys his father. The Father had gotten Jesus into the wilderness; the Father will get Jesus out. Meanwhile, Jesus would simply trust the Father's Word of baptism: heaven is open above him, the Spirit is alive within him, he is loved as a Son; he'll be all right.

Jesus' first ministry to the church, then, is to be our prophet, teaching us to find God's will in God's Word and sacrament. Jesus has taught us in the first temptation that God's nourishing will is discoverable in God's Word, present to us in the church that reads Scripture like bread. Where the church feeds voraciously on the gospel of Scripture she will be given the guidance she needs to minister to her time. (Jesus' main first-century opponents, the scribal Bible teachers and the separatist Pharisees, can serve as a warning to the church that a *mere* Bible zeal, uninformed by or uncentered on the biblical Christ, can minister death. *Christ*-centered, *gospel*-centered Scripture study is the great need. Cf. John 5:39–40.)

B. The Second Temptation. Spectacularism (The Scripture Test)

4:5-7 *"Then the devil took Jesus into the holy city and placed him atop the pinnacle of the temple and said to him, 'If you really are the Son of God, throw yourself down from here; because it is in writing that "God will give orders to his angels to protect you, and they will carry you around with their hands so that you won't even stub your toe on a rock."' Jesus said to him, 'It is in writing in another place in Scripture, "You shall not test the Lord your God."'"*

The second temptation is full of holy things. Jesus is taken to the holy city, placed atop the holy temple, and is read the Holy Scriptures. Holy, holy, holy. Where the first temptation smelled like a bakery, the second has the aroma of a Greek Orthodox liturgy at Easter. Where the devil in the first temptation had tried to reach Jesus through his weak spot, his hungry stomach, he now tries to reach Jesus through his strong spot, his faith in God's Word (by which Jesus had held off the first temptation). If the evil one cannot make us carnal perhaps he can make us fanatical; if he cannot make us supersecular by seeking wonder bread, perhaps he can make us superspiritual by suggesting leaps of faith.

We learn something of the strategy of the satanic from the sequence of temptations (in Matthew; Luke has a different sequence, Luke 4 A). The first technique is to aim at our weakest spot, where obviously it is easiest to make a person fall. But the second technique, surprisingly, is not to aim at our next weakest spot; more cleverly it is to aim at our strength. This is a kind of spiritual jiu-jitsu. For if it is easiest to get us where we are weakest, it is next easiest to get us where we are strongest. This is so because strength is not an obvious problem. Perhaps we sin as often through attempting strong or great things as we do in succumbing to sins of weakness. (Peter's *curriculum vitae* in the Gospels indicates that this is in fact the case with serious disciples.)

In this temptation Jesus is confronted with Scripture. The *devil* says "it is written." This temptation teaches Jesus—and the church—that the devil is not only sensual; he is also spiritual. Jesus' major historical opponents were, in fact, spiritual people and Bible-believers. In this temptation Jesus experiences one of the most surprising sources of radical evil in the world: the perverse use of Scripture. The devil is not only at work in the wilderness; he is at work in the temple, too.

The temptation takes a biblical form because Jesus is now being tempted to prove, in deed, a faith in "every Word from God's mouth" that he had just claimed in speech. "Put your money where your mouth is." God has clearly promised to give special protection to his people—such promises, as we know, abound in the Psalms. It is at the heart of faith that "the Lord knows"—that is, that he deeply enters into and protects—"the way of the righteous" (Ps 1:6).

"You believe *in* the Word of God? Then step out *on* it. Dare the risk of faith; *live* by faith. I do not ask you on my own authority to do this, nor do I invite you now to get anything for yourself. I only ask you to glorify God by showing that you really do trust him. And I am not asking you now to trust him generally or theoretically. I am asking you to trust him specifically and practically, where you and I know he can be trusted, in his 'every Word.' Surely God's promises to his people will hold for *you*, his own Son!"

Jesus' obedience to this tempting use of Scripture would at best have gotten him an additional assurance of what he already had in baptism: the knowledge that he is the Son of God. That the temptation intended a spectacular miracle (an air walk) for the impressing of the people around the temple is doubtful, though possible (for this possibility cf. Jero., 1:98; Beare, 110f; Gund., 56). But the ambience of the miracle seems less an evangelistic meeting for others than a confirmation class for Jesus. It is the *third* temptation that will appeal explicitly to Jesus' public, missionary, and people relations. This second temptation appeals to the springs of Jesus' relation with God (Schl., *Der,* 107; Bonn., 45). Before Jesus is asked to be a missionary, he is asked to be a practicing believer, to be a *faith* missionary, a man who is willing to trust God for everything, without (literally) any visible means of support.

4:7 "Jesus said to him, 'It is in writing *in another place* in Scripture, "You shall not test the Lord your God."'" Here Jesus exercises the first Christian biblical criticism. He puts one Scripture over another. He in fact counters the devil's crass literalistic exegesis with a more careful theological exegesis (Bonn., 45). The devil had used a Scripture that enlisted daring faith in God's promises. Jesus uses a Scripture that teaches reverent caution before God's holiness. "Satan had suggested that it was impossible to put too much trust in God. Christ points out that testing God is not trusting Him" (Pl., *Luke,* 114). There are times for daring faith; there are times for careful faith. There are times when Psalm 91 that urges daring faith has its day; there are times when Deuteronomy 6 that teaches the faith of reverence has its day. The whole counsel of God needs to be canvassed when important decisions are made. The believer must ask, "Is this a time for bold faith or for cautious faith?" Scripture testifies to both faiths and to several variations in between. Which is right now?

Cautious faith is no less faith than bold faith. Both look to God. But Jesus felt now that to leap into the arms of God without any good reason (or useful service) except to leap into the arms of God, or to get a second blessing, or an additional, surer proof of what he had already been given once in baptism, was presumptuous. To *require* a proof from God is one thing (Jesus calls this, in so many words, a "playing with" God); to expect God's gracious protection (the real teaching of Psalm 91) is another thing. Jesus believed Psalm 91 no less than he believed Deuteronomy 6. But he believed Psalm 91 rightly used—as a text of God's protecting love—did not teach believers to throw themselves around recklessly, nor did it teach that God is liege-servant of our leaps. The real question is, "Do we follow God or must God follow us?" Who works for whom? For Jesus to leap and expect God to come to his rescue is requiring God to follow him. Jesus considers this kind of faith not faith at all but simple *chutzpah*.

That Jesus puts one text over another—in this case Deuteronomy over a Psalm—permits believers to do the same whenever they are challenged by persons using Scripture. There is a hierarchy of truths in Scripture. Every text needs to be looked at in relation to the others. Is this text itself used rightly? What does the center of Scripture—the gospel, the messianic witness to God's promise—say about this? Psalm 91 is fine; but does it really teach leaping from high places? In short, we learn from this encounter of Jesus to ask of every use of a biblical text: Is this what the text itself really says? In the use of this text is God treated like Lord or like lackey? ("You shall not test *the Lord* your God.") Will God be obeyed or commanded if I use this text as suggested? Will God be followed or following?

The whole of the Gospel of Matthew will teach Jesus' repugnance for spectacles and the spectacular (cf., e.g., his disdain for signs, 12:38–42; 16:1–12). It is just such a spectacle or sign that Scripture is being used now to induce. When Scripture is ever used to encourage behavior that most of the rest of Scripture, or the heart of Scripture, *dis*courages, we can tell we are in enemy territory.

Two convictions emerge from Jesus' use of Scripture in the Gospels: (1) Jesus adores Scripture (the verb is not too strong); and (2) he has freedom with Scripture. He gives both attitudes to his church. Scripture, Jesus teaches us again and again, is nothing less than God's own words. But precisely because there are many words in the books of Scripture, and because at times they are in tension, as here, Jesus teaches us how to move among these words in reverent freedom, giving now this word, now that, the priority. Matthew's Gospel will supply us with several of Jesus' rules for Scripture interpretation. This temptation gives us one of the first.

It is also important to see how Jesus practices biblical criticism. He does not fight back by saying "the Bible is wrong," or "that text is inferior," or "even if the Bible says that, the Holy Spirit, reason, experience, tradition teach. . . ." Jesus' single great source, even in Scripture-criticism, was Scripture: "The *Bible* also says." Thus when we are tempted by the false use of Scripture "let us borrow weapons for the defence of our faith from no other source than Scripture" (Cal., 1:141).

Everything depends on Bible interpretation. In this sense, Jesus was a biblicist. But he was an intelligent biblicist. Jesus tried to see Scripture in its sweep and sense. As we will study later in more detail, Jesus saw the whole of Scripture dangling from two great pegs in the middle of Scripture, the double command of plenary love for "the Lord your God" *and* "the person you're with" (22:37–40). With Jesus, every text in Scripture was subject to this double interpretive rule: "Does it honor God? Will it help the other person?" (Leaping from temples does neither.)

Thus in this second temptation Jesus the messianic king teaches us to be loyal subjects to God's Word and to obey God without great display. In this temptation Jesus teaches us that God is God.

Jesus cannot be gotten at the point of his weakness in hunger, nor can he be gotten at the point of his strength in Scripture. What is left?

C. The Third Temptation. Successism (The Salvation Test)

4:8–11 *"Again the Tempter took Jesus up a very high mountain, and he showed him all the kingdoms of the world and their glory, and he said to him, 'I will give all of these to you if you will just fall down and worship me.' Then Jesus said to him, 'Get out of here, Satan! Because it is in writing, "You shall worship the Lord your God, and to him only shall you give religious service."' Then the devil left him, and look, angels came up and waited on his table."*

It is interesting to notice that the devil leads Jesus higher and higher: first from the wilderness and its rocks to the top of the temple and now, explicitly, to "a *very* high mountain." The *Holy* Spirit led Jesus *down*—into the easily misunderstood baptism of John, and then down still farther into the wilderness of temptation. The evil spirit leads Jesus farther and farther up. The Holy Spirit's way is not so much up into the fascinatingly holy, as it is down into the ordinarily lowly and into the way of the cross and of suffering. We will find that it is a frequent fact in Matthew's Gospel that everything exalted is brought low and that everything low is exalted, that those who seek to advance their lives lose them, and that those who lose their lives in the service of the gospel find them. (This is the introductory theme of the Sermon on the Mount in the Beatitudes, for example.) It is part of the cleverness of the devil that he leads us up—to heights. It is part of the modesty of the Dove-Spirit that she leads us down—into simple things.

4:8–9 "And he showed him all the kingdoms of the world and their glory, and he said to him, 'These things—all of them—I will give to you if you will just fall down and worship me.'" After life itself (test one) and after God's Word (test two) there is one spot left in Jesus for temptation— his center: his love for God's world. "God so loved the world that he gave his only Son" (John 3:16). This temptation promises Jesus the main thing he wanted and came to get: the salvation of the world. This is the temptation of salvation or success. It is the social (or world-related) test as the second temptation was the spiritual (or God-related) test.

In a way, the other temptations were less ultimate. One should not do something simply to satisfy one's appetites, and one should not do just anything to save one's life—we can see the temptation of carnality or selfishness in the first temptation. One should not do anything that will violate God's honor or force God's hand—one can see the temptation of superspirituality in the second test. But can one refuse anything that will help other people? Isn't half the double-love command a command of the service of others? We know how frequently the theme "love conquers all" appears in entertainment. The question (we are told) is not, "What is the (abstract) principle to follow here?" It is, "Will I be showing love here or not?" Love for persons, it is said in certain ethics, is the only binding law; and where this law is in force it may be quite legitimate to genuflect for just a moment if the end will be salvation, help, or love for another human being.

It is with just such a temptation that Jesus is faced here. Does Jesus want to save *the whole world* of human beings? The baptismal Voice had assured him that he is the beloved Son of God; and at baptism he had experienced the descent of the Spirit. To a serious auditor of the Old Testament, as Jesus was, this combination of baptismal events could mean only one thing: he had been given messianic office. And messianic office means the salvation of the world. Thus Jesus is confronted in this temptation with more than a mess of pottage or a daring leap. This time Jesus is confronted with his very purpose in coming. The one thing with which Jesus' heart burns most ardently is the desire deeply to obey his Father by saving his people in the world.

The third temptation is the temptation to make our work God. This is the most powerful and subtle of all temptations. Jesus' work as Messiah was to win the world. His work can now be successfully accomplished if he will just bow one knee.

It is very difficult for serious Christians to distinguish between (1) their work for God and (2) God. We are constantly tempted to think that if one succeeds the other succeeds as well; and if one is defeated the other is defeated. Therefore we will sometimes do absolutely anything to keep our work for God from failing. But the moment we do *absolutely anything* to keep our work for God from failing we have made our work God and, perhaps without realizing it, we have worshiped Satan.

Jesus was tempted to do absolutely anything to make his work of world mission successful, but he realized that this particular form of devotion to his work of world mission would compromise his exclusive devotion to God. Only God is God. Our work, however important, is not God and must never be treated as God. We must not seek to be successful at any price or else we have made success our God. This is the main lesson of the third temptation.

Love for people can overwhelm us, too. For example, seminary students are sometimes faced with a dilemma like this: their family has sacrificially provided a seminary education; their church is looking forward to their return and service; the work of the gospel beckons; and only one obstacle stands in the way—the examination. What is one piece of concealed paper next to a lifetime in the work of the Lord? The student doesn't intend to be a life-time cheater. And he or she loves people. Every believer who lives life in this world is faced with this temptation in some such form. It is the question, on the one hand, of good ends—my family's honor or security: what can be more important? My children's education: what is more basic? More money for the church and her mission: what is more Christian? On the other hand, it is the question of (comparatively) trivial means—a minor scruple here, a "using of one's head" there.

Our text presupposes a doctrine more familiar in John and Paul than in Matthew: that the devil has some kind of kingship over the world. "The prince of this world" or "the ruler of this age" are the devil's titles in the literature of the other apostles (cf. John 12:31; 14:30; 16:11; 2 Cor 4:4; Eph 2:2, etc.). It may be that the devil is lying in this text, that he claims to be able to deliver what he has no power to deliver. (Gundry, 58, says Matthew replaces Luke's [or Q's] phrase "all this authority" with "all these things" in the record of this temptation in order "to avoid the implication that the Devil *has* 'all this authority.'" Similarly, Jero., 1:160. See Matt 28:18 for the situation now.) But I think this temptation is a temptation in the full sense of the word because the devil is doing more than talk: he *does* have some kind of awesome power over the world (McN., 41; Schl., *Der,* 109). This is what makes this temptation, at least to the mind of Matthew, the final temptation. (Luke received or put the temptations in a different order.) When we are tempted not just for ourselves but for others the temptation is keener.

Jesus is not asked to spend his whole life at the devil's feet. He is given a real bargain: one momentary bow—the verb is aorist, suggesting one single act. And the promise is this time breathtaking: the whole wide world. What is one gesture when the planet is in the balance?

4:10 Jesus must have felt this temptation, otherwise it would not have been recorded as a temptation. The love of the whole world of persons is the meaning of not only Jesus' ministry as Son, as we all know, but of God the Father's as well. ("God so loved the world . . .") But, and this is a crucial point, Jesus' love for persons is a love in obedience to a ruling love: "Then Jesus said to him, 'Get out of here, Satan! Because it is in writing. "You shall worship the Lord your God and to him *only* shall you give religious service"'" (4:10). Even love for persons does not justify absolutely anything.

The saying "love is always the will of God" is questioned by this temptation. It is often true that an act of love is an act of God; but there can be acts done in love that are demonic if they are not controlled by a higher love. The adulterous lust, the lethal liberation, the lying success may all be done out of, and even deliver a certain love to someone else, but they are not biblical acts of love in the depths nor are they helpful to persons at length. Jesus is ruled by a conviction higher than the immediate situation or even the other person, and that conviction is God in his Word.

The Zealot party in first-century Judaism was the false liberation theology of the period. Matthew indicts Zealotism in this temptation. Cf. Bonn., 46; Caird, 79–81; Schw., 58–60.

"But what does it profit a man if he gains the whole world but loses his own soul?" (16:26) In the third temptation Jesus, like the good high priest he is, teaches us the exclusive worship of God.

*　　　　*　　　　*

The ruling passion perceptible in all three of Jesus' answers to the temptations is a sense of God. (1) "Man shall not live by bread alone but by every single Word that comes pouring out of the mouth of *God.*" (2) "You shall not test the Lord your *God.*" And (3) "You shall worship the Lord your *God* and him only shall you serve." In all three answers the central word and reality is God, the God who had engaged Jesus in Word and baptism. Twice the word *monō*, "only, alone" appears ("not by bread *alone*"; "him *alone* you shall serve") meaning that, contrary to all appearances, God is to be taken into account. But were the Zealots "the realists who would get the results while the visionary was still dreaming his dreams?" And Caird, 80, answers his own question: "It is good to be realistic, but the greatest reality is God."

A sense of God is dim in our time. Some church teaching tells us that Jesus was "the man for others," "the poor man," which he clearly was and is. But if the church forgets that Jesus was not only first of all, but constantly, the man for God, she forgets everything. We cannot make Jesus into a *mere* humanist. It is true that Jesus combated superspiritual religious separatism his whole life; it is true that he was much more humanist than is generally recognized in the church; and it is also true that he gave a priority to the human person that has never been exceeded. But it is just as true that the engine for Jesus' humanism was a theism, that Jesus' horizontalism sprang from a living verticalism, and that Jesus was able to be a man for others because he lived first for God.

The temptations stand at the head of Jesus' adult career (after his baptism, the prelude to the temptations) to teach the church, among other things, Jesus' doctrine of God. If one gives only perfunctory attention to Matthew chapter 4's temptations in order to concentrate on Matthew chapters 5 to 7's better known Sermon on the Mount, one unwittingly tears the tree from its roots, and removes the water from its spring. The commands of the Sermon on the Mount will in a certain sense be focused on the second table of the law in general and on the Sixth Commandment ("you shall not kill") in particular, directing our special attention to other people and their protection. But the second table of the law gets its force from the first table, and the Sixth Commandment will only be sovereign in those persons for whom the First Commandment is first ("You shall have no other gods before Me"). The Sermon on the Mount's person-centeredness follows the temptations' God-centeredness. The three temptations are Jesus' lived commentary on the first table of the Ten Commandments (i.e., no other gods or idols; care for God's name; time for God). The white-hot focus of each temptation is Jesus' burning determination to treat God as God. We cannot have the humanism of Jesus without the piety of Jesus nor his Sermon on the Mount without his temptations in the wilderness. Jesus' faith in God led him into the modesty where rocks stayed rocks, where Jesus walked back down the stairs of the temple and nothing striking happened, and where the winning of the kingdoms of the world was left to a long death march—a steady, historic walk to a cross—instead of an evangelistic *Blitzkrieg*.

To put this point in another way, before Matthew gives us a portrait of Jesus' hands and feet and his relation to others in chapter 5, he gives us an x-ray of Jesus' heart and soul and his relation to God in chapter 4. By way of these three temptation scenes, Matthew has given us an incomparable view into what made Jesus Jesus. It is God.

Jesus especially believed God's Word. In all three temptations, Jesus got his victory by using the source accessible to the rest of us in Holy Scripture. Jesus did not resort to a direct line to heaven to get help from God. Instead (and this helps the church that follows him), Jesus used the same old source we have: Hebrew Scripture. Jesus really believed that this book gives God's Word.

We will learn from the final lecture of Jesus in this Gospel—Matthew 25 on the Great Judgment—that whatever we do for the least significant person is done for Jesus and hence for God. But the prior question is, "Where did Jesus get the desire and power for this identification with people?" Matthew's answer stands at the beginning of Jesus' adult career: Jesus' power for persons came from God's gifts to him (the theme of Matt 1–3, preeminently baptism, 3:16–17), *and* from Jesus' gift of commitment of God (the theme of Matt 4's temptations and services). God was real to Jesus. And Jesus decided under, against, and through temptation to be real with God.

Jesus' God-centeredness may sound commonplace, but it is not. Without Jesus' God the entire Gospel is fundamentally misunderstood. Some theologians try to give us a Jesus who found his ultimate commitment only or mainly in other people or the poor. This theology will not be able to face Matthew chapter 4. A Christian liberationism that tries to make the church only or mainly poor-centered won't work. It ignores the roots of Jesus' own ministry in his baptism and temptations.

The problem involved here can be illustrated by a recent liberation theology, Richard Shaull's *Heralds of A New Reformation: The Poor of South and North America* (Maryknoll,

New York: Orbis Books, 1984). The false in the following excerpts from the book is not so much what is said as it is what literally is *taken for granted,* which taking-for-granted can effectively cancel what is said. "What is distinctive about Christianity is its belief that we are saved through the death and resurrection of a human being, Jesus of Nazareth, a man of flesh and blood. The liberation theologians take all this for granted but insist that we must speak much more concretely about it: we are saved by the death and resurrection of a poor man, who shared the lot of the poor and was killed because he took up their cause against the wealthy and powerful. . . . Here too the Latin American theologians, while taking this perspective [of Christ the Logos] for granted, insist on greater concreteness. If God redeems the world through a poor person and if the central event in this salvation history is the crucifixion of Jesus because of his identification with the poor in their struggle, *then the poor and their struggle must be at the very center of our interpretation of what is happening in nature and history"* (p. 70, emphasis his).

However, one must reply, we must be careful that we do not take the concrete Jesus Christ so much *for granted* that we turn him into an idea for or a symbol of what we think is "more concrete." A Jesus made more concrete has historically meant a Jesus molded by ideological interests—see, e.g., Jesus the Supersalesman in contemporary Success Seminars in the First World. The "concrete Jesus" is a wax nose; the biblical Jesus is sufficiently concrete himself.

Notice in the following citations from Shaull how the poor, finally, take Christ's mediating place: "As Cussiánovich puts it: 'The poor are the centerpiece in salvation history, the necessary mediating link in the relationship between God and human beings, between human beings themselves, and between human beings and nature'" (p. 71). "God will *become* our God as we struggle for and move toward greater justice for the poor. Miranda emphasizes this point in his discussion of the text in Jeremiah about the new covenant that Yahweh will establish with the chosen people: 'The heart of the matter is that men will not have Yahweh as their God unless they love their neighbor and achieve justice completely [!] on the earth. God will not be God until then. The God whom we claim to affirm when we prescind from the realization of justice is simply an idol, not the true God. The true God is not; he will be'" (p. 38).

When Shaull reviewed the ministry of Jesus I was surprised by the short shrift given to, almost the complete marginalization of, Jesus' temptations (they are only touched, really, at p. 44). But the temptations of Jesus are fatal to Shaull's program. Shaull is right when he attacks the First World's spiritualization of the gospel—"the thorough and complacent depoliticization of Jesus" (p. 49). But the attempted repoliticization of Jesus by liberation theology will not work either. The gospel of Jesus' grace that enables Shaull to function so laudably for the poor is introduced by Shaull in an account of his own personal struggle late in his book (pp. 92f); why doesn't he give this very same gospel room in his liberation appeal for the poor? It would work. Why is the very concrete biblical Jesus himself so frequently "taken for granted"?

Jesus' *God* is concretely poorward (the Beatitudes, the Psalms, the Prophets), and this God must come first, as he comes first for Jesus, or else we lack power to move toward the poor. A faith relation with God through Jesus must never be taken for granted in the church or else the poor will be.

"Even if we cannot believe that God is dead, it is clear that something has died. And that is the capacity of most of us for conducting our daily lives as if He were about, as if His existence and His interest in our affairs were fairly probable. This incapacity may have already had drastic consequences. It may be an honest explanation of the barbarism and confusion that attack our politics, and it may help to account for the turbulence in the private climate of the age." (George Steiner, "God's Acres," *The New Yorker* [October 30, 1978], 161.)

There are two Reformed God-Alone texts that may be heard as the church's commentary on the temptations. The original Scotch dialect communicates the correct emphases in the first source: "We confesse and acknawledge ane onelie God, to whom onelie we must cleave, whom onelie we must serve, whom onelie we must worship, and in whom onelie we must put our trust" (*The Scots Confession*, 1560, [Schaff, 3:438], art.1, opening words; note the exclusive terms). Cf. *The Heidelberg Catechism*, 1563, Q. 94.

4:11 "Then the devil left him, and look, angels came over, and they waited on his table" (4:11). This is the second time that we have the little phrase, "then he left him," *tote aphiēsin auton*. It first occurred at John's baptism when Jesus had urged John to baptize him, and there the phrase is translated, literally, "then he let him" (3:15). This time the phrase is used right after Jesus has said, "Get out of here, Satan," and we read again, literally, *tote aphiēsin auton*, "then he left him" (4:11). The words and point are exactly the same in both texts: when Jesus talks, things happen. Friends like John are made obedient, and enemies like Satan are removed. Jesus' Word has the power to make persons and things serve the seemingly unlikely will of God (as in the case of baptism) and to move them out of the way (as in the case of temptation). Jesus' power resides mainly in his Word. We will see this fact abundantly in his miracles. The Word of Jesus is a moving force.

"Satan is called the master of a thousand arts, but what shall we call God's Word, which easily conquers and discomfits that master with all his wile and power?" (Luther's Preface, *Large Catechism*, 9)

"And, look, angels came over, and they waited on his table" (*diēkonoun*). Jesus hadn't asked for food or angels. But he got both. "Both the food and angelic help, which He had refused (4:4, 7) when they involved sin, were now given to Him as victor" (McN., 42; cf. Bonn., 46). The church's ministry is to learn here that when ministry seeks first the kingdom of God—which the three temptations define as the all-importance of God—earthly necessities and heavenly gifts are added (Matt 6:33).

This is now the second time that the adult Jesus has gone down and has afterwards been lifted up. (1) When he had gone down into John's baptism, he received God's best gifts coming up (3:16–17). Now (2) in the wilderness, he has stuck with God's low Word rather than do anything devilishly sensational, spectacular, or speedy, and when it was over he dined well and with a good conscience. Jesus is learning obedience by the things he suffers (Heb 5:8). Jesus is learning the value of staying, simply, with God. The Christian ministry is to learn the same.

Martin Luther's *Large Catechism* (1529) discussion of the meaning of the First Commandment—"You shall have no other gods"—is the finest commentary I have found on the meaning of Jesus' temptations. In Scripture the most helpful commentary is this: "Because he [Jesus] himself has suffered and been tempted, he is able to help those who are tempted. . . . For we have not a high priest who is unable to sympathize with our weaknesses, but one who in every respect has been tempted as we are, yet without sinning. Let us then with confidence draw near to the throne of grace, that we may receive mercy and find grace to help in time of need" (Heb 2:18; 4:15–16 RSV).

Are the temptations historical? Did they actually happen as described? How did the disciples and evangelists learn Jesus' temptations when they were not there? It is possible, given the church's doctrine of the inspiration of Scripture, that the church was spiritually given an insight into the temptations that attacked Jesus throughout his life and that the fruit of this insight is our present temptations story, Matt 4:1–11. The inspiration of Scripture, in other words, makes it possible to believe that the temptations of Jesus present pictorial rather than literal truth, that the temptations are historical in the sense that they happened *like* this in Jesus' whole life-history (German *Geschichte*), but that they are not historical in the sense that they happened *exactly* like this in desert, temple, and high mountain (German *Historie;* for this view cf. J. Dupont in Bonn., 424). The older view was that Jesus told his disciples later about his experiences in the wilderness. This does not seem plausible today and is rarely advanced in scientific commentaries, but it does not have to be dismissed with contempt. Caird, 76, even argues that "the pious ingenuity of the early church could no more have created these stories [of Jesus' baptism and temptations] than the parables of the Good Samaritan and the Prodigal Son."

The best discussions of the *meanings* of the temptations, in my opinion, are, as often, in the sermons of Martin Luther and the commentaries of Adolf Schlatter. Luther preached to his parishioners that when the devil tempts believers, they can be encouraged by the fact that they know Him who has conquered the devil for them. Thus, for example, when believers are fighting impurity in themselves or the desire for revenge or for glory, and are driven almost crazy by these lusts, they can be deeply encouraged when they realize that "this is the devil making me so hot," and the battle is half won. "Then fall down and say, 'O Christ, who has overcome the devil, help me!' Then [the devil] must soon fall" (W² 12:1270–1277). We learn from the temptations that Jesus does not have many goals, but only one: to treat God as God and to honor him by believing and obeying his commands (Schl., *Der*, 110).

II. THE THREE SERVICES: THE MINISTRY OF THE SON AND SERVANT OF MAN (4:12–25)

In the first half of Matthew chapter 4 we saw Jesus as the Servant-Son of God; in the second half we see him as the Servant-Son of Man. In the temptations Jesus proved that he lived from and for God. In the services Jesus will show how, living for God, he lives for other people.

In the section before us—the second half of chapter 4—Matthew introduces us in brief ways to Jesus as (1) the Light of the Nations (vv 12–17), (2) the Lord of the Church (vv 18–22), and (3) the Life of the Body (vv 23–25), that is, to Jesus' person, Word, and work, respectively, the later foci of the developed christology of the Gospel of Matthew (Matt 5–7; 8–10; 11–12).

"In his right hand he held seven stars [the ministers of the church's Word], from his mouth issued a sharp two-edged sword [the double-work of salvation and judgment], and his face was like the sun shining in full strength [the person of Christ, Light of the world]." (Rev 1:16 RSV)

A. Jesus the Light of the Nations (The Service of His Person) (vv 12–17)

4:12–17 *"When Jesus heard that John had been arrested he withdrew to Galilee. He took leave of Nazareth and came and settled permanently in Capernaum, the city that is* *right next to the lake in the territory of Zebulun and Naphtali. By doing this, the Word spoken through Isaiah the prophet was filled full of meaning, the Word that says:*

> '*Land of Zebulun and land of Naphtali,*
> *On the road to the sea, on the other side of the Jordan,*
> *Galilee of the nations!*
> *The people sitting in darkness*
> *Have seen a great light.*
> *And those who sit their lives away in the region and shadow of death*
> *On them has light risen.'*

"*From then on Jesus started to speak out and to say, 'Turn your lives around, because here comes the kingdom of heaven!'*"

Galilee is a strange place for a Messiah to work. There is no early rabbinic reference to the Messiah's appearing or working in Galilee. Galilee was not just geographically far from Jerusalem; it was considered spiritually and politically far, too. Galilee was the most pagan of the Jewish provinces, located as it was at the northernmost tier of Palestine. This distance from Zion was not only geographic; Galileans were considered by Judaeans to sit rather loosely to the law and to be less biblically pure than those in or near Jerusalem. Finally, Galilee was notorious for being the nest of revolution and the haunt of Zealot revolutionary movements. Just a few years before Jesus' birth, Sephoris, capital city of Galilee, had been led in revolt by Judas of Galilee against the Roman government and had brought Galilee into defeat and many of the people of God into shame. (On Galilee, see Str.-B., 1:153, 160–61; Davies, 299–300; Conz. 18, 30; Grund., 105.)

Therefore when Jesus "retreated to Galilee" he did more than head north, he seemed to go wrong. We know from other accounts in the New Testament that Jesus' being a Galilean and doing his work of ministry mainly in Galilee was a charge frequently leveled against him (e.g., John 7:41f, 52; cf. 1:45f).

Matthew wanted to show that Jesus' career in Galilee was not proof against Jesus' messiahship, it was proof for it. By Jesus' living in Galilee, and particularly by his moving right up next to the Lake of Galilee to begin his public ministry, "the Word spoken through Isaiah the prophet," according to Matthew, "was filled full of meaning." *Isaiah* meant that northernmost Galilee, the first part of Palestine taken captive (in 737 B.C.), would be the first part of Palestine to experience release from exile (Jero., 1:102; McK., 69; Gund., 60). "The Galileans are now compensated for their previous disadvantages" (Bengel). The "fillment" of Isa 8–9, if we may put it this way, happened at the end of the exile. But for Matthew, the *full*-fillment of Isaiah's old Word occurred when the real Light, personally, came to live in Galilee. Every Old Testament text has its partial "fillment" in its immediate historical context; it has its full-fillment in the history of the Messiah, the deeper context of every Old Testament text. (Cf. Cal., 1:153–54.) This was the way Matthew read his Old Testament. When Matthew ran across this text in Isaiah mentioning the blessing of despised Galilee, he was sure that what the text really meant was Jesus. (Cf. Bonn., 48.)

Matthew feels free here and elsewhere to change words in the text. Isaiah had meant the Mediterranean when he said "by the sea"; Matthew has it mean the Sea of

Galilee (Stend., 774; Gund., 60). Isaiah had written "the people who *walk* in darkness"; Matthew changes this to "the people who *sit* in darkness" because Matthew believes spiritual darkness is so thick it immobilizes. "The verb 'to sit' aptly denotes a sluggish attitude" (Beng.; cf. Schl., *Der,* 115).

"Galilee of the nations." This was the nickname for Galilee, something like "America the melting pot" today. Jesus worked where Judaism touched paganism, where the Nation intersected the nations, where light met darkness. Jesus lived among the marginal peoples, on the frontier (cf. the theological project of Paul Tillich). This choice of venue suggests the missionary Jesus (Beare, 114; Gund., 59–60). "Jesus' move to 'Galilee of the gentiles' demonstrates God's amazing initiative towards those who had never ever been considered. Like the four women in the genealogy and the astrologers in the birth narrative at the beginning of this section, the gentiles stand at the end [of this introductory section, Matt 1–4]" (Schw., 68).

Jesus is called the Light of the Nations here; Jesus will later call his disciples the light of the world (5:14). The disciples' light will be the reflection of Jesus' light: he is the sun, they are the moon. Because he is the light and they are in discipled fellowship with him, they are light, too.

The nations are not by themselves in the light. They are, in Matthew's reading, so in the dark that they are not even able to move. They *sit* in darkness. In Matthew's opinion the nations are in paralysis until Jesus comes to them; they sit enshrouded in night until Jesus' sun rises on them. The New Testament picture of the world without Christ is not bright; it is shadowy. Some current theology attributes to the non-Christian religions the possibility of salvation whether there is explicit faith in Jesus Christ or not. (Representatively, Hans Küng, *On Being a Christian,* New York: Doubleday, 1976, pp. 91–97, 103f, 167, 447, but cf. 387, 394–96.) Generous as this opinion is, it is not the apostolic conviction. Persons apart from Christ the Light are in a world of night; they are not able by themselves to open themselves to God. They sit under the shadow of death; they need Jesus to live and to see. I will take up the question of contemporary theological universalism later in greater detail. I wish simply here to point out that in this first explicit reference to the nations, light is not what the nations are or have in themselves; it is what comes to them in Jesus.

"Then implying that they did not of themselves seek and find, but that God showed Himself to them from above, he saith to them, 'Light is sprung up;' that is, the light of itself sprang up and shone forth: it was not that they first ran to the light" (Chrys., 14:1:87). Luther: "The prophet Isaiah said, 'The people that walked in darkness have seen a great light.' Don't you think that this is an inexpressible light which enables us to see the heart of God and the depth of the Godhead? And that we may also see the thoughts of the Devil and what sin is and how to be freed from it and what death is and how to be delivered. And what man is, and the world, and how to conduct oneself in it. No one before was sure what God is or whether there are devils, what sin and death are, let alone how to be delivered. This is all the work of Christ" (in Bainton, 220). "And then, into this tasteless heap of gold and marble, He came, light and clothed in an aura, emphatically human, deliberately provincial, Galilean, and at that moment gods and nations ceased to be and man came into being . . ." (Boris Pasternak, *Dr Zhivago,* cited in Waetjen, 13).

4:17 "From then on, Jesus started to speak out and to say, 'Turn your lives around, because here comes the kingdom of heaven!'" (4:17). It is important to notice that we have gone almost four full chapters into this Gospel and Jesus has not yet preached. Even here we have only a tantalizingly short summary of what he said. Matthew intends for this single sentence to be a summary of Jesus' whole message. It will be well for us, therefore, to investigate the sentence carefully.

Jesus' name is emphasized by its location in the Greek sentence: "Jesus himself started to speak out" would be a translation capturing this emphasis. Matthew may want us to be surprised that Jesus preached at all. Messiahs don't have to preach; they can perform great acts of power and so do their work. Preaching means persuasion; it means the importance of the word; it means the importance of listening and learning. Great acts of power can be done without any need to persuade or inform. But preaching honors people, it takes them seriously, it addresses them, and it seeks and enables their response.

The verb used to describe Jesus' preaching activity is *kērussein*, from which the several modern forms of kerygma come, and it means "to speak out with authority, to announce as a herald, to proclaim, to assert with emphasis, to make a royal declaration." The word stresses factual assertion. Jesus' preaching is in fact characterized by a large element of simple fact-telling, of simply telling people with authority what actually is. We learn from the color present in the word *kērussein* that preaching should in considerable measure be in the indicative mood; that is, it should first tell people, in a dignified way, the great facts of the gospel: of who Jesus is, of what he has done, and of who, therefore, God is, and of what we may expect from him and do for him.

"Turn your lives around, because here comes the kingdom of heaven!" Jesus' message, as Matthew here summarizes it, is not one whit different from John the Baptist's (3:2). There, too, John preached, "Turn your lives around, because here comes the kingdom of heaven!" The first significance of this identical message is that, to Matthew's mind, Jesus did not arrive on the scene of history as the great innovator. Matthew stresses this fact through the exact repetition of John's words, suggesting that Jesus found John the Baptist's message, with its twin themes of repentance and kingdom of heaven, impressive. Jesus kept John's message and passed it on. Jesus will be original in his own way; but his is not the originality that despises what others have done before (cf. Schl., *Das*, 45). Even the terms Jesus uses here for his message are old, deeply familiar terms to Judaism: repentance and the kingdom are as familiar to Jewish ears as words such as "saved" and "the blood" are to the Christians in the revival tradition. Jesus' originality will not consist in striking new words. Jesus liked even John the Baptist's vocabulary and kept it.

We are now ready to study the sentence itself. "Turn your lives around, because here comes the kingdom of heaven!" *Metanoeite* renders the Hebrew *shuv* and means "turn around," literally "con-vert," colloquially "get converted," or simply "change." There is nothing tricky about its meaning. It does not tell what to turn from, specifically; the emphasis is on turning from our preoccupations (sins *or* goods) toward God. Whatever keeps one from turning *toward* the coming kingdom is that *from* which one should turn. The very objectlessness of what is turned from stresses the simplicity and so the urgency of the turning.

Repentance is not merely a change of mind or regret; it is a complete change of direction— ⌐ —enabled by the Word and thus our responsibility. The article on *metanoeite* in the TDNT is exemplary; cf. also Str.-B., 1:162, 170. The story of Lot in Gen 19 is the most vivid Old Testament account of the several meanings and dynamics present in the divine call to and the human responsibility of repentance; Luke 15's three parables give, in my opinion, the best New Testament definitions of repentance, and they too stress the divine initiative.

The words "here comes the kingdom" announce a *fait accompli* and could suggest that there is not much we can do about it. But when Jesus attaches to his kerygma the word "turn around," Jesus honors us. He helps us, telling us there is something we can do about it; indeed, that there is something we must do. Good theology will always teach that this "can do" or "must do" of persons is enabled by the Word of God that commands it. God's Word never returns void (Isa 55:11). Therefore, when Jesus here says "turn around," he releases with that Word—even to us who hear that Word today—the spiritual power to turn around or the power to ask for power to turn around.

The giving character of the divine Word is the reason for the New Testament's presenting repentance as a *gift* of God in most of its uses of the word (cf. 2 Tim 2:25–26: "God may perhaps *grant* that they will repent"; Acts 5:31: "God exalted him at his right hand as Leader and Savior, to *give* repentance to Israel and forgiveness of sins"; Acts 11:18: "Then to the Gentiles also God has *granted* repentance unto life." See also who *effected* the repentance spoken of in Luke's trilogy of parables, Luke 15:3–7, 8–10, 11–32, esp. v 17). Whenever a believer hears or reads any Word of God from Scripture—for example, Paul's "grace and peace" in his salutations, or any of the invitations or commands of Scripture—he or she may believe that the power to *receive* or do the Word is tucked inside the Word and that as the Word sinks into the ear its power comes into the heart. So, then, the word "turn around" is not a mere word, it is *God's* word and therefore Word.

Words, even human words, *do* things, as we all know. "I am sorry" *does* something to the one who hears the words with belief; "I love you," spoken from faith to faith, does something, too. There are many such examples of performative (doing) words in contrast to merely informative (saying) words. God's Word (written, preached, administered with sacraments, lived) is performative. Whatever Jesus says is pregnant with the power to perform it. The Roman, Orthodox, Lutheran, and (some) Reformed and Anglican churches, for example, believe that Jesus' words of institution in the Lord's Supper, spoken just once about the year 30 in our era, still work, when passed on in church services, to change ordinary bread and wine on a thousand tables into the real body and blood of Jesus Christ today. Jesus' Word *changes* people and things. It per-forms, re-forms, trans-forms, and con-forms whatever it touches. It enables what it commands. It gives what it calls for.

The vexed question of the fulfillability of the difficult commands of the Sermon on the Mount begins to be addressed here (and at the gifts of baptism). Hans Windisch, 113, wrote that the "ability truly to obey [the Sermon on the Mount] is increased . . . by the fact that a new messenger appears . . . with a new message. . . . We have to include the programmatical proclamation saying of [Matthew] chapter 4:17 [our present text] among the presuppositions of the Sermon on the Mount. The faith in the Kingdom that is . . . kindled by Jesus' proclamation is . . . the particular attitude that releases the willingness and the power to obey these new Kingdom commandments."

It is important to see that Jesus does not say "Turn around *so that* the kingdom of heaven can come," which would suggest that human action enables God's. Rather, "repent, *for* here comes." God's kingdom *is* coming; it is en route; it is breaking through now in Jesus, *therefore* repent. Both John's and Jesus' preaching had this sequence: "Repent because." This may have been the main fact Jesus liked in John's preaching: that it based human response on divine initiative.

Thus Schl., *Der*, 116; Schn., 34, and most other commentators. The kingdom of heaven is first gift, then (in the power of that gift) demand. While the terms *kingdom of God* and *kingdom of heaven* do not occur in the Dead Sea Scrolls, they are present everywhere in the Gospels. Indeed, Davies, 432, believes that the distinctive element in Jesus' teaching was his awareness "that, in his ministry, the Kingdom of God was actively at work."

"Because here comes the kingdom of heaven." What is the kingdom of heaven? The word "heaven" is first a circumlocution for "God," spoken in good Jewish reverence for the divine name. But "heaven" also indicates the place from which the kingdom comes to earth, the kingdom's provenance, the powerful locus of God's own personal residence. Kingdom of *heaven* indicates the superearthly forces discharged on earth when the kingdom comes. The word "heaven" also means that the kingdom is beyond human reach and that the kingdom comes to earth not as a human acquisition but as a divine gift. "Kingdom of heaven" means "kingdom beyond our reach," the kingdom that comes from God.

"The *kingdom* of heaven." The word "kingdom," as used by Matthew, denotes both a place (the king's *dominion*) and a power (the *king's* dominion); it is both a space-word horizontally and a time-word vertically. The idea of space is by no means secondary. The kingdom is a place entered, where people sit and eat and drink at table; it is also a place from which people are ejected or not allowed to enter; it is, in short, a house, a state, a realm—a king*dom*.

The kingdom is also an activity in time—God's sovereignty, reign, rule, indeed, even God's person—*king*dom. The *basileia* (the Greek word used) is the personal rule and presence of the king himself. The kingdom is the king at least. The kingdom is wherever Jesus is. (Origen called Christ the *autobasileia*, "the kingdom in person.") But in Matthew especially, the kingdom is (like Jesus himself) both space and time, both social place and historical person; it is the society or household of the king. It is a very social, a very spatial word—it is thingish as well as personal, social and not just the individual's union with God. The kingdom is God's government, his state, his "fourth world," his new society. When we pray "thy kingdom come" we are praying, then, for the coming of a marvelous activity—the merciful personal presence and rule of God in the history of persons—and at the same time we are praying for the coming of an entirely new society and state-of-things, for a community's settlement, for the building of a new city and a new world.

The peril of the personal-temporal understanding—reign or rule of God—is the peril of so individualizing the kingdom that it is no longer a society. The peril of the social-spatial use of the word—realm or dominion of God—is the peril of so communalizing the kingdom that it is no longer personal. Both moments belong in the word, and I will suggest, for balance's sake, that we think of the word kingdom in the sense of both its syllables: as the rule of the *king* in his *dom*(inion).

For the kingdom as both spatial and temporal, realm and reign, see the excellent sources: Str.-B., 1:172–73, 180–84; Lohm., 66–67; and Conz., 68–81.

"Here comes the kingdom of heaven!" The word I have rendered "here comes," *ēggiken*, has exercised many interpreters. Does it mean the kingdom is near, or does it mean the kingdom is present? Does it suggest a future or a present kingdom? It means both: it is on its way, it is just about to break in, in fact it *is* breaking in, in some way, as Jesus' very words are spoken—"here comes!" The translation "here comes" keeps the kingdom from being a static object either in heaven ("is near") or on earth ("is here"); it protects the kingdom from the desecration of being so present it can be taken for granted and from the irrelevance of being so future it doesn't matter. The word *ēggiken* moves—"here comes"; it presents the kingdom as in motion, as dynamic, as a kind of quantum of energy, a wave, rather than as a merely present ("here") or a removed ("near") object of inert matter. "Here comes the kingdom" means the kingdom is breaking in right now through Jesus' person and Word like a great landslide or like lightning from heaven, that the kingdom is vital, alive, moving, breaking in. Yet the kingdom, as *God's,* is always partly (and even mainly) future at the same time, anchored in its source and giver.

A comparison of *ēggiken,* "*here comes* my betrayer" in Matt 26:46 with the very next verse's "while he was still speaking, look, Judas *came,*" Matt 26:47, best illustrates the *immediate* futurity of the word *ēggiken,* and the power of Jesus' catalytic Word. The Gospel of John's idiom, "The hour is coming [future] and now is [present]," e.g., at 4:23; 5:25, is also a good synonym for *ēggiken:* it also speaks of a future that enters the present.

We might render the old expression "Repent, for the kingdom of heaven is near" with the following expression and catch its force: "Move! Here comes the whole new world of God!" Almost every word is nuclear. This thematic sentence tells us that we had better change *now,* get out of the way *now*—or, more precisely, get in the way new—because in Jesus' Word God's mighty new world is on its way toward us and is even now crashing in. "Change! Here It comes!" This is the sense of the expression.

It needs to be emphasized again that change is *not* the condition of the coming; it is the commanded consequence of, or response to, an already commenced coming, inaugurated by Christ's coming, and made available ever since his coming in his Words as they are passed on by his church. "It" is coming, Jesus is coming, whether we change or not. If Jesus meets us unchanged we can only expect judgment. If Jesus makes us and so meets us changed we can expect salvation. Every time Jesus' words are released, the kingdom lives and jumps in those words. When we hear these words, if *we* jump, if we allow his words to change us, we are ready for the kingdom.

Every Bible class, every little family Bible reading, every individual Bible study, and in a special way every worship service, every liturgical exercise, every congregational gathering around the Word of God should start with at least the sense, preferably with the sound of the urgent words, "Turn your lives around! Here comes God's kingdom!" This sentence is Jesus' perpetual call to worship. In Jesus' words, the kingdom of heaven is now *so* near that the power for the possibility of repentance is present; yet until Jesus' Second Advent, even when we believe Jesus with all our heart, the kingdom is only inaugurated, it is not yet consummated (Hill, 105).

The word "kingdom" has been understood by the church in four distinct ways: (1) as in heaven, (2) as in the homily (or sermon), (3) as in the heart, and (4) as in history.

K. L. Schmidt's ten pages in TDNT, 1:581–90, are the best short description of the scholarly consensus on the meaning of Jesus' word "kingdom."

(1) The kingdom of heaven is *heaven;* that is, it is the entirely future world, the next life, the wholly other. Therefore, when we pray "thy kingdom come" today, we are praying for the final coming of Jesus Christ, for the end of present history, and for the inauguration of the entirely new world. This understanding of the kingdom is held by the best current New Testament scholarship, interpreting the kingdom, as it is said, eschatologically; this heavenly understanding is also held by adventists of all types who believe that the kingdom is that which comes with Christ's Second Coming. The kingdom of God understood in this heaven-sent way is not just an alteration of the present world, of its individuals, its societies, or even its churches; it is the whole new world itself, the new heavens and the new earth.

(2) Then, the kingdom is in the *homily;* that is, the kingdom is God's other world breaking into this world *now* through the spoken Word of the gospel. This was the major view of the Reformation, and it is still the view of the churches loyal to the Reformation rediscovery of the gospel. Here the kingdom is present in the gospel story.

Here the focus is not so much on heaven, however, as on the church; not so much on the end as on the means to the end; here one looks not so much outside the church in longing as one looks inside the church's worship in learning—though in the learning we are made to long. And here one does not so much expect the next life as one expects, through the Word, power for this life in preparation for the next. Here one thinks of the text in particular where Jesus says, "the harvest is huge, but there are very few workers. Pray the Lord of the harvest that he will send forth workers into his harvest" (9:37f). Here we pray, "Lord, raise up students and others who will go into the richly varied forms of Christian ministry and mission and speak and live your Word in all purity of doctrine and life." (See the Reformation catechisms on the second petition of the Lord's Prayer, "thy kingdom come," for this appreciation of the kingdom.)

(3) The kingdom is in the *heart* in the sense that wherever Jesus rules in an individual's or group's heart, there the kingdom of God is. Where Jesus is Lord the kingdom is present. This understanding of the kingdom has always been congenial to spiritually serious Christians. Here the kingdom is understood not so much as a change of worlds or as changes in the world as it is a change in the hearts of individual believers. Here, where "thy kingdom come" is prayed the church thinks of persons changing, being converted, turning around, accepting Christ as Savior and Lord, and letting Jesus rule in their personal lives.

(4) The kingdom, in the final understanding, is God's presence in *history;* that is, the kingdom is something in *this world* and it occurs wherever there is a breakthrough of peace and justice in human society. This has been the predominant idea of the kingdom in the thought and work of socially serious Christians. God is still the author and source of the kingdom here, but human beings may serve as God's agents, too. Here people may be used by God to build the kingdom; they bring it

provisionally into being by doing justice and by working for peace. If God's kingdom is truly set up in the heart it will move out into the feet and hands in good works and thus out into society in good legislators, laws, and structures. In this fourth understanding the kingdom is as much this-worldly as in the first understanding it is other-worldly. In the kingdom-as-heaven it is God and God alone who brings the kingdom, and the kingdom comes as the end of this world, not as its repair. In the kingdom-as-history the kingdom is not only something given, it is also something done; it is not only something believed in, it is something lived out. The writings of American Christians from John Woolman to Martin Luther King, Jr., are especially important here. See Ronald C. White, Jr., and C. Howard Hopkins, *The Social Gospel in America* (Philadelphia: Temple University Press, 1976).

These four views of the kingdom focus Christians' attention, respectively, on the next life, the preached Word, the believer's heart, and this world. It would not be a bad idea to let all four ideas play on the imagination. Each view has its one-sidedness. Each view has its contribution. Where our attention is too earthly, the heavenly look is salutary. Where our concerns are too individualistic, the historical look is wholesome. Where one is too other-worldly, the homiletical look provides a corrective. And where attention to the sermon inclines to clericalism, or the look to society to secularism, then the look to the heart reminds the Christian constantly of one's *own* needs.

(1) The kingdom in the full sense comes with the end of the age; (2) the major present agent of this kingdom is God's Word, which awakens (3) the obedient response to it; then this obedient response—faith issuing in love—(4) works in and through groups and structures for justice in the world. All four dimensions of the kingdom have their place. The idea is to see them all, and, at the same time, to allow the Dove-Spirit to focus our attention on that dimension of the kingdom she wants us to see at any particular moment.

Jesus is the Light of the Nations. Wherever he goes darkness recedes. He is the one great hope of the peoples of the world. We do not place our hopes in the nations themselves or in their political, economic, or social kingdoms or constructions, however well wrought, however hopeful. We remember the tower of Babel (Gen 11). Our hope is entirely King Jesus, who is robed entirely in his Word. His Word is a lamp unto our feet. How this lamp casts its light *in particular* is the special contribution of the next service of Jesus.

B. Jesus the Lord of the Church (The Service of His Word) (vv 18-22)

Jesus did not just come, teach here and there, die, and then rise. He came and *made disciples*. This discipling work of Jesus is very important to Matthew's understanding of the gospel. Consequently, right after focusing on Jesus' own presence in the Word, Matthew turns our attention next to Jesus' very pointed *use* of his Word in calling particular disciples to share his ministry.

In Matthew's Gospel one of Jesus' important services is to create a ministry of workers by which to shape his church to engage the world. Through Jesus' way of making ministers and Christian workers *then* we learn how to make ministers and Christian workers *now*. Just as Jesus' own baptism and temptations taught the church the meaning of her baptism and temptations, so now Jesus' forming of ministers in-forms ours.

4:18–20 *"Jesus was walking along the beach of the Sea of Galilee when he saw two brothers—Simon, called Peter, and his brother Andrew. They were throwing their net into the lake; they were fishermen. And Jesus said to them, 'Follow me, and I will turn you into fishers of people!' And they immediately left their nets, and they followed him."*

Jesus will not be content merely to preach; he will give a great deal of attention to working closely with those to whom he preaches, and especially to a core group of persons—the disciples. We call the first group of disciples, rightly, the apostles. We learn here how the apostolate originated. At the same time we learn how the apostolate is carried on historically in disciple-making. We learn apostolic succession.

Calvin, 1:157, insists that this passage on the Call of the Four Brothers is not a general description of how *all* Christians are called. It is a particular description of how ordained ministers are called, for Christ does not call all Christians to leave their work (similarly, Bonn., 50). Ministry, even professional ministry, is the meaning of the text, but everyone called to Christ is called to some form of ministry, some kind of fishing. (The lay academies in Europe and, in my experience, the emphases of Howard Butt, Howard Hovde, Eddy Sears, and their associates at the Laity Lodge in Texas, and the work of Edward Schroeder and Robert Bertram in Crossings out of St. Louis, are exemplary.)

What made these men disciples? Is it, as we sometimes hear, something Jesus *saw* in Peter and Andrew, some potential, some sincerity that singled them out? Nothing of the sort is recorded. Matthew forcefully directs our attention *away* from anything in the disciples and *toward* the effective Word of Jesus, which does everything. Jesus called, they followed. Jesus said, "Follow me," and they dropped *(aphentes)* their nets and followed him. Once again we meet the same Greek word that appeared as effect in Jesus' two earlier encounters (with John and with Satan): *aphentes*, "let," "leave." When Jesus said "let us," John "let"; when Jesus said "leave," Satan "left." The same effect, by the same word, is recorded now a third time. Jesus calls persons to discipleship, and they "left" their nets. Matthew repeatedly underlines the "lefting," "letting," nuclear power of Jesus' Word. "He commanded and they were created" (Ps 148:5).

What makes disciples? The Word of Jesus and that alone. The power that makes disciples is not the human potential of Peter and Andrew; it is the spiritual potency of the Word. We have in our mouths and in our hearts, in the Word of Jesus, incalculable power. When Jesus' story is told with God's blessing, confidently and inviting confidence, it "lets" people, it causes people to "leave" that to which they were previously clinging, it disengages and engages, it gives what it asks for. The Word is strong. "'The speaking doth it. When this Speaker saith something that He will have, it must be so'" (Luther in Barth, *Church Dogmatics*, I/1, 144; cf. 194, 196–97).

"Follow me" meant, in rabbinic speech, "become my students, be apprenticed to me, join my school, live with me." Students lived with their rabbis; they did not merely hear their lectures. Discipleship was study-in-residence; it was a live-in arrangement in a home and with a teacher.

The unusual feature in Jesus' enrollment, however, is that *Jesus* asks the students to join him. Ordinarily, students came asking for the privilege of studying (and living) with the rabbi. But Jesus is no ordinary rabbi. He is Lord. And no one comes to this Lord by one's own initiative; the Lord comes first. Yet Jesus is a servant Lord, too; he is not too proud to go seeking his own students. (On rabbis and their students, see Davies, 421–22, 455.)

Theologically, something of importance is at stake here. It is what the evangelist John describes when he heard Jesus say, "You have not chosen me, but I have chosen you" (John 15:16). In Matthew's Gospel when a person becomes a disciple of Jesus it is because Jesus calls the person and not because the person calls Jesus. We owe our discipleship—our conversion, our call, our baptism, and whatever else we have in Christ—to the initiating Word and work of Jesus and not to any potential, sincerity, or spiritual instinct in ourselves.

What makes a disciple? Jesus' Word.

"Come be my students, and I will turn you into fishers of people!" Jesus furnishes his invitation with an exciting promise. It is the promise of catching persons, of being effective with people. This addresses our core. At the epicenter of our being, more central than even the sex drive, is the desire to influence others. We are socially constituted to make a mark. Jesus promises that mark. "I *will* make you fishers of people."

It is of first importance, then, to observe that in this the Gospel's first evangelistic encounter, Jesus calls two men not to an experience of personal salvation but to a school—to the extension (or continuing studies) school of discipleship; Jesus' evangelism is durative as much as it is instantaneous. For example, he does not say, "follow me, and I will save your souls." There may be a place for speech of this kind, but it is not the speech Jesus uses in this his first and model evangelistic call. Jesus calls two men to school, and even in this school his promise is not their salvation but others'. Jesus promises help, through disciples, to others; not, first of all, bliss for disciples. Jesus in fact offers no bliss here except that of being a help. We want to help people deeply. Jesus promises to supply precisely this want to those who join him in his ministry. "I *will*. . . ."

We sometimes worry, and rightly so, about the ambition that burns within us. We want to be something, somebody, and to do things; and it is not always easy to sort out how much of this wanting is selfish and how much Christian. Yet Jesus unapologetically addresses our main ambition: "Do you want to make something useful of your life, to have a life that is catching? I will give this to you."

This is Jesus' initial evangelistic approach to specific persons in the Gospel, and it is full of instruction. Jesus calls people to *himself*: "follow *me.*" He calls them to a walk rather than to a single act: "*follow* me" (the Greek verb is in the *present* tense imperative, which stresses continuity and means "live a life following me"). And Jesus uses fresh, secular language that fishermen understand, the language of their trade. He does not tell fishermen that they will become, say, "healers of people," language more appropriate to doctors than to fishermen. Finally, the promise Jesus suffixes to his call is full of social and not merely individual significance; it is the promise of reaching outside ourselves to *others*.

The ways we catch people are not immediately indicated. I believe, however, that the Sermon on the Mount that follows is Matthew's main way of showing us what it means to follow Jesus and thus to catch people. Jesus' main evangelistic method is Jesus' ethic. We should not understand this method in a worldly or sensational way. The temptations of Matt 4 stand sentry over every subsequent Gospel Word. There are very different ways to be catching, some quite unlikely.

4:20 "And they immediately left their nets, and they followed him." The catalytic power at work in this sentence is not the zeal of the disciples; it is the energy of the Word. In the Gospel, ministry is *created* by Jesus' Word and *evidenced* by the disciples' decision. Everything depends on getting the story out. Where this Word is released and its story told, people are given the motive power and the will power to drop their nets and leave their preoccupations.

4:21-22 *"Jesus went on a little farther, and he saw two other brothers, James, the son of Zebedee, and John his brother. They were in the boat with Zebedee their father, repairing their nets. And Jesus called them. And they immediately left [aphentes] their boat and father and followed him."*

To reinforce the seminal evangelical truths of Word and will, of cause and effect, of invitation and decision, Matthew tells the same story and uses almost exactly the same words a second time. This Hebrew parallelism, this saying of a thing twice, is the biblical way of underlining. Whenever we meet with repetition in Matthew's Gospel or anywhere in Scripture it is appropriate mentally to underline the words repeated, for they are what the author is trying most emphatically to say.

Once again in this second missionary encounter the call of Jesus causes the "leaving" of discipleship. And this time what is left is even more dear and therefore more difficult to leave: not just nets but a father (and a boat, cf. Gund., 62). Here Matthew pictures discipleship's wrenching effects, its disruptive influences, and not only (as in the first story) its effectiveness. But there is positive teaching, too: the power of Jesus' Word overcomes the power of even family ties. Jesus is sovereign not only over habit and property (story one), but also over blood and genes (story two).

And so we are in a doubly enforced position for answering our initial question in this section. What makes disciples? Jesus' Word. What, then, are we to do when we hear his Word? Give him our selves as his followers. This gift of self is not something we can work up inside. It is something that comes to us with kingdom force from the Word that is spoken to us in the fellowship of praying Christians. The principal need is for this Word to be released; the Word does the rest. Disciples who hear Jesus' Word on continual Sundays (and whenever else) find new power to will, and will power to leave what they should leave. Then for another week disciples are influential, helpful, and (whether they know it or not) catching. This is the rhythm of the Christian apostolate. "Come be my student continually ["continually" is the force of the present tense verb], and I will make you catching with people."

The magnetic attraction of Jesus' fascinating sentence is the connection of the summons ("follow") with the promise ("people"). To follow Jesus is to catch people; to give the will to Jesus in a life of close discipleship is somehow, mysteriously, to move other people to give their wills to him, too; apprenticeship to Jesus is mission to the world; following is fishing; commitment is contagious.

In the first service, the Light of the Nations, we saw the person of Jesus as the subject or noun of ministry. Now in the second service, the Lord of the Church, we have seen the Word of Jesus form disciples as Jesus' own predicates or verbs of future ministry. Jesus is the Light of the World (4:16), but he calls people to himself for ministry and so he makes them, too, the light of the world (5:14). Jesus is Subject. But he wills to "predicate" us, to use us, to move us to become living subjects of his ministry. By "subjecting" us to himself he turns us into free subjects, into verbs of his freeing work in history.

C. Jesus the Life of the Body (The Service of His Work) (vv 23–25)

In the final paragraph of the fourth chapter of Matthew we see Jesus mainly as healer. This paragraph is really the introduction to the Sermon on the Mount and needs to be read in connection with the Sermon. Indeed, this summary paragraph introduces the whole of chapters 5 through 9—Jesus as the Word-Messiah appears in chapters 5 through 7 (the Sermon on the Mount) and Jesus as the Deed-Messiah appears in chapters 8 and 9 (the Ten Miracles). When these two great units are complete, Matthew has given us his essential Word-Deed christology. The very same words used to introduce this twin section at 4:23—"And Jesus went around the whole of Galilee teaching in their synagogues and preaching the Good News of the kingdom and healing every disease and every malady of the people"—are repeated almost verbatim at 9:35: "And Jesus went around all the cities and villages, teaching in their synagogues and preaching the Good News of the kingdom and healing every disease and every malady." This is Matthew's way of bracketing; his way of writing chapters. Everything between these two thematic sentences is a single section in his Gospel. Between 4:23 and 9:35 Matthew has drafted an incomparable portrait of Jesus the Christ, delivering the world's major sermon and releasing history's main healing forces.

Thus our present paragraph is really introductory to the next chapter. And yet it serves my systematic purposes in this chapter, too, by introducing another important feature in Jesus' *ministry* (the theme of this chapter), untouched till now, and specially developed in a moment (chapters 8–9): Jesus not only talked, he healed. In fact, he often healed by talking.

4:23 *"And Jesus went around the whole of Galilee teaching in their synagogues and preaching the wonderful news of the kingdom and healing every disease and every malady of the people" (4:23).*

Jesus' itineration honors free course evangelism (Gund., 63); Jesus' teaching in synagogues honors established ministries and meeting places. The first site for Jesus' first recorded teaching ministry was the usual site of Jewish ministry—the synagogues. In this sense, as in so many others, Jesus was not sectarian, private, or esoteric; he was institutional, public, and normal. Jesus taught where people were supposed to teach.

Three verbs stand out in this sentence: teaching, preaching, and healing. (1) The word "teaching," as distinguished from preaching, usually indicates instruction in the will of God—what we call ethics or discipleship—and finds its classic form in the Sermon on the Mount that follows. (Cf. McN., 47; Schl., *Der*, 120–23; Davies, 408, 424–25; Bornkamm, "End," 38 n. l; and Rengstorf, *didaskalos*, TDNT, 2:153–57.)

(2) The special theme of Jesus' "preaching" is indicated in the following phrase: "and preaching *(kērussōn)* the wonderful news *(to euaggelion)* of the kingdom." Preaching, kerygma, as we have seen, indicates authoritative announcement, proclamation, statement of fact. What Jesus preached is called here—for the first time in

Matthew—"wonderful news," "the Good News." The message of the kingdom is exceedingly good news, glad tidings, thrilling fact. It is the news of God's society and of God's coming with it. The word "preaching," as distinguished from teaching, usually focuses on *God's* activity and the announcement of it; it has as its content or subject the divine work, and is the unifying melody (leitmotif) discernible within the music of both Jesus' teaching and healing. While teaching gives us our ethical responsibility—"turn your lives around"—preaching tells us "here comes the king-dom of heaven." Indeed, the preaching brings the power to obey the teaching. Preaching God's work enables our doing God's will.

(3) The third and final verb used in the series and the one emphasized in the paragraph is "healing *(therapeuōn)* every disease and every malady in the people." Jesus taught what we must do (change), because of what God is doing (coming), and then he gave presents to people who couldn't do much of anything until they were released from their crippling problems—he healed the sick. The healthy can be taught whom to believe and whom to follow, and so can the sick, of course. But the sick are sometimes so overwhelmed by their sicknesses that it is hard for them to see through them. Jesus cared about this overwhelming fact and did something about it. The church learns from her Messiah throughout this Gospel that special attention must be given to the sick and overwhelmed of all kinds because they are special to God.

The "alls" of Matthew's present sentence are important to Matthew and indicate something of importance, too. Jesus circulated in *all* Galilee, and he healed *all* diseases and *all* maladies of the people (4:23). The last two alls mean that Jesus is Lord not only of wills, as in the call of disciples, but of bodies too, as here in the healings. Jesus is Lord of the whole person, right down to the body. Jesus' sover-eignty is not only psychological, affecting *psychai* (souls); it is also somatic-physical, affecting nervous systems and bones. There is nothing beyond the reach of Jesus' Lordship; he is Lord of all. There is nothing within the human experience that Jesus is unable to touch and wholesomely to affect, whether it is death at the outer limit of human life, or the will in the innermost sanctuary of human life, or the body with its cells wrapping the will.

Thus in Matthew chapter 4 as a whole, Jesus is not only utterly for *God* (the temptations, 4 A); he is also utterly for *us*—for the whole of us and for all of us (the services, 4 B).

4:24 *"And his fame went out into the* whole *of Syria and they brought to him all* who *were sick with various sicknesses and possessed by various torments and demons, and epileptics and paralytics, and he healed* (etherapeusen) *them."*

In this long central verse we see Jesus the therapist at work on the whole range of the human problem: he heals those with organic, with psychic, and with nervous diseases. He heals anyone in torment. Jesus is not only the Savior of the international macrocosm—the Light of the Nations—he is also the Savior of the human micro-cosm down to the most minute cells: he is the Life of the Body. We do not learn here how Jesus heals or even why; we hear only that he heals "all." (Particulars await the Ten Miracles of the eighth and ninth chapters.) Thus the church is stretched to look at *all* that sullies people, and in fidelity to her Lord to reach out—as far out as nations, as far in as bodies.

4:25 *"And big crowds* followed *him from Galilee and the Ten Cities and Jerusalem and Judea and from beyond the Jordan."*

We have just learned that following is the special obedience Jesus wants of people ("follow me," 4:19). When Jesus has healed someone's malady (our present text teaches), the response is often that one wishes to give one's whole life to Jesus in following him. Touched, one follows. The "big crowds" (*ochloi polloi*) who follow Jesus here and often elsewhere are "the crowded out," the marginated people, the little people of Israel and beyond.

We have been witnesses to the birth of the church in these unlikely little sentences. Jesus now has several specially and specifically called followers: (1) the two sets of brothers-fishermen in the middle of the chapter who comprise, as it were, Jesus' Ministry (capital M) or core apostolate. (2) Jesus is also followed by those he has just healed. We have here the embryo of a little church with a staff consisting of the senior Minister, Jesus, four associate or assistant Ministers—Peter, Andrew, James, and John—and a congregation of wounded healers—lay ministers—all touched by Jesus at the point of their deepest need. The Ministry and the lay ministers all follow the single Minister in perfect equality (cf. Matt 23:8–12 for emphasis on equality in ministry).

Touched by the summoning Word and the healing hands of the Lord, the church starts to be. Jesus now has real people, willing persons, explicitly following him. To at least a portion of this people he has given the explicit promise that, following him, he will make them catchers of still other people. To all of them he gave a wholeness of life they had not known before Jesus met them. The Israel of God is re-born and re-formed here from rather humble, ordinary, even sick stock. This people is ready now for a formal constitution, for a service of ordination and dedication, and for instruction in what it means in practical terms to follow Jesus and catch people. The majestic address that follows is intended to supply all followers of Jesus with the innermost meanings of, and equipment for, the grace of being Christian ministry.

The current normative discussion of ministry is the third section of *Baptism, Eucharist, and Ministry* (The World Council of Churches' Faith and Order Paper No. 111, 1982), pp. 20–32. While the ordained ministry is rightly honored in this important document—and Protestantism especially needs this honoring for the spiritual and psychological health of her ordained ministers—one regrets the still underdeveloped doctrine of the ministry of the whole Christian *laos*, the whole people of God, in this summary of years of study.

Chapters Five, Six, and Seven
The Teaching Messiah: The Sermon on the Mount
Introduction to the Doctrine of Discipleship

Until now the Gospel of Matthew has been mainly introduction. With the Sermon on the Mount, Matthew reaches his first main speech. For Matthew, Jesus has not only given us great atonement benefits by his death and resurrection, though surely these are Jesus' major gifts, and like all other good evangelists Matthew will devote the climax of his Gospel to their exhibition. But Matthew's Jesus has also given us great ethical benefits by his historical life. And this life is mainly in his Word. Matthew is the moral evangelist. He sees Jesus known and experienced not only through mystical union with Jesus' person, but especially by moral obedience to Jesus' commands. In his commands Jesus is alive; in believing response to Jesus' commands people come to life. For Jesus' words are not just words, they are Word; they are not merely human verbs, they are divine Verbum, and as such they are alive with enabling power.

"The Word possesses such power wherever seriously considered, heeded, and put into practice, that it never remains barren of fruit. It always awakens new thoughts, new pleasures and devotions, and cleanses the heart and its meditations" (Luther, *Large Catechism*, 43). Paul rightly emphasizes Christ's death for us: "God shows his love for us in that while we were yet sinners Christ *died* for us" (Rom 5:8). Matthew rightly emphasizes Jesus' teaching of us: "Thus whoever hears these *my words* and does them will be compared to a wise man who built his house upon rock" (Matt 7:24).

The Sermon on the Mount as it has come to us from Matthew's hands is divided into six distinguishable parts, two for each of its three chapters, and may be outlined accordingly:
1. The Blessings (or the Beatitudes and the two You Ares), Matt 5 A;
2. The Commands (or the Antitheses), Matt 5 B;
3. The Devotions, Matt 6 A;
4. The Goals, Matt 6 B;
5. The Sums, Matt 7 A;
6. The Warnings, Matt 7 B.

It is a collateral design of the sermon to give a portrait of *disciples*. The sermon describes their person in the Who of the Blessings (5:3–16), their work in the What of the Commands (5:17–48), their method in the How of the Devotions (6:1–18), their ends in the Where of the Goals (6:19–34), their focus in the Wherefore of the Sums (7:1–12), and their ground in the Why of the Warnings (7:13–27). To read the Sermon on the Mount is to discover what it means to be a disciple of Jesus; to read it with faith is to receive the power to *be* a disciple.

Chapter Five
The Call of Mercy

"When he saw these crowds [following him], he went up on the mountain, and when he sat down his disciples came up to him" (5:1).

Lohmeyer, 75 n. 2, sees that the three phrases in this first verse all begin with the pronoun "he." The person of Jesus is as front and center at the beginning of the sermon as he is at the end (7:28–29).

One wonders at first why Jesus left when he saw big crowds. Or to put the question in another way, why does Jesus cease a successful healing ministry to undertake a teaching one? It is the question in our time of why interrupt action with talk?

The first answer, I believe, is that Jesus wants to practice preventive medicine, not only curative. Jesus wishes to do public health work and not just surgery. In life as in Scripture the relation of words to deeds is often the relation of cause to effect. Good words, as we know from experience, literally put us back together again; they integrate, help, and heal us. Wrong words, as we also know from experience, disintegrate us; they make us literally sick; they hurt and break us. Second, Jesus wants to incorporate disciples into his ministry of preventive medicine and public health. When they believe and obey this sermon they become the major antibodies in a sick world. Jesus' Sermon on the Mount teaches saving health.

The Old Testament Word of God, when kept, was seen as literally healing, too. "If you will diligently hearken to the voice of the Lord your God. . . , I will put none of the diseases upon you which I put upon the Egyptians; for I am the Lord, your healer" (Exod 15:26). "O my soul praise Him, for He is thy health and salvation."

That Jesus gives this message specifically "on the mountain" calls to mind all the great mountains of God in the Old Testament, especially Sinai, and in particular the great blessings promised by Isaiah from a messianic mountain.
"It shall come to pass in the latter days
   that the mountain of the house of the Lord
shall be established as the highest of the mountains,
   and shall be raised above the hills;
and all the nations shall flow to it,
   and many peoples shall come, and say:
'Come, let us go up to the mountain of the Lord,
   to the house of the God of Jacob;
that he may teach us his ways
   and that we may walk in his paths'" (Isa 2:2–3; cf. 25:6–10).

I. THE BLESSINGS (5:2–16)

"And Jesus opened his mouth and was teaching them, saying,
'God bless the poor in spirit, because theirs is the kingdom of heaven.

'God bless those who mourn, because they will be comforted.
'God bless the gentle, because they will be awarded the earth.
'God bless those who hunger and thirst for righteousness, because they are the ones who will be satisfied.
'God bless the merciful, because they will find mercy.
'God bless the pure in heart, because they will see God.
'God bless the peacemakers, because they will be called the children of God.
'God bless those who are persecuted for the sake of righteousness, because theirs is the kingdom of heaven.
'God bless you when people ridicule you and persecute you and say all kinds of evil things about you, falsely, because of your devotion to me. Rejoice and be very happy, because your reward is huge in the heavens; this was exactly the way they persecuted the prophets before you.'"

" 'You are the salt of the earth; but if salt loses its tang, how is it ever going to be salty again? It is good for absolutely nothing except to be thrown outside and trampled under people's feet.

" 'You are the light of the world. A city sitting on a hill cannot be hid! People do not keep a lamp burning only to put it under a basket; they put it right on top of the table, and there it shines in the service of everyone in the house. Let your light so shine out in the presence of other people that they will see your kind of good works and thus give honor to your Father who is in heaven.'"

Introduction

"And Jesus opened his mouth and was teaching them, saying . . ." (5:2). The sermon begins solemnly with this deliberately impressive formula. The "them" whom Jesus teaches are, as the preceding verse has prepared us to understand, the disciples. Jesus increases his ministry of healing now by going not only deeper in Word, but also by reaching wider through disciples. In Pauline language, Jesus is forming his body the church.

There is a debate among interpreters about whether Jesus is teaching only his disciples here, or whether he intends to include the crowds. Verses 1 and 2 favor the disciples; 7:28–29 favor disciples *and* the crowds. (Disciples only: Lu., *SM*, 106f; Trill., 30 n. 55; not for disciples only: Chrys., 15:1:91; Aug., *Harm.*, 125; Schn., 39. Harvey K. McArthur, *Understanding the Sermon on the Mount* (1960), 71–72, believes that Jesus originally gave the teaching here to both groups, but that in Matthew's design, vv 1–2, the sermon is intended to be instruction for disciples only.) Most Christian teachers, following Jesus, address disciples but hope thereby also to disciple those who hear.

"And he was *teaching* them." Teaching, as we have seen, has as its special object what we today call ethics, and what Jesus called "the will of my Father in heaven." Teaching focuses on what people are to do. But it is impossible to describe Jesus' teaching as merely ethical in the ordinary sense, for Jesus saw right human doing as the divinely enabled response *brought by* the inbreaking divine kingdom. "Repent, *for* here comes the kingdom of heaven" (4:17). The incoming kingdom, through the proclamation of the Word, enables the ethic of repentance.

A. The Need Beatitudes of Faith (B 1–4), 5:3–6*

1. The First Beatitude (B 1), 5:3
"God bless the poor in spirit, because *theirs* is the kingdom of heaven."
The "theirs" in the original text is at the beginning of the subordinate clause for emphasis and says that it is precisely for *them,* the spiritually poor, that the kingdom exists and, in fact, that it is *of* them (the word is a genitive of possession) that the kingdom consists. The emphatic "theirs" is also exclusive: Those not poor in spirit are not in the kingdom. Who then are the "poor in spirit"?

It is well known that Luke, who also begins his Sermon on the Mount (or Sermon on the Plain) with a series of Blessings, makes Jesus' point more sharply and, it could seem, less spiritually than Matthew's Jesus. For Luke's Blessings begin like this: "Blessed are the poor, because yours is the kingdom of God; Blessed are those who are hungry now, because you will be filled; Blessed are those who cry now, because you will laugh" (Luke 6:20–21). Luke's Beatitudes look physical, Matthew's spiritual (Luke's "poor" vs. Matthew's "poor *in spirit*"; Luke's "hungry" vs. Matthew's "hunger and thirst *for righteousness*"). There is something important in this contrast. Luke's Beatitudes single out the really *poor,* hungry, and crying, and it is good that we have a social evangelist who heard Jesus point the gospel in the social direction. The gospel is for the really and not merely the spiritually poor, hungry, and crying. Luke does us the service of preserving the earthly side of Jesus.

But Luke can be over-interpreted to mean "how good to be poor, hungry, crying, because in the next life it won't be so bad"; that is, Luke can appear to be canonizing a social class, to be sanctifying miserable situations, to be so physical as to be cruel. Luke's Jesus can be misunderstood to mean, "It is wonderful to be poor." That is why we need Matthew's not superspiritual but objectively quite correct interpretation of the meaning of the Hebrew *anawin,* "poor," namely, those who are poor and who are crushed as a result, "poor *in spirit.*" Matthew is seeking to translate into Greek what Jesus originally said in Aramaic in a way that will make sense to future readers. Jesus means, in Matthew's translation, "blessed are those who *feel* their poverty" we may even say; "who *suffer* their poverty" and so cry out to heaven.

In interpreting Jesus' Beatitudes we must always avoid the Clune of spiritualization on the one side and the Conway of secularization on the other. If we say that "blessed are the poor in spirit" means "blessed are the rich, too, if they act humbly," we have spiritualized the text. On the other hand, if we say that "blessed are the poor" means "poor people are happy people," we have secularized the text. I believe that in the light of our two Gospel records Jesus said something incorporating both Matthew's spirituality and Luke's sociality, with the best of each. Just as we need two eyes to see in perspective, so with important sayings we need at least two reporters to understand in perspective.

Let us seek to define this Beatitude dialectically by moving with the two evangelists gradually toward the center. First, with Luke, it is true that Jesus blesses the really poor. Whatever Jesus says here, he certainly means to bless the physically and

---

*In this section, as a mnemonic aid, B represents Beatitude, and UR represents the "You Ares" of vv 13, 14.

not merely the psychologically poor. (I say "not merely" because the psychologically poor are, as we will see, also Jesus' poor.) Jesus puts himself in his opening address and in his opening words of that address on the side of the wretched of the earth. "Blessed" means "I am with you," "I am on your side."

Cf. Bertram, TWNT, 4:365–73. Schweizer, 79, appropriately, entitles his exposition of the Beatitudes, "God's Partiality Toward the Poor." I have translated the single Greek word *makarioi* ("blessed") with two English words, "God bless," in order to capture all three of the standard interpretations of "blessed" reviewed by Guelich, 67: the word *makarioi* means (a) a communication, "a dynamic pronouncement that *conveys* a blessing to the recipient," effecting what it announces (esp. Scandinavian scholarship); it is (b) an *exhortation* to live thus (some prominent German scholarship, e.g., Gunkel); it is (c) a *congratulation* to certain persons in certain conditions (prominent French scholarship, e.g., Dupont, 3:317–18).

I believe that Jesus' Beatitudes contain all three elements—communication, exhortation, and congratulation—and in that order in importance. Because I believe Jesus' Blessings primarily communicate what they say, I translate *makarioi* "God bless." "God bless you," said even by ordinary mortals, desires to convey a real blessing. We can imagine what happens when Jesus says it! For the realistic-communicative idea of blessing in the Bible, Isaac's irretrievable blessing of Jacob can be fruitfully studied in Genesis 27, esp. vv 27–37, where Isaac's blessing really *did* things and communicated realities, visible in the three verbs of Genesis 27:37 RSV: "Isaac answered Esau, 'Behold, I have [with my blessing] *made* him your lord, and all his brothers I have *given* to him for servants, and with grain and wine I have *sustained* him.'"

But second, with Matthew, Jesus does not mean that physical poverty is ennobling, a blessed social state, and that a person is lucky to find oneself starving. Rather, the person for whom the experience of impoverishment is a spiritual crisis, who groans in his spirit under the poverty, who is on the way down and who cries out—to *this* person Jesus announces, "Look up; I am here, taking your part, and the kingdom I bring is for *you.*" (Liberation theology has rediscovered Jesus' poor.)

The word for "poor," *ptōchoi*, which comes from the verb, *ptōssō*, "to cower, to cringe," means the abject poor, the abysmally impoverished, those completely dependent on others to make it, probably in our time including some of the much maligned "welfare poor." The gospel poor, then, are probably not those who choose to live simply or in modest poverty, though exactly such persons can be powerful evangelical witnesses, particularly in cultures of affluence; the gospel poor are society's marginated people, the city's underclass, the worldwide wretched of the earth. These people are visible especially in Luke's Jesus. When Matthew's Jesus then explicates this wretchedness as also being poor "in spirit" he wishes to say that those who have reached bottom spiritually and psychically, who cannot live without God's supernatural help (one thinks of the first two commitments in Alcoholics Anonymous and other twelve-step programs or of any who have come to the end of their tether and for whom the saving God is now an absolute necessity and no longer a theoretical postulate)—for all such "failures" God is there. Simply put, the poor in spirit are "people who recognize that they are helpless without God's help" (Patte, 101). The great enemy of the evangelical message, in the light of this first Beatitude, is successism and the teaching that says that it is the winners of the world who have God and his blessing ("Blessed are the rich," or "Blessed are the rich in spirit"). The Beatitudes set the world's value-systems on their head. Jesus is the countercultural force par excellence. (Who, in Jesus' opinion, are the really "underdeveloped"?)

To do the will of God as it is unfolded powerfully in this sermon requires an immense amount of spirit (and Spirit). To be a person of God is, by definition, to be a person with spirit. And yet the paradox of the first Beatitude is that Jesus here sides precisely with those who fail what is needed before God, and who feel this failure. Thus the opening saying in the Sermon on the Mount teaches Jesus' *grace;* the sermon begins with grace and should be read, in every succeeding sentence, in the light of this gracious preamble, "Blessed are the poor in spirit," which can be appropriately paraphrased, "Blessed are those who feel their real personal failure." Jesus blesses the spiritually *in*adequate. This holy paradox is the gospel, and Luther played this tune to distraction and distinction. It is those who feel their sin with hurt and penitence who are the really righteous, and it is those who are sure they are the righteous who need no repentance who are the real sinners (cf. Luke 18:13f; John 9:39–44). It is the *dispirited* who are often spiritual and live before God, and it is the marvelously inspired who often ex(s)pire from God's final presence (see classically Matt 7:21–23). It is the poor before God to whom God can be rich, and it is those who feel they are peculiarly rich in God who miss the kingdom altogether.

I believe it is the purpose of every command in the Sermon on the Mount to drive us back to the first Beatitude. Just as the First Commandment in the Ten Commandments is the hidden source of power and real *telos* of every other commandment, so, in a similar way, the first Beatitude is both the goal of every subsequent sentence in the sermon and the source of the ability to live it. If, as often happens, a great text were to be entitled not by its place (here, a mountain) but by its opening words (as, for example, in the Magnificat, Benedictus, or "Our Father"), then the Sermon on the Mount would be called "The Sermon of the Blessed Poor." This name would more sharply focus the meaning of this Gospel's gospel.

The Sermon on the Mount is, spiritually speaking, actually the sermon from the valley. It starts low. It starts with those who feel very unlike mountains! Further on, when we read "whoever is angry with his brother is going to hell," or "whoever looks on a woman in order to lust after her has committed adultery with her already in his heart," we will (or should) feel very poor in spirit indeed. Every command in the Sermon on the Mount taken seriously drives believing readers back into the valley of the first Beatitude and its wonderful promise of kingdom belonging and kingdom resources.

All vanguard mentalities are put in question by this Beatitude. The moment we begin to look back and down on those who have not come as far or high in consciousness or sensitivity or spirit as we, in that moment we have become rich in spirit and so fall out of the blessing of the first Beatitude.

Jerome, 1:104, believes those blessed in the first Beatitude are the *voluntarily* poor, those who have opted for the lifestyle of poverty (similarly, Lohmeyer, 82 n. 1: "poor *from* the spirit," or "with all of one's heart"). Allen, 39–40, sees the *involuntarily* oppressed as the poor here; McNeile, 50, sees especially the pious in Israel, "for the most part literally poor, whom the worldly rich despised and persecuted"; Barclay, 1:88, 90–91, in an interesting word study, sees that *ptōchos* means abject poverty, but then Barclay interprets the word spiritually. Guelich, 69, summarizes carefully: "'The poor' in Judaism referred to those in desperate need (socioeconomic element) whose helplessness drove them to a dependent relationship with God (religious element)," or again at 75, "For Matthew, the 'poor in spirit' are those who find themselves waiting, empty-handed, upon God alone for their hope and deliverance while beset with abuse and rejection by their own social and religious context." Dupont, 2:34, summarizes the lexicographic meaning of the word "poor," and at 34 n. 2, he cites F. Prat's definition of the poor man approvingly: "'The poor of Scripture—especially in the Psalms and prophets—is the man without defense, victim and toy of the tyranny of the powerful, who accepts without murmuring[?] his pitiable situation and turns toward God alone his attention and his hope. God protects the poor man; he is his refuge and his sustenance.'" Too spiritual?

Schniewind, 41, defines the poor of Jesus in the following way: The social upper class and the priestly aristocracy had been extensively conquered by pagan Hellenistic culture; but the pious who held tenaciously to the old faith in God and to the sternness of the command of God belonged almost exclusively to the lower social class; thus certain words were almost synonymous in Israel. The pious, righteous, or God-fearing were called the poor, little, or lowly. The poor were "'the quiet in the land'" (Ps 35:20). Schniewind, 42, insists rightly that Jesus did not bless these persons because of their virtues but because of their inadequacies; however, Schniewind's earlier descriptions of the poor make them appear virtuous.

In his sermons on the Sermon on the Mount, Luther, *SM*, 11–19, makes two strong points about this first Beatitude: that it is against the world's honoring of the successful (which is "the greatest and most universal belief or religion on earth," 12), and that the Beatitude requires evangelical faith to be rightly appropriated. On this second point, Luther attacks the Anabaptists who believed that Jesus in this Beatitude required the leaving of house, home, wife, and children: "No, he does not want such crazy saints. This is what [this Beatitude] means: In our heart we should be able to leave house and home . . . [be] willing to be poor here and pay no attention to temporal goods." Only the Holy Spirit and faith can create the attitude of the First Beatitude in the heart. The Beatitudes are all fruits of faith. "So this is what it means [Luther concludes]: that man is called 'spiritually poor,' not because he has no money or anything of his own, but because he does not covet it or set his comfort or trust upon it as though it were his kingdom of heaven." Is this bourgeois or balanced?

2. The Second Beatitude (B 2), 5:4

"God bless those who mourn, because *they* will be comforted."

"He has sent me to bind up the brokenhearted, . . . to comfort all who mourn" (Isa 61:1–2). "Go through the city, through Jerusalem, and put a mark upon the foreheads of the men who sigh and groan over all the abominations that are committed in it" (Ezek 9:4). "[Woe to those] who drink wine in bowls, and anoint themselves with the finest oils, but are not grieved over the ruin of Joseph" (Amos 6:6). The mourning of Ezekiel and Amos is particularly a mourning for the foul state of the unjust people of God.

We are usually warned in advanced commentaries against psychologizing this verse into meaning the mourning of only our sin. The Beatitudes (like all Jesus' teachings) are larger than the individual disciple's psyche. The very absence of an object of mourning in Jesus' Beatitude should warn us against supplying too quickly what is not offered (Lohm., 84–85; Grund., 124).

First, the simple fact of being in mourning, of being grief-stricken, is blessed. The participial form of the verb heightens the *state* of the experience. It is not those who have mourned, but it is those who (now) mourn, and even more specifically (participially), it is those who *are* mourning, who have this blessing. On Jesus' authority, in deep sadness we are in God's hands.

But Jesus beatifies mourning, not moping (cf. especially 6:16–18). He does not counsel the long face. He does, however, bless real sadness, a state that can as easily coexist with an outwardly happy life as can all the other normal contradictions of living. There is even something to be said for the beatific truth that the deepest joy resides in persons with deepest sadness. Sadness and joy are not mutually exclusive, they are often mutual conditions. (Much folk music lives from this strange but strong combination.) Jesus lends his authority to the perception that it is precisely those for whom sadness is deep that God is real (cf. Eccl 7:2–4).

Luther, *SM*, 19–21: "So also a man is said to 'mourn and be sorrowful'—not if his head is always drooping and his face is always sour and never smiling; but if he does not depend on having a good time and living it up, the way the world does, which yearns for nothing but having sheer joy and fun here, revels in it, and neither thinks nor cares about the state of God or men. . . . Therefore simply begin to be a Christian, and you will soon find out what it means to mourn and be sorrowful. . . . Outwardly, too, refresh yourself and be as cheerful as possible. Those who mourn this way are entitled to have fun and to take it wherever they can so that they do not completely collapse for sorrow."

With these qualifications, it is legitimate to suggest objects of mourning so long as we do not absolutize any one object and delegitimize all others. Schlatter, *Der*, 134–35, points out that Israel "died hard," that its mourning wall in Jerusalem symbolizes a profound fact: that it is mourning in its classic and deepest sense, the mourning of death, that is comforted here. Others suggest that the mourning meant by Jesus is the mourning evoked by God's commandments when heard honestly, specifically mourning our sinful nature (Str.-B., 1:195). This interpretation has the strength of coordination with the first Beatitude and with the context of the sermon itself. Schlatter's objection (*Der*, 135) that Israel was not taught to mourn its sin but to despise it, has the strength of moral seriousness, but the psalmists both despise *and* mourn sin (e.g., Pss 32 and 51). And is there any true despising of sin that does not grieve the fact of sin's presence?

Some apply the mourning here to the disciples' mourning under persecution (Gund., 68–69). Others, with much scriptural support, suggest that the mourning of Jesus' Beatitude is less self-centered; that the mourning meant here is the mourning for Israel or the world and for their sufferings and sins (Jerome, 1:106, for the spiritually dead; Allen, 41, for sin in Israel; Schniewind, 43, for all who suffer; Guelich, 81, for the disenfranchised, contrite, and bereaved). It is of most importance that we simply appreciate Jesus' awarding the unhappy and not the happy with his Father's comfort. For a second time Jesus puts himself on the side of the outsiders, those who don't make it, the failures. This, too, is gospel—and mission.

Scripture in both Testaments sharply contrasts godly grief, which looks to God in its need, and worldly grief, which laments only one's own loss. See, e.g., the following texts: "They do not cry to *me* from their heart, but they wail upon their beds; for grain and wine they gash themselves, they rebel against me" (Hos 7:14). "Godly grief produces a repentance that leads to salvation and brings no regret, but worldly grief produces death. For see what earnestness this godly grief has produced in you" (2 Cor 7:9–11). However, as Tholuck (in Beng., 1:103) correctly sees, Jesus' Blessing embraces "all mourners, even in earthly sorrow, who hope in God."

3. The Third Beatitude (B 3), 5:5
"God bless the gentle, because *they* will be awarded the earth."

The gentle (or meek) are the poor in spirit. The words are synonymous (see, e.g., Grund., *tapeinos*, TWNT, 8:6–7; Allen, 40–42; Gund., 69). The gentle are literally those who make no claims for themselves before God or other people—*die Anspruchslose* (in many German commentaries), *les doux* (in French commentaries, e.g. Bonn., 55–56). They are "the powerless" (Schw., 89–90), those unable to be aggressive (McK., 70), the oppressed (Schn., 42–43), particularly the unbitter oppressed (Mey., 121)—again, the quiet in the land. "The meek are they, to whom in all their good deeds, in all the things they do well, nothing is pleasing but God; to whom in all the evils they suffer, God is not displeasing" (Aug., *Serm.*, 31(81):3:354).

In all these senses the gentle are the weaker or unraised consciousnesses in the community. We rightly feel in our time that the poor must organize to claim their rights, that even Christians ought less condescendingly to do things *for* the poor, and that the propertied classes should simply learn how to get out of the way (cf. Gutiérrez, *A Theology of Liberation*, chaps 2, 10, 12). Charity is in bad odor; justice is the agenda. I think these convictions can live with our text, which at first seems to say quite the opposite: "Blessed are those who do *not* claim their rights, because *they* will be awarded the earth."

As citizens deserving full human rights, all workers must mobilize to claim their rights, to form unions and cooperatives, to strike if necessary, and to do everything within human responsibility to obtain a just measure of the community's power. These convictions are the blessed legacy of the Enlightenment and its great revolutions (1776, 1789). But Jesus' concern here (as usually) is for those left out. What of those who cannot organize, who are not allowed to strike, or who are physically, socially, or psychically deficient? What of the still degraded, the brainwashed, the spiritless, even the Uncle Toms or the cowed—those who either cannot or will not put up a fight? Are they outside the pale, enemies of the revolution, parasites on the body proletariat needing excision, the weak link in the chain requiring some kind of final solution, class enemies of the Movement who forever postpone the hour of liberation and so must be cashiered?

Zealots of all times and kinds have thought this way. For example, capital enterprise and its toady the success seminar are far from praising the unaggressive, the timid, or those who do not claim all they can get. Here extremes meet: both the new socialist man and the new and old capitalist entrepreneur agree that it is the aggressive, not the meek, who inherit the earth. In both cases, it is those who fight for their rights, not those who waive them, who get them. It is those who push, who (in the favorite word in the literature) *struggle*, who get their piece of land. "For no one possesses this earth here below by gentleness, but only by pride" (Jero., 1:106).

For a third time in the Beatitudes it appears that Jesus simply picks up the pieces. First to the dependent poor, then to the grief-stricken, and now to the unaggressive, Jesus gives everything: God's kingdom, God's comfort, and God's green earth. Yet everyone else knows that it is the psychically and spiritually self-confident (not the spiritually impoverished), the positive and possibility thinkers (not the mourners), and the dynamically assertive (not the gentle) who really get things and who get things done on earth. The gentle may inherit heaven—both the entrepreneur and the revolutionary will give the gentle heaven—but not the earth. Yet Jesus gives them the earth.

Jesus himself is the best definition of gentleness, particularly at his trial (Matt 26–27). We do not exactly see weakness there, but we do not see many claims either, and not a great deal of aggression. The overall impression of Jesus on trial is an impression of poise. It is a poise born of not having to assert oneself in order to be strong. It is the poise of faith. There is a meekness that is almighty and a gentleness that is strong. In a world threatened by nuclear holocaust macrocosmically and by the destruction of the family microcosmically the great need of the age is gentle-men and gentle-women. The third Beatitude's people are the hope of God's earth.

The promise of the *earth* in this Beatitude points to one of the most breathtaking facts in Scripture: that this earth is to be the sphere of the kingdom of God, this renewed earth, but *this earth* (like our renewed bodies at the resurrection, but our bodies nonetheless). (Cf. Schw., 90.)

If it is true that in the first three need Beatitudes we are not so much called to *will* degrading poverty, heartbrokenness, or powerlessness—these are ordinarily givens rather than choices—we are clearly called by these three Beatitudes to *be willing to be* abysmally poor, heartbroken when these are given to us. (Luther's exposition of the Beatitudes.) We are also called to care for all such.

The first three Beatitudes form a trinity of persons for whom Jesus lives, and they are all the *little* people. The fourth Beatitude also honors the needy (the starving for righteousness) and is at the same time a bridge to the second trinity of persons whom Jesus especially blesses (the merciful, the pure, and the peacemakers), and they are all *servant* people.

4. The Fourth Beatitude (B 4), 5:6

"God bless those who hunger and thirst for righteousness, because *they* are the ones who will be satisfied."

This is the last of the first series of Blessings: the need Beatitudes of faith. All four of these introductory Beatitudes present the blessed as persons *in need:* lacking in (a) spirit, (b) happiness, (c) power, and now (d) righteousness. It is to these—the dispirited, the unhappy, the powerless, and the consciously (or penitently) unrighteous—that Jesus gives his promise. In fact, properly understood, the first two need Beatitudes cannot be *done* at all. In both, the blessed are victims. How does one *do* poverty in spirit or heartbrokenness without self-contortion or caricature? The fact that one cannot do the first two Beatitudes in a sermon that has as its focus the *doing* (and not merely the wanting to do) of God's will, points to a reality of first importance: Jesus' mercy precedes Jesus' demand.

"Jesus first appeared [in this sermon], not making a demand, but offering succour, his first concern [was] not the exaction of obedience, but the proclamation of a blessing (4:23ff; 5:3–11)" (Davies, 96). The salvation of the Red Sea precedes the demand of Sinai (*ibid.*, 119; similarly, G. Barth, 123–25; McArthur, 72, 125; Grayston, "Sermon on the Mount," *IDB*, 4:284).

Students of the Sermon on the Mount are warned in many careful commentaries against moralizing the Beatitudes, especially the introductory four. These

Beatitudes are not to be turned into conditions that, when fulfilled, give grace. Rather, here at the very opening of his sermon Jesus promises divine help to those who cannot help themselves. (The "God helps those who help themselves" rule, found in various forms in the Muslim Koran and in almost all proverbial wisdom, and having some truth—e.g., don't be lazy, one lesson of the Parable of the Talents [25:14–30]—is nevertheless at bottom a rather graceless truth and is not often helpful to troubled persons.) God helps people who need help simply because they need help, not because they meet spiritual conditions. This is the truth that Jesus impresses at the opening of his great sermon. In other words, the Sermon on the Mount begins with divine mercy.

At the present fourth Beatitude we begin to move into the more active moral mood of the remainder of the sermon. The first three Beatitudes do not so much summon our strength as they succor our weakness. There is a healthy externality, physicality, and reality about the first three: they simply bless real people who are down; and the first two in particular do not yet summon to great deeds. They preach gospel before they preach law.

But to hunger and thirst for righteousness in this Gospel is very clearly to hunger and thirst to be a *doer* of the will of God as taught especially in Jesus' commands. Righteousness in Matthew is not only a divine gift, or the divine vindication at the last judgment; it is also and especially right conduct.

Luther, *SM*, 26, especially stresses that the righteousness of Matthew's Jesus is the righteousness of conduct, active rather than passive righteousness. The main modern proponents of this conduct interpretation of righteousness in Matthew are Windisch, 87–88; Schrenk, TWNT, 2:200; Bornkamm, "End," 16–17; and, with force, Strecker, 156–57 and Mohrlang, 227–36.

Yet here the hungry-for-righteousness are blessed not for their possessed but for their desired righteousness; they are blessed not because they are righteous or because they feel righteous but, in harmony with the other need Beatitudes, because they feel starved for and empty of the needed content. Jesus does not bless those conscious of their righteousness, the self-consciously successful, the achievers, the people of the victorious life. Rather, God's promise is given here to people for whom righteousness, victory, vindication, and right conduct seem painfully missing.

The meaning of starvation and thirst here is this: these persons do not believe they can live unless they find righteousness. These people long for what is right; they crave justice; they cannot live without God's victory prevailing; for them right relations in the world are not a luxury or a mere hope, but an absolute necessity if they are to live at all. They long for the vindication of God's justice in the world.

In recent exegesis the word used most frequently to explain the righteousness sought in this Beatitude is the word *vindication*. The blessed here long for the divine vindication of the little people in the day of judgment: McN., 51; Stend., 775; Schw., 91–92; Bonn., 57; Gund., 70. The spirit that seeks this vindication is explained most often as a deep, even physical longing for a painfully missed righteousness. Even older commentators saw this, though less socially: e.g., "It is not sufficient that we merely want righteousness [*iusti-tiam*], unless we have a downright famine for it, which by this very image means that we are never sufficiently righteous persons but that we are always famished for the works of righteousness [*iustitiae opera*]" (Jero., 1:106). "'Who hunger and thirst' [means] who perceive that of themselves they have not the righteousness by which they may approve themselves either to God or man, and eagerly long for it. *Faith* is here described, as is fitting at the beginning of the New Testament" (Beng., 1:104). Along these same lines in modern exegesis, Schn., 44–45; G. Barth, 123–24. "Man's supreme perfection is to be in need of God" (Soren Kierkegaard, in M. Schmidt, "Perfectionism," *ELC*, 3:1880). But are all these interpretations not excessively individual? Righteousness includes justice.

Is the righteousness sought here mainly right relations with people or with God? It is sometimes said that Matthew stresses human relations, Paul divine. Is righteousness in Matthew's Gospel, then, the righteousness of human relations? The two errors most frequently combated in scientific commentaries on this sermon are the errors of psychologism and of imported Paulinism. We have already tweaked the nose of the psychologizing error (for example, the error of turning "poor in spirit" into an achievable psychological or spiritual condition). The Paulinist error is said to occur when we make Matthew's Gospel sound too much like Paul's Epistle to the Romans, when we too promptly "grace" what Matthew means morally, when we transpose Matthean terms and usages into Pauline meanings, so that moral Matthew ends up as gracious Paul. The danger is real, and I may have occasionally or frequently succumbed to it.

I think we can say that Matthew's approach to Christian life is sufficiently different from Paul's to make Matthew really interesting. Classically, Protestants have found Jesus Christ in his grace most deeply in "The Fifth Gospel," the gospel according to Paul. We do not feel that anyone has so succeeded in making clear the underlying sources of life made available by the coming of Jesus Christ as did the great apostle to the gentiles. But we do a disservice to Matthew if we do not allow his distinctive piety to work on us, too. And I will suggest that in the use here of the word "righteousness," the key word also in Paul's anti-Judaistic letters (Romans and Galatians), Matthew and Paul shake hands. It is true that within the entire context of Matthew's Gospel, "righteousness" is primarily a term with moral content; this meaning is present in Paul, too, but it is secondary in importance. Paul's "righteousness" is supremely the gift of *God*. Matthew's "righteousness" is predominantly a moral righteousness in *disciples* (and the plural "disciples" here and the plural verbs in all the Beatitudes are important and social).

But righteousness both here in the fourth Beatitude and in its other main use in this sermon—"Seek first the kingdom of God and *his* righteousness" (6:33)—is not just disciples' righteousness (though it wants to become that); it is significantly in both texts a *sought* righteousness, given by another. Righteousness in these major Matthean sentences, then, is not, first, an intrinsic righteousness. (In Matthew's Gospel, e.g., the disciples are never called "the righteous." 10:41; 13:43; and 25:37 are not exceptions.) In Palestine, righteousness always had a primarily divine dimension: there was no such thing as a righteous person who was not righteous with God. A righteousness that could be separated from one's relationship with God is unknown to Jewish piety (Schl.); indeed, the indispensable foundation for human or social righteousness was a person's right relation with God (see, for example, the sequence in the Ten Commandments, Exod 20, Deut 5).

In turn, any righteousness claimed before God that did not show itself in human righteousness or social justice brought down prophetic wrath (see especially Amos).

Matthew's Jesus will unforgettably hammer away at this prophetic requirement of personal and social righteousness in text after text. In this Gospel only the truly godly and humane get into the kingdom (e.g., 5:20). In Paul's gospel, however, God "justifies the *un*godly" (Rom 4:5).

It is just here, however, that Matthew approaches Paul, for as we have seen in all the need Beatitudes it is precisely the unright or unrighted who are righted, it is the out who are brought in, and now it is those who want a righteousness they do not have who are promised it. To say this is not to Paulinize Matthew; it is to see Paul and Matthew meeting at center: *God* is the giver of the kingdom and its righteousness. This kingdom is still largely future, but in Jesus' Word the kingdom breaks into now. All four need Beatitudes say this; all four Beatitudes—now I audaciously Paulinize—preach justification by grace; all four give God to those who are unable to get God by themselves.

But it would be fair to Matthew to stress that the righteousness longed for in his Gospel is not only heaven-sent (Paul's great contribution); it is also and distinctively earth-centered (Matthew's great contribution). Paul colors righteousness sky blue, dignifying its source; Matthew colors it earth brown, honoring its goal. Paul the doctor of divine grace and Matthew the doctor of human mercy meet at center: in their deep appreciation for the gift of God. But one teaches in an unparalleled way that gift's source, the other that gift's end: both are needed, both canonical, both Christian.

So we do not Paulinize Matthew when we say that the righteousness of which Jesus speaks here is a righteousness that is out of human reach and that comes as a gift. But we are most assuredly Matthean when we say that the righteousness sought here, in a way that I do not believe Paul would have felt safe to say, is a human righteousness, a rightness of relationship with all reality, especially with other people. This righteousness comes perfectly when the kingdom comes finally; it comes provisionally when the kingdom comes evangelically through Jesus' disciple-creating Word.

More than is the case in the first two Beatitudes, the fourth Beatitude's hunger for righteousness can be prayed for. (Can—should—one ever pray to be spiritually or physically impoverished or to be brought to grief? I think only a false theology of the cross teaches these kinds of mortification. The first two Beatitudes cannot usually, in their root meanings, be prayed for. The third Beatitude—gentleness—can. The fourth—passion for righteousness—must.) And so we find ourselves in the Beatitudes *in motion:* from the margin in the first two need Beatitudes, toward the center in the last two; then, in turn, from a kind of fate in these four need Beatitudes to a kind of responsibility in the following four help Beatitudes; from a being completely thrown upon God, helplessly, toward a being completely given to people, helpfully. The fourth Beatitude is the bridge connecting the God-directed need Beatitudes of faith (B 1–4) to the world-directed help Beatitudes of love (B 5–8).

Guelich, 84, reviews the three main interpretations of *righteousness* in Matthew: (a) as vindication, (b) as divine grace, and (c) as conduct. Righteousness as the divine vindication is the most neglected interpretation in modern preaching. On the whole, I feel that the danger in the interpretation of the fourth Beatitude is the danger of being insufficiently eschatological, by which I mean being insufficiently heavenly-minded, insufficiently awaiting the great return of Christ with the full kingdom of God and with his righteous judgments and vindications in the whole world and church. Guelich, 109–10, makes this point with reference to the preaching of the Beatitudes generally: "Even within the Church one generally hears the Beatitudes preached as exhortations for Christian conduct. Rare is the occasion when one hears any of the Beatitudes without being left with a sense of guilt or inadequacy. . . . [But] the Beatitudes are viewed by Matthew as Jesus' declaration, an announcement of congratulations, in the sense of Isaiah 61:1 rather than [as] a demand for conduct."

I would only say that Guelich's final phrase—"rather than [as] a demand for conduct"—should be altered to read "rather than as *only* a demand for conduct," since there is a moral cast to almost every word of Matthew's Jesus, and it is to the credit of Windisch, Strecker, and Mohrlang that they emphasize this. Schniewind, 45–46, believes that the reason for the prevailingly moralistic interpretation of the Beatitudes is the forgetting of God: "When the Beatitudes have been turned into a list of human virtues it is because Christian preaching has largely forgotten the final question of God. Precisely 'Christian virtues' have often characterized a warped and powerless Christianity that lacks the joyfully fruitful deed. . . . But the Beatitudes do not give us virtues that people are supposed to practice; they give us a posture that comes from God." (While Schniewind's emphases are correct, Matthew's Jesus gives Beatitudes that are *also* virtues to be practiced, esp. B 3–8.)

In my opinion, the most well-rounded study of the Beatitudes—especially the first Beatitudes in their original, pre-Matthean form—is the multivolumed work of the French scholar, Fr. Jacques Dupont. Here are Dupont's balanced conclusions, 2:50–51, 90, which I commend: Jesus' original opening Beatitudes were all meant to describe people in miserable situations; they were not in the first instance intended as descriptions of persons with praiseworthy spiritual dispositions. Dupont goes on to point out that commentaries often transfer the beneficiaries of the Beatitudes from the social to the spiritual plane because they do not want to see the Beatitudes treated as social manifesto rather than religious message.

"We do not doubt the essentially religious signification of the Beatitudes," Dupont summarizes, "but we do not believe that it is possible to express that [religious] signification by a psychologizing exegesis that discovers in the Beatitudes a simple exhortation to certain attitudes of the soul." In the Beatitudes, he believes, we find instead a proclamation of the divine design of salvation, a revelation of the grace of God. "Parenesis [i.e., ethic] is not the only way to have a religious value." The parenetic (ethical) note is unquestionably dominant in the Beatitudes as they have been edited now by Matthew; but the original, unedited form of the Beatitudes (as found particularly in Luke 6) follows a model quite different from Matthew's. The "great reversals" heard in the original Beatitudes ought to be taken seriously: the kingdom of God belongs to the despised weak people who are unable to defend themselves. The marvelous consolation of the world to come is promised not to those mildly uncomfortable with the present world who seek refuge in a dream, but to people who suffer, weep, and sigh. "'God shall wipe away every tear from their eyes'" (Rev 7:17).

The Beatitudes turn the value-systems of the world upside down. "The blessedness of which Jesus speaks," Dupont concludes, "is attached precisely to situations that the world judges disastrous. It is people really and concretely miserable whom Jesus declares blessed. To search here for a pious exhortation to detachment or confidence in God would be to evacuate the paradox and finally to justify the judgment of the world. . . . Let us content ourselves with establishing that the Beatitudes can have a religious sense without having to make the terms 'the poor,' 'the afflicted,' and 'the famished' (cf. Luke 6:20–21] mean anything else than what these terms naturally describe." Thus far Dupont.

B. The Help Beatitudes of Love (B 5–8), 5:7–12

In the second set of Beatitudes the human will is required as vigorously as in the earliest need Beatitudes it was not. The help Beatitudes, without ever leaving their rootage in the divine gifts of the need Beatitudes and presupposing those gifts, definitely focus on the disciples' moral responsibilities. Good theology will always believe and teach that even the Beatitudes of moral responsibility (B 5–8) are *Beatitudes*, that is, divine blessings and thus, in their depth, divine gifts. But it is the Jesus of Matthew who more seriously than any other biblical figure enlists his disciples in the working-out of God's gift of salvation in human, moral, and social terms.

Guelich, 115, notices that "the function of these additional Beatitudes [i.e., B 5–8, Matt 5:7–12] appears to be primarily introductory." Indeed these active Beatitudes of love introduce the antithesis-commands that immediately follow. "Blessed are the merciful" prepares us for the Monday Command of Mercy; "Blessed are the pure in heart" introduces us to the twin Tuesday and Wednesday Commands of Purity and Fidelity; and then "Blessed are the peacemakers" (with "Blessed are [the] persecuted," the active and the passive sides of a single reality) serves as the perfect motto for the final troika of the Thursday, Friday, and Saturday Commands of Truth, Peacemaking, and Enemy Love. (We can even say that the Fourth Beatitude, "Blessed are those who hunger and thirst for righteousness," introduces us to the introductory Sunday Command of Piety, 5:17–20.)

1. The Fifth Beatitude (B 5), 5:7
"God bless the merciful, because *they* will find mercy."

When we speak of moral Matthew we must always immediately qualify the word "moral." The fundamental equation in the Gospel of Matthew, ethically, is this: moral = merciful. When I think of the moral I ordinarily think of a certain grim seriousness—of dispassion rather than compassion, of coolness rather than warmth, of contraction rather than extension. And this thinking is sometimes correct, as we will see. But the morality of Matthew's Jesus is predominantly the morality of extension, of width, of forgiving. The gospel merciful are the understanding, the under-standing, those who put themselves under others to support them, to serve them, and to be sensitive to them.

What is morality? In Matthew it is first of all having a heart, showing mercy. Twice in this Gospel Jesus cites the great Hosea 6:6 text, "I want mercy, not sacrifice" (9:13; 12:7). There is a piety that hardens, that makes one more severe with others the more one has learned to be severe with oneself. This is a frequent route of sacrifice-centered, disciplinary, and perfectionist or higher-life (and some consciousness-raising) ethics. But the first test of obedience to *Jesus'* ethic is not whether obedience makes one morally tougher but whether it makes one humanly tenderer—merciful.

The promise given to the Beatitude of mercy is, surprisingly, mercy. This is the only Beatitude in which the promise corresponds exactly to the state.

In the need Beatitudes we felt ourselves without mercy and empty, but we got mercy; now in the help Beatitudes it is the mercy-*full*, those who give what in the need Beatitudes they were given, who are blessed. Fullness of received mercy exists to be passed on, not stored up. Everywhere in the teaching of Jesus the test (and even sometimes, reflexively, the source) of one's relation with God is one's relation with other people. The deep source of one's relation with God, to be sure, can only be God. But once God has delivered mercy to believers, God intends for believers to deliver this mercy on to others. When they do they are rewarded with still more of God and God's mercy. Mercy begets mercy, which in turn begets still more mercy.

The merciful are those "who come to the aid of the needy" (Aug., *LSM*, 15), those "who are not only prepared to put up with their own troubles [B 1–4], but also take on other peoples' [troubles]" (Cal., 1:171). The beautiful gospel fact, as Schlatter, *Das*, 52, has shown is this: people who are poor (B 1), troubled (B 2), meek (B 3), and repentant (B 4), are precisely those who learn to have a heart for the fall and need of others, B 5, while it is the curse of the rich and satisfied that their situations make them harder toward others.

But, and here is the gospel in the Beatitudes in general and in this Beatitude in particular, "once the outstretched hand of mercy has been grasped [B 1–4], the selfsame grace, according both to gospel teaching and personal experience, creates in us the will to good and to show mercy" (Windisch, 177). It is very important to realize here that Jesus "is declaring, not exhorting, the 'merciful' to be 'blessed'" (Guel., 89). But gospel declaring becomes also exhorting, and we must learn to hear both from Matthew's Jesus.

"Blessed are the merciful, for *they* [emphasized] shall receive mercy" also means that the *un*merciful and the *un*forgiving will *not* receive mercy or forgiveness, and this fearful corollary is taught in several emphatic places by Matthew's Jesus: in the fifth petition of the Lord's Prayer (". . . *as* we forgive our debtors") and in Jesus' single postscript commentary on the Lord's Prayer (6:12, 14–15), implicitly in the warning to judge not (7:1–2), and explicitly in the Parable of the Unforgiving Servant (18:21–35), where failure of a forgiven person to be forgiving resulted in the once-forgiven person's condemnation.

Salvation or forgiveness is unmerited and by grace (the first four Beatitudes, and see 18:25–27 specifically), but where this salvation and forgiveness are not then passed on to others there is judgment (this Beatitude, 18:28–35, and all the texts mentioned above). Being a merciful, forgiving, or loving person is not a condition for God's grace, but it is a necessary consequence. Only this conclusion makes sense of this fifth Beatitude, of the fifth petition of the Lord's Prayer, and of Matthew's entire moral Gospel.

2. The Sixth Beatitude (B 6), 5:8

"God bless the pure in heart, because *they* will see God."

It is surprising to see what Jesus blesses. The rabbis of Jesus' time blessed especially the study of the Torah, and then faithfulness in observing it, most visibly on the Sabbath and then particularly in all sorts of carefully prescribed good works. But in all the Beatitudes, remarkably, it is difficult to put one's finger on a specific *activity* that is blessed, on any concrete doing, like Scripture study, or like social work, or even like kneeling in prayer. In the Beatitudes God blesses people at center where they live. This absence of concreteness in the Beatitudes is all the more surprising when we realize how concrete Jesus is everywhere else. But in the Beatitudes Jesus does not bless persons at their hands so much as he blesses them at their heart.

"Heart" (*lēb*, *kardia*) in Hebrew psychology is, literally, human center, the home of personal feeling, willing, and thinking (heart, will, and mind are all covered by the biblical term "heart"). We can translate "pure in heart," therefore, as "clear at center," meaning that the personal center is directed toward God.

"Because *they* will see God." These centered persons will be given the inestimable gift of the knowledge of God. How? By clearer knowledge of Jesus. Jesus' doctrinal ministry does not teach the expectation of theophanies (Schl.). Instead, "*only the Son* knows the Father and those to whom *the Son* chooses to reveal him." Therefore, Jesus continues in the same passage, "come to *me* . . ., learn from *me*" (11:27–29). The disciple is promised revelation of the Father (in the important eleventh chapter passage) not beyond Jesus, but in him and from him, exclusively.

In this sixth Beatitude of purity we are very near to the teaching of the Gospel of John on the Holy Spirit of truth (see the Paraclete or Comforter texts on the Holy Spirit, scattered throughout John 14–16). In John's Gospel, the command-keeping Christian (meaning the serious believer) is promised the Spirit of truth and is particularly promised the Spirit's gifts (1) of making the person of Jesus more real and clear, (2) of reminding disciples of Jesus' teachings, and (3) of showing them fresh ways to apply Jesus' truth to new situations. Matthew's Gospel teaches this truth in a moral way by saying that every struggle for purity through obedience to Jesus' commands is an investment in a clearer knowledge of God through Christ.

Believing hearers of this Beatitude know themselves enlisted by it. Purity is not only a gift; all Christians who live in the world know that purity is also a struggle. In the help Beatitudes the disciples' will is vigorously seized. The power for purity of heart is supplied by the in-breaking kingdom that comes through the in-press of Jesus' words. But the will thus mobilized can and will grasp the power given. And the promise makes the effort of purity worthwhile: knowing God!

Augustine, *Serm.*, 3(53):7–11:267–69, believes that the purity of heart blessed here is faith, according to Acts 15:9 ("purifying their hearts by faith")—not just any "faith," but Paul's sincere "faith which works by love" (Gal 5:6), especially love toward others (so also Schw., 93). The whole Reformation was a struggle to get Augustine's understanding of Paul exactly right here, because both vapid (or intellectualistic) faith on the one hand, and "faith plus" as a means of salvation, on the other, are subevangelical conceptions.

Commentators, in my opinion, are often too eager to assure readers that the purity of heart in this Beatitude is not, at center, sexual purity (e.g., Green, 77–78, though see here Green's good remarks about Jewish *yetzer* and Freud's *libido;* pro Goulder, 259). But since Jesus in his commands that follow gives two especially sexual commands (C 3–4) we can assume that the purity Jesus blesses is at least sexual. This Beatitude, in fact, serves as the introduction to and as the motto for the Tuesday Command of Purity (5:27–30), the Wednesday Command of Marital Fidelity (vv 31–32), and perhaps even for the Thursday Command of Truthtelling (vv 33–37).

Calvin, 1:171–72, intriguingly, gives a *commercial* interpretation to this Beatitude, contrasting sharp dealing with honesty in business. The promise of seeing God is variously understood by interpreters, but there is near unanimity among scientific commentators that this seeing refers, as Jesus' future tense shows, to future and final things: seeing Jesus at his Second Coming (Gund., 71), finding acceptance by God at the last judgment (Guel., 91), or experiencing admission into God's presence (Bacor 272; Bonn., 57).

The two most fascinating interpretations of this Blessing in my reading were the knowledge of Christ interpretation of Schlatter, adopted above in my exposition, and the sovereignty of the Word of God interpretation of Luther, a portion of which I will give below. Schlatter, *Das,* 53, says in summary: We will "see God" in the sense that God will reveal his glory in and on Jesus; i.e., God will reveal Jesus Christ's relation to our lives, church, and world in a new way, a way in which we had not yet known him. But Schlatter's Jesus promises this new eye of faith only when we guard our hearts from all that stains and separates us from God. Luther, *SM*, 32–38, insists, that the purity Jesus praises here is not Jesus' call away from unclean occupations (such as the government's necessary punishing of criminals, farmers' carrying manure, or parents' changing the pants of dirty children) to "pure" occupations in so-called spiritual callings. Instead, Jesus' purity of heart means "you should be on your guard against any ideas that you call your own, as if they were just so much mud and filth." The pious person, who is meditating on deity according to one's own ideas about deity, for example, is sitting (in Luther's vivid language) in a pit of dung. "For he is proceeding on his own ideas without the Word of God."

Luther continues, "What is meant by a 'pure heart' is this: [a heart] that is watching and pondering what God says and replacing its own ideas with the Word of God." So long as a person "sticks to these two—namely, the Word of faith toward God, which purifies the heart, and the Word of understanding, which teaches him what he is to do toward his neighbor in his station—everything is pure for him, even if with his hands and the rest of his body he handles nothing but dirt." Not everything considered dirty is dirty. For example, "so it is when [a man] looks at his own wife or fondles her, as the patriarch Isaac did (Gen 26:8), which a monk regards as disgusting and defiling." Jesus' promise that the pure in heart will "see God" means to Luther, evangelically, that the pure in heart will see God's fatherly, friendly heart through faith; whoever believes, and yet regards God as angry, is not seeing God correctly. "In Scriptural language 'to see His face' means to recognize Him correctly as a gracious and faithful Father, on whom you can depend for every good thing. This happens only through faith in Christ. . . . It is a wonderful thing, a treasure beyond every thought or wish, to know that you are standing and living in the right relation to God."

3. The Seventh Beatitude (B 7), 5:9

"God bless the peacemakers, because *they* will be called the children of God."

We can almost translate the key word here, "peacemakers," with the word "wholemakers." Peace, in Scripture, is a situation of comprehensive welfare. In English the word *peace* usually refers either to an inner tranquillity—peace of mind—or to an outward state—the absence of war. But biblical *shalom* conveys the picture of a circle; it means comprehensive well-being in every direction and relation. The person in the center of the circle is related justly to every point on the circumference of the circle. While the English word *peace* tends either to be a tiny inward *point* or a very external *space*—i.e., either a period or a line—the Hebrew word depicts a circle that embraces the whole community, internally and externally, and puts persons who are at peace in right relations with the whole world of realities. If we could translate "blessed are the circle makers" and make sense, we would. To bring peace, in Scripture, is to bring community. Peacemakers are reconcilers.

There are many unnoticed, unheralded people in the world who are beneficently at work at some particular point in the distorted circle of life; all those who give their lives to rounding the circle, creating community, and bringing reconciliation are dignified by Jesus with membership in the family of God. (Cf. Matt 25:31–46 where this astonishingly "liberal" truth is exactly the point.) Everyone's part in the sphere of life is crooked or warped at some point—for many today it is at the point of social well-being. Where persons work to round out that warped sphere, specifically to bring jobs and justice and to eliminate poverty, they are called children of God by Jesus. Isn't this salvation by works? It is very near it, indeed. But we must notice *who* says this Beatitude and *how* he interprets it in the rest of his Gospel. Meanwhile, with all its difficulties, "Blessed *are* the peacemakers, . . . they *shall* be called the children of God."

We are being told increasingly by liberation Christians that we bring solid peace today when we enlist people in warfare against evil structures. They point out that conciliatory work is often palliative, and that what we need is struggle, confrontation, and partisan engagement (Gutiérrez, *A Theology of Liberation,* chap 2, "Liberation and Development"). I do not believe that this liberation position can be contested from the biblical perspective of *shalom.* For as I have suggested, biblical peace is hardly touched when it is described as inward tranquillity; the circle of right relations that is peace will often, in a crooked world, be relations that pass through struggle and confrontation.

Where liberation conflict becomes hate, however, the Christian community protests. Indeed, it will be the disciples' responsibility to inseminate liberation movements with the ingredient of heart and to show how heart can be present without diminishing vitality or partisan commitment. The call to vigorous encounter with unjust structures and persons in Gutiérrez's theology of liberation is a serious call to peacemaking, but in an unexpected way. Everything depends, of course, on whether the conflict proceeds in a christic, nonviolent way, *or* whether the real momentum of the movement is captured by forces not afraid to use the violence that is used against them. The Christian conflict will in present circumstances have to be as much against one's overzealous fellow conflictualists as against the enemy. For the enemy is invariably as much we ourselves as it is others, and any strategy that locates all evil outside oneself and outside one's circle ceases to be discipled. Christian conflictualism will be as vigilantly self-critical as it is social-critical.

Especially in chapters 9 and 12 of this Gospel, which consist mainly of conflict stories (even in the technical language of New Testament scholarship), and also in the events leading up to the passion, Jesus' ministry *was conflictual.* Jesus brought a certain peace (contrast 10:34), but this peace rather frequently had to pass through a spiritual war with family, the very devout, and Bible teachers.

Peacemaking for Christians, in other words, is classically defined by the life and death of Jesus. The way Jesus did peace shapes the way we do it. This way was rough. As far as we can tell, Jesus did not seek to conciliate the Pharisees. Jesus had *to argue* with them. What is remarkable and loving about Jesus' relation to the Pharisees is that he apparently gave them much of his time, if only in controversy. Jesus was often obliged to be quite cool toward his opponents, and sometimes even very hot (cf. Matt 23).

But Christians will let Jesus, and not recent or current heroes, determine what conflict is and how it is to be carried out. To substitute other lords of conflict because we think Jesus irrelevant is to commit the romantic, psychologizing error from which we are all trying to escape, the error of believing that Jesus' ministry was mainly spiritual, internal, and individual. (Believe it or not, this is the way the most influential Marxist Christians that I know understand Jesus. Jesus, they say, left political decisions up to us; Jesus was spiritual.) Jesus is Lord, even of conflict, and Lord on this earth, and of our politics, and of the way we do our politics. We will not need to be afraid of conflict if we allow it to occur under the aegis of Jesus. But if conflict goes to school to macho masters rather than to Jesus of Nazareth, if it is success- or effective-centered rather than Sermon-on-the-Mount-centered, if it is "Marxized" more than baptized, it becomes demonic. There is a false conflict just as there is a false irenic, and Christians must fight on both their left and right flanks if they are to remain Christians and be called children of *God*.

Augustine, LSM, 20, is an example of an interpreter who understands Jesus too psychologically, and therefore too individualistically: In peacemakers' internal lives, he writes, "everything is in order and there is no emotion to rebel against reason." (Augustine's recent editor has shown, LSM, 180 n. 21, how the church father later retracted the "everything is in order" perfectionism of this interpretation.) Luther, SM, 40, 43–44, understands this Beatitude in its correct social breadth—the Beatitude is against quarrelsome leaders who want revenge and who fight at the drop of a hat; the Beatitude is against all warmongers. At the same time, Luther brings home the Beatitude to the local congregation, which is the most important front in peacemaking (Bill Creevy): "Be a reconciler and mediator between your neighbors. Carry the best to both sides; but keep quiet about the bad, which the devil has inspired, or explain it the best way you can. But if you must talk about an evil deed, do as Christ said: go straight to the party and admonish (Matt 18:15)."

Why, then, does Luther rail at the Pope? Because, Luther answers, we are to keep quiet for as long as we can; but when evil is manifest, we must speak right up, especially if it is our office. Schlatter, *Das*, 53, recognizes from this Beatitude and from the whole of Jesus' teaching that Jesus wants people to flee fighting and to stop it. But how? Schlatter's evangelical reply is: By means of the preaching, teaching, and living of the gospel, which looses us from our usual preoccupations with our own honor and with earthly things and which makes us obedient to the one Lord. In other words, authentic evangelism is the most effective peacemaking. Stendahl, 775–76, is struck by the nonmilitant character of true disciples of Christ and refers to James 3:18. Many commentators notice that Jesus does not just bless peaceloving or peacewanting, which can remain passive, or even peaceliving, which can remain individual, but peace*making*, which is fully active and social and necessarily involves other people (Barc., 1:109–10; Guel., 91–92). Guelich, 107, is surely correct when he criticizes the evangelical view that sees this Beatitude encouraging a narrowly-defined evangelism of peacemaking between only God and people and not also of people with people. But is he correct when he says "pacifism is nowhere in sight"?

The Rev. Bill Creevy's wide-ranging ministry has made especially clear to Presbyterians that peacemaking is not just stopping violence in order to restore a status quo ante of injustice; rather, peacemaking is necessarily justicemaking, and this takes Christians very far indeed. Creevy is equally convinced and convincing in teaching that peacemaking (which is the uprooting of patterns of violence planted everywhere in the world and in our own lives) best begins (a) in a place where attitudes are changed (b) in such a way that public policy will be changed—eminently in local congregations (remember the ministry of Martin Luther King). See "Peacemaking: The Believers' Calling: The Task Force Report of the 192nd General Assembly (1980) of the UPCUSA," and Pope John XXIII's evangelical *Pacem in Terris*, especially the thematic, "If you want peace seek justice," and the Pastoral Statement of the U.S. Conference of Catholic Bishops, *The Challenge of Peace* (1983). This peacemaking Beatitude is the introduction to and the motto for the Friday and Saturday Commands of Peacemaking and of Love for Enemies (5:38–48).

*   *   *

With the peacemaking Beatitude we have completed the trinity of the main help Beatitudes: mercy, purity, and peace. In each of these, we are called to *help*. In the preceding need Beatitudes certain people *needed* help, but now in the help Beatitudes certain people *give* help. In clear progression the inaugural need Beatitudes called us to faith, and now the central help Beatitudes call us to love—to the love that true faith creates. We are first placed on our knees in faith, then on our feet in love.

It can be said fairly, I think, that a certain post-Reformation exegesis stressed the need Beatitudes too much, emphasizing that the Sermon on the Mount was intended to drive us to our knees, to our sense of need, to our impotence before the law of God. This exegesis did take seriously the almost insuperable difficulty of living the Sermon on the Mount, and it took seriously the central content of the gospel's Cross and Resurrection. Yet Jesus calls us not only to our knees, and the purpose of his sermon is not only to make us feel weak. Half the purpose of his sermon is to set us on our feet again and to give us the strength to go out *and be a help*. The help Beatitudes belong as much to Jesus' teaching as the need Beatitudes, and deserve equal time.

God helps those who cannot help themselves (the need Beatitudes), and he also helps those who try to help others (the help Beatitudes), but he does not in any Beatitude help those who think they can help themselves—an often ungodly and antisocial conception. Jesus wants faith and love. Only faith justifies, only love proves faith real. There is no contradiction between the fact that God helps the helpless (that is God's free mercy) and that he helps the helpful (that is God's justice). The Beatitudes reward not only *helplessness*—Reformation exegesis has always delighted in knowing this; the Beatitudes also reward *helpfulness*—we have been reluctant to see this from a fear, often enough legitimate, that a teaching of merits might creep in. But if we can stick closely to *Jesus'* definition of the righteous deed in the Beatitudes, and see the exact nature of that deed—that it involves people at center and not first at their works—we will be half way to freedom from new legalisms.

The need Beatitudes engage us deeply with God; the help Beatitudes engage us deeply with people. The need Beatitudes enlist us in all that we are not. The help Beatitudes enlist us in all that we are. In the need Beatitudes we are salted (passively); in the help Beatitudes we *are* salt (actively). In the need Beatitudes we are picked up from the earth; in the help Beatitudes we are thrown into it. What happens to us when we hit earth is described in greater detail in the final double Beatitude.

4. The Eighth Beatitude (B 8), 5:10–12

5:10 "God bless those who are persecuted for the sake of righteousness, because *theirs* is the kingdom of heaven."

When we are *really* in the earth we will be put down by it. Jesus' life is exemplary in this connection. It surprises us that the goodness described thus far in the Beatitudes will be rewarded with trouble, for on the whole, human experience would suggest that the better one is the less trouble one has. And yet this Beatitude and the commentary Beatitude that follows teaches that Christians should expect unpopularity if they are Christians. For Christians have to say no often to a hating and impure world, and they will be hated for this. "Bloodthirsty men hate one who is blameless, and the wicked seek his life" (Prov 29:10). We remember two men who took the Christian ethic of nonviolence seriously—Gandhi and King.

In our time even the simplest commitment to the cause of the poor raises the shackles of the Far Right. At the same time, an insistently *Christian* commitment to the poor galls the Far Left. Conservatives dislike the partisan character of the commitment; radicals dislike the nonviolent character. On the one hand it is felt that discipled Christians have sold the gospel out to social gospel interests and no longer really believe in the Lord; on the other hand it is said that such Christians have sold radical commitment out to petty bourgeois class interests and no longer really believe in the Movement. And so Christians, if real, lose both ways.

It is important that we get in trouble for the right reasons: "for righteousness' sake." How can we tell if our persecution is for righteousness' sake? By no other way than by a constant checking with the Word of Jesus in the company of the catholic community that gathers around it.

Jesus then forms a commentary Beatitude for his eighth Blessing in order to clarify his meaning. It is sometimes, though imprecisely, called the ninth Beatitude.

5:11–12 "God bless *you* [for the first time the disciples themselves are explicitly introduced into the sermon] when people ridicule you and persecute you and say all kinds of evil things about you, falsely, because of your devotion to *me* [the first time that Jesus has explicitly put *himself* in the Beatitudes]. Rejoice and be very happy, because your reward is huge in the heavens; this was exactly the way they persecuted the prophets before you."

"Once again," Schweizer, 96, notices, "the passage extols not the strong, who, to the admiration of all, heroically defend their faith, but those who are defamed and go down to ignominious defeat."

In the eighth and commentary Beatitudes, disciples are *victims* again. The Beatitudes have reached full circle. In the first seven Beatitudes we saw Jesus' Blessings going *up*, from the depths of personal poverty and need to the worldwide reaches of helpful mercy and peacemaking (↗). But now, finally, when Christians really get into the world they get into trouble, and they are put *down* again (↘). Yet even here Jesus introduces a measure of the resurrection "up": "Rejoice and be very happy," he commands. Commands! "Joy is not only the experience, but also the duty of a Christian" (Beng., 1:105). "This was exactly the way they persecuted the prophets before you" (v 12c). Being put down for righteousness' sake, then, is proof that we are in the company of the prophets and the real people of God through the ages. Surprisingly, Matthew's Jesus twice elsewhere explicitly calls his disciples, who are the sent people of God, "prophets" (10:41; 23:34).

Bengel, 1:105, in his German Version of the Bible, noted by his editors in the *Gnomon*, has this interesting insight into 5:12c, "for thus they persecuted the prophets who were before you": "'Before you'—he says not 'before us.' For He [Jesus] was before the prophets" (cf. John 8:58). Appropriately, Bultmann, 358, sees Matthew 5:11–12 as containing sayings that raise the stature of Jesus into the divine, as sayings of the exalted one (cf. also Streck., 150).

It is interesting how unobtrusively Jesus in this commentary Beatitude puts his name in the place where, in the eighth Beatitude, the word "righteousness" stood. Righteousness in its depths and Jesus in his person are ultimately the same thing, and so to be persecuted for *righteousness'* sake and to be persecuted for *Jesus'* sake are the same thing. We must nevertheless ruthlessly see through our inherent tendency to put Jesus on our side, since our capacity for self-deception is practically infinite, and we almost always think we are on the side of God. "Every way of a man is right in his *own* eyes, but the Lord weighs the heart" (Prov 21:2).

Calvin, 1:172–73, gives a social-justice interpretation to this Beatitude: Jesus speaks of suffering for righteousness' sake "because in their concern for equity and justice [disciples] oppose evil causes, and defend the good, to the best of their powers." (Barclay, 1:118, explains this cause-and-effect helpfully.) "Justice," in fact, may even be the best translation of this word "righteousness."

A survey of the seven commands that follow the eight Blessings illustrates in practical terms how believers can suffer persecution for righteousness' or justice's sake: in obedience to Scripture, disciples will be called fanatics (C 1); in seeking reconciliation they will be called cowards (C 2); in struggling for sexual purity they will be considered Puritans (C 3); in fidelity to the marriage partner they will be called foolish or out of date (C 4); in speaking only the truth, as simply and unostentatiously as possible, they will be considered obstructionist or unfaithful to the group's success (C 5); in responding nonviolently to provocation they will be called disloyal to the cause or to the country (C 6); and in loving enemies they will be considered traitors by their friends (C 7). Church history gives a fascinating array of examples.

To this Beatitude's promise of the kingdom of heaven, Calvin, 1:173 (with my emphasis), comments: "As throughout this life the way of the godly is most *miserable*, Christ duly lifts our thoughts to hope for the life of heaven." Calvin has been traditionally interpreted as teaching that the predestined have evidence of their election in their successes, lack of misery, and prosperity; his comment on this Beatitude and his entire *Institutes* show that this interpretation is a caricature. See McNeill's comments in his excellent edition of the *Institutes* (LCC 21) at II. x.12 n. 11. Calvin's doctrine of the Christian life agrees with that of the pastoral epistle: "all who desire to live a godly life in Christ Jesus will be persecuted" (2 Tim 3:12) for, among other reasons, according to the wisdom of the Old Testament, "he whose way is straight is an abomination to the wicked" (Prov 29:27).

The connection of this persecution double Beatitude to the preceding peacemaking Beatitude is this: it is not always possible to get peace between warring parties, and thus this Blessing prepares peacemakers for their hard war of persecution (Schl., *Das*, 53). Jesus wants the persecuted to know that their sufferings are not novel, accidental, or absurd, for as the Old Testament shows, God's witnesses have always suffered, and New Testament teaching underlines this fact (cf. Matt 21:33–46; Acts 7:51–53; 1 Pet 4:12). "The unity of the Old and New Testaments is marked by the persistence of human opposition to the witnesses of God" (Bonn., 58).

Summary. The Beatitudes as a Whole: Jesus Saves

None of the Beatitudes, except the commentary Beatitude (B 9, vv 11–12), explicitly mentions Christians. All eight Beatitudes reach into and beyond the church and the Christian name. I do not believe that this fact should be used as grist for the questionable enterprise of theological universalism (i.e., the teaching that all will be saved, independent of faith in Christ). Explicit faith in Jesus Christ, sealed by baptism in the Triune God, is the revealed way of salvation. Yet, the promises of the Beatitudes are universal; they have no explicitly Christian or ecclesial conditions or specifications; they are extraterritorial and immense. We must let Jesus reach wherever he wants—to *all* miserable, grieving, and powerless persons—and these Beatitudes tell us that he does reach them, whether we permit him to or not. Jesus saves.

Schlatter, *Der*, 142, finds the Beatitudes especially helpful because they are promised not only to the church, but describe the help Christ brings to *all* human beings.

The Beatitudes encircle the world. It is interesting that at the very beginning of Jesus' teaching ministry here in chapter 5 and at the very end of his formal teaching ministry in chapter 25 in the famous scene at the last judgment ("inasmuch as you have done this to one of the least of these"), the Matthean Jesus reaches beyond the explicit Christian name. I find this interesting because Matthew in almost every text between chapters 5 and 25 seeks to invite all persons to explicit faith in the very Jesus who says these wide things. Certainly the invitation to faith in Jesus is the center of the gospel. And yet precisely this Gospel, at its outer limits (chapters 5 and 25), reaches in the Word of Jesus beyond the explicit name of Jesus and embraces the extremes of the human condition and all persons in them. There is a Christ-centered universality that is not theological universalism; there is a universal reach of God that does not wipe out Jesus Christ (as theological universalism invariably does). For it is *Jesus* who says chapters 5 and 25; it is *his* promise; and it is only true as his Word and by virtue of his saving work. Jesus saves.

Jesus' central Word still stands true: "No one knows the Father except the Son, and the person to whom the Son chooses to reveal him. . . . Come to *me* . . ." (11:27–28). If anyone is saved it is exclusively by the blood, atoning mediation, and sovereign will of the Lord Jesus Christ. Matthew clearly agrees with John's Jesus that "*No* one comes to the Father except by me" (John 14:6). The impoverished, grief-stricken, and powerless of the Beatitudes will get God not because they properly behaved but because Jesus graciously wills to save such persons. The merciful, pure in heart, and peacemakers will get God not because their mercy, purity, or reconciliation merit God and thus do not need Jesus' meritorious death and resurrection, or because they adequately cooperated with grace, or were sufficiently sincere, or lived up in their own minds to the precepts of their particular religion or to standards of human decency—as much theological universalism (and some theology of liberation) in very Pelagian ways often says (see below, 156; and notice the *surprise* of the saved in Matt 25:46ff; they do *not* feel deserving). The needy (B 1–4) will be helped not because they helped themselves or God by their need but simply because, Jesus reports, they desperately needed help and God wants to help. The helpful (B 5–7) will be savingly helped because Jesus says so. (The Beatitudes are astonishingly conservative *and* liberal.)

This wide mercy is no argument for relaxing Christian mission. We are commanded to bring this deep and wide Word of Jesus Christ to all nations and to disciple everyone we can (28:18–20). The question we are constantly to ask ourselves in the matter of salvation is not, What *can* God do? for he can do anything he wants, by definition; the question is, What has God *commanded*? His command is clear in the Son's Great Commission at the end of this Gospel: "Go and disciple all nations" (Matt 28:19; cf. K. Barth, CD I/1, pp. 54f).

Thus to say that the Beatitudes reach beyond the name of Jesus is only half a truth, for *Jesus* says the Beatitudes (as he also says the story of the last judgment of the helpful and unhelpful at Matt 25:46ff). But the Beatitudes do teach us, clearly, that God's kingdom is at work savingly everywhere in the world wherever there is degradation, grief, and powerlessness (B 1–3), or mercy, purity, and peacemaking (B 5–7). God is not bound by Christians, but Christians are bound by God and his Word. ("God is not bound to the means of grace but we are," is the classic and wonderful formula. Cf. Cal., *Inst.*, IV, i.5.) Jesus *saves*.

Universalism in Liberation Theology

The belief that God reveals himself savingly in general history and in variously identified historical events or truths in this general history, and not exclusively in the history of Jesus Christ and in his church that proclaims his saving history, and that all persons can be saved by their openness to this general revelation and its specific manifestations, is theological universalism. This teaching has been combatted decisively by the church through the centuries, most recently, confessionally, in the appearance of "the German Christians" in the 1930s and their condemnation by *The Theological Declaration of Barmen*, 1934. Since Barmen, the most virile form of the teaching of theological universalism in our time occurs in the powerfully appealing social-justice movement known as liberation theology. I found this theology the most fascinating of the several forms of dynamic Christian faith in the Philippines in the 1960s and 1970s. We may listen to its witness in its best representatives.

Theology starts for liberation Christians not with bookish revelation and church tradition but with *facts* and with questions from the world and history (Gustavo Gutiérrez, *A Theology of Liberation*. Maryknoll, N.Y.: Orbis, 1973, p. 12; José Míguez-Bonino, *Doing Theology in a Revolutionary Situation*. Philadelphia: Fortress, 1975, p. 165); theology is done not from an armchair, but by "sinking roots where the pulse of history is beating at this moment and illuminating history with the word of the Lord of history" (Gut., 15). What is "fact," and where is this pulsating history? For the liberation theologians the great fact is the poor and their oppression, and the where of living history is not so much the traditionally understood churchly proclamation of the gospel, but earthly solidarity with the poor, which solidarity is itself the most authentic proclamation of the gospel. For the Bible reveals a God who reveals himself in historical, not ecclesiastical, events (Gut., 154).

But where in this history do we find *salvation?* We find it in God's ongoing work of *creation* and by our *own* creative and working identification with whatever God is doing in creation to liberate the poor from oppression; in this creative way human beings regenerate themselves: "Salvation—totally and freely given by God, the communion of men with God and among themselves—is the inner force and the fulness of this movement of man's self-generation which was initiated by the work of creation" (Gut., 159; cf. x; Míguez-Bon., 166).

Human beings, therefore, must take their *own* destiny into their own hands as it is offered to them by history, and cease waiting for a church to mediate it to them; *self*-creation and autonomy are the orders of the day, almost the *ordo salutis* (Gut., 173; Míguez-Bon., 166). For the Holy Spirit of God does *not* just dwell in Christians or in the church, but this Spirit dwells in every human being and in all of history: "The Spirit sent by the Father and the Son to carry the work of salvation to its fulfillment dwells in every man" (Gut., 193); "since God has become man, humanity, every man, history is the living temple of God" (Gut., 194). Ernst Bloch has taught us that the Bible is not so much a book about human sin and ecclesiastical salvation as it is a book about humanity's limitless possibilities, and thus when the serpent told the woman that if she ate the fruit "you will be like gods," he was offering liberation and delivering to humanity the fundamental affirmation of the Bible (Bloch in Gut., 240 n. 16).

Thus, practically speaking, we need to uncenter the church's consciousness of herself as the exclusive place of salvation and, Gutiérrez urges, become as sensitive as the early church was to the work of Christ *beyond* the church's frontiers and open to the possibility of salvation at work in every man (Gut., 256). It is not so much the world that needs to be evangelized by the church as, on the contrary, it is the church that must turn back to the world and be evangelized by it, for it is in the *world* that Christ and his Spirit are really present and active (Gut., 260–61).

> In sum, Gutiérrez's liberation theology reaffirms an old truth, freshly dis-
> covered: There is "the possibility of the presence of grace—that is, of the
> acceptance of a personal relationship with the Lord—in all people, be they
> conscious of it or not. . . . an anonymous Christianity . . . a Christianity
> beyond the visible frontiers of the Church. The advent of a 'Christendom
> without the name' . . . [However inadequate these expressions may be, they
> all point] to a reality which is itself indisputable: all men are in Christ effica-
> ciously called to communion with God" (Gut., 71). "Man is saved if he opens
> himself to God and to others, even if he is not clearly aware that he is doing
> so" (Gut., 15, citing the Second Vatican Council's main pronouncements in
> this direction, *Lumen Gentium*, 16, and *Gaudium et Spes*, 3 and 22).
>
> Juan Luis Segundo, S.J., traces the theological roots of this generous uni-
> versalism, autobiographically, in a fascinating excursus in his *Theology and the
> Church* (1985), pp. 73–85 (L. Malevez, K. Rahner). For a sympathetic account
> of Brazilian liberation theology *in situ* with disciples of Leonardo Boff, see
> Jane Kramer, "Letter from the Elysian Fields," *The New Yorker* (March 2,
> 1987), pp. 40–75.

Liberation theology's power is its commitment to the poor. Liberation theology's weakness is its abandonment of evangelical center—the urgent necessity of faith in Jesus Christ, the *only* Savior of the world and of the world's poor and oppressed. When a Protestant reads the largely Roman Catholic liberation literature, especially since the Joseph Cardinal Ratzinger *Instructions* on liberation (1984, 1986) and the passionate responses to them, one is struck with a certain déjà vu: this is, theologically, the Protestant Fundamentalism-Modernism Controversy a half-century later! Both parties in the modern Roman dispute need Augustinian-Reformation theology with its catholic substance and its secular-ethical thrust.

And what, after all, are the real "facts" to which liberation theology appeals, facts beside and beyond biblical revelation? Aren't they, finally, the liberation theologians' politics? Is Jesus a fact worthy of comparison with contemporary facts? One of several? Where is the pulsebeat of history, really? Is Jesus himself not that pulse? Is it profound, is it even true to say, as all liberation theologians seem to say, that "God reveals himself in history," and reveals savingly, when that revelation is not understood as Jesus himself as he came in the flesh (1 John 4; 1 Cor 12)? Isn't a generally or even a specifically understood message of "God reveals himself in history" precisely the error of all political faiths, from the Zealots in the first century to the "Movement of German Christians" and civil religion in the twentieth? Do we regenerate ourselves (!) by joining current movements in our countries? Is that Christian

faith? Is the Holy Spirit dwelling in everyone, according to the witness of the New
Testament? Is all history the temple of God? Isn't the serpent's message of autonomy, "you shall be like gods," the message of the *enemy* of God, and isn't Bloch's
calling this Genesis text the fundamental affirmation of the Bible (and Gutiérrez's
approval of this designation) not instead a sober indication of the bankruptcy of this
understanding of the Bible and of this theology's theological moorings?

Where in the early church, outside her weaker teachers, was there the alleged
sensitivity to the saving work of Christ *beyond* the church's frontiers? Isn't the early
church in her finest representatives—Ignatius, Irenaeus, Athanasius, Chrysostom,
Augustine—not, rather, characterized precisely by her blazing christocentrism and
the corollary, love of the catholic church? Did the early church sit as loosely to the
doctrines of the exclusivity of Christ and the cruciality of the church as these
liberation authors say? Did the early church actually preach salvation by identification with *creation?* Did she really proclaim the possibility of salvation at work in
every man, independently of the church's message? Justin Martyr's "spermatic
Word" and some of Origen's universalistic formulations *(apokatastasis pantōn)* did
teach these doctrines, but don't we see *these* teachers and teachings as warnings of
how *not* to do theology? "Salvation is the *Lord's.*"

No, this message of anonymous Christianity will not work, and the church needs
to be warned again of the latest siren calls of the newest universalism on the world's
stage. We do not recognize the voice of this shepherd (John 10).

The subtleties of liberation theology are removed when we listen to North America's more outspoken liberation theologians:

> God's presence does not appear just in one time and place "once for all," but
> wherever reconciliation is established and man glimpses his unity and the
> unity of the world with its transcendent foundation and meaning. A religious
> culture may pick out a particular place where this appearing is seen
> "normatively"; i.e., Jesus or the Torah or Buddha, but this doctrine of
> "incarnation" is not just "about" this one place or person, but this one place or
> person operates as a norm for discerning the nature of this "presence"
> wherever it happens. . . .
>
> It seems that that last heresy that must be let go of is precisely that
> "Christocentrism" that presumes that all that is messianic and revolutionary
> can be mediated only by the historical Judaeo-Christian tradition. We must
> perhaps be willing finally to see that God is the God of all men and is reveal-
> ing himself to all men in their histories (Rosemary Radford Ruether, *Libera-
> tion Theology* [N.Y.: Paulist Press, 1972], pp. 10, 191).

Cf. Hans Küng, *On Being a Christian* (N.Y.: Doubleday, 1976), 185–91, 337f, 505f, 555–
70, who shows that Jesus was not a Zealot (and so was not an ancestor of, though he was
near to, liberation theology); but then, with Karl Rahner, *Theological Investigations*
(1966), 5:97–134, building on openings provided by the New Testament and the Second
Vatican Council (especially on the Church [*Lumen Gentium*], [1964], 16), Küng, with
many other progressives in and outside the Roman Catholic Church, boldly concludes:
"Non-Christians too as observers of the law can be justified. In fact, then, there is salvation outside the Church. In addition to particular, there can be seen a general, universal
salvation history" (91; see also in this vein, his 93, 97, 103f, 125, 167, 394–96 [contrast
99 and 396], 447).

But on the contrary, see our churches' Confessions. *The Theological Declaration of Barmen* (1934), Thesis one: "'I am the way, and the truth, and the life; no one comes to the Father, but by me (John 14:6). 'Truly, truly, I say to you, he who does not enter the sheepfold by the door but climbs in by another way, that man is a thief and a robber. . . . I am the door; if anyone enters by me, he will be saved' (John 10:1, 9). [Then, in my translation, the thesis continues:]

"Jesus Christ, as he is attested for us in Holy Scripture, is the one Word of God which we have to hear and which we have to trust and obey in life and in death.

"We reject the false teaching that suggests that the church could and should have to recognize as a source for its preaching, apart from and beside this one Word of God, still other events and powers, figures and truths, as God's revelation." Still other events: current liberations and revolutions; still other powers: the world's religions and ideologies, human work, *praxis,* Marxist analysis; still other figures: the poor and all progressive spirits; still other truths: God in history.

The Scots Confession (1560), chapter 16: "Out of this Kirk there is neither life nor eternal felicity. Therefore we utterly abhor the blasphemy of those who hold that men who live according to equity and justice shall be saved, no matter what religion they profess."

The Heidelberg Catechism (1563), Q. 29. "Why is the Son of God called *JESUS,* which means *SAVIOR?* A. Because he saves us from our sins, and because salvation is not to be sought or found in any other." Q. 30. "Do those who seek their salvation and well-being from saints, by their own efforts, or by other means really believe in the only Savior Jesus? A. No. Rather, by such actions they deny Jesus, the only Savior and Redeemer, even though they boast of belonging to him. It therefore follows that either Jesus is not a perfect Savior, or those who receive this Savior with true faith must possess in him all that is necessary for their salvation."

C. The You Ares: The Ordination of Disciples to World Service (UR 1–2), 5:13–16

1. The Salt Shaker (UR 1), 5:13

"*You* are the salt of the earth. But if the salt loses its tang how is it ever going to be salty again? It is good for absolutely nothing except to be thrown outside and trampled under people's feet" (5:13). The initial "you" is strongly emphasized in the Greek sentence both by being placed at the head of the sentence and then by being used at all (since in Greek, pronominal subjects do not have to be expressed). "*You* are the salt. . . ." We have seen that ever since at least the concluding commentary Beatitude (vv 11–12) the disciples themselves have been blessed by God. Jesus now explicitly gives disciples the next best blessing of all: the knowledge that they are of use to the world. The deepest desire of Christians is to be used by God. Jesus here assures them that they are used by God, and used on the widest possible scale: "the salt *of the earth*" (not just of Galilee or Palestine).

Salt preserves, purifies, flavors, and kills.

"Salt . . . seasons food (Job 6:6; Col 4:6), and prevents corruption (Lev 2:13; Ezek 43:24): human life would be both insipid and corrupt but for the presence of good men" (McN., 55).

Disciples who bring the Word and will of Jesus into history preserve, purify, flavor, and convict human society in incomparable ways. Salt does not exist for itself. Christians do not exist for themselves either. Salt's main purpose is penetration of food; Christians' main purpose is penetration of earth. Salt a centimeter away from food is of no use; Christians who do not live and work for persons outside themselves are worthless.

It is remarkable that Jesus should give this unprepossessing group of disciples such a global ministry. Even by the time Matthew wrote these words the church was not important in the Roman Empire. It was very near presumption, then, not only for Jesus to say these words but for Matthew to record them. Yet their fulfillment proceeds apace. The witness of these first disciples—we call it now the apostolic witness—gives testimony to Jesus today on all seven continents. (Cf. the final chapter in Jaroslav Pelikan's *Jesus Through the Centuries* (1985): "The Man Who Belongs to the World.")

Christians who are Christians *are* the salt of the earth. This is the tenth straight statement of fact in the Sermon on the Mount. (Each of the eight or nine Beatitudes, note well, is a statement of fact, and the two You Ares do, indeed, say, "You *are.*") In ten straight sentences, Jesus has simply asserted what is; he has not yet commanded anything (except for the ejaculatory "rejoice and be very happy" in the promise of the commentary Beatitude). This priority of assertion to injunction means that Jesus supports before he challenges, that he tells disciples who they are before he tells them what to do.

Jesus does not say that disciples should be, ought to be, or must be salt; he says, apodictically, "You are." We are blessed, *as we are,* before we are asked to be what we are not. Christians are, by the simple fact that they are in contact with Jesus, the salt of the earth. Simply to hear his Word with faith is to be salted.

But salt can either pursue its function—enter the food—and so be salt, or it can deny its function, either by not entering the food at all or by entering the food and ceasing to be salt there. Thus the warning that immediately follows the salt assertion—"but if the salt loses its tang"—is meant to shake Christians up. While Christians are not challenged to *become* salty—their saltiness is a gift of Jesus' Word—they are challenged to *stay* salty, that is, they are challenged to be real Christians. There are pressures at work all around us and within us not to be too Christian, not to take our faith too seriously, to relax the war with what is despicable in us and with what is vicious in the community. Though we are salt, there is the constant pressure to be insipid salt, prudent Christians, and "normal" people. Some of this is the work of the Dove Spirit who makes Christian people normal, human, and gentle; but some of this is the work of the spirit that makes people cowards, inhumane, and temporizing.

The Christian ethic, it has been often pointed out, is an ethic of "become what you are" rather than the Greek ethic of "become what you should be." In Jesus' teaching "wholeness stands as God's gift at the beginning and not at the end" (as a result of my performance; compare over and against this the ethics of Aristotelianism and Scholasticism). (Conz., 61)

But we are now in the presence of the first of many warnings in the sermon, to this effect: Blessing is given to believers that they become, in turn, blessing to the *world* (cf. especially the seminal Abrahamic promise of Gen 12:1–3 and Jesus' primary call to fish *people*, Matt 4:19); salt is made salt in order to be salty in meat.

Jesus takes us here by the collar and says, "I have made you into something, now be it." We are put on notice that while it is from nothing (*gratis*) that we have been made into salt, it is not *for* nothing (*frustra*). We are to live for other people. Christians, we learn here for the first time explicitly, are in danger if they do not live right. They are in danger of losing what has been freely given them. This is what is meant by the warning "it is good for nothing except to be thrown outside and trampled on by people." Here is *deserved* persecution. This kind of persecution most often takes the form of simple contempt or complete disinterest; these Christians are not jumped on, ambushed, or attacked; they are merely ignored or shrugged off. They are so insipid that they are hardly worth persecuting. It is a form of persecution no Christian should be proud to have.

Schlatter, *Der*, 146, stresses the importance of this You Are: to receive Jesus' Word only for one's own blessing is perverse. When Jesus says that disciples are the salt of the *earth* he means that their calling has no boundaries, it reaches to all humanity. Thus Jesus' final word in this Gospel, "go and disciple all nations" (28:18), unites with his early "you are the salt of the earth" (5:13) to teach world mission. All messianism, even Jewish, had universality in it—to speak of the Christ was to speak at the same time of the universal. Thus when persons have a true encounter with the Christ they become inevitably mission-minded. In a way the You Ares are as characteristic of Matthew's Jesus as the I Ams are of John's Jesus (Lohm., 99), and both sets of sayings share high christology and universal mission. Cf. Psalm 2 and Darrell L. Guder, *Be My Witnesses* (1985), chap 1

2. The Light House (UR 2), 5:14–16

"*You* are the light of the world. A city sitting on a hill cannot be hid. People do not keep a lamp burning only to put it under a basket; they put it right on top of the table, and there it shines in the service of everyone in the house. Let your light so shine in the presence of other people that they will see *your* kind of good works and thus give honor to your Father who is in heaven."

Once again this little band of disciples is given surprisingly cosmic significance; they are here called literally the light *tou kosmou*, "of the cosmos." In this passage Jesus ordains his original disciples and thus all his followers; each one is made an ordained Christian worker, a commissioned missionary, a world force. Christians *are* the world's light. How they let this light function is another question. Beyond question is the reality that Jesus believes disciples are universal history's most luminous fact.

Earlier, Jesus himself had been called the light of the nations and a great light (4:16); now the Light passes on his light to the disciples. In the disciples' reflection of Jesus, like the moon's of the sun, disciples are something too, and when they face him and take him seriously they reflect his light into the world. "A city sitting on a hill cannot be hid" (5:14b). Where the salt Word had a warning (the danger of saltlessness), the light Word has a promise: the impossibility of uselessness. Disciples need both warning and encouragement: warning so that they remain disciples, encouragement so that they not think their being effective is up to them. (Schlatter, *Das*, 58, points out that in the You Ares two needed admonitions are given disciples: in the salt saying an admonition against unbelieving sloth, and in the light saying an admonition against unbelieving busyness.)

This city Word is intended to lift Christians into a self-esteem, into a self-consciousness which at first might seem far removed from the poverty of spirit celebrated in the inaugural Beatitudes but which in fact is related to that spirit. Persons who find themselves and their worth in Jesus (and not primarily in themselves) are given the gift of feeling themselves of worldwide worth. The humility of faith and a sense of significance in mission are not contradictions; they are cause and effect. "He who loses his life for my sake *finds* it" (16:25b).

If we will be serious Christians (the intent of the salt Word), *Jesus promises* to take care of the strategies and techniques of our effectiveness (the intent of the light Word). Thus the salt Word and the light Word hang together like the command and promise of the fishing Word: "Follow me [command], and I will make you catching with people [promise]." If *we* follow him, *he* will make us catching. Being catching is *his* promise and so his responsibility. Our responsibility is only to stay close to the really Big Fisherman; his responsibility is to make us salty, catching, and interesting, or in theological language, to be missionary, evangelistic, and relevant.

5:15 "People do not keep a lamp burning only to put it under a basket; they put it right on top of the table, and there it shines in the service of everyone in the house." What no one does with lamps, the Lord will not do with disciples. He will not light us, make us disciples, beatify us, and twice tell us that we are something, and then stick us under a basket. What no one in a right mind does, the Lord will not do. One of the biggest and most understandable problems of Christians is knowing where to go in order to be most useful. We worry about where we work. This Word removes us from the unbelieving anxiety that one's missionary success is up to oneself, one's skills in strategy, or one's friends in power. Jesus is in the Christian enterprise too, and is interested in seeing light reach the whole house. The one who lights us will also put us on the table.

5:16 "Let your light so shine in the presence of other people that they will see *your* kind of good works and thus give honor to your Father who is in heaven." Three words in this important sentence make Jesus' command intelligible. (This is only the second command in the Sermon on the Mount so far.)

First, we notice that Jesus' proximate purpose with us is "that they will see *your* kind of good works." The "your" is emphasized in the Greek sentence and is meant to contrast the disciples' good works with traditional pieties. There is to be something special about Christian works. This specialness, I think, is to be their modesty (the need Beatitudes) and mercy (the help Beatitudes). In the light of the Beatitudes, the disciples' works will not be more spectacular works, they will be simpler. The muted luster of Jesus' own light—the Jesus who initially got baptized rather than who baptized others, and who rejected sensationalism so decisively in the temptations—will be upon disciples and on their works.

Second, the word "good" (*kala*) in the expression "good works" (*kala erga*) is a word that usually describes the attractive *form* or appearance of a thing rather than the good content of a thing, for which there is another word (*agathos, agatha,* etc.). The *way* commands are done is important to Jesus (chap 6).

Third, we observe that Jesus' ultimate purpose with his disciples is "that they will see your kind of good works and give honor to your *Father* who is in heaven." Christian works are to be transparent, revealing less their agent than their source. Here for the first time in the Gospel disciples are told that Jesus' heavenly Father is *their* heavenly Father. This is the supreme honor, and Jesus will seal this act of adoption formally when he gives his disciples the Lord's Prayer—the "Our Father."

The purpose of our lives (the meaning of the Hebraic expression "good works" is the English "our lives") is to remove the veil from the Father's face and to display something of his glory to the world. It should no longer be necessary to ask the purpose of life. The purpose of life is the glory of God.

There is a certain tension between this text that asks us to let our light shine before others *so that* (*hopōs*) they will see our kind of works, and the first verse of chapter 6 that warns us to be very careful *not* to do our righteousness before people *so that* (*pros to*) they will see us. The decisive difference is purpose; here in our text the purpose is the glory of God; in chapter 6 the purpose of works is our own glory. The distinction is easy to make but difficult to live. It is enough if we know there is a right and wrong way to do good works, a right and wrong way to live a Christian life. We must pray for God to show us the difference.

"In their setting in Matthew . . . the verses in [Matthew] 5:13–16 [the You Ares] clearly transfer to the new Israel the functions demanded of the old" (Davies, 249). We may cite Deuteronomy 26:19, the many Isaiah texts on light, and Ezekiel 5:5 as examples. Jesus gives *disciples* "the promised role of Israel to the nations" (Guel., 130). The You Ares mean, in a word, the church is the Israel of God in the world. This is very exciting.

Luther, *SM,* 61 sees Jesus applying the You Ares to the *apostles* in very special particular, making them Christendom's exclusive authority. (This is important for the doctrine of authority.) "Thus," Luther says, "He subjects the whole world to the apostles, through whom alone it should and must be enlightened. . . . Because He calls them a 'light of the world,' their teaching alone must be authoritative and adequate to enlighten the whole world. Therefore, no other light is necessary; indeed, anything apart from their teaching is sheer darkness." Luther, *SM,* 64, concludes that the light of apostolic teaching is the most despised teaching in the world, for "no other teaching is so dangerous. . . . This teaching meets universal opposition because its intention is to step forward and to show up the worthlessness of the world's light and teaching." (When Jesus says, "You are the salt of the earth and light of the world" he means that "the earth of itself is without salt, the world without light," Beng., 1:106.) Luther's more doctrinal than ethical interpretation of the You Ares has been criticized in the literature. But see recently, Guel., 124–25. An interesting feature of Luther's interpretation of Matthew 5:16 is his subordination of ethical Matthew (and of the other synoptic Gospels) to the doctrinal (and christocentric) John and Paul (*SM,* 65). Immediately after Luther's doctrine of hierarchical Scripture here (i.e., his preference for the biblical books that stress the priority of faith to works), we hear equally important words from Luther about the doctrine of salvation and the praise of good works here in Matthew and elsewhere in Scripture: "But you dare not look at the statements and instructions about works in a manner that separates faith from them, the way our blind theologians mutilate them. You must always connect them with faith and incorporate [the works] in [faith], making [works] a result and a concomitant of faith, praised and called 'good' for [faith's] sake, as I have often taught" (*ibid.*). Ethical Chrysostom comes at Scripture from a different angle than doctrinal Luther, as the following comment by Chrysostom on our text will make clear: When our non-Christian neighbors "see us building ourselves fine houses, and laying out gardens and baths, and buying fields, they are not willing to believe that we are preparing for another residence away from our city. . . . Hearest thou not Christ say that He left us to be for salt and lights in this world, in order that we may both brace up those that are melting in luxury and enlighten them that are darkened by the care of wealth?" (12:5:79). Luther listens for *faith* in every text in Scripture, Chrysostom for *morals.* Luther is more Johannine-Pauline, Chrysostom more Matthean-Jamesian.

Summary: The Blessings as a Whole
How the Sermon on the Mount Starts: The Foundation of Ethics

In the Beatitudes we are given God's love; in the You Ares we are sent to share this love with the world. In the Beatitudes we are united with Christ for the world; in the You Ares we are united with the world for Christ.

The Sermon on the Mount begins with almost unqualified mercy. "For nothing," *gratis,* and "from nothing," *ex nihilo,* we are made into something. The power of the remainder of the sermon flows from its beginning. The momentum for keeping the following commands flows from the drive of the preceding Blessings. Just as Yahweh in the Old Covenant only gave his commandments to Israel *after* he had led her across the Red Sea, so now in the New Covenant Jesus only commands his disciples *after* he blesses them. The Ten Commandments begin significantly with this boost of grace: "I am Yahweh your God, who brought you out of the land of Egypt, out of the house of bondage" (Exod 20:2). Only after God has assured Israel that "I am . . . yours" does he command "You shall not. . . ." Similarly in the Sermon on the Mount, only after Jesus has both blessed and "you are'd" us does he give us the great commands of the antitheses. Thus the peculiar and powerful sequence of biblical ethics is the sequence of blessing *and then* command, of support before challenge, of indicative before imperative. "Before the imperative 'be perfect' (5:48) stands the indicative 'you are the light of the world'" (Trill., 214).

All disciples know that power for good living comes from Jesus' having seized them first. It is because Jesus takes people to himself that they find the biblical ethic unonerous. There is a friendliness about Jesus' ethic that takes its heaviness away. "My yoke is easy and my burden is light" (11:30). By themselves, isolated from the Blessings, the commands of Jesus are not at all easy and light.

The Beatitudes are not dispensable knowledge or merely preliminary fluff before the all-important commands; they are foundational, formative, basic for the living of the Christian life and its commands. Therefore they stand at the beginning of the New Testament and of New Testament ethics. We cannot go directly into the *doing* of the ethics of Jesus' commands without passing first through the receiving of the *being* unconditionally loved in his introductory Blessings. We cannot be a blessing until we have been blessed.

It is important to keep first things first, to lay foundations right. The foundation of Christian existence is the grace of God (to use Paul's language), it is the Beatitudes (to use Matthew's). The Beatitudes are not the mere preface of the Sermon on the Mount, they are its engine. We will only read the commands that follow in the right spirit if we read them in the power of the Beatitudes.

II. THE COMMANDS (5:17–48)

For catechetical and educational reasons, I will transmute the following seven paragraphs (the introduction and the six antitheses) into a week of commands, into a little Christian Heptalog (Seven Words). I have the feeling that Matthew's Jesus would like disciples to give the kind of attention to these seven paragraphs of commands that the old people of God gave to the old Ten Commandments (Decalog, the Ten Words). (In the interest of clarity, I will from now on call Jesus' commands "commands" and the Old Testament's commands "commandments.") This Gospel ends, significantly, with Jesus commissioning the eleven to teach the discipled nations "to keep all that I have *commanded* you" (28:20a). In Matthew's Gospel, Jesus is as present in his commands as in Paul's gospel Jesus is present in his grace. The commands of Jesus are Matthew's special contribution to the church.

Because of the emphasis on Jesus' commands there is an ever present danger of legalism and moralism in Matthew's Gospel. This has to be admitted. It is important that Paul's epistolary gospel is in the New Testament. But Matthew's Gospel of teachings itself is full of delegalizing Words—from the Beatitudes that begin the sermon, through the controversies with the first-century legalists in the middle of the Gospel, to the Lord's Supper at the end. It is a narrow reading of Matthew, not the Gospel itself, that is responsible for legalistic misreadings.

It is just as true to say that there is an ever present danger of laxity and immorality in Paul's gospel. The fault is not Paul's, it is the carnal reader's. But Matthew's "Gospel of the Sermon on the Mount" stands guard at the head of our canonical New Testament against every immoral misunderstanding of the Good News of the rest of the New Testament (W.D. Davies). Matthew's enthronement of Jesus' commands keeps the church morally serious. "Moral Matthew" must not be misconstrued as moralistic Matthew. The gospel *is* moral. A careful reading of Paul shows that his gospel is moral too, though in a different way from Matthew's Gospel (Rom 6–8; 12–15; and the great "be not deceived" texts: 1 Cor 6:9f; Gal 5:19–21; Eph 5:5f). The church of our time badly needs the magisterial morality of Matthew's Gospel.

Recently a student told me something that nicely explains the relation between the Beatitudes on the one hand and the commands on the other: "God loves me enough to accept me the way I am [the Beatitudes], but too much to leave me that way [the Commands]."

A. Introductory. Scripture Day: The Sunday Command of Biblical Piety (C 1), 5:17–20

"Do not ever think that I came to destroy the law and the prophets; I did not come to destroy but to fulfill them. For Amen, I tell you, until heaven and earth pass away, not one dot of an i, not one cross of a t, will drop out of the law before it all happens. So whoever loosens up even one of the least of these commands, and so by this behavior teaches others to do the same, will be called 'Least' in the kingdom of heaven. But whoever does and teaches these commands will be called 'Great' in the kingdom of heaven. Because I want to tell you something: Unless your righteousness is greater than that of the Bible teachers and the Serious, you will never even get into the kingdom of heaven."

The sense of this passage—Jesus' only book review—is Jesus' mandate to love Scripture and to live to keep it. (The day for Christians to give special attention to this command is Sunday, the Lord's Day.) When Luther in his Small Catechism asked the meaning of the Sabbath commandment in the Decalog ("Remember the Sabbath day, to keep it holy"), he taught believers to answer, "We should fear and love God, and so we should not despise God's *Word* and the *preaching* of the same, but deem it holy, and gladly hear and learn it." Luther's answer captures exactly what Jesus' first command, and what Sundays, are for: the glad learning and doing of God's preached Word in Scripture.

The four verses of this paragraph (vv 17–20) are the preface or introduction to the six commands that follow. These verses are not usually considered one of the commands themselves. But in fact verses 17, 19, and 20 are three sides of one great command: the command to take Scripture very seriously. In these verses Jesus tells us how he feels *about* God's law before he proceeds to deliver his exposition *of* that law at six salient points. A command to take God's law seriously is a command, too. Jesus wants us to appreciate "what was said of old" before he gives us his imperious "but I say to you."

There are two "I say to you" remarks by Jesus in this paragraph, vv 18 and 20, making the whole unit a veritable antithesis. Arguments for understanding 5:17–20 as a command can be found in Chrysostom, 17:1:115; and Schlatter's comment, *Der*, 279, is apt: Jesus' "New Command" "begins with his confession of Holy Scripture, Matthew 5:17 (–20)."

5:17 "Do not ever think that I came to destroy the law and the prophets; I did not come to destroy but to fulfill them." Because of Jesus' freedom—glimpsed already in the Beatitudes, where the usual strict conditions are not present (Torah study, Sabbath observance, temple reverence, almsgiving, prayer, fasting)—there was some suspicion of Jesus' scriptural orthodoxy. Since Jesus explicitly referred disciples to the great traditions of Israel (such as Torah study) so little; since he blessed almost "on his own," as it were, it began to be thought that Jesus was secretly and not so secretly against the Torah. This question lived then, and it lives still. In the history of the church from Marcion to Bultmann it has been seriously asked if Jesus and the religion inspired by him ought not to be freed from the Old Testament and its myriad difficulties.

Jesus wished promptly to correct this suspicion. He had not come to set aside Hebrew Scripture or to make it unimportant. He had come to "fulfill" it, which means to "do" it, to "fill it full" (full-fill) with obedience and meaning, to set it on its feet, and not to set it aside. (The expression "the law and the prophets" was the way one said "Scripture" in Jesus' time; law and prophets were the Hebrew Scriptures' two main parts, and they circulated on separate scrolls. Cf. Gutbrod, TDNT, 4:1059; Trill., 137, 172–74.)

Matthew felt that it was important both for the old and new people of God to know that Jesus was not anti-law or anti-Scripture. Israel would not be able to take a Messiah seriously who flaunted God's gift of Torah. But Jesus did not flaunt this gift; he lived from it (we saw how deeply in the temptations) and for it (we will see this throughout the rest of the Gospel). He "came" (mysterious word, as though from another planet) to fulfill the Torah and its classic companion, the prophets. So far from Scripture being an indifferent thing to Jesus, it was what gave him life's directives. (The root meaning of the Hebrew word *Torah* is to point, direct.) For Jesus, Torah and prophets were Word of God. Jesus will authoritatively *interpret* the Old Testament Word of God; but this Old Testament is still for Jesus, unmistakably, the Word of God.

This verse instructs Christians to be careful about any teaching that sets Jesus (and so Christians) against the Old Testament. Emmanu-El certainly was and is over the Old Testament, just as divinity is over all persons and things; but Jesus is not against the Old Testament, and his way of being over it was first to be under it and for it. A disciple is not above his or her Lord; if Jesus lived in a lifelong love affair with the Old Testament, how can anyone dismiss the Old Testament and still call oneself Jesus' disciple?

Our love for the Old Testament might increase if we occasionally called it "Jesus' Bible" instead of "Old Testament." The Old Testament was Jesus' personal library; it was his shelf of books. The only glimpse we get of Jesus in his youth is while he is sitting with the Bible teachers asking and answering questions about these books (Luke 2:41–52). Jesus' ministry in Matthew reveals a remarkable prior immersion in Scripture. Thus in owning an Old Testament we have the exciting privilege of owning Jesus' personal library. The purpose of this entire paragraph of verses about the law and the prophets, which we understand as Jesus' first command, is clear: it is to infect us with Jesus' enthusiasm for Hebrew Scripture.

Jesus' life cannot be adequately described as an "unbooked" life. Jesus was a Jew, and Jews are first and foremost People of the Book. In our time book learning is frequently looked down on by the pragmatic, and book religion is often put down as beneath progressive Christians. But good Jews have never been misled from respect for books, and so while the *goyim* go running off to "the real world" in frantic projects, the Jews burrow into books and change the world. To be antibook is, of course, to be anti-intellectual, but in the light of Jesus' first command, to be antibook is to be anti-Christian, too. One of the purposes of this first command is to marry us to a book.

"Jesus saw his entire life-calling in the Scripture—it was not marginal but absolutely central to his life. . . . His whole will was consumed with this: to do what each commandment commanded. Here is the one man—the first in history—who not only knew the Word but did it" (Schl., *Das*, 61).

While I have adopted the interpretation that understands Jesus' "fulfillment" of Scripture as his *doing* it, there is a responsible exegesis that believes Matthew's Jesus' fulfilling of law and prophets was Jesus' authoritatively *interpreting* Scripture, i.e., that 5:17 is to be understood more of Jesus' public teaching than of his personal obedience (e.g., Born., "End," 29; cf. Guel., 138–42, for a review of interpretations; also Trill., 210). I understand Jesus' *teaching* to be an important part of his doing. In addition, Jesus' yes to the law of God in this verse is not contrary to his frequent criticism of the law-mongers in the rest of the Gospel. Paul could speak critically of the law in the interest of faith (as in Galatians and Romans, especially), but Paul, too, writes: "Do we then overthrow the law by this faith? By no means! On the contrary, we uphold the law" (Rom 3:20). Romans 4 then shows how Paul understood faith's upholding law.

On Jesus' provocative "*I came*" (*ēlthon*), even the skeptical Beare, 141–42, comments that "the words 'I came' imply a claim of Messianic status, and indeed of heavenly origin, on the part of Jesus; for they carry the sense of 'I came down to earth'—'I came from heaven.' There is a high christological claim for Jesus here, and we may well question whether Jesus himself ever spoke of his mission in terms like these." Most Christians, however find Jesus' "I cames" congruent with his mysteriously authoritative way of speaking. If Jesus' "I came" implies heavenly origin, then Brown's arguments against Jesus' preexistence in Matthew, discussed at Matthew 1, are put in question.

5:18 "For Amen, I tell you, until heaven and earth pass away, not one dot of an i, not one cross of a t, will drop out of the law before it all happens." (Cf. Guelich's, 134, translation: "not even the slightest detail of the Law will ever become passé.") The law will last as long as heaven and earth last. Interestingly, the law does *not* last as long as Jesus' own Word, for in chapter 24 Jesus says, "Though heaven and earth pass away, my words will *never* pass away." Thus, the law has a long tenure—as long as heaven and earth's—but Jesus' reign is longer! The point of v 18 is that in the present world *the law remains in force*. There has not been "any abrogation of the law in Christ's coming, for the rule of holy and devout life is eternal" (Cal., 1:180).

We all know, from having read the rest of the Gospel—indeed, from even having read the rest of this chapter—that Jesus exercises a sovereign freedom *over* law. His royal "But *I* say to you" after he has just quoted Scripture will indicate this fact no less than six times in this chapter alone. Moreover, Jesus' own personal displacement of the temple (chap 12), his alteration of Old Testament food and cleanliness laws (chap 15), his higher criticism of an Old Testament permission for divorce (chap 19), all indicate (less radically than Mark but still) that Jesus was not a slave of the dotted i's and crossed t's. Jesus will exercise, and he will give his church the authority to exercise, a sovereign freedom with the Old Testament. And yet in Matthew's opinion it is very important that before Jesus grants this freedom he commands a prior respect. On reaching maturity a child obtains freedom from its parents, but it is important that the child first learned to honor parents. In the context of prior honor, freedom is not dangerous. Similarly, in the commands, Jesus first teaches high respect for Scripture. Where this respect lives—and it is the central purpose of this first command to inculcate respect—later freedom is responsible.

One of the more difficult expressions to interpret in this sentence is the enigmatic "before it all happens" at the end. Does this mean, "until the end of the world," like the earlier "until" in the same sentence, or does it mean "until I fulfill [the law] in my passion" (which would have the effect of *shortening* the law's reign)? It is difficult to say. The first "until" clearly says that the law will remain in force until the end of history; the second "until" makes us wonder if (in Matthew's understanding, like Paul's) a certain fulfillment of the law isn't given already in Jesus' passion (thus Schl., *Der*, 157; especially Gutbrod, *nomos*, TDNT 4:1062; Guel., 260, and often). It is my guess that Matthew intended the ambiguity and wishes us to know through this curious sentence that the law is still Sacred Scripture in the church (the first "until") but that when Jesus dies and rises, Scripture undergoes a profound preliminary fulfillment (the second "until").

It has been pointed out that this verse, which seems to contradict other parts of his Gospel, indicates Matthew's fidelity to even uncongenial parts of the tradition handed down to him. He heard on good authority that Jesus said this; and therefore even though it does not really fit his overall picture of Jesus in this Gospel, he includes it. This might be the case. On the other hand, when one sees how often Matthew alters the tradition handed down to him, one can believe that this command of respect for Scripture was not embarrassing to Matthew. It serves to enhance Jesus' biblicism, his reverence for Scripture, and his desire for his church to be a biblical church.

Jesus' first "Amen, I say to you" occurs in this verse. An "Amen, I say to you" from Jesus carries the highest authority, and hearers may underline what Jesus says after it. The phrase's appearance in this paragraph supports the thesis that we are already dealing with Jesus' commands in this introduction. On the special meaning of Jesus' emphatic "Amen, I say to you," or "I say to you," Bengel, 1:107–08, is good: "The prophets used to speak in the third person . . . , ['Thus] saith the Lord'; the apostles, 'It is written';

but Christ, in the first person, 'I say unto you.' . . . Christ seldom quotes passages of Scripture, and not without special reason: He rests with becoming dignity on His own authority."

Schlatter, *Der*, 156–57, interprets this verse with his usual incisiveness: In this saying Jesus announces his unreserved allegiance to the divine origin of Scripture; "until heaven and earth pass away" means that for as long as persons live in nature—in this world— Scripture reveals the will of God to them; the position Jesus takes toward Scripture in these verses harmonizes with what we have seen of him in the temptations (4 A): here as well as there, the first thing Jesus wants is the obedience that fulfills Scripture. Cf. Schlatter, *Das*, 62: Jesus makes the commandment of Scripture his command, and thus disciples now know how they may obey him: by doing what Scripture says.

5:19a "So whoever loosens up even one of the least of these commands, and so by this behavior, teaches others to do the same, will be called 'Least' in the kingdom of heaven." Where verse 18 had taught a theology of Scripture—it is authority—verse 19 teaches an ethic of Scripture—it is to be obeyed. We have another puzzling phrase before us in this verse, too: "one of the least of these commands." What are these "least" commands? Schlatter, *Der*, 157–58, thinks that the expression refers to the commandments in the Decalog, especially the shorter ones such as "You shall not kill, You shall not commit adultery," and the like (also Grund., 149; Michel, TDNT, 4:656 n. 40). It is well known that the commandments of the first table of the Ten Commandments, the commandments regulating relations to God, are relatively longer than the commandments of the second table that regulate relations to neighbor.

Still others see the "least" as referring not to the Old Testament commandments at all but to Jesus' own teaching. They say that this is why the expression reads, "one of the least of these command(ment)s," where the "least of *these*" points ahead to *Jesus'* commands in the immediately following exposition (thus Beng., 1:109; Lohm., 110; Schw., 108). This suggestion is attractive because we do in fact learn that Jesus' commands are to assume sovereignty in the church (see the last Warning of the Sermon on the Mount, in particular the "my" in 7:24, 26, and the meaning of the transfiguration, especially 17:5, the last word). The Great Commission at the end of this Gospel concludes with the important words, "teaching them to keep everything *I* have commanded you" (28:20). Therefore, the expression in question here—"the least of *these* commands"—probably means "the least of *my* commands," i.e., "Respect my commands, even the seemingly least significant ones."

Green, 81, is judicious: "The original force of this saying must have had in view the Old Testament law as it stands; but the following verses, and the section it introduces, suggest rather that Matthew takes it to mean the law as interpreted by Jesus." Similarly "both/ and," Patte, 107. Thus in summary we may say that v 17 honors both the OT and NT, that v 18 honors especially the OT, and that v 19 honors especially the NT.

A still third possibility is that the phrase simply means "the whole of Hebrew Scripture is important, even its apparently unimportant parts; therefore read it with respect, and be prepared to obey even its most insignificant commands." This interpretation, if not pressed (say, cultically), but understood morally and spiritually, has the strength of simplicity, but look out! Jesus is simply saying for a third time now what he has been saying all along: "Hebrew Scripture is precious to me: hear it."

We can accept all three views: Jesus refers (a) to the whole of Scripture, but especially (as his exposition will show) (b) to its moral commandments, and principally, as the whole Gospel will teach, (c) to his own exposition of these commandments, which wants to be nothing more than true exposition of the central meaning of the Old Testament.

But in the context of this whole command (vv 17–20), a command delivering Jesus' high doctrine of Scripture, the main office of this particular verse is to drive the church to spiritual and ethical seriousness under Scripture—to piety. The Scriptures are not only to be held sacred in the realm of ideas; they are sacred because they are to be kept in life. In the following of Jesus we are not left to subjectivist whims, we are directed to Scripture teaching and reading for our counsel. Jesus warns us solemnly that if we *belittle* Scripture (which is what the verb "loose" here means), we will ourselves become "little" in the kingdom.

In the church's necessary controversy with the biblical inerrantists it is not always easy in the heat of controversy to avoid a belittling relation to Scripture. We must be on our guard that the hyperorthodox do not make us unorthodox with Scripture. "'Least'— . . . As we treat the Word of God, so does God treat us" (Beng., 1:109). Cf. the solid writings of P. T. Forsyth in this connection.

When teachers loosen Scripture their loosening has the effect of teaching others to do the same. This is the meaning of a connection that is barely visible in this verse: "Whoever looses . . . and *so* [*houtōs*] teaches others." The "and *so*" means that our way of living with Scripture teaches others, by example or anti-example, how to live with Scripture. Therefore Jesus says, be warned: if you live with Scripture in loose or noncommittal ways you teach others to live that way too, and the consequence is that what you have done to Scripture here on earth is what will be done to you after this life: minimilization.

It has seemed curious to many commentators that these "minimalists" even get into the kingdom: "they shall be called 'Least' *in* the kingdom." Is this verse to be understood literally, or does it mean that belittlers won't get into the kingdom at all? It probably means they won't get in at all (thus, e.g., Aug., *LSM*, 29; Bonn., 62; contra Schn., 55; Streck., 145 n. 6). This verse warns us, in short, against the temptation to dismiss Scripture, to relativize it arbitrarily, to get out from under its difficult texts cheaply, to evade obedience through sophistry. This verse means take Scripture seriously and beware of every "loosening" of a text's simple meanings. (Cf. this spirit in Deut 4:2, as well. Thus Matt 5:17–19 calls us to honest exegesis.)

5:19b "But whoever does and teaches these commands will be called 'Great' in the kingdom of heaven." One of the deepest drives in a human being is the drive to be great in some way. The desire to be great is eminently human and can be easily perverted. Jesus takes hold of this desire and gives it new space. "Do you want to be great?" he says in effect. "Then here is how: Live to do (and so) to teach Scripture." The person who wants to be great in *this* way is promised the name "*rab,*" meaning "great," in the coming kingdom. Thus ambition is harnessed and attached to an exciting star: make your life goal the translation of Scripture into life, and you will be given the award of being called Great in the kingdom.

We have already seen how doing is itself teaching and vice versa. But Jesus was also aware that life is lived in community and that an important part of public responsibility is *communicating* truth. Therefore, teaching has a dignity all its own. "Whoever does *and teaches*," Jesus thus says a second time. We are reminded again of the conclusion of the Gospel in the Great Commission, "*teaching* them to keep all that I have commanded you" (28:20).

Some interpreters believe that Matthew is not only directly attacking all antinomians but obliquely attacking *Paul* and his law-free message in this verse, too (recently, Mohr., 40, 85; Beare, 141, following Manson and J. Weiss; contra Davies, 340; *idem, SM,* 92–100). Schniewind, 55, believes this verse presupposed that there will be ranks and differing dignities in the kingdom of God and cites Luke 12:47b; Mark 10:40; Revelation 20:6. Schlatter, *Das,* 63: only that person has honor in the kingdom of God who has sincerely lived in relation to the divine law; Jesus counts all human greatness that is won contrary to the divine commandments as worthless. True greatness is won only through obedience. When we, then, *teach* others to do evil and when we present God's commands as invalid we fall under even greater guilt. Part of our loyalty to God is not only to *do* God's commands but also in our life together to teach others to do God's commands.

This paragraph on the doctrine of Scripture began with Jesus' own relation to Scripture: fulfillment not abolition (v 17). It moved to the durability of Scripture (v 18), and it has now come to what we can call the ethic of Scripture (v 19), warning us of a loose relation to it and encouraging us to piety toward it. But when Matthew puts together units of Jesus' teaching it is his characteristic to end the unit with warning. This is part of the bracing unsentimentality of Matthew's moral Gospel.

5:20 The final verse in the command takes us up short and tells us how urgent a right relation to Scripture is. "Because I want to tell you something: unless your righteousness is greater than that of the Bible teachers and the Serious you will never even get into the kingdom of heaven." Here we learn that our relation to Scripture is not only a prudential matter, it is finally a saving matter. By this time the paragraph has moved us entirely from an only theoretical consideration of Scripture. We have seen that between verses 17 and 20 the command has moved gradually from the theoretical to the practical. Now finally Jesus leaves us with this supreme warning: If Scripture does not make us righteous, righteous beyond the righteousness of the most serious people in the community of the old people of God—the Bible teachers and the members of the separatist *Pharisaim*—we won't get in the kingdom. The purpose of Scripture, finally, is not so much a right doctrine of it as it is a personal obedience to it. The goal of Scripture is the piety of obedience. The point of the dotted i's and crossed t's is the behavior of those who read them. This final verse in Jesus' doctrine of Scripture is completely moral and even salvific. Jesus warns us that if Scripture does not reach its end *in* us— righteousness—it will be the end *of* us. Life or death depends on our response to this Book.

The pitch in these verses has gotten higher and higher. Protestant interpretation has often heard the pitch and found it excessive, even shrill. In this command it appears that we are increasingly called to do the very thing that the gospel according to Paul everywhere warned us against: to find a righteousness of our own, a righteousness built upon our obedience to the law of Scripture rather than upon a righteousness residing exclusively in Christ, received exclusively by faith (cf., e.g., Rom 9:30–10:4 and Phil 2:9, 12–13; 3:9, 12–14).

One frequent way of escape from this seeming works-righteousness has been to understand the "righteousness" urged upon us here as not our own righteousness but as actually the righteousness of Christ. But this interpretation stands in clear contradiction to the words of the text: "Unless *your* righteousness exceeds," and the "your" is even emphasized in the Greek text, meaning "your very own." It has been objected that the Christian's own righteousness is *not* one's own, but Christ's, and, it is then urged, this is the only way realistically that our righteousness can ever exceed the righteousness of the Bible teachers and the Serious. I find the intention of this argument praiseworthy—the intention of preserving the gospel of free grace and faith. But the exegesis is wanting. Much as I might wish that Matthew would make Christ's own person and righteousness more central in this text, as Paul always did in his texts, such is not the case. Matthew has another way of presenting the gospel.

If we will be patient with Matthew and not try too quickly to baptize him in Paul, we will find him teaching a gospel. Right now Matthew's Jesus is urging on us a real, personal righteousness. We will see soon enough that the "much more" of right- eousness asked of us in this Gospel will often drive us to the Beatitudes and to prayer for divine help. Matthew's word "righteousness" is an evangelist preaching our need of salvation.

What is this higher righteousness? In this Gospel it is obedience to Jesus' commands, to his mercy toward the underprivileged (5:1–6; 8:1–17), to his "I desire mercy and not sacrifice" (9:13; 12:7), to his summons to love (5:21–48; 22:34–40)—to become little ones (18:1–5; 19:14)—to humility (23:8–12)—and to suffering (10:16–39; 16:24–29). "All [these] describe the 'better righteousness' (of 5:20), the fruits which will be asked about in the judgment (25:31–46), the perfection of which the end of the antitheses of the Sermon on the Mount speaks (5:48)" (Born., "End," 37).

"Qumran demanded more obedience, Matthew deeper" (Davies, 212), or "broader" (Patte, 107 n. 22). Even Paul comes finally in the heart of his gospel to a personal, "Matthean" view of righteousness, after Paul's magnificent understanding of reckoned righteousness, when, e.g., "according to Romans 8:4, the righteous demands of the law (Rom 13:8–10) are fulfilled '*in* us'; Paul does not say either 'for us' or 'through us,' because he is thinking of the operation of the Spirit" (Schw., 108). Matthew notoriously speaks less of the work of the Spirit and more of the Word of Jesus. But according to Mohrlang's excellent study of Matthew and Paul, 229, "both writers are convinced that ethical living on the highest plane is indeed possible for Christians (Matt 5:48; Rom 8:2ff); but whereas Matthew sees [ethical living] as the result of heightened obedience to the ultimate demands of the law, Paul insists that it is the result rather of being freed from the law to live by the Spirit. Matthew would bind the Christian more tightly to the law, Paul would free him from it." One of my disagreements with Mohrlang is his view that Matthew's Gospel does not provide us with the same rich resources for living the Christian ethical life that Paul's gospel does with its doctrines of grace and the Spirit, that Paul is more concerned than Matthew with how one finds power for a life of moral goodness and that Matthew does not even raise the question of resources (Mohr., 224– 25). But what, respectfully, are the meanings of Matthew's Beatitudes, Lord's Prayer (Matt 6:9–13), and the teaching on prayer throughout the Gospel (not least in the prayers in the miracles that follow the Sermon on the Mount, chaps 8–9)?

At the very least this verse challenges us to be good if we will be God's. There is no cheap grace in Matthew. The way to be good, this command teaches us, is to follow Jesus in obedience to Scripture's commands. This paragraph has tried to make us lovers of the Bible and People of the Book.

If we sit loose to Scripture and do not let it make us serious we are going to hell. That, in English, is what this paragraph has been trying to teach. I am grateful that Paul's literature is nearby in the canon to save us from a serious misunderstanding. Paul, more comprehensively than Matthew, shows us the source of divine righteousness. But Matthew, more clearly than Paul, shows us the goal of Christian righteousness. Let us allow Matthew's Jesus to work on us. It may be that he will drive us, in the quest for personal righteousness, to the first Beatitude; "Blessed are the poor in spirit, for theirs is the kingdom of heaven."

*   *   *

The following texts from the church's confessions and creeds clarify the relation of believers to the *law* of God in Scripture. In the Lutheran tradition, *The Augsburg Confession* (1530) adds to the great articles on justification and ministry an important article on the new obedience of justified believers:

"It is also taught among us that such faith [we may say, the faith of the Beatitudes] should produce good fruits and good works and that we must do all such good works as God has commanded, but we should do them for God's sake and not place our trust in them as if thereby to merit favor before God . . . (Luke 17:10)" (art. 6).

And in the *Apology of the Augsburg Confession* (1531), in the comment on the article of justification, this kind of remark is frequent: "We are justified *for this very purpose,* that, being righteous, we might begin to do God's will and obey God's law" (art. 4, 348 emphasis added; cf. art. 12, 131).

In the Reformed tradition, Calvin's *Geneva Catechism* (1541) asserts that the law of God has a special use in believers, and Calvin's law is like Matthew's commands.

"First, in that [the law] shows them that they cannot justify themselves by their works, it *humbles* them and disposes them to seek their salvation in Jesus Christ (Rom 5:18–21). Secondly, inasmuch as it requires of them much more than they are able to perform, it *admonishes* them to pray unto the Lord, that He may give them strength and power (Gal 4:6), and at the same time reminds them of their perpetual guilt, that they may not presume to be proud. Thirdly, it is a kind of *bridle,* by which they are kept in the fear of God" (228, emphases added). Cf. *The Heidelberg Catechism* (1563), Q. 3.

Craig's Catechism (1581) asks, "What profit do the faithful derive from the Law?" and replies, "It puts them daily in remembrance of their sins." Then, "What good fruit comes from that? Answer: Humility and earnest reliance on Christ." The *Westminster Confession of Faith* (1647), in its discussion "Of the Law of God" in chapter 19, especially sections 5–7, seems to me to be too rigorous. Cf. the *Westminster Shorter Catechism* (1647), cf. QQ. 2, 39, and 44.

Again the opening sentence of the position in the second thesis of *The Theological Declaration of Barmen* (1934) summarizes everything perfectly, the first clause giving the truth of the Beatitudes, the second the dignity of the commands.

We may let Augustine, *LSM*, 42, conclude our consideration of the Sunday Command of Biblical Piety. "Now, who agrees with Divine Scripture save the one who religiously reads or hears it, according it the highest authority in that what he learns there does not make him hate [it] because it thwarts his sinning? . . . and if he finds anything [in Scriptures] obscure or what appears to him absurd, he does not forthwith start a contest of contradicting but he prays for further knowledge and he bears in mind the reverence and good disposition of soul that is to be shown so commanding an authority."

B. Mercy Day: The Monday Command of Temperamental Mercy (C 2), 5:21–26

*"You have heard that it was said to the people of old, 'You shall not kill,' and 'whoever kills will have to face the judgment.' But I say to you that everyone who nurses a grudge [*orgizomenos*] against his brother will have to face the judgment; and whoever says to his brother, 'You idiot!' will have to face the supreme court; and whoever says, 'You liar!' will have to face the fire of hell.*

*"So if you are bringing your gift to the altar, and you remember there that your brother has anything [*ti*] against you, leave your gift right there in front of the altar, and go first [*prōton*] and get right with your brother, and then come back and offer your gift.*

*"Make friends quickly [*tachu*] with your opponent while you are still with him on the road, lest your opponent hand you over to the judge, and the judge hand you over to the jailer, and the jailer throw you into jail. Amen, I tell you, you will never get out of there until you have paid your last pretty penny."*

The scope of Jesus' second command is good relations with people, especially brother and sister Christians. As the first command directs us seriously to God, so the second command directs us seriously to people. (It is appropriate, therefore, that after the Lord's Day, the first day of the work week, Monday, be devoted to repairing relations with others. Monday is Mercy Day.) Our first work in the world, as the fruit of biblical piety, is the work of reconciliation with people. Nothing dignifies the primacy of human relations quite like the fact that Jesus' six antithesis-commands in his great sermon are commands regulating the way we live with other people. (Lohmeyer, 121, sees the historical situation into which this saying of Jesus was spoken as that of the revolutionary Zealots who turned against their own and alien authorities with hate and violence.) Jesus' ethic is not heroic in that it is geared to unusual situations; it is heroic in that it asks us to be unusually Christian in all the usual situations.

5:21–22 Jesus' first antithesis (as this command is called) is not really an antithesis at all. An "anti-thesis" means, technically, a counter-thesis, a contradiction or rebuttal. A true antithesis, for example, would run, "You have heard 'You shall not kill,' but I say to you, 'Kill.'" (To the thesis of not killing a true antithesis would be killing.) But what we have here, and in several of the antitheses that follow, is, really, Jesus' *epithesis*, his intensifying or deepening thesis. To the thesis of not killing, Jesus adds the epithesis of not despising. Jesus has not canceled the commandment, he has full-filled it, filled it full of meaning, deepened it, and clarified its meaning at its roots, for at the core of the commandment against killing is the divine displeasure with all human contempt for other human beings. The real meaning of this command is "Don't nurse hate." The root of killing is contempt.

Having penetrated to the heart of the command, Jesus gives two additional examples of what may spring from a disordered heart, the words "idiot" and "liar." The first word, *hraka*, simply means, like it sounds, "stupid," and questions the mental competence of the other person. The second word, *môre*, pierces still deeper and questions the moral competence of the other (Str.-B., 1:279; Schl., *Der*, 169–70).

So Jesus has given three examples of how we break the commandment against killing: grudge bearing, idiot saying, and liar calling. "Whoever is angry with his brother" is the usual translation of *orgizomenos*, the first of the three terms. "Anger" is an orgy, a temporary madness. (It is significant that in English everyday speech we speak of anger as a "being mad.") The grammatical construction used here, however, is more extensive than the usual translation "is angry"; *orgizomenos* is a present tense participle and so literally means "is *being* angry," "bears anger," "carries anger," or in our idiom, "nurses a grudge." The present participle does not point to a single *moment* of anger—it would be inaccurate, for example, to translate *orgizomenos*, with "gets angry"; the word points to a *carrying* of anger, to a kind of portable anger. "Resents" might give a better meaning, for resentment is a continued anger. Resentment is anger prolonged, anger carried around.

The word *orgē* itself represents more than temporary anger. Barclay, 1:138, contrasts the two main Greek words for anger—*thumos* and *orgē*. The Greeks said *thumos* is "like the flame which comes from dried straw"—it quickly blazes up and just as quickly dies down. *Orgē*, on the other hand, was described "as anger become inveterate . . . long-lived anger; . . . the anger of the man who nurses his wrath to keep it warm."

It is this attitude of carried anger that Jesus confronts with judgment. This attitude must go. And this attitude is not *just* an attitude or an inner matter, an emotion that is not yet a deed; this carrying around of anger presupposes a decision to carry it, and such a decision constitutes a deed, a decision for a way to live. New Testament scholarship has shown us that the Sermon on the Mount does not teach a mere attitude-ethic or a purely inward morality. Jesus commands deeds. Jesus shows us that the attitudes we decide to bear are already public acts, real deeds, and as such, answerable before the judgment of God.

Twice Jesus calls the angry person's victim in these illustrations "his brother." We may understand this term in two ways. First and mainly, it applies to the actual Christian brother or sister. The first test of Christians is their relation with other Christians. It is notorious that this relationship is the most difficult of all. Another Christian is, by definition and baptism, a real brother or sister, whether we like it or not, whether we are happy with God's adoption policies or not. We get angry with Christians the easiest because we expect of them the most. But "by this shall all people know that you are my disciples, if you love *one another*" (John 13:35). The chief missionary fact is Christians forgiving each other and getting along well.

The second and subordinate meaning of "brother" is, as Jesus will teach elsewhere, *anyone* (e.g., 25:31–46; and cf. esp. Luke 10:25–37 and Jesus' redefinition of neighbor). Every other person is baptized "neighbor," "brother," or "sister" by the New Testament Jesus. I can love an abstract brother, but when this abstraction gets filled up with the sometimes difficult person I am given in the church and in the course of my day, the plot thickens.

The first visible fruit of inward resentment is the word of irritation or exaspera-tion—"You idiot!" ("hare-brained," Jero., 1:114). The next act of bottled anger is a word that tells a person whom we dislike exactly what we think of him or her: "liar" or "rat" or a comparably degrading word captures the sense of this word, and it says that a brother or sister lacks not only mental strength but moral substance. Jesus confronts this word with hell itself. Words, as we know from painful experience, have power to hurt. The school yard taunt, "sticks and stones may hurt my bones, but names will never hurt me," is not true. There are many people in mental wards because a hateful name or word is lodged in the psyche like a bullet in the spine. A word that questions our intelligence or, especially, our character, deeply hurts. Words that throw our mental ability into question, or that consider us morally vile, reach places in our nervous systems that even lasers cannot touch.

Grundmann, 155–56, shows that what is new in this command is that beyond the law that protects *life* ("you shall not commit murder"), Jesus now protects *persons*. God's will is injured in every angry confrontation. Calling others abusive names in Jesus' time was not thought to be very evil; Jesus, on the contrary, says namecalling deserves the severest judgment. Words that take from persons their honor before other per-sons are placed under God's wrath of judgment (Schl., *Das*, 67). Jesus is the classic advocate of human rights at the deepest levels, as each of the antithetical social com-mands in this chapter will show. (Guelich's view, 188, that Jesus is ironic not literal in 5:22 weakens the command.) Schweizer, 118, believes that other-centeredness is the common denominator in Jesus' commands: "The crucial point is that attention is no longer focused on us, and our striving to be beyond reproach, but on the *other* person, and how his living is whittled away by our conduct, even if only by an angry heart. This shift from personal righteousness to the protection of one's fellowmen is characteris-tic of the antitheses [commands]."

The *source* of all these injuries is *orgizomenos*, "orgying," grudging. Out of this cesspool hisses the careless or the bitterly critical word, and both the pool and its effusion poison others and in some cases actually lead to death. Resentment and hard words kill people more swiftly than cigarettes and alcohol. There are more pollutants than we recognize. Jesus performs a major act of public health when he bans from the community this source of sickness and damnation. When Jesus left the sick at the end of the last chapter and began teaching, he did not cease healing; he began to heal at the depths.

Jesus' surgical method is almost literally to scare hell out of his hearers. He confronts the bitter pool and its vapors with the still more bitter pool of divine judgment. Jesus' love teaching is not delicate. In Palestine, local communities held their own courts; but for more serious cases the local provincial heads and their councils held court. The worst place in Palestine, however, was the Geh (Valley) of Hinnom, just below Mount Zion, where a fountain once sprang and where Israel used to do despicable things when she followed Canaan's religious practices. In times of reform this idolatrous valley was turned into the city dump. And just as all city dumps are constantly on fire, so geh-Hinnom. Thus "Gehenna" became a sym-bol of the last judgment of hell.

So Jesus threatens the resentful and the verbally violent with three graduated sentences: the community sentence, the provincial sentence, and the city dump, and all three "mean what they mean," that hate gets judgment. (John the Baptist had said that the Messiah would baptize with fire, Matt 3:11, and now Jesus consigns to the fire of Gehenna the disciple who dishonors another, Schl., *Der,* 171.)

It is worth noticing that Jesus' vocabulary is contemporary, using the town court, the supreme court, and the city dump as his figures of speech for final realities. We are thus instructed to use similar, familiar expressions from our own environments for our teaching. Unimaginative hell preaching does little good. Preaching that uses familiar terms of social dissolution is more apt to make the point. But more than rhetoric is involved here. We do not know the topography, temperature, or very much else of hell. One is wise to be skeptical of even those who claim to know that hell "is not a place but a condition." How do they know so much? One thing we *do* know is that behind Jesus' picture words there is some kind of awful judgment for people who hurt other people.

A careful review of Jesus' teaching shows that he spent a great deal of his time warning people, particularly disciples, of the seriousness of judgment. We do not do a mythical love or the Master of love any honor by omitting references to judgment. We do a disservice to Jesus, however, when we merely rant or pound the pulpit or use florid language. Some hell preaching can actually be the preacher's grudge-bearing and verbal violence ecclesiastically camouflaged. But the abuse of a thing does not make wrong its use. Jesus teaches everywhere that serious ethical instruction should be undergirded by serious warnings. The holiness of God is at war with all bitterness and hatred and hurting. And where this holiness collides with our hostility the crash is called the wrath of God. God's wrath is God's war of love against everything that unnecessarily hurts others. God's love would not be love if it did not work to remove all that ungraciously hurts. The wrath of God is the proof of the love of God; God's love is a love that is not merely sentimental, for it grapples with inhuman forces.

The New Testament references to hell are not antithetical to New Testament references to love. It is love that warns of hell. "God hath threatened hell, not in order to cast us therein, but that He might persuade us to flee" (Chrys., 1:15:7).

"You shall call his name Jesus, for he himself will 'Jesus' (God-Save) his people from their sins" (1:21). The first social "Jesusing" is liberation from the sin of bitterness. The bitter person will not see God; he or she will go to judgment. This is Jesus' clear teaching here. The disciples' eyes do not have to be turned outward to find this bitter person. The venom is in our own breasts, waiting only the slightest provocation to come spewing out, hurting others, and so hurting ourselves.

Therefore, where these words of Jesus are heard with faith they slay us. If our anger is as bad as these two verses say it is, then we are not as surely enroute to the kingdom as we thought. Thus the first thing a serious hearing of these verses does is drive us immediately to the Beatitudes of need and to the company of the dispirited and grieving. Few words introduce us as effectively to the need for the doctrine of salvation by grace as Jesus' words of damnation by anger.

5:23–24 "So if you are bringing your gift to the altar and you remember there that your brother has anything against you, leave your gift right there in front of the altar, and go first and get right with your brother, and then come back and offer your gift."

Jesus' commands drive us not only to despair; they also drive us to doing. Every command of Jesus first humbles, but then it lifts. Thus while Jesus *begins* this command with a set of examples on how we break the old sixth commandment (grudging, belittling, demeaning), he *concludes* it by giving us two examples on how we can keep the commandment (immediate reconciliation, prompt meeting).

It is important that we know, first, that we *do* break God's command so that we will be disabused of self-righteousness and introduced to the *first* Beatitudes (poverty of spirit, grief, and meekness). But it is just as important that we know that we *can keep* God's command, at least retroactively, by immediately seeking reconciliation with those whom we have hurt and so be introduced to the *central* Beatitudes (mercy, purity, and peace). Perhaps it is impossible never to nurse anger or to say hard words, though Jesus is certainly seeking to make these disobediences more difficult. But it is possible to get right again or at least, from our side, to seek to get right again, with those we have hurt. Jesus is not content with just showing us up and bringing us down. He concludes his second command by teaching us what to do when we go wrong.

The first obedience, then in *keeping* the Monday Command is to make friends with the aggrieved brother or sister, and that as soon as possible. If it is sometimes impossible to keep our temper it should not be impossible to make amends for having lost it. Jesus' concluding contribution in this command is not the gift of a technique for controlling temper, but the gift of a reconciling will. That the two illustrations following Jesus' damning Word are illustrations of making up indicates that Jesus takes our weaknesses seriously.

"So if you are bringing your gift to the altar, and you remember there that your brother has anything against you . . ." (v 23). The illustration Jesus uses is the illustration of going to worship. This is not accidental, for one of the major purposes of worship is to remind us of our relationships. "In the performance of a sacred rite, the remembrance of offenses arises more naturally than in the noise of human affairs" (Beng., 1:113). For at worship we are at center; and at center we are reminded of circumference.

"That your brother has anything [*ti*] against you." The little unaccented particle *ti* (pronounced tee) indicates even by its smallness the possible insignificance of the "anything" the brother holds against us. The *ti* may be any "thing," it may even be something for which we are not to blame. The source, cause, or nature of the "thing" is not at all in Jesus' view; all that is important is that *some* thing is wrong.

"And He said not, 'When thou hast suffered any of the greater wrongs, then be reconciled'; but, 'Though it be some trifle that he hath against thee.' And He added not, 'Whether justly or unjustly'; but merely, 'If he hath aught against thee'" (Chrys., 16:12:113). Jerome, 1:114, correctly observes that Jesus does not say "if *you* have anything," he says "if *he* has anything," "in order to impose on you the greater seriousness of the obligation of reconciliation." Stier in Bengel, 1:114, therefore adds, "It is not enough to say, 'I have naught against him,' and so justify myself." Lohmeyer, 122, however, shows that Jesus' saying is so plastic that the "brother" here could even be the guilty party, and Jesus can even be commanding the *injured* party to seek reconciliation.

"Leave . . . the altar." The Lord does not want to talk with a disciple who does not want to talk with a brother. One reason some Christians' prayers are not answered is indicated here. Jesus makes it clear elsewhere in this sermon that if we will not forgive people who have failed us, our failures will not be forgiven us (6:12,

14–15). Thus in this saying Jesus teaches us that if we do not seek reconciliation with people we have hurt we come to the altar in vain.

"Leave your gift right there in front of the altar, and go first [*prōton*] and get right with your brother" (5:24). The rabbis had debated whether a commenced duty should be interrupted to do a neglected one, and they had concluded that each case depended on a calibrated evaluation of duties. A higher duty (e.g., toward God) takes precedence over a lower one (e.g., to a creature). Thus in the illustration that Jesus gives, the orthodox would have counseled, "First complete your worship to God, then go and be reconciled to your brother," for God is more important than human beings (Str.-B., 1:284). That Jesus occasionally reversed the traditional order indicates the behavior that got Jesus in trouble with his contemporaries. For more than once in his ministry it appeared that Jesus put people before God.

In our time one of the big debates in the churches is the debate between evangelicals and (as they are called) social activists (or, sometimes, ecumenicals). Evangelicals say that we must put Christ, his Word, and reconciliation with God first, and then people, the world, and reconciliation in society second. Ecumenicals argue for the greater integrity of the reverse order (or for serving God *by* serving others). There is something to be said for each decision when one consults the whole of Scripture. But the paradox is this: When Christians decide to put Christ and his Word first (Jesus is Lord), they soon discover that he often, as here, bids us put the other person first. We should be social *because* we are evangelical.

The church today is surrounded with a "Third World" (in all three worlds) that has a host of legitimate grievances against the ancient and modern imperialisms of the church and of the so-called Christian West. One thinks immediately of working people everywhere. The church that makes Jesus Lord will make the reconciliation with these historically neglected brothers and sisters *prōton*, principal, primary, first. Social reconciliation today is not a Christian elective, an evangelical afterthought; it is the order of the day.

"And then [*tote*] come back and offer your gift." It belongs to the wholeness of Jesus' illustration that he does *not* say, for example, "Go first and be reconciled to your brother, and then your worship is accomplished." In order both to worship and to be sensitized anew to fresh grievances, we are "then" to return to where we first began and where most beginnings, even of social justice, begin again and again—to the altar.

In my limited experience, many Christians engaged today by the social question were first confronted by Jesus Christ in evangelical churches. "At the altar," in an evangelical experience, they came to love Jesus Christ and his causes. Before long they discovered the depth of these causes, and soon they were on the streets. We like to think that we have moved beyond our earlier somewhat socially obtuse evangelical churches and their narrow conservatism. But if we are honest, it was there at those often narrow altars that the whole matter first began to make sense; it was there that Jesus Christ became a reality to us. We owe loyalty to those altars. I am inclined to think that Jesus' admonition, "then come back," means for many of us to return to that deep evangelical worship of God, to that priority of Jesus Christ first taught us in our evangelical churches where, or after which, we learned to care about his causes and about the priority of others. The fact that social concern does not seem to happen to all of our evangelical brothers and sisters at their altars is a problem for itself. Jesus Christ must not be made to suffer because his followers disappoint us. Jesus Christ at his altar—that is, in his church—is the power for all continuing social sensitivity and we neglect this altar at our own risk.

5:25–26 Jesus uses one more illustration to urge us to the importance of right relations with others. "Make friends quickly [*tachu*] with your opponent while you are still with him on the road, lest your opponent hand you over to the judge, and the judge hand you over to the jailer, and the jailer throw you into jail. Amen, I tell you, you will never get out of there until you have paid your last pretty penny."

The accuser is the aggrieved other. In this illustration he is not called "brother," and this allows us to understand the aggrieved as anyone. The judge, jailer, and jail can be understood both sociologically and theologically. When the *ti*-tied other is not immediately sought out, problems suddenly proliferate. The aggrieved person tells first one and then another about the grievance, and before one knows it one is caught in a cat's cradle of social hostilities. Jesus advises us to consider our own interests and so teaches that it pays to break the grievance chain at the earliest possible moment. But this is to see the story at only a certain level. At its deep level in Jesus' teaching the judge in the story is the living God, and the jailer and jail are pictures of God's justice, a justice that works both in this life and in the next, and in this life not infrequently at the level described mundanely above—at the level of increased social enmity.

The key word in this story, *tachu,* "quickly," like the key word in the immediately preceding story, *prōton,* "first," stresses the *urgency* of social reconciliation. Speed is of the essence in Jesus' teaching on anger and so in all subsequent Christian teaching. "Do not let the sun go down on your anger" (Eph 4:26–27); "when personal relations go wrong, in nine cases out of ten immediate action will mend them" (Barc., 1:145).

Jesus' final word in this paragraph is a word of warning. (Ending teaching with warning is often the case in this Gospel.) It is the warning that if we do not *quickly* seek out our accuser we are going to pay *lengthily* for our tardiness. If love (the motive of Jesus' first illustration of the worship service) cannot move us, then perhaps fear (the motive of Jesus' second illustration of the jail) can. Both motives are loving, for both seek to save us from our own damnation and others from hurt. Jesus warns us that the result of a dilatory response to a troubled relation is deeper and deeper judgment and exponentially increased bondage. "The sinner receives God's forgiveness only through the repentance that ends injustice" (Schl., *Das,* 70).

But "Jesus Saves," and here he very practically saves anyone who receives his command of social reconciliation with faith. All three central Beatitudes are fulfilled in obedience to this Monday Command: "Blessed are the merciful, for they shall obtain mercy"; "Blessed are the pure in heart, for they shall see God"; and "Blessed are the peacemakers, for they shall be called the children of God." In those who listen with faith, Jesus' command calls upon *and creates* the will to mercy, the passion for pure relations, the resolutions of reconciliation. Jesus' commands in Matthew are a form of his gospel. To receive Jesus' *commands* with faith (and so obedience) is very practically to be saved from proximate sins, just as to receive Jesus' *promises* with faith is to be saved from ultimate ones.

The spirit of the Monday Command is an exuberant concern for the welfare or peace of the other person. This command puts a bubble of protection around everyone the disciple meets, for the disciple, too, carries the plague of original sin within, that deep pool of bitterness. The soul of Jesus' command is almost perfectly and unconsciously commented on by Tarrou's conclusions in Camus' novel, *The Plague*:

Each of us has the plague within him; no one, no one on earth, is free from it. And I know, too, that we must keep endless watch on ourselves lest in a careless moment we breathe in somebody's face and fasten the infection on him.

* * *

The ethics of both East and West (Confucian and Greek ethics, for example) are built upon *self-respect*. (The heroic in epics is, in fact, a direct function of self-respect.) But self-respect, absolutized, is the mother of anger and hate, as the Greek epics show in general and as Achilles shows in particular. The characters in the *Iliad*, as C.M. Bowra, *Homer*, 113, shows, are so frequently angry *because* they jealously guard their self-respect—"that self-respect which rejects anything unworthy of heroic honour. They face their problems bravely and squarely and say exactly what they mean about them. . . . This brave candour reflects the self-regard which inspires heroic behaviour." Heroes in modern entertainment reflect these ancient and pagan notions, too. We see in pagan self-respect the meaning of Jesus' ethic of self-denial more clearly. Some of the vast biblical wisdom on anger is summarized in the following passages: Prov 12:16, 18; 19:11; 20:3, 22; Rom 12:18; Eph 4:31–32; 6:4; James 1:19–20.

Two of the wisest church parents summed up Jesus' command on anger this way: "Think not therefore that these sayings are in any wise hyperbolical, but consider the good done by them, and admire the mildness of these laws. For there is nothing for which God takes so much pains, as this; that we should be united and knit together one with another" (Chrys., 16:11:111; cf. 16:14:115).

"Let us then understand, Dearly beloved, that if no man can tame the tongue (James 3:8), we must have recourse to God, that He may tame it. . . . That the horse, and ox, and camel, and elephant, and lion, and viper, may be tamed, man is sought for. Therefore let God be sought to [*sic*], that man may be tamed. . . . Why, then, brethren, should we doubt that the Lord will make us gentle, if we give up ourselves to be tamed by Him? Thou hast tamed the lion which thou madest not; shall not He tame thee, who made thee? . . . Shall the image of God tame a wild beast; and shall not God tame His own image?" (Aug., *Serm.*, 5(55):2–3:273).

Particularly interesting in the Reformed understanding of this command is its active, even political reading. To keep the commandment not to kill means in fact "to save the lives of the innocent, to repress tyranny, to defend the oppressed." *Not* to keep this commandment is the same as "to murder, or to consent thereto, to bear hatred, or [most interesting of all] to let innocent blood be shed if we can prevent it" (*Scots Confession*, 1560 chap 14). This is good liberation theology.

The Confession of 1967 summarizes the Monday Command's positive meaning (and, incidentally, its relation to the prior Sunday Command of Piety) in this way: "The church disperses [from worship] to serve God wherever its members are, at work or play, in private or in the life of society. . . . The quality of their relation with other persons is the measure of the church's fidelity" (37).

C. True Day: The Tuesday Command of Sexual Purity (C 3), 5:27–30

"You have heard that it was said, 'You shall not break marriage.' But I say to you, every man who is staring at a woman in order to lust after her has already broken a marriage in

his heart. So if your right eye is causing you to sin, yank it out and throw it away from you, because it is much better that one part of you perish than that your whole body be thrown into hell. And if your right hand is causing you to sin, chop it off and throw it away from you, because it is much better that one part of you perish than that your whole body go off to hell."

The goal of the Tuesday Command is sexual purity and the will to wage decisive warfare against unfaithful lust. Lust is like anger in that it seeks mastery over another person. Both anger and lust put other people down, though by seemingly polar opposite emotions—by hatred and by desire. But the emotions of anger and lustful desire unite, finally, in their egoism, in their enjoyment of power over other people. People are used in both. (In Greek mythology, Ares, the god of war, is Aphrodite's lover.) Jesus declares war on both the secular gods of anger and of lust. Discipleship's first *social* forms are patience and purity. In the Tuesday Command, the disciple seeks to be true to Jesus and so to the other person by avoiding even subtle sexual seduction.

After murder, Jesus discusses the sexual relation in two successive commands (against lust and, in a moment, against divorce). Bonnard, 65, believes that it was in the sexual area that the shock of the Christian message was greatest in the demoralized Greco-Roman world, and he refers to the two Corinthian letters for documentation. Barclay, 1:153–56, has helpful examples of Rome's lamentable conquest by Greece in the realm of the sexual, an experience paralleled today in the Third World's gradual capitulation to Western eroticism, particularly through the influence of the all-pervasive media. Muslim fundamentalism is a last ditch attempt to secure the fortress. Disciples, too, must enlist in a warfare against cultural license, without the frequent legalisms of the Moral Majority. Tertullian's little tract "On the Shows" (about A.D. 200) cannot be read by Christians of any generation without pangs of conscience. And Chrysostom's cry, 37:8:249, must not be dismissed as fourth-century fundamentalism: "For whence are they, tell me, that plot against our marriages? Is it not from this theatre? Whence are they that dig through into chambers? Is it not from that stage? . . . So that the subverter of all things is he that goes to the theatre; it is he that brings in a grievous tyranny."

Christians today go to theatres, watch television, and read novels, but with a wise selectivity, a constant vigilance, and often with a vigorous repudiation. Being a disciple has always required Christians to be cultural atheists, publicly disavowing Aphrodite, Ares, and the myriad other gods of popular life. *Caveat Christianus.*

Jesus follows the exposition of the Decalog's commandment against killing, which protects life, with his exposition of the commandment against adultery, which protects marriage. Rather than command "You shall not break marriage," ascetic religion of all types has had commands such as, "You shall not get married at all," or even, "Leave the marriage you have and seek the spirit." In Theravada or classical Buddhism, for example, one forswears marriage and *all* desire when one wishes to be a truly holy person (to be an arhat-monk). In Hinduism, too, the higher and later holinesses of the *ashramas* (or stages of life) requires the forsaking of the marriage bond (cf. Gandhi's career).

But the God of Abraham, Isaac, and Jacob commands his people not ever to break or disparage marriage and, in fact, from the opening chapters of Genesis we have been taught, in Yahweh's own words, "It is not good that man should be alone; *I* will make a helper [*ezer*, literally "a savior"] for him who will be just right for him" (Gen 2:18). The biblical God loves marriage, institutes it, and now in his Son singularly protects it. It is therefore entirely natural that the creation stories of our Bible climax with a joyous and even erotic love song: "At last, this one is bone of my bone and flesh of my flesh!" (Gen 2:23). Hebrew religion, instituted by Yahweh, is thematically nonascetic. *Not* to be married was considered shameful in Israel. (Matthew's Jesus characteristically alters this, honoring the single life, 19:10–12.) Marriage was prized by the old people of God and so its breaking was prohibited.

"But *I* say to you" [*egō de legō hymin*—the *egō*, "I," is strongly emphasized in the Greek sentence]. That Jesus should put *himself* next to the Word of Yahweh in such a self-conscious way is already remarkable. The prophets began their messages with "thus saith the Lord." Jesus never used this prophetic formula. Instead, he regularly asserted, "But *I* say to you," or, "Amen, I say to you." Jesus was at least a prophet (cf. 21:11–16). But in his words there rings something clearer than the prophetic: we feel somehow that we are in the presence of the very Word of God itself, directly. Who of us, for example, would dare regularly to say, "The Bible says this, but *I* say to you"? The all-sufficient reason for the keeping of this difficult command of purity is Jesus' imperial, "But I say to you." No other reasons are necessary for a disciple.

"But *I* say to you, every man who is staring at a woman in order to lust after her. . . ." I have translated the present participle of the verb "to look," *blepōn*, as "staring" in order to bring out the force of the participle (Gundry, 88, translates "the leering look"). It is not just a look at another person that is condemned; it is a willful, sustained looking—what we in English call "staring." Looking at a beautiful person is a drive given in creation; staring or leering is a drive given in the fall from creation. All staring has a purpose, and the staring that Jesus condemns here, specifically, is lustful staring, staring with the intent to possess or at least to burn. The other person is no longer really a unique human *being;* she or he is now simply kindling, tinder, thing; a way for one to enjoy oneself, to express oneself, to feel one's powers. Jesus' concern is the human being and her or his valuation. Jesus' ethic is not first of all an ethic of self-development or self-culture; it is an ethic of other-honoring and of other-protection, flowing from the primary relation of obedience to the God present in Jesus (cf. Bonn., 65).

It is important to point out that despite some translations Jesus does not condemn looking "*with* lust" (the word "with" is not in the verse); every look at an attractive person is inevitably combined with at least some element of desire. Jesus condemns looking "*in order to* lust."

The Greek construction *pros to* with infinitive means purpose, "in order to": Chrys., 17:2:116; Aug., *LSM*, 43; Mey., 134; Lohm., 127 n. 1, *both* the goal-purpose ("in order to") *and* the result ("so that"); also McN., 64, with a preference for result; Grund., 160 and 160 n. 53, adducing Matt 6:1 where the same idiom in the context clearly means purpose; and recently Guel., 175, with the majority of interpreters. Jesus' command, then, is severe, condemning not only lustful looking but also looking that can lead *to* the awakening of lust (Lohm., 127 n. 1). Disciples, therefore, will often avoid those activities that excite such looking. But Jesus, unlike the Pharisees and rabbis, not only did not forbid the presence of women, he encouraged their presence, as Luke's Gospel especially celebrates.

The difference between looking with lust and looking in order to lust may seem subtle. But something important is protected by the difference: to see a person *with* desire is the result of a God-given drive (Gen 1:27–28; 2:18–24), to be enjoyed in the marriage relation; to stare at another person *in order* to desire that person is proscribed, for it uses another person, and it takes what God has given in creation—the created desire for the opposite sex—and uses it outside God's plan of marriage. The lustful stare goes beyond the desiring look like hate goes beyond prophetic anger or like theft goes beyond admiration.

And yet avoiding the second look, or the stare, and avoiding the strong irrational desire beneath most staring, are very difficult obediences. Thus for many this is the most difficult of all the commands of Jesus. The purity called for here is nothing short of heroic. This had *better* be a Word of Jesus—that is, a divine Word with power in it to do what it says—or else the case is hopeless.

We have all heard people, often psychologists, say in public that it is impossible to expect people, especially young people, to control sexual drives. Exegetes sometimes say the same thing, e.g., Beare, 152: "If this is to be taken as a 'demand' of Jesus, then it must be said that he is demanding the impossible, for it is the universal experience that the sexual impulses are uncontrollable" (similarly, Guelich, 242–43: "We are faced again with the human impossibility, the absurdity of meeting such a demand"). Yes, but "what is impossible with human beings is possible with God" (19:26), and thus it is *also* the universal Christian experience that sexual impulses *are* controllable. There are faithful marriages, and there are young premarried persons who are able to control their sexual drives. The fatalism of the social sciences is subject to the power of the universal lordship of Christ. Luther, "Treatise on Good Works", *LW* 44:105–06, is right: "In the matter of chastity a good strong faith is a great help, and more noticeably so then in almost any other [good] work. . . . Where a man has faith like this the Spirit tells him in no uncertain way how to avoid evil thoughts and everything that opposes chastity. For just as the certainty of God's favor toward us never ceases to live and be active in us, so too, that certainty never ceases to warn us in those matters pleasing or displeasing to God."

I do not think it is an evasion of this Word's power to say, first of all, that it drives its serious hearers to the Beatitudes of need: "Blessed are the poor in spirit . . . the grieving . . . the lowly . . . the longing to be righteous." For this hard command displays, as few other commands do, our lack of the spirit to check ourselves by ourselves, the state of our selfish hearts, the unjustified pride in our Christian character, and the absence within us of the respect that God and other people deserve.

This command levels. A person blessed with a good temper, for example, might be able to read the other commands of Jesus in this chapter and feel oneself a pretty good Christian. But this command slays. One might not readily believe in original sin—that is, in a depth sinfulness that lies beneath all sinful acts, shooting up like volcanic lava, deeper even than the level of our will—if this command were not here. ("The chief function or power of the Law is to make original sin manifest and show man to what utter depths his nature has fallen and how corrupt it has become." Luther, *Smalcald Articles*, 3:2:4, 1537.)

The sincere attempt to keep the command of purity reveals oneself to oneself. This command is the thorn in the flesh for many persons, especially men. If a man takes this command seriously, every new, attractive (or even half-attractive) woman shows him his fresh need for the strong grace of God. The commands of Jesus are the best evangelists because like few preachers they show us that without the forgiving help of Jesus Christ we are lost. Reformation exegesis of this command is the primary exegesis required if this command is to be heard in its deepest tones: *the commands of Jesus damn.* That is the first comment that needs to be made if we are to look this demand in the face.

Interestingly, the initial rhythm of the Beatitudes is the exact opposite of the initial rhythm of the commands. The Beatitudes first pick us up and then move us out (B 1–4, then B 5–8); the commands, on the other hand, first knock us down in order that we might seek to be picked up and moved on. The commands are in fact fitted to the Beatitudes: to drive us to them so that there, in the gospel, we might be picked up and empowered to do the commands (and not merely to bewail our inability to do them). Blessed are the poor in spirit, because theirs is the *power* of the kingdom. Blessed, too, are the pure in heart, for they shall *experience* God.

The Sermon on the Mount is not a legalistic message, antithetical to the gospel, as has often been felt. Nothing quite drives to the gospel like an attempt to keep the Sermon on the Mount. To take this sermon seriously is to feel that without the gospel of the undeserved grace of God the situation is hopeless. Nothing makes the gospel according to Paul more necessary than the Gospel according to Matthew. For if Matthew's Jesus is telling the truth, we badly need a justification or forgiveness that reaches down beneath our will, underneath our sinful acts, and that touches and covers our sinful *nature,* our subterranean *drives,* our *original* sin, our depths. If Matthew's Jesus is true, then Paul's Jesus is necessary.

Matthew was given a profound charisma for showing the *need* of the gospel, for teaching that bad news about ourselves that is absolutely essential if we are to seek the good news about God at all. Without Matthew's going before Paul in the canon, Paul could seem superfluous. Matthew's way of bringing us to the grace of Jesus Christ is a different route than Paul's, but it is a route equally calculated to bring us to the goal. Let us listen to what this Gospel is saying to us and seek to do what it says. In no other way will we experience Jesus Christ in this Gospel.

The obedience asked of us in Tuesday's Command, then, is the obedience that for the sake of Christ and for the honor of the other person controls sexual lust. This obedience is very difficult because it runs contrary to the pleasure principle (Schl., *Das,* 72–73). It is pleasurable to lust, to "enjoy" the other sex. This pleasure, left to itself, has enslaving power, and many a person experiences internal bondage to the presence, fantasy, or opinion of attractive others. For many people the real gods of daily life are members of the other sex, and much of one's day is spent trying to impress them. Thus this command, too, is a command seeking our liberation, a Word emancipating us from idols. Its first power is its ability to show us we are in chains.

5:29–30 Jesus intends this Word to *free* us from our chains in the command attached *to* it. Just as Jesus rounded out his anti-anger Word with a *reconciling* Word, so now he does not prohibit lust without equipping us with a *disciplining* Word. "So if your right eye is causing you to sin, yank it out and throw it away from you, because it is much better that one part of you perish than that your whole body be thrown into hell. And if your right hand is causing you to sin, chop it off and throw it away from you, because it is much better that one part of you perish than that your whole body go off to hell."

The central meaning of Jesus' advice is to take decisive, drastic action against that habit, thing, or person that, though pleasurable and perhaps even seemingly necessary, is in fact ruining life. Jesus does not advise cautious, gradual action; he counsels surgery, immediately. He does not advise Band-aids; he commands amputations. "Desparate cuts require desparate cures." The meaning is clearer if we think of another person, the famous third party. (Chrysostom, 17:3:118, and Schlatter, *Der*, 179, believe that Jesus is, in fact, talking here of the cutting out of intimate but compromising relationships.) The relationship may be tender; it may even seem necessary to life; but if it is known to be wrong, *"cut it out."* (Very often in such cases one knows what is right and wrong, but there are so many extenuating circumstances: it is the right eye, it is one's very own hand, etc.) The third party is a person, too, we tell ourselves, and we don't want to hurt her or him. So we suggest to ourselves that we make a break gradually. All such gradual breaks are ill-considered and, in the light of this command, disobedient. Jesus commands a swift, brutal, and seemingly uncivilized "tear it out and throw it *away."* But like the surgical emergency amputation, in the long run this mercilessness is the greater mercy. Mistaken compassion in disease can be fatal. "No half measures!"

The "right eye" may be almost literally something visual, a propensity for a certain literature or for certain entertainments. It is best for the interpreter not to go into much detail here. Jesus remains purposely vague: the conscience of disciples knows the erring eye or hand. Jesus' counsel is disarmingly simple: "Be tough with yourself; be completely decisive; in moral matters immediate action is nine-tenths the cure; in sexual purity decisiveness is everything."

The motive Jesus uses to secure this decisive action is again the motive of Geh-Hinnom, the garbage pit, complete destruction. Jesus advises that it is far better to undergo the extremely painful but still only partial self-destruction that the plucking of an eye or the cutting off of a hand dramatizes, if it means avoiding the total destruction of the valley of damnation. Better to go limping into heaven than leaping into hell.

It is well to notice Jesus' realism. He does not say that the sacrifice required for the purity of sexual relations is easy. A right eye is no cheap possession; a hand is a hand and there are only two of them. Jesus explicitly tells us by these words that he knows the sacrifice we make to keep our conscience and relations clean will be very hard and painful. Yet Jesus honors us by even thinking we can make the attempt. He dignifies us by asking such a decisiveness of us.

Large as the loss will be, Jesus says it cannot begin to compare with the disintegration of one's *whole* life. The maiming that moral life requires will be a thousandfold repaid with the wholeness of selfhood and the life with God that comes with amputation. "Blessed are the pure in heart, for they will see God!" Obedience will mean a maiming; we may feel we are being robbed of harmless pleasures and of personal independence when we are told to stop staring, cease lusting, and to cut out offending practices. But Jesus says that it is better to be maimed and alive than whole, dead, and eternally damned. It is better to limp and have integrity than to swing and be destroyed.

The use of "body" in Jesus' parable shows that with Jesus we are never dealing with the soul alone. Jesus' teaching is always a body-and-soul matter (Bonn., 67). Bengel, 1:115, accents the word "one" used twice here by Jesus for emphasis and comments, "Many, indeed, have been destroyed by neglecting the mortification of one member, [such] as the gullet."

Jesus' command of purity has been criticized for emasculating men, idealizing women, and for being supermoral, rigoristic, and perhaps worst of all, utterly unrealistic. But I think it must be said first of all that Jesus' command serves Christians deeply by teaching them the depth of their sin, by showing up the large measure of unreality in their Christian lives, and therefore by driving Christians also to repentance. Then, this command has the power of being one of the few words from important persons which protects marriage on its sexual side. It is evident everywhere that marriage is in danger in our time, and that sexual laxity is one of the main causes of this danger. In this command and the next, Jesus places himself unequivocally on the side of the purity and permanence of the marital relationship; Jesus' Tuesday and Wednesday Commands stand like lions before the door of the home. The Christian who is serious will never be able to sit loose to sexual or marital morals after hearing this sermon. Many spouses have come home at night faithfully because these commands were alive in them and others. This command does not emasculate. It requires—and gives—integrity, especially in a key context, the home and the married relation. It is a good command; it belongs in the Good News.

In its original form in Matthew's Gospel, this command protects women from men. It is a feminist text, defending women's rights (Grund., 159–60; Schw., 121). Expositors today correctly teach the command from the other side, too. For women also lust. It is true as well that if a person is guilty for inordinate *looking* at another person, then the man or woman is also guilty who seeks inordinately to *draw* the look (cf., e.g., Isa 3:16—4:1; Schl., *Das,* 72). All seduction, active or passive, is damned by this text. Popular culture thrives on the theme of seduction and would grind to a thundering halt without it. But the Jesus of this command is not as pleased as culture is by titillation.

The Psalm joined in the church's lectionary with the exposition of Matthew 5:21–24, 27–30, 33–37, includes this catechetical question and answer, "How can a young man keep his way pure? By guarding it according to thy word" (Ps 119:9). The Christian is called to a continual war: "If you live according to the flesh you are going to die, but if by the Spirit you constantly put to death [*thanatoute,* present tense, meaning repeatedly] the deeds of the body, you will live" (Rom 8:13); "Put decisively to death, [*nekrōsate,* aorist, in a bold act], therefore, what is earthly in you: immorality, impurity, passion, evil desire" (Col 3:5, my translations; cf. Eph 5:3–4).

"Here there is need for heroic courage" (Aug., *LSM,* 46; similarly Cal., 1:188–89; Mey., 135). But Luther, *SM,* 88, is right: "We should not make the bowstring too taut here, as if anyone who is tempted and whose lust and desire for another woman are aroused would be damned for it. . . . 'If an evil thought is involuntary (as the theologians say), it is not a mortal sin.' It is impossible to keep the devil from shooting evil thoughts and lusts into your heart. But see to it that you do not let such arrows (Eph 6:16) stick there and take root, but tear them out and throw them away. Do what one of the ancient fathers counselled long ago: 'I cannot,' he said, 'keep a bird from flying over my head. But I can certainly keep it from nesting in my hair or from biting my nose off.'" The flip side of Jesus' command is really to love one's wife. Even severe old Chrysostom, 17:2:117, saw this: "If thou desirest to look and find pleasure, look at thine own wife, and love her continually." Similarly, Lu., *SM,* 89.

*   *   *

In his *Small Catechism* (1529), Luther taught the church to remember the commandment against adultery in this simple way: "We should fear and love God, and so should lead a chaste and pure life in word and deed, each one loving and honoring his wife or her husband." *The Heidelberg Catechism* (1563) rightly interpreted the commandment against adultery to teach that "all unchastity is condemned by God and that we should therefore detest it from the heart and live chaste and disciplined lives, whether in holy wedlock or in single life" (Q. 108). *The Confession of 1967*, 47, devoted one of its four great social paragraphs to the theme of sexual relationships.

D. Wedding Day: The Wednesday Command of Marital Fidelity (C 4), 5:31–32

"You have heard it said, 'Whoever divorces his wife should give her a written document of divorce.' But I say to you that any man divorcing his wife for any other reason than sexual infidelity drives her into adultery, and whoever marries a divorced woman commits adultery, too."

The goal of the fidelity command is the lifelong love of marriage partners. In marriage matters Jesus is in special earnest. This is his second straight command protecting marriage (and he only gives six commands in this series). In exposition the positive goal of the command should not be left unfocused: Jesus wants disciples to love their marriage partners deeply. (On Wednesdays, we may say for catechetical purposes, obedience buys flowers, goes out to dinner, celebrates the marriage partner.)

The prohibition in the command is difficult, and in our time, for many reasons and for many persons, painful. I will spell out the problems involved in obedience to this command partially here and fully when we come to chapter 19 where marriage, divorce, and remarriage are treated in much greater detail (19:3–12).

Jesus' command of fidelity has only two provocative sentences. But in these two sentences we have a summary of Jesus' essential feelings about the marriage relation. The Mosaic requirement of a bill of divorce (in Deut 24, summarized here in 5:31) was a civilized act at the time, for the old people of God were dismissing their wives too easily. From Deuteronomy 24 forward a man must provide the woman he divorced with at least the dignity of a document indicating the divorce was his decision, not hers, thus declaring in a formal way that the woman could be married again. Deuteronomy 24's divorce legislation, Jesus later teaches (19:8), was concessionary legislation. Deuteronomy 24 was intended to dam the eroticism of a male chauvinism that dismissed wives to the street without legal rights and then thought it could take them back at pleasure. The paper of Deuteronomy 24's concession at least put a legal right into women's hands, if not a sense of self-respect into their hearts. In the next sentence (v 32), Jesus proceeds to put rights into women's lives, and before the Gospel is done Jesus will have honored women in several more ways.

But even Deuteronomy 24's concession was abused by male chicanery (cf. Schw., 123). As we learn in detail in chapter 19, Jesus penetrated the sexist stratagems of his times and returned believers from Deuteronomy's concession to Genesis' intention, to the original will of God in instituting marriage at all, namely, the equal dignity and permanent union of one man and one woman in marriage. Jesus here places himself foursquare on the side of the legally weaker party (in this case, the woman) and against the concessionary legislation of Deuteronomy (as read by the laxer party in Jesus' time, the party of Rabbi Hillel). Jesus reinstitutes God's original creation plan of inviolable marriage.

Deuteronomy 24:1–4 should be kept open by the student of this text. The all-important first verse begins by saying, "When a man takes a wife and marries her, if then she finds no favor in his eyes because he has found some indecency in her, and he writes her a bill of divorce and puts it in her hand and sends her out of his house, and she departs out of his house . . ." (RSV). (Verses 2, 3, and 4 then continue by saying that if the thus divorced woman remarries and her *second* husband divorces her or dies, "then her former husband, who sent her away, may not take her again to be his wife, after she has been defiled; for that is an abomination before the Lord. . . .")

Several preliminary problems must be solved before we can understand Jesus' difficult teaching of his fourth command in Matthew 5:32. (1) First, Jesus in v 32 seems to place himself *against* the teaching of Deuteronomy 24:1–4 (summarized in Matt 5:31) in two ways: (a) Deuteronomy 24 *allows* a man to divorce his wife, which Jesus clearly seeks to prevent in Matthew 5:32a and in every other text, *unless*, Matthew's Jesus adds, there has been sexual infidelity; (b) Deuteronomy 24 allows a divorced woman to *remarry*, which Jesus seems to forbid in Matthew 5:32b (Guel., 245–46). According to Matthew 5:31–32, even if an innocent (i.e., nonadulterous) husband divorces or even separates from an innocent (nonadulterous) wife, without either party intending a second marriage, he "drives her into adultery" (in the severe formulation of Matthew's Jesus in Matt 5:32), and so the divorcing husband is no longer innocent (Lohm., 129 n. 1). Thus Jesus is not merely contravening or even relativizing the lax *rabbinic* interpretation of the text of Deuteronomy 24; he appears to be countermanding the very text of Deuteronomy 24 itself.

(2) Second, the battle over the interpretation of Deuteronomy 24 was fought in the first century between the schools of Rabbis Shammai and Hillel, and the battle can be summarized as a war over two words in Deuteronomy 24:1: "if then she finds no favor in his eyes because he has found *some indecency* [*ervath davar,* literally "nakedness of a thing," *BDB,* 789] in her," etc. The liberal Hillel stressed the word "some" [*davar,* "thing"], and said Moses meant "any" indecency such as bad housekeeping; the conservative Shammai stressed the word "indecency" [*ervath,* "nakedness"], and said Moses meant only the ultimate indecency of marital infidelity. (Rabbi Aquiba stressed the still earlier words in Deuteronomy 24:1 that said "if then she finds *no favor* [ḥēn, i.e., grace, beauty] in his eyes because he has found some indecency in her." He interpreted this to mean "if she no longer seemed beautiful to him" or if another woman seemed more beautiful to him, he could divorce. On these several rabbinic interpretations, cf. Str.-B., 1:313–14.)

Matthew's Jesus sides with the conservative Shammai, particularly with "the Matthean exception" in 5:32 (and 19:9)—divorce is prohibited "except on the [very serious] ground of unchastity" (RSV).

(3) Third, as Green, 248, is especially helpful in making clear, in the thought of the old people of God, *men did not commit adultery against women;* rather, either (a) a woman committed adultery against her husband, or (b) a husband committed adultery against another husband. *Husbands,* in other words, were the only victims of adultery. Jesus reverses this conviction drastically in this his earliest teaching on marriage. "Any *man* [*hos an,* masculine] who divorces his wife and marries another woman commits adultery *against her* [*ep autēn,* i.e., against his first wife]" (Mark 10:11; cf. Luke 16:18). A woman is a person full of dignity in Jesus' teaching; she is not property. A husband can be as guilty as a wife in adultery, according to Jesus (Guel., 201). And thus Jesus shows that a *woman,* not just a man, can be a victim of adultery.

In protecting the woman, Jesus is recovering a portion of the Old Testament, the poignant Malachi 2:13–16 paragraph, where the Lord no longer accepts certain offerings "because the Lord was witness to the covenant between you and the wife of your youth, to whom you have been faithless, though she is your companion and your wife by covenant. . . . 'I hate divorce, says the Lord the God of Israel . . .'" (RSV).

5:32a "But I say to you that any man divorcing his wife *for any other reason than sexual infidelity* drives her into adultery." Matthew alone of the evangelists includes what is called the "Matthean exception," the little clause that allows divorce: "for any other cause than sexual infidelity [*porneia*]." In a case of sexual infidelity, Matthew's Jesus says, the disciple does not so much divorce an unfaithful spouse as he or she recognizes a fact: a divorce has already occurred; the unchaste spouse simply does not live as a true marriage partner any longer. A divorce has already happened in reality (*de facto*); thus a legal (*de jure*) divorce recognizes in law what is already true in life. In obedience to Jesus' prior command of mercy, the offended disciple will seek reconciliation, repentance (the partner's and one's own), and mutual forgiveness—and seek these for as long as possible. But there are limits.

When infidelity has occurred, Luther, *SM*, 96, gives this advice "to those who really want to be Christians": Try to stay together. If the guilty party is humbled and reformed, the innocent party should try to forgive. But if there is persistently loose behavior, Christians should *not* forgive, for "one oversight is still pardonable, but a sin that takes mercy and forgiveness for granted is intolerable." Luther, *SM*, 97–98, citing 1 Timothy 5:8, believes desertion is also a ground for divorce. (Desertion is a form of sexual infidelity.) But apart from sexual infidelity (i.e., marital immorality) and desertion, all other faults and foibles in a partner should be borne, in Luther's conviction, with Christian forbearance.

The fact that fornication or marital immorality (*porneia*), which I have translated "sexual infidelity," has such separating power is stressed by Augustine, *LSM*, 61: "However, in this part of the Gospel nothing is to be noted with closer attention than that fornication is so great an evil that, while in wedlock people are bound to each other by so strong a bond, this one reason for breaking it is excepted." For an excellent review of biblical teaching on fornication, adultery, divorce, and remarriage, I recommend Elizabeth Achtemeier, *The Committed Marriage* (Philadelphia: Westminster, 1973), especially chapter 7, "Is the Tie Blessed that Binds?" pp. 109–31. The interpretation that sees *porneia* as marriage contracted in forbidden degrees of consanguinity (e.g. with a cousin), following Baltensweiler, *ThZ* 15 (1959), 340–56, and represented, e.g., by Bonn., 69–70, and Guel., 209, has not convinced me or most other interpreters (cf., e.g., Schw., 125; Gund., 91).

In Mark (our earliest evangelist) and Luke, there is *no* exception at all in Jesus' teaching on fidelity in marriage. "Any man who divorces his wife and marries another woman adulterates his wife, and if she who has divorced her husband marries another man she commits adultery" (Mark 10:11–12). "Every man divorcing his wife and marrying another woman commits adultery, and he who marries a woman divorced from her husband commits adultery" (Luke 16:18).

It is interesting to notice that Roman Mark, in contrast to Palestinian Matthew, heard Jesus discuss divorce from a woman's side as well as from a man's (notice the reversal of roles in the second line of Mark, above). Of still greater interest is the fact that, unlike Matthew, neither Mark nor Luke heard Jesus give an *exception* to lifelong marriage. If, as in Matthew, the historical Jesus *gave* an exception, then it would not seem to be true (or complete) to report that Jesus gave no exceptions, as in Mark or Luke. If on the other hand the historical Jesus gave *no* exceptions (as in Mark and Luke), then it would not seem to be true (or accurate) to say that there is an exception, as in Matthew. This *prima facie* irreconcilability has to be appreciated before we can seek to understand the texts together. Are there or are there not exceptions to the rule of marriage's inviolability?

First, it is important to introduce as collateral testimony the famous "Pauline privilege," as it is called, Paul's' independent understanding of an exception to the dominical rule. (We notice in Paul's text that he clearly understood what Jesus, "the Lord," had said; Paul just as clearly and candidly says that he, Paul, and *not* the Lord, had a supplementary understanding: the Pauline exception.)

> To the married I give this ruling, which is not mine but the Lord's: a wife must not separate herself from her husband; if she does, she must either remain unmarried or be reconciled to her husband; and the husband must not divorce his wife. To the rest I say this, as my own word, not as the Lord's: if a Christian has a heathen wife, and she is willing to live with him, he must not divorce her; and a woman who has a heathen husband willing to live with her must not divorce her husband. . . . Otherwise your children would not belong to God, whereas in fact they do. If on the other hand the heathen partner wishes for a separation, let him have it. In such cases the Christian husband or wife is under no compulsion; but God's call is a call to live in peace. Think of it: as a wife you may be your husband's salvation; as a husband you may be your wife's salvation (1 Cor 7:10–16 NEB).

Here is how the case stands: Mark and Luke heard Jesus give no exception; Matthew heard Jesus give a moral exception, and Paul, in his authority as an apostle, felt authorized to give a spiritual exception. Again our question is a simple one: Are there or are there not exceptions to the rule of marriage's indissolubility?

With the help of the historical-critical study of Scripture we can hear the witness of the diverse texts as the Lord's Word in the following way. Mark and Luke, without the exceptions, heard what was said *by* the Lord in his historical ministry as Jesus of Nazareth; Matthew and Paul, with their exceptions, heard what they heard *in* the Lord, in their capacity as evangelist-apostles of Jesus. In Mark and Luke we are closest to Jesus' original teaching; in Matthew and Paul we hear the risen Jesus' supplementation of his original teaching by means of the creative thought of his spokesmen. In Mark and Luke we have Jesus, 1; in Matthew and Paul we have Jesus, 2. Disciples should hear these texts in this order, too: first giving the most serious attention to Jesus' original historical teaching in Mark and Luke, then giving equally serious attention to Jesus' inspiration of his evangelist and apostle in the supplementary teaching of Matthew and Paul. All four texts are inspired; all four texts come from overlapping but different traditions; but all four texts come ultimately from the same Lord.

I learned this distinction from Lohmeyer, who speaks of sayings *kyriou* (*of* the Lord) and sayings *en kyriō* (*in* the Lord). There are other ways to assert virtually the same thing: by saying (a) that "the Christian Church, with its authority to bind and loose ([Matt] 16:19;

18:18), early made the exception to meet a pressing ethical need; and since the need has not ceased, the exception is valid today" (McN., 66)—binding and loosing involves the church's right to interpret Scripture, under the aegis of the Lord, for changing situations; (b) that "the phrase 'apart from the matter of immorality' comes from Matthew, not from Jesus, as an editorial insertion to conform Jesus' words to God's Word in the Old Testament" (Gund., 90). Through the centuries the church's doctrine of the inspiration of Scripture has enabled Christians to be reverently attentive to *every* text in Scripture; the church's more recent historical-critical study of Scripture has enabled Christians to be completely honest in *distinguishing* texts and to ask rigorous questions of them.

The next feature to see is this: while the Jesus of Matthew 5 sees divorce as forcing the woman into adultery, the Jesus of Mark and Luke, where we are closest to Jesus' historical teaching, unites with the Jesus of Matthew 19 (not Matt 5) in seeing adultery committed *not* with divorce, but with remarriage (while the other partner is still living). We may listen one more time to Mark, "whoever divorces his wife *and marries another* commits adultery against her" (Mark 10:11), then to Luke, "everyone divorcing his wife *and marrying another* commits adultery" (Luke 16:18), and finally to Matthew in chapter 19's fuller teaching, "I say to you, whoever divorces his wife for any cause other than immorality, *and marries another*, commits adultery" (19:9). According to these three witnesses, it is remarriage, not just divorce, that adulterates.

This clear threefold teaching about divorce and remarriage means that there are situations where living together under the same roof is not possible: for example, where the situation for the children or for one or both spouses is so destructive that living together is wrong, the termination of legal life together is not a sin but the obedience of discipleship. In short, separation or divorce is not always infidelity to Christ; it can be Christian fidelity. A divorced person can be a true disciple.

The discipleship of the faithful divorced is one of the world's most difficult kinds of discipleship. (It is not accidental, therefore, that Jesus' full teaching on marriage and divorce in Matthew 19 is in the midst of Jesus' three predictions of his *suffering*—16:21; 17:23–24; 20:17–19—*and* in the midst of his successive calls to *suffering discipleship*—16:24ff; 17:24ff; and 20:20ff—i.e., it is not accidental that Jesus' teaching on marriage and divorce is under the sign of the cross.) The point to stress is that in Jesus' teaching there is a discipled divorce and an undiscipled divorce, a right divorce by a violated person, and a wrong divorce consummated in anger or in order to marry another person.

It is important to see next that Matthew, who intends to be more systematic, has not altered Jesus' original point of marriage inviolability with his famous exception. Once we have seen that none of the other biblical texts records divorce per se as adultery, Matthew's exception brings clarity—and stringency. Matthew's Jesus, by allowing separation or divorce in exceptional cases, is simply saying what the Jesus of Mark, Luke, and Paul (as in 1 Cor 10:11–12) would say when (as in Matthew) confronted with the case of the unrepentantly promiscuous spouse: This marriage is of course over; divorce is necessary and not just possible, if repentance and reconciliation cannot happen. Matthew's exception is stringent, not, as is often thought, permissive, in that immorality is the *only* ground for divorce that Matthew heard allowed, whereas in the other evangelists divorce may be possible for *other* reasons.

Contrast Strecker, 132, who says that Matthew's exception is not rigoristic at all but permissive, since the· earlier church did *not* see infidelity as a cause for divorce. But Schniewind, 64, agrees with Schlatter, *Der*, 179–80, that in the ears of the old people of God it was impure to say that marriage is unbreakable even when an affair is continued; Schniewind cites 1 Corinthians 7:10–16 (cited above) as a text expressly presupposing that there can be justified cases of divorce.

But when the marriage is over, the disciple's fidelity is not. This hard fact deserves special treatment. The overwhelming central conviction of all three synoptic evangelists and of the apostle Paul in reporting Jesus' relationship to divorce is that married, separated, or divorced, the disciple will seek to remain faithful to the other person "till death do us part." The *marriage* may be over; marriage *fidelity* is not. ("What is common to all these Gospel texts, including 1 Corinthians 7:1–40 and especially vv 10–11 with reference to the 'Lord,' is the polemical accent against any divorce. The famous Matthean 'exception' must be seen in this context," Bonn., 68.)

This forced divorce of Matthew's exception *is* life under the cross; this is (in some cases) "love of enemies" to an eminent degree; this is discipleship of the highest order. For this reason the faithful divorced disciple needs the church's special support, not disdain.

Jesus does not want divorce (5:31–32); but if there must be divorce, Jesus does not want remarriage (Matt 19; Mark 10; Luke 16; 1 Cor 7). We cannot summarize the New Testament's teaching here any more clearly—or less painfully. (In the exposition of Matthew 19 in *The Churchbook*, the second volume in this commentary, the text requires me to come to somewhat different conclusions.)

In a succinct note, the always careful Schlatter, *Das*, 74 n. 1, summarized by saying that because of 1 Corinthians 7:11 there can be no objection to state law permitting some persons to dissolve a relationship, but that remarriage goes against Jesus' Word.

Matthew's continuation of his abbreviated teaching here in chapter 5 is worth noting. The man (Matthew heard only this side) who divorces his wife "involves her in adultery" (NEB). The focus of the text is compassionately riveted on the endangered woman. We are not even specifically told in this Matthean command that the man who divorces the woman is *himself* an adulterer. (Is this a survival in Matthew of the old, sexist point of view?) Moreover, adultery in this command only seems technically to happen where there is remarriage while the other partner is still living. (Sexual immorality, *porneia*, is a wider category than adultery—adultery technically means the breaking of a *marriage*.) In Jesus' teaching, a divorced person is terribly vulnerable to adultery. Jesus here recognizes the primitive power of the sexual drive. Jesus is not blind to reality or pre-Freudian in the sense of sexual naiveté.

5:32b Jesus' marriage-protecting teaching concludes by saying, "and whoever marries a divorced woman commits adultery, too." His teaching here gets harder, and the danger for the expositor is to push Jesus' words from hard to harsh. So precious is the marriage union in Jesus' sight that whoever takes home someone else's (even divorced) marriage partner contaminates not only that person and partner but oneself as well. Whoever touches the divorced person—and this command sees this touching as almost (but not necessarily) inevitable—adulterates not only the divorced person (and the already contaminated divorcer), but oneself as well. So sacred is the marriage bond that even when it is externally broken it lives on with a kind of inward taboo power, with a kind of *mana*, contaminating anyone who dares to break what God's own hands have joined together. Is this too harsh?

Jesus' command draws a definite circle around a married (and around even a divorced) couple and writes beside them: "*Do not touch.*" This couple belongs together for life, even when they are not together. There are three dead or dying persons in this Wednesday Command: the husband who starts the death of the divorce, the wife who is almost mortally wounded, and the third party who touches her and so is mortally wounded himself. This Word ends like a Shakespearean tragedy.

The intention of these simple but full two sentences is to underline in a dramatic way that divorce is ordinarily inimical to the will of God and that remarriage (while the other partner is still living) is extraordinarily inimical. Unfaithful behavior pollutes. Expositors can speak more subtly and with greater grace when they come to Jesus' complete teaching on this delicate topic in the nineteenth chapter. But we do not do justice to the text before us if we introduce too promptly a grace that is patently not yet here. A misguided charity must not lead us to dismiss a clear fact: Jesus abhorred divorce and remarriage. Malachi 2:16 was also in Jesus' Bible, "'For I hate divorce, says the Lord the God of Israel. . . . '" The Wednesday Command places Jesus' unconditional "No" over any tampering with the marriage bond, even by a seemingly innocent outsider who would marry a divorcée. This command blazes with the holiness of the marriage union and with death to all who fool with it. If this Word cannot drive men and women to the Beatitudes, what can?

In the *Beatitudes*, as in the rest of the Gospel, there is forgiveness of sins. Who fits the Beatitudes more perfectly than the person who feels one's own sin or failure *in marriage*, the closest of all relations? "Blessed are the poor in spirit, . . . blessed are the brokenhearted." Blessed are the divorced who are deeply sorry; yes, blessed are the divorced and remarried who acknowledge their sins, repent of them, and believe the gospel of full forgiveness of sin. Teaching Jesus' divorce sayings is unpleasant work because it often hurts and puts down people who have been hurt and put down enough.

Here the church must openly ask the question: "Can God's blessing rest upon a remarriage?" One answer to this question, surely, must be: "Is there forgiveness of sins in the church?" And the answer to both of these questions is yes. Yes, there can be God's blessing on a second or even subsequent marriage because, yes, there is forgiveness of sins for the sincerely repentant person in the gospel of Jesus Christ proclaimed in his church. But the forgiveness of sins is the forgiveness of *sins*. There is no forgiveness of anything less serious than sin; if we try to remain above sin ourselves, however ingeniously, by excusing ourselves or accusing mainly the partner or someone else, or if we try, however subtly, to say *we* had no sin, or little sin, then it must be made clear that for unsinful persons there can be (by definition) no forgiveness of *sins*. Thus there should be no remarriage of such persons in the church. Jesus Christ forgives only sins and sinners. He does not forgive mistakes or mistakers or those who seek prematurely to forgive themselves. There is forgiveness of sins in the church only for those who truly repent of their sins.

But real sins and real sinners, Jesus can forgive. There are churches that permit the divorced or the divorced-and-remarried to become church members but not church officers. This does not seem right for it is close to saying "we will forgive, but we will not forget." What God forgives, he fully forgives and thus forgets. So must the church.

One of the major problems with teaching the Gospel texts on divorce is that the divorced and remarried are so visible. The sins of the rest of us are more conveniently invisible; we are not always sure who are impious (C 1), bitter (C 2), philanderers (C 3), liars (C 5), revengeful (C 6), haters (C 7), vainglorious (Matt 6 A), careerists, or money-grubbers (Matt 6 B). We cover our sins rather effectively. Is divorce, or are divorce and remarriage, more deeply sinful than the anger and revenge that Jesus condemns in his surrounding commands? Are divorce and remarriage the unforgivable sins? But don't we sometimes give the impression in the church that we think they are?

We must always remember that the *text* of Jesus' commands (including this one on marriage) lies within the *context* of Jesus' gospel, a gospel that says, for example, "Blessed are the merciful, they shall receive mercy" (B 5). The church is always to teach faithfully both text and context, both Jesus' commands and Jesus' Blessings, both Jesus' antagonism to sin and his forgiveness of sin wherever there is true repentance and amendment of life. Jesus' hard texts must be taught with just the right measure of hardness but always in the context of the infinitely gentle gospel. Jesus' marvelously freeing message of plenary forgiveness of sins for the sorrowing penitent must be taught *con brio* but without ever dismantling Jesus' high commands. For both Jesus' gospel and his commands have the same end: the deep helping of people, the salvaging of lives, salvation. God-Saves is Jesus' name, and he saves both by his tough commands and by his forgiving Blessings. Disciples must be careful to keep faith with both.

In this Wednesday Command, Jesus is protecting the exploited party in his culture—"the disposable woman." It is Jesus' way, we learn repeatedly in the Gospels, to side with the oppressed. In our culture, some divorced persons now need Jesus' protection. And the repentant and forgiven remarried disciple in our time deserves Jesus' protection, too. Everything Jesus teaches about forgiveness and renewal in the rest of the Gospel delivers this protection. A pastor (Bill Goff) was asked for counsel on this difficult subject. His response was helpful: "God hates divorce, but God loves divorced people." God *saves* the repentant divorced.

Thus we have come full circle—to almost the teaching of Deuteronomy 24 (as read by its serious interpreters in the school of Rabbi Shammai). Matthew, even with his antitheses, would not have wanted readers to think that Jesus flaunted Old Testament law. The reverent attentiveness to Hebrew Scripture that Jesus' Command of Biblical Piety taught us can be extended even to Deuteronomy 24. McArthur, 146–47, believes that Jesus probably understood even Deuteronomy 24:1–4's permissions to be *divine*, and not just mistaken Mosaic modifications. "Any other attitude on the part of Jesus would involve a view of the Pentateuch almost without precedent in Jewish circles." Jesus believed, McArthur continues, that God's unconditional will (in Genesis 1–2) said "no divorce," while God's conditional will (in Deut 24) said "divorce under some circumstances." "I can only state my conviction," McArthur concludes, "that [Jesus] would have assumed that the circumstance which justified the modification of the unconditional divine will in the Mosaic period would, if repeated, lead to the same conclusion in the first century. In other words, [Jesus] did not say: 'I am withdrawing the concession made [by Moses] because of human weakness.' On the contrary, he said: 'You must not assume that the concession made to human weakness represents the original or unconditional intent of God.' . . . I am suggesting that Jesus would have expected this small distinction [between the Genesis unconditioned and the Deuteronomic conditioned will of God] to be applied in other areas of his ethic, specifically in the Sermon on the Mount. The way of true obedience may be to follow the conditioned will rather than the unconditioned— because of the hardness of men's hearts. But the conditioned will which we follow must never be confused with the unconditioned, which remains as the final guide."

McArthur's two-storied truth honors (a) Jesus' double tribute to the Hebrew Scriptures and (b) Jesus' superceding or fulfilling of the Hebrew Scriptures in the New Testament gospel. In his recent study, Guelich, 248, comes to conclusions rather similar to McArthur's: "As sinners with 'hard hearts' God's Law on divorce [in Deuteronomy] still obtains. Just as Paul and the early church recognized the presence of sin in one's experience and adapted the divorce sayings [of Jesus] accordingly, so today we must also recognize that divorce was also given by God as part of the Law to protect individuals for whom the element of sin has destroyed the marriage relationship. One must recognize that situations exist in which God's accepting forgiveness [in the gospel] and the divorce Law [in the Old Testament] offer opportunity for one to seek God's intended wholeness in another relationship."

The most helpful answer I have encountered to the question, "Is divorce *ever* possible for a follower of Christ?," is in the book referred to earlier, Elizabeth Achtemeier, *The Committed Marriage*, 128–31, where, after a faithful survey of the high biblical teaching on marriage, she concludes: "Divorce is never the intention of God for our marriages. We can make such a general statement on the basis of the Biblical evidence [just reviewed] . . . Christ could heal our marriages; there is no doubt about that. He has conquered our sin by his death and resurrection. . . . Divorce is never 'good,' never 'right,' and never 'justified' in the eyes of God" (128). In divorcing, we can only believe we are doing wrong, with deep anguish and repentance (129). But with such an attitude, "there is indeed forgiveness and acceptance and the opportunity of a new life, even in a new marriage, offered by the gospel. God tells us that he can make all things new (Rev 21:5)." The church's self-righteousness and shunning of divorced or remarried persons is sin (130), but so is the casual remarrying, "live and let live" attitude toward divorce of some clergy and laity—see Revelation 21:8 (131).

*   *   *

In the first set of three commands (after the introductory spiritual command of piety), Jesus has taught his church to banish enmity, eroticism, and infidelity from her midst. We can call this set Jesus' *social* commands. Jesus' disciples are to be characterized socially by a countercultural warfare against their own and society's temperamental and sexual laxities.

Anger and unfaithful lust have been the enemies in the social commands. What unites these disobediences? In anger we would like to prove to ourselves and to others that we are right; in lust we would like to prove to ourselves and to others that we are attractive. In both we manifest a deep uncertainty about ourselves. In both we seek a "justification" of our selfhood. Cheap popular culture teaches us that the angry person is the vital person and that the seductive person is the real man or woman. But in fact deep personal uncertainty of one's own vitality unites the drives of anger and unfaithful lust and prompts us to seek to bring others under our control. By the angry feeling or word we can put others in their place; by the lustful stare, act, and stratagem we hope we can bring others under our power. And if we can succeed in doing these things, we succeed, provisionally, in validating ourselves to ourselves. These disobediences are both "justifications by power."

But without explaining why, Jesus places a protective covering around every person we meet. He says, in effect, "Don't touch the honor of other persons by hurting them with your anger; and don't touch other persons by your egoistic lust either."

There are civil ways to state our anger in conversation which allow us honesty and which at the same time treat our opponent with humanity—Jesus made this clear by concluding his Monday Command with two mandates to conversation (5:24–26). There is a legitimate, God-created lust, made for marriage and its enjoyment (Gen 2:18–25). Jesus' commands are not simple repressions; they are commands that seek the *civilized* expression of drives.

Does Jesus do irreparable harm, however, when he makes people feel guilty about ever being angry or lustful? Thoughtful psychiatrists and psychologists raise this question, and we know what they mean. We should always beware of saying more than Jesus says. Meanwhile, Jesus here clearly seems more interested in describing the hurts of anger and lust than he does in describing the hurts of suppressing anger and lust, and we should listen.

See a modern reaction against the psychological conventional wisdom that suppressed anger is more harmful than creatively controlled anger: Carol Tavris, *Anger: The Misunderstood Emotion* (New York: Simon and Schuster, 1982, especially the summaries at pp. 26–27, 45, 102, 143–45). Tavris's dismantling of some psychology's "ventilationism" is thorough. It is a pity, however, that she does not know the difference between the Old Testament and the New Testament when she writes, 27–28, "Is [anger] a human blessing, or a bestial sin? (The Bible does not answer, now recommending the furious smiting of the unjust, then the ameliorative turning of cheeks.)"

An immense respect for human rights—for human *beings*—emanates from Jesus' commands. Jesus is not content with the simple absence of immediate killing or direct adultery. He goes to the roots. He wants the banishing of, or at least warfare with, the two great sources of the destroying of nations, persons, and families: inveterate anger and unfaithful lust. He intends to begin this warfare in his disciples, and in this way to make disciples the salt of the earth and the light of the world (5:13–16). Disciples are to be the world's advocates of the Rights of Man. This passion for the *humanum* unites not only the first three social commands; it unites Jesus' whole mission.

Luther was impressed in the commandment against adultery with, "first, how highly God honors and glorifies the married life, sanctioning and protecting it by his commandment." And a little later he sees its special value in relation to the family and the raising of children (*Large Catechism*, 1529, 1:206–09).

Among the creedal discussions of marriage and divorce, the revised *Westminster Confession of Faith*, chap 24, says what needs to be said here most beautifully, and is quoted at the end of the full discussion of Jesus' teaching on marriage and divorce at Matthew 19.

E. Truth Day: The Thursday Command of Spoken Truth (C 5), 5:33–37

"Again, you have heard that it was said to the people of old, 'You must not break your sworn oaths,' but 'You must do what you swore to the Lord you would do.' But

I say to you, Do not swear at all, not even by using the name 'heaven,' because it is God's throne, nor 'by the earth,' because the earth is God's footstool, nor 'for the sake of Jerusalem,' because it is the city of the great King, nor by swearing by your own head, because it is not you who turns hair gray or dark. Instead, let your yes mean yes, your no mean no. What goes beyond these simple words is from the Evil One" (5:33–37; cf. James 5:12 for a clear cross reference).

The command of truth seeks to protect speech in the community as the immediately preceding two commands sought to protect sex. The trustworthiness of what we say is as important to a community's welfare as the trustworthiness of our temperament (C 2), or our morals (C 3–4). Discipleship applies to speech, too. In this command Jesus seeks to make our speech simpler, less exaggerated, more down to earth, and even (in a certain sense) less outwardly spiritual, or less filled with spiritual formulae.

On Thursdays we may think especially of the ways we communicate. Honestly? Simply? Clearly? Do we use God's name (or spiritual equivalents) too blithely? Are we scrupulously concerned about the truth of what we say?

The sequence in Jesus' commands is instructive. The Sunday Command of Piety summarizes the first table of the law, i.e., the *first four* commandments regulating our duties toward God. The Monday Command of Mercy summarizes the Sixth Commandment against murder. The Tuesday Command of Purity and the Wednesday Command of Fidelity summarize the Seventh Commandment against adultery. (The rabbis understood the Eighth Commandment against stealing in three ways: as a commandment against [a] deception, [b] theft, and [c] kidnapping, Str-B., 1:810–11. In a sense, adultery is all three. Thus Jesus' Wednesday Command of Fidelity can also be understood as Jesus' comment on the Eighth Commandment.) The Thursday Command of Truth is Jesus' commentary on the Ninth Commandment of the Decalog against false witness (Stend., 777).

As a command against deception (in the rabbinic understanding seen above) this command of truth can also be understood as Jesus' commentary on the Eighth Commandment against stealing. Will it then be possible to understand Jesus' last two commands (vv 38–48 against revenge and against hate) as his commentary on the last two commandments of the Decalog (against false witness and against coveting)? Not without strain—and we have already been straining a bit. The point is that Matthew's Jesus *is* commenting mainly and authoritatively on the Ten Commandments. The Ten Commandments are the Old Testament summary of God's will; Jesus' Sermon on the Mount commentary on the Ten Commandments is the New Testament summary of God's will, and it is the authoritative ethic today for the people of God. (Lest one wonder if Jesus comments at all on the Fifth Commandment to honor parents we can refer to Matthew 15:3–9 where Jesus pays that commandment special homage.)

The words introducing our present command of truth—"Again, you have heard that it was said to the people of old"—repeat for the first time the same *full* formula used at the beginning of Jesus' command of mercy (C 2, 5:21). By this repetition Matthew signals that Jesus is starting a new set of three commands. Because of their ramifications the present set of three commands, C 5–7, can be called Jesus' *political* commands just as the prior set, C 2–4, contains Jesus' *social* commands. (The first command, C 1, on our obedient relation to Scripture, is the fountain or spiritual command from which all the other commands receive their force.) Thus both the Beatitudes (B 1–4, 5–8) and the Commands (C 2–4, 5–7) are divided into two great sections. Cf. Grund., 163. On Matthew's catechetical love for sets of threes (three divisions in the genealogy, three temptations, two sets of three petitions in the Lord's Prayer, three devotions, three sets of three miracles, three passion predictions, three prayers in Gethsemane, three denials by Peter, etc.), see Allen, lxv, and Bult., 188, 314.

This command of Jesus not to swear at all seems to be a full-blooded *antithesis* to the many Old Testament commandments to swear (e.g., the commandment Jesus used in warding off the third temptation says, in full, "You shall fear the Lord your God; you shall serve him, *and swear by his name,*" Deut 6:13; cf. also, "offer to God a sacrifice of thanksgiving, and pay your vows to the Most High," Ps 50:14).

At first, Jesus' command against oaths seems to be the least weighty and least relevant of all his commands. How can taking oaths compare with taking life or breaking marriage? And yet the more one studies this command the more one is impressed with its range. Did Jesus realize that this command not to swear *at all* would put us in tension with governments, all of which require oaths? With this command, we first decisively enter—and question—the political order.

Civil life at its critical junctures is knotted with oaths; thus Christians at these same junctures are asked to be wary. Jesus' command stands peremptorily above all subtle distinctions and declares, summarily, "But I say to you, do not swear *at all.*" Like other commentators, I will seek to explain how we make our way through the maze of civil requirements and their oaths. But my conscience is always somewhat uneasy when I do. I think that if Christians read this command with a deserved fiduciary obligation and then face an oath, they will always ask themselves, "Can I say yes or no here? Must I take this oath?" Obedience to this command of truth will require our consciences to be rubbed raw again and again. This command politicizes.

Jesus was not alone in condemning oaths: Others included Sophocles, Philoctetus, Pythagorus, Epictetus (except for emergencies), Philo (except for emergencies), and the Essenes (except for entering the order). Cf. Lohm., 132 and Grundmann, 165–66, who adds that in the rejection of oaths Jesus brought the human-ethical sensibilities of classical antiquity to fulfillment. In many ways, Jesus fulfills not only Hebrew Scriptures but antiquity's wisdom as well.

A craven legalism can take root in the disciple at this point, too, of course. The *Schwaermerei* of fanaticism and ostentatious obedience can ruin any command. But so can ingenious evasions. One clear goal of Jesus' command is the dismantling of the whole lying structure of oaths and of oath-taking, at least in the church and (as befits mission) at length in culture. Jesus' command has the perpetual possibility of civil disobedience inside it. Society requires people to be swearing all the time. Disciples must uncomfortably question society's doing this and ask at times respectfully for permission not to comply. I can see no other way with good conscience to begin to interpret this at first seemingly innocuous but finally very penetrating command.

Strathmann concludes his informative article, "Oath," in the *Evangelisches Kirchen Lexikon* (1:1032) with a program that illumines the sharp edge in Jesus' command more clearly than I have read anywhere else:

"Eminent juristic authorities from F. Liszt to Kahl and Ebermeyer have held that the legal oath has become completely outdated. But even from the Christian standpoint, decisive reservation must repeatedly be registered against the whole nature of oaths (and has been registered for a long time, again and again, by significant theological and philo-sophical ethicists), not only where the oath is required of persons who do not really believe in God, but also because of one's own convictions. For one thing, the one who swears assumes for oneself a certain power of attorney for God which one does not have. For another, the oath is a misuse of religion for profane ends, ends we seek to reach, lacking other means, by using the 'metaphysical ass's-ladder of the jurists' (to put it in Schopenhauer's words). But it is entirely unacceptable that the one who takes the oath should be obliged to block the divine forgiveness and to pawn one's eternal salvation for the sake of any conceivable earthly obligation. But that is the implication of the formula, 'so help me God,' . . . [etc.]. The objection that is always raised against this standpoint, that our church-confessional writings allow the oath that is required by the government, and that the Bible is to be interpreted in the light of our confessional writings, is not supportable. For 'God's Word should make articles of the faith, and no one else, not even an angel' (Luther's *Smalcald Articles*, 1537, 2:15 M 304) . . . The texts of Holy Scrip-ture treated above—Matthew 5:33–35 and James 5:12—leave, however, little to be desired in the way of clarity."

We have to be proud of Jesus for so long ago having seen through the oath and for having put this teaching in the center of his commands. Taking this command seriously makes disciples politically salty. I have the feeling that Jesus gave this command, among other reasons, to make disciples always question the state and their relation to it. This command is not as irrelevant as it at first seems.

5:33–34a "'You must not break your sworn oaths,' but 'you must do what you swore to the Lord you would do.'" (Guelich, 249, shows two kinds of oaths in Jesus' summary: an assertive oath [v 33a] "by which one affirms or denies having done something [in the past], and a promissory oath [v 33b] by which one swears to do/use or not to do/use something [in the future]. . . . The former has to do with one's honesty, the latter with one's faithfulness." "But *I* say to you, do not swear at all" (v 34a). Jesus' opposition to oaths is opposition to the faulty presupposition of oaths, namely, that there are two kinds of statements: those supplied with oaths—these, of course, must be kept unconditionally; and those unaccompanied by oaths—these, too, should be kept, but the obligation to keep them is not as great. Jesus resists all split-level truth (Hunter, 55).

One is reminded of comparable Old Testament wisdom: "You shall not have in your bag two kinds of weights, a large and a small. You shall not have in your house two kinds of measures, a large and a small. . . . For all who do such things, all who act dishonestly, are an abomination to the Lord your God" (Deut 25:13–16). The New Testament is full of statements like the following: "Therefore, putting away falsehood, let every one speak the truth with his neighbor, for we are members of one another" (Eph 4:25).

Jesus is fighting for the integrity of all speech, sworn or unsworn. A community is not stable when words cannot be trusted. It is important to Jesus that disciples' words be invested with an almost sacred significance. It is a veritable Confucian "rectification of terms," a sanctification of speech, that Jesus is effecting here.

5:34b–36 The devout tried to avoid the careless use of the divine name by swear-ing "by heaven" or "by Jerusalem" or even "by my own head." But Jesus indicates the obvious: "everybody knows what you mean when you say heaven; and when you invoke Jerusalem you are simply invoking the aura of God's great institutions." Jesus also tells us that when we swear by our own head or life, we have not left God behind. For even our physical life is not our own; it is in God's hand when our hair turns gray. In other words, we are quite presumptuous to think we can enlist even ourselves as warranty for our promises, as if we had final control over our lives. Even when we swear by ourselves we are in fact invoking God since it is God who will either keep us in the picture or take us out of it altogether.

A Christian's simple yes is to be the equivalent of a pagan's string of oaths. A Christian's no is to mean no.

The meaning of Jesus' command is "that disciples should avoid as far as possible the use of unnecessarily strong expressions of affirmation. . . . For [the Christian] Yes and No should be sufficient. His ungarnished statements should carry with them the authority of truthfulness" (Allen, 53).

Christian speech is not to be characterized by its greater or more unctuous use of the divine name. It is to be characterized by the twin features of simplicity and honesty. Honesty, in fact, leads to simplicity. ("The more sincerely we speak, the more simply may we speak, for others will learn to believe our word alone;" Stier in Beng., 1:117.)

How then can we justify our oath-taking when Jesus seems so clearly to forbid it? First, when Jesus was placed under oath at his own trial and commanded by the incumbent authority in the name of God to tell whether or not he really was the Christ, he responded—simply (26:64; cf. Paul too at Gal 1:20; Rom 1:9; 2 Cor 11:10–11, etc.). The Christian learns from Jesus' own behavior at his trial that when *others* in authority place us under oaths we can respond as Jesus did, as simply and as unelaborately as possible. Here, too, if possible, we can say simply yes or no, or I do, or an equivalent, as Jesus did. Jesus is Lord. Second, Jesus addresses disciples, not the state, in the Sermon on the Mount. He outlaws *Christians* swearing, but he has not outlawed civil oaths. The distinction is subtle but necessary. "Give to Caesar what is Caesar's . . ." (Matt 22:21). The disciple practices civil obedience where possible and Christian obedience always. We may *take* oaths from authorities, as Jesus did innocently; but we may not *make* oaths independently, without disobeying Jesus' command.

See Luther's exposition of this command, *SM*, 98–104, in the following sentences: Jesus does not intend to interfere with secular life or government here, Luther claims, for Jesus and Paul used oaths; swearing is forbidden in exactly the same way that killing and lusting were forbidden in the prior commands: i.e., lust is wrong *except* with the woman God has given you, and anger is wrong *except* that which is demanded of you in your office by law (101). Jesus (in Matt 23) and Paul (in Gal 1) were obliged even to curse. If one has authorization from God, one has the right to swear. For example, if the prince demanded an oath of allegiance, or a judge demanded an oath from a witness, it would be our duty to take that oath, on the basis of Rom 13:1 (102). But, Luther finally asks, what about Jesus' forbidding us to swear *at all?* "Here it is not you that is swearing, but it is the judge who is ordering you to do so. . . . Now, Christ is neither prohibiting nor prescribing anything for the government here, but He is letting this realm take its own course as it should and must. What He is forbidding is unauthorized, capricious, or habitual swearing. Similarly, when He forbids you to draw your sword (Matt 26:52), He does not mean that you should disobey the government if your territorial prince needs you or summons you to go to war" (102). Even the modern, critical Conzelmann, 65–66, agrees with

Luther's assessment: "Jesus does not demand that the oath as an institution be abolished, but he forbids swearing (Matt 5:33ff, cf. 23:16ff), i.e., He commands truthfulness. This makes swearing superfluous. Truthfulness is possible where I am relieved of anxiety about myself [as one is by Jesus' teaching], and mistaken machinations to save myself are no longer necessary."

5:37 The "make-take" distinction (making oaths is wrong, taking oaths is possible) is present, some say, even in the final sentence of Jesus' command: "What goes beyond [a simple yes or no] is from the Evil One" (5:37b), i.e., oaths are necessary in a fallen world. But Jesus' sentence first of all and more simply means what it says, that all speech that moves beyond the clear yes or no has its source in the devil. This yes or no clarity also means that there is something devilish about all pedantic or painted speech that seeks to impress with its learning, cleverness, or even devotion. The devil is the author of both extremely abstruse and of extremely pious speech. We saw the devil at his "holy work" in the temptations, quoting devoutly from Holy Scripture (4:6). Jesus means here, first of all, that speech that goes beyond yes or no simplicity is speech infected by the Evil One (cf. Schl., *Der*, 183–84).

The boldness of Jesus' saying that oaths come from the devil (or from evil), when the Old Testament said that they came from God, should not be missed (Lohm., 134–35). Thus Jesus' Word "forbids oaths and demands unconditional truthfulness in speech, while the righteousness [of Moses and that of the Pharisees] is satisfied with the prohibition of perjury and with the command to be true to one's sworn word" (Wind., 69). Jesus' command this time is not epithesis but antithesis (cf. Schl., *Der*, 181). Schlatter sees this unique Matthean text as being dangerously near the later heresy of Marcionism, but as avoiding Marcionism's slandering of the Old Testament because Matthew "saw the devilish work in lies, not in natural things" (*Der*, 183–84).

Yet as Schniewind, 66, suggested, Jesus' words may have a more subtle meaning: "What goes beyond these simple words is from the Evil One" or (as the hidden gender can also be translated) "from evil," or "from the evil world." Whenever speech is supplied with oaths, as it was in Jesus' trial for example, the source of this fact is the evil condition of a world in and to which oaths seem a necessity if citizens are to be impressed with the special seriousness of their words in court.

We are obliged to sign many legal and civil documents under oath; the whole of civil life is a series of oath-supplied statements. Christians, too, take these oaths. The source of these oaths (and the reason they are necessary) is the evil condition of the world and, ultimately, the Evil One himself, the ruler of this world. Christians take oaths simply because an evil world requires them, but they take them, as it were, under duress. They give back to Caesar what Caesar gives to them, even if it is tainted. "Let every soul be in subjection to the ruling authorities," the apostle commanded us (Rom 13:1). Christians, like Jesus before them, are under both secular government *and* authoritative oaths. But Christians (unless in government vocations) are not to *make* oaths themselves or to require them of others. Thus the Magisterial Reformation taught that Christians, like their Lord, *take* some imposed oaths not because they approve them but because they suffer them.

The positive focus of Jesus' command of truth, then, is this: the *whole* of Christian speech is to be invisibly oath-laden, transparently honest. When a Christian says, "I will be there," the Christian will be there. When a Christian says no, the Christian means no. When a Christian joins a group or enrolls in a course or accepts an invitation, the Christian fully means what that act entails and is, simply, faithful and there. Yes means yes. By obeying this little command, a Christian's whole life is invested with the seriousness of an oath. ("Evangelical truth does not admit an oath since every word of a believer is considered an oath," Jerome in McN., 67.)

Luther felt that there were good grounds for believing that all monastic vows by which people swore the impossible were rendered invalid by this command. The church should at least seek to remove oaths from her *own* life, even if she cannot yet make society do so, because a Christian vow is often a contradiction in terms. For example, a vow in God's name to perpetual chastity, or to obedience to other persons, comes close to playing God, or allowing others to play God, and can at times fly in the face of Jesus' explicit command here to *disciples* to avoid *making their* oaths.

There is a host of vows in some churches: choir vows, youth vows, officer vows, and other kinds of membership vows. One can question their legitimacy in the light of this command. The state may require marriage vows, and the Christian may submit to this requirement (Rom 13; 1 Pet 2:13f; Matt 22:21). But even here the Christian's submission, like that of Jesus, can be in the form of a simple yes or I do. The only kind of explicit vow that would seem to be countenanced in the apostolic writings is the baptismal vow, but it too might better be called a "prayer for a good conscience," as one apostle put it (1 Pet 3:21). Ordination vows should be a reaffirming of the fundamental baptismal commitment.

On the whole, Jesus' Thursday Command means that disciples should beware of making big promises to God (cf. Peter at Matt 26:31–35). They should seek to simplify all solemnities and the speech used in them, and to make promises as *un*deity-laden as possible and all responses as susceptible as possible to simple yes or no answers.

Without a quibbling legalism, for the sake of simple obedience to Jesus, and for the purification of language, the worshiping church should investigate her speech to simplify and "de-oath" her services. For speech is the basic way persons have communion with each other, and worship is the basic way we have communion with God. Where speech in church services can be simple, trustworthy, and relieved of excessively unctious references to deity the congregation's life will be more pleasing to God and more straight with people. Jesus' command of truth is a command for perpetual liturgical renewal.

The *Constitution on the Sacred Liturgy (Sacrosanctum Concilium)* (1963) of the Second Vatican Council put what Jesus seeks here beautifully: "The [liturgical] rites [of the church's worship services] should be distinguished by a noble simplicity; they should be short, clear, and unencumbered by useless repetitions; they should be within the people's powers of comprehension, and normally should not require much explanation" (34).

The command of truth combines the central commandments of both the first and second tables of the old law, namely, the commandment (in the first table), "You shall not use the Name of the Lord your God in a wrong way," and the commandment (in the second table), "You shall not bear false witness against your neighbor." We love God (the great concern of the first table) by that reverence for his Name that, paradoxically, keeps us (in oaths or in other ways) from using the Name too much. And we love other people (the great concern of the second table) by being trustworthy, even without oaths, in our speech to them and about them. In a certain sense, all four of Jesus' last commands are united by a desire for good faith toward other people: by avoiding that which hurts them (unbridled anger), toys with them (unbridled lust), sits loose to them (infidelity in marriage), or fails to be trustworthy with them (oaths).

In all of these commands we see Jesus' concern for *persons*. When we let these commands work on us we begin to see that every single person—lumpenproletariat or bourgeoisie, Philistine or sophisticate, mass man or elite—*every* man and woman is important to Jesus, and therefore important to disciples, too. God's law in its exposition by God's Son—the Sermon on the Mount—is humanity's real Bill of Rights.

*   *   *

In the *Large Catechism*, Luther addresses the problem of false oaths and in so doing shows rather (or too?) provocatively how closely related the Wednesday and Thursday commands of marital fidelity and verbal truth are to each other:

"If one party in a dispute swears falsely, he will not escape punishment. Though it may take a long time, nothing he does will in the end succeed; everything he may gain by the false oath will slip through his fingers and will never be enjoyed. This I have seen in the case of many who broke their promise of marriage; they never enjoyed a happy hour or a healthful day thereafter, and thus they miserably perished, body, soul, and possessions" (1:67–68).

The thirty-ninth article of the Anglican *Thirty-Nine Articles* (1562; 1801), "Of a Christian Man's Oath," is typical of the Reformation and Catholic position with the permitted "take" of civil oaths and the proscribed "make" of most other oaths:

"As we confess that vain and rash Swearing is forbidden Christian men by our Lord Jesus Christ, and James his Apostle, so we judge, that Christian Religion doth not prohibit, but that a man may swear when the Magistrate *requireth*, in a cause of faith and charity, so it be done according to the Prophets' teaching in justice, judgment, and truth." (Schaff, 3:513–14.)

The Heidelberg Catechism (1563), question 101, asks, "May we not swear oaths by the name of God in a devout manner?" and answers:

"Yes, when the civil authorities *require* it of their subjects, or when it is otherwise needed to maintain and promote fidelity and truth, to the glory of God and the welfare of our neighbor. Such oath-taking is grounded in God's Word and has therefore been rightly used by God's people under the Old and New Covenants."

Craig's Catechism (1581), in the commentary on the commandment against bearing false witness, succinctly summarizes Jesus' intention in this command of truth: "Q. What is the end of this commandment? A. That the simple truth remain among us."

The Westminster Confession of Faith (1647) goes to great lengths to defend oaths in its chapter, "Of Lawful Oaths and Vows." As so often, in my judgment, the Westminster "protesteth too much." But the following sentence captures its main emphasis: "Yet as in matters of weight and moment an oath is warranted by the Word of God under the New Testament as well as under the Old, so a lawful oath, being *imposed* by lawful authority, in such matters, ought to be *taken*" (chap 22:2; emphases added).

La Bible de Jérusalem (rev. ed., 1973) has a lucid note on the meaning of the final sentence of Jesus' command of truth, which may be translated like this, "Let your conversation be 'Yes? yes,' 'No? no'; when one says more than this, it is because of the Evil One" (v 37):

"This formula . . . [the French Jerusalem Bible comments] can be explained in several ways: (1) Veracity: If you mean yes, say yes; if you mean no, say no. (2) Sincerity: Let the yes (or the no) of your mouth correspond to the yes (or the no) of your heart. (3) Solemnity: [When the Greek is translated, as literally it most easily can, "Yes, yes, or no, no"] the repetition of the yes or no would be a form of solemn affirmation or negation that should suffice of itself and dispense with recourse to an oath that engaged divinity" (*ad loc.*).

F. Friend Day: The Friday Command of Peacemaking (C 6), 5:38–42

"You have heard that it was said, 'An eye for an eye' and 'a tooth for a tooth.' But I say to you, do not try to get even with the evil person; instead, when someone slaps you on the right cheek offer him the other also; and if someone wants to take you to court for your shirt, let him have even the coat off your back; and if someone bullies you to go one mile, go with him two. Give to the person who asks from you, and do not turn your back on a person who wants to borrow."

The command of peacemaking is Jesus' command against revenge. "Have a heart," not because people are basically so lovable or because they are made in God's image (an argument that Jesus does not specifically use, though the feeling for it is there) or because it will pay off later in conversions, but again simply because Jesus commands it. All other motivations are secondary. (On Friday, catechetically, we seek a relation of friendship with the unfriendly because of Jesus' command.)

This command is meant, first of all, in the basic I-Thou relations (see the four second-person *singular* examples in vv 39b–42, suggesting that obedience to this command is, first, personal and individual). Yet publicly and politically, as in the civil rights movement of nonviolent resistance led in the United States by mainly black Christians (M.L. King), this command can also be obeyed creatively in *We-You* relations. I say "creatively" because at first glance resistance seems to be exactly what this command forbids, even if the resistance is nonviolent. And yet in "The Little Sermon on the Mount" (Matt 18–20), Jesus explicitly commands us, "If your brother sins, *confront* him!" (Matt 18:15). Matthew 18 nuances Matthew 5 to say that nonviolent confrontation is not necessarily revenge (similarly the fundamental Lev 19:17). The point in introduction is this: Jesus' command of peacemaking is even politically relevant. Where dared, it has changed the face of even national life (cf. Gandhi's truth, convicting because it was Christian truth practiced by mainly non-Christians).

Jesus' command is vulnerable to dangerous distortions. Jesus does not say, "If someone slaps your *neighbor* on the right cheek, offer the other as well." When Jesus' command against revenge has been used as a command against community defense, against police and armed forces, mischief rather than obedience has happened. If British militia had not (finally!) defended Gandhi's nonviolent resisters the carnage would have been far worse. We need the pacifist conscience in our midst to keep us honest and to make us ask uncomfortable questions. Arms have always been one of the easiest national idolatries (see the prophets). Yet it needs to be insisted that Jesus' command is not a command to civil magistrates to disarm; it is a command to disciples to seek to make peace in all difficult personal and public relations.

If judges cease to fit punishments to crimes ("an eye for an eye"), if authorities turn the *community's* other cheek by not penalizing criminals, havoc occurs. Our text has historically been as often overinterpreted by pacifist zealots as underinterpreted by militarist bourgeoisie. The results have been fair neither to the text's meaning nor to the community's welfare. Obedience to this command is hard enough as it is; when this obedience is turned into a program of hateful resistance to, or disrespect for, legitimate governance, Jesus' mission has been badly misunderstood.

5:38 It is important first to notice (as in the murder, adultery, and even divorce legislation of Moses earlier in this sermon) how good the *old* commandment was that Jesus commented upon and that he now revises and puts in a new edition. The old eye-for-an-eye commandment did two things: It checked wild revenge, and it taught the administration of justice. Prior to this commandment it was possible that injury to a member of one's family would be avenged by a family's killing or maiming one or more persons from the offending family. One still witnesses so-called "Sicilian justice" in many contemporary situations (cf. *The Godfather*). An eye is avenged by a vendetta. Moses said that it must not be that way in Israel. The punishment must fit the crime. Therefore an *eye*—not a life—for an eye, a tooth for a tooth. This Word was civilized, advanced, and just.

The "law of the tooth," *lex talionis,* was widespread legislation in the ancient world, and was at least as old as the eighteenth-century B.C. Code of Hammurabi. Cf. Schl., *Der,* 184–85; Green, 85; Gund., 94.

Justice continues to be required by law in all civilized communities today. As in Jesus' treatment of the earlier commandments against killing and adultery, this commandment against injustice is not abrogated by Jesus, it is deepened. Political society must continue to keep the old commandment of justice. The gracious and just Old Testament "law of the tooth" is still legitimate civil legislation and will forever remind the community that God *wants justice* and is not pleased when the taking of an eye goes unpunished. It is a part of love, an important part, that there be justice. The old commandment stands guard forever against all sentimental interpretations of love. Chrysostom, 16:8:109, defends the much maligned Old Testament God here: "Whereas thou sayest, 'Because He commanded to pluck out "an eye for an eye," therefore He is cruel'; I say, that if He had not given this commandment, then He would have [been cruel]."

5:39 But disciples go farther. In a life that constantly experiences injuries to honor (the meaning of the slap example), unfair or litigious treatment (the meaning of the shirt example), exploitation (the meaning of the forced mile example), and most mundanely, just plain being taken advantage of (the meaning of the borrow example), disciples are to render justice in a surprising way: by the suspension of justice and the rendering of magnanimity. The peacemaking command is the command of a radical rejection of self-assertion.

The apostle Paul gives one classic rationale for this command: "'Vengeance is *mine,*' says the Lord, '*I* will repay'" (Rom 12:19, citing Deut 32:35). Justice has not died in the world; "the Lord lives"; there *will* be divine justice on every hurtful, unfair, exploitive act in history (see C 2). One meaning of the "judgment according to works" taught everywhere in Scripture, and by Paul no less than by Jesus, is that there will be a cosmic "eye for an eye," a last judgment *lex talionis;* there will be justice on earth.

It is a common experience in daily life that, moved by a sense of justice, we try to "get even" when others treat us unjustly. The other person needs (as we say) to learn a lesson, and so we deliver the lesson in the several well-practiced forms of angry justice in our repertoire. One reason for our frequent anger is the created instinct for justice that burns in the breast of each of us. We feel deeply within that injustice should get its due. One reason Americans found themselves desiring the full punishment of the Watergate criminals was the feeling common to all that proud injustice needs strict justice. This feeling for justice is by and large created and correct, though it is always corrupted by our fallen nature. But when individual Christians are treated badly, when in daily life their superior is verbally abusive or fellow workers inconsiderate or family members thoughtless—the hundred and one experiences of Everyone—disciples are to be "surprising people" (Bonhoeffer). They suspend judgment. They respond with grace, giving the other cheek, the other garment, the other mile. (Cf. "the prodigal father" and his undeserved love for both his prodigal and prideful sons in Luke 15.)

Grundmann, 170, sees the difference between this command and the preceding ones to be this: In the preceding commands we asked, How may a disciple protect the right of *others* (the point of C 2–5), but in this command we ask, How does one act when one's *own* rights are attacked (C 6)? And the answer is: With a radical undefensiveness. (The eighth Beatitude comes to mind: "Blessed are those who are persecuted for righteousness' sake.") Schlatter, *Das*, 79, reminds us that all who are called to govern and protect others—parents with children, judges with criminals, etc.—are granted the use of coercion in Scripture. But recent studies encourage those who work with children and others to see Jesus' teaching of gentleness here as not merely idealistic but as eminently reasonable (cf. Kuhn in Berger, 161 n. 44).

Frequently, Christians are public persons in official capacities, representing and defending others, and these Christians' responses to injustice in such cases, while gentle and peace-seeking in form, may be firm and severe in effect. Persons in authority must defend their communities from exploiters of every kind, not avert their eyes or turn other people's cheeks. Sexual harassment requires women to pursue their rights from authorities; racial and other discriminations require minorities and those exploited to seek judicial redress. Jesus' command is not a command of irresponsibility or cowardice, it is a command for disciples to seek peace. As noted earlier, Jesus' famous "other command" is still in the Gospel: "If your brother sins, confront him" (Matt 18:15; Lev 19:17). It takes a fine-honed Christian conscience to discern when one is a private person and so commanded to make *peace* without justice, and a public person and so commanded (for the sake of others) to seek *justice* with peace. Paul himself wrestled with this question, and sometimes sought justice: "To decline legal justice would often involve injustice to others; [so] St. Paul did not scruple to appeal to it [i.e., to legal justice] (Acts 16:37; 24:10–21; 25:8–12)," e.g., in his famous appeals to Caesar (McN., 69). On two famous occasions neither Jesus nor Paul turned the other cheek (John 18:22–23; Acts 23:3; see the discussion in TDNT, 8:265–67).

I can introduce so many Old and New Testament exceptions to Jesus' command here and so many other reasonable considerations that I can take the teeth out of Jesus' straightforward teaching. Then I become that "loosener of the commands" against whom Jesus warns us in his first command (v 19). Schlatter, *Das,* 79, puts us on track with Jesus' central intent in this sixth command: "In every ostensibly holy zeal for justice there arises an endless quarrel; [this zeal] is an ever-renewing fountain of injustice, and, rather than bringing an end to injustice, it simply continues it."

Jesus in this command mounts his own war against Maccabean-Zealotic wars against evil, i.e., against many wars of liberation, particularly those that invoke Jesus' name and teaching (cf., classically, and I believe correctly, Luther's reasons for opposing the Peasants' Rebellion of 1525, *LW,* 46:5–85, and recently Baumbach in Grund., 171 n. 106). Behind the undefensiveness of Jesus' sixth, peacemaking, command stands the figure of the suffering Servant of God (Isa 50:4–9, esp. LXX), who offers his cheeks to be slapped because he knows that *God* stands at his side as his helper and provides him with a justice he does not have to seek for himself (TDNT 8:265–66; Grund., 173). The bravery frequently required in our time is the bravery of not having to appear brave.

What does Jesus specifically command here? First he lays down a broad principle: "Do not withstand [literally, *antistēnai; anti-,* against, *stēnai,* stand] the evil person" [literally, *tō ponērō,* "the evil"]. The word "withstand" usually referred to law court situations and meant "go to court with" or "stand up in court against" (cf. Gund., 94; Guel., 219–20). It then came to mean, and means here more generally, do not resist, do not "hold court" or "mete out justice." ("So far from seeking to injure his oppressor by calling in the aid of the law to inflict penalties. . . , the Christian disciple should quietly submit to wrong," Allen, 54; the classic New Testament example is 1 Cor 6:1–8.) I translate, "Do not try to get even."

It is important to notice that Jesus has already judged the aggressor in this command: Jesus specifically calls him or her "the evil person." This name means that evil persons will get the justice that evil persons deserve. But the (unofficial) *disciple* is not the one to give this justice. Dispensing justice in the form of punishments is not the disciples' business, unless they are called to this publicly by vocation, emergency, or for the sake of others (as with Paul, above). The simple fact that Jesus calls the not-now-to-be-prosecuted person "the evil person" indicates sufficiently (and comfortingly) how *Jesus* judges the acts here of slapping, suing, exploiting, and taking advantage. (Cf. Schl., *Der,* 187.)

There is exegetical debate about the meaning of the two words "the evil" in v 39 (*tō ponērō*). Chrysostom, 18:1:124, suggests that they refer to a masculine "evil *one,* " the devil: "He did not say, 'resist not your brother,' but 'the evil one,' signifying that on his [the evil one's] motion men dare so to act; and in this way relaxing and secretly removing most of our anger against the aggressor, by transferring the blame to another"; also at 87:4:518f, Chrysostom counsels, "Consider that he who is insolent is beside himself and mad, and thou wilt not feel indignant . . . , since *the possessed* strike us, and we, so far from being provoked, do rather pity them. . . . [For they are] held in subjection by a dreadful monster, rage, by a grievous demon, anger" (emphasis added). Lohmeyer, 137, believes a neuter "evil *power* " rather than a masculine "evil one" is present in *tō ponērō,* a cosmic evil power, and thus we see why Jesus forbad resistance to it, "for it is not within man's possibilities (otherwise than in Rom 12:21) to overcome this domineering earth-and-man-covering power." (Similarly a neuter: Aug., Cal., Ewald, Tholuck: "das Übel"; tentatively, TDNT 6:562.) The devil and the evil power meanings do not finally, greatly differ, and both may well be present in *tō ponērō.* But the immediate context suggests to most interpreters that "evil person" is the best translation (cf. Mey., 139f; Bonn., 73).

The words "Do not try to get even with the evil person" (5:39a) are the covering letter for the bill of particulars or four examples that now follow (vv 39b–42). "When someone slaps you on the right cheek offer him the other also" (v 39b). It is worth noticing that Jesus does not say, "When someone knocks out your right *eye*, offer the other." Jesus is not asking us to be stupid or to offer ourselves for mutilation. The slap here refers to a considerably depotentialized situation: the insult, something people encounter frequently. In such situations Jesus specifically commands us neither to cower nor to get even. Jesus commands us to confront the attacker bravely and calmly with still another opportunity to hurt. What is required here, in a word, is the poise (or faith—they are the outside and inside of the same thing) of Christian discipleship.

Nietzsche considered Jesus' ethic effeminate and weak and wished to see instead a morality of blood and iron. But Nietzsche's disciple, Oswald Spengler, had to admit that "it takes blood to check blood," that it takes power to control power, strength to subdue spirit. "He who rules his spirit is mightier than he who rules a city" (Proverbs).

McKenzie, 72, believes that the principle of self-defense is categorically rejected by Jesus here. This conviction turns on the interpretation of the word "slaps." Does the word convey an attack on a person's honor or a person's health? Most interpreters believe it represents an attack on honor and so do not see here the rejection of self-defense. But there is clearly the rejection of defensive*ness* (cf. TDNT 8:263). Thus some interpreters prefer to the usual translation of 5:39a, "Do not resist the evil person" (which expresses a passivity that Jesus never practiced), the translation, "Do not encounter evil at all in its way" (Machovec, *Jesus*, 126–30, cited in Berner, 164 n. 12). Jesus advocated *an active quietism* that went directly against the passion of the patriotic-nationalistic Zealots of his time, and which just as sharply confronts some patriotisms, nationalisms, and liberation theologies of our time. (For Jesus' time, against the Zealots, cf. Hare, 7–8.) In Jesus "there is a battle against evil, but not the pathos of anger" (Conz., 58). But Matt 23?

5:40 "If a man wants to sue you for your shirt, let him have your coat as well." (NEB). The text speaks of the two major garments worn in Palestine: the long underwear (shirt) next to the body with sleeves, and the loose-fitting coat that went over it and in which the poor man slept at night. These were the only two pieces of clothing most persons wore. What is asked for here, then, is drastic. If someone wants to take you to court for your clothes, let him have your overcoat too—in short, you would rather go naked than fight. Where the cheek Word addressed disciples at the point of honor in connection with their persons, the coat Word addresses them at the point of honor, too, in connection with their possessions.

Augustine, *LSM*, 72, is too quick to see this command as an allegorical address to the heart and not as a call to real action. The setting here is clearly legal—the defense of oneself in court (Mey., 140; Bonn., 73). Disciples are to be as undefensive about their *things* as they are about their "face." In both cases "Jesus is saying this: 'The Christian never stands upon his rights. . . .' There are people who are forever standing on their rights" (Barc., 1:167). The anarchy feared by some commentators here (e.g., Guel., 224) is checked by the Scriptures' high view of government. Government has the divine calling to defend citizens (Rom 13), and if a motive of revenge is absent disciples may occasionally and legitimately appeal to government for protection.

This obedience is discussed brilliantly by Calvin, *Inst.*, IV.xx.17–21: "If it is to no purpose that [the magistrate] has been given by the Lord for our defense unless we are allowed to enjoy such benefit, it is clear enough that the magistrate may without impiety be called upon and also appealed to" (17), "but having in mind only to prevent the efforts of a destructive man from doing harm to society. . . . For . . . the magistrate's revenge is not man's but God's . . . (Rom 13:4)" (19). In 1 Corinthians 6, Calvin points out, "Paul inveighs against that mad lust to go to law, not simply against all [legal] controversies. . . . But when any man sees that without loss of love he can defend his own property, the loss of which would be a heavy expense to him, he does not offend against this statement of Paul, if he has recourse to law" (21). Cf. also Luther's discussion of Matt 5:38–42, *SM*, 105–15. We must still be vigilant lest we so "loosen" Jesus' tough commands that we earn the censure he gives to such looseness at Matthew 5:19.

"Eagles catch no flies." Disciples are above revenge. There are too many other important matters in life—Christian mission most of all. In this whole command it appears that disciples have their center of gravity outside themselves. The disciple is so focused on Jesus as Lord, so concerned to do Jesus' bidding and accomplish his mission in the world, that insults are taken as invitations to mission, and troubles are the opportunity to prove oneself an honest follower of Jesus. Jesus takes away defensiveness when he commands the turning of the other cheek; he takes away litigiousness when he commands giving up the coat.

5:41 "And if someone bullies you to go one mile, go with him two." The New English Bible renders the "someone" with "a man in authority" because the word used for "bullies" or "commandeers" or "forces" is a military word indicating the Roman soldier's right to make a colonial subject carry his baggage for a mile, often by means of the victim's beast of burden. The old people of God considered this service to the hated heathen occupation army especially degrading. In fact, all three illustrations used so far in this command—cheek, coat, and journey—are united as studies in degradation. In cultures awakened by legitimate nationalist and anticolonial feelings, accompanied by the quest for a new pride and self-respect, this particular "colonial" illustration of the forced march is the most offensive of all the commands in the Sermon on the Mount. Give in to the exploiter? Let the imperialist run all over one? Give *him* an extra mile? To ask redblooded persons in exploited situations to live like this is to ask them to give up their soul. Here at this Word Jesus is strangest and most offensive. Everything Franz Fanon so nobly asks for in his moving book, *The Wretched of the Earth*, goes against everything Jesus asks for here in his Sermon on the Mount. (See the work of Martin Luther King, Jr., as commentary.)

One needs to be reminded again, however, that Jesus is not asking disciples to acquiesce in letting an evil person slap *someone else's* cheek, rob someone else's property, exploit someone else's labor. All three illustrations are one-on-one, second person "thou words," not third person "they words." I do not know where Jesus commands us to stand by as *others* get hurt. One recalls in fact that the Great Judgment will ask us what we have done for the hurt and neglected (Matt 25:31–46). But here the *individual* disciple is addressed at the core (*se*, "you," is singular and emphasized in vv 39b–42).

"Here Jesus explicitly dissociates himself from the extremist policy of all-out resistance to the Romans" (Green, 86). Jesus' Word here "is the precise opposite of what the Zealots advocated doing in their revolutionary sedition against the Romans. . . . Jesus' concern again is to destroy self-consciousness, here the self-pity of the persecuted. . . . Therefore one must never under any circumstance adopt the style of one's opponent, not even to gain a worthwhile end. . . . The use here of the second person singular instead of the plural [*se*, not *hymas*] is not accidental: the decisions involved are the most intensely personal" (Schw., 130–31; cf. TDNT 2:886).

In the Philippine national anthem there is a line that says, "*sa manlulupig, 'di ka pasisiil,*" which means, "to the exploiter you will not submit." Politically, socially, there is something to this. But personally, individually, Jesus' command says the opposite: "to the exploiter who forces you to go one mile, go with him two." The "*'di ka pasisiil*"—"you will not submit" of the anthem—has its place in national defense and in the courageous defense of others. But *all* individuals guard their own honor jealously; all persons fight back somehow when insulted. Jesus asks the disciple to be different from everyone else: more poised, less threatened, more relaxed, and less unbelieving. This behavior is possible only for the person who believes in God; but for the believer this behavior really is possible—"all things are possible for the person who believes" (Mark 9:23). The Philippine nonviolent revolution of 1986, led by Christians, is a parable of this truth even nationally.

Jesus stands almost alone with this Word and will find few followers; the way of the liberators is the way of the many; the way of the Liberator is always the way of the few (7:13–14). Yet the Christian knows inside that this is the way to live. Jesus' commands carry the ring of truth; they are self-authenticating. If it is not possible to live this way naturally, it is still clear that this is the only way to try to live supernaturally.

5:42 "Give to the person who asks from you, and do not turn your back on a person who wants to borrow." This Word is anticlimactic after the increasingly painful series of exploitations just described. In this Word we are "let down" again into ordinary life where our usual exploiters are simply pushy people or undependable borrowers. But by using this illustration last, Matthew's Jesus teaches us again that the usual tests of discipleship occur in daily, unheroic situations.

Augustine, *LSM*, 79–80, wisely pointed out that this text does not say "give *whatever* you are asked," but "give to *whomever* asks," meaning that if persons ask us for something unjust or excessive, we do not have to give *that* to them, but we do have to give them something, if only an explanation or time. The command is person-centered, like most of Jesus' ministry. It is not the *what* that is in question in this command, it is the *who*—not things but persons. ("'To him that asketh'—what! A knife to a murderer? No. The Spirit teaches the exception. Thus the broad, plain terms of our Savior's popular language count everywhere upon the Spirit for an interpreter, and are not otherwise to be interpreted." Tholuck in Beng., 1:118.)

We should see this fourth and last picture (in the four pictures of this command) as a species of obedience to Jesus' genus command of peacemaking. This "asker" is one of two kinds: (a) another type of the "evil person" in the sense of being violent or unjust in the asking, careless with what is loaned, or irresponsible in returning or paying back (thus Bonn., 73–74; TDNT 1:191 n. 12; cf. Gund., 95–96); or (b) the asker may be simply any needy person, and the "evil" in view here is our own egoism (Mey., 141; TDNT 7:721; cf. Luther, *SM,* 117: Jesus "is not saying that we should give and lend to everybody, but 'to him who begs from us,' that is, to the one who really needs it, not to the one who develops a whim that he would like to take something from us by force").

There is something to be said for both views: the context favors the former, good sense the latter. The Spirit and disciples' conscience give discernment. The most helpful commentary on this borrow command is Deut 15:7–11, though Jesus widens the boundaries. Jesus gives direction, not directions; a compass, not a map (Manson).

The four pictures of this command are four portraits of the real Christian. The evangelistic techniques suggested in this command are not four spiritual principles for leading others to decision; they are four interpersonal examples leading disciples to discipleship.

The watermark on all four portraits in this Word is that of *degradation*. It is normally possible for persons to be willing to be degraded only if they have been previously upgraded. In classical theological language, only when persons know themselves to have been justified before God will they usually be willing or able to be treated unjustifiably by people. Therefore disciples will seek to live as much in the first half of this chapter, in its justifying Beatitudes, as they will in the second half in its sanctifying commands. There is no living of Jesus' commands where there is no prior receiving of Jesus' blessings. "He who has been forgiven little, loves little" (Luke 7:47). Paul's theology of justification is the best extra-dominical equipment for living Jesus' ethic of sanctification.

Jesus' commands ask for almost the impossible—for "the new man" and for "the new woman," for an almost entirely different breed of human being. Jesus' commands clearly require a miracle because they are impossible for us as we are to keep. Luther with his usual clearsightedness saw this: "This Word [vv 38–42, C 6] is too high and too hard that anyone should fulfill it. This is proved, not merely by our Lord's Word, but by our own experience and feeling. Take any upright man or woman. He will get along very nicely with those who do not provoke him, but let someone proffer only the slightest irritation and he will flare up in anger, . . . if not against friends, then against enemies. Flesh and blood cannot rise above it" (in Bainton, 46). Another evangelist heard Jesus describe the miracle required with these words: "Unless you are born again, you will never see the kingdom of God" (John 3:3). Jesus commands the impossible, but there is good hope, for there is a God who gives new life.

In ancient, classical, and medieval culture, as in modern culture, the hero is always a person of "honor," which means, of revenge: "Honour, when wounded, calls for something to restore it, and this Achilles unerringly and inevitably seeks" (C.M. Bowra, *Homer* [1972], 99). Cf. the medieval Beowulf (in which, one editor observes, "men seem to be caught in a vast web of reprisals and counterreprisals from which there is little hope of escape," NAEL); and recall Christian resistance to the duel in the "Age of Enlightenment" (e.g., personally, by the commentator Beng, 1:117).

For the wild revenge of the vendetta see Buck's description of a feud to Huck Finn:
"'What's a feud, [Buck]?'
'Why, where was you raised, [Huck}? Don't you know what a feud is?'
'Never heard of it before—tell me about it.'
'Well,' says Buck, 'a feud is this way: A man has a quarrel with another man, and kills him; then that other man's brother kills *him;* then the other brothers, on both sides, goes for one another; then the *cousins* chip in—and by and by everybody's killed off, and there ain't no more feud. But it's kind of slow, and takes a long time.'"
And cf. the modern John Wayne's life motto, "Never apologize; never say you're sorry. It's a sign of weakness" (from "She Wore a Yellow Ribbon"). The noble exception to the

rule in classical culture is the Socrates of Plato's *Crito:* "One must not even do wrong when one is wronged, which most people regard as the natural course" (49b).

There is a treasury of biblical parallels to our command. Only a selection needs to be given: Lev 19:17–18; Isa 35:8–9; 50:6–7; 53:7; Prov 12:16; 19:11; 20:3, 22; Matt 27:6. The important Rom 12–13 passage is discussed below. Cf. 2 Tim 2:24–25; Jas 1:19–20; 1 Pet 2:19, 23; and Stählin, TDNT 5:420 n. 277.

Biblical and Traditional Material on the State and the Problem of Coercion

The person who understood the meaning of Jesus' mission best and who has provided us in Scripture with the most inspired commentary on the sense of Jesus' Sermon on the Mount and this particular command in it is the apostle Paul. In the last paragraph of the twelfth and the first paragraph of the thirteenth chapters of Romans, Paul summarizes both his own and, I think, Jesus' ethical teaching, while at the same time answering the pressing question: Where, then, does *justice* come in?

In the last paragraph of Romans 12 we notice the personal spirit of nonviolence that gives God what is God's (i.e., the exercise of vengeance); then in the first paragraph of Romans 13 we notice how, without contradicting himself, Paul affirms the God-given right of the state to use the sword that gives Caesar what is Caesar's (i.e., the temporal administration of justice and vengeance). The key matter to see in these two paragraphs, laid out below, is how wrath and revenge are denied *individual* Christians and are permitted the *state* (and of public Christians in the state), by God's will and command.

The individual Christian is to be as pacific as possible toward all persons, avenging no evil to oneself; but civil authorities are called to be as vigilant as possible in resisting all evil toward others for the sake of the community and the individuals in it. The individual disciple should be an interpersonal pacifist; the disciple called into public or police service should be undefensive in person but a public defender, a soldier, in office.

Christians, of course, live in both Romans 12 and Romans 13 at the same time; both texts are Holy Scripture; both texts ask us to love others—in Romans 12 by stepping aside and letting God's wrath punish evildoers, in Romans 13 by deferring to (or being) government officers who exercise God's justice and wrath in the world. Government authority is (as Paul says three times in this text) *God's own servant* (Rom 13:3 [twice], 6) instituted to punish and protect. We all know the painful occasions where government officials are the main *opponents* of God, punishing the good and protecting the evil. There are times when contemporary disciples must say with the earliest disciples "we must obey God rather than men" (Acts 5:29). We know that Revelation 13 with its portrait of malignant government is also in Scripture. But the ordinary rule for Christians is still Romans 13's command of subjection. Christians should study both Romans and Revelation, for rule and exception respectively, but in that order: Romans, Revelation. And even in Revelation the disciples' behavior is nonviolent and Christian.

When a disciple is called into military service, he or she is that moment given the responsibility to be God's good public servant by doing precisely what as a private Christian one has no right to do: use coercive force when necessary to protect the community and to punish those who hurt it. Both Romans 12 and Romans 13—

Romans 12 privately and Romans 13 publicly—serve the law of love. Disciples must regularly pray that God will lead them in the very difficult decision of knowing when they are private Christians, when public ones, when to give Caesar what is Caesar's, and when to know that Caesar is playing God and can only be refused. The careful reading of Romans 12 C and Romans 13 A—the apostolic form of the two kingdoms doctrine—will help disciples make the proper distinctions. (See especially that what is taken *out* of Rom 12:19 is placed *in* Rom 13:4 italicized below.)

Romans 12:17–21; 13:1–7 (TEV): 17 If someone has done you wrong, do not repay him with a wrong. Try to do what everyone considers to be good. 18 Do everything possible on your part to live in peace with everybody. 19 *Never take revenge, my friends, but instead let God's anger [orgē] do it. For the Scripture says, "I will take revenge, I will pay back, says the Lord."* 20 Instead, as the Scripture says: "If your enemy is hungry, feed him; if he is thirsty, give him a drink; for by doing this you will make him burn with shame." 21 Do not let evil defeat you; instead, conquer evil with good.

[Then, Romans 13 immediately follows:] 1 Everyone must obey state authorities, because no authority exists without God's permission, and the existing authorities have been put there by God. 2 Whoever opposes the existing authority opposes what God has ordered; and anyone who does so will bring judgment on himself. 3 For rulers are not to be feared by those who do good, but by those who do evil. Would you like to be unafraid of the man in authority? Then do what is good, and he will praise you, 4 because he is God's servant working for your own good. But if you do evil, then be afraid of him, because *his power to punish is real* ["*for he does not bear the sword in vain*," RSV]. *He is God's servant and carries out God's punishment on those who do evil* ["*he is the servant of God to execute his wrath (orgēn) on the wrongdoer*," RSV]. 5 For this reason, you must obey the authorities—not just because of God's punishment, but also as a matter of conscience.

6 That is also why you pay taxes, because the authorities are working for God when they fulfill their duties. 7 Pay, then, what you owe them; pay them your personal and property taxes, and show respect and honor for them all.

Cf. Helmut Thielicke, *Theological Ethics*, 2:322, for discussion of the two kingdoms doctrine.

The doctrine of the two kingdoms became a systematic principle in Luther's theology, but it is older than Luther. Augustine, e.g., in his letter to Publica (Letter 47; cited in McArthur, *Understanding the SM*, 177 n. 29), wrote: "As to killing in order to defend one's own life, I do not approve of this, unless one happens to be a soldier or a public functionary acting, not for himself, but in defense of others or of the city in which he resides, if he act according to his commission lawfully given him, and in the manner becoming his office."

The official Lutheran position toward the kingdom "of God's left hand," civil government, is spelled out in *The Augsburg Confession* (1530), article 16 (cf. the rather drastic formulation in the Latin version at art. 28:1–11).

Melanchthon, in his *Apology of the Augsburg Confession* (1531), explains the Lutheran doctrine of the two kingdoms with all desirable clarity in his commentary on *The Augsburg Confession's* sixteenth article.

In the Lutheran *Formula of Concord* (1580) antistate errors of the Anabaptists were condemned, *Epitome,* art. 12: 12–16.

A selection of texts from Luther's sermons on the Sermon on the Mount (1530–1532) (*LW* 21), where he discusses this present command of peacemaking, will illumine the classic Reformation position: "This text [Matt 5:38–42] has also given rise to many questions and errors among nearly all the theologians who have failed to distinguish properly between the secular and the spiritual, between the kingdom of Christ [e.g., Rom 12] and the kingdom of the world [e.g., Rom 13]. Once these two have been confused instead of being clearly and accurately separated, there can never be any correct understanding in Christendom, as I have often said and shown. . . . [Christ] is not tampering with the responsibility and authority of the government, but He is teaching His individual Christians how to live personally, apart from their official position and authority. . . . We say, therefore, that all [this command] does is to proclaim to every Christian that he should willingly and patiently suffer whatever is his lot, without seeking revenge or hitting back. . . . You must always pay attention to the main point, which is, that Christ is addressing His sermon only to His Christians and seeking to teach them the kind of people they should be, in contrast to the carnal ideas and thoughts that still clung to the apostles. . . .

"This distinction [between the two kingdoms] enables us to take up this text [Matt 5:38–42] and to apply each of its parts. *A Christian should not resist any evil; but within the limits of his office, a secular person should oppose every evil.* . . . In short, the rule in the kingdom of Christ is the toleration of everything, forgiveness, and the recompense of evil with good. On the other hand, in the realm of the emperor, there should be no tolerance shown toward any injustice, but rather a defense against wrong and a punishment of it, and an effort to defend and maintain the right, according to what each one's office or station may require.

"But you may say: 'All right. But still Christ says here in plain words: "Do not resist evil." It sounds obvious that this is being absolutely forbidden.' Answer: Yes, but pay attention *to whom* He is saying this. He is not saying: 'No one should ever resist evil'; for that would completely undermine all rule and authority. But this is what He is saying: 'You, you shall not do it.' Now, who are these 'you'? They are the disciples of Christ, whom He is teaching about their personal lives, apart from the secular government" (*SM,* 105–14, emphases added).

In his important treatise, *Temporal Authority: To What Extent It Should Be Obeyed* (1523), Luther summarized his convictions in this way: "Thus the word of Christ [about nonresistance] is now reconciled, I believe, with the passages which establish the sword, and the meaning is this: No Christian shall wield or invoke the sword for himself and his cause. In behalf of another, however, he may and should wield it and invoke it to restrain wickedness and to defend godliness" (*LW* 45:103).

John Calvin, in his influential twentieth chapter on "Civil Government" in the fourth book of the final edition of his *Institutes* (1559/1560), argues similarly for the two kingdoms. He argues, for example, against Anabaptist perfectionists who believe the world can be ruled now by the Sermon on the Mount alone, without civil government, and who "think that nothing will be safe unless the whole world is reshaped to a new form, where there are neither courts, nor laws, nor magistrates, nor anything [that] in their opinion restricts their freedom. But whoever knows how to distinguish between body and soul, . . . will without difficulty know that Christ's spiritual Kingdom and the civil jurisdiction are things completely distinct" (IV.xx.1).

Magistrates, Calvin insists, are *God's* ministers of justice according to Romans 13. They are not private vindicators.

"But here a seemingly hard and difficult question arises: if the law of God forbids all Christians to kill (Exod 20:13; Deut 5:17; Matt 5:21) . . . how can magistrates be pious men and shedders of blood at the same time? Yet if we understand that the magistrate in administering punishments does nothing by himself, but carries out the very judgments of God, we shall not be hampered by this scruple. The law of the Lord forbids killing; but, that murders may not go unpunished, the Lawgiver himself puts into the hand of his ministers [the magistrates] a sword to be drawn against all murderers. . . . They are ministers of God, to execute his wrath, avengers of wrongdoers (Rom 13:4). . . . [For] 'he who justifies the wicked and he who condemns the righteous are both alike an abomination to the Lord' (Prov 17:15). . . . Should [magistrates] sheathe their sword and keep their hands clean of blood, while abandoned men wickedly range about with slaughter and massacre [?]. . . . During the reign of Nerva it was . . . said: it is indeed bad to live under a prince with whom nothing is permitted; but much worse under one by whom everything is allowed" (IV.xx.10).

But Calvin, like the Wittenberg Reformers, was always careful to include the great "apostolic exception" to political submission: "We must obey God rather than men" (Acts 5:29). Jesus Christ is King of Kings. "In that obedience which we have shown to be due the authority of rulers, we are always to make this exception. . . . How absurd would it be that in satisfying men you should incur the displeasure of him for whose sake you obey men themselves! . . . Daniel denies that he has committed any offense against the king when he has not obeyed his impious edict (Dan 6:22–23). For the king had exceeded his limits. . . . Conversely, the Israelites are condemned because they were *too* obedient to the wicked proclamation of the king (Hos 5:13)" (IV.xx.32, emphasis added).

The more recent anti-Nazi *Theological Declaration of Barmen* (1934) explicitly endorses the coercive role of states:

"5. 'Fear God. Honor the emperor' (1 Pet 2:17). Scripture tells us that, in the as yet unredeemed world in which the Church also exists, the State has by divine appointment the task of providing for justice and peace. [It fulfills this task] by means of the threat and exercise of force, according to the measure of human judgment and human ability."

The Confession of 1967 expresses itself in this way: "The members of the church are emissaries of peace and seek the good of man in cooperation with powers and authorities in politics, culture, and economics. But they have to fight against pretensions and injustices when these same powers endanger human welfare" (25). (Much depends, of course, on how the "fight" of the last sentence is carried out.) And then in one of its four serious social statements the Confession declares: "The church . . . is called to practice the forgiveness of enemies and to commend to the nations as practical politics the search for cooperation and peace. This search requires that the nations pursue fresh and responsible relations across every line of conflict, even at risk to national security, to reduce areas of strife and to broaden international understanding. Reconciliation among nations becomes peculiarly urgent as countries develop nuclear, chemical, and biological weapons, diverting their manpower and resources from constructive uses and risking the annihilation of mankind. Although nations may serve God's purposes in history, the church [that] identifies the sovereignty of any one nation or any one way of life with the cause of God denies the Lordship of Christ and betrays its calling" (45).

Two sections from Karl Barth's thorough treatment of the subject Life in his *Kirchliche Dogmatik*, III/4, 55.2 (1951) are relevant here, 488–99, 515–38 (on killing in self-defense, and on war). As for the whole question of nuclear war in our time, I commend to the reading of church members, as an introduction, Jonathan Schell's *The Fate of the Earth* (New York: Knopf, 1982) and *The Abolition* (Knopf, 1984).

G. Sanctiday: The Saturday Command of Enemy-Love (C 7), 5:43–48

"You have heard that it was said, 'You shall love your neighbor and hate your enemy.' But I say to you, love your enemies, and pray for those who persecute you so that you may really be the children of your Father in heaven, because he shines his sun down on bad

people and good, and he sends rain down on the righteous and unrighteous. For you see, if you are just loving toward the people who love you, what kind of reward do you expect for that? Aren't even the collaborator-tax-collectors doing the same? And if you just give warm greetings to your spiritual brothers and sisters only, what are you doing that is so special? Don't even the pagans do the same thing? So you must be a perfectly mature people just as your heavenly Father is perfectly mature."

In this command Jesus frees behavior from calculations. ("Enemy" is at first anyone with whom the disciple has hard relations, and may even be a member of one's own family.) We worry about how warm to be to the undeserving or hostile, how much we ought to love certain people, whom to love unconditionally, whom conditionally. This command makes clear that Jesus wants to abolish all such calculations and distinctions. Disciples are to love even enemies unconditionally. This is real liberation. Jesus "knows that when love no longer has to wait on the performance of others . . . an immense transformation has taken place" (Schl., *Der*, 195).

We have risen considerably since the sermon began. At the beginning of it we were with the poor in spirit; here at the end of the chapter we are called to perfection. There we were in the valley, here we are called to the summit. In the Beatitudes we were in deep need, in the commands we are on high assignment. (The movement from the beginning to the end of Matthew's fifth chapter, as Grundmann, 181, has pointed out, is similar to the movement "in the Gospel according to Paul" from Romans 1 to Romans 8.) And yet the two ends of this Matthean chapter, while spatially distant, are not so distant spiritually. The shortest distance to the first Beatitude is taking this seventh command seriously. As we have seen, it is one of the purposes of Jesus' Sermon on the Mount at every sentence to drive us back to the Beatitudes. "We move forward by going back."

(On Saturday we are called to the sanctity of love for even our enemies. On Saturdays we can make it a point particularly to pray for our spiritual, personal, national, and political enemies and for a more generous and large-souled relation to them: for the gift of a new angle on them and for new power to think better of them, or for grace, in us, them, or others, to bring about conversion and a right mind.)

Even the most radical critics of the synoptic texts—Bultmann and Braun, for example—consider the command of enemy-love to be the authentic teaching of Jesus. Here, it is said, we hear the real Jesus, and here Jesus is absolutely unique. (The Talmud, e.g., counsels patience under injury, but not love to enemies, McN., 71.)

5:43 The first thing to be said about this text is that The Old Testament does not have the words "You shall hate your enemy." Matthew's Jesus has summarized the Old Testament teaching at several points, the teaching that encourages believers so to love God that they hate the godless. Psalms 58 and 109 most notoriously, and the ends of Psalms 137(:7–9) and 139(:21–22), the so-called Psalms of vengeance, speak of enemies in what can only be called a hating manner. We are familiar with the commands of Canaanite extermination and the prayers of the pious for the destruction of the impious. The other side of a burning love for God is often a burning desire for the end of all those realities that resist God; passion for God is matched with a perfectly comprehensible passion against everything against God. "You shall hate your enemy," understood as "You shall hate the enemy of God," a psychologically and even spiritually comprehensible command, is now altered by Jesus.

In classical culture, fierce loyalty to friends and fierce hatred of enemies is precisely that which is considered noble in heroes. Cf. C.M. Bowra, *Homer,* 113.

Does the Old Testament really teach us to hate our enemies? The answer, I think, is yes, it teaches us in places to hate the enemies of God and of the people of God. One could multiply texts in documentation, but let just two serve here: Deuteronomy 23:3–6; 25:17–19. Windisch, 92, believes Matthew's antithesis "and you shall hate your enemy" is unfair to Judaism, even in its Old Testament form, because it overlooks such humane teachings as Exodus 23:4–5 and Proverbs 25:21–22. But contrast Schlatter, *Der,* 191–92, who points to the pervasive Old Testament contempt for Canaanites; also Gund., 96–97; Beare, 161; and Guel., 227.

Davies, 275, believes Matthew's command is written in part in response to first-century Judaism's *Birkath ha Minim* against Christians (contained in the prayer of the twelfth benediction of the Eighteen Benedictions): "'For persecutors let there be no hope, and the dominion of arrogance do Thou speedily root out in our days; and let Christians and *minim [wa–ha–nozirim wa–ha–minim]* perish in a moment, let them be blotted out of the book of the living and let them not be written with the righteous.'" Even the ancient Old Testament command to love the *neighbor* is not understood as a command to universal love but to love of fellow countrymen (Str-B., 1:353–54).

Various Jewish groups saw in their fellowship the true remnant of the Covenant, and so they limited the love-commandment to those belonging to their group (Grund., 175–76). Many commentators see Jesus' antithesis directed against especially the Qumran communities' express command to hate all sons of darkness (cf. 1 QS 1:3–4, 9–10, etc.; discussion in Davies, 245–49; Streck., 24 n. 5; Green, 86). In Qumran there was great love for all within the group, great hatred for all outsiders (Grund., 178–79). In-group love, out-group contempt is a mark of sectarian mentalities. But even those of us in the so-called mainline churches must beware of a sectarian mentality that hates sectarians (or independents).

In the final analysis Jesus' enemy-love command is profoundly ecumenical and inclusive, calling the church to join to her distinctive and indispensably christocentric exclusivity, theologically, an all-embracing love, ethically. Ecclesiastical fellowship lies precariously between the demands of truth and the demands of love because we can only honestly consider fellow-Christians those who hold the central tenets of the Christian faith (as summarized classically in the great catholic creeds). Yet the balancing act to which this command of Jesus calls us is the love with agapic warmth of even those who oppose, subvert, and persecute our precious Christian faith. This balancing act calls us to combine a conservative with a liberal spirit, true faith with true love, evangelicalism with ecumenicity, doctrinal orthodoxy with ethical universality.

5:44a From now on disciples read the Old Testament differently. When one comes to a hate passage one thinks: "I know the intention of this text: it intends the wholehearted service of God, and that intention I must honor. But I can no longer permit the form this intention takes—the prayer here for the destruction of God's enemies—to be the form my prayers take." With Jesus' command, Christian readers are given a new set of glasses for reading, "Jesus glasses." They will never again be able to read vengeance texts as binding. Jesus' "But I say to you" has become the disciples' major critical principle, and from now on the Old Testament is a different book. In fact, the spectacles that Jesus now places on his disciples will be useful not only in reading the Old Testament but in reading all literature, even Christian liberation literature. The disciple simply will never again be able to enter crusades dominated by a burning hatred—whether against oppressors, exploiters, Communists, capitalists, or whomever. (Muslim *jihad* is seen here critically.)

To be sure, we will be tested for Christian reality by our zeal for justice—this will become particularly clear when we reach Jesus' crowning appeal at the end of Matthew 25. But Jesus lays down, as a first principle: Authentic discipleship is not expressed as often as we think it is in zeal against the enemies of God. (The problem with hatred is that it sees others as the great problem: self-righteousness infects all crusades.)

In Jesus' enemy-love command he takes away every limitation and classification by which people usually divide themselves from others, even our confessional divisions by which we distinguish ourselves spiritually and in which we find our identities (Grund., 177). Schweizer, 132, observes that in both the Old Testament and Qumran "as in all militant movements, what is meant [by "you shall hate your enemy"] is not hatred directed against the individual personally, but hatred of godlessness or [e.g.] capitalism or communism or whatever is being cast in the role of devil, a hatred that uncompromising battle seems to demand." The whole command, as Allen, 56, shows, "is aimed at definitions of the word 'neighbour' which would limit its application to a particular class who must be treated [with love], whilst others not included in [the command] might be treated in a different way."

Again, it is *poise* that strikes one as the covering word for Jesus' final two commands. In the preceding nonviolence Word we encountered temporary enemies of sorts: a passing insult, an unjust suer, an exploiting imperialist, and an irresponsible borrower. And in the face of these sporadic provocations disciples were counseled to keep their poise and to respond with the hilarity of faith and magnanimity. There we encountered occasional evil persons, but here in this command we encounter more entrenched enemies. Since the poise visible in this command is more sustained, I think we can call what is asked for in this command to be the poise of maturity. Another way of saying the same thing is to observe that in the previous command we were in special relation with what we might call social enemies, but here we are especially (though not exclusively) related to spiritual enemies.

See Foerster, TDNT 2:814; Bonn., 74, 428–29; Gund., 96–97; and Guel., 228–29 for evidence that the "enemy," both in the context of this command (persecution) and in its usage elsewhere in Scripture (Ps 31:6; 139:21; Rom 5:10; Col 1:21; 2 Tim 3:15; Jas 4:4, etc.) is not only the personal, national, or military enemy, but especially the persecutor of the faith, the spiritual enemy. Bonnard, 438–39, using 1 John (2:9, 11; 3:15; 4:20), shows how even self-consciously advanced Christians in the early church came to feel the hate of religious contempt for simple believers. Sectarian Christians today, too, doubt that there are *real* Christians in groups other than their own. ("Enemy," finally, is anyone with whom we have very difficult relations—understood thus, an enemy could be someone under our own roof.) But "enemy" is primarily a spiritual title in Scripture.

The highest seriousness in the face of enemies is to relax. We must defend the church from ungodly *doctrine* (see chap 23 in this Gospel and almost all of the New Testament epistles), but we must show respect to ungodly *persons* and teachers, and even be gracious to them (Matt 23 poses real problems in this connection). Enemy-love is unprecedented in spiritual controversy, since in spiritual matters we characteristically feel that the greatest issues are at stake, and they are. Here, we feel, no ground should be yielded. Here charity stops. (Even some

New Testament literature teaches this: cf. 2 John 10–11.) Yet Jesus demurs. With enemies, distinctive Christian life comes to its true testing ground.

Matthew 23's severity is hard for the student of Jesus' ethic. "There is . . . an unresolved antimony between Jesus' commandment to pray for the persecutors of one's faith [Matt 5:44] and his woes and invectives [e.g., Matt 23], and there is nothing that can be done about it" (Wind., 103; cf. *idem*, 140; Mohr. ix).

5:44b What does it mean to love our enemies? Jesus' first explanation is, "Pray for those who persecute you." Often the only effective way we can love our enemies is to pray for them. Often they are either so hostile to us or so separated from us that our only access to them is through God. Or when we do have access to them we find it humanly impossible to do anything but heartily to dislike them. It is hard, if not impossible, to love evil people. Thus often the only realistic possibility is prayer, and so Jesus immediately adds the command to pray to the command to love. (The fifth petition of the Lord's Prayer, "as we forgive our debtors" [Matt 6:12], will keep constantly before us precisely this one person— our enemy—as the highest test of the reality of our faith. Jesus prayed for his enemies from the cross, Luke 23:34.)

There is an alchemy present in prayer that can only be described as miraculous. More than psychological forces are at work in prayer for enemies; slowly but surely real spiritual energies are inserted into the will until—as surprisingly for disciples as for enemies—something like a little actual love for the other person begins to come flowing (or dripping!) out.

A frequent dodge must be noted. It is sometimes said that the agape-love commanded by Jesus is not eros-love; that is, that agape means to wish or to will well, but not (as in eros) to like or to feel affection for. By means of this distinction disciples are allowed to continue to dislike or despise their enemies, to feel absolutely no affection for them at all, and yet by a kind of steel-cool Stoicism toward the enemy to believe that they are keeping Jesus' command.

But while agape is much more than eros, it is nothing less. For it is not true that eros is a hot thing and agape cold. We are not to be satisfied that we have kept Jesus' love command when we are able merely to treat our enemies with semicivility. We are to pray and to pray some more until we are able to feel something of God's own agape love for problem people. Granted, a miracle is required for this to happen, but God is good at miracles. Therefore, we must beware of all counsel saying "you can love without liking." Disciples will permit God's own powerful agape so to effect them that they will find themselves with actually warm feelings, and not just steel wills. (Jerome, 1:134–36, warned us already in the fourth century against this universal evasion: "Many people, measuring the commandments of God by their own weaknesses rather than by the power given to the people of God [*sanctorum viribus*], think that we have been commanded to do impossibilities and say that it is enough for our powers if we do not hate our enemies, but that to love them is a command surpassing the possibilities of a human being. But . . . David did this to Saul and Absalom; and Stephen . . . prayed for his enemies who stoned him.")

We are not asked to love the enemy's *deeds*. Exploitation, such as that described in the Friday Command of Peacemaking, or hurtful emotions, words, and acts as depicted in the five preceding social and political commands, are all hateful to God.

Jesus has already taught that such deeds and their unrepentant doers are condemnation bent. Evil remains evil and therefore en route to judgment. Disciples do not like to see either the honor of others or the cause of God harmed. And yet they are asked to pray for the *person* of the harmer.

The old wisdom, "Men give themselves friends, God gives a neighbor" (Lohm., 142–43) has been broadened by Jesus to become, "God gives us not only our neighbors but our enemies, too." "The person whom earthly life has given to me as an enemy, that person has in the strictest sense been given to me by God as a 'neighbor,' as the friend of my existence" (Lohm., 145).

In Jesus' command two reasons for love are supplied: (1) that we might really be in act what we have been made in fact—sons and daughters of the Father, and (2) that we might receive the reward of being recognized at the judgment as true children of God. The motives for love are placed entirely within the disciples' relation to God and are not located in the person or circumstances of the enemy or in the advance of the mission.

5:45 We are urged to live in this unprecedented way "*so that you may become* sons and daughters of your Father in the heavens." We *are* by grace sons and daughters of our Father (notice the words "of your Father"); we are now by an answering obedience to *become* sons and daughters of our Father; that is, again, we are to become what we *are*.

Chrysostom, 18:4:126, read his Greek text to say *homoioi* ("like") instead of *huioi* ("sons"), thus "that you may become *like* your Father" (v 45), and so he urged his hearers to welcome persecution and hatred as so many opportunities for acquiring likeness to the Father (18:5–6:127; 18:11:130; on the Greek, see BDF 183 [4]). Lohmeyer, 146–47, shows how Jesus here abolishes the old idea of the *Volk* or people of God: it is no longer the *Volk* for whom the promise occurs; instead, the way to validate membership in the people of God is enemy-love.

For the Father shines his sun and sends his rain not only on the good but on the bad, too. The Communists and the capitalists, the rebels and the reactionaries, the reds and the rednecks, the whole lot, get just as much sun and just as much rain as the devout and the dedicated, the Bible students and the evangelists, the pray-ers and the socially involved. By this even-handedness God displays his maturity to the world, *and his will to disciples.*

It is important to notice that the rule of righteousness is maintained in this paragraph. Jesus calls evil people evil, unrighteous unrighteous ("he makes his sun to shine on the *evil* and the good," etc., Schl., *Der*, 194). Yet how does the Father treat evil people? As far as we can read from nature, he lets his sun shine as much on them as on his own; he rains on their houses as much as on the houses of the godly. God's maturity is so great that he gives himself as generously to the bad as to the good. God's sons and daughters are asked to be no less mature. (We are to be very good to undeserving people simply because God is this way. Cf. Schw., 135.)

"If God sent earthly gifts to His friends and withheld them from His enemies (in the [love-hate] spirit of v 43), the natural world would be chaos; in so far as His sons fall short of His nature, the spiritual world is a chaos." McN., 71.

Not just behind, but in and through nature, it is the Father himself with whom we have to do in the world. Very often what we honor as nature is honor rightfully belonging to the Father (cf., classically, Calvin's discussion, *Inst.*, I.v. 5). It is the Father who "rains," and it is the Father who points the sun. (Jesus looks through the catastrophes of nature and sees the one important fact: the God who loves human beings, Lohm., 48, a truth we woefully neglect in all the good seasons.)

In Marxism-Leninism, class warfare is the fundamental law of existence. History is the history of class warfare, as the beginning of the Communist Manifesto teaches us. There is enough truth in this observation to deserve a Christian's serious study. We *are* all members of different classes, and our class origins do determine to a large extent our views of life (and our interpretations of Scripture). And it is well to know this and to do all within our power to eliminate, or at least always to recognize, the slanting effects of class. Something of this self-criticism is commanded in Jesus' signature word, "Change" ("Repent").

The command of Jesus to love our enemies, however, wipes out any possibility of Christians forwarding class *warfare*. Class analysis, yes; class warfare, no. One normally fights, one normally carries on warfare, with those one hates. And those to be fought are those who belong to the oppressor class—the real enemy. The double law of the serious Communist is, "You shall love the party, and you shall hate the class-enemy." But to this law of distinctions Jesus opposes his, "But I say to you, You shall love your enemy, you shall pray for those who [oppress] you."

Here some political militancy disappears. In the East and West, to be a militant in the usual sense (there is a discipled militancy) is, in Jesus' reckoning, to be immature, for such militancy fails to imitate the Father's impartial sun, rain, and compassion toward even those who are evil. The word *class* in the East or *Communist* in the West is able to hide the awkward fact that behind a class and a Communist stand human beings. If the militant Marxist-Leninist or the militant anti-Communist is able to be convinced that another person belongs to a certain class or group he is able to justify his contempt, since members of certain classes and groups are by definition enemies of the people or of God. The effect of Jesus' enemy-love command is to wipe out this subterfuge, to wipe out the justification of hatred for an opponent. Where Marxism-Leninism mobilizes class warfare (and so the limitation of love) or where the West marshals anti-Communism (and so the disqualification of love), Jesus mobilizes maturity (and so the expansion of love).

In the first two centuries "loyalty to Jesus' command to love one's enemies undoubtedly produced a sharp cleavage between Christians and political activists. . . . [Christians'] central allegiance was not to the nation and its political destiny but to Jesus, their risen Lord" (Hare, 7).

5:46–47 Jesus now uses two examples to explain what he means. First, *all* persons, even collaborator-tax collectors (the *comprador* class who put themselves in the service of alien exploiters) love those who love them. The principle of treating well those who treat us well is thoroughly secular and has nothing special about it at all. Mutual geniality, warmness in the presence of the warm, friendliness in the in-group—this is the way of the world and of even the most spineless in the world. Jesus asks, "What kind of reward can you expect for love-for-love conduct?" What makes

Christians distinctive, salty, different, and useful in the meat of the world is their breaking the world's law of love-for-love, good-to-good, evil-to-evil reciprocity, and their countergrain, countercultural love for the undeserving, the unloving, and even the positively hostile. This imbalance, this contrariness, this nonconformity is the only truly nonconformist, revolutionary, and deeply subverting activity in history—all else going by the name of revolution is simply, in the literal sense, reaction, that is, acting back (re-) what has been acted out.

Jesus' question, "What is so special about that?" (v 47), uses the same root (*periss-*, "special," "more") found in v 20, "unless your righteousness *goes beyond (perisseusē)* that of the Bible teachers and separatists," etc. Our righteousness will go beyond that of the separatists (v 20) and secularists (v 47) when our love goes beyond our group and embraces enemies. Cf. G. Barth, 80; Grund., 179.

"And if you just give warm greetings to your spiritual brothers and sisters only, what are you doing that is so special? Don't even the pagans do the same thing?" (v 47). This greeting example is used last in the Saturday Command as the borrowing example was used last in the Friday Command, to show that Jesus is asking not for exceptional or heroic behavior but for behavior as routine as greeting other people. We meet people all day long; and, as we know well from experience, we reserve our especially warm greetings for our especially close friends, and we calibrate our greetings down a very exact calculus from friend to foe. Greetings are almost our only personal contact with a large part of the daily world. Jesus here lifts greetings into a prominent place; by our greetings we can exercise a considerable discipleship. The greeting is to be to the Christian what sun and rain are to the Father: a means of fructifying the world. And like the Father's sun especially, the disciple's greeting is to be warm, impartial, and wide reaching. Maturity is the gift of oneself to every person, even the enemy, in a complete way.

The Hebrew greeting and response was *Shalom alekah* (or, plural, *aleychem*), "Peace be with you," and was considered an important religious duty. A question was raised here, however, in the Judaism contemporary with Jesus: Since *shalom* was also a name for God, should this sacred name be placed indiscriminately on heathen? One answer was that on the days of heathen feasts the true Israelite should give non-Israelites an unclearly spoken greeting (Str.-B., 1:380–81)! But in Jesus' understanding, a greeting is a benediction ("Peace be with you"), and as a prayer it is meant even and sincerely for the religious enemy (Grund., 179; cf. Bonn., 75). In fact, the greeting is the practical expression of the prayer of v 44 for those who persecute us (Allen, 55).

5:48 "So *you* must be a perfectly mature people, just as your heavenly Father is perfectly mature." The "you" (plural) is strongly emphasized: *disciples* are going to be special people. The Greek future tense verb, "you shall be," is to be seen first of all in its ordinary sense: as a promise! "You disciples *shall be* a perfectly mature people." Disciples have thrilling prospects. The verb is then also a clear command. (On the dual promise-command character of the future tense *esesthe* used here, cf. Schl., *Der,* 197; Grund., 180; Bonn., 75.) "You shall be—you *must be*—a perfectly mature people." The especially emphasized "you" answers the previously emphasized "I" of the commands. What the "I" commanded, the "you" will do: such is the power of Jesus' Word.

The plural "you," referring to the disciples as a group, is so strongly emphasized that I have stressed it in the translation above. Ever since the salt and light Words in the middle of the chapter we have seen that it is a large part of Jesus' purpose to give his disciples confidence in themselves. Jesus intends not only to convict us through his Word—though this is one of the two main purposes of his sermon—he intends also and especially, by the same Word, to build us up again. In fact, Jesus convicts us only to reconstruct us. Jesus is making something of his people in the world.

It is Jesus' intention to *save* his people (1:21) and make them complete human beings. To do this he has put his arms around them (the need Beatitudes), locked arms with them (the help Beatitudes), ordained them to special world service (the You Ares), and now, in seven great charges, commanded them to be a mature people.

The word translated "perfectly mature" here—*teleioi*—is the word that Jesus' contemporary Josephus used to describe persons come of age, the adult as contrasted with the minor (Schl., *Der,* 197). Ever since his Beatitudes, Jesus has been describing adulthood. And in the commands we learn especially that adult disciples love obedience to God's Scriptures (C 1), zealously seek to keep communications open with everyone around them (C 2), fight off lust like death (C 3) and infidelity like murder (C 4); they seek to avoid dramatic oath-like statements (C 5), are undefensive and poised (C 6), and are enabled *even* to love their enemies (C 7). The seven commands define Christian maturity.

The word *teleioi* is usually translated "perfect" instead of, as here, "perfectly mature." But the noun "perfect" seems to me to be too cold a word to carry the warmth, weight, and humanity of *teleioi.* "Perfect" seems to designate "faultless, impeccable," and other somewhat superhuman or at least semifanatical connotations that are neither pleasant nor true to Jesus' sense. When Luke, in his version of this sermon, comes to this saying in his Gospel, he renders it, "Be *merciful* [*oiktirmones*] as your Father is merciful" (Luke 6:36; Calvin, 1:200, prefers Luke's rendering to Matthew's). Luke's translation is apt. The kind of perfection to which Matthew's Jesus refers, as the context shows, is the perfection of mercy, of whole- or wide-heartedness, not the perfection that we usually associate with strict behavior. (Thus the New English Bible, for example, renders Matthew's verse this way: "You must therefore be all goodness, just as your heavenly Father is all good.")

It is the maturity of goodness that Jesus promises to and commands of his people in this summarizing sentence. In the context in which Matthew's *teleioi* occurs, the context of the universally sun-shining and rain-producing Father, the word is stretched even wider: to be *teleioi* as our heavenly Father is *teleios* is to be as indiscriminately good in society as the Father is in nature. *Teleioi* is a width word like mercy rather than a height word like perfect. Christian perfection is the width with which disciples are able to embrace others, it is not the height to which they themselves are able to climb. Jesus' prophetic motto, "I want mercy and not sacrifice," might even be translated, "I want width, not height," or even, "I want social maturity, not personal perfection." (For good discussions of biblical perfection, cf. Bonn., 76 n. 1; G. Barth, 101; Grund., 180; Schw., 135.)

The fact that Matthew's Jesus can promise this maturity ("you shall be") indicates what Matthew thinks about the vexed question of the fulfillability of the Sermon on the Mount. Jesus expects that his Word and his personal presence in his Word will enable disciples to live the way he has directed in his Seven Commands.

Because the nouns, pronouns, and verbs relating to disciples in this verse are all plurals, not singulars, I have added the word "people" to the translation in order to give Jesus' sentence its intended communality. Jesus is not only seeking perfectly mature individual disciples, though he is seeking that, too; he is especially seeking a perfectly mature community of disciples, a people of, in, and for the world. This enemy-love command of Jesus is as broad as it is deep; it seeks community as well as character.

The depth of all Jesus' commands in this chapter is remarkable. In the old social commandments discussed by Jesus in this chapter, as Schlatter, *Das,* 81, shows, there was still room left for evil; e.g., we should not kill, but we may hate; we should not commit adultery, but we may lust; we should not break an oath, but we may otherwise lie; we should not be too hard in revenge, but we may counteract in law; we should love, but we may hate certain hateful persons. Jesus makes love entire.

Maturity, adulthood, then, is a whole-souled commitment—for Jesus' sake, before all other motives—to the protection of every other person. Maturity is looking at every person we meet and saying, at least to oneself, "I will never, God helping me, do anything to hurt you": neither by angrily lashing out at you, lustfully sidling up to you, faithlessly slipping away from you, verbally oiling you up, protectively hitting back at you, or even justifiably disliking you. This high life is attained only by faith. ("To willingly bend before evil means really to trust God," Lohm., 139.) The just person of the Sermon on the Mount, too, *shall live by faith.* We simply will not be willing to live the way Jesus commands unless we believe that Jesus is God's Son teaching us the truth, and God's Savior enabling us to live it. The height of the Sermon on the Mount is clearly love; its depth is clearly faith.

There are two other emphases in Jesus' commands (in addition to the focus on the protection of the other person) that need finally to be underscored if an adequate vision of the first half of Jesus' Sermon on the Mount is to emerge. These are the realities designated by the words "I" and "you." The other person is the focus of the Sermon on the Mount, but Jesus is the one who teaches and enables us to focus on the other person. Jesus' imperious "But *I* say to you" is a performative, creative Word that, like all divine Words, creates what it says, bequeathing power over anger and unfaithful lust. The engine for the motor of the Sermon on the Mount is Jesus' Word, Jesus' "I." This "I" is the key that opens up the Sermon on the Mount and makes it possible; it is the Rosetta Stone that deciphers every word of the sermon. Jesus is the key to the Sermon on the Mount.

"*You* are the salt of the earth. *You* are the light of the world. Let people see *your* good works. For unless *your* righteousness exceeds their righteousness . . . But I say to *you* . . . therefore *you* shall be perfectly mature." "You" is the other important word of the sermon. If the other person is the focus, and if Jesus is the focuser, disciples are the lens. Between the "I" of the Lord and persons in the community stand the "you" of disciples. Disciples are Jesus' "middlemen" in history. Jesus' "I" gets to the world's "him, her, and them" through especially the "you" of real disciples. Hence Jesus can take the name given to him—the light of the nations (4:16) and confer it on the disciples: "*You* are the light of the world" (5:14). For Jesus shines on the world in a special way through his people. Where there are real Christians the world is helped.

(1) The other person, (2) I Jesus, and (3) you disciples are the elements in the atomic power that is the Sermon on the Mount.

Christian perfection is like Huck Finn's raft: "I was powerful glad to get away from the feuds, and so was Jim to get away from the swamp. We said there warn't no home like a raft, after all. Other places do seem so cramped up and smothery, but a raft don't. You feel mighty free and easy and comfortable on a raft."

The Relation Between Faith and Works (Beatitudes and Commands) in the Reformation Tradition

The Augsburg Confession (1530) defined the Reformation's teaching on the relation between faith and good works (we can say, between Beatitudes and commands) in this way:

"Consequently this teaching concerning faith is not to be accused of forbidding good works but is rather to be praised by teaching that good works are to be done and for offering help as to *how* they may be done. For without faith and without Christ, human nature and human strength are much too weak to do good works, call upon God, have patience in suffering, love one's neighbor, diligently engage in callings which are commanded, render obedience, avoid evil lusts, etc. Such great and genuine works cannot be done without the help of Christ, as he himself says in John 15:5, 'Apart from me you can do nothing'" (art. 20, 35–39, emphasis added).

Luther's *Large Catechism* (1529) discussion of the difference between the Creed (or, as in German, the Faith) on the one hand and the Ten Commandments on the other can be transported almost bodily into our discussion of the relation between the Beatitudes and the commands. The Beatitudes are the Creed.

"Now you see that the Creed [*der Glaube:* the Faith] is a very different teaching from the Ten Commandments. The latter [the Commandments] teach us what *we* ought to do; the Creed tells what God does *for* us and gives *to* us. The Ten Commandments, moreover, are inscribed in the hearts of all men. No human wisdom can comprehend the Creed; it must be taught by the Holy Spirit alone. Therefore the Ten Commandments do not by themselves make us Christians, for God's wrath and displeasure still remain on us because we cannot fulfill his demands. But the Creed brings pure grace and makes us upright and pleasing to God. Through this knowledge we come to love and delight in all the commandments of God because we see that God gives himself completely to us, with all his gifts and his power, to help us keep the Ten Commandments: The Father gives us all creation, Christ all his works, the Holy Spirit all his gifts" (2:67–69).

An influential part of the Reformed tradition approached good works (or in our terminology, the commands) through the door of "Thankfulness," as the third and final section of *The Heidelberg Catechism* (1563), and especially the first question in this section, shows (with my emphases):

"Q. 86. Since we are redeemed from our sin and its wretched consequences • by grace through Christ without any merit of our own [—the Beatitudes], why must we do good works [—the commands]?

"A. Because just as Christ has redeemed us with his blood he also renews us through his Holy Spirit according to his own image, so that with our whole life we may show ourselves grateful to God for his goodness and that he may be glorified through us; and further, so that we ourselves may be assured of our faith by its fruits *and by our reverent behavior may win our neighbors to Christ* ["Follow me, and I will make you fishers of men"]." Cf. *The Westminster Confession of Faith* (1647), chap 19, secs. 6–7, for a good discussion.

The Theological Declaration of Barmen (1934) summarizes best:

"As Jesus Christ is God's assurance of the forgiveness of *all* our sins [the Beatitudes], so in the same way and with the same seriousness he is also God's mighty claim upon our *whole* life [the commands]. Through him befalls us a joyful deliverance from the godless fetters of this world for a free, grateful service to his creatures" (thesis 2).

Finally, Luther's two kingdoms understanding of the love-of-enemies command, expressed for example in his sermons on *The Sermon on the Mount* (1530–1532), raises important questions and deserves a special hearing.

"What is to be said about the fact that the Scriptures often talk about holy men cursing their enemies, even about Christ and His apostles doing so? Would you call that blessing their enemies? Or how can I love the pope when every day I rebuke and curse him—and with good reason, too? The answer, put as simply as possible, is this: I have often said that the office of preaching is not our office but God's. But whatever is God's, that we do not do ourselves; but He does it Himself, through the Word and the office [of preaching] as His own gift and business. Now, it is written in John 16:8 that it is the office and work of the Holy Spirit to convince [convict] the world. But if He is to convince it, He cannot act the hypocrite or play the flattering gentleman and say what it would like to hear. He must rebuke it vigorously and attack it—the way Christ pronounces 'Woe!' upon His Pharisees (Matt 23); the way Paul says to Elymas (Acts 13:10): 'You son of the devil . . . full of all villainy!'; the way Stephen reads a hard and sharp text to the high priests (Acts 7:51–53); and especially the way St. Paul (Gal 1:8) puts it all on one pile and calls everyone *anathema,* that is, excommunicated and cursed and sentenced to the abyss of hell, who does not preach the pure teaching about faith . . . In other words, our love and service belong to men. But they belong to God above all; if this is hindered or threatened, love and service are no longer in place. For the command is: 'You shall love *your* enemy and do him good.' But to God's enemies I must also be an enemy, lest I join forces with them against God" (*SM,* 119–22, emphasis added).

In the opinion of many Christians, Luther is the finest expositor of Scripture the church has been given, and by Protestants Luther's testimony is taken with special seriousness. There is an uncanny perceptiveness in Luther that sees into the heart

of Scripture. But Jesus stands before us in the seventh command to love our enemies, demanding a deeper love for the doctrinal *enemy* (not the *doctrine* but the
doctrinal enemy) than I ever see Luther admitting. Surely the major enemies of the
disciples whom Jesus addresses in this command will also be *God's* enemies, or will
be perceived as such by the disciples. (Luther's distinction between our enemies and
God's is too facile.) The seventh command requires of disciples the extremely difficult feat of loving even the enemies of God. It is the virtue of Luther's exposition
that it sets Jesus' command in the context of the whole biblical witness to enemies.
And Luther is correct in his interpretation of these other biblical texts: We must
fight false doctrine and, in that way, false teachers, vigorously (see Matt 23). But
this fight must always be waged under the banner of Jesus and his seventh command
which means, practically speaking, that we must indeed fight false teaching (out of
love for the endangered people of God), but we must also pray for and show love to
false teachers. The tension between these two requirements—of fighting false
teaching and of loving false teachers—is too much for human beings to bear or to
obey. Yet nothing less is required of disciples than, at the same time, a deeply
committed evangelicalism combined with a high-minded ecumenism. "Jesus looked
at his disciples very intently and said to them, 'With human beings this is impossible,
but with God absolutely everything is possible'" (Matt 19:26).

Chapter Six
The Call to Faith

I. THE DEVOTIONS (6:1–18)

Jesus defined and gave righteousness to his disciples in the fifth chapter in the Blessings and then taught and empowered his disciples to live this righteousness out in thoughtful relations to others through obedience to his commands. Righteousness is a right relation with God (the inaugural Blessings) and with people (the social commands), gift and demand.

Chapter 5 taught mainly mercy; chapter 6 teaches mainly faith (cf. Aug., *LSM*, 2:1:1:92). Chapter 5 taught the *what* of the Christian life; chapter 6 teaches the *how* (see an excellent discussion in Chrys., 19:1:130). In Jesus' teaching it is important that persons not only do what is right but that they do what is right in the right way and from the right resources. The how of righteousness is as important as the what. Righteousness that is overly conscious of itself, love that is impressed with its sacrifices, mercy that seeks attention or purity done for show are all unright and unrighteous. And Christian life that looks mainly to will power for its resources and not, for example, to the Lord's Prayer (Matt 6:9–13), is doomed to frustration.

"Watch out that you do not do your righteousness in front of other people to be noticed by them; if you do, you won't have any reward from your Father who is in heaven" (v 1).

Jesus begins this section of his sermon by warning against theatrical righteousness. "Watch out that you do not do your righteousness in front of other people to be noticed by [*theathēnai*, to be theater to] them." Theatrical righteousness is a righteousness that is concerned to do good in a way that is dramatically noticeable. Jesus rejects the motive of notice—but in a unique way: "if you do this, you won't have any reward [that is, "notice"] from your Father who is in heaven" (v 1).

We are made to want notice. One of the most characteristic remarks of the child is "Watch me!" The child's verbal "watch me" becomes the adult's more unspoken (but just as deep) "notice me." This drive to be noticed is not only the result of our sin, it is also a part of the image of God. We were made to notice and to be noticed by God, to imag(e)-ine and image his pleasure.

I will submit that in Matthew's Gospel the desire to be noticed by the Father is what the Christian tradition calls faith. I believe the sixth chapter of Matthew is largely a sustained call to faith as the fifth chapter was largely a long call to mercy. In the fifth chapter Jesus mainly asked us to have a heart, horizontally, for others; in this chapter Jesus asks us mainly to have a soul, vertically, toward the Father.

There is an apparent contradiction between Jesus' thematic Word in the middle of the fifth chapter—"Let your light so shine before people that [*hopōs*] they may see your good works and glorify your Father who is in heaven" (5:16)—and the opening Word in this section—"Watch out that you do *not* do your righteousness in front of other people to be [*pros to*] noticed by them" (6:1). How can these two sentences be reconciled? It is right to do good works in such a way that when people see them they think of God; it is wrong to do good works in such a way that when people see them they think of us. The difference can only be prayed for.

I think that there is still a further way to relate 5:16 and 6:1. In the earlier 5:16 we have a strongly emphasized you-plural (*hymōn*, "your," placed emphatically before "good works"). "Let your light so shine before people that they may see *your* good works and glorify your Father in heaven." The emphasized "your" is intended to contrast Christian good works with other kinds, to suggest that the substance and style of Christian good works will be different from the substance and style of usually praised good works, which were (as a rule) rather striking. The kinds of good works that Jesus then commands in 5 B are not visually striking and are not the kinds of good works that are usually considered spectacular; they are, instead, quickness to reconcile, sexual circumspection, nondefensiveness in the face of provocation, and warm relations with hard people. These practices in fact are often seen by many people as so many varieties of weakness. These obediences are often scorned as pollyanish, Puritan, or prudish. Christian good works are not works that set the Christian so much above others as they do beneath them.

There are two other recent solutions to the tension between 5:16 and 6:1. W. D. Davies, 250–51, 290, sees 5:16, like 5:13–14, "to have been originally a critique of the withdrawn piety of the [Qumran] Sect. . . . While the New Israel [of the church] as a community is to shine forth among men by their 'good deeds' and not to withdraw under a bushel, individual Christians [according to 6:1] are, at the same time, not to be ostentatious in their piety." Similarly, Gundry, 101, sees no contradiction between the two texts because in 5:13–16 "Matthew was concerned with the temptation to hide one's discipleship in order to escape persecution (cf. 5:10–12)," whereas the issue in 6:1ff is showing off.

In this sixth chapter Jesus gives three examples of personal devotion to make his appeal for unostentatious righteousness vivid: almsgiving (we may call it giving money or helping the poor), prayer, and fasting. In the thought of the people of God if one wished to go beyond the commandments or to make amends for possibly broken commandments—to secure extra merit or to assure a larger balance of righteousness—Halakah recommended the three activities of charity, prayer, and fasting. Giving money, praying, and fasting were not explicitly mentioned in the Ten Commandments, the core of the Torah. They were the works, we might say, of spiritual overtime, extra works, works available to the Israelite who wanted to be sure (cf. Grund., 191–92). For Matthew's purposes these three activities illustrated righteousness in its three main relations: to others (giving money), to God (prayer), and to oneself (fasting) (cf. Beng., 1:120).

A. Giving Money (D 1), 6:2–4

"Thus when you give money, don't sound a trumpet in front of you like the phonies [hypokritai] do in the synagogues and in the town squares so that they may be honored by people. Amen, I tell you, they already have their reward. But when you give money, don't even let your left hand know what your right hand is doing, so that your giving may be in secret; and your Father who sees what happens in secret will reward you."

6:2 Of the many illustrations that Jesus could have selected for relations to others he chose that of giving money. (The word "alms," translated "money" here, really means any good deed intended to serve others Schn., **77**.) We learned in chapter 5 that Christian righteousness is marked by a deep concern for the other person. But now it is important that we be warned against showing that concern in irresponsible ways. For example, the gift of money can help persons. But it can also hurt them. If a gift is given in an ostentatious way it is delegitimized by Jesus. What could have been a help to another—a right thing—is turned by its demonstrativeness into a wrong thing. There is a goodness that is too good.

"Care for the needy constituted an important part of Jewish religious life" (Guel., 302). Thus the very generous in Palestine were sometimes literally summoned to the front of the synagogue alongside the rabbi to be publicly honored. This led Schlatter to suspect that trumpets were actually blown to announce to the congregation that an especially generous person was being brought to the front (*Der*, 201–02; cf. Bonn., 78; Hill, 133). Jesus wishes to put an end to this bad handling of a good work. The work of God needs money, and giving money is a good thing. But it is a great pity when giving is spoiled by theatrics. The spiritual leader in such cases is as much to blame as the "actor" (*hypokritēs* means, literally, actor), for it is the leader who has the trumpets blown. Human glorification does not often work divine glory. Where people are made too much of up front, God leaves by the back.

Jesus' realism is evident in his observation, "Amen, I tell you, they already have their reward." He does not say, as we might have expected, "Amen, I tell you, they will not have any reward at all." For Jesus knows that celebrated people are celebrated, and impressive people impress. They do get their reward. Matthew uses the commercial term then current for business transactions: "paid in full" (*apechousin*) (Grund., 194; Schw., 143). The reward of the demonstrative is to be paid then in full, meaning that they get what they then want, but there is no reward left from the Father; they have all the reward they're ever going to get, right now, in the reward of people's admiration. "For good deeds cannot merit more than one reward; to gain it from man is to lose it from God" (McN., 73).

6:3 "But when *you* [emphasized] give money, don't even let your left hand know what your right hand is doing." The emphasized "you" (this time singular) indicates that Jesus wishes to form special people. Christians are to be nondemonstrative people. Keeping the left hand from knowing what the right hand is doing means, first, seeking to be unself-conscious and unself-impressed (Schl., *Der*, 202; Schn., 77). Specifically, our financial generosity (the one hand) should not be credited to the account of our spiritual standing before God (the other hand). Not only should there be no external trumpets or public flurry; there should not even be any internal music, not even violins in the background which might comfort us by suggesting the self-contentment that says, "I am, after all, a pretty decent fellow." Jesus' left-hand right-hand picture tells us that beyond avoiding the attempt to impress others we should not even seek to impress, or internally justify, ourselves.

The left-hand right-hand relation might also apply to one's spouse or closest friends or neighbors ("best friend," Grund., 194; Gundry's literal interpretation here seems forced, 102). However understood, Jesus wishes to liberate us from the bondage of having to be impressive to other people or even to ourselves.

6:4 "So that *your* [emphasized] giving may be in secret; and your Father who sees what happens in secret will reward you." When not even our left hand knows what our right hand is doing—that is, when our contribution has been private—the Father has noticed. It is as if God the Father is "blinded" by dazzling, spectacular deeds and "cannot" see them; but when the deed is muted by privacy, when it does not dazzle, he sees it. Or to use another analogy, the invisible God has a certain affinity for invisible deeds. The Father sees what is done in secret; *he* is impressed by the unimpressive. Just as a human father can *see* the fumbling magic trick that his child tries to perform for him, so our Father can see our fumbling attempts to do the magic (or invisible) tricks of modesty and anonymity.

And the Father is impressed. This is the meaning of the doctrine of rewards. Rewards posit a living, reciprocal, mutual relationship between the Father and his children. But precisely because the relation is between the *Father* and his *children*, the commercial factor falls away from Jesus' doctrine of rewards. (What father pays for his child's magic tricks?) A father's reward to his child is, first of all and primarily, himself; the reward, however expressed, is the father's closeness. Jesus' doctrine of rewards is decommercialized by its grammar of family. (Cf. Conz., 65.)

Reformation Protestantism, wishing to avoid the idea of merits in rewards, has at times gone to the extreme of making the Father unresponsive to the deeds of his children. In the desire to preserve the grace of God, a grace that does not wait to respond but that hurries to give—an entirely laudable and biblical desire—Protestantism has sometimes been reluctant to teach that God rewards anything people do at all. The old Roman doctrine of merits sometimes chased Protestants away from Jesus' doctrine of rewards. We "escaped Clyde and drowned in Conway."

But it is important that believers know that the heavenly Father *notices* what they do and that he notices not merely in a deistic way, like a distant, benign grandfather, but that he notices in a highly personal, lively way, like a living Father—i.e., that he rewards. It is important that disciples know that their sacrifices are worth it, that their bucking public opinion, or visibility, gets a response somewhere. Human beings are so made that they have to be noticed. Persons were created to be response-making and response-receiving—i.e., responsible—persons. This is a part of the image of God. We cannot live without responses. That is why the child's "watch me" is such a primeval call. Jesus, unlike the Buddha, does not demolish this *tanha*, this passion to be noticed; he redirects it. He says, in effect, "Focus your deep desire to be noticed in the right direction—toward your Father. And your Father *will* notice; he will reward you."

The mystics speak of loving God for God's sake, disinterestedly, and moralists urge persons to do good for its own sake, without any crass notion of rewards (cf. the good discussions in Bonn., 76, and Streck., 164). But Jesus knows human nature. It is foolish, Schlatter says, to think that God calls his people to almost superhuman sacrifices and then fails to react, respond, reward. The biblical God is personal, responsive, and rewarding. "Heaven" in Jesus' vocabulary is not a chronological but a spatial term, and so when Jesus says our reward will be in heaven he means our reward will be good relations with God now, and not just later at the judgment, though the final judgment figures massively in Jesus' teaching. Both now and then, the person obedient to Jesus' commands *is rewarded*, "knowing that whatever good anyone does, he will receive the same again from the Lord" (Eph 6:8).

The human drive to be impressive to people is so deep-seated that Jesus knows it can only be countered by the still deeper drive to be impressive to the Father. (The close correlation between faith and being impressive is captured by the penetrating question of the evangelist John's Jesus, "How *can* you believe, who receive glory from one another and do not seek the glory that comes from the only God?" [John 5:44].) The drive in Matthew's Gospel to be noticed only by the Father is what Paul's gospel, in particular, calls faith. Jesus' teaching of rewards is Paul's doctrine of faith. In each the person is asked to look away from the desire to be humanly impressive—even impressive to oneself—and to look to the Father alone as our reward, as our "noticer" (in Matthew) or justifier (in Paul). The Epistle to the Hebrews unites in one sentence both Paul and Matthew, both a theology of faith and a theology of rewards, showing that the two are not mutually exclusive: "Without faith it is impossible to please [God]. For whoever would draw near to God must *believe* that he exists and that he *rewards* those who seek him" (Heb 11:6, RSV).

Chrysostom's *Homilies on St. Matthew* ranks with Luther's sermons on Matthew and Schlatter's commentaries on Matthew in helpful interpretation of the Gospel. One weakness in Chrysostom's homilies is a doctrine of what I can only call justification by almsgiving (cf., e.g., for one of many discussions, 47:5:295). The strength of Chrysostom's emphasis on almsgiving is that it relates the discipleship of faith to the discipleship of money, a concern everywhere evident in Jesus, especially the Jesus of Luke's Gospel.

Surprisingly, Luther exults in the biblical doctrine of rewards, and nowhere more expansively than in his "Explanation of the Appendix to the First Commandment" in the *Large Catechism* (1529). The Reformed doctrine of rewards is best explained in the *Second Helvetic Confession* (1566), chapter 16, "Of Faith and Good Works, and of Their Reward, and of Man's Merit."

B. Prayer (D 2), 6:5–15

"And when you pray, don't be like the phonies; they love to stand praying right out on the streets and at the main intersections so that people may notice them. Amen, I tell you, they have already received all the reward they are going to get. But when you pray, go into your supply-room, lock the door, and pray to your Father who is in secret; and your Father who sees what happens in secret will reward you" (vv 5–6).

An old rabbinic rule forbade people to pray loudly in public. One spin-off of this rule was that it made possible a quiet praying in public—what we today associate with the Muslim practice of public prayer or Jewish prayer at the Jerusalem Wailing Wall. The old believer could have his prayers right out on the street, since they were to be done low volume anyway (Schl., *Der*, 203). Jesus had noticed this practice and was repelled. He felt that public private devotion was a contradiction in terms: it was a piety directed both toward God and people. No doubt the direction of this piety could be justified; praying like this in public was a kind of witness to the priority of God. Some Christians today feel this way about table grace in public restaurants. They believe that observable prayer before meals is not a bad idea; in fact, in addition to thanking God, such prayer also reminds observers that God is important. (Table grace in public can be done appropriately, but disciples guard against ostentation.)

Jesus was not happy with prayer that tried to be a witness. Prayer is not a form of evangelism, addressed to other people. Prayer is addressed to God, exclusively (unless one is praying with or leading others in prayer, a practice that Jesus in no way contests here or elsewhere; Jesus urges prayer meetings, in fact, as a major means of spiritual power at, e.g., 18:19–20; 21:22; 26:41, in all of which the plural verbs point to group prayer). But group prayer thrives only where private prayer lives (Schl., *Das*, 90). Thus Matthew's Jesus' earliest teaching on prayer, here, stresses privacy. Prayer must be vertical to be honest. Directing an activity that is supposed to be directed to God into an activity that can also make a good impression on others, Jesus calls phony.

Luther, *SM*, 140, spoke powerfully for prayer meetings: "Such prayer is a precious thing and a powerful defense against the devil and his assaults. For in it, all Christendom combines its forces with one accord; and the harder it prays, the more effective it is and the sooner it is heard. . . . Thus it is certain that whatever still stands and endures, whether it is in the spiritual or in the secular realm, is being preserved through prayer."

There are subtle ways of showing others we pray. In conversation we can casually say, for example, "When I was praying this morning, I realized . . ." or, "Last night in prayer the Lord showed me. . . ." These elliptical references, intended often as witness, are inauthentic because they make public what should remain private. Charity and devotion are to be guarded by privacy if they are to be real.

6:6 "But when *you* [emphasized and singular!] pray, go into your supply-room, lock the door, and pray to your Father who is in secret; and your Father who sees in secret will reward you. . . ." The supply-room was the only room in poor Palestinian farms that could be locked (Schl., *Der*, 205; Schl., *Das*, 89; Schn., 77f; Schw., 145). In one sense it was seemingly the least sanctified place in the house: it was used to store feed, small animals, tools, and other supplies. But the furnishings of the room were its least important fact; it could be locked, it could be private, and that was the supreme consideration. In a single sentence Jesus has revised the whole Old Testament cultus. It is no longer the Holy of Holies that is the special meeting place between God and believer; it is the room with the lock. Sacral space is replaced by secular space, if the door can be closed.

Of course, God is near at all times, but Jesus knows that the believer is only able to draw near God in a particularly serious way when one has a little privacy. The well-known saying, "Life is prayer," was familiar to the pious of Israel. But they also knew, as Jesus now confirms, that only the life that gets aside, that closes the door occasionally, is able to live prayerfully. The life-is-prayer formula can be used as an excuse for not praying at all. Prayer for Jesus was not only living with a *sense* of God; it was real talking to God with words. Prayer is conversation; it is the attempt to say words. Much true prayer, of course, is often a stammering for words (cf. Rom 8:26), but this stammering occurs while really trying to say something.

1. How Not to Pray (Wrong Prayer) (6:7–8)
Matthew 6 A, which we call the Devotions, is divided into three precision-shaped parts—charity, prayer, and fasting—each with exactly the same form. These three parts, placed side by side, conform in the smallest detail. Into this arrangement, Matthew the systematician has now inserted special dominical teaching on prayer—Matthew's Prayer Catechism (vv 7–15). This special teaching can be subdivided into two sections: "How Not to Pray" and "How to Pray"— "Wrong Prayer" and "The Lord's Prayer." Here Jesus first disabuses us of widely held but wrong conceptions of prayer; then having cleared the foundation of rubble he builds the edifice of the disciples' special prayer.

The first misconception of prayer that Jesus attacks is the belief that there must be much prayer before prayer works. The pagan rule concerning prayer says "much"; Jesus' first antirule, on the contrary, is "*not* much."

Jesus says,

6:7–8 *"When you pray, don't go on and on like the pagans do, because they think that the more they talk, the more likely they will be heard. Don't you be like them, because your Father knows the things you need before you even ask him."*

The quantitative idea of prayer is pagan (cf. Seneca's "fatigue the gods," *Ep.* 31:5, and Martial's "Let each one wear himself out with his petitions," 7:60:3). Pagan counsel rests on the conviction that God is reluctant to listen to prayer unless it is long, and that only when the pray-er has proven oneself sincere by spending time in confession, praise, or even quiet, does the divinity begin to listen. This belief de-deifies God by making God a grudging Giver, and it dehumanizes persons by turning them into beasts of burden. Jesus attacks the "much" conception of prayer mercilessly. It is unworthy of both God and human beings. It empties both of their distinctive character. God is made a taskmaster and people monkeys.

At first glance, Jesus' attack on quantitative prayer seems to be unsound pedagogy. When he discourages quantity in prayer is he not discouraging prayer itself? Here, too, the shortest distance between two points is not always a straight line. The paradox of prayer is that only when we are relieved of the burden of the *necessity* of much will we experience the freedom to do much (or even little). People who pray much because they believe that they have to before they get a hearing may not really be praying at all, in the serious sense of praying; they may be earning merits for their own conscience, marking time, or proving their sincerity to themselves in order, they hope, finally to get through. But with these ideas in the heart, is prayer really prayer?

What became the beautiful standard Jewish "Eighteen [Petition] Prayer" was first prayed twice daily, then three times a day, and represented a huge accomplishment. When combined with the twice daily She'ma Confessions, table prayers, and the doxologies at every opportunity, the people of God in Jesus' time were confronted by Jesus not as a prayerless community but as a people overburdened with prayer. Jesus brought measure (Schl., *Der*, 206–07). Jesus released his people "from having to make a special effort to guarantee access to God. He turns prayer once more into children's conversation with their father" (Schw., 147).

It is an immense relief to know that the heavenly Father to whom prayer is addressed is not a reluctant listener. It is good to know that the Father does not require certain initiation rites to be performed before we get passage. (Calvin's treatment of prayer has this problem, *Inst.*, III. xx. 1–14.) Few facts encourage the outpouring of prayer like being released from the burden of praying much. Luther's discovery, shared at this text in his sermons (*SM*, 143), is faithful exegesis of Jesus' warning: prayers should be "brief, frequent, and intense."

In the practical matters of Christian life such as prayer, Matthew's Jesus teaches grace no less effectively than does the apostle Paul. Jesus knows grace. Old Testament wisdom knew what was involved here, too: "Be not rash with your mouth, nor let your hearts be hasty to utter a word before God, for God is in heaven, and you upon earth; therefore let your words be few" (Eccl 5:2). But this wise old man speaks with a touch of resignation, whereas Jesus' words are a message of joy closer to the Lord of Isaiah's "Before they call I will answer, while they are yet speaking I will hear" (Isa 65:24).

It will be objected that the New Testament elsewhere says "pray without ceasing" and that there are parables, particularly in Luke (chaps 11 and 18), that encourage us to importunate prayer. I believe that the rule to pray without ceasing (1 Thess 5:17) can be kept only when we are first freed from the false idea that we have God by means of our activity instead of by his mercy. In a moment, Matthew's Jesus, too, will teach us to "Ask . . . , seek . . . , [and] knock" in persistent prayer (7:7–11). But he first wishes us to know the foundational truth of prayer: that it is not how much or how frequently we pray that earns us the right to be heard. Once this is known, we are free to hear the commands to pray without ceasing and to be askers, seekers, and knockers.

It is another question to ask what "pray without ceasing" means. Does it mean to continue in an attitude of prayer throughout the day—"prayer is life"? Impressive as this idea in itself is, I do not believe that it is the author's meaning. I believe we may effectively interpret "pray without ceasing" by saying "keep your times of prayer faithfully," or "be continually at your prayers," meaning that we should not permit business or the press of life's necessities to crowd out the paramount necessity of daily fellowship with God in prayer. I believe, in other words, that it is not so much Brother Lawrence's practicing the presence of God that is meant here—though this practice is not a bad idea if one has this aptitude—but it is the devotional keeping faith with the Father through regular prayer. Jesus did not shrink from using drastic illustrations to make his point. His point in the eleventh and eighteenth chapters of Luke on importunate prayer is to teach that the Father is *unlike* the cranky friend and heartless judge. Luke would be completely misunderstood if he were read to mean that God *is like* these portraits—sleeping, grudging, reluctant. Jesus' point, in the Gospel's own words, is "*how much more* will your *heavenly* Father give the Holy Spirit to those who ask *him*" (Luke 11:13).

We can be encouraged to importunate prayer *after* we have been assured, as we are in Matt 6, that our importunity is not the basis of prayer. The basis of prayer is the good Father, not good disciples. If Luke 11 and 18 are placed before Matthew 6, the meaning of prayer is endangered; if they are placed after it (as they are in our canon), they are "graced"; Luke's teaching in *this* sequence is even necessary, for we tend to sloth. (Cf. Augustine's "Remove from prayer much speaking, not much praying," *Ep.* 130 in McN., 76; cf. Chrys., 19:5:133; Cal. 1:203.)

Jewish prayer, as has been pointed out (the "Eighteen Prayer"), is impressive but it is long and had to be recited more than once daily by the devout (Schw., 146). Muslim prayers in the Koran are sublime, but I still recall my disappointment when I learned that they must be repeated at each of the five appointed times of prayer in order to be properly executed. Hindu and Buddhist prayers in particular depend on the principle of "much equals much," that is, on the principle of repetition; indeed, it is felt that the repetition of certain mantras, words, sounds, or syllables (Om, hari, the nembutsu, etc.) can identify one with (or transform one into, or move one to realize that one is) the deity invoked or the reality recited. In each case, repetition is the soul of prayer. Jesus' words confront this conviction like a stone wall: "They think that they will be heard because of how much they say. Don't you be like them." (When one compares Jewish and Essene rigor in prayer, one has to be impressed that there are no prayer *times* in the Gospels. Bonnard, 80, speaks of *la sobriété évangélique.*)

6:8 "Don't you be like them, because your Father knows the things you need before you even ask him." If the first "antiprinciple" of prayer is "not much," the second is "he (already) knows." And for a second time it could seem that this principle is more apt to inhibit than to encourage prayer. For if God already knows our needs and what we are going to pray, then why pray at all?

That God is God is the first principle of all right thinking about God. To say that only if God does *not* already know our needs does prayer make sense may be logically plausible but it is theologically inadmissible. In personal relations it is precisely with those human beings who already know us, with those who know our needs better than we know them ourselves, that we in fact talk most freely. Therefore, the words "he knows" do not inhibit prayer. For if the Father did *not* know, he would not be God, and precisely the fact that he knows encourages us to come to him. Prayer is not an intelligence briefing for God; it is intelligent conversation with him.

When Jesus' two antiprinciples of prayer are taken to heart—when we believe that "not much" is required of us before we have much of the Father, and that "he knows" our needs before we pray—if we believe both these disabusing truths—we are liberated to pray, and to pray more simply and less heavily. "Not much" frees us from the amount of time we think we have to spend in prayer, and "he knows" frees us from the amount of information we think we have to give to get through. Christians are freed from the double burden of lifting either "much" or "news" to the Father. Instead, they can just talk honestly. "Much" is not the mediator, Jesus is. And "news" (the new or unknown) is not absolutely necessary since God is God and knows already. Neither a mediatorial-quantity nor an informative-preliminary is required of Christians before they can pour out their hearts to the Father. Because the Father is *good* the much is not required, and because the Father is *God* the information is not necessary. A lot of honest prayer is simply groaning.

Luther, *SM*, 142–43: "The gentile delusion [is] that prayer meant making both God and oneself tired with yelling and murmuring. . . . But the Christian's prayer is easy, and it does not cause hard work. . . . It presents its need from the heart. Faith quickly gets through telling what it wants. . . . And because He [the Holy Spirit, Rom 8:26] knows that God is listening to Him, He has no need of such everlasting twaddle. . . . Therefore the ancient fathers have said correctly that many long prayers are not the way. They recommend short, fervent prayers, where one sighs toward heaven with a word or two, as is often quite possible in the midst of reading, writing, or doing some other task. But the others, who make it nothing but a work of drudgery, can never pray with gladness or devotion. . . . [But] the man who is serious in his intentions and takes pleasure in prayer neither knows nor feels any toil and trouble; he simply looks at his need, and he has finished singing or praying the words before he has a chance to turn around. In other words, prayers ought to be brief, frequent, and intense."

2. How to Pray (The Lord's Prayer), 6:9–15

"*So you should pray like this:*
'*Our Father who is in the heavens,*
Hallowed be your name.
Your kingdom come,
Your will be done,
    on earth as it is in heaven.

Give us this day our bread for the next day;
And forgive us our debts
    as we, too, have forgiven our debtors;
And lead us not into temptation,
    but snatch us from the evil one' " (vv 9–13).

A major problem of prayer is not knowing what to say or, what is the same thing, not being sure that what we pray is right. Having liberated us from a false certainty—from the carnal certainty that only much praying gets much answer—Jesus now liberates us into a true certainty, into a set of requests that we are sure are heard and are the right petitions to pray. Jesus not only releases our hearts from false, burdensome notions of what prayer is, he puts on our lips the prayers to pray.

It is impressive that Jesus' Lord's Prayer does not remove the mind, as some mysticisms do, but engages it. For Jesus gives six rational petitions to pray, six sentences, not six ways to eliminate thinking and to induce being. Jesus does not give mantras, he gives petitions. The Lord's Prayer is one of the major proofs that Jesus is not an irrationalist or an anti-intellectual.

The prayer Jesus gives us is a short prayer. It can be prayed, even slowly, in less than a minute. It is simple. And yet it contains all the petitions that Jesus says we should ask. Matthew's Jesus says "pray *like* this," teaching us that this prayer is not a law but a pattern; Luke's Jesus, who gives us almost the same prayer, says "when you pray, *say*" (Luke 11:2), teaching us the equally important truth that it is not wrong to pray exactly this prayer, verbatim.

We are therefore either to pray this prayer in Matthean obedience by using each phrase as a kind of handrail along which to proceed in forming our own words, or to pray exactly this prayer in Lukan obedience by using the very words thoughtfully. However we use the prayer, it is important that we appreciate that one of Jesus' greatest gifts to his church was this prayer. For we do often wonder if we are praying as we should. The Lord's Prayer also "helps us when our ideas run out" (Cal., 1:205). Jesus' atonement enabled us to have fellowship with the Father at all, but once in the Father's presence this prayer teaches us what to say.

6:9a Matthew emphasizes the "you." "So *you* should pray like this." In context, the emphasized "you" is meant to contrast with the "polylogic," "muchist" prayer ideology of pagans (Mey., 147) and of the old synagogue (Davies, *SM*, 87). *Christian* prayer is characterized by attention to six petitions.

In these petitions disciples are taught what prayer, constructively, is. Jesus now teaches *positively*. (But what Jesus just before taught negatively—How Not to Pray— is almost as important, for the gifts of privacy, brevity, and assurance are the air by which prayer breathes.)

When we look at the Lord's Prayer as a whole we notice that it is divided into two almost exactly symmetrical parts. The first three petitions all include the word "your"; the last three petitions include the word "our" or "us." The first half of the prayer is about God the Father (the divine petitions), and the last half is about us (the human petitions). (Though of course what concerns the Father also deeply concerns us, and what concerns us concerns the Father.)

a. The Address, 6:9b

"Our Father who is in the heavens."

There were many names for God in Judaism. In the religion it is customary to collect the names of the deity (the ninety-nine beautiful names in Islam, for example). Jesus' name for God here and throughout the Gospel accounts is strikingly simple and uncomplicated: "Father." It is important for us to notice that the phrase "Our Father" is an expression that Jesus gives *us* to use; "our Father" is never Jesus' own expression in his prayer or conversation. He always talks of "my Father" or absolutely of "the Father," and when he talks to the disciples of the Father, he calls him "your Father." He never speaks to them of "our Father." This very clear distinction is carried through even in the Gospel of John where, classically, we hear Jesus telling Mary Magdalene to "go tell the disciples that I am ascending to your God and to my God, to your Father and to my Father" (John 20:17).

The meaning of this distinction is simply that which the church confesses in its creed: "I believe in Jesus Christ, his *only* (*unicum*) Son, our Lord." Jesus' relation to the Father is absolutely unique. He and he only is God's Son by nature; Christians are his children by adoption. He and he alone is God's Son by right; we are God's children by grace. Jesus' unique relationship with the Father is pointed to everywhere in the Gospels and is clarified in the creeds. He is *the* Son.

Therefore, when Jesus gives us the right to call on his Father as our Father, he is passing on to us his own priceless relationship. This is Jesus' greatest gift in the Lord's Prayer. Without much celebration, in this simple text, we are adopted into the family of God. We are allowed, we are even gently commanded to pray "Our Father." This is an inexpressible gift (Schl., *Der*, 208–09). The Old Testament also referred to God as Father, usually in expressions "like a father" (yet see "our father" in Isa 63:16; 64:8 NEB). For Jesus, and now for his church, God is not simply like a Father behind whom stands a more awesome God. God is the Father.

Israel's introduction to Yahweh was similar. God's opening words on the mountain were "I am Yahweh, *your* God" (Exod 20:2; Deut 5:6). The simple possessive pronoun "your" on Sinai and now the simple possessive pronoun "our" on the New Testament mountain join the people of God to deity. God was not introduced to Israel coldly and formally as "Yahweh, the God," but graciously and warmly as "Yahweh, your God." And now in the same spirit, God is given to us not only as the Father, but as *our* Father. The "our" means belonging, mercy, home. It is a *possessive* pronoun meaning that God the Father is ours and we are his. In the "our" is contained the joy of the whole gospel. We will never be able to calculate the honor that has been done us by being allowed to pray "Our Father."

The word for "Father" used by Jesus, *abba*, was the intimate term used by little children with their fathers, and it comes close (as the sounds *ab-ba* themselves suggest) to the child's reference to a father in all languages: *papa, fatie, tatay, daddy*, etc. (But *abba*, "unlike its English equivalents, . . . remained in use during adulthood," Grund., 105.) *Abba* is a word of love and affection. It is the most warm of the Aramaic words for father. (The modern "Our Parent" simply will not do.)

At the same time, the word *father* carried stronger connotations of authority than we today associate with the word. The father was the one *responsible* for the child: He was not only the child's friend; he was the child's progenitor, guardian, provider, and lord. The word, therefore, has elements of strength in it beyond its more obvious elements of tenderness.

The word "our" is significant, finally, because it turns individual prayer into prayer for others. The "our" teaches that when we address the Father we address him for the rest of us, too. ("Our" means that "in prayer, each speaks for all the children of God," Beng., 1:122.) The "our" means that in a sense even our most private, bedside prayer is public and includes the rest of the Christian family. After having made our prayer very private with his storeroom Word (v 6), Jesus now makes our prayer very public with his "our." True private prayer will be public prayer. "He setteth the solitary in families" (Ps 68:6 RV). ("It is very significant that in the Lord's Prayer the words *I, me,* and *mine* never occur," Barc., 1:202.)

Here a question is often raised. Does the "our" refer to all people as God's children or does it refer only to those who by faith in Jesus Christ have been especially adopted into the family of God? In John (for example, John 1:12–13) and Paul (Gal 4:6) it appears that those only enjoy the privilege of being called the children of God who have been adopted as such by grace through faith, that being sons or daughters of God is not so much a right of birth as a gift of grace. In Matthew's Gospel this distinction is not as clear. I think that the Christian may include both fellow-Christians *and* the whole world in the "our" (thus also Cal., *Inst.* III. xx. 38: "all men who dwell on earth"). The world may not yet recognize and may even fight the Father, and in this sense the Father is not yet in the full subjective sense, *their* Father. Nevertheless, because the Father created them and the Son died for them in order to make them fully conscious children of his Father, we can include them in the "our." It seems gracious to do this. If this Father is the Father we met in the last chapter who sends his rain and sun beneficently on the unrighteous as well as the righteous (C 7), then it would seem unnatural and ungracious to exclude the world from the prayer's "our." But the "our" most appropriately fits the Family who recognizes him as Father; it is for the worldwide church, the *communio sanctorum,* soul brothers and sisters, that the prayer to our Father is most natural.

The "our" in the "Our Father" will also fight classism in disciples. Aug., *LSM*, 2:4:16:106: "Here there is also an admonition to the rich and to those who in the eyes of the world are well-born, that when they become Christians they are not to lord it over the poor and lowly, because they are one in saying to God, 'Our Father,' which they cannot say with true piety unless they recognize that they are brothers." Aug., *Serm.* 8 (58):2:284f: "But we say all in common, 'Our Father.' How great a condescension! This the emperor says, and this says the beggar: this says the slave, and this his lord. . . . Now let not the lord disdain to have his slave for a brother, seeing the Lord Christ has vouchsafed to have him for a brother." Cf. also in this vein Chrys., 19:6:134. The Lord's Prayer plants a democratizing time bomb in culture. The Lord's Prayer is both leveller *and* elevator.

All over the world the family of the church prays this prayer, together and in private, and so in a special way offers its part of the world to this Father. The "our" of the Our Father should always remind us of, and draw us toward, the whole catholic church on earth, and then toward the whole world for whom the Father formed the church.

"Who is in the heavens." In most modern translations the Greek's plural "heavens" is rendered by the singular "heaven." The Greek singular *ouranos* means simply "sky" and is thought of artlessly as that which is above us. I believe that the original plural "heavens" (or "skies") preserves something of importance. The sky immediately visible over my head at the moment stretches for about a hundred kilometers or more from my western to my eastern horizon. That is "my sky." But there are other skies over other people, and the Father is in those skies, too. Thus when one prays "Our Father who is in the skies," one is addressing the God in all the skies of earth, on all the horizons of everybody. (Chernobyl taught the unity of skies.)

Therefore, "Our Father who is in the heavens" can give us roughly the same feeling that the opening words of our classic creeds give us: "I [or "we"] believe in God the Father *almighty* (*patrem omnipotentem; patera pantokratora*)." The expression "in the heavens" stretches the idea of the Father we address. He is not only intimately "our Father"; he is also universally the great God of the whole earth. That is to say, he is not only love, he is also almighty; he is not only close, he is great; he is not only gracious, he is sovereign; or in classical theological language, he is not only merciful, he is holy. "Father" gives us the most essential fact about God: his goodness; "heavens" gives us the most essential background fact about God: his holiness. Lest we become too chummy with the Father, the qualifier "in the heavens" tells us that the Father is *God*. Lest we become too selfish with this Father, "in the heavens" tells us that he is God not only in my sky but in all the skies of all the world.

b. The First Petition (LP 1), 6:9c
"Hallowed be your name."

The root of the word for "hallowed" (*hagiasthētō*) is *hagios*, of which the anglicized words *holy, holiness,* or the Latinized words *saint* and *sanctification*, are translations. The word means to set aside—or better today—to make central. I say that "to make central" is better today because with our sense of space it is preferable to see God at center rather than to one side.

Christians, called "saints" consistently in Paul's literature, are those who have been brought to center, drawn to the center of things (and not set aside, which today can mean "made marginal"). Therefore, when we pray "hallowed be your name," we are asking God to be central, to be God to us, to his church, and to his world. The fact that Jesus made this petition our first petition indicates its importance to his mind. Our main concern in life should be that God be treated as God. Moreover, the prayer to the heavenly Father for the hallowing of his name is a petition that *God* will *himself* make himself central and God under all skies. Since our great need, without reservation, is the knowledge of God as real, it is deeply encouraging to know that we can ask God to do this most important of matters for us. Behind the passive voice of this "hallowed *be*" petition is the active God who is asked to do the hallowing, the centering, the making real, the glorifying.

The biblical word "glory" translates the Hebrew noun *kavod,* which in the adjective means "heavy" (von Rad, TDNT, 2:230f; BDB, 458). God is "heavy," significant, (literally) weighty. The great need of the world is to know this and so, in knowing the primal fact, to be made weighty and significant itself. For without the proper reference to its center, to its own depth, the world is centrifugal, torn, and fragmented.

The world's major need, though it hardly appreciates it, is to know God. Jesus' first petition teaches this need classically.

And to know God as he is, and not just as he is thought to be, leads us to the significance of the word "name." The name is one's real, as opposed to one's supposed, identification; one's real identity or character as opposed to rumors or fabrications; one's revealed nature as opposed to one's surmised. When we pray "hallowed be your name," therefore, we are praying that God-as-he-*is* and as he has revealed himself to be will be known and honored as such, that God's real character will be revealed again, that God's reputation in the world will improve, that God will be known, as he has classically been made known through Jesus Christ, as "Our Father."

Indeed, though Jesus' modesty prevents him from saying so, I believe that the *meaning* of this first petition, when seen in the context of the whole Gospel's revelation, is that people will know Jesus of Nazareth. For historically "no one really knows the Father except the Son and any one to whom the Son chooses to reveal him" (Matt 11:27b). The name is hallowed where the Son is followed. To know Jesus Christ is the way to know his Father.

Compare John 14:7–9: "'If you have really known me,'" Jesus says, "'then you will know my Father.' Philip said to him, 'Lord, show us the Father, and that will be all we need.' Jesus said to him, 'Have you been with me for such a long time, Philip, and yet you have never really known me? The person who has seen me has seen the Father.'" Yet in Matthew's Gospel Jesus does not place himself in the prayer (Schl., *Der*, 209). It should be pointed out, however, that behind the aorist tense of the petition is the desire for the hallowing to happen once and for all, namely, by the cataclysm of the kingdom's coming at the end of the age, which in the New Testament is always coincidental with the coming of the Son of Man. This end-time coming is understood as the great revelation and as the definitive hallowing of God. This first petition, then, is in theological language eminently "eschatological" (McN., 78; Schw., 151; Guel., 289). It is thus eminently christological since the Christ ushers in the eschaton.

"Hallow thy name" would be too direct and almost presumptuous a prayer for a reverent Jew to pray, and thus Jesus the Jew teaches his disciples to pray "hallowed *be* thy name." (We do not pray directly "Hallow thy name, Bring thy kingdom, Do thy will"; instead, as in the Beatitudes God is spoken of and to indirectly, reverently, carefully. This is the fruit of the Third Commandment not to take God's name in vain, as it is the fruit of Jesus' Jewishness and his love for God. Cf. Schn., 81f) The passive voice ("hallowed *be*") instead of the active ("hallow") preserves God's sovereignty and prevents the prayer from being a command. The prayer *is* a prayer, an asking, a petition (it is not a doxology, like "Blessed be thy name"), and the petition specifically asks God in the most reverent way, "Please make your real identity known so that we and others will recognize you as central and weighty." "Please sanctify your dishonored name in the world." (See Ezekiel for this emphasis in the Old Testament, e.g., Ezek 36:23; 39:7.) "Please prove yourself holy, by judgment and grace, through overcoming sin" (Str.-B., 1:411f).

We are not taught to pray "let *us* hallow your name," though by extension this meaning can be present (Jero., Aug., Chrys., and Lu., all place believers near the center of the petition). But in none of the first three petitions are *we* mentioned; we are put one remove away, and properly we ask the only one who really can handle God's name, kingdom, and will to do so. The prayer is sheer theocentric prayer; we not only ask God to be God; we ask God to cause God to be God.

Each of the petitions, then, "asks for the establishment of the Kingdom of God by God for us, not by us for God" (Stend., 778), or by God for the world, not by the world for God. Our part is asking that this happen. And since asking means wanting and wanting means seeking, there is a sense in which we are asking that we, too, may have a part in the hallowing of the Father's name. But that is not the major point in this petition and so should not be made primary (as it is, for example, in Patte's structural interpretation, 102, but contrast 103–04). The major point is that we make our chief concern in life, our first petition, that the Father reveal himself in his glory.

It should encourage us to know that when we pray this prayer for the centrality and reality of God we have given the *doing* of the petition to God. Only God can reveal God. "'Leave to God the privilege of knowing himself; for it is he only who is able to bear witness of himself who knows himself by himself alone. And we shall be leaving him what belongs to him if we understand him as he declares himself, and ask nothing at all concerning him except through his word'" (Hilary of Poitiers in Cal., *Inst.*, I. xiii. 21, in F. Wendel, *Calvin*, 152). Hilary of Poitiers' motto was "God is to be believed insofar as he speaks of himself [*Ipsi de Deo credendum est*]" (Pelikan, *Jesus*, 65). The first petition is the prayer for God's self-revealing *Word*. (See in this connection both of Luther's Catechisms on the first petition and the Reformed *Heidelberg Catechism*, Q. 122.)

c. The Second Petition (LP 2), 6:10a

"Your kingdom come."

(The first petition, common to the Old Testament, is brought into the New Testament; the second petition is "in some sort peculiar to the New Testament," Beng., 1:123.) Few words are as difficult for pastors and teachers to understand as the words "covenant" in the Old Testament and "kingdom" in the New. Those who teach Scripture read something new on the subject of the kingdom almost every year and often come away from their reading as confused as when they began. What are we really praying when we ask "your kingdom come"?

I reviewed the meanings of kingdom at 3:2 and 4:17. Let me briefly restate my present understanding of kingdom.

1. *The Kingdom as Heaven.* The most sophisticated biblical scholarship on the one hand and the most ingenuous adventist faith on the other combine, correctly, in believing that when Jesus taught his church to pray "thy kingdom come," he taught her to pray for the coming of the new heavens and the new earth, for the end of history, and thus (as we now know) for Jesus' own Second Coming. Here we are not praying merely for changes in history. We are praying for a complete end to history and for the new world of God. Our century began with the rediscovery of the eschatological (J. Weiss, W. Wrede, A. Schweitzer, etc.), and it has become increasingly clear that the New Testament is fundamentally misunderstood where it is not read under the sign of the more or less eager expectation of the near end of the world and the coming of the kingdom. "*Maran-atha*" ("Come, Lord!") is the spirit with which almost every sentence in the New Testament literature was written and should be read. Indeed, the whole Lord's Prayer (as the punctiliar aorist tenses in the petitions especially show) is "an extended Maranatha," one great prayer for God's final coming (Stend., 779).

I must confess that this eschatological or adventist understanding was at first the most difficult of the four major meanings of the kingdom for me to appropriate. For on the one hand I would like to live a while longer and write and see my family grow. On the other hand I have been inclined to think, rightly or wrongly, that the coming of the kingdom in the final sense would mean the end of evangelistic and missionary opportunity and therefore the uncertain destiny of the majority of the people of the world. Thus both for selfish personal reasons and (I hope) for unselfish missionary ones, the heavenly meaning of "thy kingdom come" was hard for me at first to adopt. Yet I am convinced that I need more of the hope of the coming kingdom of God, and that my faith and life suffer when the dimension of divine hope is absent. I have read far too many New Testament passages about hope without any organs of reception, and this "hope-less" reading is bound to take away the fulness of faith and love. Thus every time one prays the petition "thy kingdom come," one should in the same breath pray, "Lord, please make me *want* your kingdom to come."

2. *The Kingdom of the Heart.* This understanding of the kingdom prayer is, I believe, more widespread and popular in the churches. Here it is prayed that God will come and be king of our hearts, that *he* will reign in our lives and not our own designs and desires (cf. this understanding as far back as Jero., 1:130 and in Cal., *Inst.*, III. xx. 42).

Here it is prayed that God will become the king of the hearts of others, too. While the heavenly understanding of the kingdom pictures the kingdom as a great future reality heading toward us from the future, the heart understanding looks especially for an inward, internal reign of God in the present. While the heavenly understanding might be called adventist, the heart understanding may be called pietist—and I am using the terms unpejoratively. To pray for God to be king of the heart is not a hard prayer for most disciples to pray because they know their need. Certainly if we pray for the kingdom in any other sense but omit this sense we fool ourselves. It is surely not right to pray for God to be king of everyone else but to believe that we need no change in our own hearts. The heart understanding of the kingdom prayer is the basic minimum understanding, and without it the prayer becomes external and unreal.

Only two modern scientific interpreters of Matthew, to my knowledge, understand the coming of the kingdom in a slightly less than eschatological way, and so deserve mention here. Trilling, 134, believes we pray here not for "the powerful appearance [of the kingdom of God] at the end of time, but [for] the gradual penetration on earth" of that kingdom. Gundry, 106, appreciates the eschatological interpretation, but in light of the *presence* of the kingdom (especially in Matt 12:28 and Luke 11:20) and other factors Gundry sees here "a prayer that at the present time more people become children of God through taking on themselves the yoke of discipleship and so do the will of God on earth as it is done in heaven."

3. *The Kingdom in History.* The word "kingdom" is a social word. Thus it has rightly been felt in the church that merely to pray that God be king in "my" heart or even in the hearts of fellow Christians is to pray too narrowly and to miss the larger meaning of kingdom. For at the end of the first three petitions, embracing them all, is the codicil "on *earth* as it is in heaven." Significantly, we are not taught to pray "in my heart as it is in heaven," though of course the heart is part of earthly history. The scope of our Lord's concern in this prayer as in his whole ministry is nothing less than the whole earth. Thus movements have constantly appeared in the church to remind us that when we pray for the coming of God's kingdom we are praying for something larger than human hearts, however proper and necessary prayer of this

sort is; we are praying for a worldwide fact, for a fact stretching far beyond the interior space of piety and reaching into the uttermost parts of the earth.

The historical understanding of the kingdom prayer, therefore, has usually translated "kingdom" with words such as justice, peace, and love. This understanding of the kingdom has been as congenial to liberal Christianity as the heart understanding has been to conservative Christianity. And it must be admitted that this breadth of concern does catch something of the breadth of Jesus himself. The dangers of this historical understanding of the kingdom can be its abstractness, generality (love, peace, justice), and its human-centeredness. However, heaven and the heart can be abstract and anthropocentric, too. Sometimes advocates of this historical view speak of *humans* bringing in the kingdom, which is so far from this petition's meaning that it almost contradicts it. "Thy kingdom *come!*"

The social gospel movement still has something of importance to say to the church. Liberation theology is in some ways the movement's extension into the present. But as Conzelmann, 69f, has shown, summarizing majority New Testament scholarship, in Jesus' teaching the kingdom of God is not brought, or even hindered at all, by human activity. "The only possibility of man's intervening in the course of events is to pray that the kingdom 'come.' The word 'come' contains the aspects of direction (from 'beyond'), suddenness [the aorist], and certainty of its arrival."

4. *The Kingdom as Homily.* The Reformation, especially, teaches that when we pray "thy kingdom come" we are praying for the purity and increase of the Word of God in the world as the indispensable *means* by which the kingdom now is present at all. For Christ becomes king of our hearts and king in history wherever the Word of God is faithfully preached and obeyed. The other two understandings of the kingdom might be called *end*-understandings—in the future and in the heart—but this present homiletical understanding is, like the history understanding that stresses obedience, a *means*-understanding: here is *how* God reigns eschatologically, existentially, and historically. The prayer for the kingdom is the prayer for the Word. To pray "thy kingdom come" means praying what Jesus will later teach his disciples to pray, "that the Lord of the harvest will send workers into his field" (9:38). For the kingdom of God is most surely at work wherever the Word is being preached in evangelical homilies, and it achieves its sovereignty over individual hearts and in historical situations by means of the presence and preaching of faithful Christian workers. Thus the prayer for the kingdom is also the prayer for an increase in Christian ministry and vocations to it and for a greater fidelity on the part of all God's people to Christian witness at home, at work, and in the world. In this petition we should pray especially by name for our pastors and teachers in church and school.

Luther never tired of saying that we must pray zealously that God will give to our ministries greater and greater purity of doctrine, for only where teaching is genuinely apostolic does the kingdom really come in truth and in power. The Reformation prayed more than we are accustomed to praying for right doctrine. The Reformers believed that the church's homilies, sermons, lessons, and lectures could only be authentically kingdom-expectant where they were faithful, and they could only be faithful where they were biblical, and they could only be biblical where they were Christ-centered, and they could only be apostolically

Christ-centered where they were thoroughly informed by the right understanding of the differences between law and gospel, i.e., our doing and God's doing.

Three of the four understandings of the kingdom surveyed here are present in Kingsbury's threefold interpretation (*Story*, 60–64) of the meaning of kingdom in Matthew's Gospel: (1) the "salvation-historical" is what I call the heavenly understanding, which is mainly future, (2) the "cosmic" is what I call the homiletical understanding, which stresses mainly the growth of the kingdom through proclamation, and (3) the "existential" is what I call the heart understanding, which deals mainly with the crisis of personal decision. New Testament scholars are rightly reluctant to include what I call the historical (or social gospel) understanding, which if used at all, must be under the control of the main three.

The meaning of "kingdom" will be particularly enriched by Jesus' kingdom parables in chapter 13 of the Gospel, where the single major theme is the definition of this key term. Here in this second petition, as in each of the first three petitions, it is wise to point to the important pronoun "thy" or "your." "*Your* kingdom come" (and no one else's!). We are praying that the kingdom of the Evil One be displaced and, in fact, that the sovereignty of every other even laudable person or impression or conviction or movement will be displaced by the sovereignty of *God* the Father himself and alone. "Let God arise, let his enemies be scattered; let those who hate him flee before him" (Ps 68:1 RSV).

In the context of Matthew 6, where the Lord's Prayer lies embedded, one is strongly inclined to translate the word "kingdom" with the word "all-importance," for each of the three surrounding Devotions (almsgiving, prayer, and fasting) teaches that Christians need a sense of God's reality and importance that exceeds their natural sense of the reality of other people and of their importance. Only when God is more real and more important than people will the Christian be able to overcome the almost irresistible temptation to impress others with one's generosity, prayer life, or discipline. Only where God assumes all-importance is the Christian able to live the modest Christian life that is the theme of the first half of this chapter. "There is *one* who is good" (19:17).

It may be, too, that "kingdom" is one of those rubber words that can mean whatever a particular paragraph in Scripture portrays to us of God and his truth. For example, the text in our Philippine seminary community today as I write these words is the first paragraph in Acts chapter 6: "it is not right for us to leave the Word of God for waiting on tables" (6:2). Therefore, we should "devote ourselves to prayer and to the ministry of the Word" (6:4), while, at the same time we should be careful to see that our churches have adequate diaconal ministries to serve the physical needs of our communities (6:3, 5). When we pray "thy kingdom come" today, therefore, we will especially pray that we will never allow the priority of the Word and prayer to be displaced by other needs (precisely for the *sake* of those needs), that God will be sovereign in that sense, and finally that we may be careful not to neglect the imperatives of social justice but to see to it that the finest persons are directed to these tasks. Thus "kingdom" means everything Acts 6 teaches. And so throughout Scripture, whatever has been proposed to us for faith and life that day or week in the Word, we use to reshape afresh all our prior understandings of the kingdom. In the final analysis the kingdom is the king himself; Christ is God's messianic kingdom in person, and this kingdom is present to us in infinite richness in Scripture.

"If you want to know [the kingdom of God] and find it, you must not seek for it on the basis of your own ideas. You must hear His Word, as the foundation and cornerstone, and see where He directs you and how He interprets it" (Lu., *SM*, 204–05). Luther's central conviction about the kingdom is that it is not a matter of outward things like eating or drinking (Rom 14:17), "nor other works that we can do. . . . Rather, it means believing in Jesus Christ." This believing in Christ, which is the kingdom come in faith, will then naturally lead to "practicing and applying the Gospel, to which faith clings" (*loc. cit.*, 204). The most helpful current commentary discussion of the kingdom of heaven, in my opinion, is in Green, 232–37. The most helpful article is K. L. Schmidt's *basileia*, TDNT, 1:579–90.

d. The Third Petition (LP 3), 6:10b
"Your will be done."

What is the will of God? In the context of this sermon I believe that it is the Sermon on the Mount itself. "Your will be done" means, then, "your Sermon on the Mount be done." And the will of the Sermon on the Mount thus far is (1) the blessing of the poor and merciful, and the apostolic witness in the world (the Beatitudes and the You Ares, 5 A), (2) respect for persons (the Commands, 5 B), and (3) faith in the reality and all-importance of God the Father so that we may be able to live single-minded Christian lives (the Devotions, 6 A). In the light therefore of everything the sermon has taught us to this point we may say that "your will be done" means "may everything you have taught us be effected." We do not pray "May *we* do your will," though this is certainly wanted. Rather, we pray that *God* the Father will do his will, that *he* will supply the power for his will to happen on earth. *How* his will is done is not in focus.

It may be pointed out again that in each of the first three petitions the words "we" and "us" do not appear. And while it is right and even necessary that we include ourselves in each petition if our prayer is to be real, it is just as important that we know these petitions are bigger than we, that God can hallow his name, bring his kingdom, and do his will without us, and that it is not true that "he has no other hands than ours." We should be as careful as Jesus to keep ourselves from center in these petitions. The "we" and the "us" will get their due in the second half of the Lord's Prayer, but in the first half the focus is vigorously theocentric. We are asking *God* to hallow his name, bring his kingdom, and do his will. If he chooses to do these through us, and we hope he will, it is all to the good; if he chooses to do these things in some other way through other people, that is his privilege.

The witness of the church teaches a more human view of the third petition than I have given it. "Thy will be done" is not to be understood as a fatalistic sigh. "God's will is done when men carry it out" (Schw., 152; also Bonn., 84–85). God is the primary doer, but human beings are the secondary (Trill., 191). So also Aug., *Serm.* 6(56):7:276; 7(57):6:281; 8(58):4:285; and Luther's Catechisms. Matthew's parable of the talents (25:14–30) and Luke's parable of the pounds (19:11–27) were also given to the church to guard her from an irresponsible theocentrism.

When we take the whole of the apostles' witness in the New Testament and put it together we know that the will of God is that Jesus Christ be trusted—that is the single great will of God, out of which all other good wills flow. Jesus has been too modest to put it this way. But the Father himself, the two times he speaks directly from heaven (in the synoptic Gospels), directs us *not* to himself, "in the raw," as it were, or to anyone or anything else than to this: "This is my very dear Son; I am deeply pleased with him; listen to *him*" (Matt 17:5; cf. 3:17). The Father's will to "be done" is that we give heed to his Son.

Thus "thy will be done" has almost as many meanings as "thy kingdom come," for both "kingdom" and "will" are words with epic scope and application. The Father's will can most concretely be discerned in the text the church gives us in Scripture each week. It is also found, as this Gospel particularly teaches, in the persons who surround us and in those persons' special needs. Jesus often makes the will of God attention to the person or persons with whom we are involved at any particular moment. But even here in emphasizing the importance of the other person I am emphasizing a truth constantly impressed upon us by *Scripture*. Taking Scripture seriously teaches us to take people seriously.

In "thy will be done," Luther in his Catechisms saw Christians marshaled in warfare against the unholy trinity of the devil, the world, and the flesh. Moreover, the Reformer insisted, as in the first petition we prayed especially for *pure* teaching, and as in the second for *trust* in this teaching, now in the third we pray for *perseverance* in pure teaching. *The Heidelberg Catechism*, Q. 124, understands the prayer "thy will be done" to be a prayer especially for vocational fidelity: we do God's will when we are faithful in our callings.

"On earth as (it is) in heaven." (6:10c)

I believe that this simple little extension applies to all three of the preceding petitions: as your name is hallowed in heaven, may it now be hallowed on earth; as your kingdom and importance are known and present in heaven, may they now be on earth; and as your will is practiced in heaven, may it come into effect, too, here on earth (similarly McN., 79). We do not pray "in my heart as in heaven" or even "in the church as in heaven," though these will be important desires in Christian prayers. "On earth as in heaven" girdles the globe; it makes the Lord's Prayer cosmic. Thus whenever we come to this phrase and pray it carefully we experience a "mid-course correction." It is the unavoidable and almost magnetic tendency of our prayers to be taken up primarily with *our* duties, and it may be all right that this is initially so. Yet the little word "earth" will serve as a corrective and encourage the pray-er to find a healthier width. The word "earth" teaches us that the Father's concerns are earth-wide, bigger than ours, and that because he is a larger God than we think, we should pray more largely than we ordinarily do. We are praying *big* things when we pray the Lord's Prayer. Somehow our little prayer for God's honor, rule, and will touches the whole wide earth with effect; the phrase "on earth" enables us to believe this and invites us to this daring confidence. (According to Chrysostom, Jesus here has urged each of us who prays "to take upon himself the care of the whole world. For [Jesus] did not at all say, 'Thy will be done' *in me* or *in us,* but everywhere on the earth," 19:7:135, emphasis his.)

The expression "as in heaven" teaches us again that God has some kind of lively enterprise going with angels and spirits and that the earth is not all there is to history (cf. 2 Kgs 6). There is some kind of exciting invisible world at work in perfect obedience to God, where God's name, kingdom, and will are treated with the respect they deserve. Moreover, this phrase asks us to believe that something like heavenly worship and obedience can touch earth. Indeed, the simple and bold "as" permits us to believe that this heavenly worship and obedience *can* somehow happen on earth. We are not to ask too specifically how, just as we are not to inquire too curiously about the nature of the heavenly activities; we are simply to pray that the name, kingdom, and will of God the Father shall all come to rights here on planet earth. (I prefer this interpretation of the "in heaven," cf. Jero., 1:130, to the view that we are praying here *against* resistance to the will of God in heaven, as in Beare, 174, and as considered but not adopted by Bonn., 85.)

We have completed the first table of the Lord's Prayer—the three petitions addressed to the great concerns of God: "your name," "your kingdom," and "your will." Using Paul's triad of faith, hope, and love as a summary, we can say that (a) in praying for the hallowing of the divine name we are praying mainly for faith, (b) in prayer for the coming of his kingdom we are praying mainly for hope, and (c) in prayer for the doing of God's will we are praying mainly for love. Using Matthew's triad of mercy, justice, and faith (Matt 23:23; cf. 1 A), we are praying for good faith in the first petition, divine justice in the second, and human mercy in the third.

Paul's prayer for the Ephesians (1:17–19) contains almost exactly the first table of the Lord's Prayer. Paul prays "that the God of our Lord Jesus Christ, the Father of glory [The Address], may give you a spirit of wisdom and of revelation in *the knowledge of him* [LP 1], having the eyes of your hearts enlightened, that you may know what is *the hope* to which he has called you, what are the riches of his *glorious inheritance* in the saints [LP 2], and what is the immeasurable greatness of his *power* in us who believe, according to the working of his great might [LP 3]."

e. The Fourth Petition (LP 4), 6:11

"Give us this day our daily bread."

In the second half of the Lord's Prayer, "us" and "our" and "we" are as significant as the "yours" were in the first half. Where the theological concerns of the first table of the Lord's Prayer are principal and real, the human concerns of the second table will never be merely secondary or peripheral. "The second will be like unto" the first (22:39a). The worship of God *can* be socially irrelevant (consider the complaint of all the prophets). But the worship of God that Jesus teaches is, when received, a force that makes for humanity and sociality.

It is important to notice, moreover, that Jesus was not satisfied when we prayed only for the most important things: God's honor, rule, and will. Jesus felt it important that we give equal time to those matters that some suggest are beneath God's time and trouble: bread, forgiveness all around, and rescue from evil forces. That Jesus gives a second table to the Lord's Prayer at all teaches that it is not selfish to pray about physical, social, and personal problems. It is in fact Jesus' command that we pray for these things. ("This petition is of extreme value as showing that material things do not lie outside the region of prayer," McN., 79.)

The prayer for bread in this fourth petition should be allowed to remain a prayer for bread. At times in the church's exposition the bread has been turned into spiritual bread (cf. the Vulgate's *panem supersubstantialem* with Aug., *LSM*, 114–15, and Jero., 1:130, 132, who believe that here we are praying especially for him who says "I am the living Bread"; but see Jero. at Luke 11:3). It is possible to be more spiritual than God. Why should Jesus who fed his five thousand not want us to pray for our five billion? And while Jesus said that man does not live by bread alone, he was too realistic to say that man does not live by bread at all. We may pray, certainly, for spiritual bread (and this was done in the first three petitions), but here in the fourth petition we pray for real bread for real people.

Bread costs money, money requires work, work requires good government, good business, and good labor. Thus when we pray for bread we are praying at the same time for money, jobs, government, business, labor, good crops, good weather, roads, justice, and for everything economic, political, and social. The fourth petition is the politico-economic petition. Here Jesus teaches us to pray for the economic order and for everything that goes into the just production, distribution, and purchase of bread and rice.

We are not told to pray for daily cake. We may be grateful, of course, when cake is given. But we may only legitimately pray for bread; that is, we pray for necessities.

"Feed me with the food that is needful for me, lest I be full, and deny thee, and say, 'Who is the Lord?' or lest I be poor, and steal, and profane the name of my God" (Prov 30:8–9). Chrysostom, 19:8:135, points out that even this physical prayer for bread is spiritual, for we do not pray here for riches, affluent living, or costly clothes, "but for bread only . . . and for 'daily bread.'"

Are we in fact praying for our "daily" bread or for our bread "for the morrow"? The scholarship that represents the second view has impressed me most (Mey., 150; Schl., *Der,* 211–12; Schl., *Das,* 94; Schw., 153). Prayer today for tomorrow's bread seems responsible and implies that we are not asking carelessly and at the last minute for a goose to be dropped in our mouth (in Luther's colorful expression). The Greek word in the text is ambiguous and lends itself to either interpretation.

We do pray once "give us *this day*" our bread, putting an urgency into the prayer and a day-by-dayness into even our economic dependence upon God. Those of us who have never gone hungry learn from this petition how much we have to be *grateful* for. Thus we will rarely be able to pray this petition without saying immediately "thank you very much." At the same time few of us can pray this prayer without *guilt* for being able to enjoy bread abundantly while such a large number in the world lives miserably. Hence when we have prayed this petition we will often find ourselves also praying "I am very sorry," and "please show us what to do." This petition forms a kind of thorn in the flesh for its comfortable pray-ers. ("No Christian can be content to have too much while others have too little," Barc.) Something is wrong in world production and distribution. Something is out of joint economically. This petition should stick in the throat when prayed by full Christians; it reminds us of the wretched of the earth.

The "our" in this petition serves two other useful purposes: it teaches us to pray for other people's bread and not just our own (Cyprian in McN., 79); it also teaches us to work, because the "our," as Stier notes, "points to needful labor, Gen 3:19, without which we eat not *our* . . . bread, but another's," in Beng., 1:124.

We live in "the time of the fourth petition," for there are so many hungry people in the world. Where the first three petitions are prayed seriously, and thus where mission is prosecuted vigorously, the fourth petition is partly answered. For the most economically and socially significant event in the world is gospel preaching in it. The gospel *includes* economic-social prayers like this, and gospel preaching is unfaithful when it fails to include a lively concern that there be bread. The fourth petition, then, is the prayer for social justice.

It is important that this petition for bread precedes the petition for forgiveness. A person can only stand when one has had enough bread. Then one can only stand straight when one has been forgiven. It is of central importance that persons be able to stand straight; it is of first importance that people be able to stand at all. Thus the Christian church has never been able to live with a good conscience when she has not prayed and worked hard for bread in the world. The fourth petition will always keep the church's conscience next to the grindstone of earthly reality and will teach her never to be more spiritual or less physical than the Lord who gave her this prayer.

Organizations that distribute food to those who hunger have the deep respect of all people. Three features stand out in Luther's Catechism exposition of the fourth petition: that we pray especially for the gift of a thankful heart, that we pray for all earthly necessities, and that we pray especially for government, "for chiefly through them [in government] does God provide us our daily bread and all the comforts of this life [and] . . . we cannot retain any of them or enjoy them in security and happiness unless he gives us a stable, peaceful government" (*Large Catechism*, 3:72–74). As we pray in particular for our pastors and teachers when we invoke the second petition for the coming of the kingdom, we should pray especially for our government leaders by name when we pray this fourth petition. In his *Geneva Catechism* (1541), Calvin says that the words "daily" and "this day" teach us to ask "that we may learn to be content, and not to covet more than our need requires."

f. The Fifth Petition (LP 5), 6:12

"And forgive us our debts as we, too, have forgiven our debtors."

In rabbinic thought every sin created a certain deposit of debt before God, the accumulation of which formed a kind of separating wall between the person and God. On the other hand every righteous deed contributed to the believer's accumulation of assets before God and so created a kind of bridge. Sins were demerits that separated; righteous deeds were merits that connected. The corporate name for these separating demerits was "debts." Jesus takes this well-known word and the set of ideas connected with it and tells us that we can ask the Father to *wipe out* our debts!

The petition is audacious on the face of it. It is shameless for a debtor to approach a creditor and ask for remittance of debt. Yet Jesus teaches us to approach God in this "shameless" way. In Jesus' thought the Father was consummate compassion. To the person who turned to this Father for pardon Jesus here promises complete removal of debt and of the separation debt creates (cf. 1 John 1:9).

Matthew does not embellish the grace of God in the way that Paul's gospel does; however, this should not make us overlook the abundance of grace in the simple deeds and words of Matthew's Jesus—as here in this remarkable petition. To be able to ask God the Father simply to remit debt and to overlook sins is breathtaking.

In Luke's version of the Lord's Prayer we ask that our *sins* be forgiven (Luke 11:4). We can say catechetically that in Luke's word "sins" (or "trespasses") the focus is on our act of *commission* and that in Matthew's word "debts" the focus is on our acts of *omission* and that the two taken together instruct us to ask for forgiveness both for committing "those things which we ought not to have done" and for omitting "those things which we ought to have done," and so to confess with the whole church that "there is no health in us." (The meaning of all three words used in connection with this petition in the two evangelists—debts, sins, trespasses—"clearly refers to one's *failure* before God," Guel., 312, emphasis added; thus also Schn., 86. "Forgive us our failures.")

In the second table (or human side) of the Lord's Prayer the order of petitions is interesting. We pray first for food, then for forgiveness, and then for guidance. There is sanity in Jesus' sequence. Sometimes in Jesus' teaching the physical (or social) precedes the spiritual (for example, C 2: "go *first* and be reconciled with your brother; then come back and offer your gift to God"). A starving person needs forgiveness, but he first needs food. A sick person needs eternal life, but in this Gospel the sick ask first for healing, and Jesus honors this asking.

Most of Jesus' *miracles* show the seriousness with which Jesus took the order of creation—first the physical and then the spiritual; the second table of the Lord's Prayer now carves this order into the consciousness of the church. Most of Jesus' *teachings* show us how seriously he took the order of redemption—first the spiritual and then the physical; the first table of the Lord's Prayer engraves this order.

"Give" and "forgive"—these are humanity's two great petitions of God. Please give us physically what we need in order to live like humans, then please forgive us spiritually those things that we do or don't do, in order to live free of guilt. "Thou art giving and forgiving, Ever blessing, ever blest." Please give us food so that we may stand up; please give us forgiveness so that we may stand up straight. Food is a human being's priority need, but forgiveness is a human being's profoundest need.

In our time it is sometimes said that forgiveness does not play the role in life that it did in the Middle Ages and the Reformation. However, the omniverous contemporary craving for self-esteem can make us question this assumption. We may not be as aware of our need for forgiveness as our church parents were (which does not mean that we are not as in need of forgiveness as they were). In the industrialized and industrializing world the felt need is said to be meaning. But when meaning is supplied by the gospel the believer sooner or later finds that the deepest need of life as well as the deepest resource of the gospel is the free forgiveness of sins provided by the God of Jesus Christ in several ways (Word, sacrament, fellowship) and here unostentatiously offered in the fifth petition of the Lord's Prayer.

"As we, too, have forgiven our debtors."

The verb "forgiven" here is in the aorist (perhaps Semitic perfect) tense, signifying either completed action (thus Green, 91; Schw., 155) or continuing action. One gets the impression that the ideal petitioner has just come from a conversation of reconciliation with a "debtor," with a formerly alienated person, and that this experience of friendship, enabled by God, encourages the request for a renewal of God's friendship.

In chapter 5 in the Monday Command, Jesus taught his disciples to go *first* and be reconciled with an aggrieved brother or sister and *then* come to the altar (C 2). This "first-then" sequence, another illustration of Jesus' frequent first-social-then-spiritual mandate, is imagined here in the fifth petition, too. Believers are not to seek divine forgiveness if they have not given human. We are not conscientiously to seek God's friendship where we have not sought our wounded brother's or sister's. We cannot honorably try to be on speaking terms with God the Father where we have not sincerely sought to be on speaking terms with some problematic other. This reality-sequence is an expression of honest faith and is not a difficult justification by works. The conscience that is able to ask for forgiveness without giving it is not a conscience living in faith. Jesus forms the parable of the unforgiving servant in chapter 18 of the Gospel to teach exactly this truth (18:21–35). Forgiveness received and not passed on (the force of the parable), or forgiveness requested of God but denied to others (the force of this petition), is faithless forgiveness and unreal.

Schlatter, *Das*, 95: There is no serious prayer for forgiveness except on the lips of a forgiver; this is no contradiction of justification by faith: as if a revenge-seeking heart could be said to believe in God's forgiveness of sins!

It has understandably troubled the church that this apparent *condition* of human forgiveness is attached to the reception of divine forgiveness. But a prior massive forgiveness precedes and makes possible believers' praying the Lord's Prayer at all. We would not even be able to address God as Father if we had not first been *given* the Father and then authorized to ask him for the several gifts of this prayer. The Father's forgiveness mediated to us here through his Son makes it possible to pray the Lord's Prayer at all.

In particular, the privilege of praying for the Father's forgiveness—the meaning of the first part of this fifth petition—is placed by Jesus *before* the rider of *our* forgiveness of others. This means that Jesus reminds us of our standing privilege of access to the Father before he reminds us of our standing responsibility to be forgiving with our neighbor. This order, this sequence, makes me prefer the expression "consequence" to "condition" for the clause "as we, too, have forgiven our debtors," though the consequence is close to being a condition.

The strongest case for the conditional understanding of our petition is in Strecker, 149, where it is shown that forgiveness of sins is not mentioned at Jesus' ministerial appearing in 4:17, nor is Jesus' ethical demand ever expressly related to a preceding divine forgiveness (but I must ask about 18:21–35). Thus Strecker concludes that in Jesus' teaching in Matthew the divine forgiveness of sin is not the point of departure; it is the goal of Jesus' ethical demand. Mohrlang argues similarly in his dissertation on Matthew and Paul. Cf. Patte, 89.

Schniewind, 85–86, on the other hand, contends against the conditional and for the consequential interpretation. However we decide the case, the fifth petition's rider clearly reminds its pray-ers that we illegitimately ask for a mercy that we refuse to give. If *without* forgiving someone (who is or could be repentant) we then pray "forgive us *as* we have forgiven," do we realize what we have prayed? We have prayed a curse on our own heads. "He asks eternal vengeance on himself, who offers this prayer with hatred in his heart" (Quesnel in Beng., 1:125). "In no way can thine enemy so hurt thee by his violence, as thou dost hurt thyself if thou love him not" (Aug., *Serm.* 6 (56):14:278). Luther, *Large Catechism*, 3:95–96, calls the rider a "comforting clause." For, he argues, when we find ourselves able to forgive others we have a kind of sacramental (spiritual-physical) evidence that God's forgiveness is alive and at work in us, and this should encourage us. Cf. the *Heidelberg Catechism*, Q. 126: "We also find this witness of Thy grace in us, that it is our sincere intention heartily to forgive our neighbor."

I think it is fair to say that in the New Testament Paul is the theologian of privilege par excellence, Matthew the premier theologian of responsibility. Yet each theologian, being a Christian and having experienced both the privileges and responsibilities of forgiveness, stresses that side of the great truth of forgiveness that seemed most important for his community to hear. Each theologian had special gifts, and it was Matthew's to stress Christian responsibility without neglecting Christian privilege, while it was Paul's to stress Christian privilege without neglecting Christian responsibility. In both theologians, certainly, the privilege of God's free mercy preceded the responsibility of our good life. (Matthew's call [4:19] precedes the commands (chapter 5); and in Paul's Romans, chapters 1 to 11 precede 12 to 16.) Yet it seems accurate to say that Paul has been unexcelled in highlighting the gospel's privileges while Matthew has been unexcelled in highlighting the gospel's responsibilities. Let us allow each his gifts without making them enemies.

g. The Sixth Petition (LP 6), 6:13

"And lead us not into temptation, but snatch us from the evil one."

In the second table of the Lord's Prayer, we may say in pedagogical summary, the petition for bread was a prayer for the present, the petition for forgiveness a prayer for the removal of a bad past, and now the prayer for leading is a prayer for a good future.

This petition follows naturally from the preceding prayer for forgiveness. For when we ask for forgiveness we almost instinctively ask next to be kept from the very temptations and evil that made our prayer for forgiveness necessary at all. We rarely feel real when we ask only to be forgiven; we feel real only when we ask that we might not fall into the same faults again. So the sixth petition follows the fifth like wanting to be good follows sorrow for failing to be good.

It is interesting to notice that the petition which in our private and group prayers we usually pray first—"Lord, lead me" or "lead us"—is in the Lord's Prayer put last. We might think that the first and main thing we need is leading and guidance for the future, but such thought reveals a certain superficiality. Though we rarely appreciate it, the past is as important to the future as the pure future is. The prayer "lead us," all alone, can also betray a certain selfishness, a too quick desire to get on with it, and an unwillingness to face up to God and to God's major concerns (LP 1–3) or to our own present needs, responsibilities, and past guilt (LP 4–5). There may be things more important than *our* leading—such as the honor of the Father's name, the presence of God's kingdom, the performance of God's will, the feeding of the hungry, or right relations and mutual forgiveness in the community. All these matters can well be more immediately important than our future. The Lord's Prayer teaches priorities.

Yet it would not be correct to say that the farther we go in the Lord's Prayer the less important the petitions become. The sixth petition's prayer for leading is another way of praying for the Father's name, kingdom, and will; it is another way of praying that we (the petition, we should remember, is still prayer for the community) be led into the future.

The picture in this petition is of a people walking through something like a minefield; we pray that we will not be led *into* a mine of overwhelming temptation. To come *into* something is to enter its sphere and so come *under* its influence. Walking *in* and through a myriad of temptations, we pray amid these temptations that we may never come *into* or under any of them.

"Temptation is always in the way: Wherefore we pray, not that it may not exist, but that it may not affect or overpower us. Matt 26:41; 1 Cor 10:13" (Beng., 1:125; also Aug., *LSM*, 2:9:32:119–21; Gund., 109). But contrast McN., 81.

"But snatch us from the evil one." The word for snatch is the very strong, even violent word for rescue or seize. It suggests that the evil one is constantly luring us toward his mines and pits and that only the Father's constant and more powerful snatching, seizing, and rescuing can free us from destruction (Bonn., 87).

It is only in so being constantly seized that we will be able to honor the divine name, experience the kingdom, and do the will of the Father. The fulfillment of the first three petitions in us occurs only when we are constantly rescued by the Father from the machinations of the evil one.

Is this evil from which we pray deliverance the evil *one* or moral evil (i.e., is the Greek noun here masculine or neuter)? Grammatically, the construction does not tell us. But we are safest when we see both meanings present: evil here is both the evil one (the devil) and evil deeds. The understanding of evil here as personal evil—as the devil—is the more comprehensive understanding. The devil's work, however, *is* moral evil—what Matthew calls "lawlessness"—and so we are praying that we may be rescued *both* from the evil one's person and from his work, which in this Gospel is especially the lawlessness of lovelessness.

We may bring together the first and second halves of the sixth petition by a slight change of figures: *temptation* is a pit into which we fall, *the evil one* is the power whose influence draws us into the pit and dominates us in it. In this petition we are asking, "Dear Father, please lead us in such a way that we will be able to resist the temptations that both consciously and unconsciously surround us; please constantly swoop down and rescue us from all the wiles of the evil one and all his evil works—we need your help."

The sixth petition keeps us from thinking of ourselves as spiritual heroes. We do not pray, "Bring on temptation!" We do not go looking for tests of strength. More modestly we pray for protection and guidance. Especially in view in this petition, many commentators tell us, is the great test of the end—of the eschatological time of troubles (Matt 24), of the special persecution of Christian mission (Matt 10), and of death.

Luther's Catechisms, following the Roman tradition, see two petitions here—a sixth and a seventh. Most interesting in the sixth, against temptation, is the way Luther sees the seminal temptation as unbelief. In the seventh, against evil, Luther sees believers grappling especially with the great enemies of death (in the *Small Catechism*) and the devil (in the *Large Catechism*).

h. Summary

And so the Lord's Prayer stretches from the Father at the beginning to the devil at the end, from heaven to hell, and it embraces in between in six brief petitions everything of importance in life. The prayer originally ended with the ominous words "the evil one." But early on it was felt that this ending was too abrupt and negative, and so the more polished ending was added, "for thine is the kingdom," etc., which teaches valuable truth. We should allow the prayer to end roughly when we pray it privately. It seems characteristic of Jesus' thought in this Gospel that he begins messages with mercy and ends them with warnings. The Sermon on the Mount itself commences with a ninefold benediction and concludes with a ruined house; the Sermon of Parables (Matt 13) begins with a liberally sown field and ends with the separation of bad fish, and now the Lord's Prayer begins with the intimacy of a God who is Father and concludes with the urgency of an evil one who threatens our lives. Matthew's Jesus honors us in this prayer both by freely giving us his Father as ours and then by taking us with such seriousness that he both warns us of the dangers of a misled life and gives us a prayer for warding off the devil.

The Lord's Prayer is the Christian's daily companion and prayer book. In it we have Jesus' own priorities in prayer; by it we learn how to form our prayers into closer conformity to the divine will; through it we are assured that prayers circling these six themes are prayers according to the will of God and so, surely, heard. It is a short prayer, but when chewed like cud it can fill a good half-hour. It can be prayed word for word or thought by thought. After each day's Scripture reading or church message the great terms of the Lord's Prayer can be freshly defined by the themes of the day's text: for example, the name, the kingdom, and the will of God are, respectively, the Lord, the doctrine, and the point of each biblical text. The bread for which we pray is the creaturely material of the text. The debts from which we pray remission are the sins revealed in the text, and the temptations from which we pray deliverance are the dangers revealed in the text.

We are also able to contribute, even from afar, to the feeding of the millions. We are empowered to ask for, and to receive, the remission of the sins of many and, at the same time, to pray for the reality of common Christian forgiveness in every-day reconciliations. We are also able to pray for the rescue of Christendom from its omnipresent dangers and its hereditary foe. These are major privileges. Our ancient church parents audaciously believed that the world is held together by the prayers and pray-ers of the Lord's Prayer, and that the earth is upheld by the company of those who in good faith pray this simple prayer.

It hardly needs to be added that where this prayer is prayed in good faith its petitioners are given marching orders. Who can pray for the honor of God's name without believing that one must seek this honor? Who can pray for common bread and not feel obliged to work for it? I think that to stress this point too much, however, is to labor the obvious, which is another way of saying that it is to moralize. This prayer is not mainly or even subtly a program of human action, however laudable. There will be space enough devoted to human action elsewhere in Jesus' teaching. The Lord's Prayer is not a program of Feuerbachian self-suggestion or a dominical mantra, a set of latent commands for our implementation (or formulae for our absorption into deity). To think in these ways is seriously to misinterpret Jesus. The Lord's Prayer is *a prayer,* directed to the living God.

So we will believe that when we pray the Lord's Prayer we are moving the living God—who in it asks to be moved—and thus that we are moving world history at its central junctures. To think anything less is to be guilty of what Jesus everywhere calls "littlefaith."

i. The Postscript, 6:14–15

"For if you forgive people their failures, your heavenly Father will also forgive yours. But if you do not forgive other people their failures, neither will your Father forgive yours."

It is noteworthy that the only petition in the Lord's Prayer to which Matthew's Jesus adds commentary is the fifth on forgiveness, and in particular he comments on the "consequential" part, on *our responsibility* to forgive.

Here Jesus soberly underlines the truth that the unforgiving Christian becomes, *by that fact,* the unforgiven Christian. Consequently, this reading of the Lord's Prayer teaches Christians that there should be no praying of this prayer at all where there has not first been the attempt by its pray-ers, "as far as in you lies" (Rom 12:18), to be on good speaking terms with everyone else in the community. To speak to God without first having sought to speak to someone from whom we are alienated (near or far) is to speak to the air. Thus wherever the Lord's Prayer goes up in the Christian community, where Jesus' attached commentary here is in conscience and in force, there we have a sign that the community is reconciled and that no one who prays it is at enmity with anyone else who is praying it or, for that matter, with anyone else in the community outside, as far as this is in Christians' power or responsibility. "If you do not forgive, do not think that God forgives you" (Lu., *Large Catechism*).

This "forgiveness P.S." perpetually reminds churchpersons of the great theological privilege and the great ethical responsibility of forgiveness. Forgiveness is almost a single-word summary both of the Christian gospel and of the Christian ethic.

"I desire that in every place the [people] should pray, lifting up holy hands *without anger or quarreling*" (1 Tim 2:8 RSV). "Surely, we must not indifferently pass over the fact that of all those texts in which the Lord has commanded us to pray, He declared that special emphasis should be laid on the petition which has to do with the forgiveness of sins. . . . For in no other text do we pray in such a way that we, as it were, *enter a contract* with God, saying as we do: 'Forgive us *as* we also forgive.' If we lie in that contract, the whole prayer has no value" (Aug., *LSM*, 2:11:39:127, emphases added). "He who cannot overcome breakdowns in love loses prayer" (Schl., *Das*, 97).

C. Fasting (D 3), 6:16–18

"And when you fast, do not be like the 'performers' who put on a very pious face. They screw their faces up so that it can be clearly noticed by people that they are fasting. Amen, I tell you, they have their reward in full. But you, when you fast, anoint your head and wash your face so that people won't notice that you are fasting at all, but only your Father who is in secret. And your Father who sees in secret will reward you."

The twice repeated "when you fast" in this paragraph indicates to most commentators that Matthew's Jesus wanted fasting (Schl., *Der,* 219; Bonn., 88; Streck, 189 n. 2; good summary in Conz., 67: "Jesus does not abolish the Jewish practice of fasting (Matt 6:16ff), but he demands no ascetic practice."). Verse 17's Greek is catching: literally, "they *disfigure* (*aphanizousin*) their faces so that they may *figure* (*phanōsin*) to people." For Jesus' fullest teaching on fasting, pro and con, see 9:14–17, below.

If we substitute the word "disciplining" for the word "fasting" (a species under the genus of discipline), we see contemporary situations. It is a great temptation for the Christian to advertise, ever so subtly, one's personal disciplines. The motive is often genuine enough: to be a witness and so perhaps to encourage others to be more disciplined Christians. But we have already seen under the heads of charity and prayer that Jesus is not interested in that sort of witnessing. Jesus apparently feels that he can move people to self-discipline by other, more effective, and less ostentatious means.

The pious or grave look, the slightly creased forehead, can be used as means of witness to Christian seriousness. But Jesus does not approve of performances, however well intentioned. He fears that too often this witness is addressed more to the attention of others than to the attention of God. In fact, isn't all witness, by definition, the attempt to move *people*? And isn't evangelism, by definition, the attempt to move people to decision for God? Then how else can we do evangelism than by directing our attention to people and people's attention to us? Nevertheless, in his three Devotions Jesus rigorously excludes charity, prayer, or fasting from being *visible* or intentional means of evangelism or of Christian witness. "The fact stands that Jesus laid down no regulated lifestyle for his disciples which would distinguish them from the public" (Conz., 35).

"But you, when you fast, anoint your head and wash your face" (v 17). In other words, look normal. It was the practice of the people of God to anoint their heads and wash their faces not only for festivals and other especially joyful occasions, but also for everyday personal hygiene (Guel., 300). Thus Jesus is asking *his* disciples— the "you" is again stressed in the Greek—to be normal in appearance precisely when they are fasting in practice. Is this not hypocrisy? Isn't hypocrisy the appearing to be what we in fact are not? Not always. To appear before people as normal and happy when before God we are fasting and mourning is not hypocrisy, but civility. Precisely when the "performers" would dishevel their hair and disfigure their faces in order to be a witness, Jesus urges *his* people to comb their hair and wash their faces so that no one will notice they are fasting—except the impressionable Father. (Interestingly, a meal—the Lord's Supper—"rather than a fast became the earmark of the early church's public worship. The good news brings joy rather than remorse," Guel., 300.)

The normalcy of Jesus in matters of lifestyle is astonishing. He is not impressed by the demonstrative. This is a liberating fact. By this fact disciples are freed from feeling that they have to appear pious if they wish to be so. This is not to say that Christians are to be the well-known hail-fellows well met, a class of Christians who particularly afflict student work. There is an hypocrisy in attempting to be worldlier than thou. Both superspiritual and supersecular lifestyles are often acts, and Christians are asked in the Devotions of Matthew 6 to give up all acting—specifically, to give up attempts to seem impressive to others. Jesus prefers that we demonstrate discipleship by solid social relations (as we see in the Commands of chapter 5) rather than by visible spiritual practices (as we see in the Devotions of chapter 6). This must not be taken to mean that Jesus is not as interested in the giving of money or prayer or fasting as he is in human relations; he will in fact later teach us that the use of money is a signal mark of discipleship, that prayer is faith in the act of breathing, and that fasting is a real possibility for church people. Yet precisely because all three of these inevitably throw so much light on their agents, Jesus prefers them to be practiced mainly in private.

II. THE GOALS (6:19–34)

A. The Two Treasures (G 1), 6:19–21

"Don't keep making big investments for yourselves here on earth where moth and rust corrupt and where thieves break in and steal. Instead, make big investments for yourselves in heaven where neither moth nor rust corrupt and where thieves do not break in and steal. For where your investment is, there will your heart be as well."

We see immediately the connection between the Devotions that preceded and the Goals that follow. The point of all three Devotions was that we seek the Father's praise rather than the world's. The three Devotions gave us examples of *how* to do this. The Goals now finesse the Devotions by teaching us *where* to aim our life goals; rather than seeking the goal of the treasure of human popularity, disciples seek the treasure of the Father's esteem.

This text on laying up treasures "is to be understood as speaking not only of money but of all passions. [For example], the god of the gourmand is his stomach; . . . the treasure of the sensual is banquets, of the licentious, shows, of the libertine, luxury. 'Everyone is a slave of that which dominates him' (2 Pet 2:19)" (Jero., 1:134). Bonnard, 90, shows that "moth, rust, and thieves do not mean the perishability of riches, but the fragility and vanity of human appreciation."

The text before us provides one of the most striking examples of the value of interpreting texts in their context. If this treasures-in-heaven story is understood, as it often is, of money only, its context is ignored. The context is the quest for esteem, not money. And while it is certainly true that one main way we seek esteem is by money, the financial quest is by no means the only form of human treasure-seeking. We want money because we want the esteem it wins.

Chrysostom, 20:2:141–42, sees the connection between the Devotions of 6 A and the Goals of 6 B this way: "Thus, after He hath cast out the disease of vainglory [6 A] . . . He seasonably introduces His discourse of voluntary poverty [*aktēmosunēs*] [6 B]. For nothing so trains men to be fond of riches as the fondness for glory."

The reasons Jesus annexes to his goal of heavenly treasure are worth noticing. Treasures on earth either rot by nature or are taken away by history. It is well known that fame is fickle. Last Saturday's hero is next season's nobody. This year's financial success is next year's bankrupt. It is not because Jesus is a misanthrope that he discourages the quest for success; it is because he loves human beings. He urges them to avoid the inevitable despair that comes with evanescent glory. Doing well—financially, professionally, socially, personally—doesn't last, and Jesus does not want his disciples disappointed.

Schlatter, *Das*, 99–100, comments on this: We want treasures because they give us security. But because of decay (moth, rust, thieves, etc.) treasures lead us to security's opposite, anxiety. Because our riches bring us into a constant war with decay, they do not bring us rest. It is a great service of Jesus, therefore, to liberate us here from anxiety about gain. Schlatter, *Das,* 98, appropriately entitles the last half of Matthew 6: "Liberation from Greed and Anxiety." The gospel of Jesus' ethic is true liberation theology. Luther, *SM,* 166–67, noticed, too, that "whenever the Gospel is taught and people seek to live according to it, there are two terrible plagues that always arise: false preachers who corrupt the teaching, and then Sir Greed, who obstructs right living. . . . [S]piritually . . . [the great problem is] the false teaching that corrupts faith; physically, it is the greed that corrupts its fruit." Chrysostom, 81:4:489, saw clearly that the covetous do not really enjoy what they have for two reasons: "by reason of not feeling confident about the security of them, and because with their whole mind they are [still] intent upon what they have not yet seized." Ezekiel saw this even earlier (Ezek 7:19).

Even lofty aspirations, if they seek mainly human esteem, will go the way of all flesh. If my passion for reading exceeds my passion for the pleasure of the Father, blindness will bring everything crashing down around my ears. Even the desire to preach the gospel can be a desire for earthly treasures if it is a desire that is linked to earthly (or even missionary) success. The purpose of evangelism must be the honor of God and not even, legitimate as it might seem, the maximum number of converts, or else we will be deeply disappointed. Life lived for human impression is life misspent, and Jesus would liberate us from misspent life.

The moth represents *nature's* corrosions eating away, the rust (or worm, Guel., 321) represents *time's* corrosions eating away, and the thief represents *humanity's* corrosions eating away—and all three together represent the insecurity of life lived for the accumulation of wealth or honor.

> "Do not toil to acquire wealth;
>   be wise enough to desist.
> When your eyes light upon it, it is gone;
>   for suddenly it takes to itself wings,
>   flying like an eagle toward heaven" (Prov 23:4–5).

"All compound things are impermanent." The Buddha was right. But where Gautama Buddha was led to jettison all desire, Jesus goes another way.

6:20 "Instead, make big investments for yourselves in heaven." Jesus does not remove desire; he redirects it. Rather than uproot all human ambition and passion as the Buddha had taught, Jesus counsels us to make it our ambition to be a success before the Father, to impress him, to accumulate the rewards and treasures of his notice and esteem. Every person has a ruling ambition, treasure, or investment somewhere. That fact is not disputed or even combated by Jesus. What is decisive in Jesus' teaching is the *where* or *what* of the ambition or investment (Bonn., 90), or perhaps, most pointedly, the *whom*—whom are we really trying to impress?

Jesus does not quash ambition; he elevates it. The Christian *is* to be ambitious, passionate, acquisitive, enterprising, zealous—for the treasure of the Father's approval, for the "well done" of God's final judgment. Thus Jesus' ethic is not so much a tepid asceticism as it is a vigorous athleticism. Jesus is appealing for the adventure of faith.

Schlatter, *Der,* 220, believes Matthew 6:19–34 is the only section in the sermon where Jesus turns the community's attention to the Eighth Commandment on property ("Thou shalt not steal"). Persons, not possessions, are Jesus' primary concern as the whole fifth chapter showed. Schlatter, *Der,* 221–22, also points out that the idiom "in heaven" does not mean "after this life," but means "with God." Thus to have treasure in heaven means to have the living, giving, working God on one's side, now. Nevertheless, Schlatter concludes, it will be only visible in the next world how rich God's grace has made a person. Augustine appropriately warns against one of the commonest excuses for laying up treasures and investments on earth: to say that we are laying them up *for our children.* "It is a great duty of natural affection (it will be said) for a father to lay up for his sons; rather it is a great vanity, one who must soon die is laying up for those who must soon die also" (*Serm.,* 10 (60):3:291).

Luther's feelings here, *SM,* 185, parallel Augustine's: "See to it that greed does not take you in with a sweet suggestion and lovely deception like this: that you intend to advance yourself or your children into a higher . . . social position. The more you get the more you will want; and you will always be aiming for something higher and better. No one is satisfied with his position in life." What do we do with our money, then? Later in the Gospel Jesus will reply, "Give to the poor, and you will have treasure in heaven" (19:21).

Augustine comments on the meaning of this: "Transport goods then" (*Serm.,* 10 (60):7:292), namely, by living for the poor. Inventive love will find ways to do this. Luther's counsel here, *SM,* 172, is that "in your outward and secular life you may lay up as much as your relation with God and your honesty permits, not for your own pleasure and greed but for the need of other people." But how does one get the power to live this way? Once again, Chrysostom, 20:5:145, comes through with the needed perception: "Even this cloud [of the love of money] may be easily scattered and broken, if we will receive the beam of the doctrine of Christ; if we will *hear* Him admonishing us, and saying, 'Lay not up for yourselves treasures upon earth.' 'But,' saith one, 'what avails the *hearing* to me, as long as I am possessed by the desire?' Now in the first place, there will be power in the continued *hearing* to destroy even the desire" (emphases added). The power to *do* the Word comes from faith in *hearing* the Word.

6:21 "For where your investment is, there will your heart be as well." That is to say, where your goal is, there will your heart be also. If one's goal is to impress others, one's center of gravity will be people and their admiration; if one's goal is to please the Father, one's center of gravity will be the Father and his honor. In every enterprise the setting of goals is of first importance. Goals determine action. A person's goals are in fact very often a person's gods. And the Old Testament's "Thou shalt have no other gods before me" is paralleled now by the New Testament's more subtle "Thou shalt have no other goals before me," for "where your goal is there will your heart be also." Ask a person's goals and you find a person's gods. Our goals can be laudable, but if they are not lodged somehow in a real relationship with God himself, then we are going to be disappointed either by the moth of nature, the rust of time, or the thievery of people. Even the desire to be an outstanding Christian preacher, or teacher, or writer, or to be an impressive Christian person—goals that are too often determined by whether others find us outstanding or impressive—will not do. Only a goal that seeks exclusively to please the heavenly Father is saved from human vanity and historical decay.

The major god of the world is Success or Successism. In the light of this fact, the many biblical warnings against idolatry become contemporary: cf., e.g., Jer 25:6; Exod 34:12–15; and the summary of Col 3:5: "covetousness, which is idolatry," which can be translated more relevantly as "successism, which is idolatry." "With their lips they show much love, but their heart is set on their gain" (Ezek 33:31).

A *too* great concern for people (and a great concern for people is a major theme of chapter 5) will lead us not only into getting help to them, but also mislead us into seeking esteem from them, and then we have gone too far. Chapter 5 needs the sixth chapter, mercy needs faith, neighbor-love needs love for God if the Christian life is to have bearings. Serving people (chapter 5) must be kept distinct from impressing people (chapter 6). We are to love people but "cursed is the man who trusts in man and makes flesh his arm" (Jer 17:5). The third temptation taught us the perils of a love for people that exceeded the bounds of the Lordship of God. "You shall worship the Lord your God, and him *only* shall you serve" (T 3; 4:10).

In a time when a great deal of necessary emphasis is given to the service of others we will have to be alert lest the worship and faith belonging exclusively to God be shifted subtly to "the toiling masses," the poor, or to "the people," however portrayed. A strong theme in several revolutionary forms of Marxism is the call to trust or serve the people. Where this is meant as respect for the people, sensitivity to them, and learning from them, this theme is useful; where it is meant as a confidence in their unshakable integrity or "historic mission" or something similar, it becomes messianic, and messianic confidence belongs only in one place. A great deal of foolish talk about trusting the people is spoken today by Christians who should know better.

Jesus is not embarrassed to urge us to treasure God, not least because God treasures people. But only where God is treasured above all will people be treasured at all or for long. "Teach me thy way, O Lord, that I may walk in thy truth, *unite* my heart to fear *thy* name" (Ps 86:11).

B. The Two Eyes (G 2), 6:22–23

"The light of the body is the eye; so if your eye is sound your whole body will be luminous. But if your eye is bad your whole body will be darkness. And if, then, that which is supposed to be light in you turns out to be darkness—what a great darkness that is!"

The original meaning of this parable is elusive. In its context one can paraphrase the word "eye" with "goal" and the word "body" with "life" (cf. Cal., 1:217–18). Then we get the following helpful teaching: "The light of one's life is one's goal; if your goal is sound your whole life will be luminous. But if your goal is bad your whole life will be darkness. . . ." Jesus is then saying in a second way what he had said in the preceding parable of investments: Goals determine life.

"If a man divides his interest and tries to focus on both God and his possessions, he has no clear vision, and will live without clear orientation or direction" (Filson, 100, in Hill, 142). The bad eye is allowing any other masters than God alone "to dictate one's vocation" (Patte, 92). The eye of the disciple is sound (or simple or single) in that it seeks nothing but obedience (Bonn., 91). "Let your eyes look directly forward, and your gaze be straight before you" (Prov 4:25). The good eye also means generosity, the evil eye loveless greed (Allen, 62; Stend., 779; Gund., 113); therefore be liberal in helping the needy. This can mean, at the most prosaic level, the willingness to be taxed. Luther, *SM*, 185, has a stimulating interpretation of this parable. He believes it is a warning to beware of human ideas and doctrines and an admonition to look straight at the pure doctrine of the gospel. "Apostasy from the Gospel must make a man so possessed by the devil that he simply cannot be greedy enough. And on the other hand, whoever really has the Gospel in his heart becomes mild. Not only does he stop scratching, but he also gives everything away and is willing to risk whatever he can and should."

Another interpretation sees in this saying the almost literal significance of the human eye. "The eye has one language everywhere." According to this understanding, it is possible to detect in the eye whether one gives gladly or halfheartedly (Schl., *Der*, 222). Where the eye reveals coldness, superiority, or unreality the person is exposed as false. The intention is in the eye (Aug., *LSM*, 132). This parable, then, teaches the importance of a right disposition in the doing of good; otherwise we ruin every good thing we do (Schl., *Das*, 101). The eye becomes the decisive way to help other people, since in the eye what is in a person comes out (Grund., 212).

The picture of the bad eye reminds of palace gifts for the indigent, favored by dictatorships and feudalisms everywhere (e.g., by the former Marcos government in the Republic of the Philippines); the good eye reminds of every sincere act of Christian love. A worker with the poor was counseled by his father always to ask the poor's forgiveness when giving them help. As we know, a look in the eye cannot be manufactured; it is either there or it is not. We are thrown again on the mercy of God and on the prayer for a good eye, one of God's best gifts. "Incline my heart to thy testimonies, and not to gain! Turn my eyes from looking at vanities; and give me life in thy ways" (Ps 119:36–37).

C. The Two Lords (G 3), 6:24

"No one can serve two lords; because he will either hate one of them and love the other, or he will be devoted to one and look down on the other; you cannot serve God and Gain."

In context, this saying means that the attempt at the same time to win people's attention *and* God's is an impossibility. Either human esteem or divine esteem is lord. There is great danger that where the esteem of people rules our life there God is no longer Lord. We sometimes wonder why we feel a certain grudge against God—or more deeply, why we cannot seem to believe in God. One of the sources of unbelief, this saying tells us, is that the real lord of our life is human praise. "How *can* you believe, [you] who receive glory from one another and do not seek the glory that comes from the only God?" (John 5:44).

By this series of goals-sayings Jesus is saving his people from spiritual schizophrenia. The commonest god in the world is Success, and the Christian no less than others wants to be successful in some ways—but not in all ways or by all means. But this particular saying teaches the Christian that to be even a part-time devotee of the god Success is to lose one's fellowship with the Lord God. We cannot work largely for God and then moonlight for Success—it is one or the other. ("The ambitious man says, I shall not stop serving God, even though I apply the good part of my mind to pursuing positions of honour," Cal., 1:219.) Thus once again disciples are asked to give their faith either to God or to People, to his praise or theirs, to his rewards or society's. For Jesus "makes it clear that whoever fails to do his duty as he should on account of Mammon—money or pleasure, popularity or favor—will not be acknowledged by God as His servant but as His enemy" (Lu., *SM*, 188).

The god of humankind is given a curious name in this particular story: *mamōna,*

Mammon. Mammon means, literally, possession, or property. Today we might legitimately say things, money, gain, or success. (The word does not mean wealth
or affluence; it means "worldly possessions, however few," Beng., 1:128; cf. Schl.,
Der, 225.) The god Mammon is left with his pagan name to remind us that he is a
spiritual force who works with tremendous attracting power to draw us into his
orbit of influence and out from under the exclusive service of Christ.

For we will do almost anything to succeed. And since one of the major badges of
success is the possession of fine things or money we will often find ourselves in the
train of the worshipers of Mammon. Jesus wants us to be aware of the power of this
god and of the countervailing power of faith in the one God. The decision of faith is
an either/or decision, tolerating no double-dipping, no side-glances at the bitch-
goddess Success, no smuggled incense at alien altars. For it is *impossible*—the word
is used twice in this single verse—to have two lords. (Chrysostom, 21:2:147: When
God has said it is impossible, don't say "it is possible.") "Trying to get ahead," a
seemingly harmless pastime and a normal one for a person with drives, conscience,
or family, is playing with fire—it is in real danger of being, if it is not already, the
"covetousness that is idolatry" (Col 3:5; Eph 5:5). We cannot serve both God and
Making It.

Beginning with Jerome, 1:136, commentators have pointed out, e.g., with Luther, *SM*,
189, that "the emphasis here is on the little word 'serve.' It is no sin to *have* money and
property, wife and children, house and home. But you must not let it be your master. You
must make it serve you, and you must be its master" (emphasis added). Luther, *SM*, 186,
also pointed out that this text is misapplied when "No one can serve two masters" is
understood to forbid obedience to earthly government. "He is referring to two masters
that are opposed to each other, not to those that govern together."

On the same passage, Luther, *SM*, 192, insisted that Jesus does not teach here that it is
wrong to *acquire* money and property as the "crazy saints" teach. "He lets you get rich;
but He does not want your heart to cling to your riches, as David taught and as he proved
by his own example, saying, (Ps 62:10): 'If you acquire riches, do not set your heart upon
them.' " Only with a miracle from God is this possible.

There is some New Testament corroboration for this approach to money, perhaps
most clearly at 1 Timothy 6:17–19: "As for the rich in this world, charge them not to be
haughty, nor to set their hopes on uncertain riches but on God who richly furnishes us
with everything to enjoy. They are to do good, to be rich in good deeds, liberal and
generous, thus laying up for themselves a good foundation for the future, so that they
may take hold of the life which is life indeed." But the *Gospels* are critical of the quest for
wealth. The classic Gospel discussions of money, in addition to our present Matt 6;19–34
texts, are Matt 19:15–30 (The Rich Young Ruler) and the whole of Luke 16. Luke's social
Gospel in its entirety is challenging to the commercial soul. Success seminars of all sorts
must face Jesus' indictment. For appalling illustrations of successism see "The Executive's
Wife" cited in Elizabeth Achtemeier, *The Committed Marriage* (Philadelphia: Westminster
Press, 1973), 37.

The New Yorker ran a *Fortune* magazine ad picturing a chauffeur holding the door of a
limousine, with the caption: "Drive yourself today/ and tomorrow you will be driven."
There follows this pitch: Hard work "is the straight route to the top and all the perks that
go along with success" (and, then, read *Fortune* to learn how). Jesus teaches disciples a
number of times in his gospel that the goal of (hard) work is not to be personal success or
the top, but the service of others—a drive downward rather than upward. Christians
must set their faces resolutely against the gods of culture, not the least of which is
successist ambition. "Take heed to yourself, lest you make a covenant with the inhabitants

of the land whither you go, lest it become a snare in the midst of you. You shall tear down their altars, and break their pillars" (Exod 34:12–13).

Jesus is not asking disciples to make a decision for fanaticism or for professional or social suicide; he is telling them to be rational. For he does not say that it is *unwise unwise* or *unspiritual* to serve two masters; he says, more matter of factly, "you *cannot* serve God and Mammon." Jesus does not want us to waste our lives practicing the impossible. The prudent, sensible course for a Christian to follow is simply to make the basic decision that one will no longer allow one's life to be determined by the perquisites of Success, awards, appointments, salaries, things, or Mammon. We are asked by this story to turn our backs resolutely on the god of the world, to be the *real* atheists of our time, to deny the gods to whom most give unquestioning fealty and to serve only the Living God.

"But those who desire to be rich fall into temptation, into a snare, into many senseless and hurtful desires that plunge men into ruin and destruction. For the love of money is the root [*hriza*, anarthrous, better translated "*a* root," but placed at the front for emphasis] of all evils; it is through this craving that some have wandered away from the faith and pierced their hearts with many pangs" (1 Tim 6:9–10, RSV). "But immorality [Matt 5] and all impurity or covetousness [Matt 6] must not even be named among you, as is fitting among saints. . . . Be sure of this, that no immoral or impure man, or one who is covetous (that is an idolater), has any inheritance in the kingdom of Christ and of God. Let no one deceive you with empty words, for it is because of these things that the wrath of God comes upon the sons of disobedience" (Eph 5:3–6).

D. The Two Anxieties (G 4), 6:25–34

"In summary, then, I tell you, stop being so anxious about your life—about what you will eat or what you will drink—or about your body—about what you will wear. Isn't life a greater thing than food, and the body a greater thing than clothes?" (v 25).

False prophets inundate us with questions like, "How are you going to eat (well or poorly)? How are you going to dress (well or poorly), if you don't give yourselves to ambition and success?" We are in fact counseled on every side to make immoderate secular investments (G 1) in order to give our lives security; the world seduces our eyes to this or that goal (G 2) in order to advance our lives; we are taught incessantly to give ourselves to the pursuit of Success (G 3) so that we can have lives happy and free of anxiety. But our anxiety is only increased as we seek these means of relieving anxiety. The more we have the more we fear its loss—to moths, rust, or thieves, and so the more we want, and so on and on. At the root of the money question is the anxiety question, and thus Jesus moves now to that root. (Cf. Schl., *Das*, 103.)

Jesus frees us from this world's obsession with how we're doing (how we're eating and dressing) by giving us the liberating obsession of concern with how God is doing: "Seek *first* the kingdom and righteousness of *God,* and all these other things will fall into place in your lives" (6:33). Jesus supplies us with the *necessary* physical, psychic, and professional securities—"all these other things" that we wrongheadedly pursue—but he supplies us these things not by the regular route (namely, by pursuing them), but by the route of seeking that God be king and his righteousness manifest in the life of our communities.

At first glance, this command not to be anxious about food or clothes offends us. As a missionary in the Philippines I was convinced that this is a text that cannot be preached to the poor—it is cruel to tell the poor not to be anxious about getting enough to eat or wear. And I have often thought that this text should not be preached in the well-to-do West either, for it will only confirm the comfortable bourgeois prejudice that spiritual values should be placed above material ones—for example, that social concern for food should be a secondary matter. (The comfortable often feel, too, that they are comfortable because they sought first the kingdom of God; they believe that spiritual success *leads* to material success.)

But we must ask what the text actually says. It does not tell disciples to be unconcerned about whether *others* have enough to eat or wear. Jesus' whole ministry teaches that the opposite is the case. When we pray for human needs, the second table of the Lord's Prayer tells us that we pray first of all for food (the fourth petition of the Lord's Prayer); when the four and five thousand are hungry in the Gospel, Jesus commands his disciples to give them *bread* (chaps 14 and 15); and at the end of his formal teaching ministry Jesus specifically tells his disciples that at the judgment day we will be told, "I was hungry and you gave me (or you did not give me) something to eat" (25:35). No, the text before us does not say "Do not be anxious about others' lives, with what they shall eat, or with others' bodies, with what they shall put on," because precisely a care for these matters is the quest for the righteousness of God that Jesus commands at the end of this Goal.

Instead, we are commanded to take our eyes off our *selves,* off *our* lives, off our own selfish anxiety with our desires for good things for ourselves, and to look around God's world for a place where we can throw ourselves into the cause of God's righteousness. All four goals-sayings are attempts to turn our eyes from ourselves to God. There and there alone will our eyes receive the light and our bodies the illumination that will make us of use to others at all, even socially.

The Christian world in the West is on the whole a fat world, too concerned with food; it is a superficial world, too occupied with clothes. Jesus intends to liberate us from these obsessions with inanities and to lift our lives to the nobility of caring about things that matter. Our surfeited world must learn that God's gift of *life* is much more important than eating well, and that the gift of the *body* is much more important than dressing well. He who gave these more important gifts may be quietly trusted to provide the less important—that is the force of Jesus' comparisons here (v 25b).

Only when we have been liberated from anxiety about our own food and clothes—a liberation devoutly to be desired in Western Christendom—will we give necessary attention to the food and clothing of the Poor World around us. Thus Jesus' text is not antisocial; it is antiselfish. It does not tell us to be unanxious about others' food, but to be unanxious about our own. It does not preach indifference to society; it preaches a rejection of Christians' unbelieving anxiety about themselves and their circumscribed obsessions. Anxious care is the denial of God; it is acting as if we are alone in the world and that either there is no God or that he does not care (Schl., *Das,* 104).

6:26 "Look around at the birds of the sky; they don't sow, they don't harvest, and they don't even put things aside for safekeeping, and still your heavenly Father feeds them. Aren't you worth a lot more than they?"

This is a second example of the famous rabbinic method of arguing *a fortiori* from the lesser to the greater (*a minori ad maius*): "If God takes care of birds, won't he take care of you?" (The first example of this method was in the preceding verse, If God gives you life and bodies, doesn't he care that they be fed and clothed?) Here again we are asked to have faith in the Creator. The God who made birds and who miraculously keeps them stocked with food is the same God who made us and who is able also miraculously to keep us in food. It is to this Creator Father that Jesus constantly directs us. (The haunting question of a hungry world still rankles.)

This is still one more call to faith in a chapter full of such calls. (Indeed, the sermon itself is one long call to faith.) In *natural* needs, where natural means are required, it is easier for humans to believe that God is irrelevant (Schl., *Der*, 233). Here in natural matters, we are told or we tell ourselves, one must use one's head, and the name "God" seems a pious obfuscation. But it is precisely this conviction— the conviction of the irrelevance of the Creator in the sphere of the natural—that Jesus everywhere challenges. *Iesus contra mundem.* For Jesus, God is *God,* and as such is competent in the world of the natural. God made it. God sustains it. It is God who is over the economic activity of even birds, and Jesus reminds us of this seemingly trivial fact. (In the First and Second Worlds, we *must* assimilate Jesus' teaching; but can it be done in the hungry Third World?)

Of course it is true, as Fr. McKenzie has reminded us, that the sparrow is one of the busiest creatures in nature and that therefore this Word about the birds of the sky is only rightly understood if it is seen as counsel against anxiety, not as counsel for indolence (*labor exercendus est, sollicitudo tollenda,* Jero., McN; 87: "The birds are an example not of idleness but of freedom from anxiety"). And yet Jesus is not asking here that we be as busy as sparrows, though the seeking of righteousness that he commands in a moment includes seeking the righteousness of faithful work. If Jesus' reference to the birds is not pro-indolence, neither is it pro-industriousness (Gundry, 116, correctly sees this) it is first of all and fundamentally pro-faith. We are asked not to limit our faith in the Father to spiritual things; we are asked to believe that the Father is active in economic matters, alive to physical need, and a provider of food no less than of mercy. We are asked, in a word, to believe that God is God. And as God he is not only Redeemer; he is Creator.

A major purpose of the Feeding Stories (Matt 14–15) is to teach the church that Jesus cares about hunger and uses his disciples to feed the hungry. "Trust and Obey." "We have as many teachers and preachers as there are little birds in the air. . . . Their singing of Lauds and Matins to their Lord early in the morning before they eat is . . . [so] pleasant. They sing a lovely, long Benedicte and leave their cares to our Lord God, even when they have young that have to be fed. Whenever you listen to a nightingale, therefore, you are listening to an excellent preacher" (Lu., *SM,* 197).

In other words, Jesus asks us to believe that the heavenly Father sees not only our private, secret, and *spiritual* lives (giving money, prayer, fasting—6 A), but also that he superintends our public, secular, and *natural* lives as well (money, food, clothes—6 B). We are simply asked throughout this chapter to believe that Jesus' Father is God, "the Father *all*-mighty, maker of heaven *and earth.* "

6:27 "And who of you by being anxious can add one single day to his life?" This must have been said tongue in cheek. For the fact of the matter is that anxiety shortens life.

6:28-29 "And take clothes: Why are you so worried about them? Study the flowers out in the field sometime, and notice how they grow. They don't agonize, and they don't even weave. But I tell you that not even Solomon in all his glory was decked out like one of these little wildflowers."

The Creator Father *clothes* his creatures, too—and beautifully. He is the omni-competent Creator and serves his creatures not only as their farmer and baker, but as their tailor and beautician as well. The Father can be trusted: from the filling of creatures' insides to the dressing of their outsides. The Father is not to be left out of a single one of our concerns—least of all from the physical concerns where we might think that he is too busy to be bothered or too spiritual to be debased. To think that the Father is not really relevant to basic economic needs, Jesus instructs us, is to think God's deity away. The living God lavishes every single wildflower in every distant field with all the beauty of Solomon's court—this God has plenty of time left over, then, for us. (The birds and the flowers "sing and preach to us and smile at us so lovingly, just to have us believe," Lu., *SM*, 200.)

This Word of Jesus is strikingly antiascetic. If Jesus had intended to create in us a suspicion of the beautiful, or even a contempt for the aesthetic, he would hardly have used Solomon's court as a favorable comparison. This text "means that Jesus' warfare with self-seeking was not mixed with that tendency that sought to reduce the means of life to the smallest possible quantum" (Schl., *Der*, 232). The God and Father of our Lord Jesus Christ, this Word teaches us, is not only the Creator of basic things; this God is the Creator of beautiful things, too. This love of beauty was already apparent in the Creation stories of Genesis 1 and 2. God made the trees "which are beautiful to the eyes" as well as delicious to taste (Gen 2:9). The heavenly Father is aesthetic. ("All thy works with joy sur-round Thee, Earth and Heaven reflect thy rays.") Solomon's historical glory here is singled out for comparison, but the Father's glory in the natural world is the real point of reference in Jesus' observation. This text has important aes-thetic ramifications.

6:30 "But if God so adorns the grass of the field that is here today and is thrown in the fire tomorrow, won't he take much more care to clothe you, you little faiths?" The Father's concern for his people does not stop with their souls; it continues on down into their stomachs; but it does not even stop there in the inner person, spiritually or nutritionally; it then extends even to outer adornment. God the Cre-ator of body and soul is God the Provider for both. No one must push God into a spiritual corner where alone God is allowed to be God. It is precisely this limiting of God's reach, belittling God's interests or abilities in the real world, that Jesus calls "little faith" (Schl., *Der*, 233). God lives. To learn this takes a lifetime, but the sooner disciples enroll in Jesus' little course here on the Deity of God the sooner their maturity and their helpfulness in the large natural world.

6:31-33 "So don't get all excited saying, 'What are we going to eat?' or 'What are we going to drink?' or 'What are we going to wear?' because it is all of these questions that obsess the secular world. But your heavenly Father knows that you need these things—all of them. So make your first care his kingdom and righteous-ness, and all these other things will be added to you as well."

We have noticed throughout the Sermon on the Mount that Jesus wants his disciples to be different from the world around them—different not so much in diet or clothes or appearance (he specifically commands us to "look natural and normal" in the third Devotion), but different in deed (Matt 5) and motivation (Matt 6). It is characteristic of the secular world to be obsessed with economic questions, to be almost entirely engrossed by consumer concerns, to be preoccupied with finding and getting better and better *things*. The prizes on television game shows, lotteries, and the near hysteria surrounding them, illustrate this preoccupation unattractively. The world has a religion: acquisition, getting, Mammon. Jesus will not have his disciples believe in the world's religion or be possessed by the secular demon of possession. Jesus wants us to know that there is already a God who gives attention to the legitimate subconcerns of possession. His name is "your Father." (Chrysostom, 22:3:152: Jesus does not say "God," but "your Father," to show that he will not leave his children in the lurch.)

Thus Jesus commands us to turn our backs on the god Possession and to turn our primary attention to the quest for the Father's royalty and righteousness. This is not a counsel to seek spiritual things instead of material things, or inward things instead of outward things; it is counsel to seek God's things rather than our own (Schl., *Der*, 226–27). For God's kingdom is to come *on earth* as it is in heaven, and God's righteousness (in Matthew) is deeds outwardly done. Jesus creates higher loves in us (for the righteousness of God) in order to drive out lower loves (for dressing well) (Schl., *Das*, 106–07). Luke's Rich Man is the best commentary here, Luke 16:19.

The "his" of this sentence—"seek first *his* kingdom and righteousness"—is a key word and applies to *both* nouns: righteousness as well as the kingdom belong to the Father and are *his* to give. In this command we are not told that we are to seek *our* righteousness or a kingdom for ourselves or even that we might be able to *bring* his kingdom or righteousness. Rather, we are to make it our care that God the Father bring his kingdom and his righteousness to the world, that he vindicate his people and get himself a name now and at the end of history. When this care—let us call it faith—is in place, it determines our lives and makes us obedient.

In Matthew's Gospel there is no sincere seeking of God's righteousness where we do not seek to do right ourselves. Yet the emphasis in Jesus' sentence is certainly on *God's* righteousness, and at this point Matthew and Paul agree. The righteousness we are taught to seek here is an alien righteousness, the Father's righteousness, and not first of all our own.

"And all these [necessities] will be added to you as well" (v 33b)—as a kind of bonus. The economic goods that fill the whole horizon of the secular world are not to fill the disciples' whole horizon. Goods are to be received as gifts, not sought as acquisitions. For disciples, goods are by-products not goals. While disciples seek God's kingdom in the front or living room of their lives, possessions are brought in the back door and deposited in the kitchen. The front door of disciples' lives is open to human need and the divine glory; disciples are there for the important matters of Christian discipleship and human existence; meanwhile the Father has a special delivery service that brings to the back door the very things for which the secular world spends its whole time shopping.

Our text does not say, "Your heavenly Father knows that you *don't* really need these earthly things"; on the contrary, it says that he "knows that you *need all* these things." The same word Jesus used in order to remove repetition from prayers—"he knows"—he now uses to remove anxiety from economics: "He knows your need" (cf. vv 8, 32). The Father of Jesus Christ is an intelligent Father, aware of the realities of human life. He can be trusted to provide for his children.

Socrates' teaching is as similar to Jesus' here as anywhere (e.g., Plato, *Apology,* 30 a–b). This similarity indicates that the unique contribution of Jesus to the world is not so much his teaching, which has its parallels, or even his death understood as a martyrdom, which Socrates again parallels, but his unexampled bodily resurrection from the dead. Yet for the Christian, even when Jesus' teaching can be paralleled, as in this text, there is a scope and an aim in each saying of Jesus that leads cumulatively to the conviction of the incomparability of Jesus' teaching.

6:34 "So don't be obsessed by tomorrow; tomorrow will have its own worries; today has enough problems."

This sentence seems anticlimactic after the noble sentence about seeking the kingdom and righteousness of God. And yet it is consistent with Jesus' realism and with his already observed tendency to end units of teaching with warning.

This entire paragraph (indeed, the whole chapter) is devoted to *focus.* The disciples' eyes are to be directed singly and simply to the honor of God—and, our present Word adds—to today. We cannot get the honor of God tomorrow, for tomorrow is a promise, not a possession. It is a characteristic of anxiety that it is peculiarly futuristic, tomorrow-centered, and thus often unrealistic and wasteful of energy.

Luther, *SM,* 207–09, has these fascinating observations on time in connection with this verse: "If God is kindly disposed to a man and gives him success, he can often accomplish more in one hour without care and anxiety than another man in four whole days with great care and anxiety. . . . Thus no one can accomplish anything except when the hour comes that God gives as a free gift without our anxiety. It is vain for you to try to anticipate and with your concern to work out what you think are great schemes. . . . What He does is this: when He sees someone fulfilling his office diligently and faithfully, being concerned to do so in a God-pleasing way, and leaving the concern over its success to God, He is generous in His gifts to such a person."

The *kakia,* "evil," "trouble" (RSV), or worry that the text tells us will be our lot today is not the objective evil of the satanic against which the Lord's Prayer warned us (*ponēros,* the "evil" at the end of the Lord's Prayer means *objective* evil before God); *kakia,* the "evil" here, is subjective evil, evil in the less ultimate sense of the inconvenient, the daily "troubles" and distractions that keep us, we think, from devoting our time to God's work (Schl., *Der,* 236; Stend., 779–80; Hill, 145; cf. Chrys., 22:5:153).

Nothing bothers serious disciples quite as much as the many distractions that keep them from devoting themselves to the few matters that really count. It is these bothersome "troubles" that Jesus here calls evil in the subjective sense. Discipleship learns sooner or later, however, that it can pursue God's kingdom and righteousness right in the middle of these daily "evils." Brushing the children's hair, grading students' papers, going to committee meetings, entertaining unexpected visitors, and doing the thousands of other earthly things that seem to distract us from more important things and from the one thing needful, can all be forms of kingdom-seeking when viewed in faith. Thus when Jesus tells us that "sufficient unto the day are the evils or interruptions thereof," he means that it will be by our mastering these irritating daily gremlins that we learn to be disciples. For the grading of students' papers thoughtfully, while it takes the teacher away from writing and reading, helps students considerably. The parent's brushing of the children's hair, though it takes one from more elevated tasks for the moment, may be the only chance a parent and child have to touch each other that day. These "evils," then, may be "sufficient" in quite unexpected ways.

The Dolomite Chant, found in many hymnals, is a commentary for the First and Second Worlds on the spirit of Jesus' teaching in this chapter on anxiety.

> Not so in haste, my heart! Have faith in God and wait;
> Although He linger long, He never comes too late.
>
> He never cometh late; He knoweth what is best;
> Vex not thyself in vain; Until He cometh, rest.
>
> Until He cometh, rest, Nor grudge the hours that roll;
> The feet that wait for God Are soonest at the goal;
>
> Are soonest at the goal That is not gained by speed;
> Then hold thee still, my heart, For I shall wait His lead.

*   *   *

The whole of the sixth chapter has been a call to faith. The key word of the first half of the chapter is "secretly" (rather than demonstratively); the key idea of the second half of the chapter is "singly" (rather than doubly). Paul wrote that "to those who by simple steadiness in well-doing seek glory and honor and integrity [from God], there is life eternal" (Rom 2:7). Normally Paul prefers to talk of faith as a receiving rather than a seeking, but in the verse just cited he sounds like the Jesus of Matthew. Matthew's Jesus in the Sermon on the Mount is asking us through a whole series of illustrations to make only God God, to value only God's awards and emoluments, and to stop flirting with the world.

A quiet simplicity of lifestyle is what chapter 6 is finally all about; the disciples' charity is private, their prayer is secret, their disciplines are hidden, and their treasures, goals, masters, and cares are simply God the Father himself and his coming rule and present righteousness in the world. An utter theocentricity marks chapter 6 in the life of the disciple as it marked chapter 4 in the temptations of the Lord.

How can one find the power to love as the fifth chapter commands us to love? By living a private devotional life with the Father (6 A) and a single life of faith in him (6 B) as the sixth chapter teaches. Faith is the how of love. God-centeredness is the fuel making other-centeredness possible. The Lord's Prayer is the way to the world's service. The sixth chapter is the how of the fifth chapter. God is the how of godliness. Chapter 6 supplies us inwardly and spiritually with what chapter 5 asks us to do outwardly and socially. Chapter 6 is not an alternative lifestyle for people who cannot make it in the world; it is the depth with God that provides disciples with the means for living in the width of the world of chapter 5. Luther's *Large Catechism* on the First Commandment says exactly what needs to be said on the meaning of faith, the theme of chapter 6.

Chapter Seven
The Call to Justice

I believe the first four stories of Matthew 7 summarize the preceding sermon so I call them "the Sums." The last four stories of the chapter warn us about the seriousness of keeping the sermon and so are called "the Warnings." From the chapter's opening call not to judge so that we will not be judged, to the concluding warning of the house that will fall in its day of judgment we find ourselves in this chapter face to face with God's justice and with the special *seriousness* of Jesus' Word. Chapter 5 called us to the width of mercy, chapter 6 to the depth of faith, and now chapter 7 calls us to the height of justice. The themes of the Sermon on the Mount are "the weightiest themes of Scripture: justice, mercy, and faith" (Matt 23:23).

I. THE SUMS (7:1–12)

A. Don't Judge (S 1), 7:1–5

"Do not judge so that you will not be judged" (v 1). This is simply the fifth Blessing in summary and in reverse, "Blessed are the merciful, for they will receive mercy." "Don't judge" also summarizes the content of the second, sixth, and seventh commands in the heart of chapter 5 concerning anger, revenge, and hate. "Don't judge" recapitulates in fresh language the point of the fifth petition of the Lord's Prayer in the middle of chapter 6: "forgive us our debts, as we have, forgiven our debtors." In a way, then, the command not to judge summarizes the heart of both the preceding chapters. In every sense Jesus' will is clear: "I want mercy and not sacrifice" (9:13; 12:7).

"Don't judge" is open to several interpretations. It certainly does not mean "do not have discernment" or "do not think," for the second Sum will immediately ask us to discern "dogs" and "pigs" from whom to keep the Word, and the Warnings at the end of the chapter will tell us that we can and must discern false from true prophets by their fruit. All discernment involves the formation of judgments. Jesus does not ask us to surrender the judgment of discernment. (We are forbidden *Ver*urteilung, not *Be*urteilung, i.e., damning, not discerning, Grund., 219.)

The judgment we are asked to surrender is the judgment of condemnation (i.e., snatching from God the verdict of the last judgment, Bonn., 96). We are not to make final judgments on anyone, to speak assuredly of people's real character, to pretend that we know *God's* verdict on other people's lives at the final judgment.

There is still another sense in which the word "judge" is understood. The Old Testament "judges" were, in fact, conquerors, champions, liberators, and saviors (see the Book of Judges). In Jesus' teaching we are not permitted to be what we might think Christian disciples should be: conquerors for God, "judges" in this heroic sense. The parable of the weeds in Matt 13, Matthew's own special contribution to that chapter's parable collection, specifically forbids disciples what they might have thought to be their responsibility: the uprooting of evil persons, the "judging" of weeds, the seemingly liberating removal of rotten fruit from the field of God. "Judging," then, in its form as violent power is disallowed disciples. (Paul clarifies and amplifies the meaning of this Sum in Rom 2:1–11; Jesus protects this Sum from irresponsibility in Matt 18, especially vv 15–20.)

"So that you will not be judged." The passive construction of this phrase masks, as it often modestly does, the person of God. To resist damning criticism is pleasing to God and is rewarded with his not damning us. "Blessed are the merciful for they shall receive mercy" (B 5). In the Gospel of Matthew our relation to persons definitely conditions our relation to the Father. This "don't judge" summary, then, is saying that where criticism or conquest is suspended by disciples on earth it is suspended from us by the Father in heaven.

There is a lesser, psychosocial sense in which this "don't judge" word is also understood. Critical persons feel (psychologically) and receive (socially) the same devastating criticism they dispense, and these experiences are the source of much psychic and social distress. Jesus would save us from these wounds, too.

7:2 *"For the ruler you use on others will be used on you, and with the very cup that you measure out to others you will receive your measure."* This is a strong argument for generosity. The slide rule that we apply to approved and unapproved behavior in our circles is taken from our hands in God's judgment and is applied to us. The size of the cup we use in dispensing little or large signs of disapproval is the size of the cup that the Father uses in his righteous dispensation of judgment to us. We sometimes think we have the *responsibility* to disburse disesteem in the measure we feel people deserve, and we think these disbursals contribute to social equilibrium and justice. For with signs of disapproval the wayward are chastened. But this command tells us to beware of our calculus. Jesus' words amount to an attack on perfectionism.

Nothing less is called for here than forgiveness, that gift enshrined in the center of the Lord's Prayer in the middle of the sixth chapter. The mercy of understanding, the main theme of chapter 5, is what our present summary Word seeks to shock into us a final time. For the threat of God's judgment can often move us where appeals to God's love cannot. Jesus is not afraid to warn of judgment because he knows the character of God and of God's burning justice. We are not to live in the delusion that God forgives our sins when we do not forgive the sins of others (cf. both LP 5, "forgive us . . . as," and 18:21–35).

But are disciples not to struggle for *justice?* And if they are, doesn't this mean that they must also struggle to *dispense* justice? Here is the rub.

Disciples are to work for justice *as disciples* (and not as warriors), but (unless called vocationally to the administration of justice) they are forbidden the logical next step of actually being dispensers of justice in the punitive or retributive sense. It is this lack of logic that infuriates consistent Marxist-Leninists. Disciples must have the courage to leave to God's sovereignty (sometimes exercised by the state—Rom 13 and Acts *passim*—but sometimes not, Rev 13 *et passim*) the earthly *final* judgments and the conquests of coercive justice. The disciples' role is the more modest and seemingly less effective one of doing everything *for* justice up to but excluding its actual leveling. Disciples *qua* disciples simply cannot be dispensers of divine judgments in society unless called to do so by vocation. To be sure, they will be called in chapter 18 to bar unrepentant sinners from the community, but unless they occupy offices of justice (police, soldiers, judges, government positions), they are individually not given the privilege of measuring out specific, graded punitive judgments to errant people.

Jesus' proscription of judging here poses serious questions for the church's penitential practice as well as for her frequent temptation to crusade, to play God or liberator, to "participate fully and unquestionably in the people's struggle against the oppressors." Whether from the left or the right, the logical conclusions of "the struggle" ("struggle" is a favorite word in all messianic-romantic movements, e.g., *Mein Kampf*), namely, physical conquest and the execution of divine judgment, are not, apart from divine office, permitted disciples. "No promise of any future justifies . . . the murder [we may translate, "the final judging"] of inconvenient people" (Bergen).

7:3–5 *"How is it that you are so able to see the sawdust in your brother's eye but the log that is sticking out of your own eye you don't even notice? How can you possibly say to your brother, 'Come here, I'll take care of that sawdust in your eye,' and look, all the time there is a log hanging out of your eye? You phony. First get rid of the log in your own eye and then you will have the vision necessary to get rid of the sawdust in your brother's eye."*

It is a law of life that we consistently undervalue the size of our own faults and overvalue the size of others'. "Every way of a man is right in his own eyes, but the Lord weighs the heart" (Prov 21:2). In all conversation the disciple should be aware of this law, this "critical law of gravity," which persistently inclines us to judge in our own favor. We have the eyes of Argus with the faults of others; we are blind as moles with our own. "The absent are never without fault nor the present without excuse."

An excessive eagerness to help others is also questioned here by Jesus. "Come here, I'll get rid of that sawdust in your eye," *can* be a feature of missionary consciousness in helping younger churches or less mature Christians or correcting what may indeed be faults. But perhaps the log in the missionary's eye is nothing else than the log of fault-finding, the twenty-twenty vision (perhaps objectively correct in itself) into the faults of others. Because logs are big, gifted persons are often unable to notice that precisely their gift is their problem. Their perceptiveness into everything (but themselves) is what is resented; their very other-centeredness disturbs recipients no end, because these great big bears of charity cannot smell their own breath or see their own matted fur.

The unnoticed log is often the critical spirit itself. The log may be others' faults, of course. But Jesus' major purpose in this Word is to make disciples conscious of the law of critical gravity that always perverts their assessment not so much of others—in this case the brother *does* have sawdust in his eye—but their assessment of themselves. The tragicomic feature in this story is a log-eyed reformer saving a speck-eyed sinner, a Redwood teaching a shrub to be low profile. Thus this saying of Jesus has turned in upon itself: "Judge not" has become "judge *yourselves*," "get rid *first* of your own Redwood."

"And *then* you will have the vision necessary to get rid of the sawdust in your brother's eye." Self-criticism is to end in finally helping the other get rid of the sawdust. This Sum has too often been used as a cover for moral laxity, for indifference to evil, and for toleration of falsehood. But sawdust in the eye hurts, and it impairs vision; problems in fellow Christians and churches impede the Christian mission. It is legitimate and even urgent, after all is said and done, to help others remove specks from their eyes—but this assistance will be especially appreciated where it is accompanied by the assistants' sense of their own wood. Genuinely *self*-critical aid can be tolerated; aid with *other* kinds of eyes, eyes that have never been diseased, eyes that purport to be much sharper than the aid's recipients, expert eyes, eyes of "developed countries" or of "mature churches"—these eyes are intolerable. They are the kinds of eyes Jesus earlier spoke of as filled with darkness rather than light. Only convalescent, that is, not yet completely perfect eyes can help other eyes. In this sense, what the world needs more than the perfect is the consciously imperfect. Only wounded healers have a right to heal (Nouwen).

We may correct others, "but not as a foe, nor as an adversary exacting a penalty, but as a physician providing medicines. For neither did Christ say 'stay not him that is sinning,' but 'judge not'; that is, be not bitter in pronouncing sentence" (Chrys., 23:2:158).

The first Sum of chapter 7, then, is a summary seeking by a negative formulation ("don't judge") to enlist what all of chapter 5 taught positively—mercy. "Faults are thick where mercy is thin." Therefore, by all means, get mercy.

B. Don't Push (S 2), 7:6

"Don't give the holy to dogs, and don't throw your pearls before pigs; if you do, they are going to trample what you give them under their feet, and they will then turn around and tear you to pieces."

Disciples eager to *help* brothers and sisters—encountered in the previous story—are also eager, of course, to *convert* others and so to help people in the deepest possible sense. But once again, strangely, Jesus checks the zeal of disciples. (Allen entitles this Sum "Perverted Zeal," 66.) If all attempts at help must first of all be self-critical (S 1), this should not mean that we are to use no discernment with others at all (S 2). Some people have harmless specks in their eyes; others have harmful clubs in their hands. This command counsels disciples not to be stupid. We are not only to be harmless as doves, we are to be wise as serpents (10:16).

There is a form of evangelism that urges Christians to use every opportunity to share the gospel. Unfortunately, insensitive evangelism often proves harmful not only to the obdurate whose heart is hardened by the undifferentiating evangelist, but harmful also to the gospel that is force-fed. Pressure evangelists tell us that "the fear of man is a snare" and that when a Christian worker is filled by the Spirit he or she will turn dogs into puppies and pigs into piglets and that there will be a decision and not a disaster at the end of a Spirit-filled encounter.

Jesus is more cautious and sane. He positively commands us not to give the holy to the insensitive. Incidentally, the requirement here to discern (in Jesus' colorful language) dogs and pigs, reconfirms the conclusion that "don't judge" does not mean "don't think." The disciple is supposed to notice whether people are receptive or closed (dogs), and in the latter case Jesus' counsel is "don't push." To be "urgent in season and out of season" (1 Tim 4:2) means, in some cases, to pray rather than to talk.

As assistance is sometimes insensitive to its own need of assistance (7:1 , so evangelism is sometimes insensitive to other persons' unwillingness to be evangelized (7:6). In both activities there is a kind of imperialism of the spirit that impedes the work of the gospel. Aggressive evangelism gets converts and counts them, but we are never able to count those turned away from the gospel for the numbers of the offended are never tallied.

Jesus' methods of assistance and evangelism in the Sermon on the Mount seem curiously cautionary, unaggressive, and to be so many species of nonpositive thinking. Jesus would not have made a very good car salesman. How is the gospel going to grow if we don't push it, and how are we going to help other people if we are constantly paralyzed by our own problems? Nevertheless, Jesus believes that the slower path of self-criticism in aid and of personal sensitivity in evangelism will grip persons more dependably than aggressive techniques.

Bengel, 1:131, believed that in the first two Sums we avoid two extremes: "to judge those who are not to be judged, and to give holy things to dogs; too much severity and too much laxity." Gundry, 119, 122, believes that the prohibition against judging is balanced in this text "by a precautionary note that nondisciples ought to be barred from the fellowship of the church." This Sum, then, "warns against easy conditions of entrance into the church." Schlatter, *Der*, 109, observes that the first Sum teaches us not to impute sin, the second not to impose holiness.

The second Sum of chapter 7, then, summarizes negatively ("Don't push") what chapter 6 teaches positively—the sensitivity and modesty of *faith*. Chapter 6's Devotions attacked ostentatious witnessing; chapter 7's second Sum forbids insensitive witnessing.

"He who corrects a scoffer gets himself abuse, and he who reproves a wicked man incurs injury" (Prov 9:7). "Conduct yourselves wisely toward outsiders, making the most of your time. Let your speech always be gracious, seasoned with salt, so that you may know how you ought to answer every one" (Col 4:5–6). Chrysostom, 23:3:159–60, understood the dogs and pigs as the incorrigible, and cites excellent cross references: 2 Tim 3:5, "Avoid such people"; Tit 3:10, "As for a man who is factious, after admonishing him once or twice, have nothing more to do with him." See also Chrysostom's disciplined approach (behind closed doors) to the Lord's Supper.

On the early church's warfare against lax communion (seen by some as the scope of this text, Matt 7:6) see Barc., 1:266–67. Jerome 1:142, referred approvingly to those who said "dogs" were those who had believed in Christ and had then returned to the vomit of their sins (cf. 2 Pet 2:22; Prov 26:11), while "pigs" were those who had not yet believed the gospel at all and who wallowed in the slime of their unbelief and sins. Luther, *SM*, 225–26, believed that this verse in Matthew taught separation from schismatic spirits. It is also possible that our v 6 simply says in another way what vv 1–5 were saying already: "Don't throw your Christian life to the dogs by being hypercritical." Then 7:1–6 would be one long Sum. Cf. Patte, 96.

C. Ask (S 3), 7:7–11

"Ask, and you will receive; seek, and you will find; knock, and it will be opened to you. Because everyone who asks receives, and everyone who seeks finds, and everyone who knocks gets openings" (7:7–8).

As chapter 5 had presented us with demands that required the power of the faith and Lord's Prayer of the sixth chapter, so in chapter 7 the commands not to judge or push are enabled by this new promise of prayer. (This third Sum gives us the mercy to practice the first Sum with believers, the patience to practice the second with unbelievers, Schl., *Der,* 239, and the wisdom to discern which is which, Grund., 223; Schw., 172.)

In chapter 6 Jesus began his systematic instruction on prayer by discouraging repetitive prayers (6:7–8). Such praying he called pagan, and he contrasted the verbosity of pagan prayer with the omniscience of the Father. Brevity, simplicity, privacy, faith—these were the hallmarks of Jesus' initial instruction in prayer. But lest we think the Father asks us to be brief because he does not want to waste time with us, or that prayer should be "not much" because the Father wants not much of us, Jesus gives fresh teaching on prayer. This Sum, then, does more than summarize. Where the Lord's Prayer taught us prayer content, this teaches us prayer responsibility (Schn., 98).

This famous Ask passage is noteworthy because of the unconditioned character of its promises. Ask *what?* We are not told exactly. The promises are astonishingly open-ended. Whenever this passage is read with simple faith it will take the breath away. Six different times in six different ways Jesus almost begs us to pray, and promises solemnly that simple asking *receives,* seeking *finds,* knocking *opens.* (The English "Ask," with its three letters, helpfully outlines the first letter of the main verbs used here: *a*sk, *s*eek, and *k*nock.) Here disciples are encouraged to pour out their hearts before the Father (Ps 62:8) and the open-ended promises are like huge gift baskets beckoning us to come and take.

This great Ask passage is the most encouraging biblical passage on the subject of prayer with which I am acquainted, for it promises almost unconditionally that simple asking receives, simple seeking finds, and simple knocking gets in. And as if this were not enough, Jesus goes through the list of promises still once again: "For *every* person who asks, receives, and the seeker finds and the knocker gets openings," as if to say "this is law: the way to receive from the Father is asking."

The irony, of course, is that, as Schlatter, *Das,* 111, has pointed out, we carry around within us great bundles of wishes that never become askings. We *wish* that our relation to those with whom we work were better or that we might be able to do this or that; but when did we make the wish a prayer? We talk to ourselves about our problems in the form of much thought, worry, and sleeplessness; we might talk about our problem with those close to us, too, but even we Christians are strangely reluctant to talk frankly about our problems with the Father, proving again that our faith needs robustness. Jesus opens the doors of faith as widely here as they will ever be opened again, and he promises us unconditionally a fruitful audience with the Father—for the simple asking.

This text has its problems, for we all know of asking that to all honest observation did not receive what it asked. People have been hurt here (see Wind., *The Meaning of the Sermon on the Mount,* 205–07). Why, then, is Jesus' promise so dangerously absolute? I believe it is because Jesus is convinced that his disciples have an appalling lack of faith (and so, of prayer, faith's exhalation). "When the Son of man comes," he says in another place where he is teaching prayer, "will he find faith on earth?" (Luke 18:8), Schweizer,

173, acknowledges that Jesus' open-ended teaching on prayer can be abused, but Jesus "is not concerned about the chance of being misunderstood . . . [by someone who] would transform the gift into an instrument for his own designs. . . . He is not concerned that his hearers might misuse [the gift of prayer], only that they have it."

In my opinion it is not good form to stress that the verbs Jesus uses (ask, seek, and knock) are present tense imperatives in the first series and present tense participles in the second, meaning, in both cases, "continually ask." For it is understood that asking will be in a living, that is, in a continuing relation to the Father—we talk even with our earthly loved ones more than once about the things that matter to us. If continuity is stressed, however, we are back to the repetitiveness and burdensomeness that Jesus took from our backs in his initial lesson in prayer (D 2). Since our text does not stress the laboriousness of asking, but the grace of the Giver, it is best for us to read the text in the least strenuous way. In fact, the exhortations—ask, seek, knock—are all one-worded (in Greek, too), as if to stress simplicity, while the promises are all more elaborate as if to stress the multiplied assurance of provision.

The point of this powerful invitation is simply, in the words of the hymn, "O what peace we often forfeit, O what needless pain we bear, All because we do not carry Everything to God in prayer." We need to be reminded that asking is *not* (as some spiritual teachers tell us) more selfish than praise, which is more God-centered, or than intercession, which is more neighbor-centered, or than thanksgiving, which is more humble. All six sentences of the Lord's Prayer are petitions, askings; and the right way for disciples to appear before God is not as givers to a divine Egoist, but as humble receivers from a generous Father. There is sometimes more self-centeredness in the giving or praise understanding of worship, which assumes that we are the important actors and God the recipient, than there is in the receiving understanding of worship, which lets God be God and us be human beings. It is not selfish to ask—it is selfish not to ask—if God is God.

With human beings, importunate asking, seeking, and knocking are considered rude, "troublesome and disgusting," but with God, *not* to come asking eagerly is displeasing (Chrys., 23:5:160). Barclay, 1:270, cites the rabbis: "'A man is annoyed by being worried by the requests of his friends, but with God, all the time a man puts his needs and requests before him, God loves him all the more.'" On worship see V. Vajta, *Luther on Worship*.

Luther said that in the monastery he was never really taught to *ask* in prayer. But the discovery of justification by grace, which puts a person's feet on the ground, taught him afresh the marvelously uninhibited and normal way we may approach the living God—as askers, as human beings who are in need. Asking is what prayer is; this passage and the Lord's Prayer together carve this gracious fact into the doctrinal conviction of the church. If this passage can succeed in making disciples prayerful, the Sermon on the Mount (which is the will of God) is on its way to fulfillment "on earth as it is in heaven." Jesus does not leave his church with a great deal of equipment, but he knows (as we will see more than once in this Gospel) that if he can leave her with the simple, open-ended gift of prayer, he has already met most of her need.

Jesus' main gift to his people will be his Word, by which the Father continually speaks to us; this is the first and main gift of Jesus to his church. His other gift is the privilege of our speaking to the Father. By these two means—the Word and prayer—the church makes her sure way through the world. The sacraments, incidentally, are divinely instituted extensions of the Word; they are not competitors with it. The seventeenth chapter of Matthew teaches the Word and prayer doctrines classically. "By this [Sum] Jesus intends to teach [his disciples] that, second only to the office of preaching, prayer is the chief work of a Christian" (Lu., *SM*, 228).

7:9–11 "Tell me, who of you will give your son a rock when he asks you for bread? Or if he asks for fish will give him a snake? If you, then, who are evil, know how to give good gifts to your children, how much more will your heavenly Father give good things to those who ask him?"

The relation of parent to child is one of the most precious in human experience, and Jesus appeals to it to reinforce the power of his promise. If human parents want to give their children the best, just imagine "how much more" (the key words in the story) the heavenly Father will respond to *his* children. A parent's heart is tuned to its child and lives to help it. No parent, asked for bread, would give its child a stone to choke on.

Jesus intends to shock us by these illustrations. He says, "You who are evil"—an interesting reflection, incidentally, on Jesus' sober estimate of human nature *and* of his own—he does not say "*we* who are evil." (Bengel, 1:132, calls our verse "an illustrious testimony to the doctrine of original sin." Bonnard, 100, contests C. H. Dodd's idealism about human nature here: "The a fortiori reasoning ["how much more"] does *not* start with the general goodness of man in order to lift itself to the generosity of God; it starts with the wickedness of man . . . to make comprehensible the incomparable generosity of the heavenly Father.") This human analogy intends to buck up our wavering, unbelieving, reluctant-to-pray spirits and to encourage us to start *asking!* Jesus is trying in every way he can—whether by repeating an open-ended promise six times (as he did in the Ask sentences) or by appealing now to the universal love of parents—to bring us by any means possible to the Father, hands out and mouths open. We are not supposed to have a dumb relation with God in which he is so divine that he shouldn't be bothered by our talk or in which we are so sinful we shouldn't try. *Jesus wants us to ask.*

This parable of bread, rock, fish, and snake is also designed to disabuse believers of the well-known (and consciously or unconsciously racist) fear that if we come to God with the asking of faith in full surrender, "he'll send me to Africa" . . . "he'll hurt me." Jesus fights a morbid fear of God in many of his parables.

The power for *doing* the Sermon on the Mount is put in the Beatitudes at the beginning, in the Lord's Prayer in the middle, and in this prayer Sum near the end of the sermon. Like three deep springs beside a trail these three texts empower those who walk the high mountain of this sermon. The refreshing, empowering purpose of this third Sum (called "The Answer to Prayer Colophon" in Bacon, 278) is taught nicely by Chrys., 23:4–6:160–61 and by Aug., *LSM*, 2:21:71:159. Cf. also Schl., *Der*, 245; Grund., 223. For this reason I find it hard to agree with my colleague at Whitworth College who writes, in his otherwise excellent study of Matthew and Paul, that Matthew is a Gospel "almost totally devoid of explicit reference to God's aid in the moral-ethical realm" (Mohrlang, 209; cf. 224).

Matthew's version of this story invites us to ask for "good things" from the Father; Luke's, to receive "the Holy Spirit." The meaning is the same, with Matthew focusing on deeds and Luke on their source. Matthew's "good things" to ask certainly include the living of the Sermon on the Mount, especially in the form codified in the petitions of the Lord's Prayer—each petition is a very good thing (Schn., 99; Grund., 225; Schw., 174). The good things of the Blessings and obedience to the Commands (Matt 5) are also right askings, as are the right ways of the Devotions and the right seekings of the Goals (Matt 6). The Matthean phrase "good things" limits prayer, too, in that prayer for the not good is forbidden (Mey., 163). Hence every good thing taught in every paragraph in Scripture is something we can ask for in prayer. The emphasis in the text is on the Father's breathtaking readiness to give his asking children what is good for them. To awaken a simple, uncomplex faith in the Father is the goal of this Sum, as it was the goal of the whole sixth chapter, especially that chapter's Lord's Prayer. As "don't judge" summarized the central intention of mercy in chapter 5, so "ask" summarizes the central intention of faith in chapter 6.

"I was *ready* to be sought by those who did not *ask* for me; I was *ready* to be found by those who do not *seek* me. I said, 'Here am I, here am I,' to a nation that did not *call on* my name" (Isa 65:1). "You do not have, because you do not ask" (Jas 4:2). "First, we must know that it is our *duty* to pray because God has commanded it [in the commandment, "You shall not take the name of the Lord your God in vain."]. . . . [But] the human heart is by nature so perverse that it always flees from God, thinking that he is averse to our prayers because we are sinners and have merited only his wrath. In opposition to such thoughts, I say, we should give heed to this commandment, and turn to God in order to avoid aggravating his anger by such disobedience. By this commandment he makes plain that he will not thrust us aside nor cast us out because we are sinners" (Lu., *Large Catechism*, 169–70:96–97, emphasis added).

D. Be Generous (S 4), 7:12

"*So the way you want people to treat you is the way you should treat them: this is what the Bible is about.*"

The "so" of this saying (the Golden Rule) is at first puzzling. The previous Word spoke about prayer, but this Word speaks about conduct. Perhaps the connecting link between the two Words is the idea of *generosity.* Then the "so" means that just as we should live in a relation of asking with a generous Father so we should live in a relation of generous helpfulness with our neighbor (thus Chrys., 23:6:161; Schl., *Das*, 112).

The simplicity of this rule is deceptive. For as Schlatter, *Der,* 112–13, has taught us to see, this rule liberates the church from the reign of experts. In Jesus' time people were often counseled to go to sages, rabbis, and seers in order to know exactly what was required of them. But Jesus refers a believer anxious for a rule in social or ethical conduct to the simplest source of all, oneself. In personal relations, all that believers need usually consult is their own feelings—how would I like to be treated in this situation?—and in the answer to this question one has a rule.

"It was certainly clever of Christ to state it this way. The only example He sets up is ourselves. . . . The book is laid into your own bosom, and it is so clear that you do not need glasses to understand Moses and the law. Thus you are your own Bible, your own teacher, your own theologian, and your own preacher" (Lu., *SM,* 236–37).

This sensitivity, Jesus goes on ingenuously to assert, is what the Bible (literally, "the law and the prophets") is all about. (Luther noticed that Jesus did not say that this was what the *gospel* is all about, *SM*, 240; cf. Cal., 1:232.) We know of course that the Bible is also about *divine* generosity (grace and faith) and not just about human generosity (the just preceding Ask story told us this). Yet throughout Matthew we see Jesus teaching an astonishing humanism. Sensitivity to the humanity of our neighbor, Jesus says here, *is* the law and the prophets, *is* the Old Testament, *is* the Bible. Jesus comes close to saying that what is taught about God in Scripture is for the sake of relations to people. Theology is for the sake of ethics, and the truth of God is for the service of persons.

It is almost as if God makes himself a means to the service of people. We say "almost" because Jesus' own life teaches us important exceptions. While the gospel must come close to being a radical humanism if it is to find its original shape, the perils of an unbridled humanism or human-centeredness were taught the church classically by the temptations at the threshold of Jesus' ministry. Yet serious disciples who have come this far into the Sermon on the Mount will need to be guarded at the other extreme from an unbridled spiritualism that fails to see that we are on earth in large measure in order to be human with other human beings and that this humanity pleases God. "So the way you want people to treat you is the way you should treat them: this is what the Bible is about."

Experts in Scripture and counseling, specialists in doctrine and ethics, pastors and teachers, scholars and Christian leaders, will always be useful in the church. But Jesus does us no little service by liberating us in many ethical questions from an abject dependence on the leadership of others. Disciples can know the will of God for their relations most of the time by consulting their own interest, by "the inventiveness of love" (Bonn., 101). This liberation from expertise, from hierarchies, and from outer-directedness—into personal autonomy, generosity, and creativity is another of Jesus' considerable gifts in the Sermon on the Mount. Jesus gave us the Father in the Lord's Prayer; he gives us ourselves in the Golden Rule.

Finally we need not fear that in taking the Golden Rule seriously we will be leaving God behind. When Jesus teaches faith rambunctiously in the immediately preceding Ask Word, he is not afraid to teach human relations uninhibitedly in the Golden Rule.

Luke placed this rule in the middle of Jesus' love-of-enemy command (Luke 6:31). "Matthew appears to have removed it to this point to form a general conclusion to the main body of his Sermon" (Mc., 93), i.e., to make it a summary. See how the phrase "law and prophets," early at 5:17 and now here toward the end at 7:12, brackets the body of the sermon. The Blessings at the beginning are the sermon's prologue, the Warnings at the end its epilogue. The Ask Sum taught *the love of God* and faith; the Golden Rule Sum teaches *love of neighbor* and sensitivity, and so together they summarize disciples' two main duties (22:34–40). On the summary character of the Golden Rule in Matthew's design see also Schw., 172.

*　　　*　　　*

In the four Sums the two major texts, quantitatively and qualitatively, are "don't judge" and "ask," summarizing, respectively, the mercy of the fifth chapter and the faith of the sixth. We are now ready for four concluding Warnings where the Sermon comes to its sharpest point.

II. THE WARNINGS (7:13–29)

A. The Two Gates (W 1), 7:13–14

"Enter the narrow gate, because the gate is wide and the way pleasant that leads to destruction, and most people enter this wide gate; but the gate is narrow and the way tough that leads to real life, and very few people find this narrow gate."

Luther, *SM*, 241: "Our dear Lord has now finished preaching. Finally He closes this sermon with several warnings to arm us against all sorts of hindrances." McNeile, 93: "Like the Book of the Covenant (Exod 20–23), the Deuteronomic code (Deut 12–28), and the Law of Holiness (Lev 17–26), the Lord's commentary on the Law closes with warnings and exhortations."

Jesus began his sermon with unqualified tenderness, embracing in the Blessings those who felt least embraceable. He concludes with unqualified toughness, warning us that his sermon is not an intellectual option, a set of suggestions we may take or leave, one philosophy of life among several others, but that it is the exclusive way to life.

Because this sermon is so wide and humane in mercy, it surprises us to hear Jesus describe his way as "narrow." In what sense can the width of the Beatitudes and the breadth of the promises of the Lord's Prayer and of the Asking invitations be considered narrow? Let us follow the text to find the answer.

"The gate is wide and the way pleasant that leads to destruction, and most people enter this wide gate" (v 13). Life outside of loyalty to Jesus Christ, which is the life of the secular world, *is* a life full of the alluring width of moral permissions and of the tempting delectations of a seemingly fuller life (cf. the psychology of Gen 3:5–6). The life of discipleship, on the other hand, passes through the narrow gate of the decision to obey Jesus' commands against anger, defensiveness, and hate, and it then passes along a still narrow defile of almost unheard of purity and fidelity in sexual relations and marriage. Disciples are asked to choose this way of obedience to Jesus because it is a way that supplies, not subtracts, life. The Word of Jesus is the way to, not the loss of, vitality.

Some commentators stress that Jesus is appealing in this Warning for *la décision évangélique*—not so much for a long walk (at the end of which is salvation) as for a once-for-all decision (where salvation, then, is already present). Thus Bonnard, 102, and Michaelis (whom Bonnard cites) in TWNT 5:72: "'He who has passed through the narrow gate has already entered, he is already at the goal.'" Bonnard, 102, continues: "Here the idea is not so much that of a gate so small, so low, that one must stoop down or lower oneself in order to pass through, as it is that of a gate ignored by the greater number of people, as the end of v 14 indicates. The dominant idea is this: in order to enter Life, it is necessary to make a personal choice no longer to follow the anonymous crowds but, on the contrary, 'to find' and to follow the Christ." While I like the evangelical christocentricity of Bonnard's exposition and believe he correctly interprets the gate and the (aorist) once-for-all force of the verb to "enter" (and the truth that a personal relationship with Christ precedes everything), I feel he fails to do justice to the "way" in the saying and to the (participial) continuing force of the other verbs in the sentences. Matthew's Jesus is appealing *both* for an evangelical decision (the gate) *and* for an ethical endurance (the way). Taken together, then, the narrow gate and the tough way are simply the difficult choice for Jesus *and* the constantly challenging decisions for discipleship to him. Similarly, Patte, 99. The first Psalm is the perfect commentary on this first Warning.

There is no need to fool ourselves by saying that Jesus' ethic is not difficult. Jesus' Sermon on the Mount requires red blood and moral investment. It is a tough way. But its destination is life, its way is vitality, and its experience is meaning. The successism of both secularity and superspirituality lacks the moral fiber and intellectual meaning found in life lived in obedience to Jesus' demands.

An emphatic feature in the parable of the two gates is the "many" who go the wide, easy way and the "few" who find the narrow, rough way. Jesus warns us thereby that the way of the majority in morals will not often be the way of discipleship. To be a disciple is to be in the moral minority. "Everybody does it" will not be a very helpful criterion in Christian ethics. ("The 'wide gate and spacious way' represents the popular decision, the choice of the majority," Guel., 388). Disciples must fight the temptation to look around to see how many persons are going their way. For "when you do what the majority does you destroy your life" (Schl., *Das*, 114). They must not take heart from the number of persons agreeing with them.

Disciples must be prepared to go the way of the little flock rather than the way of the great herd, the way of persecution rather than the way of least resistance, of ethical rather than antinomian discipleship (cf. Gund., 127).

The way is tough. And yet this arduous way will not only lead *to* life, it will be the way to live now. Discipleship is the true nonconformity; its low way the real "high." Discipleship meets the ideals of the classical desire for the "exercise of vital powers along lines of excellence in a life affording them scope." Discipleship is far from being actually narrow; it is the epic way to live. But few will believe this.

Surprising in this story is the final verb: "and very few people *find* this narrow gate." It is as if the narrow gate is so tiny, so miniscule, that a person can hardly see it. The minuteness of the gate indicates the razor sharp character of decision. The decision to follow Jesus is a decision of minute precision; it is a decision of "moment." Jesus invites us through this Word, as he has been inviting us with every preceding Word, to take him with a final seriousness and then to follow him the rest of our lives. Where the decision is made to take him seriously the way to life is found.

Luther, *SM*, 246: "Christ Himself and the whole heavenly host are at my side and have traveled this very same way, preceding me to heaven in a beautiful and long procession. Until the Last Day all Christendom will be travelling on the same road. . . . 'It is a yoke and a burden for the flesh, [Jesus says], and it is called a hard way and a narrow gate. But just cling to Me, and I will make it nice for you, pleasant and easy, giving you enough strength to travel the road with ease.'"

B. The Two Trees (W 2), 7:15–20

"Watch out for false prophets who come to you all dressed up like sheep, but who inside are vicious wolves. You will be able to recognize them by their fruit. Can grapes be picked

from briars, or figs from thistles? In the same way, every good tree just naturally produces good fruit and every rotten tree naturally produces bad fruit. It is as impossible for a good tree to produce bad fruit as it is for a rotten tree to produce good. Every tree not producing good fruit is chopped down and thrown into the fire. Thus I say you will recognize them by their fruit" (7:15–19).

In the first of his Warnings Jesus separated us from the majority into the community of the few; now in the next two Warnings he will separate us from even those within our little Christian community who are not real. And in the final Warning, Jesus will separate us from even things within ourselves that incline us to hear but not to do the words of Jesus. A kind of refining process goes on through these Warnings. Jesus sifts us down to reality.

If we are not to enter upon the Broadway leading to destruction we will need to be liberated from those who beckon us to it, from the hawkers of the Broadway. Jesus now tells us how to defend ourselves from all advocates and prophets of false ways.

False prophets wear sheep's clothing, that is, they have *Christian* ways. Sheep are a symbol of believers (cf. 10:18, etc.; Davies, 200; G. Barth, 73; Green, 96; Hill, 151). This presents us with a difficulty: what is the difference between a gracious appearance (sheep's clothing) and a gracious effect (good fruit)?

It is the first subtlety of false prophets that they *appear* Christian. False prophets rarely wear wolves' clothing. They are often (not always) sheep-like, Christian, seemingly in earnest, apparently real. This is why Jesus has to warn us at all; for if the wolves came on as wolves there would be little need to be alert.

Jesus does not want Christians to feel helpless before false teaching. Twice in this paragraph he confidently asserts that we *will* be able to recognize false prophets by their fruit (7:16, 20). "Fruit" means "what is produced," what people actually teach and do, how they really live, and thus their effects on their hearers and the kinds of life and teaching they encourage in others (Str.-B., 1:466; Schl., *Der*, 254–56; Schl., *Das*, 115–16). First, do they encourage faith in Christ alone, the narrow gate, or do they "lead others into *everything else*"? (Beng., 1:102, his emphasis; cf. in this christocentric direction, too, Lu., *W²*, 11:1402–21; Lu., *SM*, 248–65; and see, especially, the important cross reference in John 10:1–2: "Truly, truly, I say to you, he who does not enter the sheepfold by the [*tēs*, the single] door but climbs in by *another* way [*allachothen*], that man is a thief and a robber; but he who enters by the [single] door is the shepherd of the sheep." The first thesis of the Theological Declaration of Barmen uses this John text, too.)

Second, do they teach or ignore, make important or trivialize the "way" or road of Jesus' hard social commands, for example, by a false appropriation of Paul that says "grace is all and obedience is not important"; are they so relational in their theology that obedience to Jesus' demands is not emphasized, and God's judgment is not preached—that is, are they antinomian? The tests of gate and way—of faith and love, of *solus Christus* and discipleship—are tests that will penetrate sheep's clothing and good appearances. If we are honest, these tests will test us, too, for only the unreal are unself-critical, as this chapter's opening text taught us (7:1–5).

The church fathers often spoke of the twin tests of truth and life. "You can judge the quality of their faith from the way they behave. Discipline [meaning: discipleship] is an

index to doctrine. They say (for example) that God is not to be 'feared.' So everything is
free to them and unrestrained. But where is God not feared except where he is not
present? Where God is not present, there is no truth either; and where there is no truth
[i.e., right doctrine], discipline [i.e., discipleship] like theirs is natural" (Tertullian, *The
Prescription of Heretics*, 63).

In the second century, false prophets such as the Marcionites came to churches
bringing a message of the love of God where God did not have to be feared because
he was only love and not judgment. But the fruit of this seemingly sheep-like teaching was undisciplined life and unbridled moral behavior. The merely outward
Christian message of false prophets breeds un-Christian morality. Matthew's Jesus
is simply convinced that the good are good (cf. 1 John 3:7) and that the bad will
reveal themselves as bad. The moral suggestion of the teacher's *message* and the
moral direction of the teacher's *life* mutually influence each other and will be
the means by which disciples will be able to tell true from false.

The New Testament's famous doctrinal texts apply here, too: Does the teacher
teach Jesus Christ as both human (1 John 4 A) and divine (1 Cor 12 A)? Does he or
she preach the gospel at all? The way Jesus Christ is preached will be the root—the
fruit-producing tree—of ministry. If a Christ without judgment is preached, the
tree will produce bad fruit; if a Christ without true human nature is preached,
the tree will produce Christians who do not take human nature seriously and who
practice the immoralities associated with superspirituality (see the Corinthian correspondence in the New Testament, especially 2 Cor 10–13). One of the values of
church history is the acquaintance it gives with a wide variety of trees (messages,
prophecies) and their fruits (morals, effects). The docetic Christ (excessively spiritual) leads to docetic (antimaterial) ethics; an ebionitic (onesidedly human) Christ
leads to a secularism without serious spiritual content, and so on.

The sum of the matter is that false prophets invariably claim and appear to be
Christian, even specially Christian (see the very next paragraph in Matthew), but
the test of their reality is not how they come on but how they come off; not how they
appear but what they produce; not how they seem but the theological and moral
influence of their teaching and life on the community. Thus the prayer at the end of
the Lord's Prayer, "deliver us from evil," also means "deliver us from false prophets
and their amoral, immoral, or supermoral messages."

Some commentators see Jesus combating the Zealots (the first-century liberation movement in Israel—Masada) in special particular in this second Warning: Schl., *Der*, 251–54
(but contrast G. Barth, 74); Grund., 232; McK., 75. There is no unanimity about the
nature of the false prophets' falseness: is it false teaching (Aug., Jero., Lu., Cal.) or false
living (Chrys., Beng., Mey., Bult., Schw.)? Why not both, since doctrine and life interpen-
etrate? (See Guelich's survey, 391.)

C. The Two Doers (W 3), 7:21–23

*"Not everyone who says to me, 'Lord, Lord,' will get into the Kingdom of heaven, but only
the person who is doing the will of my Father who is in heaven. Many people will say to me in
that day: 'Lord, Lord, didn't we teach marvelously in your name, and didn't we, by means
of your name, cast out demons, and didn't we, through your name, perform many miracles*

and mighty works?!' And then I will have to confess to them, 'I never ever really knew you; get away from me you workers of lawlessness.'"

In Jesus' first Warning he separated us from the secular majority; in his second he separated us from attractive false prophets in church or culture; and now he separates us from a group in the church who might deserve special respect: those who seem to have the greatest ministries! Here we are confronted with Christ-centered Christians (note carefully their threefold insistence that all they did was "in *your* name"), Christians who preached *him*, exorcized explicitly through *him*, and performed miracles *in his name*, which means, they believed they ministered by his power. If it is true that "by their fruits you will know them," then certainly here we have people with real fruits: great preaching, effective healing, and many miracles. The air roils with the impressive.

But where in this sermon has Jesus commanded any of these impressive things? (The gift of healing is discussed in Jesus' *next* sermon, chap 10.) To be sure, it is a gift of God when anyone can preach effectively, cast out devils, and do miracles, as Jesus later teaches; nevertheless, significantly, these fruits nowhere appear in this principal sermon as commands of Jesus or as the will of God. The fruits Jesus commanded in this sermon are much less sensational and much simpler: revering Scripture's commands, the casting out of one's own anger, the miracles of sexual purity and marital fidelity, the spiritual speech that does not overuse God's name and that does not defame the other person, and most deeply, the heart that extends itself even to persecutors and enemies (C 1–7). These are the miracles or fruit that Jesus commands in his opening address as the will of the Father and that, apparently, he missed in these charismatic believers.

The people in the preceding "Two Trees" story were loving (sheep's clothing) but doctrinally-morally noxious (bad fruit); the Christians in the present "Two Doers" story are doctrinally christocentric (the double "Lord, Lord" and the threefold "in your name") and spiritually charismatic (prophecy, exorcism, miracles), but they do not do the will of the Father. (Not doing the will of the Father means, in the context of the Sermon on the Mount, not keeping Jesus' commands.)

Thus it is not sufficient for the Christian community to ask "are they Christ-centered?" They must also ask "do they themselves seek to keep, and do they lead others to keep, the moral commands of Jesus?" Nor is it enough for the community to ask "do they win others to Christ?" They must also ask, "Do they themselves seek to do and to move others to do the will of the Father as this will is taught us in Jesus' *teachings?*" "Do they honor the Sermon on the Mount?" Neither the Christ-*like* (sheep's clothing) nor the Christ-*centered* (Lord, Lord) are necessarily Christ's. For the Christ-like may teach violence, and the Christ-centered may live in hate, lust, or greed. All of us are in the dock here.

Remarkable in the present story of the Two Doers is the *way* the Christ-centered Lord-sayers live their Christian lives: sensationally. Their works are all out of the ordinary: prophecy is spiritual speech with power (Mey., 167); exorcism and doing many mighty miracles are spiritual acts with power. We have no reason to doubt that these special people actually did what they claimed, and that they believed, too, that they did all of this by the power of Christ's name. I believe that we are in the presence of actually successful Christian workers. Yet Jesus disowns them. "Get away from me."

Bengel, 1:135: "'Many'—even of those, perhaps, whom posterity has canonized, accounted blessed and saints. . . . 'We have prophesied'— . . . Add: We have written commentaries and exegetical observations on books and passages of the Old and New Testaments, have preached fine sermons, etc."

They own Jesus and Jesus disowns them; they honor him and he dishonors them; they work for him and he separates himself from them. What can this mean? Does it not seem to mitigate the mercy that we were coming to associate with the person of Jesus?

We learn from this story that it is possible to work *for* Jesus and yet not work *under* him. We can be intoxicated by the power of Christ's person and yet be indifferent or even hostile to keeping his hard commands where they pinch us. It is possible to be powerful for Jesus and yet not allow Jesus to be powerful in oneself. "I never knew you; get away from me you workers of *lawlessness."* They hate God's law. They believe that *they* know Jesus, but they never gave *him* a chance to know them ("I never knew *you*"), that is, they never gave him a chance intimately to come into contact with their real life (the force of the biblical word "know"). It is strangely possible to serve and even to glorify Christ and yet in actual life not to obey him. The fact that "many" will present their christocentric-charismatic credentials at the judgment and that even then they will not be admitted should be genuinely frightening to all of us. It means that just as a loving manner (sheep's clothing) is not necessarily the real thing so, similarly, a Christ-glorifying ministry ("in your name, . . . in your name, . . . in your name") is not always the real thing either.

When a gracious personality teaches violence or encourages immorality (perhaps by influence as much as by word), that gracious personality is unveiled as a front for rapine. Where a christocentric charismatic wins others to Christ or the Spirit, but cherishes hatred for one's rivals or unrepented lust for other women or men, that christocentricity and spiritual success count for nothing at all. In each case Jesus wants reality. He wants disciples whom he can *know,* that is, over whom he can be Lord. He wants to be Lord of both their message and their morality. And Jesus' major teachings are not complex or spectacular; they are laid out in bright clarity in this great sermon, and they require the simplicity and singularity of life that Paul calls faith and that Matthew's Jesus calls doing the will of the Father.

Finally we must take note of the fact that the self-consciousness of the christocentrics in this story is too high. They are too aware of both their piety ("Lord, Lord") and of their successful ministries ("Didn't we . . . perform *many* miracles and mighty works?!") Their sense of devotion seen in the double divine name and their sense of success seen in the review of their three major fruits all indicate that they are too impressed with their work. But are any of Jesus' Beatitudes present in their three ministries? Is there any poverty of spirit here? Any mourning? Any meekness? Any hungering and thirsting for *righteousness* (there is a hungering and thirsting for powerful spiritual impact)? Is there mercy here, or purity of heart, or making of peace? Is there any suffering of persecution?

Christians believe that prophecy, exorcism, and mighty works can be gifts of God and that they need not be evil. But it is surprising in Matthew's Gospel that these great gifts are rarely called the *will* of God.

The minimizing of the spectacular is only a little less true in the theology of Paul (though Paul praises prophecy especially in 1 Cor 14). There is a remarkable connection between this Warning in Jesus' teaching and 1 Cor 13 A in Paul's teaching (cf. Grund., 235). Chrysostom, 24:2:167–68, connects this Warning explicitly with 1 Cor 13 A and asks relevant questions: Were these false disciples living immorally before, during, or after their miraculous activity? Augustine, *LSM*, 2:25:82:170ff, believes that the magicians of Pharoah's court prove that false faith can also work miracles. Cf. Matt 24:24. Luther's discussion, *SM*, 268–77, is typically trenchant: "It is a frightening judgment, that no one is deeper in hell than the great servants of God" (268); the Lord-Lord-sayers "'are always busier and more energetic . . . than the genuine Christians'" (269). See much sectarian, cultic, and super-Christian activity.

The express and clearly defined will of God in Jesus' Sermon on the Mount is the discipleship emblazoned into the clear Commands, Devotions, and Goals of the sermon—the obediences of mercy (chap 5), faith (chap 6), and justice (chap 7)— these obediences are not so much spectaculars as they are simplicities.

In the Two Trees and Two Doers stories Jesus has been effecting a purge of his community from two dangerous elements in it. The elements are dangerous because at first glance they seem so Christian. The sheep's-clothes Christians seem to *live* in such a Christian way—their lifestyle, perhaps their poverty, their solidarity with the poor, their gracious, modest, unassuming manner—all seem to point to the Master of us all. Yet it is precisely from these that bad fruit can and historically has sprung up to infect the whole church, from the austere Ebionites and earnest Pelagius to some engaging social and liberation Christians of our time.

Progressive and radical Christians of all sorts are able to take social elements of Jesus' message and make them their own while disowning Jesus' clear spiritual teachings. There is no honest way that Jesus can be made an old or a new Zealot. No matter how sheep-like the advocates of this way appear, the church will penetrate beneath impressive lifestyles into less impressive life-messages and life-influences to see fruits that do not come from the root of Jesus.

But while the Two Trees saying divides us from certain progressives whose seemingly Christian lives mask an un-Christian message, the present Two Doers saying divides us from certain evangelicals whose Christian message hides un-Christian life. These enthusiastic Christians emphasize Christ and his miracle-working power—even for *others,* as in healings—and they seek to make Christ known; but they do not seek to be known *by* him *themselves;* instead, they live "lawless," that is, loveless, and so, immoral lives.

So in two consecutive warnings Jesus separates the church from her falsely radical and from her falsely charismatic wings. The one seems so right in life but is wrong in message; the other seems so right in message but is wrong in life. And Jesus warns us that neither is finally Christian, neither does or says the simple will of the Father embodied in the clear teaching of Jesus.

Fellowship with Jesus is present only where moral norms remain sacred (Schl., *Der*, 259). The greatest danger for the Christian community arises precisely from those who call Jesus Lord and who even do great spiritual works in his name (Schn., 105). Astonishingly, here the Jesus of Matthew attacks his own community. Thus the Two Ways teaching is not so simple: "Lord, Lord" is heard also on "Broadway" (Matt 7:13–14) (Schw., 189).

D. The Two Houses (W 4), 7:24–27

"So everyone who hears these my Words and does them can be compared to a thoughtful person who built a house on a rock. And the rain came down and the rivers came up and

the winds blew and they hit that house and yet it did not fall because it had been built on rock. And everyone who hears these my Words and does not do them can be compared to a stupid person who built a house on sand. And the rain came down and the rivers came up and the winds blew and they hit that house and it fell, and its fall was great."

In the Two Ways Jesus divided us from the immoral majority; in the Two Trees he divided us from attractive false prophets; in the Two Doers he divided us from powerful false evangelicals; in the present warning of the Two Houses he divides us from what is false in those still left. He has of course been dividing us from the false *in ourselves* in all four warnings. For in all four, Jesus is addressing *us* and asking us to separate from that in us which is falsely secular, falsely prophetic, or falsely evangelical. But in the fourth Warning the knife is sharpest and its bite deepest.

"Everyone who hears." Hearing the Word is the indispensable first step toward doing it (see, e.g., Luke 11:28 and the two key verbs). How can we do a Word we have not heard? Or have power to do God's will without hearing God's Word? But as indispensable as hearing the Word is, Christians must not fool themselves into believing that hearing good teaching or studying the Bible is all by itself the whole doing of the will of the Father. The Father's will is that his Son's Word be heard in such a way that it be *done;* that the Word so penetrate the ears that it reach the heart and so the hands, the lips, and the feet.

The problem is as old as the people of God: "They sit before you as my people, and they *hear* what you say but they will not *do* it; for with their lips they show much love, but their heart is set on their gain" (Ezek 33:31).

Jesus *first* compliments and encourages those who do hear and do his Word. He compares them to thoughtful persons. People who make it their life work to *do* the words of Jesus are people who build their houses on solid foundations. When inevitable troubles hit a house built on that kind of foundation, the house stands. Jesus does not say that a house built on his words will, for example, glow in the dark or miraculously expand into a mansion, or in any way be particularly impressive. The only impressive fact about this house is that it will still be standing when the storm is over. "But the person who sticks to the end will be saved" (Matt 10:22; 24:13). Matthew's Jesus almost always describes the Christian life in terms of survival rather than sensation.

Nor are we told that life built on the foundation of Jesus' words will be *spared* rains, floods, or winds, as though Jesus' teaching were a kind of talisman against trouble. Realistically, Jesus says the same storms hit thoughtful disciples as hit thoughtless ones. Obedience to Jesus' words, then, is not so much a protection from troubles as it is a protection in them—just as rock under a house does not shield from storms, it supports during them.

By this parable disciples learn not to assign Jesus' teaching to the limbo of things too impractical to be taken literally. Jesus wants disciples to *do* and not merely to hear or even admire his words. And he wants this not only for his sake, which he disregards for a moment, but for ours and for the sake of the stability of our lives. Our very lives depend on the seriousness with which we do Jesus' words—where seriously, there rock; where unseriously, there sand.

In the phrase "these my Words," the word "my" is stressed by its position in the Greek sentence. Jesus does not refer us to the words of the law or the Word of God in the prophets; he refers us to "these *my* Words," as if these words of his were the Word of God in the final sense (cf. Gund., 133f). The power of the Word of Jesus is Jesus' real presence in his Word. Jesus is alive; he has risen from the dead, and he lives on in his Word. The Sermon on the Mount cannot be lived apart from a living relationship with its speaker. The Sermon on the Mount is not mere philosophy or ethics; it is the Word of the God who became a man and of the man who rose from the dead, of the living Lord, and therefore this Word needs to be appropriated religiously.

But the sermon does not end on the note of joy for those who build intelligently. It ends to the sound of the crash of those who build thoughtlessly. (Interestingly, Jesus does not contrast good and bad in this parable but thoughtful and foolish. There is a morality in intelligence.) It is important to notice that the story of the Two Houses is about two kinds of Christians, not about Christians and non-Christians. The house that crashes is not the house of pagans or of those who did not hear Jesus' Word at all. The house that crashes is the house of Christians who find Jesus' words important enough to hear but not realistic enough to live. For such Christians the Sermon on the Mount is not practical enough for the demands of modern life, or it is dispensationally limited, or it is too naive for contemporary fast-lane business, or too spiritual for the national democratic struggle, or, perhaps most commonly of all, it is just too hard. For whatever reason, Jesus' Word is only heard; it is not done. And Jesus sees this chemistry of hearing plus non-doing as forming a compound of sand. Nothing very different happens to the house built on sand: it gets hit with the same rain, flood, and wind that hit the rock house. But when the storm is over the house is gone.

"And the fall of it was great." It is interesting that the last word of the Sermon on the Mount is the word most cherished by Jesus' major historical enemies: the word "great" (*megalē*). Greatness, we learn from Jesus, was his enemies' major goal in life, the major reward they sought, and even God was used to make this goal transcendent and impressive. Jesus' war against greatness, a war that filled his teaching career, is one of the most impressive features of Matthew's Gospel. Yet here is the term "great" as the final and emphasized word in Jesus' major sermon. This could suggest that the only finally great thing about greatness-seeking Christians is the greatness of their fall. The quest for greatness rather than for righteousness, for the sensational rather than the simple, for doing the charismatic rather than the ethical, for speaking prophetically rather than compassionately, for being up-to-date at all costs rather than a loyal disciple of Jesus in all cases, is a quest that will end only by crashing greatly. The crash may be postponed as late as the last judgment, and to all outward appearances sand houses may appear to stand. But one day "a *hard* rain's gonna fall."

Jesus prefers the last illustration in his sermon to be an illustration of warning rather than of encouragement. (Bengel, 1:136, gathers from Jesus' concluding illustration this homiletical wisdom: "Thus it is not necessary for every sermon to end with consolation.") *Not* to have been enlisted to do Jesus' words, Jesus warns, is tantamount to having already *done* something else: to have built an entire house (a life) and to have placed it on sand (a philosophy of life). The decision *not* to do Jesus' words, for whatever reason, is already a decision to do a great deal. It is the decision to live by someone else's words, for we all live by someone's words. The decision not to do Jesus' words is the foolish conviction that, all in all, the main thing is to *hear* Jesus' words, to be around enough to do *that*, and that whatever goes beyond this is either fanaticism or naiveté.

"He who keeps the commandment keeps his life; he who despises the word will die" (Prov 19:16). Psalm 119 is the great Old Testament commentary on—and prayerbook for—the Sermon on the Mount. Luther's concluding remarks on the Ten Commandments in his *Large Catechism* apply, *mutatis mutandis*, to Jesus' authorized commentary on the Ten Commandments which is the Sermon on the Mount: "Thus we have in [these words] a summary of divine teaching. They tell us what we are to do to make our lives pleasing to God. They show us the true fountain from which, and the true channel in which, all good works must flow. No deed, no conduct, can be good and pleasing to God, however worthy or precious it be in the eyes of the world, unless it accord with [these words]. Now, let us see what our noted saints find to boast in their holy orders and the great and difficult tasks which they have invented for themselves. . . . My opinion is that we shall have our hands full in keeping these commands—in practicing gentleness, patience, love towards our enemies, chastity, kindness and whatever other virtues they may include. Such works, however, are not important in the eyes of the world; for they are not unusual or showy, they are not restricted to particular times and places, customs and ceremonies, but are common, everyday duties toward our neighbor, with no show about them."

*   *   *

7:28–29 "And when Jesus had finished these words the crowds were amazed by his teaching; because he had been teaching them as if he were a person with authority all by himself and not like their Bible teachers."

What Matthew believes is of greatest importance to point out at the end of Jesus' sermon is the impact of *Jesus himself*. Of main importance is not, first of all, the content of the sermon or its ideas, but who delivered it. This teacher's sense of authority, his sense of office, his conviction that his words determined destinies, his sense that at the final judgment "many will say to *me*" (7:21), his almost apodictically assigning blessings to certain persons in the kingdom of heaven as if he knew, or, in a word, his practically identifying himself as in some kind of kinship with the one he calls his Father in this sermon—these were the impressions that Matthew wanted most deeply left in our consciousness at the end of the sermon. Jesus himself, his authority—today we would call it his deity or dignity—this is what makes the Sermon on the Mount permanently impressive.

It is in fact fascinating to proceed through the sermon and note the personal pronouns in it, and watch them uncover the sermon's most astonishing dimension: that Jesus believed himself to be, as we say, "something else."

Barclay, 1:392, gives us the special prayer composed for the Lambeth Conference of Anglican Bishops of 1948. The prayer seems especially appropriate at the end of the Sermon on the Mount. "Almighty God, give us grace to be not only hearers, but doers of thy holy word, not only to admire, but to obey thy doctrine, not only to profess, but to practice thy religion, not only to love, but to live thy gospel. So grant that what we learn of thy glory we may receive into our hearts, and show forth in our lives: through Jesus Christ our Lord. Amen."

Assurance and Warning, Certainty and Insecurity in Reformation Theology

The Warnings of Jesus at the end of this sermon raise the question—Can a Christian fall from grace?—and so return us to the controversies surrounding this question in the sixteenth-century Reformation. Against the Roman teaching that it was presumptuous to have an assurance of one's salvation at all unless one was given special revelation, the Reformers steadfastly insisted, as Luther put it against Erasmus, that "the Holy Spirit is not a skeptic." The Spirit works a deep assurance in the heart of the believer that he or she really is a child of God, can come to God boldly and confidently in prayer, and can have an assurance of perseverance in faith and salvation until the end. "No one shall snatch them out of my hand" (John 10:28). This doctrine of assurance was one of the most precious fruits of the Reformation. It restored the note of joy to the evangel, the "Good" to the "News." The Reformation doctrine of assurance must not be surrendered.

At the same time, the Lord, his evangelists, and his apostles knew how to warn. In some evangelical churches there is a doctrine of eternal security that teaches "once saved, always saved" in such a way that it is said that if a person has had or has professed a conversion experience nothing can prevent that person from entering the kingdom of heaven. This teaching has worked moral chaos. Scripture knows how to combine the assurances of forgiving grace and the warnings of the loss of grace, and a church obedient to Scripture will learn how to be obedient to both these themes without surrendering the truth of either.

1. Assurance and Certainty

In the momentous contest with Erasmus about human ability, Luther made clear why he preferred the doctrine of the bound will to that of the free will: the bound will puts salvation exclusively in God's hands; the free will puts it in human hands. But if salvation is exclusively in God's hands, then a believer can rest in a deep assurance of salvation. If, however, salvation is partly in the believer's hands, then the believer can never have assurance and is damned to a life of uncertainty. Where is there any gospel, any good news, in a message of uncertain salvation? (Cf. esp. Lu., *BW* [1525], 6:328.)

Calvin's understanding of assurance flows from his understanding of faith. Faith is "a firm and certain knowledge of God's kindness toward us, based on the truth of the freely given promise in Christ, both revealed to our minds and sealed upon our hearts through the Holy Spirit" (*Inst.* [1559/60], III.ii.7; the key terms are "firm and certain" and "sealed upon our hearts"). Thus Calvin takes strong exception to the "half-papists" who mingle assurance with uncertainty on the basis of our unworthiness.

The Roman Council of Trent had clearly ruled, for example, that, if we regard our own weaknesses, we must fear:

> "For even as no pious person ought to doubt of the mercy of God, of the merit of Christ, and of the virtue and efficacy of the sacraments, even so each one, when he regards himself, and his own weakness and indisposition, may have fear and apprehension touching his own grace; seeing that no one can know with a certainty of faith, which cannot be subject to error, that he has obtained the grace of God." (*The Canons and Decrees of the Council of Trent*, sixth session [1547], Chap 9; cf. Canon 15: "If any one saith, that a man, who is born again and justified, is bound of faith to believe that he is assuredly (*certo*) in the number of the predestinate: let him be anathema." In Philip Schaff, *The Creeds of Christendom*, 2:98–99, 113.)

Calvin rejoins that if we are *uncertain* of God's love toward us our blessedness is turned into misery (*Inst.*, III.ii.28). It is indisputable that no one is loved by God apart from Christ: "This is my beloved Son" (Matt 3:17); but in Christ we *are* really loved. What kind of confidence can I have, Calvin asks, if I believe God is favorable to me on the basis of the purity of my life? (*Inst.*, III.ii.38). But the Council of Trent anathematizes it as rash presumption "if anyone saith, that he will for certain, of an absolute and infallible certainty, have that great gift of perseverence unto the end—unless he have learned this by special revelation" (Canon 16). But the Holy Spirit who has been given to us (1 Cor 2:12), Calvin counters, is not a Spirit of uncertainty or ambiguity (*Inst.*, III.ii.39). Romans chapter 8, especially vv 38–39, is for Calvin the great proof of the right of Christian assurance. There, Paul writes, "for I am *persuaded* that [nothing] . . . shall be able to separate us from the love of God in Christ Jesus our Lord." And the truth of Romans 8 was not just a special revelation given to Paul alone, as St. Thomas argued; it was truth written by inspiration to all believers (*Inst.*, III.ii.39–40). *Not* to be sure of grace, the Roman Cochlaeus had said, was a matter of Christian modesty and humility. But Calvin rebutted that not to be sure of grace dishonors the trustworthiness of God's promises. "Glorying" is not contrary to modesty or faith; it is an important part of true faith in the *good* news (*ibid.*)

2. Warning and Insecurity

At the same time, without at all denying the *certitude* of faith, Reformation teaching believes that Christians must take the warnings of Scripture with great seriousness. For example, there is a set of "be not deceived" texts in the literature of the great doctor of the assurance of faith, the apostle Paul, which deserves to be heard. (And this group of texts, it should be remembered, was written to *churches* and to *Christians*.)

> Do you not know that the *unrighteous will not inherit the kingdom of God?* Do not be deceived; neither the immoral, nor idolaters, nor adulterers, nor homosexuals, nor thieves, nor the greedy, nor drunkards, nor revilers, nor robbers will inherit the kingdom of God. And such were some of you. But you were washed, you were sanctified, you were justified in the name of the Lord Jesus Christ and in the Spirit of our God (1 Cor 6:9–11 RSV).
>
> Now the works of the flesh are plain: immorality, impurity, licentiousness, idolatry, sorcery, enmity, strife, jealousy, anger, selfishness, dissension, party spirit, envy, drunkenness, carousing, and the like. *I warn you,* as I warned you before, *that those who do such things shall not inherit the kingdom of God* (Gal 5:19–21 RSV).
>
> Be sure of this, that *no immoral or impure man, or one who is covetous (that is, an idolater), has any inheritance in the kingdom of Christ* and of God. Let no one deceive you with empty words (Eph 5:5–6 RSV).

While Paul teaches that good works do not get us *into* the kingdom, he just as clearly teaches that the unrepentant practice of evil works will bar us *from* the kingdom. God's grace will make men and women good, and in this graced sense it is true to say that only good people will enter the kingdom. "Be not deceived."

Matthew's Gospel is much more pervasively insistent than Paul's that immoral practice removes a person from the way to the kingdom. We see this so consistently on every page of Matthew that it would be redundant to cite texts here. The just studied four Warnings of Matthew 7 make no sense apart from this assumption of danger; they are four separate underlinings of the important moral truth of responsibility. Believers, disciples, men and women called, converted, and used by Jesus Christ need the warnings of Scripture no less than they need the promises. Warnings are not just for other people, for non-Christians, or bad Christians; they are especially for serious Christians, who, almost by definition, are in real spiritual danger of pride or smugness. (See the urgency of the last petition of the Lord's Prayer, for example, and the warning postscript to the Lord's Prayer, 6:13–15.)

Therefore in the Reformation teaching of Luther and the Lutherans especially an abhorrence of any doctrine of carnal "security" parallels and coexists with a doctrine of the blessed assurance of salvation for believers. *Certitudo* (certainty), yes! *Securitas* (smug security), no! There is a difference.

There are three emphatic loci in the Lutheran Confessions where the idea of an immoral, smug, or careless security is vigorously rejected: (1) the foundational *Augsburg Confession*, art. 12; (2) Luther's *Smalcald Articles*, 3:3:42–45; and (3) the *Formula of Concord*, Epitome 4:19; False antithesis 3. Cf. also Luther's many *Catechism* warnings.

Reformed teaching also takes the biblical warnings seriously, but the doctrine, begun by Augustine and reinforced by Calvin, of an unconditional perseverance of the saints, leads directly into the problematic (because careless) once-saved-always-saved teaching that plagues some evangelical churches today. It is interesting to notice the decline, as I see it, from (1) *The Scots Confession* (1560) chap 13 with its vigorous denial of unsanctified Christian life, through (2) the other Reformed confessions to (3) *The Westminster Confession*'s (1647, chap 17) denial of the possibility of ever finally falling from Christian life.

Donald Bloesch's short comparison of Luther and Calvin is provocative. "On the question of certainty of final salvation or eternal security, Luther's position was that our eternal security is with Christ in heaven. We have this eternal security by faith. It is ours so long as we believe and continue to believe. Unlike Calvin, Luther maintained that the Christian could fall from grace into condemnation, and that this was a distinct possibility throughout life" (*Essentials of Evangelical Theology* [1978], 1:236f). But what of Luther's *The Bondage of the Will* above, p. 292?

The best way to end this review of Reformation teaching on assurance and warning is to take the beautiful thirteenth chapter of the *Scots Confession* (1560) and to hear in full what we heard a moment before in part: its witness to the dialectical truth of the *certain* work of the Holy Spirit in believers, giving deep assurance, and at the same time the truth of "that continual battle" of believers with the flesh and so our need of *warnings*. I believe it is possible, indeed I believe it is necessary, for Christians to live with two layers of consciousness: the deeper layer of the *assurance* of a complete salvation, independent of the work of our wills and as firm and sure as the work of Christ, the witness of the Spirit, and the will of God; and an upper layer of full *responsibility* for the conduct of our Christian lives, alive every day to the warnings in God's Word addressed precisely to us as believers—"Work out your own salvation with fear and trembling [the upper layer of responsibility]; for God is at work in you, both to will and to work for his good pleasure [the deeper layer of assurance]" (Phil 2:12–13):

The cause of good works, we confess, is not our free will, but the Spirit of the Lord Jesus, who dwells in our hearts by true faith, [and] brings forth such works as God has prepared for us to walk in. For we most boldly affirm that it is blasphemy to say that Christ abides in the hearts of those in whom is no spirit of sanctification. Therefore we do not hesitate to affirm that murderers, oppressors, cruel persecutors, adulterers, filthy persons, idolators, drunkards, thieves, and all workers of iniquity, have neither true faith nor anything of the Spirit of the Lord Jesus, *so long as they obstinately continue in wickedness.* For as soon as the Spirit of the Lord Jesus, whom God's chosen children receive by true faith, takes possession of the heart of any man, so soon does he regenerate and renew him, so that he begins to hate what before he loved, and to love what he hated before. Thence comes *that continual battle* which is between the flesh and the Spirit in God's children, while the flesh and the natural man, being corrupt, lust for things pleasant and delightful to themselves, are envious in adversity and proud in prosperity, and every moment prone and ready to offend the majesty of God. *But the Spirit of God,* who bears witness to our spirit that we are the sons of God, *makes us resist* filthy pleasures and groan in God's presence for deliverance from this bondage of corruption, and finally to triumph over sin so that it does not reign in our mortal bodies. Other men do not share this conflict since they do not have God's Spirit, but they readily follow and obey sin and feel no regrets, since they act as the devil and their corrupt nature urge. *But the sons of God fight against sin;* sob and mourn when they find themselves tempted to do evil; *and, if they fall, rise again* with earnest and unfeigned repentance. They do these things, not by their own power, but by the power of the Lord Jesus, apart from whom they can do nothing (*Scots Confession,* chap 13 emphases added).

A Summary of the Sermon on the Mount: The Relation of Faith and Works

It is precisely *doing* that prompts the final question of the Sermon on the Mount. The will of God the Father as taught us by Jesus is a will not merely to be heard or even admired, celebrated, or preached; it is a will to be done. "Thy will be *done.*" It has been pointed out by modern New Testament scholarship that the ethic of Jesus in the Sermon on the Mount is not adequately described as an ethic of disposition or of only inner attitude. Everywhere in this sermon we learn that Jesus wants the *fruit* of good disposition, the *deed* of good inward attitude, and not just these inward dispositions or attitudes themselves. Reading the Sermon on the Mount to see how often Jesus wants doing is an educational experience.

To the Christian who comes to the Sermon on the Mount from the literature of Paul there is a difficulty with this emphasis on doing. For Paul's theology of grace has shaken the foundations of all confidence in deeds (or "doings"), even in the best of deeds, namely, the deeds done in obedience to God's law, called "the works of the law" (*erga nomou*). Paul classically contrasts trust in "doing" and trust in Jesus Christ and in *His* doing, for example, in the great third chapter of Galatians. Paul's gospel of faith alone *apart from* doing, has more than once reformed and blessed the church and seems to be what the Christian gospel at its core is all about. What then are we to do with the Sermon on the Mount that asks us above all to *do* the good works of the commands of Jesus if we wish to be safe?

Luther and other Reformers have consistently urged us to hear Jesus' Word here in all its rugged force and to acknowledge this Word as the true law of God that, more than anything else, condemns us and shows us our need for a Savior. Medieval Catholicism often saw here a call to those who willed to be perfect—to the "religious"—and not necessarily a Word for *all* Christians. Christians in the radical tradition, such as Tolstoy, have seen here the one Word of God to be literally done by all who truly call themselves Christians—from eschewing every state oath and sworn contract to a giving up of all military force. There is something to be said for each of these views, but Christians cannot be left hanging between drastically opposed options. It is refreshing occasionally to meet a serious student of Scripture (e.g., Windisch) who believes that Paul and Matthew here simply collide and that at some points one or the other will have to yield. One may be doing theological gymnastics when one tries to reconcile Paul's contra-doing with this sermon's pro-doing. But let me essay the possible.

The commands of Jesus cannot be done without a relation of faith to Jesus' Father. Matthew fortifies this conviction by the arrangement of the Sermon on the Mount. The Beatitudes bless littleness before God (the meek and starving for righteousness) before and en route to blessing helpfulness to people (the merciful, the pure in heart, and the peacemakers). Moreover, the Beatitudes, which can be interpreted as Jesus' gifts of grace, precede the commands and enable them. Then the commands themselves are so hard, so high, so total that they cannot be read or kept without a swift flight to the Lord of the Beatitudes for mercy and help. No one who has tried to keep Jesus' demands can, I think, deny this flight. Then the commands are followed and backed up by the sixth chapter's one long call to faith. (Faith is especially the point of the gift of the Lord's Prayer at the heart of Matt 6.)

This is all to say that the commands to *do* in the Sermon on the Mount are preceded (in the Beatitudes) and followed (in the Lord's Prayer) by gifts. The fifth chapter's introductory Beatitudes and You Ares and the sixth chapter's faith and prayer are gifts and then commands to be believers in God. I do not see how a single line of the sermon can be read without feeling summoned to one's knees before God—to what Paul calls faith. And yet in this sermon the summons to our knees is never an end in itself; the calisthenic of this sermon is to move repeatedly from kneeling to standing. The direction of the Sermon on the Mount is *to* the deed—but *through* God; to the neighbor through the Father. This is to say that the direction of the Sermon on the Mount is to love through faith.

Where Paul carefully seeks to separate faith from deeds in order to give all the glory to God's free mercy for human salvation, Matthew's Jesus seeks to call us to such a quality of life that we will be driven to faith in God. The dynamics are different but complementary. The height of the deeds to which Jesus calls us in this sermon can only be reached by people who walk on their knees. Only the first four Beatitudes can lead us to the last four, only the little people can be big, only faith acquires love.

The key fact of the sermon is Jesus himself, as indicated throughout by the little, unobtrusive, omnipresent personal pronouns. It is the disciples' relation to *him* that makes possible the doing of fruitful living. Fruit is "done," but it is not done without organic rootage in a tree (that John calls a vine), and this fruit-bearing tree and vine in Matthew's Gospel is Jesus' Word. Only by discipleship to Jesus' Word can fruit be *done;* only by prayer to Jesus' Father can the Father's will be done. "Command what you will, then *give* what you command." Augustine's great formula, applies to the whole Sermon on the Mount.

I do not believe that the Sermon on the Mount and Paul can be made to fit each other flush. Paul's explicit emphasis on faith and his unmistakable contrast of faith and works differ from Matthew's more implicit call to faith and more explicit call to deeds. But in a certain sense the antispectacular quality—may I even say, the believing quality—of the demand of Matthew's Jesus comes very close to the Pauline life of faith. Neither Paul nor this sermon admire sensationalism or self-glorying. Both want us to look only to God for rewards. Do they meet here?

Davies, 434–35: "What we can be certain of is this: that Jesus displayed the utmost *agapē* to 'the Lost' [the Beatitudes] and demanded the utmost *agapē* of his own [the commands]. . . . Nowhere in the New Testament is the Gospel set forth without moral demand, and nowhere is morality understood apart from the Gospel." The words of the Sermon on the Mount face us with Jesus Christ himself, Davies concludes, and "[these words] are themselves kerygmatic. But emphasis on the act and person of Christ in life, death, and resurrection, central and essential though it be, is never wholly free from the danger of abstraction from life. The meaning of the kerygma for life has to become concrete. And it is the penetrating precepts of Jesus as they encounter us in the Sermon on the Mount, and elsewhere, that are the astringent protection against any interpretation of that person, life, death and resurrection in other than moral terms."

Chapters Eight and Nine
The Touching Messiah: The Ten Miracles
Introduction to the Doctrine of Salvation

Matthew has taken miracles scattered throughout Mark and with his systematic gifts placed them here in an orderly series in much the same way that in the great Sermon he gave us an ordered memorandum of Jesus' scattered ethical teaching.

The doctrine that is highlighted in the next two chapters is the doctrine of salvation—soteriology—or in simpler terms, the doctrine of God's help. Here we learn how and whom God helps. In chapter 8 Jesus not only expects much of us, which is Matthew's emphasis (chaps 5–7); but Jesus now also gives much of himself to us in our need. Here, certainly, Matthew unites with the entire apostolic witness. Matthew also is a *gospel.*

In the Sermon on the Mount we have the commanding Jesus who especially desires love; in the Ten Miracles (chaps 8–9) we have the healing Jesus who especially desires faith—and in both places love and faith are made free of all limitations (e.g., love of even enemies in the Sermon, and faith saves even the most despised in the Miracles, Schl., *Der,* 266–68). W. D. Davies says that Matthew 8–9's teaching "expresses the infinite succour available in [Jesus'] deeds, just as [Matthew] 5:1–7:28 expresses his infinite demand"; in addition, while the Sermon on the Mount expresses Jesus' authority in word, chaps 8–9 express Jesus' authority in action (Davies, 90; Bonnard, 122, too, sees Jesus' *authority* as the bond uniting the two bodies of material; on the unity of Matt 5–7, 8–9 see Streck., 175f).

The structure of chaps 8–9 is actually that of three sets of three miracles (cf. Allen, xvif; Green, 97; Beare, 201) with discipleship stories serving as dividing buffers in between (8:18–22; 9:9–17). The Ten Miracles division is catechetical, for there are in fact ten *particular* miracles (Davies, *SM,* 18; Streck., 39; Gund., 137f). The richest source for the study of Matthew's miracles is the dissertation of Heinz Joachim Held, "Matthew as Interpreter of the Miracle Stories," in Bornkamm, Barth, and Held, *Tradition and Interpretation in Matthew* (abbreviated TIM), "The New Testament Library," trans. Percy Scott; Philadelphia: Westminster, 1963, pp. 165–299.

———————

Chapter Eight
The Five Miracles of Grace
The Doctrine of Grace

I. THE LEPER (8:1–4)

"When Jesus came down from the mountain a big crowd of people followed him. And look, a leper came up to him, bowed down in front of him, and said, 'Lord, if you want to, you can make me clean.' And Jesus reached out his hand and touched him and said, 'I want to; be clean!' And immediately he was cleansed from his leprosy. Then Jesus said to him, 'Now you be sure not to tell anyone about this; but go show yourself to the priest, and bring the gift that Moses commanded so that you can be a testimony to them.'"

Lepers were considered unclean in the community and before God; they were people under a curse (Lev 13–14). They were commanded to wear disheveled hair and clothes, to cover their lower lip when near people, and cry "unclean, unclean" in order to keep the community from spiritual pollution by contact with them. Of all persons in Israel they were the most ostracized. For as long as they retained the disease they lived outside the camp, away from others (Lev 13:45–46). Lepers were excluded from all walled cities in Israel and so, of course, were absolutely excluded from the holy city and its temple of worship. Rabbis kept six feet between themselves and lepers. Lepers were the classic outsiders. (The leprosy of the Bible is not always the leprosy—Hansen's Disease—of contemporary medical science; it is some kind of skin disease. See the translation of TEV and Gund., 139. For helpful examples of behavior toward lepers see Barc., 1:296–98.)

The fact that this leper approached Jesus at all is remarkable, given the traditional inhibitions and the strictures of Scripture (cf. the more discreet lepers who "stood at a distance" in Luke 17:21). It is significant that Matthew places this particularly marginal person at the *head* of his series of miracles. (In Mark this miracle happened after two other miracle stories.) Matthew is trying to say something.

8:2 The leper's remark has been described as a perfect definition of faith from two sides: "Lord, [1] if you want to, [2] you can make me clean." First, "if you want to." Faith does not demand help as a right; it is modest and respectful, and, while bold enough (the simple fact of the leper's approaching Jesus indicates this), faith still keeps its place of spiritual distance and bows before the sovereign pleasure of the one it calls Lord. All good faith has respect in it (4:7). Super-Christians have sometimes attempted to do away with Christians even praying "if it is thy will" in requests for healing since (it is said) "it is always God's will to heal" ("Name it, claim it"). Such teaching is tactless.

Second, "you can." Though modest, faith is sure that if it is the will of the Lord he can meet the petitioner's need. This fine combination of modesty ("if you want to") and confidence ("you can") is true faith. Faith does not honestly know if the

Lord in every case intends to heal. (We finally die, faith or not.) This honest agnosticism is particularly alive in Christians since the Ascension. Paul's *unhealed* thorn in the flesh had its purposes (2 Cor 12). We cannot presume to order God to heel or to heal.

But the heart of faith is not its tact, though that is its indispensable posture or form. The heart of faith is confidence—"you can." No "you might be able to" mars the leper's petition. Indeed, on closer inspection the leper's remark is not a petition, but an affirmation: "Lord [a religious word in Matthew's Gospel], if you want to, you can make me clean."

It is surprising that the leper did not *ask* to be made clean, which would, of course, have been perfectly in order (7:7 "Ask"). A confidence that is even deeper than a question marks this man's feeling about Jesus: "If you want to, you can." We learn from this first specific healing in the Gospel that faith is not general belief in God; it is particular trust in Jesus and in his ability to help deeply. In Matthew, faith in God is faith in Jesus (Schl., *Der*, 271), "God with us."

Is there anything else in this "if you want to"? Can one hear in it a history of disappointments? "A lot of people haven't wanted to help me; I hope you're not one of them." Mark's best reading at this point—"then Jesus, filled with *anger*, reached out his hand, . . ." (Mark 1:41, the more difficult reading) would support an interpretation of bitterness. In any case, as we learn when we put the five miracles of this chapter end to end it is not the worthiness of the approach or of the petitioner that determines the measure of help; it is the worthiness of the Lord who is approached and petitioned. Whether the leper's sentence is model or morbid, the leper did approach Jesus and that is all that is required in this chapter for help.

Chrysostom, 25:2:172, admires the leper's "genuine faith and right opinion about [Jesus]. For neither did he say, 'If Thou request it of God,' nor, 'If Thou pray,' but, 'If Thou wilt, Thou canst make me clean.' Nor did he [even] say, 'Lord, cleanse me,' but leaves all to Him." Bengel, 1:137: "Faith says, 'if Thou wilt,' not, 'if Thou canst'; Mark 9:22." This modesty does not contradict the certainty of faith, as Calvin shows, 1:244. Bengel also wonders if the leper conceived his faith from Jesus' just preceding Sermon on the Mount ("faith comes from hearing," Rom 10:17), though Jerome, 1:152, doubts that the leper would have been allowed to be there. Historical-critical interpretation, aware of the *literary* character of the Gospel, no longer asks such questions or queries such connections. Theological interpretation can ask: Did Matthew have doctrinal reasons for placing the Cleansing of the Leper story immediately after the convicting Sermon on the Mount? We feel very unclean after the Sermon.

8:3 "And Jesus reached out his hand and touched him and said, 'I want to; be clean!'" If Jesus had stepped back ten paces and had only *spoken* his healing, this would be a different miracle. (When Elisha healed the leper Naaman [2 Kings 5:10–14] he did not come near him—to Naaman's well-known chagrin.) Leprosy ("a dreaded skin disease" TEV) was a frightening thing in Jesus' time, and people did not want to get near it, both for hygienic and spiritual reasons. (Medically we now know that this fear was ungrounded. Leprosy is not highly contagious. It is important, especially in certain areas of the world, to say this clearly in order to banish the ancient stigma against persons with skin diseases. Lohmeyer, 155, points out that a significant historical side-effect of this story has been that it has made Christianity the only world religion that has everywhere accepted lepers who, otherwise, have been consistently rejected from society's fellowship.)

The fact that Jesus in his milieu "reached out with his hand and *touched* the man" says volumes. The whole gospel is in that grasp. This is the easiest of all the miracles to understand. Here is a man who since first becoming ill has never been touched. Few acts would affect this constantly shunned leper like *this* man's touching him. And in that touch we have God's identifying love. It is the *gospel* that God through his Son Jesus *touches* us, enters even physically into our lives, and makes us his. (There are many persons in contemporary life who feel deprived of touch; this story wishes to minister this touch to them.) Cf. Mother Teresa.

Jesus' touching this man even before Jesus speaks to him teaches the church something of Christian work, too. Jesus did not heal the man six feet away or by Word alone. Only that talking is credible that is preceded and accompanied by a risky, genuinely meant, and serious touching. A believable ministry of the Word will always be accompanied by a compassionate touching ministry of the deed, as Christian mission at its best has always known. When Jesus reached out and grabbed the leper he gave his evangelistic method. Believable evangelists communicate their love by contact and identification with those to whom they come.

Jesus' wilfully touching a leper also contravened the law (Lev 5:3) and made Jesus technically unclean (Str.-B., 1:474 and the Excursus there). But Jesus goes beyond the law and fulfills the law's intention of wholeness in his healings in Matt 8–9 just as he went beyond the law and fulfilled its intentions of radical obedience in his teachings in Matt 5–7 ("But I say to you"). Thus Jesus did not so much contradict the law of God as he consummated it (Gund., 140; cf. McN., 102).

It is easy to believe that Jesus' touch alone healed the man. But Jesus says words, too, in order to interpret his touch. Deeds often need clarification. The deed without the word is unclear; the word without the deed is unimpressive. So Jesus says the words the man most needed to hear. And those words, supported as they are by Jesus' grip, carry conviction: "I *want* to, be clean." The main thing the leper needed to know was that Jesus *wanted* to cleanse him ("if you *want* to"); once that was known, Jesus' ability was unquestioned ("you can").

Jesus' miracles, often effected or consummated by his Word, are extensions of his authority-laden Sermon on the Mount "But I say to you" (Schl., *Der*, 269; Schn., 107; cf. Chrys., 25:2:173). "As Jesus taught by his own authority, 'not as the scribes' (7:29), so he does not even ascribe the miracle to God his Father, but performs it by his own authority: 'I will, be cleansed'" (Gund., 139).

8:3c "And immediately he was cleansed from his leprosy" (8:3c). The church learns from this story that there is no limit to either Jesus' ability or his will. Since the resurrection we must admit that Jesus has not always wanted to heal *now*—how else can we explain the fact that faith does not always experience healing? (It is completely unfair to teach, as some who call themselves healers do, that the only reason healing does not occur is that faith is insufficient. "It is not God's fault, He wants to heal. It must be your fault." Paul's 2 Corinthians 12 experience is a classic rebuttal.) There are many *believers* who are sick. Suffering is a mystery whose bitterness is not taken away by Jesus' "why" on the cross, but it is comforting to know that Jesus, too, asked why.

8:4 "And Jesus told him, 'Now you be sure not to tell *anyone* about this; but go show yourself to the priest, and bring the gift that Moses commanded so that you can be a testimony to them.'" The whole healing story comes to this surprising conclusion. We learn Jesus' modesty: He is not interested in attaching the healed leper to himself as a walking advertisement. It is not the time for this kind of witness. Once again we learn tact in this story, this time from Jesus' sensitivity to times and seasons. There is a time and a place for the several types of testimony, and the disciple is to be always on the alert to ask, "Is this a time for spoken or for acted witness?" In this particular instance the healed man is specifically counseled to postpone spoken witness and to do the traditional thing—obey Moses' Old Testament command about bringing a gift to a priest when one has experienced a cleansing of leprosy. This simple act of *traditional,* submissive, scriptural obedience will perform a witness to several important realities: (1) that Jesus came not to destroy the law but to fulfill it, in deed as well as in Word (cf. Matt 5:17–20); (2) that Jesus' work as well as his Word is the fulfillment of the Old Testament; (3) and that Jesus is the Christ. Jesus will not storm Israel with his messianic claim; he will knock quietly at its door, leper by leper, little by little.

Jesus' desire here to express his fidelity toward the law is emphasized by most contemporary commentators, e.g., Allen, 75f; McN., 102f; Trill., 127–29; Caird, 92; Schw., 211; Hill, 156f. Thus Matt 8:4 plays the role in the miracles that Matt 5:17–20 played in the teachings. Jerome, 1:154, nicely summarized the three main interpretations of the intention of this last (go to the priest) verse in the leper story: humility, to bring the priests to faith or rejection, and to show respect for the law.

II. THE CENTURION (8:5–13)

"And when Jesus came into Capernaum a centurion came up to Jesus, and he begged him, 'Lord, my servant is lying in my house paralyzed and is in terrible pain.' And Jesus said to him, 'I am coming to heal him.' And the centurion said to him, 'Lord, I am not worthy for you to come under my roof; just say the word and my servant will be healed. Because I know what it is like to live under orders, and I, too, have soldiers under me: when I say to one, "Go!," he goes, and when I say, "Come!," he comes, and if I tell one of my servants, "Do this," he does it.' When Jesus heard this he was very impressed, and he said to the people who were following him, 'Amen, I want to tell you something: I have found absolutely no one who has faith like this in all Israel. And I tell you, many people will come from east and west and sit at the banquet with Abraham and Isaac and Jacob in the kingdom of heaven. But the sons of the kingdom will be thrown out of that banquet into the outer darkness, and there will be real wailing and gnashing of teeth out there.' Then Jesus said to the centurion, 'You may go home now; everything has happened just as you believed it would.' And his servant was healed that very hour."

8:5 The first person Jesus healed was a leper, the archetype of the outsider, the person barred from participation in Israel's worship and social life. The second person he encounters in Matthew's series was provisionally barred from Israel's inner life: he was a gentile (more probably a Syrian than a Roman). Lepers could not enter

Jerusalem at all. Gentiles could, but they could go no farther than the outermost Court of Gentiles in the temple. Male gentiles, too, were considered unclean unless they became proselytes, were circumcised, and ritually washed. Only a leper was more unclean than a gentile. Consequently, Jesus' almost precipitate willingness to go to this seeking gentile's home would have struck serious people of God as careless.

8:6 It is noteworthy that the centurion, like the leper, does not in fact petition—he simply states a fact. Simply telling Jesus facts about our lives sets his saving work in motion. "Lord, if you want to, you can make me clean," confides the leper; and "Lord, my servant is . . . in terrible pain," reports the centurion. The sense of both expressions, where neither petitioner really *asks*—each simply *says* something—strikes one as characteristic of faith in the Gospels. Faith mainly *talks* to its Lord; it often hardly knows what to ask or how to ask it. Sometimes all we need to do is state the problem: the how and the what of help are the Lord's business. "Lord, my servant is in terrible pain." That's enough.

8:7 There is a debate among interpreters whether Jesus' response to the centurion should be translated as an affirmation, "I [myself] am coming to heal him," or as a question, "Do you want *me* to come and heal him?" Either is grammatically possible. The affirmative interpretation fits the immediate context of Jesus' unquestionably touching the leper; the question fits the later context of Jesus' hesitation to enter any kind of gentile mission yet (chapter 10's mission and chapter 15's Syrophoenician woman). I prefer yielding to the immediate and surrounding context of the story—the context of the chapter's unconditioned grace—and so to see Jesus' *affirmation*, his eagerness to help.

Those who see Jesus' remark as a question include Kl., 74; Bult., 38; Lohm., 155f (with lists of others); Stend., 781; Trill., 105; Held, 195; Goulder, 160 n. 19; Green, 99. Those who see an affirmation: Schl., *Der*, 247f; Grund., 251–52; Gund., 142f; and Beare, 207 who, in my opinion, correctly calls the question interpretation "oversubtle."

No sooner is Jesus approached by this second representative of all that is unclean to Israel than Jesus is halfway there—"I am coming to heal him." The word "I" is emphasized in the Greek sentence as if to say, "I don't know what the response of others may have been to your request, but *I* want to come." Once again we see a Jesus extremely eager to help—and this is the picture from this chapter that the church is to have burned into its memory about the God whom Jesus represents (Emmanuel, the God who is with us) and who, in mystery, Jesus is. The Lord we worship is almost inordinately ready to meet needs. "You just call on my name, I'll come running; you've got a friend."

Cf. The Second Helvetic Confession, 25:5:234, with my emphasis, on "The Visitation of the Sick": "Since men are never exposed to more grievous temptations than when they are harassed by infirmities . . . , therefore let [the pastors of the churches] visit them *soon*, and let them be called in good time by the sick." This wisdom applies to all Christian friendship. "He gives twice who gives quickly."

8:8 But even the centurion finds the Lord impetuous. He doesn't feel at all worthy of the Lord's coming. (Thus in fact by owning himself unworthy for Christ to enter his house, he became worthy for Christ to enter his heart, Aug., *Serm.*, 12(62):1:298; similarly, Chrys., 26:4:179.) This gentile was sensitive to the scruples of the people of God, and he did not wish to offend. He had not meant to imply that Jesus would have to break his people's legislation in order to heal his servant, and he probably intended to go on to explain what he meant. But the Lord interrupted him and was practically en route before the centurion could explain. In the two opening miracles Jesus has moved almost instantly across cultic and national barriers to help. We are reminded of the first two Beatitudes and their blessing the impoverished and the grief-stricken—other outsiders.

8:8b The key phrase of the story then follows. In Greek the phrase is in four short words: *alla monon eipe logō* which can crudely but precisely be translated "just only say (a) word." The confidence of the centurion in Jesus is a deep confidence. Jesus does not even have to be present with the sick man! He needs "just only" to say a word and the problem will be solved.

This is the first long-distance healing in the Gospel accounts. And it is occasioned by the complete confidence in Jesus of a *gentile* centurion. But something else is important. The servant is healed by Jesus via the *centurion's* faith, not the sick man's. This is an important text on intercessory prayer. We can believe for others. Jesus does not ask the centurion, "Does your *servant* believe in me like you do?" or "Has he confessed his sin?" or something similar. On the basis of the faith of the centurion, Jesus heals the sickness of the servant. The moral is that on the basis of one person's faith another person can be deeply helped—the hope of all intercessory prayer. And while it is true that the ultimate issue of faith in Jesus Christ is entirely personal and cannot be proxy, and while it is true that each individual is asked to place his or her own personal faith in this Lord, nevertheless it is also true that meanwhile other people can be deeply helped by the faith of friends who pray. It is one purpose of this particular story to teach the important doctrine of substitutionary faith or intercessory prayer. (This incident is not isolated; there are several third-party healings in the Gospels: cf. the following Matthean incidents and their parallels in the other Gospels: 8:16; 9:2, 18–19, 32–33; 14:35–36; 15:21–28, 30; 17:14–20; in the Hebrew Scriptures, out of many possible examples, see 2 Chr 30:9, 20.) When future disciples see what happens in this story, even across distances—that a ritually unclean gentile gets healing for his servant—they will be moved to pray more often for others.

8:10 Jesus is impressed with the man's faith in his Word, and he praises him. ("Our Lord praises His friends warmly where there is opportunity: 11:7; 15:28; 25:35; 26:10; Luke 7:44; 21:3," Beng., 1:139.) A pagan believes that Jesus' mere Word, all alone (*alla monon*), can heal his servant even at a distance; this is remarkable faith in anyone, but especially remarkable in a man with so little background. Jesus has to admit that he had never yet found an instance of faith in all of spiritually cultivated and scripturally instructed Israel to compare with the faith of this outsider.

Chrysostom, 26:2:177, admires the centurion's right doctrine concerning *Christ*, "for neither did [the centurion] say, 'entreat,' nor . . . 'pray . . . ,' but 'command only.'" Calvin, 1:248, admires the centurion's humility in placing Jesus, "a man from a conquered, client race, so far above himself." Verse 9's "I also" probably means "I also am the agent of another as you are of God" as well as "I have soldiers under me, as thou hast spiritual powers, healing angels, or disease and death" under thee (DeWette in Beng., 1:139, and much earlier Chrys., 26:4:179). Verse 10 has the New Testament's first explicit mention of faith. "Of all the virtues of those who come to the Lord, He is wont to praise faith alone: 15:28; Luke 7:50," Beng., 1:140. Jesus, unlike apostles and prophets, does not reject faith placed in *him;* contrast Acts 3:12; 14:15; Rev 19:10; indeed, Jesus' mission is to elicit faith in himself, which, mysteriously, he does not see as compromising faith in God alone. Cf. Schn., 109; Schw., 214.

Wherever this kind of faith in Jesus' simple Word begins to occur regularly across an entire culture, reformation happens. Gerhard Ebeling, in his lectures to all faculties at the University of Zurich, collected in the valuable book entitled *Luther,* asked, "Why did Luther's Reformation, in contrast to all prior attempts at reformation, become a reformation in deed and not just in words?" And Ebeling's provocative answer is, "Luther's Reformation became a reformation in deed and not just in words because Luther trusted only in the Word and not at all in deeds" (*Luther: Einführung in sein Denken* (Tübingen: J.C.B. Mohr [Paul Siebeck], 1964), p. 60). Luther frequently had to rebuke the zealous and fanatical Karlstadt and others in the early Reformation and to tell the newly reforming church to cease storming monasteries and unreformed churches in the attempt by the good works of iconoclasm and zeal to bring about a quicker, more thorough Reformation. Luther insisted that good sermons alone would do it—all alone. "Only say the Word." Luther's breathtaking confidence in the power of the purely preached Word of the gospel through the faithful exposition of Scripture is a confidence that grips the Lord and his miraculous competence. We, like Karlstadt, have far too much confidence in our own zeal and works. Our time, like the sixteenth century, deeply needs reformation. Jesus' Word all alone and simple confidence in it brings reformation and God-pleasing good works.

8:11–12 After praising the centurion's faith, Jesus predicts that many people will come from east and west, which means from the international communities beyond Israel, and (literally) "lie down at table," which means be present at the big festal banquet of the kingdom (ordinary meals were eaten sitting up, extraordinary meals reclining). (The centurion came seeking healing; he got heaven. Chrys., 26:5:180; Gund., 145.) Many from east and west will feast with Abraham, Isaac, and Jacob in the kingdom of heaven, while many who are *supposed* to be at the party, some of the already invited children of the kingdom, are going to be thrown into the dark, where there will be lots of regrets. Jesus' meaning, expressed often elsewhere, is that many who think they are in are going to be surprised to be out; and many who are thought to be out are going to be in. (Augustine: "Many sheep are outside, . . . many wolves within." *Tract. in Jn.,* 45:12:254.)

The church today should hear this story, as it should hear every story directed to those who believed then, as directed to us in the church. She should not hear in it even the slightest anti-Judaistic teaching. After all Jesus was a Jew; Matthew probably was; all the original disciples were. What Jesus is attacking here is that possessiveness, that sense of exclusiveness which disfigures every religious community too sure of itself. The church should feel herself questioned when she reads this story, and we should ask if we really believe, or if we merely belong or think we belong.

"But the sons of the kingdom will be thrown . . . into the outer darkness" (8:12a). "The very ambivalence of 'the sons of the kingdom,' which may refer either to Israel or to the church, helps make the present statement precursive of the warnings to the church" (Gund., 146; cf. Grund., 253f). Earliest Christianity applied the threats of hell to *herself* (5:22; cf. 13:42, 50; 22:13; 24:51; 25:30), for she too was concerned lest the salvation entrusted to her be eternally lost (Schn., 110f).

Jesus' strong words about "the outer darkness" remind us again that no one speaks as frequently or as pointedly of what the church has come to call "hell" as Jesus himself. The church is unwise to speak with confidence of the temperature or topography of hell. She is equally unwise to say that hell (and heaven) are "not places but conditions." The eagerness to say this flows as much from a skepticism about there being any ultimate judgment at all as it does from an attempt to be pastoral and contemporary.

The much more important matter to see here is that whatever or wherever hell is, Jesus warned us and warns us continually of something ultimate to avoid. There is *some* reality signified by the words "outer darkness," "Gehenna," and "Hades," a reality that the church is advised to take seriously. Jesus is telling the church that there is an awful reality, call it what we will, into which a life without good faith will be cast. Life is morally—and mortally—serious. There is an issue to the affairs of life that will be worse than death. Jesus feels that he serves us by warning us of it. "For those whom He was threatening to cast out, He threatened not in order to cast them *out,* but in order that through such fear, He might draw them *into* [himself] by His words" (Chrys., 26:6:181; emphasis added). True love warns.

8:12b The expression "wailing and gnashing of teeth" points to deep regret and self-recrimination for what was ignored and missed (Schl., *Der*, 280). ("Self-love, indulged on earth, will then be transformed into self-hate," Beng., 1:141.) "We had it in our grasp, and we let it go!" The biblical expression is meant to move people to ask, "What do we have within our grasp that we might deeply regret having ignored or taken for granted?" The church therefore will present faith in Jesus as the Great Opportunity. ("How shall we escape if we neglect such a great salvation?" Heb 2:3.) Jesus intends to be taken seriously. If wooing will not work he will try warning.

Jerome, 1:158, sees the resurrection of the *body* intimated by the weeping of eye and gnashing of teeth; this is over-interpretation. "Gnashing of teeth" is not a representation of bodily agony but of emotional (Schl., *Der*, 280).

It is important to underline the fact that all of Jesus' warnings about hell occur in messages to people who believed *themselves* heirs of the kingdom. Jesus did not preach hell to pagans; he preached it to those who thought themselves believers. Hell is not a doctrine used to frighten unbelievers, it is a doctrine used to warn those who think themselves believers.

"Gnashing of teeth," e.g., is a formula used five times in Matthew and is always used of those who have been graced with God's gifts, but in vain (Schl., *Der*, 280; cf. Allen, 78). Interestingly, Matthew has no antithetical formula for describing the ecstasy of the elect; this is due not to Matthew's morbidity (Beare, 149), but to his sobriety.

The absence of the urgency and warning dimension in the preaching of the main-line churches indicates a loss of substance, a loss of a sense of the gravity of the gospel. It is impossible to preach convincingly of the kingdom of heaven where there is no real conviction of the reality of hell; it is hard to persuade that our message conveys ultimate matters if we are not sure that it makes any final difference.

8:13 "And Jesus said to the centurion, 'You may go home now; everything has happened just as you *believed* it would.' And his servant was healed that very hour." The final point of the story, like the initial one, is that Jesus honors *faith*. It is surprising that Jesus does not say "my Word has made you whole," or "everything has happened that you asked *me* about," since the source of the servant's healing *was* Jesus' Word. The centurion's faith was, as theology rightly says, the channel through which the Lord's healing came pouring. But isn't the fountain more important than the channel, the source than the means? Yet Jesus wants to honor the faith that joins the source, the means that attaches to the end, the confidence that is placed in him. Though Jesus will not be physically present with the centurion after this event, the centurion is to know through Jesus' parting words to him that whenever the centurion has confidence in Jesus again he has Jesus himself with him (and in him, God). Trust *in* the Lord *is* the Lord with us. Faith is a portable Christ-carrier.

For studies of Gospel faith see Bult., 219, his article with Weiser in TDNT 6:174–228, and especially Held, 241–43. The classic discussion is in Schlatter, *Der Glaube im Neuen Testament* (4th ed.; Stuttgart: Calwer, 1927), esp. 94–176.

We do not believe as we should, and this is the deep source of our problem as Christians. There is no art or technique or series of steps on how better to believe. Jesus in this Gospel and, in fact, consistently in all the Gospels, actually downplays the need for great quantities of faith—faith like a grain of mustard seed will do, and by such faith Jesus will even do quantitatively great things such as move mountains (cf. 17:20, and quite especially, Luke 17:5–6). Faith is what we need most of all, since it always encounters an eager Lord.

III. PETER'S MOTHER-IN-LAW AND SEQUEL (8:14–17)

A. The Mother-in-law (8:14–15)

"And when Jesus came into the house of Peter he saw Peter's mother-in-law lying there and burning up with a fever. He touched her hand and the fever left her, and she was raised and put herself at his service."

This is the third outsider. Jewish women were not allowed as far inside the temple as Jewish men. Lepers could not get into the temple at all. Centurions and gentiles could only get into the outermost Court of Gentiles. Then came, in order, the Court of Women, the Holy Place (for Jewish males only), and the Holy of Holies where only one Jewish male, the high priest, could enter one time in the year. Women in Israel were cultically half-caste. Even in synagogues women were regularly placed behind screens to the rear, as in modern Muslim mosques. One of the Eighteen Prayers prayed by the pious Israelite male each day was a prayer of thanks that he had not been born a woman.

On the place of women in the ancient and biblical worlds see the article *gunē* by Oepke in TDNT, 1:776–89; Rosemary Radford Ruether (ed.), *Religion and Sexism* (N.Y.: Simon and Schuster, 1974); classically, on the modern American woman, Betty Friedan, *The Feminine Mystique* (N.Y.: Norton, 1963); evangelically, Letha Scanzoni and Nancy Hardesty, *All We're Meant To Be: A Biblical Approach to Women's Liberation* (Waco, Tex.: Word, 1974). The laws of the old people of God forbad the touching of a woman's hand (Str.–B., 1:299; Hill, 160), comparable to the biblical ban on touching anything unclean (Lev. 3:5). Jesus, as we saw also in the case of the leper, behaved with sovereign freedom in the area of clean and unclean (cf. Matt 15). At the end of this healing, Jesus permits the woman to serve him (8:15c), but this, too, the rabbis forbad, lest women "become accustomed to being around men" (Str.–B., 1:480; cf. Lohm., 159; Green, 100). Cf. the movie *Yentl.*

But Jesus breaks down the outer wall, letting in the leper, then the wall of the Court of Gentiles, letting in the centurion, and now the wall of the Court of Women, letting in women. At the cross he will split the veil to the Holy of Holies, letting in everyone (27:51). Jesus is the Great Wallbreaker, letting outsiders in. A leper, a centurion, and a woman; one physically excluded, one racially excluded, one sexually excluded from the innermost worship life of the community—these Jesus heals *first*. Through his opening sequence of miracles, Matthew says in effect that our Lord begins where we end (the Beatitudes at the head of the Sermon on the Mount teach the same thing); Jesus' mercy extends beyond the bounds of law and custom and reaches outsiders and helps them first. As a consequence the church must constantly be asking, "Who are the outsiders in our time?" In this way she follows Jesus. (The churches' recent investigations of their relations to homosexual persons was an example of just the kind of seeking discipleship that the ministry of Jesus wishes to encourage. The churches' decisions seem right to most disciples—ministry to, justice for, but not ordination of practicing homosexual persons, the difficult combination again of the mercy *and* holiness, width and depth in Jesus' gospel.)

It is interesting that according to this story Peter had a mother-in-law (cf. also 1 Cor 9:5). This means of course that Peter was married (and see in 1 Cor 9:5 that Peter's wife accompanied him). If Peter is later elevated in this Gospel to a position of leadership in the church (see 16:13–20, but contrast 23:8–10), it is worth noting that Jesus did not find Peter's marriage an impediment. If Peter is the "first pope" or moderator or bishop or whatever, is it not interesting that he was married? This is not the point of the story, but since the question of priestly marriage is so vexed in our time and since in some of our churches those called to religious vocations are disqualified from marriage, it is appropriate to point out that Jesus had no such scruples.

Simple center in this story is Jesus' *unsolicited* mercy in healing the fevered woman. In Matthew, the disciples do not petition for her; she does not pray. She was not asked if she *believed* Jesus could heal; Peter and his family were not even asked if they were willing to believe for her; absolutely no conditions are recorded. According to the text the woman is healed simply because Jesus wanted to heal her. We cannot know how often these unsolicited mercies happen in our experience but we may believe that they happen more often than we think. If the grace of God was transparent in Jesus' touching the leper and in his speaking the gentile's servant back to health, it is transparent in still a third way in this story:

the mercy of God often works without even being asked. We must not load the scales of faith with too much freight, as though God will not work unless we or someone else believes or prays enough—to think this would ruin free mercy. Divine mercy is such unmerited favor that it often goes into operation for its own good reasons without any connection whatever with believing (cf. Held, 169; Grund., 255; Green, 100; Gund., 148).

It is Matthew alone who is the source of this grace note because in the versions of this story in Mark and Luke (Mark 1:30; Luke 4:38), Jesus' help *is* intercessorily requested. Matthew, in my opinion, has a theme he wishes to carry through in this series of three healings, namely, that Jesus is more eager to help than we realize—and particularly eager to help outsiders; that he will move beyond all religious, racial, and sexual boundaries and walls and help precisely those who are perceived, respectively, as unclean, unworthy, or unequal. Therefore this Matthean healing is unmotivated by anyone but Jesus himself.

Matthew has also given the story a fresh christocentricity. Where the other evangelists tell us that the healed woman got up and served "them," Matthew quietly elides the plural ending and writes, "and she served *him*," or, in another translation, "she put herself at *his* service." Then it is doctrinally important to notice that it was not her service that released Jesus' grace; it was his grace that released her service. (This evangelical sequence recurs most prominently in the parables of the gems in Jesus' Kingdom Sermon, 13:44–46.) Jesus' healing kindness, uncaused by our good works, penetrates so deeply that it causes the good works of Christ-centered *diakonia* (the actual word used here of Peter's mother-in-law's service).

All three of Jesus' first personalized healings in the Gospel are grace healings of outsiders. The sequence—leper, gentile, woman—paints three portraits of capacious grace. The church's reach should be no less wide. Those whom community (or even church) sensitivities ostracize should be the first focus of the church's concern: Blacks, Hispanics, and Native Americans in North America; the so-called Coloured in South Africa; the lower castes in India; the Chinese in Southeast Asia; Koreans in Japan; Jews, dissenters, and ethnics in Russia; the Mediterranean peoples in Northwestern Europe; Christians and the bourgeoisie in Eastern Europe and Marxist countries; the Indians in Latin America; rural people in cosmopolitan areas everywhere; the mentally ill, and (more than we realize) teenage boys ("punks") in almost all cultures, and so on. One can draft one's own list; but everywhere, in every community, there are particularly disdained persons. Matthew's first three healing stories tell us that Jesus' grace will not recognize these disdainings, will reach through them, and will touch first those whom others would touch last, if at all; the loathed, "unscheduled" persons, class-enemies, the "dirty," "lazy," and "unclean" of every culture's prejudices and oppressions are first in Jesus' concern. What Jesus taught in the Sermon on the Mount about love of enemies, he now practices in love of outsiders. Jesus can ask us to be wide in compassion because he is. The one who expects so much of us in his Sermon gives so much to us in his Miracles. "Infinite demand; infinite succour" (W. D. Davies).

One other feature in Matthew's sequence of three miracles deserves particular emphasis: the decreasing directness of Jesus' healings. In the first miracle, Jesus heals the leper who comes directly to him (like this ↑). (We, too, can come directly to Jesus for help.) In the second miracle, the servant comes to Jesus, as it were, through the faith of the centurion (like this ↑). (We, too, can bring people to Jesus for help.) In the present miracle, no one comes to Jesus for help at all; Jesus comes to the woman on his own (like this ↓). (We, too, can know that Jesus helps us often not because we or others have come to him but because he, unsolicited, comes to us.) Luther once put it this way, in his earthy manner, "God brings in his kingdom while we drink our little jug of Wittenberg beer." No one poured themselves into preaching, praying, writing, counseling, or hard work more than the Protestant Reformers; yet no one rested more in the sovereignty of God and in God's gracious election than these same Reformers. In summary, the Lord's unmotivated healing of Peter's mother-in-law will keep the church from ever claiming too much for her faith, intercessory prayer, or love. This third miracle should keep the church modest.

B. The Sequel (8:16–17)

One verse now tells us of Jesus' "evening healings," and a concluding verse grounds Jesus' healing activity in the Isaiah songs of the Suffering Servant. These verses are attached to the third of the first series of triple healings as a summarizing reminder of what is going on and why.

8:16–17, with the following section on the would-be disciples (vv 18–22), serves as a kind of "buffer pericope" (Meier, 86) between the first three miracles of healing (vv 1–15) and the next three miracles of power (8:23–9:8). Cf. Gund., 138.

8:16 *"And when evening came they brought to Jesus many people who were demon-possessed, and he got rid of these spirits with a Word* (logō), *and all of those who were sick were healed."*

The key expression in this sentence is "with a Word." As we have now learned in a number of examples, all that Jesus is and does is wrapped up in his Word. It is Matthew's special concern among the evangelists to thrill us with the treasure that is ours in having Jesus' Word. (Oversimplified, Matthew treasures Jesus' Word; Mark, Jesus' works; Luke, Jesus' mission; John, Jesus' person.) And now Matthew wants to tell us that Jesus mastered even demon possession with the same sovereign means he had used to heal the leper and the centurion's paralytic servant— with the Word (accompanied in the case of the leper by the sacrament of touch). Jesus' Word is full of healing: it touches as well as teaches. No bag of tricks, no techniques, no great series of pre- or post-operative practices bring Jesus' healing: "only say the Word." The church learns that she too is healing and helpful in the community with the physically or mentally oppressed when she simply ministers his Word with his touching sacraments. Jesus' Word *does* things.

8:17 *"So that the Word was fulfilled that was spoken through the prophet Isaiah, 'He himself took our sicknesses and carried away our diseases.'"*

We know by now that Matthew loves to see Hebrew Scripture fulfilled in the career of Jesus. What is most surprising about the use of this well-known verse from Isaiah 53 is that Matthew applied it to Jesus' ministry and not just to his cross. Matthew felt that Jesus' entire ministry was a living of the cross. Until now we had not been particularly conscious that Jesus was exactly carrying anything of ours. Yet when we look at the last three stories in the light of Isaiah's Word we can see that Jesus was, according to the persuasion of his time, *taking on* the leprosy (and the cultic uncleanness of the leper) by touching him and that he was *carrying away* the disease and its ostracizing consequences. Jesus was also perfectly willing to take on the legal "sickness" of the gentile world (*and* the spiritual separatist sickness of his own religious community) by going right to and into the house of the putatively unclean gentile. When Jesus touched the feverish woman (rather than keeping his distance in order to avoid a physical infection or a legal infraction) he once again both took on and carried away the causes and consequences of the woman's uncleanness and sickness. And when Jesus exorcised demons he came into dangerous contact with the ultimately unclean. Jesus' whole life, then, and not only his cross, is to be seen as his fulfilling the role of the Suffering Servant by being willing to *take on* and to *carry away* anything wrong with us, from leprosy to demon possession. (Cf. Allen, 80; Held, 262f; Schw., 217; and Gund., 149f for discussion.)

Contrast an older view where not the Messiah, but Israel's enemies were given sicknesses: "And the Lord will take away from you all sickness; and none of the evil diseases of Egypt, which you knew, will he inflict upon you, but he will lay them upon all who hate you" (Deut 7:15). Even after the Sermon on the Mount the reader of the Gospel will have frequent occasion to hear Jesus say in effect, "You have heard that it was said of old . . . , but I, Jesus, say to you." Chrysostom, 27:2:185, with most church fathers, believed that the healing ministry of Jesus continues seminally in the church's ministry of the gospel of the forgiveness of sins; for "most of our diseases arise from sins of the soul. For if the sum of all, death itself, hath its root and foundation from sin, much more the majority of our diseases also: since our very capability of suffering did itself originate there."

Since Jesus has definitively accepted and carried away our sicknesses and diseases in the power of his ministry we may believe him for health more than we do. Jesus is the savior of the total person, body and soul. We may bring to him, therefore, *all* our needs, not only our spiritual ones. Jesus did something classical about our total human need in his thirty years in our midst. And now we are specifically and authoritatively told by the Hebrew prophet through the New Testament evangelist that God's suffering servant took on and carried away all our maladies, from demon possession in the innermost psyche to weakness in our outermost flesh. Believing this has historically done wonders for God's people. (In a hymn, the church sings, "Praise to the Lord, the Almighty, the King of creation! O my soul, praise Him, for He is thy *health* and salvation!" And in the liturgy we celebrate God's "saving health.")

Healing has been going on among Christian people from the beginning and it must not be made the esoteric specialty of particular eras or groups. Believers have always included in their faith the conviction that Jesus *heals,* too. All the Gospel stories and all of church history teach this. There is hardly a practicing Christian living who has not experienced some healing in his or her immediate family. Healing is rarely the presence of great meetings or healers; it is and has been usually the continuing presence of faith in Jesus as our savior also in sickness, in every simple Christian church. Wherever pastors, elders, and disciples have come praying for the sick in simple faith in Jesus (who is "God-Saves") they have come expecting real help, and even when the help has been entirely spiritual, the church has known and confessed the presence of the saving Christ.

The more simple and unostentatious the prayers for healing are, the more authentic they are. The church is rightly suspicious of all spectacular, and especially of all advertised healings. (Here, Matt 7:21–23 may be consulted again with profit.) Jesus does not do his work this sensational way, as his temptations first taught us, and he positively warns us in his Gospel in more than one place of the danger of spectacularism of all sorts.

But a fear of spectacularism should not inhibit a congregation from having quiet (the quieter the better), simple meetings and visits for healings. Some churches include prayers for healing and laying on of elders' hands in the Lord's Supper (see the Lutheran liturgy, for example). The Lord's Supper, in fact, seems to be the single most appropriate place for prayers of healing, bringing, as it does, the real bodily presence of Christ. To be sure, in his Great Commission at the end of this Gospel, Jesus did not specifically or explicitly give his church a healing mission. This fact should keep the church from isolating healing ministries from the regular ministry of Word and sacraments as if discipling, baptizing, and teaching (the verbs of the Great Commission) were not themselves healing ministries. The right ministry of Word and sacrament, blessed by Christ, heals by itself. (But a right ministry of Word and sacrament rightly includes prayer for the sick and needy in the congregation.)

That Jesus saves us from our sins *and* their consequences (cf. 1:21) is the burden of the sermon-and-sacrament-centered Gospel of Matthew. And so, special attention to the sick, outsiders, and the weak is an important component of Jesus' missionary theology in Matthew. Therefore the church always follows her master here, too, by praying with real faith for the sick. Prayer meetings for healing are not only right and salutary in themselves, they also give the people of God a much needed vehicle for spiritual life, fellowship, and prayer.

The pure preaching of the Word and the right administration of the Word's sacraments give the church the great *objectivities* of our faith (like this C, down); prayer in the fellowship of other believers with laying on of hands gives the church the great *subjectivities* of our faith (like this Ɔ, up), bringing us full circle into a real relationship with the living God. Compare Acts 2:42 for a description of the powerful life of the earliest church: "And they devoted themselves to the apostles' teaching [the Word] and fellowship, to the breaking of bread [the sacrament] and the prayers." There we have a whole church.

There is more healing available in Christ's Word, people, sacraments, and prayers than our little faith quite believes. We need a shove now and then, moving us out. The healing miracles of Jesus provide such a shove. *Let us pray.*

> "At even, when the sun was set,
> The sick, O Lord, around Thee lay;
> O in what divers pains they met!
> O with what joy they went away! . . .
>
> *Thy touch has still its ancient power*;
> No *word* from Thee can fruitless fall.
> Hear, in this solemn prayerful hour,
> And in thy mercy heal us all."
>   (The Hymn, "At Even, When the Sun Was Set")

IV. THE STORM (8:18–27)

The storm story has discipleship as its theme. Appropriately, then, it begins with two would-be disciples who illustrate how *not* to go about discipleship. (We recall how Jesus first taught *prayer* by showing what it is not, 6:5–8.)

A. Introduction: The Would-Be Disciples (8:18–22)

"When Jesus saw the big crowd around him, he gave orders to move on to the other side of the lake. And a Bible teacher came up to him and said, 'Teacher, I am going to follow you wherever you go.' And Jesus said to him, 'Foxes have holes and birds in the sky have nests, but the Son of Man has no "where" ever to lay his head.' Then another of his disciples said to him, 'Lord, please give me permission to go home first to bury my father.' But Jesus said to him, 'Follow me, and let the dead bury their own dead.'"

Matthew inserts these discipleship stories into his nexus of miracles to teach that faith in Jesus must always be united with obedience (Grund., 257; Gund., 150). Christians are not just patients, they are disciples. An unrelieved series of healings might have given the church the impression that her sole or main business is the priestly task of comforting, consoling, and healing. But whenever the church thinks that her almost exclusive purpose is to comfort in Jesus' name she will need to hear the gospel's discipleship stories, which teach her the rugged responsibility to obey Jesus' demands. For while the church exists indeed to comfort and to grace, she also exists no less centrally, and in Matthew's Gospel probably even more centrally, to challenge and to disciple. The commands are Jesus' main gift to the church according to Matthew's vision (Matt 28:20). A debility creeps into the church when she sees her task as mainly that of comfort—a peril to which the grace-centered Lutheran churches and all relational and suburban churches are especially susceptible. Jesus grips people not only to heal them; he grips them also to disciple them—or, as here in one case, to push them away from discipleship for a while! Jesus' love is not only tender, it is tough, and so into the healings Matthew inserts discipleship stories to keep the record straight and the gospel balanced.

It is interesting that both the Sermon on the Mount and the present discipleship encounters *begin* with Jesus immersed in ministries of healing, "seeing the crowds," and wanting to get away. In both instances Jesus felt that if the "crowds" of the world were to be helped in depth and not merely temporarily, in soul and not just in body and mind, he had to do something deeper than heal; he had to make disciples. Real disciples are the world's healthiest reality and evil's major antibodies. Christian people are the health the world most needs. "*You* are the salt of the earth. . . . *You* are the light of the world" (Matt 5). Correctly seen, discipleship training is not a detour from healing, but the best way to it. When Jesus leaves healing ministries and engages in teaching ones, he is not leaving an unimportant, merely physical sphere; he is reaching down beneath the physical into the sources of the physical in the springs of mind and heart. Teaching rearranges the depths, and healing rearranges the maladies of the person "de-ranged" by wrong relations in the depths.

An eager Bible teacher approaches Jesus to announce his readiness to go all the way in following Jesus; and he is (at least temporarily) rejected; a hesitant disciple asks Jesus for permission to go home for a while to arrange important family matters; and he is (at least temporarily) told to do nothing of the sort. In both cases Jesus rudely rejects the requests of the two would-be disciples. The rejections even reverse the normal criteria for recruitment: The eager is turned away, the half-hearted is summoned.

Why does Jesus give such contradictory advice? Because as the Greeks said, circumstances alter cases. We may find an example in Confucius's reaction in a situation roughly similar to Jesus' (*Analects*, 11:21). Two persons approached Confucius and asked, "Should I carry immediately into practice what I have learned?" and to the one Confucius said yes and to the other, no. When asked by his disciples why he gave contrary advice to the same question, Confucius replied that the first questioner was overcautious and needed to be more enterprising, while the second questioner was precipitous and needed to think first. In our Gospel stories, the men make dissimilar approaches; they want to be disciples, and they get surprisingly dissimilar counsel.

I believe we can discern clues in Matthew's careful portraiture of the two disciples and see why Jesus discouraged the zealous candidate and encouraged the timid one. "A Bible teacher came up to [Jesus] and said, 'Teacher, I am going to follow you *wherever* you go'" (v 19). The focus of the entire remark is the dedication of *the speaker*. The subject of the sentence, not only grammatically, is the Bible teacher himself ("I am going to follow you . . ."). And when listened to carefully his remark has overtones of "Jesus, this is your lucky day: I have decided to be your disciple." The man is an intellectual, as Matthew indicates by his title for the man ("scribe," Bible teacher) and by the Bible teacher's address to Jesus—"Teacher." Significantly, this educator does not approach Jesus as "Lord." Jesus, to this man, is mainly an attractive *teacher*. And since the candidate's task is teaching, too, and since apparently he had not encountered another teacher as impressive as Jesus, he now announces to Jesus—notice, announces, he does not request—that he is Jesus' man, completely.

"If he had said, '*Lord*, I will follow you wherever you go,' he would not have been rejected by the Lord; but he thinks of Jesus as but one teacher among many" (Jero., 1:160, emphasis added; Jerome thinks the scribe had seen Jesus' miracles and wanted to gain profit from them, as Simon Magus sought to do later with Peter at Acts 8:19; thus also Chrys., 27:4:186; cf. Aug., *Serm.*, 12(62):2:298; 50(100):1:420; Streck., 124 n. 2). Only nondisciples address Jesus as "Teacher" in Matthew, 12:38; 19:16; 22:16; 24:36 (Held, 203). Gundry, 151–53, is the only modern commentator I know who argues for the scribe's being "a true disciple," and for the following would-be disciple proving himself false.

The key term in the Bible teacher's announcement is the impressive "*wherever* (*hopou ean*) you go." Jesus will pick up this expression in a moment and give it a twist. Until now we have not noticed any scribe or educated Bible teachers in Jesus' entourage; perhaps the candidate has noticed this, too. This may have given even more *élan* to his announcement—"Jesus, at last you have a man with a mind."

Jesus is not terribly impressed. He tells the man—and it is all that he tells him in this tantalizingly brief record—that it is rough being a disciple of the Son of Man. "Foxes have holes, and birds in the sky have nests, but the Son of Man has no 'where' [*pou*] ever to lay his head." Jesus too had noticed the man's emphatic "wherever" and wants him to know that there isn't any such place and that a kind of total insecurity is the lot of the person who follows him. The man asserted a willingness to go anywhere; but what if there is no sure "anywhere"?

Jesus is not so desperate for disciples or for well-educated associates that he bursts with joy when one enlists. To our surprise, he puts this man under a severe scrutiny. The church can learn from this incident not to be too desperate to get followers for Jesus, as if Jesus could not do without certain kinds of people. (Some evangelistic groups are too eager to convert leaders, for example.) Jesus wants disciples—that is clear from the whole Gospel—but he does not want them at any cost; and, of most surprise here, he is reserved toward one who claims entire commitment. This man with his too academic view of Jesus, with his too generous sense of his own faith-commitment, and with his announcement of fact rather than request for consideration, has a lot to learn about discipleship.

"We should learn . . . , in his person, . . . not to make wild and irresponsible claims to be Christ's disciples, without taking any thought for the cross and the hardships" (Cal., 1:254). There is an immense literature on the title Son of Man, used for the first time in this Gospel here in v 20—"The Son of Man has nowhere to lay his head." I am most attracted by the views that see Jesus favoring the title (with one exception in the New Testament, Acts 7:56, interestingly, the title is used only by Jesus) because of its deliberate ambiguity and "as illustrative of the mysteriousness of His person" (Allen, lxxiii; cf. Colpe's long article in the TDNT 8:400–77, and Green's helpful summary, 237–41).

"The Son of Man has nowhere to lay his head" means that the follower of the Son of Man will not always or often be able to get a good rest (Schl., *Der*, 286–87), that his or her life will be a life of exhausting service to people, and of misunderstanding and persecution from a world hostile to the message. Surprisingly Jesus does not capitalize on his missionary successes so far; instead, he frightens off the overly-eager (Schw., 219–20). We learn in this important discipleship paragraph that discipleship is an insecure vocation, with many discomforts. Let everyone think twice before they enter it (cf. Luke 14:28, 31).

But the last word about this Bible teacher is an encouraging one. When Matthew introduces us to the second candidate he writes, significantly, "Then *another* of his disciples said to him, 'Lord . . .'" (8:21a). The fact that this second man was called *another* disciple can indicate that the first man became a disciple after all, though this is admittedly thin evidence (and Allen, 82, doubts the conclusion). We do not know how long the Bible teacher had to feel the cold water that Jesus had thrown on him—Matthew leaves out unnecessary details. But the text, however dimly, hints to some of us that the Bible teacher became "another disciple" at last.

8:21–22 "Then another of his disciples said to him, 'Lord, please give me permission to go home first to bury my father.' But Jesus said to him, 'Follow me, and let the dead bury their own dead.'" This man was already a "disciple," notice (Held, 202), which teaches us that discipleship is constantly renegotiated, renewed—or canceled. By *again* challenging the man to "follow me" we learn that Jesus constantly re-calls us to the totality that is discipleship (Grund., 258–59). This second man is the person whom most of us would have gladly dismissed—if he wants to go home, let him. Give us men and women who are willing to go anywhere and who are not hankering after family. But Jesus grabs this man by the scruff of his heart, shakes him a little, and commands imperiously and even a little crudely, "Follow me, and let the dead bury their own dead." Having in the previous incident squashed Mr. Bighead, Jesus now bucks up Mr. Faintheart.

At first glance this disciple's request does not seem bad. He simply wants to go home to take care of his dying or dead father (it is hard to know which of the two). Filial piety was honored in Israel almost as much as it has been in China, and one of the great expressions of this piety was a decent burial (Gen 50:5-6; cf. McN., 109; Gund., 153-54). I believe that Matthew gives a slant to this request, however, by inserting the word "first." "First" colors the spirit of the man who asked it. He does not ask to go "for a moment," or "at the end of the week," but "first," as if the thrilling firstness of his discipleship to Jesus has slightly worn off and his more familiar past begins to reassert itself. Now, the *first* consideration is taking care of his parents.

We learn elsewhere how deeply Jesus honors care for parents—in chapter 15 Jesus scores the Pharisees for using their pious Korban tradition as an excuse for dropping the fifth commandment's economic duties to their parents. Jesus is not an enemy of filial piety; he *is* an enemy of putting filial or any piety or devotion ahead of—"first" and before—commitment to himself. "No soldier on service gets entangled in civilian pursuits, since his aim is to satisfy the one who enlisted him" (2 Tim 2:4).

"Unless a man hate his father and his mother . . . and, yes, his own life, he cannot be my disciple" (Luke 14:26; cf. Matt 10:37-38). The context of the Gospel tells us exactly how Jesus means "hate," but we should not too promptly soften Jesus' strong word. When it comes to choosing between devotion to loved ones and devotion to Jesus only the clarity of "hate" will do. The word "hate" is not to be used, as the Pharisees used Korban, to abandon parents in nursing homes, or children in boarding schools (as some missions used to require), or wives in homes hundreds of miles away. Jesus is not summoning disciples to human cruelty and least of all to family callousness. "If anyone does not provide for his relatives, and especially for his own family, he has disowned the faith and is worse than an unbeliever" (1 Tim 5:8).

One is reminded of Tertullian's telling the hostile Romans why Christians could not give the emperor divine honors (i.e., treat as "first"): "Never will I call the emperor God, and that both because it is not in me to be guilty of falsehood and because I dare not turn him into ridicule; . . . Let him think it enough to bear the name of emperor. . . . To call him God is to rob him of his title" (*Apol.*, 33). When anyone, however precious, becomes first to us that person is deified and deification belongs, by definition, only to deity. Jesus is putting down this disciple's secret rebellion, not putting down his parents. I have the feeling that if the man had asked for permission, somehow, "second," to go home and take care of his father's burial that Jesus would have granted it. It was the smoldering rebellion, the implicit loss of first love, the discouragement that announced itself in this disciple's "first" that concerned Jesus.

"Follow me, and let the dead bury their own dead." Jesus' view here of secular society is not flattering. It is not a world come of age, a mature secular city, a society of persons living and coping well; secular society is a sick city, a city sick unto death and dying. Jesus looks at the world with clear eyes.

The two would-be disciples did not take a sufficiently clear look at what discipleship and the world really are. For Jesus, discipleship is tough going and the world is a place of the walking dead. The world is in mortal need of disciples who will follow Jesus into rough engagement with it. The world is death; discipleship is life.

"Your slain are not slain with the sword or dead in battle" (Isa 22:2). *Mortuus est quicumque non credit* ("Dead is anyone who does not believe," Jero., 1:160). "When unbelievers bury a dead body, the dead bury the dead" (Aug., *Serm.*, 12(62):2:299). "In other words, the only ones who are really living are those who concentrate their efforts, and all the activity of their life, upon God's obedience" (Cal., 1:255).

B. The Stilling of the Storm (8:23–27)

"Jesus then got into the boat and his disciples followed him. And look! A huge earthquake hit the lake so that the boat was covered with waves; but Jesus himself just slept. So the disciples came to him, woke him up, and said, 'Lord! Save us! We're dying!' And he said to them, 'Why are you such cowards? Littlefaiths!' Then he got up and rebuked the winds and the lake, and there was a great calm. And the people were amazed and said, 'Who in the world is this fellow that even the winds and the lake obey him?'"

8:23 Matthew uses this miracle to teach that *disciples* also need salvation. It is not just outsiders (lepers, gentiles, and demeaned women) who need Jesus' help. Disciples, the insiders par excellence, need saving, too. The fact that this is Matthew's intention is shown by his studied use in the introductory sentence of both the standard verb and noun of discipleship—"they followed" (*ēkolouthēsan*) and "his disciples" (*hoi mathētai autou*). The boat is "*the* boat" and represents the church; the rough sea and wind are figures for the world in which the church lives; and a portrait of the fearful faith of even believers is one big point of the story. (The now classic treatment of this text is Günther Bornkamm's "The Stilling of the Storm in Matthew," *TIM*, 52–57 [hereafter simply "Storm"].)

8:24 The earthquake (*seismos*, Matthew's unique word) hits the lake and covers the ship with waves; the world overwhelms disciples. Yet the Lord sleeps. This is the first surprising feature in a story of surprises. The Lord asleep? What about the Lord (in the Psalms somewhere) neither sleeping nor slumbering? Wouldn't it be more appropriate to have the Lord looking out over the storm with a steely gaze? Sleep is not for lords.

But the point of the story would not have been as dramatic if Jesus had been awake. And isn't prayer in dangerous times rather like waking a sleeping Lord? Sleep also points out to us what we had glimpsed in Jesus' interviews with the two would-be disciples: Jesus is in serene control. Storms are a part of life. Jesus can relax in storms because he knows the purposes of ship and sea. One reason the church has loved this story is that in it we see the two cardinal doctrines of Christ: his true humanity (he sleeps) and his true deity (he commands wind and sea). The Lord in heaven neither sleeps nor slumbers, but on earth, as a true man, he does.

"While the sleep and the outward appearance showed man, the sea and the calm declared him God. . . . He put forth no rod, as Moses did, neither did He stretch forth His hands to Heaven, nor did He need any prayer, but, as was meet for a master commanding his handmaid, or a creator His creature, so did He quiet and curb it by word and command alone" (Chrys., 28:1:190).

8:25 The disciples waken Jesus and, in Matthew, in three staccato Greek words, cry out their need: "Lord! Save! Dying!" (*kurie, sōson, appollumetha;* the last verb literally means "we are being destroyed"). At least Jesus is "Lord" to his frightened disciples; he is no longer just a teacher (as he was to the Bible teacher in the last paragraph). In disasters we need a lord not a teacher. "Save" is the right thing to ask a lord to do, too. The disciples do not ask for teaching on how they might save themselves. Tidal waves are not overcome by education. What the disciples need is not for the Lord to help them find a solution but for the Lord to save them. Pelagianism, with its confidence in the powers of the free human will, will always be swamped by the tidal waves of crisis. Salvation is the sovereign act of a *Lord;* from the human side it can only be cried for. "Once, twice have I heard, salvation belongs to the *Lord*."

"We're dying!" The waves are too big, the ship too little; there seems no way out. The story teaches disciples that despair in the church is as common as storms on the sea. This ancient discouragement was known to even apostles.

8:26a "And Jesus said to them, 'Why are you such cowards? Littlefaiths!'" There is something moral about faith; it is often a form of courage, its absence a form of cowardice. By impressing upon us the moral character of faith we learn that it is not simply a passive acceptance of truths, a mere empty hand, a weak resignation that "just believes." Faith is often depicted in the Gospels as a courageous confidence that Jesus is equal to the occasion. Particularly Melanchthon's Reformation conception of faith, in its legitimate interest in keeping faith from being a work, is in danger of passivity. But faith can be kept from works-righteousness—the Reformation concern—and still be robust. Disciples need to know that when they fall victim to despairing fear they are cowards and that Jesus is unimpressed.

Jesus answers his own question about why they are such cowards: "Littlefaiths!" Cowardice is a precipitate of littlefaith. Littlefaith in the Gospels is faith that wilts in crises, particularly in the face of natural dangers. In such situations disciples believe that the laws of nature are so imperious that nothing can help them from beyond nature. Jesus is not happy with confidence that trusts him only so far. He expects of us a confidence that is as extensive as his Lordship—a Lordship over absolutely everything. Jesus calls any less extensive faith by name—cowardice, littlefaith.

What should the disciples have done? Sit calmly by while their boat sank? The story comes close to suggesting this. Is it wrong for disciples in danger to come crying to their Lord for help? We know that it is not, and in this story Jesus helps his distressed, though cowering, disciples. But while Jesus helps littlefaith, he does not want to give the impression that he admires it. One could learn from the story, if one follows its logic, that sometimes in danger disciples should just walk into their room, lie down, and go to sleep. Sometimes sleep with confidence pleases Jesus more than prayer with fear.

"To wait for God's saving presence in the sea-storm: that is faith and bravery" (Schn., 115). Jesus rebukes his disciples "for failure to rest in [his] divine authority" (Gund., 156). Gundry's reasoning, 155, though, is hard to follow: "In Matthew . . . the storm does not pose a threat to the disciples. . . . In correspondence with 28:2 . . . the great shaking in the sea previews the majesty of Jesus in his resurrection." This symbolism demands too much of readers. Calvin, 1:280–81, sees the force of the text with his usual clarity, and he does not blame the disciples for being merely afraid: "Fear, in the ordinary sense, is not opposed to faith"—it is excessive fear that Jesus criticizes.

The major point is that even when our faith is excessively fearful, cowardly, weak, and worthy of rebuke, Jesus hears our cry, gets up, rebukes wind and sea, and creates great calm. Jesus did *not* say, as he might have, "Come back later when your faith is stronger and less fearful, and then I will help you." He takes us as we come; and if we come with hardly any faith at all, he cannot pretend that he is flattered, but he does go immediately to work. What really matters in the final analysis is that Jesus helps us *however* we come to him, even with littlefaith. "Even little faith is faith still" (Stier in Beng., 1:144). And that is the main point of the story. Faith—the way Jesus wants us to relate to him—is not the real theme of this discipleship story. Jesus' salvation of even weak-in-faith disciples is.

8:26b "Then he got up and rebuked the winds and the lake, and there was a great calm." "Creation recognizes its Creator" (Jero., 1:162). Jesus does here what only the Lord God does in the Psalms.

"The voice of the Lord is upon the waters; . . . the Lord sits enthroned over the flood" (Ps 29:3, 10). "Who dost still the roaring of the seas, the roaring of their waves, the tumult of the peoples" (Ps 65:7, addressed to the "God of our salvation, who art the hope of all the ends of the earth, and of the farthest seas," v 5). "Then they cried to the Lord in their trouble, and he delivered them from their distress; he made the storm be still, and the waves of the sea were hushed. Then they were glad because they had quiet, and he brought them to their desired haven" (Ps 107:28–30; cf. Ps 93:3–4). The similarities to the story of Jonah are striking (Jonah 1:4–6, 15–16), but "Jonah slept in the storm from a dead [conscience], Christ from a pure conscience; [and] the prophet's presence [in the boat] made the danger; Christ's . . . [the] deliverance" (Trench in Beng., 1:1–44).

8:27 "And the people were amazed and said, 'Who in the world is this fellow that even the winds and the lake obey him?'" This is the remark of "the people" (*hoi anthrōpoi*), which is probably Matthew's designation of the disciples who are, at least, people like everyone else. (Cf. McN., 111; but Bornkamm, "Storm," 56, believes the people are those encountered by this story in gospel preaching, Lohmeyer, 164, that they are the hardened world.)

We have to admire the disciples and their disciples later for remembering and recording these bad reviews of disciples (Beng., 1:144). The disciples did not make themselves heroes when they told their stories. The tendency of those who write literature of this sort is to omit the less attractive incidents and to give themselves some credit. But we will notice almost the complete absence of self-advertisement in the Gospels. There is an honesty in the earliest church's self-portraiture that wins respect and encourages credence. The disciples paint themselves, warts and all. The church tells us here, honestly, that she is like other people when in danger—fearful, cowardly, unimpressive—and that at such times she needs help no less than unbelievers. This story was passed on by the church because she wanted to encourage all who hear it to place their robust confidence in a good Lord whose measure of help is not our measure of faith but his of grace.

The people's question about what kind of a man this is who can even command wind and water teaches the church that Jesus is Lord not only of disease in humans (as in the first three stories) but of disorders in nature as well. The reach of Jesus' competence goes beyond the human into the structures of the natural world. Jesus is Lord of *all*.

In the last story and this one (the two would-be disciples and the storm), all part of one complex, we have our first glimpses of how *Christians* lived in the earliest church. Chapter 4 told us how they were called; the Sermon on the Mount told us how they were supposed to live; the first half of chapter 8 told us how outsiders responded to Jesus; now, for the first time, we see Christians in action—and in all three cases we see them as all too human. The first disciple-to-be was self-centered, the second was comfort-loving, and in the storm the whole band of disciples was cowardly. The fact that the first Christians gave themselves this portraiture is winning. They fish us by telling the truth.

Yet it would be wrong to conclude that the Gospel intends for Christians to be content being as human as everyone else. Jesus put the intellectual down, pulled the dispirited up, and called cowardice cowardice. Jesus wants good faith. Certainly the purpose of these discipleship stories has been not only to keep us in our place—our very human place—but also to assist us to rise to finer faith. In particular, in the more developed storm story we are urged to "play the man." Faith is a form of bravery. The disciples' will is not to be thought of as a weak, pitiable thing that can do nothing at all in the onslaught of storms. Christians are to see their wills as responsible, answerable, and healed because of the real presence of Christ; they are called to defy the realities of storms with the courage born of a greater reality. Disciples are to learn that faith is a moral act and failure in faith is failure in personal substance. And yet one must stress again in conclusion that as important as faith certainly is in the Gospel, the always deeper fact, even in this story, is that no matter how weakly or unworthily we approach Jesus and no matter how unimpressive our faith, *Jesus helps us.* Jesus' grace is more important than our faith.

> We worship Thee, God of our fathers, we bless Thee;
> Through life's storm and tempest our Guide hast Thou been.
> *When perils o'ertake us, escape Thou wilt make us,*
> And with *Thy help,* O Lord, life's battles we win.

V. THE DEMONIACS (8:28–34)

"And when Jesus got to the other side of the lake—to the Gadarene area—two demon-possessed men coming from the graveyard met him as he was walking along. They were really wild, and no one had the courage to take that particular road. And look! They screamed, 'Hey! Why are you meddling with us, O Son of God? Have you come here, before the time of judgment, just to torture us?!' Now some distance away there was a big herd of pigs feeding. So the demoniacs were begging him, 'If you are going to get rid of us, send us into that herd of pigs.' And Jesus said, 'Move!' And they came out and went over into the pigs. Then look! The whole herd went careering over the cliff and into the lake, and they died in the waters. Their keepers ran away, and went into the city and told the people there everything that had happened to them and to the demon-possessed men. And then look, the whole city came out to meet Jesus, and when they found him they begged him, saying, 'Would you mind leaving town?'"

In all three synoptic Gospels the storm-story of wild nature and the psychic-story of these wild men are told together as a pair. "The Wild Ones" would make an appropriate covering title for both stories. Jesus is Lord of nature, both physical and psychical. Whenever the natural gets unnatural Jesus is still Lord. He can still storms of sea and soul, of nature and mind.

Modern writers often separate these two miracles as a miracle of nature (the Storm) and a miracle of healing (the Demoniacs), "but by biblical standards they belong together as examples of Jesus' authority over the chaos in nature and in man" (Caird, 121). Two consecutive verses in the Psalms summarize the meanings of these two consecutive miracles in the Gospels. "Thou dost rule the raging of the sea, when its waves rise, thou stillest them" (Ps 89:9, the Storm) and "thou didst crush Rahab like a carcass, thou didst scatter thy enemies with thy mighty arm" (Ps 89:10, The Demoniacs).

We have moved in this chapter from physical to mental illness, and the purpose of the movement is to teach us that across the whole range of life Jesus is Lord.

8:28a "The other side of the lake" was pagan territory to the Jews, and we are told by commentators that even physically the rough, craggy eastern coastline compared unfavorably with the paradisiacal west coast of the people of God. Here on the eastern seashore there were demons and pigs—unclean things—and here people needed help badly (Lohm., 165). Apart from the church's self-critical corrective in the Storm Story, there is a sense in which this chapter is mainly missionary, dealing as it does with cultural outsiders of various types: with lepers, gentiles, women, and now demon-possessed pagans. (Technically, it would not be right to describe this chapter as a missionary *journey*, for in Matthew's conception—in chapters 10 and 15 in particular—Jesus' earthly mission is almost exclusively to the old people of God. When Jesus encounters gentiles it appears to be almost by accident or by their intention, not his. It is well to notice, further, that though in this story Jesus comes to the eastern side of the lake, it is the wild men who come to him.)

8:28c Matthew tells us that these men were so wild that hardly anyone dared pass that way. The violence of some forms of mental illness is well known. Mental illness in that era as in many others suggested possession by demonic powers. Physical illnesses are sometimes attributed to demons in the Gospels; what we call mental illnesses usually are. We are still extensively ignorant about the invisible forces at work in mental disorder, though psychiatric medicine progressively penetrates the mystery. Jesus' true humanity argues for his sharing his contemporaries' views of disease.

However we choose to understand Jesus, it is not good theology to say that Jesus merely accommodated himself to his contemporaries' inadequate views when he spoke of demons. Nor is it good theology to say, for example, that while he *spoke* of demons he actually *knew* they did not exist. To say such things is more a psychological wish-projection of the modern sensibility than it is a scientific analysis of the text. From a reading of the record it clearly appears that Jesus believed in the existence of the demonic. This does not mean that we must call things by the same names; it does mean that there are morbid forces at work in history and in human consciousness, by whatever name, and that any rational account of life requires their inclusion. That there are even more important considerations will appear in the course of the exposition. But an acknowledgment of Jesus' recognition of the demonic is the minimum requirement for a responsible reading of the text.

I find Caird's synthesis, 88, helpful: "Ancient opinion ascribed to demon possession any disease which involved loss of control—epilepsy, delirium, convulsions, nervous disorders, mental derangement—and which therefore suggested the presence of an invading power. . . . Modern medicine can provide other explanations for most of the symptoms, but this does not mean that demon possession can be dismissed as outmoded science. . . . To Jesus all diseases were caused by Satan (cf. Luke 13:16), though not all by possession, so that with each of his cures he was driving further back the frontiers of Satan's dominion." Cf. McK., 77–78; and Russell's *The Devil*, chap 6, "The Devil in the New Testament." I did not get as much out of Scott Peck's *The People of the Lie* as did others.

8:29 "And look! They screamed, 'Hey! Why are you meddling with us, O Son of God? Have you come here, before the time of judgment, just to torture us?!'" (v 29). Their address is more assault than petition. In the course of the eighth chapter we have moved all the way from pure faith—"If you want to, you can make me clean"—to impure faith—"Why are you meddling with us?" In the leper we have physical sickness but mental seriousness; in the demoniacs we have physical strength but mental derangement. What does their remark mean? It is not explicitly a petition for help; it is not even (as with the leper and the centurion) a statement of the problem. Rather, it is two strange questions, containing odd affirmations. (It is interesting to notice that they "scream," not speak, which also indicates imbalance.)

First of all, they don't see why Jesus should be around at all, and they definitely don't see why he should be around them—they don't see any common ground, any reason, for the meeting. "What do we have in common?" they in effect shout, adding strangely, "O Son of God." The demons recognize Jesus—a point stressed much more by Mark than by Matthew who, one senses, is not comfortable with the encounter (Matthew greatly abbreviates Mark's detailed account). Supernatural forces have a clearer view of the nature of Jesus' person than mortals—it is as if they move at an altitude where the spiritual is more perceptible. How do they intend for their "O Son of God" to be understood? Not as a compliment, and certainly they do not say it in faith. Occasionally the demon-possessed will use the name of their accoster in order to defend themselves from him (for power was believed to reside in the name), and this may be the reason why they address Jesus by his divine name (Green, 102). Greetings in many cultures are supplied with divine names in order to ward off the dangerous power of the other person. It is of course christologically interesting that the spirits think Jesus' most essential name is "Son of God," the name that baptism focused and the tempter tested (Matt 3:17–4:3, 6).

But if the demoniacs' first statement is full of curiosities—"Why are you meddling with us, O Son of God?"—the second is no less ambiguous. "Have you come here to torment us before the time?" (RSV). There are two schools of thought about this "before the time." One view holds that the demons expected their destruction at the eschatological Day but that Jesus' appearance now prematurely anticipates the last judgment (Str.-B., 1:492; Schn., 116; Schw., 223; Hill, 168). We may call this the temporal interpretation. The other interpretation, which we may call spatial, holds that the Matthean Jesus' *earthly* ministry was a mission designed for Jews, and that only after his resurrection would Jesus direct his mission to the gentile world. In this sense, Jesus' coming now to pagan territory and, in particular, to pagan demoniacs, says he has entered his gentile mission "before the time" (Stend., 781).

We learn about Jesus himself that wherever he appears God's judgment and mission appear in person and in power. The last judgment and its preparatory mission become a present judgment wherever he—or his name or gospel— appears. Time is wrenched into a "now" where Christ is preached. Thus *praesentia Salvatoris tormenta sunt daemonia*, "in the presence of the Savior the demons are tormented" (Jero., 1:164).

In the contorted cries of the demoniacs the evangelist indicates the emotional instability, the mental confusion, and the spiritual thralldom of all that is pagan or secular. The secular world does not know what is really happening, and is locked in a state of confusion about the deepest issues of life. The eastern shore needs Jesus badly. (Cf. "those who sit in darkness" in 4:16.)

8:30 Jesus gives no answer to the attack of questions. He just stands there. He lives the Sermon on the Mount he taught; he does not return evil with evil. Questions as confused as these cannot be answered. And in fact, they were questions only in form; in substance they were a pained mix of query and insult, covering a cry for help. (Adolescents are sometimes this way, and stories like this can teach us to have a heart and to keep our counsel.) There is a person somewhere down underneath all this chaos. No words or actions of Jesus are recorded by Matthew, which means (in Matthew—Mark is quite different here) that the brute fact of the *presence* of Jesus (today the presence of his Word in his church) is a preliminary exorcism. A church just sitting there on the block; a disciple just sitting there in the office; the Word just being explained there in the Sunday School class—all these by their simple existence announce, and in some deep ways project, the exorcising power of the Lord Jesus Christ.

8:31–32a Finally, their questions unanswered, the demons asked that if Jesus *is* going to exorcize them, he send them into the pigs (see how Matthew softens Mark here, Gund., 160). And then we read the simple, "and Jesus said to them, 'Move!'" (v 32). Absent are all the usual exorcizing incantations and formulae (Grund., 264). Even Matthew's choice of a verb to introduce Jesus' response is interesting: "he *said*," not "he shouted." Jesus says simply and firmly "Move" (*hupagete*), just one Greek word. The simplicity of Jesus' exorcism is noteworthy in Matthew. He requires no great effort of speech, no complex vocabulary of liberation, no special exorcizing technique. "Just say the Word." The church learns that her exorcisms too may be by the Word alone. Simply teaching the Word of Jesus exorcizes. Faithful sermons exorcize. We may consciously think of every Word of Jesus we teach as exorcizing that which is evil in our fellowship, as communicating divine powers, as liberating people. And it is not the pitch or fervor with which we say this Word that makes it effective—"he [just] *said*"—it is simply the Word itself, in which Word Jesus lives. The Word of Jesus is the exorcist. Luther's hymn "A Mighty Fortress" (a commentary on the devil) celebrates this: "And though this world, with devils filled, should threaten to undo us, We will not fear, for God hath willed his truth to triumph through us: The prince of darkness grim, we tremble not for him, his rage we can endure, For lo, his doom is sure, *One little word* shall fell him."

8:32b "And [the demons] came out and went over into the pigs. Then look! The whole herd went careering over the cliff and into the lake, and they died in the waters." The transfer in the final statement from the singular "herd" to the plural "*they* died" teaches that not only the herd of pigs died but the multiple demons that invaded the herd died as well (Grund., 264). We learn in mission that one question is of first-rank importance with people: What happens to the spirits when they leave? Will they return? Matthew teaches here that what happens to spirits is death. The Word of Jesus entirely vanquishes them. The simple Word of Jesus drowns them (Schl., *Der*, 294; McK., 78; Grund., 264; Green, 102; Gund., 160). "One little word shall fell them." Believers need not live in fear of evil spirits any longer. (Contrast the Return of the Unclean Spirit, 12:43–45.)

Does the expression "and they died *in the waters*" point to the waters of baptism by which, traditionally, evil spirits were banished? We only know that through the centuries believers have taken great comfort from the "charming" power of baptism. Luther's scouting of the devil by his writing "I have been baptized" on his desk is well-known. At baptism, believers have, as it were, a circle of protection drawn in blood around them into which the evil spirits may not come. The spirits shout over the circle to frighten us, but they cannot touch us within the circle of grace and faith. For by baptism we have been made God's family, which means he is now responsible for us—"our Father"—and we have been internally filled and equipped with the *Holy* Spirit who is not easily sullied or bullied. We have in our hearts and on our lips the powerful Name of Jesus Christ and his exorcizing Word. We are safe.

8:33–34 The story comes to a conclusion with the surprising notice that the herdsmen asked Jesus to leave. Before we too hastily criticize their action—something, interestingly, that Matthew does not do—we must remember that pigs were the herdsmen's livelihood. A few more such exorcisms could wipe out the village economically.

Does the fact that Matthew (with Mark) uses the same verb—"begged" (*parekaloun*, v 31; *parekalesan*, v 34)—in describing the demons' request to be sent into the pigs *and* the herdsmen's request of Jesus to leave, indicate that the evangelists see the herdsmen too as under the influence of the demonic? (In the herdsmen's case, of the demon Mammon?) If the evangelists do see this, they do not press it. We *are* supposed to ask whether the herdsmen valued property more than persons, economics more than human beings, their pigs more than the rehabilitation of townsmen. Jesus may have temporarily wiped out their herd, but he has permanently restored two men to the labor force, and in the long run, even economically, Jesus' presence is beneficial to the community.

It has even been facetiously suggested that perhaps the evangelists included this story precisely as a kind of evangelical bait to first-century Hebrew readers—a Messiah who wipes out *pigs* can't be all bad. In any case, Jesus' mission at first seems to be economically harmful. To people in the grip of an economic demonism Christian mission will at first appear unhelpful. Mammonized personalities will not be able to see what happens *to people*; all they will be able to see is what happens to their businesses, their bottom line, and their pigs.

Jesus left (9:1). His Word and presence are powerful and imperious, but they are not pushy ("Don't push," 7:6). Unwanted, he will leave without any other word. And the Gadarenes will be poorer, even economically, for his going. Thus the story is supposed to end rather threnodically, with a thud, because Jesus is misunderstood and because the people misread even their own best interests. World mission will in one sense be easy—Jesus' Word really is tremendously powerful. But in another sense it will not be easy—the whole world is under the quasi-demonic influence of economic passions, and it will look at times to the world as if Jesus' work and Word are against it. The church is forewarned.

Summary: The Five Miracles of Grace

When we put the five miracles of the eighth chapter together we see an interesting pattern. I am a teacher, and I like to grade. If we grade these miracles I think we will see Matthew's design (or mine, put on Matthew). The leper's faith was model—personal, modest, firm. We may give him an A in faith. The centurion's faith, too, was exemplary and was highly praised by Jesus. (It, too, deserves an A, but that would ruin my outline!) I will give the centurion a B-plus in faith. The mother-in-law's faith was neither good nor bad—she was in a fever and may even have been in a coma, or at least asleep. In any case, nothing is recorded of her faith at all—she was completely in neutral. Since she can neither be praised nor blamed, I give her a C. The disciples' faith was "barely passing." In fact, their littlefaith was accused by Jesus of cowardice. But at least they came to Jesus, at least they asked for his help, and therefore their faith did not completely fail. We give them a D. But in the final story Jesus is approached only to be insulted. His name as Son of God is used only as a defensive put-off or barrier. We cannot say that their approach to Jesus even barely passed. Their spirit was hostile. They get an F.

And yet in all five cases Jesus gave A-1 grace. This is the gospel of chapter 8. It may be the point of Matthew's arrangement of the miracles. It is not true that the measure of faith determines the measure of help. In this Gospel though Jesus always praises big faith, he never requires big faith before he will help. All he requires—and it is a very gracious requirement—is faith "like a grain of mustard seed," and to this *small* faith he promises *big* results, such as the moving of mountains (17:20). Legalistic preaching requires big faith on our part before God will deliver big help on his. ("Absolute surrender," "total commitment," "entire yielding," etc.) This demanding has little in common with the gospel. Jesus Christ will help independently of how well we approach him, as these five stories classically teach. What is needed is that we *approach him*. To approach Jesus, however inadequately, is to get help. This is certainly one of the major meanings of these five stories and of the Gospel as a whole.

This meaning is called grace in Christian theology. Grace means unconditional favor, undeserved help. Jesus helps anyone who approaches him, whether with personal openness, vicarious concern, fearful need, or even hostile confusion. To get near Jesus, *however well or badly we do it*, is to get near help. Jesus helps unconditionally.

It has been one of Protestantism's major temptations to turn faith into a meritorious work by whose quality or quantity God helps. Justification *by* faith has been turned into a justification *on the basis* of faith, or, divine help through the quality, quantity, depth, or entirety of faith. Only absolute surrender, we have been told, gets absolute help; only total commitment receives total power; only an empty vessel can be filled. But these mystic-gnostic adjectives, all of which focus on us and on the quality of our inner doings (or undoings), are to be rejected out of hand, and the focus is to be replaced on the face, hands, and Word of Jesus Christ alone. To be sure, Jesus wants great faith, and he praises it when anything like it appears, but he does not require it before he will help, as all five of these stories taken together show.

We used to criticize old Catholicism for making salvation a matter of exterior works: rosaries, novenas, satisfactions, pilgrimages, confessions, etc. But Protestant works can be even more excruciating because they have to be performed within, where it is hardest to tell how we are doing. Complete emptying, yielding, abandoning—and all other "completes," "fulls," "totals," and "absolutes"—can be cruel when imposed by uncompassionate teachers on eager candidates (cf. 23:4). Jesus loves confidence, praises it, and helps it. But he does not tyrannically demand it of us in a large, not to mention an entire measure, before he will help. These stories teach us that Jesus will help *because he wants to help*—with an astonishing eagerness (the leper and the centurion)—and all a person needs to do is to put oneself in his way.

Justification, according to the first, classic Reformation exposition of it, is *gratis propter Christum per fidem* ("by grace, for Christ's sake, through faith," *Augsburg Confession*, 1530, art. 4). And the order of words is important. God's saving help is first of all *gratis*, completely free. If we had first spiritually to pay for help it would not be free or *gratis*. Indeed, the real source of even faith— even in ordinary *human* relations—is the presence of the trustworthy other; by the grace of the worthy person, trust is awakened. *All* faith is gift. Not only must all exterior works and satisfactions be removed from the obscuring of this gracious fact, but, more subtly, all excruciating interior works (even "deeper" faith) must be taken away from our teaching so that Jesus can be everything he wants to be to us, and is, *gratis*.

Chapter Nine
The Five Miracles of Freedom
The Doctrine of Freedom

"The Lord sets the prisoners free;
the Lord opens the eyes of the blind" (Ps 146:7–8).

"Now the Lord is the Spirit, and where the Spirit of the Lord is, there
is freedom" (2 Cor 3:17).

There are five more miracles in chapter 9, and they honor faith. They are the histories, respectively, of the paralytic, the ruler's daughter, the woman who touched Jesus' garment, the two blind men, and the deaf mute. At the same time there are three full stories of freedom (in three famous controversies) that begin the chapter, that take exactly half the chapter's space, and that so thoroughly dominate the chapter's spirit that I prefer to see the whole chapter, even its miracles, under the rubric of freedom.

(1) The healing of the paralytic at the beginning of the chapter, for example, teaches Jesus' gift of *freedom from sin;* (2) the calling of Matthew the tax collector and the controversy that ensues teach *freedom from separatism;* (3) the following question about fasting teaches *freedom from scrupulosity;* then (4) the stories of the ruler's daughter and the woman who touched Jesus' garment are so notoriously intertwined in a single paragraph that we can see them teaching a single, fourth, somatic *freedom from sickness and death;* and finally, (5) the healing of the two blind men and deaf mute at the end of the chapter show Jesus giving the interpersonal, sensate *freedoms of sight and speech.*

As the eighth chapter taught the grace of Christ in helping us independently even of the worthiness of our faith, and thus stressed the *sources* of our salvation in Christ's free grace, so chapter 9 teaches us faith in Christ and the *end* of our salvation, which is the freedom of Christian persons through faith in, and discipleship to, Christ. An affirmation of the apostle Paul can serve as a motto for this chapter's central teaching: "*For freedom* Christ has set us free; stand fast therefore, and do not submit again to a yoke of slavery" (Gal 5:1 RSV).

Matthew highlights *faith* in this chapter as the great subjective way to freedom. If Jesus helps us graciously and even independently of the quality of our faith, as the five preceding miracles of chapter 8 taught us, this fact must not lead the church to think that faith itself is a matter of indifference to Jesus. Even chapter 8 taught how highly Jesus valued faith, in the first two miracles especially, but also in the fourth. Jesus wants faith, but he takes it as it comes, not imposing a tyrannical measure on it before he will come to our assistance. In order that the doctrine of God's salvation not end, however, with the conviction that faith itself does not matter much (that "God will help anyway")—in order, in other words, to avoid passivity and quietism—Matthew has given us a final ensemble of five miracles to praise faith's power and, especially, faith's freedoms.

I. THE PARALYTIC. FREEDOM FROM SIN: THE FORGIVENESS CONTROVERSY (9:1–8)

This is the first of three consecutive controversy stories, and the controversy here is about forgiveness (the next two are about fellowship and about fasting). The controversy story is an important genre in the Gospels. Jesus not only taught (5–7) and healed (8–9), he also argued (especially 9 A and 12). Matthew has compressed the miracle in this controversy, as he has in so many of Mark's original stories, into about half Mark's size. Mark's gift is to give us all the colorful details, to make a story jump; Matthew's gift is to give us only the essential details, to make a story sharp.

Together, Mark and Matthew give us a colorful (Markan) and a catechetical (Matthean) portrait of Jesus and the way Jesus works. Mark is technicolor gospel; Matthew is black and white. Mark is Luther; Matthew is Calvin. I think of Mark as young, definitely more joyful than Matthew, and in some senses even more evangelical (rather Lutheran). I think of Matthew as more serious and grave, and as most deeply concerned that we live moral lives worthy of the grace of Jesus Christ (rather Reformed, Calvinist, or Presbyterian). Each has a place in the church. Mark without Matthew might be slightly frivolous; Matthew without Mark would be too ponderous. Together, young and old, happy and serious, evangelical and moral, they give us the full Jesus Christ. (Luke adds social, John adds spiritual dimensions. Luke is Methodist, John Episcopalian—Acts is Baptist, except, in my opinion, for its doctrine of baptism!)

"And Jesus got into the boat and went back to his home town, Capernaum. And look, people brought him a paralytic lying on a bed. And when Jesus saw their faith he said to the paralytic, 'Courage, son; your sins are forgiven.' And look, some of the Bible teachers said to each other, 'This fellow is blaspheming.' And when Jesus knew their thoughts he said, 'Why are you thinking these evil thoughts in your heads? Tell me which is the easier thing to say, "Your sins are forgiven," or to say "Get up and walk"? Well, so that you will know that the Son of Man has authority on earth to forgive sins. . . .' Then Jesus said to the paralytic, 'Get up, take your bed, and go back home.' And he got up and went back home. When the crowds saw this they were really frightened, and they gave praise to the God who had given this kind of authority to human beings" (9:1–8).

9:2 If we had only Matthew we would not know that the people who brought the paralytic had been so eager to get their friend into Jesus' presence they had literally torn the roof off (Mark 2:4). All that Matthew tells us, cryptically and summarily, is that Jesus "saw their faith." Matthew's interest is always more in what Jesus does than in what eager believers do; thus Matthew drops all colorful expressions of faith, points simply to faith's presence, and spotlights the authoritative Christ.

Yet without Mark's rich details we would be definitely the poorer. Mark's details tell us that faith is bold, importunate, insistent, seemingly indifferent to social consequences (deroofing is antisocial), and that faith lives under one great compulsion: the determination to get into the presence of Jesus.

Jesus' word "courage" is instructive. It indicates that the audacious faith of the paralytic and his partners *was*, humanly, accompanied by some fear and trepidation; no one goes crashing into another's house without some fear. People in prayer often feel that to come crashing into the presence of the *Lord* is surely to take advantage of him and to be presumptuous with his grace. "Courage" corrects this impression. Nothing pleases this Lord as much as being boldly trusted, audaciously believed, and treated as if he were good. (This bold faith is the main lesson of Luke's Parable of the Widow and the Judge, Luke 18:1–8.)

Per omnia fides ad Christum penetrat ("Faith penetrates through all things to Christ, Beng.) "This [story] is a picture of how in temptations and calamities the opinions of men try to keep us away from Christ—e.g., Job's friends and those who in Ps 3:3 say, 'There is no help for him in God.' Again, it is a picture of the sentence of the law and of the accusations of one's own conscience. And it is a picture of how, through all these things, faith ought to come tearing in, so as to let itself down before the presence of Christ the Mediator" (Gerhard, *Harm. Evang.*, 43, in Trench, *Miracles*, 216 n. 1).

9:2c "Your sins are forgiven." It should be noticed that Jesus' remark is a simple statement of fact—"your sins are forgiven"—and that by putting the verb in the passive, "*are* forgiven," Jesus gives the credit to God. Jesus does not say "I forgive your sins." The way he puts forgiveness surprises us for another reason: he seems to know certainly how things stand with God ("your sins are *forgiven*"). How does Jesus know this? If one could answer this question one would have penetrated the mystery of Jesus' person.

We are surprised, too, that Jesus handles a case of paralysis by forgiveness. "Your sickness is healed" would have made more immediate sense. But when Jesus says "your sins are forgiven" we are given the impression that Jesus is doing surgery with words, that he is reaching down beneath the man's paralysis to his guilt, removing *that*, and so curing him at his roots. Paralysis, often a sickness of the nervous system, is associated readily with guilt, and so perhaps it took no great insight for Jesus to make this connection. Nevertheless, we can still be impressed by the assurance with which Jesus made his declaration of pardon.

On the connection between sin and sickness, Barclay, 1:328, puts the matter nicely, I think: "This man in the gospel story knew that he was a sinner; because he was a sinner, he was certain that God was his enemy; because he felt God was his enemy, he was paralysed and ill. Once Jesus brought to him the forgiveness of God, he knew that God was no longer his enemy, but his friend, and therefore he was cured."

The question of the relation between sin and sickness is one of the most delicate and difficult questions in theology. There is a clear connection between the two in this story (contra Beare, 222). Even if Jesus forgave sin here because the rabbinic theology of his time made the connection between sin and sickness, the connection in consciousness was—and still is—there (cf. Bonn., 125). Luke 13 A and John 9 A correct crass connections. But much Scripture, from Gen 3 to this text, teaches or presupposes a connection between sin and human ills that cannot be dismissed. Sin is the root of all our problems and the source of the ultimate sickness of death.

Doctor Roger Chillingsworth said to the Reverend Arthur Dimmesdale in the tenth chapter of Hawthorne's *The Scarlet Letter:* "He to whom only the outward and physical evil is laid open, knoweth, oftentimes, but half the evil which he is called upon to cure. A bodily disease, which we look upon as whole and entire within itself, may, after all, be but a symptom of some ailment in the spiritual part. . . . Thus, a sickness, . . . a sore place, if we may so call it, in your spirit hath immediately its appropriate manifestation in your bodily frame."

Psalm 32, the church's lectionary psalm for this Gospel text in Mark's version (Mark 2:1–12), draws the appropriate evangelical conclusions: "Blessed is he whose transgression is *forgiven,* whose sin is *covered.* . . . When I declared not my sin, my body wasted away through my groaning all day long." See Tay., 195, for exegetical-theological reflection.

It has always been appreciated in the church that with the forgiveness of sins we are at the ultimate place—we are in relation to God. (The Lord's Supper has been helpful here.) Jesus claims in our text, modestly and yet unmistakably, to be able to mediate this ultimate relation. The cleansing of leprosy, the long-distance healing of a gentile servant, the cooling of fever, the stilling of storm, the exorcism of demons, great as each is, cannot compare with the forgiveness of sins. Healers of body and mind can mediate miraculous curative powers into persons; but who, as the Bible teachers in a moment correctly ask, who can forgive sins except God alone? People cannot just go around telling other people that God holds nothing against them. To say this presupposes the most intimate possible knowledge of the real mind of God. Knowing and delivering divine amnesty comes close to presumption. Yet Jesus quietly and authoritatively tells another human being how he stands with God and how God has ruled concerning him. This is unprecedented in Jesus' ministry until now.

There can be little question that here we have reached the deepest point in the Gospel so far: a man is being placed completely right and clear before God, not by virtue of having kept, or even having promised to keep, God's law or the Sermon on the Mount, for example. Nor is this deep healing given on the basis of a prior repentance. In none of the three accounts of this healing in the Gospels is the healed man investigated. He is just put right, simply, on the basis of the faith of those who brought him. The deepest salvation is mediated to the man *gratis,* because of Christ, through faith—and the faith mainly of others ("when he saw *their* faith"). Perhaps we should not put too much stress on the faith of the others because here "their faith" in verse 2 can include the paralytic's own faith, though this is not stressed either.

Chrysostom, 29:1:195, works both sides of the street: The faith that Jesus sees is "the faith of them that had let the man down. For He doth not on all occasions require faith on the part of the sick only: as for instance, when they are insane, or in any other way, through their disease, are out of their own control. Or rather, in this case, the sick man too had part in the faith; for he would not have suffered himself to be let down, unless he had believed."

But Victor of Antioch (fifth century) believes that it was "not the faith of the paralytic, but of those who bring him," and Ephrem, therefore, urges us to "see what the faith of others may do for one." Ambrose, on the parallel text in Luke 5:20, comments that "it is a great Lord who by the merit of some forgives others. . . . If you despair of the forgiveness of great sins, cling to pray-ers, cling to the church" (all in Swete, 34). Jerome, 1:166, is similar.

Luther, W^2 11:20:24–26, evangelically, loves what he calls alien faith: "They win for this sick man with their faith a faith of his own; for this sick man at first had no faith, but afterwards he heard the Word, and Christ poured into the man a faith of the man's own, awakened him with the gospel; Jesus is accustomed to pour faith in through the Word."

Luther then combats the idea that infant baptism should occur on the basis of the church's faith—for each person must have personal faith. (Luther believes that the Word of God in baptism *gives* infants faith.) Alien faith, Luther insists, does not get anyone salvation, even if there were two whole Christendoms present at the baptism. But we preach, pray, baptize and work to the end that unbelievers and children will be given faith. Therefore, here in our present text, *first* the friends alone had faith, not the sick man; but then *he* had to come to faith, otherwise their faith would not have helped him. But with their faith they asked Christ to give the sick man his own faith. "Therefore, alien faith helps me to come to my own faith."

Calvin, 1:258, agrees: "Even though Christ is said to have been moved by the faith of others, the paralytic could not have gained the forgiveness of sins, unless he had his own faith. . . . For Christ did not so much attend to those who carried the paralytic, as He looked at the faith of the man himself." Finally, the early twentieth-century commentator, McNeile, 115, concludes: "The paralytic himself may be included in *autōn* [*their* faith] but the power of faith in obtaining blessings for another is illustrated in [Matt] 8:10; 15:28; James 5:15. It rests upon the real unity of human life." The greatest blessing to obtain for another is faith. This should encourage Christian parents.

What is clearly stressed in the text is that *faith* is the medium that receives forgiveness from God through *Jesus—sola fide, solus Christus*. We are moving farther and farther down into the root of things as we proceed in this Gospel: from the Sermon on the Mount that calls for *our* mercy and forgiveness we move into the Ten Miracles that teach *God's* mercy and forgiveness.

9:3 The Bible teachers or seminary professors ("scribes") correctly perceived that what had just been said by Jesus was spiritually unprecedented and, if they heard him correctly, blasphemous. Jesus had assumed (or presumed) the prerogatives of God. "I, I am He, who blots out your transgressions," says the *Lord* emphatically in Isa 43:25 (cf. Exod 34:6f; Isa 44:22).

9:4 Jesus sensed what was going on in their minds. And so he asked, "Why are you thinking these evil thoughts in your heads?" Theologians then as now were trained to defend the honor of God—in the final analysis that is what theology is about. They would not think that their judgment of blasphemy should be called "thinking these evil thoughts in your heads." The evil, certainly, was in the blasphemer, not in those who detected him. The only conceivable way that Jesus could have averted their judgment would have been for him to be deity or authorized by deity, and since these were (for them) clearly unproved, their judgment seemed to have had a strong basis in fact.

Taylor, 201: "When Nathan says to David, 'The Lord hath put away thy sin' (2 Sam 12:13), there is a similarity [to our text] in that his words give the assurance of a prophet of God, but not a complete parallel. Nathan reverently names the name of God with a full assurance of truth, but Jesus in His own person says 'Thy sins are forgiven' with the conviction of One who sees the paralytic through the eyes of God. Moreover, in His case it is not only a matter of knowledge, but also of action. Without implying that sin is the universal cause of sickness, He sees that forgiveness is indispensable to [this] cure, and feels Himself able to mediate forgiveness to the paralytic. The action is divine rather than declaratory, but it does not invade the prerogative of Almighty God."

9:5–6 Jesus then asked his central question: "Which is the easier thing to say, 'Your sins are forgiven,' or to say 'Get up and walk'? Well, so that you will know that the Son of Man has authority on earth to forgive sins . . . , 'Get up, take your bed, and go back home.'" (The title "Son of Man," Bonnard, 126 n. 1, says correctly, should be left in its "*accent énigmatique.*" Cf. Tay., 200; Caird, 94f, for discussion of the title and the same conclusion.) The easier thing to *say*, of course, is forgiveness, because nothing visible is needed for proof in an invisible relation with God. (Yet, to be sure, nothing is more difficult to get.) It is definitely harder to say a healing word because the truth or falsehood of this can be instantly verified. Jesus could have been accused of a cheap sensationalism—or even of making the most audacious claims (forgiveness of sins)—without having to deliver any proof whatever. So Jesus says, "so that you will know that the Son of Man has authority on earth *to forgive sins*. . . ." Jesus intends to keep the issue focused where he wants it: on his seemingly blasphemous claim. The healing will be used to prove the deeper reality of Jesus' divine investiture.

"Authority" (*exousia*) is the word Jesus uses here. "Authority" in fact is the last word used in the Gospel to signify Jesus' dignity (28:18); it is the last major impression left on the hearers of his Sermon on the Mount (7:29); it is also the word used at his first major interrogation in Jerusalem (21:23–27); thus it is apparently the word that in Matthew's conviction best unifies all that made Jesus who he is. Jesus everywhere appears with authority. He seems instantly to claim it. And he claims, moreover, to be able to exercise it "on earth" (v 6). This last fact is as remarkable as all the other remarkable facts with which this story is studded. It was assumed that the place where forgiveness was transacted was in heaven, in the presence and court of God, who was the only dispenser of forgiveness. The claim to be able to dispense forgiveness of sins *here on earth* was as audacious as the claim to be able to forgive or announce forgiveness at all. But Jesus twists the knife: he has the authority delegated to him by God, both to *forgive* (the dimension of height or heaven) and to forgive *here* (the dimension of depth or earth). And to prove it he will use the case immediately before them. He tells the paralytic to pack up and go home. The possibility of human mediation of divine forgiveness now hinges upon the most mundane of acts: if a man can roll up his blankets and walk home, Jesus has divine prerogatives; if the man cannot, Jesus stands exposed.

9:7 "And he got up and went back home." By this simple act Jesus is simultaneously vindicated—and condemned. Vindicated temporarily before God and the believing public; condemned before the theological leadership. This incident marks a watershed moment in the history of Jesus in this Gospel: something akin to deity, in a remarkable way, is present in Jesus; and yet rather understandably, I think, something very demonic could have been present in a person claiming, apart from all the traditional safeguards, to be able to grant divine largesse. The people were impressed; those responsible for God's honor in Israel were not. The issue is joined.

9:8 "When the crowds saw this they were really frightened, and they gave praise to the God who had given this kind of authority to human beings." What is meant by this curious last phrase is that to human beings such as Jesus the right, the authority, to forgive sins had been given. And Matthew intends to remind his readers that this authority has also been given to other human beings—to the disciples of Jesus—through Jesus, as Matthew will show more fully in chapters 16 and 18 (the church chapters) of his Gospel. "Human beings" (*anthrōpois*, plural) have now been given the right to forgive sins. This is a momentous fact if it is true. And the Christian community claims that it is. The first raison d'être of the church may be said to be the privilege of forgiving sins in Jesus' name through preaching the gospel and administering the sacraments.

Beare, 223f (emphasis added): "The remarkable shift to the plural 'men' [in our text] does not indicate at all that Matthew thinks of this as a *general* authority which God has granted to *all* men. The thought is that the authority of Jesus to pronounce the forgiveness of sins is now exercized by the ministers of his *church*. . . . It is a distinctively Christian rite, and the church could not fail to ascribe its origin and its ultimate authority to Jesus." Modern commentators who see here the gift of forgiveness of sins given to the church include Schl., *Der*, 301; Held, 249, 274; Stend., 781; Grund., 268 n. 12; Green, 103; Hill, 172; Gund., 165.

Still one other fact should be highlighted before leaving the story. Forgiveness of sins and the ability to move are interchangeable. By saying one Jesus grants the other. Forgiveness of sins is, practically speaking, the engine of Christian motion. To forgive a person is to enable a person to move.

The meaning for the church is that when we preach and grant, in Jesus' name, the forgiveness of sins we are enabling persons to move. Nothing is, in fact, more mobilizing than forgiveness. We know this from personal experience. Nothing moves us like assurance that we are fully pardoned by God. Every Christian community is eager to be alive and on the move; let the community not forget in her arsenal of renewal the simple power of the forgiveness of sins present in sermon and sacrament. It is a frequent error of even conservative communities to believe that the message of forgiveness is only for unbelievers. But this is too limited. The gospel of forgiveness is also—weekly, daily—for believers, too, because believers also contract guilt and guilt's paralyses, and believers, too, need forgiveness. The way for a church or for an individual Christian to move is for there to be a continuing ministry of the stories and supper of Jesus with their gifts of forgiveness received by faith.

The first, the seminal freedom of the gospel, is the freedom of Jesus' forgiveness of sins.

Luther, W² 11:2–6: The kingdom of Christ is the sentence "your sins are forgiven"; here there are no works, no merits, no commandments or law—but only pure grace and kindliness; therefore, if we want the kingdom of Christ to multiply, don't tell people to go and do this or that; when you propose works to me (as the way to forgiveness, says Luther) you are not moved by the Holy Spirit; "for the Holy Spirit goes around leading me first of all to the grace of Christ, and not to works." Luther, *Large Catechism* (on the third article of the Creed): "All appointments in Christendom have been so ordered that we should daily obtain full forgiveness of sins, through the Word and [the sacramental] signs as sources of comfort and cheer to our consciences as long as we live. And this is what the Holy Spirit does for us: Although we have sin, it cannot harm us, because we are a part of Christendom, where there is entire forgiveness of sins; God forgives us, and we forgive, bear with and help each other. Outside of Christendom, where the Gospel prevails not, there is no forgiveness."

II. THE CALL OF MATTHEW. FREEDOM FROM SEPARATISM: THE FELLOWSHIP CONTROVERSY (9:9–13)

We noticed in the middle of chapter 8 that the miracles of grace were joined and divided by the buffer-like insertion of two discipleship stories (8:18–22). Now in the midst of the miracles of the ninth chapter we meet two comparable discipleship stories in the form of controversies. In fact, the whole first half of the ninth chapter is controversy. The story we have just reviewed—the healing of the paralytic—is really as much a story of controversy with Bible teachers about forgiveness as it is a story about the healing of a man with paralysis. This chapter shows us how *opposition* to Jesus begins to build. We had the first intimation of opposition to Jesus' work in the dismissal of Jesus by the Gadarene pagans—yet their dismissal was a little understandable, as we saw. But those who contend now with Jesus at the entrance to chapter 9 are those who religiously we might have expected to be closest to Jesus: the Bible teachers in the forgiveness controversy, the Serious (*Pharisaim*) in the fellowship controversy, and the disciples of John the Baptist in the fasting controversy. All three controversies teach us that the ministry of Jesus gives believers a freedom that will not go uncontested by religious people.

9:9–13 *"And as Jesus was walking along he saw a man sitting at the tax-collector's table—Matthew was the man's name—and Jesus said to him, 'Follow me!' And Matthew got up and followed him. And when Jesus was having dinner that night in the house there were many tax-collectors and questionable people who had come and were sitting there with Jesus and his disciples. When the Pharisees saw this, they said to his disciples, 'Why does your teacher eat at all with tax-collectors and bad people?' When Jesus heard what they were saying, he replied, 'Healthy people don't have any need for a doctor; but sick people do. Go back home and read your Bibles again where it says, "Mercy is what I want and not sacrifice." Because I did not come to invite good people; I came for bad people.'"*

Tax-collectors were Palestine's quislings. We might in fact preface the noun "tax-collectors" with the adjective "collaborator" to give the right sense. Palestine was under Roman rule, and for the amoral one of the most coveted economic positions under the new regime was the office of tax-collector for the colonial power. The job usually went to the highest bidders. Marx called this class "comprador bourgeoisie." They betrayed their own people for their private interests, and so they were despised. In a sense we have gone deeper into the first century's social pit here in this story than we had even in the first three stories of chapter 8 with the leper, the gentile, and the woman: a tax-collector was considered a moral untouchable. Jesus recruits *him*. This pleased the morally serious of Jesus' time (the *Pharisaim*) as little as friendship with a collaborator with an enemy power pleases the politically serious of our time.

Taylor, 204: "Universally despised for their rapacity and low morals . . . , the *telōnai* [tax-collectors] of the Gospels were scorned on political grounds and because their work involved contact with Gentiles." Barclay, 1:330: "These tax-gatherers were universally hated. They had entered the service of their country's conquerors, and they amassed their fortunes at the expense of their country's misfortunes. . . . By Jewish law a tax-gatherer was debarred from the synagogue; he was included with things and beasts unclean, and Leviticus 20:5 was applied to them; he was forbidden to be a witness in any case; 'robbers, murderers, and tax-gatherers' were classed together." Cf. McK., 78. The *theological* meaning of Jesus' call of the tax-collector is put well by Calvin, 1:262, "in his [the tax-collector's] person [Jesus teaches] that the calling of us all depends not on the merits of our own righteousness, but on His sheer generosity." Green, 103: "Disciples included reclaimed sinners from the beginning." Schlatter *Das*, 140:

Jesus did not usually recruit those he healed immediately into his discipleship; but he does enlist Matthew the collaborator as a perpetual, walking witness to the depth of his forgiveness of sins. See Jerome, 1:168, 170, for speculation on why Levi in Mark and Luke is called Matthew in Matthew.

9.9 "'Follow me!' And Matthew got up and followed him." The same imperious Word that had unlocked Peter, Andrew, James, and John from their nets, boats, and parents (4:18–22), now liberates Matthew from his collaboration. It is the simplest Word, "Follow me." Matthew intends for us to marvel at the uncanny power of this low-key invitation. The Word that summons a person to follow Jesus is a Word invested with nuclear power. This Word has the power to tear persons away from all that which until then had been most precious to them (fishing, boats, parents) or from that which until then had most debased them (colonialism, money). The surest way to break the grip of bourgeois creature-comforts and colonial mentality is the discipling Word of Jesus. Wherever the church has summoned persons to—notice—*the following of Jesus* (and not to another creature-comfort such as, say, heavenly bliss), the church has had the power to change persons.

9:10–11 ". . . there were many tax-collectors and questionable people . . . sitting there with Jesus and his disciples." We know especially from the Book of Acts (chapters 10, 11, and 15 in particular) how tenaciously the older conceptions of holiness gripped even the disciples of Jesus. Separation from immoral elements seems required by the Word of God in Scripture everywhere in the Old Testament and in critical places in the New (2 Cor 6). The first psalm is a classic example of the biblical doctrine of separation: "Blessed is the person who walks not in the counsel of the ungodly, stands not in the way of sinners, and sits not in the seat of scoffers." (Cf. Ps, 26:4f, "I do not sit with false men, nor do I consort with dissemblers; I hate the company of evildoers, and I will not sit with the wicked.") But here is Jesus sitting with precisely these types. Who was right: Scripture or Jesus? What possible good could fraternizing with such people do to the community's moral seriousness? If one of Jesus' intentions was the moral renewal of the people of God, what kind of an example would this evening's dinner set?

It would not have been easy for persons steeped in the piety of the people of God to reconcile with Scripture the seemingly indiscriminate social habits of Jesus. It is necessary for us to feel *with* the best and most religiously serious elements in Israel before we can feel *against* them fairly or feel the pinch of this story and of similar stories. The word "Pharisees" has come to be so tainted that we can hardly feel the force any longer of the Pharisees' real (and not merely pretended) righteousness. Jesus took the Pharisees more seriously than he took any other group in Israel. The Sadducees hardly figured in his polemic—they lacked scriptural seriousness. But the Pharisees were in dead earnest; consequently Jesus gave them time.

9:12 When Jesus heard their honestly expressed question, he responded with his now classic riposte: "Healthy people don't have any need for a doctor; but sick people do." Jesus will ground this on a Scripture text in a moment (because no matter how astutely Jesus spoke, unless he could marshall Scripture he did not stand a chance with the serious). But first of all he wants to argue from common sense: "Who needs a doctor: sick people or well people? My conduct may not be as inconsistent as you think. It is precisely those persons whom you rightly consider sick with whom I rightly practice medicine."

There is some discussion among exegetes about Jesus' meaning in the use of the words "healthy" and "righteous": Is he facetious or serious? Are the Serious really spiritually healthy and righteous? We should not dismiss out of hand the possibility that they are. In his programmatic statement in the Sermon on the Mount, for example, Jesus had said that unless our righteousness exceeds the *righteousness* of the Bible teachers and Pharisee-Serious we would not enter the kingdom, conceding them a certain righteousness. It is noteworthy that the evangelists never ascribe demon-possession to the Pharisees. They are not mentally deranged or sick—they are disgustingly healthy.

Perhaps at this point in his ministry Jesus was not fully aware of the depth of the hostility in, or the spiritual sickness of, Pharisaism. In any case, Jesus appeals for understanding: doctors serve, they do not avoid, the sick. Jesus is not two-faced when he talks morally and then eats with sinners, any more than a doctor is who talks of health and then spends his day in the hospital.

The Old Testament and even Pauline doctrines of separation receive something of a correction or supplementation (not a substitution) by Jesus' new approach to the sin question and to the holiness goal. Identification with sinners becomes another way of holiness. The dangers of identification are only too apparent: doctors can catch their patients' diseases. Separation would seem the safer route, and sometimes separation is God's clear will (Ps 1 and 2 Cor 6 are in the canon).

9:13 "'Go back home and read your Bibles again where it says, 'Mercy is what I want and not sacrifice.' Because I did not come to invite good people; I came for bad people.'"

Jesus unleashes his big guns: his knowledge of the heart of Scripture. With his hospital analogy Jesus had attempted by common sense to clear the ground. But common sense among the spiritually serious is not as persuasive as Scripture. Where in Scripture does it say anything about throwing dinner parties for pagans? To tell the truth, most of the holiness code of Israel (Exodus, Leviticus, Numbers) and much of the point of the historical books (Samuel, Kings, Chronicles, and esp. Ezra and Nehemiah) seem indeed to teach the rigorous separation of the people of God from alien influences. But Jesus found in the prophets (and also in the law, as we will see later when he discusses the love of neighbor in a fundamental way) a deeper Word, a Word which, though not as frequently heard, is still there, and to which Jesus now gives priority: "Mercy is what I want and not sacrifice" (Hos 6:6), i.e., "God is gracious before he is demanding" (G. Barth, 83; see the Beatitudes before the commands). Hosea 6:6 is enthroned here by Jesus as the social point of the Hebrew Scriptures. Hosea 6:6 is the Old Testament's way of saying the New Testament's Golden Rule (Matt 7:12). It is a canon within the canon, a hermeneutical rule, an interpretive principle for the correct reading of Scripture and correct relation to people. ("We have here an axiom of interpretation . . . , the sum total of that part of theology which treats of cases of conscience," Beng., 1:148.)

"Sacrifice" calls for an act of the will and the separation of oneself from others. "Mercy" is mainly an act of (what our time calls) the heart and it seeks identification with others. It is as if Jesus had said, "I want heart and not will power," or "I want simple humanity and not your spiritual self-discipline." Wherever self-discipline has become too central in the church this mercy-Word has been a corrective. Discipline can be the most selfish of acts, calculated more to create spiritual giants than human beings. Jesus says that Scripture wants to create human beings.

Toward God, the Pharisees were generous—in almsgiving, prayer, and fasting (6 A); but God has said in Scripture, and Jesus now reemphasizes the divine decision, that he prefers generosity toward people (Schl., *Das,* 141f; Schl., *Der,* 307f). Bonnard, 131, believes that the sacrifice spoken of in this text is the strong desire for purity by avoiding society's bad elements (thus McN., 119, too)—elements seemingly condemned even by Scripture, i.e., by God (Schl., *Der,* 308). But Hosea 6:6 and Jesus clarify the will of God definitively.

9:13b "Because I did not come to invite good people; I came for bad people." The "I came" and "I did not come" passages of the Gospel point to something of the mystery and deity of the person who says them (cf. Allen, 91; Beare, 227, doubts that Jesus could have spoken this way of himself; unconvincingly). It is as though Jesus had come from a kind of preexistence to our now; the words everywhere add weight and authority to Jesus' declarations. And Jesus says that the reason he came was to invite the bad, not the good. If only the bad are the mission of the Messiah, then the consequence would seem to be either to become bad (which doesn't sound right) or to realize we're not so good (which sounds better). From now on, in any case, no serious Christian can be condemned for being with the wrong people—if it is for the right reasons. Moreover, Jesus wants his people to know that they are themselves wrong people whom he met and put right.

In this paragraph Jesus has freed his church from false separatism and from the fear that there are some people with whom we cannot mix. In the first story in this chapter, in the forgiveness of sins, Jesus united us in the depths with God in the highest; in this second story, in calling and dining with Matthew and his friends, Jesus unites us with the whole world in its width and breadth. Jesus is the Maximum Liberator.

III. THE QUESTION ABOUT FASTING. FREEDOM FROM SCRUPULOSITY: THE FASTING CONTROVERSY (9:14–17)

"Then the disciples of John came up to Jesus and asked, 'Why do we and the Pharisees fast a lot, but your disciples don't fast at all?' And Jesus responded, 'Is it really right for the best man and ushers of the bridegroom to fast while the bridegroom is right there with them? Of course, there are days ahead when the bridegroom will be taken away from them, and then they will fast. But you see, for now, no one in her right mind puts a beautiful new piece of cloth as a patch on an old dress, because its beauty and fulness detract from the old dress, and, what is more, it will only make the tear in the old dress worse. And people don't pour brand new wine into old wine bags. If they did, the bags would split and the wine would spill all over, and those old wine bags would be destroyed. No, people pour new wine into new wine bags, and this way both are preserved."

We are still around a table, the unifying symbol in both this and the former story (Lohm., 174). In the preceding story the problem was *with whom* to eat (the fellowship question); in the present story the problem is *how often* to eat at all (the fasting question). The Serious believed (rightly, in many respects) that one's company determines one's character; and both the Serious and the Baptist's disciples believed that diet also influenced character, particularly the dietary habit or spiritual discipline known as fasting.

9:14 The question of the Baptist's disciples, exactly, is "Why do we and the Pharisees fast a lot, but your disciples don't fast at all?" In almost all religions, fasting plays a role. Fasting effects and symbolizes the suppression of the body for the sake of the spirit. Consequently, that Jesus should appear as a religious teacher, recruit and train disciples, and yet not give any particular attention to fasting, seemed inconsistent and almost irreligious. How could he be serious spiritually and yet leave his disciples to eat as they did before they met him?

The problem in this and the preceding controversy-story, then, is the naturalness of Jesus: he seems to eat (1) with almost anybody and to be willing to eat (2) almost anything. Can such a person be a credible religious leader? (Bonnard, 132, believes that the preceding fellowship story and the present fasting story are united by the fact that in both Jesus is "living well," i.e., that in the opinion of his questioners he is insufficiently simple, rigorous, or radical in his lifestyle.)

One disputed word in our text raises a small alarm. It is the word "[we] fast *a lot* (*polla*)," which the twenty-sixth edition Nestle-Aland and the United Bible Societies' Greek New Testaments include between brackets in their readings (against S and B). If the Baptist's disciples said this "a lot" we are disappointed, because it indicates a wrong spirit. One detects in the word a too self-conscious pride in spiritual activity (thus Jero., 1:172), and if this was the case we have a clue to why Jesus gave so little positive instruction on fasting: fasting tends to make one too self-conscious (these fasters "were too gloom-ridden and turned in upon themselves," Cal., 1:266). What is more, fasting does not do much for the neighbor—it can be a somewhat self-centered discipline—and Jesus' ethic is conspicuously a neighbor-centered ethic, an other-person ethic; it is not an ethic of spiritual, physical, or mental self-cultivation. ("I want mercy and not sacrifice" is a way of saying "I want neighborliness and not individualism.") Jesus' ethic is humane not yogic, interpersonal not intrapersonal.

In a 1537 sermon, Luther (W^2 12:1278f) said, "I have never yet seen a right fast"; in his experience, all fasting had been done with a false trust in human works; a right fast is "carrying sadness and suffering" in a Christian manner. Caird, 96, points out that in later Judaism fasting became in fact meritorious.

Disciples are to be focused outward, first of all, on their Master—that was the lesson of chapter 8's discipleship-stories (8:18–22); and when they are focused on their Master they will notice that *his* eyes, in turn, are focused on other people and their needs—the lesson of chapter 9's controversy-stories. The eighth chapter discipleship-stories taught us discipleship's rigor; the ninth chapter controversy-stories teach us discipleship's freedom. Chapter 8 draws us in to Jesus; chapter 9 moves us out into his world. Chapter 8's discipleship-stories asked us to love our Lord with all our heart and strength; chapter 9's controversy-stories ask us to love our neighbor as ourselves. All five (the two discipleship and three controversy stories) are *discipleship*-stories in that they teach us what following Jesus means;

and all five, again, are *controversy*-stories in that they teach us to expect controversy *in* discipleship—with (1) our own ego, (2) family, (3) critical co-religionists, (4) separatists, and (5) disciplinarians.

9:15a Jesus' answer to the fasting question is rhetorical: Is it right for the bridegroom's wedding party to be sad (fasting is a form of mourning)? To fast at someone else's wedding party would not only be unnatural; it would be rude and, finally, selfish. Few things were as happy as the Jewish week-long wedding party (described in Str.-B., 1:504–06; Barc., 1:335–36; Caird, 97); it was the closest thing to a modern vacation we can imagine. One was with best friends at a party that lasted seven days, with the finest food, drink, and fun available. For one of the inner-circle of friends at the party to have fasted this week would have been a capital insult to the host, depressing for everyone else, and callously egocentric. The honorees at the wedding party are the bride and groom. Jesus does not intend for his disciples to be a company of the dour, drawing attention to themselves, their discipline, and their piety. Here, too, he wants mercy and not sacrifice.

The classic biblical commentary on Jesus' fasting controversy is Paul's moving passage in Colossians (2:16, 20–23): "Therefore let no one pass judgment on you in questions of food and drink or with regard to a festival or a new moon or a sabbath. . . . If with Christ you died to the elemental spirits of the universe, why do you live as if you still belonged to the world? Why do you submit to regulations, 'Do not handle, Do not taste, Do not touch' . . . according to human precepts and doctrines? These have indeed an appearance of wisdom in promoting rigor of devotion and self-abasement and severity to the body, but they are of no value in checking the indulgence of the flesh [margin: or, are of no value, serving only to indulge the flesh]" (RSV). Why do Christians, then, and whole denominations, make strictures about food, drink, and sabbath?

9:15b The sentence "there are days ahead when the bridegroom will be taken away from them, and then they will fast," points to two times: (1) the days of passion and burial immediately ahead when the disciples may fast (Lohmeyer, 175, believes this is the only time referred to) and (2) the church's freedom in the indefinite future to fast (see *Didache*, 8:1, very soon after Matthew, when the church was fasting again). There is a sense in which the bridegroom has been taken away from us: we cannot see him; we live by faith and hope, not by sight (2 Cor 5). His "return" is called literally his "presence": *parousia*. But there is a sense, too, and a very important one, in which Matthew wants us to know that the bridegroom is present wherever two or three are gathered together in his name (18:20) and that he "is with us always, even unto the end of the age" (28:20), in which case fasting, carried too far, is inappropriate. The sentence does give the church the freedom to fast in the future. But it is not (and this is important) a command to fast. (It is a prophecy, not a command; Swete, 45.) As with celibacy later on (19:10–12), Jesus is discreet in the area of the ascetic. Jesus leaves some matters to the conscience of disciples.

In the easy manner with which Jesus identifies himself with the Bridegroom of Old Testament prophecy (Hos 2:19), and thus with *God* in his covenant relationship to Israel (Swete, 44), Jesus may not "put forth a public claim to be the Messiah," but "He silently implies it, and the claim is for those who have ears to hear" (Tay., 211). Jesus' reply "makes the highest christological claim imagineable" (Beare, 229). Jesus appears to believe that some of the feasting of the kingdom of heaven has already begun. The kingdom, in some sense, has already been inaugurated and is now present in the world. Gundry's interpretation of the text as meaning "there is no excuse for failure to fast now" (55; cf 168–70) seems to me to miss the direction of the text.

9:16–17 The patch-parables of dress and wine bags are among the most difficult and diversely interpreted parables in Jesus' teaching (see Bultmann's problems with them, 98). This much is clear: Jesus, his freeing Word, and the discipleship that he forms are the new; separation, fasting, and other disciplines are the old. The two do not conveniently mix. One cannot often blend the best of ancient religious disciplines (such as fasting), spiritual as they might be in their way, and real discipleship to Jesus; either the venerable practices are mangled in the process or the dramatic freshness of Jesus is spoiled.

"The sentiments [that these two parables] express are revolutionary, since they affirm that a new message must find a fresh vehicle, if it is not to perish and to destroy existing institutions" (Tay., 212). "'People will not accept new things unless they have become new persons'" (Hilary in Swete, 47, who believes that *this*—conversion—is the point of these parables). Jerome, 1:174, 176, also believes that Jesus' message here is the need for spiritual *rebirth* in order to be able to carry the tough commands and austerities of the Christian life.

Disciples have different disciplines for the living of their diverse discipleships. Jesus with real dignity refuses the invasion of this privacy. "In brief, not all are to be compelled to lead the same pattern of life, for their conditions are not the same, and everything does not suit everybody" (Cal., 1:268). This story is a Bill of Rights for disciples and a classic of Christian liberty.

Jesus' Word here is a mandate to alertness, a command to be open to fresh forms of discipleship. Just as the preceding fellowship-controversy story taught us to be more open to *people* than we had earlier thought appropriate, so the present fasting controversy-story teaches us to feel free to serve people in *ways* that earlier some might have thought not useful. Jesus in these two stories gives discipleship an exciting relation to the world. The discipleship-stories of Matthew 8 (vv 18–22) taught us to be careful of worldly influences; the controversy-stories of Matthew 9 teach us to be open to world service—a nice balance.

We have now completed the three controversy-stories in this chapter. (The next set of controversy-stories—three again—will complete the doctrine of the person of Christ and fill up the whole of chapter 12.) In freeing us from sin in the forgiveness controversy, Jesus gave us spiritual freedom (like this: ↑); in freeing us from separatism in the fellowship controversy, Jesus gave us social freedom (like this: ↔); and now in freeing us from scrupulosity in the fasting controversy, Jesus gives us self-freedom (like this: ↻), the freedom to be ourselves, to develop our own set of disciplines and scruples, as situations, needs, and the divine Lord determine. We are freed "every which way" by Jesus. Salvation is by grace (chapter 8) into freedom (chapter 9).

One of the blessings of discipleship to Jesus is that while it binds us to rigorous obedience to him, at the same time and because of this binding, we are set marvelously free. "Make me a captive, Lord, and then I shall be free." There are many gods loose in contemporary culture who only bind; they do not simultaneously bind and free. Jesus is the best of all gods, the liberator par excellence. These three freedom stories teach an evangelical liberation theology.

IV. THE LEADER'S DAUGHTER AND THE WOMAN WHO TOUCHED JESUS' ROBE: FREEDOM FROM SICKNESS AND DEATH (9:18–26)

The next two miracles are always intertwined in the synoptic tradition, similar to the linking of the miracles of the "wild ones" in chapter 8 (the storm and the demoniacs). The two present stories might be called the desperation or *in extremis* miracles (the Vulgate rendering of the Mark 5:23 parallel is, in fact, "My daughter *in extremis est*"), for in both cases the principals are at the end of their tether: the leader's daughter is dead or dying, and the woman with the hemorrhage has been trying for years to get healing and has not gotten it. Both these cases came to Jesus in deep need. And in both, faith got Jesus' help. (Faith is the focus of the healing stories at the end of this chapter as freedom was the focus at the beginning. The master study of faith in the Matthean miracles is Held, esp. 180, 241–46, 274–88.)

9:18–19 *"While Jesus was talking, look, a Jewish leader came up to Jesus, bowed down worshipfully at his feet, and said, 'My daughter has just died. But when you come and lay your hand on her, she will live.' And Jesus got up and followed him, and the disciples came along."*

This man has faith indeed. He believes that Jesus can raise his dead daughter. (Matthew has again telescoped a longer story in order to get to the point. In Mark and Luke the daughter is dying, not dead; in them she dies while Jesus and the father are en route to her.) Matthew drops all details in order to concentrate his attention on the central teaching in this incident: faith in Jesus conquers even death.

The weight in the leader's remark tends toward the word "but": "My daughter has just died. *But* when you come. . . ." To say "dead *but*" requires extraordinary confidence. (Gundry, 172, shows how Matthew's editorial work here enhances faith.) The man does not believe that Jesus is helpless before the last and most intractable human problem. Confronted in this bold way, then, Jesus is placed before the question: "Shall my ministry stop short of the final problem? Shall death be the only enemy I am unable to conquer?" (Schlatter, *Der,* 317; *idem, Das,* 147, makes the observation that in healing the daughter of this community *leader* (*archōn*), Matthew shows how Jesus had help ready for *every* person in the city, regardless of class. Jesus is for, but not only for, the poor.)

This miracle teaches us that Jesus' ability to help is limitless. There is absolutely nothing that can separate us from the love of God in Christ Jesus our Lord—even death must now learn this. The first two *healings* of chapter 9, then, reach right down into humanity's two fundamental problems: first, sin and its forgiveness (the paralytic); now, death and its conquest (the leader's daughter). In the eighth chapter miracles of grace we saw Jesus healing *out*casts—the dimension there was breadth. In the ninth chapter miracles of faith we see Jesus healing, let us say, "*down*casts," that is, persons trapped within the abysmal sicknesses of guilt and death. Here the dimension is depth. In chapter 8 Jesus reaches out; in chapter 9 he reaches down; in 8 he embraces those whom nobody else wanted to touch; in 9 he rescues those whom nobody else thought human beings could touch.

9:19 When a person comes to Jesus with the kind of confidence this elder brought—"dead but"—a remarkable thing happens: Jesus "follows"! Matthew uses the word that until now he has used for human following: "And Jesus got up and followed him." Where faith comes, Jesus follows—willingly, immediately (on the uniqueness of this story, see Allen, 77). We caught something of this truth in the opening two miracles of chapter 8 when Jesus immediately reached out his hand and touched the leper and, again, when Jesus overwhelmed the centurion by announcing his immediate coming to his home. Now Matthew wants to reassert this evangelical doctrine: Where people have confidence in Jesus, Jesus immediately follows. Faith has almost divine powers. (Cf. Luther on the First Commandment in his *Large Catechism*.)

9:20–22 *"And look, a woman who had had a bleeding problem for twelve years came up behind Jesus and touched the tassel at the corner of his robe. She did this because she kept saying to herself, 'If I can only touch his robe I'll be all right.' Jesus turned around, saw her, and said, 'Courage, daughter, your faith has made you completely well.' And the woman was indeed made well that very hour."*

What Mark told in ten verses Matthew tells in three: that faith in Jesus deeply helps. And while Mark had given us a physical, almost chemical view of Jesus by having the woman's touch draw power from Jesus, Matthew locates the power entirely in Jesus' *Word*. Compare Mark's rendering without Word, and Matthew's emphasis on the Word:

> *Mark:* "And immediately [after the woman's believing touch], the fountain of her blood was dried up, and she knew in her body that she was healed of her affliction. And immediately Jesus sensed in himself that power had gone out of him . . ." (Mark 5:29–30).
>
> *Matthew:* "[After her believing touch] Jesus turned around, saw her, and *said*, 'Courage, daughter, your faith has made you completely well.' And the woman was indeed made well *that very hour*" (v 22).

Mark will later hear Jesus tell the woman that her faith saved her. But in Mark's account the simple physical touch helped the woman, first, without either the conscious or verbal accompaniment of Jesus' will. Matthew silently corrected this and so teaches that power does not flow out of Jesus without Jesus' will and Word bringing that power. In Mark, Jesus then begins to question the crowd to ask who caused this outflow of power: "Who touched my clothes?" (5:30). This view of power is naïve, fresh, and perhaps even useful at times, but Matthew does not want us to think that just by touching sacred objects, without a *personal* relation to Jesus, healing can be communicated. In Matthew, therefore, Jesus' Word, in a conversational relation ("daughter"), is the agent of healing.

But in both Gospels the point of the story is the power of faith. Mark may have communicated the message a little colorfully, but we get the point: touching Jesus with faith helps deeply. Matthew teaches the same truth with more sophistication (or inhibition).

With the artist's touch he had used a few verses earlier—"dead *but*"—Matthew describes her thoughts with an "if I can *only,*" and in writing this way he underlines his major lesson in this chapter: the freeing power of faith in Jesus. Yet in all three Gospels the woman's faith seems slightly superstitious. She does not say, "If I can only talk with Jesus"; she seems to believe that it is Jesus' *garment* that will heal her. Her faith is near magic.

But we need to appreciate the nature of the woman's problem. We are told that her flow of blood was probably a chronic menstrual disorder, rendering her and all whom she touched unclean according to the law (Lev 15, especially 15:25ff). Thus according to Scripture when Jesus was touched by the woman he became impure before God—unless, somehow, Jesus is above Scripture. By now in this Gospel we have learned that this is, in fact, exactly the case: Jesus is above Scripture.

Whatever we make of the person of Jesus, the healings of the leper and of the centurion's servant have taught readers that Jesus crosses Scripture's ritual barriers. But this woman may not have known that, and by coming up behind Jesus she seeks to avoid compromising Jesus' relation to his Scriptures and people. "Though she was bound"—even isolated—"by her affliction, yet her faith had given her wings" (Chrys., 31:2:207). The woman's decision to come up behind Jesus (stressed in all three Gospels), rather than, as ordinarily, before him, and to touch his clothes rather than, as ordinarily, to address his person, may have been prompted more by her sensitivity than by her superstition. (Chrysostom, 31:2:206, points out that this is the first woman who came *to* Jesus in public, "having heard . . . that He heals women also, and that He is on His way to the little daughter that was dead.") If the woman's act is slightly superstitious (and is the faith of any of us free of all superstition?), perhaps the church ought to learn here, without in any way commending superstition, at least to have patience with its appearance and to correct it as sensitively as Matthew's Jesus did. (Calvin, 1:271, shows pastoral sensitivity here to the problem of superstition. There is helpful discussion of the woman's problem in Barclay, 1:346.)

9:20b The woman believed contact with Jesus desperately necessary and so she was driven to her awkward expedient: "[she] came up behind Jesus and touched the tassel at the corner of his robe." This passing sartorial reference gives us interesting information about Jesus: he wore the four little tassels on the corners of his robe prescribed by the law as memory-aids in recalling God's saving deeds and words in Holy Scripture (Num 15:38; Deut 22:12). It was these tassels that Jesus later says the Serious had made especially long and noticeable [23:5b]; in their minds, no doubt, to be a witness; in his mind, clearly, to make an impression. The fact that Jesus wore these tassels underscores a fact we have already noticed—that Jesus was conservative. He revered the law, and as far as possible sought to live by it. What Jesus had earlier said about the law in the Sermon on the Mount in his laudatory review (C 1, 5:17–20), we see him practice now in the Ten Miracles—from his sending the leper back to his priest according to Moses' instructions, to his present wearing of the law's prescribed tassels. Jesus loved the Hebrew Scriptures and sought to make them the guide of his life. Even this casual reference to his clothes confirms this.

Mark continues the story with characteristic verve (Matthew will edit most of these details away): "Jesus turned to the crowd and was saying, 'Who touched my robe?' And the disciples were saying to him, 'Look at this crowd crushing you on all sides, and you say, "Who touched me?!"'" (Mark 5:30–31) Rather than leaving the miracle impersonal, Jesus makes it whole and personal by seeking and finding conversation (Trench, *Miracles*, 206). One reason Matthew may not have cared for this part of Mark's story is the sarcasm of the disciples' remark. They don't precede their observation with the respectful "Lord," and they command Jesus to look around at how many people are touching him.

It is as if they were saying, "What do you mean 'Who touched me?' *Everybody's* touching you in this thick crowd!" But Mark tells us that Jesus kept looking around to see who really had "touched" him. For there is touching and there is touching. The majority of the persons around Jesus touched Jesus *throngingly;* only one person touched Jesus *needily.* It is this latter "needing-touch," that is faith and so receives help from Jesus. When need comes this way to Jesus it invariably gets some kind of help. Simple interest, mere curiosity, social pressure, mere proximity, and even trying one's luck were factors in the thronging touch of the majority.

We might say that Jesus is still "touched" this thronging way by many. But the Gospels teach us again and again that the only touch that counts with Jesus is the touch that comes (1) in need (2) with expectancy. This is the spirit with which to come to church, to read the Bible, to come to the Christian group; it is "needy expectancy"—faith—that puts us in vital touch with Jesus. In the gospel, "faith" is never general belief in the existence of God; gospel faith is getting in touch with Jesus by bringing one's major need to him with the expectation that Jesus can do miracles.

Therefore, in spite of the disciples' sarcasm, Jesus continued to look for the person who had *really* touched him. *Mark* tells us that this interrogatory look of Jesus troubled the woman; she was afraid that she was going to lose everything that her body had just now healingly gained. She no doubt feared that Jesus might make public her embarrassing illness; perhaps she also feared that she would be rebuked for her literally "backward" or slightly superstitious approach, or for her failure to approach Jesus from the front candidly, personally, and publicly. This whole ensemble of fears may have assailed her as Jesus continued his search for the source of the touch. We read then in Mark that the healed and fearful woman "approached him, fell down in front of him, and told him the whole truth" (Mark 5:33). Augustine, *Serm.,* 12(62):5:299: "And they answer, 'The multitude press Thee.' And the Lord would seem to say, I am asking for one who touched, not for one who pressed Me. In this case also is His Body now, that is, His Church. The faith of the few 'touches' it, the throng of the many 'press' it." (Victor and Bede, similarly, in Swete, 104f) Trench, *Miracles,* 205: "Many 'thronging' Christ; His in name; near to Him outwardly; in actual contact with the sacraments and ordinances of His Church; yet not *touching* Him, their not drawing nigh in faith." Cf. the English proverbs (ODEP): "Many go to Church who say not their prayers," and "Not all Stuarts are sib to the king."

9:22 At this point Matthew rejoins Mark. Jesus' response to the woman was a bracing "Courage, daughter, your faith has made you completely well." (All three evangelists have the words "Daughter, your faith has saved you"; only Matthew adds the admonition "Courage.") For Matthew, as we saw especially in the storm story, faith is a courage, it is a *keeping* faith with Jesus. Jesus' "courage!" to this woman, then, is his call to her to *keep on* living the life of expectancy she so boldly began when she touched Jesus so believingly—"if I can *only* touch!" Courage is keeping in touch.

It was thoughtful of Jesus not to mention her disease—what she was saved *from.* (Jesus is also the helper of private need, of the prayer that cannot be expressed publicly because modesty forbids it, Schl., *Der,* 317.) It was also modest of Jesus not to say that *"I* have saved you and don't forget it." He gives the credit to her faith because he wants her to know that in her faith in Jesus she has perpetually within herself the connecting-link to him; in faith she has Jesus' "number." Faith is a portable Jesus-receiver. Jesus is present wherever there is faith in him.

Augustine, *Tract. in Jn.,* 49:19:276, is good on this: "If there is faith in us, Christ is in us. For what else says the apostle: 'That Christ may dwell in your hearts by faith' [Eph 3:17]. Therefore thy faith in Christ is Christ himself in thy heart." The time element is important in Jesus' words too: Jesus does not say "Your faith *will* save you," but "your faith *has* saved you" (Jero., 1:178). The salvation of wholeness can be a present experience for believers. Jesus attributes the experience entirely to the woman's faith, not the tassel on the robe, not even the touching of the robe's tassel (Schl., *Das,* 148). In Jesus' opinion, faith is almost everything.

For faith is nothing less than the means of contact with Jesus' real presence. It is the continuing sacrament. That is why, so equipped, the woman can be dismissed by Jesus (according to Mark and Luke) with the words "Go in [literally, "into"] peace" (Mark 5:34; Luke 8:48). The life of faith is the life of peace.

Taylor, 293: "Jesus attributes the woman's cure to her faith. . . . This explanation cannot be watered down to the hypothesis of auto-suggestion, since the consistent New Testament view of faith is that it derives its content and virtue from the object in which it rests." *Idem,* 289: "The suggestion of the narrative, that the cure was due to faith energized by the personality of Jesus, is the best explanation of a story which cannot be completely rationalized."

In Mark and Luke "while Jesus is still talking" to the woman, as both evangelists stress, an embassy from the leader's home arrives to tell him not to bother "the teacher" any longer—the daughter is dead. The father could have been tempted to be resentful of Jesus' lingering with this semisick but living woman when he had a dying daughter with whom Jesus had a prior appointment. Jesus instantly intercedes: "Don't be afraid; only believe" (Mark 5:36). Jesus places his arms underneath the falling father to pick him up; Jesus instantly and pastorally supports the father's sinking faith by telling him not to do that which faith is constantly in danger of doing in the light of realities: to fear. "Don't be afraid" is a variation on Jesus' frequent "courage" theme and means not to take realities more seriously than reality.

Jesus makes the man's responsibility simple. "Just sustain the courage that brought you to me in the first place; believe that I am able to attack death as well from the rear as from the front, after its effects as easily as before. Just believe me: I will not let you down." This simple message, told in hundreds of ways, is close to the heart of the Christian gospel.

9:23–25 *"And when Jesus came into the house of the leader and saw the flute players and the crowd of people mourning and wailing, he said, 'Please step outside; the little girl is not dead, she's just sleeping.' The people really laughed at him when they heard him say that. And when the crowd had been put outside, Jesus went into the girl's room, took hold of her hand, and the little girl got up. And the news about this case went all over that part of the country."*

Again Matthew has substantially abbreviated the story. Mark and Luke tell us that Jesus not only removed the professional mourners from the room, but brought in his disciples

(Peter, John, and James, according to Luke), as well as the girl's father and mother. Mark and Luke also tell us that Jesus raised the girl by speaking—*"Talitha cum"* (says Mark)—while Matthew, the great emissary of the Word, speaks surprisingly only of Jesus taking the girl's hand (which the other evangelists *add to* Jesus' Word).

9:24a Only Matthew gives us Jesus' rather abrupt remark to the mourners, "Step outside" (*anachōreite*). Even the poorest funerals in Israel were supposed to hire at least two flute players and one female wailer in order to join the neighborhood people in crying, singing pathetic rounds, and clapping sadly (Str.-B., 1:521; Allen, 96; Gund., 175). Jesus encounters this mourning situation when he arrives. And he asks the people to leave. All three evangelists join in hearing Jesus say that the little girl "is not dead, she's just sleeping."

"'She is not dead but sleeps' because to God all things live" (Jero., 1:178). "To men who could not quicken, she is dead; to God she is asleep" (Bede); "Where faith in the resurrection is present we do not have a species of death but of resting" (Ambrose); "In truth, when He had come, death was from that time forward a sleep" (Chrys., 31:3:207). "Our Lord . . . means to teach that *bodily death* is not essentially *death,* but in his hands as but *sleep* to all the children of men" (Stier in Beng., 1:150f). Trench, *Miracles,* 195, believes there are two reasons for Jesus saying "sleeping": to strengthen the father's weak faith and to veil His divine work with the double significance of the word *sleeping*. Taylor, 295, wrestles impressively with the meaning of the whole incident and concludes: "It is clear that the saying [about "sleeping"] is one of great ambiguity. If, as is probable, Mark himself regarded the incident as one of resurrection, he has related the story with great objectivity in that another interpretation is possible. . . . [Everything] suggests that the case was one of *apparent* death" (emphasis added). Bonnard, 136, has another view: "If Jesus says that the little girl 'sleeps,' it is not because he believes she is still living, nor that death is just a sleep for him; he means that God, by [Jesus'] ministry, is going to show that death is not that absolutely irreparable thing of which men are so frightened." Green, 105, observes that the joyful certainty of death's nonultimacy "continued to distinguish Christians from their Jewish and pagan neighbors in the ancient world." (Cf. Athanasius, *On the Incarnation of the Word,* 27, 47.) Victory over fear of death is one of the most exciting and prominent themes in the literature of the early church fathers.

All three evangelists add the mourners' response, "the people really laughed (*kategelōn*) at him" ("*kategelōn* is a clear sign of literary dependence [among the evangelists] since the expression is so bold and the verb is not used elsewhere in the New Testament," Tay., 296). The mourners' swift change in mood is striking, and incidentally shows the superficiality of their mourning (while emphasizing the fact of the girl's real physical death, Cal., 1:274). Perhaps their laughter is partly embarrassed, prompted by Jesus' curt dismissal; but the evangelists also intend for us to hear in the laughter the secular derision that often encounters Jesus' message of resurrection.

If Jesus had been a showman, or had had a drop of fanatical blood in his veins, he would have challenged the disbelievers to come *into* the room, rather than to get out of it, so that he could prove to them what he could do ("I'll show you something you've never seen before"). But for the Jesus of the synoptic Gospels, healing is not a show; it is not even intended to be an advertisement or attraction (Schl., *Der,* 319). As often as possible Jesus wants healing to be unpublic. Thus here as elsewhere Jesus asks unbelief to leave, and he brings only faith into the room. In this circle of confidence, without any incantation, without, in fact, a single word (in Matthew's telling) the girl is quietly gripped and raised from her sleep of death (without even a prayer; contrast the Old Testament Elijah and Elisha raisings of the dead, 1 Kgs 17:19f; 2 Kgs 4:33). The story is told as simply as it is possible to tell a story of resurrection from the dead, and for this we must credit the professionalism of Matthew and the dignity of the ministry of Jesus that Matthew's Gospel reflects.

A father believed that Jesus was stronger than death. That father's confidence was honored. We do not believe that Christians should try to raise the dead today. But the expectant hope, which is faith, believes that Jesus will raise the dead on the last day; this hope is at the heart of the Christian message. The death-defying faith of this father teaches that Jesus' reach is as deep as death.

V. TWO BLIND MEN AND A DEAF MUTE: FREEDOM TO SEE AND SPEAK (9:27–34)

The two miracles are combined in the treatments of Schl., *Das*, 149 (with the title "The Results of the Miracles of Jesus") and Schw., 230. "Matthew here inserts two miracles which illustrate Christ's power to quicken defective physical senses" (Allen, 96). "The reason for Matthew's insertion of the two miracles after 9:18–26 was probably to complete a triplet [of miracles]" (McN., 129), recalling that chaps 8–9 contain, strictly and structurally, three sets of three miracles: 8:1–17; 8:23–9:8; and 9:18–34 (where 9:18–26 is considered one miracle), buffered by discipleship stories in between. The unity of the two miracles before us, a catechetical artifact, is characterized well by Waetjen, 127: "The restoration of seeing, speaking, and hearing establishes the possibility of communication and therefore also of community." These are social miracles.

A. Pursuing Faith: The Healing of Two Blind Men (9:27–31)

"And as Jesus was walking along, two blind men followed him and were shouting, 'Have a heart for us, O Son of David!' And when Jesus came into the house, the blind men came up to him. Jesus said to them, 'Do you believe that I can do this?' And they said, 'Yes, Lord.' Then Jesus touched their eyes, and he said, 'You believe; you have it.' And their eyes were opened. And then Jesus very sternly and strictly told them, 'Now you watch out that you don't let anyone know about this.' But they went out and spread the matter all over that part of the country."

This story may be a doublet (that is, a recasting) of the story of the healing of the two blind men in chapter 20 (20:29–34), placed in this ninth chapter setting to impress the chapter's thematic truth of the freeing power of faith. (The story of the healing of the blind *men* in Matthew 20 is a story of the healing of a blind *man*, Bartimaeus, in Mark and Luke. It is a curiosity of Matthew that where the other evangelists have one demoniac Matthew has two; that where Jesus rides one donkey in Mark and Luke, two animals are included by Matthew; and now we have a similar doubling of the blind men. Matthew's doubling must be due to something deeper than his own or his sources' double vision. Perhaps Matthew wished to say something communal or social about these healings. The reason for these twos still escapes me.)

9:27 The initial curiosity in the story is the fact that these blind men are the first persons in the Gospel to call Jesus by his official name, "Son of David." "Son of David" was the popular way of saying "Messiah" (cf. the important chapter Pss Sol 17; Str.-B., 1:525; McN., 127; Grund., 277 n. 7). The Son of David was the person promised David by the Lord through the prophet Nathan in 2 Sam 7:12–13 and 1 Chr 17:11–12—a son who would be a king *forever*. Ever since this Davidic promise, Israel looked forward to the coming of this royal figure, this eternal "Son of David," and significantly it is two *blind* men who are the first to "see" Jesus' royalty (Schl., *Das,* 149; and see esp. John 9:39).

The Serious would hear the name "Son of David" as an alarming provocation here where we, long accustomed to considering Jesus the messianic Son of David, simply hear another title of Jesus. But these two blind men were claiming nothing less than that Jesus is the Christ, and as we know from all the Gospels, this was both a perceptive and, for a time, a dangerous thing to claim.

9:28 Jesus kept on walking. For the first time in Matthew Jesus seems not to respond to faith. Everywhere else faith had found Jesus instantly, even eagerly turning to it, "following" it, helping it, touching it, and reaching across culture's deepest chasms to heal. But Jesus now seems impervious to faith, and uncaring.

He went into the house—perhaps his own house—in Capernaum. The blind men come pursuing and walk right in. This pursuing fact is close to the center of the story. The blind men were not put off by Jesus' failure to respond—they followed him until they had him cornered (not easy for blind to do). This pursuing faith becomes a worthy companion of the other vital faiths in this chapter: the bold faith of the paralytic's friends, the touching faith of the unclean woman, and the deathless faith of the father. In each instance the faith has been extremely eager. Eager faith, contrary to initial impressions, is never disappointed. Jesus immediately turns to the blind men and asks them not what they want (as he will in chapter 20). Instead, in this chapter of faith he asks them, summarizing in a way the combined messages of all the chapter's stories, "Do you *believe* that *I can* do this?"

Jesus could have healed them without asking them this question of faith, of course. But as often as possible Jesus wants to have a personal relation with those who come to him. Thus rather than automatically and impersonally healing them, he begins a conversation (Held, 265f). And he begins the conversation with a concern that has carried us for two chapters: "Do you believe that I *can* . . . ?" (The leper in the first miracle had said, "If you want to, you *can.* ") Apparently an approach of "you can" deeply pleases Jesus. "You can," said to Jesus, is faith. Jesus had heard the blind men shouting, "Have a heart for us, O Son of David." But it is one thing to shout pious phrases and another to believe that Jesus can meet one's need. Jesus' question both does research and gives hope.

Jesus' question does not ask, "'Believe ye that I am able to entreat my Father, that I am able to pray,' but 'that I am able . . . ?'" (Chrys., 32:1:211). Thus McNeile, 127, correctly observes that Jesus' question "did not merely seek information, but was a spur to their faith." Indeed, the blind men's "Yes" was only able to be expressed "as a *response* to Jesus' *question;* this faith, then, is a creation, a gift of the presence of the Word of Jesus" (Bonn., 138, emphasis added). "Faith comes by *hearing*" (Rom 10:17).

Their reply is simple: "'Yes, Lord.'" Though they cannot see Jesus, their "Yes" puts them in front of him, and their "Lord" puts them at his feet. "Yes, Lord" is the right place to be. With their "Yes" they make themselves open to Jesus' grace; with their "Lord" they make themselves open to his power. "Yes, Lord," is what the Jewish people meant with their word—"Amen." The liturgical "Amen" means "Yes, Lord." Every time we say "Amen" we are saying "I believe you can do it."

Chrysostom, 32:1:211, notices that in the men's "Yes, *Lord*" they no longer call Jesus "Son of David," but "soar higher." Son of David, interestingly, is mainly the title of a healer in Matthew's Gospel (Kingsb., *Struc.*, 100, 103; Brown, 184 n. 17).

9:29a "Then Jesus touched their eyes." This touching is as impressive as the touching of the leper. We are told that Near Eastern eye diseases were particularly repulsive, not greatly different in popular opinion from the skin diseases called leprosy. That Jesus should have touched these diseases and not merely spoken to them teaches us again how intimately Jesus establishes solidarity with us. If we are oppressed in skin, eye, or anything, Jesus touches us at the point of our oppression; he does not merely talk to us.

9:29b Jesus spoke as he touched their eyes and summarized the meaning of the whole series of miracles, literally (and woodenly), "according to your faith, it has happened for you," which I have translated, "You believe; you have it." He did this in order to remove any quantitative or meritorious notion from faith (Bonn., 138; Hill, 180; contra Mohrlang, 100f). Where there is faith in Jesus there is Jesus. This is the law of the gospel. And Matthew taught us in chapter 8 that where there is not even recorded faith (the fevered mother-in-law, for example) or where the faith is pitiful (the terrified disciples in the storm) or even contemptible (the demoniacs), Jesus is still there, and he still helps.

In a sense, then, in at least three of the miracles of Matthew 8 Jesus could have said, "according to my grace, not your faith, it has happened to you." Yet Jesus wants faith, and Matthew 9 exists to teach that. Though Jesus helps even where faith is weak—and that important evangelical truth and teaching is a function of chapter 8—nevertheless this gracious fact must not be interpreted to mean that Jesus is indifferent to faith. There is nothing that means more to Jesus or to which he responds more promptly than simple confidence that "he can." Jesus loves faith. Every person who got help in this chapter got it because of *someone's* confidence in Jesus. If disciples wish to please Jesus they may learn from this chapter that one of the best ways is to trust him.

9:30–31 "And their eyes were opened. And then Jesus very sternly and strictly told them, 'Now you watch out that you don't let anyone know about this.' But they went out and spread the matter all over that part of the country." The disobedience is not impressive. The men may have thought that Jesus was trying to be modest, that surely like everyone else he would like to be better known. This seemingly parenthetical incident can teach us something important about discipleship. It is not always true that if one experiences the grace of God one becomes obedient. We sometimes teach that all people need is an experience of God's grace, a sound conversion, and then they will do what is right; that what we need is not new laws but new persons, that if individuals could experience Christ's grace, then social justice would happen. (This is often heard in various conservative-evangelicalisms.) But the blind men had just experienced Christ's healing grace in a direct way; they had just said and meant, "Yes, Lord"; these men had had real faith, and Jesus had been honestly impressed, and had honored their faith.

Yet not even Jesus believed that his grace was all that was needed for their correct behavior, as his explicit warning shows. And if this warning were not enough, their disobedient behavior should convince us that while grace and faith can heal us, they do not instantly or spontaneously sanctify us or make us wonderful people or good disciples. Matthew's Gospel, especially, works hard to teach the church that obedience to the warning ministry of Jesus is perpetually necessary if we are to be true Christians. True faith should lead to simple obedience, but it does not automatically do so, as this story dramatically shows. The trust of the blind men in Jesus' healing words should have been spontaneously followed by their obedience to Jesus' warning words. Instead, they trusted their common sense—"this fellow can't be serious"—or they trusted the logic of their own wonderful evangelical experience—"how can I help but share what the Lord has done for me?"—or they trusted their own rational conception of how Jesus can be served—"I know if we tell others about this that it will increase, not decrease, Jesus' ministry." But all these trusts, good as they may seem in themselves to be, are so many failures to trust the seriousness of Jesus' clear command, and it is this command that must reign over common sense, evangelical experience, and rational insight.

"There is forgiveness with thee, that thou mayest be *feared*" (Ps 130:4); it is this wholesome fear of the Lord that the healed blind men lacked. According to Jerome, 1:182, while Jesus desired to avoid vainglory, the blind men spoke up anyway "because their remembrance of his grace is overwhelming." But grace should not overwhelm Jesus' commands, as Calvin, 1:245, 276, correctly sees. In the nineteenth century, Trench (in Beng., 1:151) noticed intriguingly that "the disobedience of these men is praised by nearly all Roman Catholic expositors; a most characteristic fact, based on deep differences." What does Trench have in mind? Von Rad, *Genesis*, 88, commenting on Gen 3:4–5, has the perfect word for out text: "Man's ancient folly is in thinking he can understand God better from his freely assumed standpoint and from his notion of God than he can if he would subject himself to [God's] Word."

In Christian theology we believe that where persons place their trust in Jesus Christ and receive his grace, they receive at the same time the gift of the Holy Spirit. This story should instruct us that even when we have had an experience of grace, or reception of the Spirit, obedience to the simple *commands* of Jesus is not dispensable or legalistic. The Christian life is not first of all lived in the glow of a wonderful experience; it is lived more soberly first of all in simple obedience to Jesus' commanding Words. Our experience, our feelings, our best thinking, even some leading from (we think) the Holy Spirit, should not move us to contradict Jesus' commands.

It is well known that in some of those areas where the Bible is most insistently *believed* and where Christ is most ardently and experientially preached—for example, in some Bible churches in America, in the conservative, sometimes independent, sometimes denominational Christian churches in East and West, and in some seriously Reformed and "orthodox" Calvinist churches in South Africa—that the Bible is most flagrantly *disobeyed*. It is disobeyed in simple, basic obediences to Jesus' commands of interracial and intersexual civility and elementary human and civil rights. These churches teach that one must believe in Christ and believe the Bible, and they frequently excoriate those who do not believe as fervently as they do. But this Christ has clear commands about human relations and social ethics, too, commands that deserve trust as much as his Words about healing and salvation. Unfortunately, many who have been (as they say) saved in such churches have not been saved enough to believe the whole Christ and the whole Bible, the Christ and Bible who want obedience and not just devotion, the Christ and Bible who command obedience and ethics just as much as they minister grace and healing. If this story of the healing of the blind men does nothing else for us but disabuse us of the received wisdom that conversion is all people need, then it serves its purpose.

One mystery remains. Why did Jesus pass the blind men by? The law of faith that we have seen operative everywhere else has taught us that Jesus is immediately present to the call of need. Yet here Jesus walked past, and it was not until the blind men pursued that he began to help. Why? The clearest answers are, I believe, (1) messianic, (2) modesty, and (3) the testing of faith.

The theme of the messianic secret is particularly important in Mark's Gospel. In Matthew the theme is peripheral and may at times only represent Matthew's appropriation of Mark's tradition. Yet in Matthew, too, Jesus does not want to be known, yet, as the Messiah. As we have seen, the expression "Son of David" was the popular way of talking about the Messiah and meant "Messiah." The name "Son of David" was fraught with political content and appealed as much to the romantic side of the people as it did to the religious.

Jesus did not publicly respond to the call "Son of David," then, because he wished to avert the danger of being understood as a political Messiah. This is the first reason why Jesus seems to violate the law of faith. (Cf. Schl., *Der*, 320f; Lohm., 179; Kingsb., *Struc.*, 103; Schw., 231; and Grundmann, 278, who writes: "for precisely in connecting Jesus . . . with this national political hope (expressed in the messianic name) the [Christian] community has its major temptation." This is relevant to national political theologies.)

Second, Jesus' modesty—closely connected, thematically, to his understanding of his messianic task (see the temptations for example)—led him often to go actually or figuratively indoors when he was called to heal outdoors. We have already noticed that Jesus sought to avoid show in his healing ministry. Jesus removed, not imported, spectators at his raising of the dead girl in the immediately preceding miracle. Jesus might have been willing to respond outdoors to the leper because the leper's appeal was not to the Son of David, and it was spoken, not shouted. But when Jesus is screamed at as the Son of David in public the case is altered. Jesus will heal, but not under any circumstances. Jesus deplores religion that does show business (see Matt 6 in the Sermon on the Mount for documentation). Jesus' modesty is, I think, a fair second reason why Jesus seemed here to act contrary to the rule of faith. (Cf. Chrysostom, 32:1:211, "lest any should suppose Him to be rushing upon these miracles through vainglory.")

Third, Jesus may have thought "if these men are serious they will follow me." Jesus can, if he wishes, test our faith or at least hold it in animated suspension or require its pursuit of him—not arduously, legally, or cruelly, but normally—in order for faith to be brought into more intimate contact with him (cf. Cal., 1:275, and, most impressively in Scripture, the Abraham stories of Gen 12–25).

In the text before us, tested faith did nothing else than follow Jesus into his house (into the church!). Faith should pursue Jesus into his house when it gets no answer from him. Jesus' "passing by" seems only to require that the bypassed ones *stick with him,* follow him into his home, and just wait there before him quietly. They have already made their need known; they have already (somewhat awkwardly) addressed him ("Son of David, have a heart for us"). And now the fact that they have quietly followed him home attests to the reality of their faith.

Inside the house Jesus can converse with them. And the main thing he wants to know is this: Do they believe he can do what they want? This is still the first thing Jesus wants to know of us in his church (it is not the only thing, as his added command showed). Jesus does not correct their Son of David christology; he does not ask them to approach him next time more quietly. It is important even to notice that he does not *require* faith of them in order for them to be worthy of help. "Required faith" can collide with grace, have legalistic coloration, and should be used only with caution in careful evangelism. Jesus has simply asked if they *had* faith (without adjectives) in his ability to help them—and they did—and that was all they then needed. No worked-up faith was made necessary.

Jesus did not even ask if they will in the future always obey his Word before he will heal them. As we know now in retrospect, this would not have been a bad question to ask. All Jesus asked about was their faith in his ability. Neither conditions prior or posterior are required by Jesus before he will help, neither the proof that we are worthy now nor the promise that we will be worthy later are asked. Jesus helps faith; the gospel is that simple and fundamental.

At the same time, the whole gospel asks us to continue to *live* by the faith with which we began our relation with Jesus. How? By giving his commanding Word the same faith we give his healing person. For in Matthew's Gospel the command and person of Jesus are inseparable.

B. Pursued Faith: The Healing of a Deaf Mute (9:32–34)

"And when they were leaving, look, people brought a man to him who was a deaf-mute and demon-possessed. And when the demon had been exorcised the choked-up man spoke. And the people marveled and said, 'We have never seen anything in Israel like this!' But the Serious were saying, 'He exorcises demons through the power of the ruler of the demons.'"

That the Greek word *kōphos* represents a man with a double-problem—unable to hear and thus unable to speak—has been recognized since Jerome, 1:182; cf. Bonn., 139; Hill, 181; Gund., 179–80; and contrast Schw., 231. Lohmeyer, 180, sees the original link between this deaf-mute story and the preceding blind men story in the gift of sight being complemented with the gift of speech, "for seeing and speaking lift persons into the image of God."

This is a slightly told miracle. It has no middle (Lohm., 180). There is no recorded conversation, the central feature in most miracles. Conversation is impossible with a deaf-mute anyway, though Jesus knows of other ways to communicate (cf. Mark 7:33). We are not told whether Jesus healed by Word or by touch; we are not even told of the man's faith, the subtheme of the entire chapter (the *theme* is freedom). Everything in this healing story is subordinated to the division that arose in Israel over the meaning of Jesus. It is almost as though the miracle is told in order to get *ten* miracles and then, particularly, in order to feature this climactic split in the faith of the people of God. (Thus Lohm., 180; Held, 247–48; Schw., 231–32. Jerome, 1:182, believed, incorrectly, that the good crowds represented the gentiles, while the bad Pharisees represented the Jews.)

In this chapter, Matthew has presented us with (1) bold faith, (2) touching faith, (3) deathless faith, (4) pursuing faith; now *he* pursues his readers themselves, asking, (5) "and *your* faith?" "Are you, like the people, impressed by Jesus, or are you, like the people's leaders, unimpressed?" Matthew, like all good evangelists, is asking at the end for a decision. This miracle is told so that the evangelist can pursue *our* faith. He presents this tenth miracle in order to fashion, as it were, an altar where those who have been attracted by Jesus through these stories may come and confess their readiness to believe. In this miracle it is *we*, the listeners to the story, who, if mute or tongue-tied, are invited to spoken decision for Christ.

Held, 248, shows that this conclusion to the miracles indicates that Matthew arranged the miracles of chaps 8 and 9 in order that the person of Christ be center stage. We saw the same arrangement in Matthew's ending of the Sermon on the Mount at 7:29. "At the conclusion of both chapters 5–7 and 8–9 Jesus is seen as greater than Israel's previous history" (Grund., 281).

Poignant in the story is the fact that the simple people are beginning to be impressed: "We have never seen anything in Israel like this!" The cumulative effect of Jesus' miracles has moved Israel to the threshold of faith. They are about to be persuaded that Jesus is a prophet bringing God's Word to them, perhaps even (in a way that Jesus will have to cleanse and reinterpret) to believe that Jesus is the Christ. Jesus at this point in Matthew's outline does not ask for anything more than this openness, this readiness to be impressed, this respect before the fact.

But the people's leadership rejects Jesus in a thoroughly decisive way. It is interesting to notice that the leadership cannot and does not deny Jesus' power, but it does deny that his power comes from God. In chapter 12 Matthew will document in a systematic way the "Spirit Controversy" that occurred between Jesus and the leadership of the people of God; it is enough now for the decisive theological question to be raised: Where does Jesus' authority, his miraculous power, come from? Readers are asked to take sides and so to allow Jesus' impact upon them to heal them of *their* speechlessness, to confess Jesus and so to become themselves the Tenth Miracle.

> Who is like thee, O Lord, among the gods?
> Who is like thee, majestic in holiness,
> terrible in glorious deeds, doing wonders? (Exod 15:11 RSV).

Summary: The Ten Miracles of Prayer (Matt 8–9)

In chapter 8 the five miracles of grace taught the width of Jesus' reach to those farthest out: to lepers, gentiles, women, cowards, and demoniacs. In chapter 9 the five miracles of freedom taught us that the way people come to freedom is through faith in Jesus: whenever Jesus sees faith, is touched by it, approached by it, pursued by it, or is allowed to awaken deep impressions of who he is, then Jesus' grace touches human need and people are freed.

The most striking characteristic of faith in the ninth chapter's series is faith's *audacity*. In a single-minded way, the father of the dead girl, the bleeding woman, the blind men, and (in Mark's version, especially) the house-crashers, all determined to get into the presence of Jesus. No matter what other people thought, no matter what was thought possible, the important matter was the presence of Jesus: this, above all other considerations, was sought. And this mindset, this determination to be in the presence of Jesus, this resolution to bring one's deepest need to him with the confidence that he could meet that need—this is gospel faith.

And gospel faith is prayer. For prayer is faith bringing need to Jesus. Faith is coming to Jesus with two things: with one's need, and with confidence in Jesus' "can do," in Jesus' ability to meet need. Without need, faith is vague, abstract, and unreal—need is almost as central to gospel faith as Jesus himself. To come to Jesus "generally" is not faith in the New Testament sense. Faith is coming to Jesus specifically with a particular need, with a real life problem. Without need, faith is ghostly and too spiritual. (This does not mean we cannot come to Jesus unless we are hurting. It does mean that we do not have to feel our problems are obstacles to prayer; they are its stuff.)

Accompanying need is an expectant confidence that Jesus can meet the need. Quantitative measures are not used with faith in this chapter. *Big* faith, *total* faith, "absolute surrender"—or similar words that can, unguarded, turn faith into a work—are all absent. It is not so much the quantity of faith that is highlighted in this chapter as it is faith's singleness: this faith *will* get in touch with Jesus. If a ceiling has to be removed, or a crowd penetrated, or death ignored, or propriety pushed aside, no matter—faith will get in touch. It is not the absoluteness of human faith so much as it is the simple, single will to touch Jesus, however slightly ("even the tassel of his robe"), that is crucial. For faith, even when it is central (as it is in this chapter), must not be required to be heroic before Jesus will look at it. The point of the stories is not that Jesus does not pay attention to people unless they are spiritual heroes; the point is that people who simply *will* get in touch with him, however slightly, *will* be helped. We must not dictate the form this help takes (Paul's "thorn," 2 Cor 12). Meanwhile, faith will not let itself be put off by a hundred obstacles, by all kinds of natural considerations, or by any other so-called realities. To faith there is one overwhelming reality in life and that reality is Jesus Christ.

And so chapters 8 and 9 have presented us with a little theology of prayer. The Lord to whom we pray is not a reluctant listener, but an eager, zealous Savior (the whole eighth chapter). If we will simply have the wisdom to set aside the thousand and one natural obstacles that impede prayer and make it inconvenient even today to get in touch with this Lord or to have (even the most modest amount of) time for prayer and prayer meetings we will be helped deeply (the lesson of chapter 9). These chapters ask us to believe that such a Lord actually exists and then to take the next logical step—to seek frequently to be in touch with him, by way of our needs, in prayer and prayer meetings, the great neglected resource. These two chapters are one long invitation to pray: to a gracious Lord (8) with faith (9). We are asked, as we saw, to be ourselves the tenth miracle, "deaf mutes" so freed by Jesus that we can talk again. And the best form of talk is prayer. Let us pray.

The Gratis propter Christum per Fidem Teaching of Salvation in Reformation Theology

We are put right with God according to the fourth article of *The Augsburg Confession* (1530) *gratis propter Christum per fidem,* that is, "by grace [*gratis*] for Christ's sake [*propter Christum*] through faith [*per fidem*]" This conviction has been illustrated in the preceding two chapters. (1) The unifying theme of especially the eighth chapter is Christ's helping us *gratis,* graciously, freely, even independently of the quality of our faith. (2) In both chapters 8 and 9, in all 10 miracles, we were helped "because of *Christ.*" (3) The human way to be in touch with the graciously Touching Messiah is *faith,* as chapter 9 taught especially.

It is not entirely true that God accepts us as we are, as we often hear in contemporary preaching and teaching. A price must be paid to live in the presence of the holy God. God in Christ has paid this price. All God's "frees" come to us through Jesus' "costlies." All God's grace comes mediated through Christ's work. All responsible teaching of God's free acceptance (or the *gratis* of grace) must be immediately accompanied, therefore, by the teaching of the costly price—the *propter Christum*—that God paid in the person of his Son, if the teaching is to be credible to consciences, or Christian at all. Our conscience, rightly, will simply not believe that we are acceptable to God as we are. But if we hear the *propter Christum* in the power of the Holy Spirit, clearly, we can believe the gospel that now, because of Christ, we really are accepted as we are. (Indeed, God *so loved us* "as we are" in the first place that he sent his only Son to make atonement for us. Cf. Aug. in Cal., *Inst.,* II.xvi.4.)

We are accepted and helped freely, *gratis;* but Someone Else paid a high price to make our "freely" a possibility. The apostles Paul and John stress the costliness of Christ's incarnation and death; Matthew, the costliness of Christ's life and ministry. "He himself took our sicknesses and carried away our diseases" (8:17). Now we know that God does not wink at sin and sickness or take them lightly. He pays their consequences, himself, in his own dear Son.

In our time we suffer from the preaching of a *gratis* that is not fortified by a *propter Christum.* We have retreated from the preaching of Christ's substitution in our place and his vicarious satisfaction of God's holiness and wrath, partly because the fundamentalist preaching of these truths has been unsavory, but partly also for craven reasons of our own acquiescence in culture's liberal prejudices.

In the gospel we get God freely because God in his Son shed costly blood: that is the right way to put together the *gratis* and the *propter Christum.* And the right way to receive God's freely given pardon and help is *per fidem,* "by faith." In the Augsburg formula, faith is placed last, appropriately, lest it be thought that our faith precedes or merits God's grace or Christ's mediation. We are not put right with God "*because of* faith"—that would be works-righteousness all over again. The only "because" of salvation is the *propter Christum,* the person and work of Jesus Christ, not the person and work of the believer. It is not *because of* faith, it is *by* faith, that we receive the free grace merited by Christ, and given to us through sermon and sacrament.

Faith is the sigh of relief that this is so. Chapter 9 stressed *per fidem* as chapter 8 stressed *gratis* and as both chapters taught *propter Christum.* The Ten Miracles are ten pictures of God's one way of salvation.

A. The Roman *Confutation* and the Reformation *Apology*

In the Reformation of the sixteenth century the Roman Catholic Church combated Reformation church teaching at the doctrinal level primarily through its own doctrines of merit and what was called "formed faith," faith internally filled with love (*fides charitate formata*). It is useful to record the historic objections. (The Second Vatican Council and subsequent Roman theology have changed a number of emphases. I do not record this sixteenth-century controversy over salvation in an unecumenical spirit, but in the hope that exposure to the original texts will cause reflection in both Roman and Reformation traditions and so increase the impetus for ecumenical work.)

In the first draft of the Roman *Confutation* of the fourth and fifth articles of the *Augsburg Confession* (in M. Reu, *The Augsburg Confession* [1930], pp 334–36), we read:

Merits are worthy through the grace of God. In this way righteous men render themselves worthy of eternal life by their good works. . . . On the other hand, when they say that we are justified by faith, this is the great and principal error of the [Protestant] preachers. For to faith alone they ascribe that which is proper to charity and to the grace of God. . . . For, that faith alone does not justify, Paul expressly testifies, 1 Cor 13, 'If I should have all faith so as to move mountains, but should not have charity, I am nothing.' . . . St. James [also] destroyed this [faith alone] error in his epistle. . . . And as far as Paul's words in praise of faith are concerned, Galatians 3, they must be understood of faith which works through charity, Galatians 5. This faith the theologians have correctly named *fides formata* [formed faith], because it is clothed in grace and charity, acceptable to God, etc.

According to this Roman teaching, faith (that receives) needs to be filled with love (that gives) in order to be authentic and so be worthy of God's grace. The Reformers insisted that to speak of faith this way and of faith being thus *worthy* of God's grace makes grace meaningless and faith a work. (See Matthew 8's unworthy faiths and Romans 4's arguments.)

The Roman *Confutatio Pontifica* is more carefully formulated than the first draft *Confutation*, but says essentially the same things (in Reu, 351).

It is entirely contrary to Holy Scriptures to deny that our works are meritorious. . . . Nevertheless, all Catholics confess that our works of themselves have no merit, but that God's grace makes them worthy of eternal life.

To these Roman objections the whole body of Luther's works addresses itself eloquently. In Lutheran confessional literature the most solid reply to the opponents is Melanchthon's detailed *Apology of the Augsburg Confession* (1531), chapter 4. The next fourteen paragraphs summarize the major arguments of *Apology* 4, in defense of the Reformation theology of justification. (The numbers in parentheses document *Apology* 4.)

1. Melanchthon begins by pointing out that "in this controversy the main doctrine of Christianity is involved; when it is properly understood, it illumines and magnifies the honor of Christ and brings to pious consciences the abundant

consolation they need" (2). The decisive structural fact of Scripture is its division into two chief doctrines: law, on the one hand, and promises (or gospel), on the other (5). The force of *law* goes up (like this ↑) from us to God, commanding us what to do to please God; the *gospel promises* come down (like this ↓) from God to us, giving us gifts. "Faith is that worship which receives [↓] God's offered blessings; the righteousness of the law is that worship that offers [↑] God our own merits" (49).

2. Furthermore, there is the important human fact that it is existentially impossible to love a God whom we know to be angry with us; not until we know God's free forgiveness of sins and have already received this forgiveness by faith can our hearts begin to be filled with the *caritas* required in the old Roman system of love-filled faith (36).

3. But our deepest reason for believing that works of love are not the way of salvation is Scripture's clear teaching. "If [salvation is] of works," Paul said explicitly, "[it is] no longer by grace" (Rom 11:6), and then "faith [is] null and the promise void" (Rom 4:14) (41–42). "Faith sets against God's wrath not our merits of love, but Christ the mediator and propitiator" (46). Reformation faith does not exclude love and good works; it excludes trust in their *merit* (74). Christ himself, and all alone, is the sole meritorious cause of all salvation.

4. The problem with *our* merits is simply this: If salvation requires them, "we could never determine whether we had merited enough" (84). Our salvation would be built on the shifting sands of our subjectivity. How can I tell that I have loved *enough* to merit grace? But when we know that Christ has done *all* the meriting necessary for salvation and that this is *all* ours by just believing this wonderful substitutionary fact, then our salvation is placed upon a solid rock, for Christ's merits are sure and eternal. The only enough (*satis*) ever done (*facio*)—*satis-facio*—is Christ's.

5. When the opponents say that Paul's formula of salvation apart from works means "apart from *ceremonial* works," they miss the whole point. For Paul was talking about the *whole* law when he said we were justified apart from "the works of the law" (87). Paul did *not* say "apart from the works of ceremonial law." Even our *moral* works of the law are excluded from God's way of putting us right. That is *real* grace. For our real problem is not ceremonies; it is being good enough morally. Not only *can* we not do the good works that merit God's salvation; we should not even try. God wants to merit our salvation all alone by the work of his Son. Relieved from trying to earn God, we can start concentrating on the truly good works of loving other people out of a deep gratitude for God's prior costly love for us in the substitutionary ministry of his Son, effective by faith alone.

6. "It is surely amazing that our opponents are unmoved by the many pages of Scripture that clearly attribute justification to faith and specifically deny it to works" (107). And when they say that the faith of which Scripture speaks is "faith filled with love" (*fides charitate formata*), they in one stroke abolish the promise (which says nothing about our faith having a sufficient measure of love in order to be worthy faith) and return us to the law (109–10). "If faith receives the forgiveness of sins on account of love [*propter charitatem*], the forgiveness of sins will always be unsure, for we never love as much as we should" (110). Trust in love, rather than in Christ, means completely abolishing the gospel of *free* forgiveness (110)—and Christ's necessity at all.

7. The law cannot be satisfied; it always accuses us [*lex semper accusat*]. It demands things of us constantly, and our conscience just as constantly tells us that we fall short. "Who loves or fears God enough? . . . Who does not often wonder whether history is governed by God's counsels or by chance? Who does not often doubt whether God hears him?" (167)

8. Then what about all the strong commands of God in Scripture, which seem to teach that our salvation depends upon our keeping the commandments (e.g., Matt 19:17)? "Augustine says very clearly, 'All the commandments of God are kept when what is not kept is forgiven'" (172; *Retractiones*, 1:19:3). "Against the Pelagians, Jerome writes, 'We are righteous, therefore, when we confess that we are sinners'" (173). It is easy to refute the opponents' objections, Melanchthon summarizes, when the fundamentals in this issue—the distinctions between law and gospel—are acknowledged (183).

9. What about the opponents' citation of *1 Corinthians 13*, where faith seems surmounted by love ("and now abide faith, hope, and love; but the greatest of these is love")? Answer: "In this text Paul is not discussing the mode of justification. He is writing to people who, upon being justified, needed urging to bear good fruits lest they lose the Holy Spirit. Our opponents proceed in reverse order. They quote this one text in which Paul teaches about fruits, and they omit the many other texts in which he systematically discusses the mode of justification" (220–21).

"No one can draw anything more from this text than that love is necessary. This we grant. It is also necessary not to steal. It would be a fallacy to reason that because it is necessary not to steal, therefore not stealing justifies; for justification is not the approval of a particular act but of the total person" (222). "If it is love that makes men perfect, Christ, the propitiator, will be unnecessary" (231).

10. What about *James*, who wrote unambiguously, "You see that a man is justi fied by works and not by faith alone" (Jas 2:24)? "The context demonstrates that the works spoken of here are those that follow faith and show that [faith] is not dead but living and active in the heart. James did not hold that by our good works we merit grace and the forgiveness of sins. He is talking about the works of the justified, who have already been reconciled" (246). James had already written (Jas 1:18) that regeneration takes place through the gospel (247). Faith in the gospel brings us a whole new life and therefore necessarily produces new impulses and works in us. (Luther saw James more critically.)

"Accordingly, James is correct in denying that we are justified by a faith without works." But he does not mean we are regenerated by works, or that propitiation is due in part to Christ, in part to our works. "Nor does he describe the *manner* of justification, but only the *nature* of the just who have already been justified and reborn" (250–51). In a word, both 1 Corinthians 13 and James discuss not the cause of justification but the effect, not the root but the fruit, not the necessary conditions but the necessary consequences.

11. The hard evangelical texts such as "forgive and you shall be forgiven" (Matt 6:14–15) and "unless your righteousness exceeds the righteousness of the scribes and Pharisees you shall never enter the kingdom of heaven" (Matt 5:20) all "require a new life" (259). But this new life simply does not come about by any other way than by believing the gospel and, so, receiving the Holy Spirit who begins this new life in us.

12. *Maintaining* faith in the gospel is not easy and involves a constant struggle

with our own flesh and reason, which do not natively believe God, but resist him. Faith that really believes in grace and the free, undeserved forgiveness of sins "does not come without a great battle in the human heart. Sensible people can easily see that a faith which believes that God cares for us, forgives us, and hears us is a supernatural thing, for of itself the human mind believes no such thing about God" (303).

13. What, finally, *is* faith? "Faith is not merely knowledge in the intellect but also trust in the will, that is, to desire and to accept what the promise offers—reconciliation and forgiveness of sins" (304). Faith is not just knowledge *that;* it is trust *in,* reception *of.* And this faith is always married to personal penitence and the constant struggle with sin (348, 350, 353).

14. Melanchthon summarizes the whole argument of the Reformation against its opponents like this: "They interpret grace as a disposition by which we love God, as though the ancients meant to say that we should put our confidence in our love, which [love] we know by experience is weak and unclean" (381). Only confidence in *Christ's* gracious love will do. The good news is that God's way of salvation is *gratis propter Christum per fidem.*

B. Reformed Statements

My favorite single description of salvation in the Reformed (or Calvinist) creeds is question 60 of *The Heidelberg Catechism* (which I will cite in the old Schaff translation with which I am most familiar).

Question 60.   How art thou righteous before God?

Answer: Only by true faith in Jesus Christ; that is, although my conscience accuse me that I have grievously sinned against all the commandments of God, and have never kept any of them, and that I am still prone always to all evil, yet God, without any merit of mine, of mere grace, grants and imputes to me the perfect satisfaction, righteousness, and holiness of Christ, as if I had never committed nor had any sin, and had myself accomplished all the obedience which Christ has fulfilled for me, if only I accept such benefit with a believing heart.

The realities in the Heidelberg 60 that I find deeply encouraging are (1) the present tense verbs, describing the believer's state not "then" or "once upon a time," but today and tomorrow too—"my conscience accuse(s) me" (not, accuse*d* me) "that [and now note all the present tense existentials] I *am still prone* always to *all* evil"; (2) the marvelous turning point at the heart of the answer—"yet God"; (3) the bells of *gratis*—"without any merit of mine, of mere grace"; (4) the *propter Christum* with its beautiful corollary, the doctrine of imputed righteousness, a doctrine meaning that I am not righteous before God because I am righteous within, but I am righteous because God *considers* me righteous, which is infinitely settling—"God . . . grants and imputes to me the *perfect* satisfaction, righteousness, and holiness of Christ"; (5) the breathtaking view of myself that I can now have, since God has it of me (and this is far more important than what I think of myself)—"as if I had *never* committed nor [even] *had* any sin, and had myself accomplished *all* the obedience which Christ has fulfilled for me [the *propter*

Christum again]; and (6) the gentle admonition at the end just to believe all this good news—"if only I accept such benefit with a believing heart."

This thrilling doctrine of salvation can be graphically plotted in two contrasting sets of three, this way, reading down the columns:

Although
My conscience accuse(s) me that
(1) I have grievously sinned against all the commandments of God, and
(2) have never kept any of them, and
(3) that I am still prone always to all evil,

Yet God
Without any merit of mine, of mere grace
(4) grants and imputes to me the perfect satisfaction, righteousness, and holiness of Christ,
(5) as if I had never committed nor had any sin, and
(6) [as if] I had myself accomplished all the obedience which Christ has fulfilled for me,
if only I accept such benefit with a believing heart.

* * *

Lutheran and Reformed theologies have caught the joy of the Augustinian-evangelical doctrine of salvation as it appears on almost every page of the New Testament and as it appears, as it were, in *picture* form in the Ten Miracles of Matthew 8 and 9.

Chapter Ten
The Sermon on Mission
The Doctrine of Evangelism

The authoritative teaching and touching of Jesus are not meant simply to astonish us as great marvels of the past. Jesus' mission of Word and Work goes on—through disciples. The tenth chapter of Matthew shows how.

The church today is not as enthusiastic about mission as she was in the nineteenth and early twentieth centuries. There are historical reasons for this. The Age of (political) Imperialism is over, or is supposed to be over, and this has affected the missionary enterprise. Yet there is never good theological reason for diminished commitment to mission. Jesus still has a heart for the wide hurting world; Jesus still has praying disciples; Jesus still equips his church with missionary gifts. Thus there is no true believer in Jesus who is not instinctively concerned about mission and evangelism. I sense that while mission passion has been sobered by the great decolonialization experiences of the postwar period, mission concern is no less present today than it was in the nineteenth century. Many Christians and churches long to be in missionary harness again, afire with a cause, and alive with zeal. "Without a vision the people perish," and without a mission churches languish. "The church lives by mission as fire by flame" (Emil Brunner).

Jesus' Sermon on Mission has this outline:
I. Mission Sources (9:35—10:4)
II. Mission Instructions (10:5–39)
    A. Travel Instructions (10:5–15)
    B. Trouble Instructions (10:16–25)
    C. Trust Instructions (10:26–39)
III. Hospitality Awards (10:40–42; 11:1)

The tenth chapter Sermon on Mission begins with the final four verses of chapter 9 where Jesus is healing needy people (as the Sermon on the Mount began with the healing of needy people in 4:23–25). Both great addresses of the first half of the Gospel—the Sermon on the Mount and the Sermon on Mission—begin with Jesus immersed in the "sickening" needs of people. Moved by the people's helplessness, by their physical and spiritual desolation, Matthew's Jesus forms two major speeches: the first to teach Christian life, the second to teach Christian mission—the inhaling and the exhaling, respectively, of Christian existence.

I. MISSION SOURCES (9:35—10:4)

"And Jesus was walking around to all the cities and villages teaching in their synagogues and heralding the wonderful news of the kingdom and healing every disease and every sickness. And when he saw the crowds of people his heart really went out to them

361

because they were harassed and helpless like sheep without a shepherd. Then Jesus said to his disciples, 'The harvest is huge, but there are hardly any workers; so pray the Lord of the harvest to thrust workers into his harvest.' And when Jesus had summoned his twelve disciples he gave them authority over unclean spirits so that they could cast them out and heal every disease and every sickness.

"And these are the names of the twelve apostles: first, Simon, who was nicknamed Peter [Rocky], and Andrew his brother; and James the son of Zebedee and John his brother; Philip and Bartholomew; Thomas and Matthew the tax-collector; James the son of Alphaeus and Thaddeus; Simon the Zealot and Judas Iscariot, the man who betrayed him."

In these two introductory paragraphs of the Sermon on Mission we learn the sources from which the church may draw in order to be perpetually missionary. Where these sources are alive in the church's consciousness, mission thrives. The sources are four: (1) the heart of Christ, (2) the prayer of disciples, (3) the gifts of ministry, and (4) the fellowship of the church. (Lohmeyer, 181, calls Matt 9:35—10:4 "Pre-Message." Grundmann, 284, shows how the twofold introduction of 9:35–38 and 10:1–4 goes beyond the original Galilean situation and applies Jesus' missionary instructions to the church everywhere in every time.)

The opening verse—"And Jesus was walking around . . . teaching . . . heralding . . . and healing" (v 35)—is almost a word-for-word duplication of the sentence that introduces the Sermon on the Mount (4:23). This striking replication indicates that these two sentences (4:23 and 9:35) are meant as parentheses embracing all the material between chapters 5 and 9 (called *inclusio*, an author's way of marking sections; cf. Beare, 237). Chapters 5 through 9 give us the first installment of Matthew's christology—Jesus Christ, the teaching and touching Messiah. We are now entering a second unit of materials (chaps 10–12) that, like the first, will give us first a message from Jesus (the Sermon on Mission, 10), and then a series of his deeds (the Six Portraits, 11–12). We have graduated from Matthew's first semester of christology—Christ's Word and Work (5–9)—to a second semester—Christ's Mission and Person (10–12). The chapters on the person of Christ (11 and 12) are intended to round out the disciples' full knowledge of Jesus: What Jesus says (5–7), how he helps (8–9), and the way he sends (10) are completed by lessons on who he is (11–12).

The Jesus of Matthew's first semester, our summary verse (v 35) reminds us, was a peripatetic preacher, a circuit rider, an itinerant evangelist-doctor, moving about the whole province of Galilee, going into every town and village, teaching and preaching the wonderful news of the kingdom. (That Jesus went into not only the cities but the *villages*, too, impressed Jerome with Jesus' humility, 1:182, 184.)

A. The Heart of Christ (9:36)

"And when he saw the crowds of people his heart really went out to them because they were harassed and helpless like sheep without a shepherd." Why is there mission? First, because Jesus' heart goes out to people. The Greek verb here means, literally, "to feel in the viscera," and in colloquial English can be rendered "feels for." Jesus hurts when he sees people, he "feels for" them, they "grab" him down deeply, they "reach" him. The first reason for Christian mission is the fellow-feeling of Jesus, which we can formally call Jesus' compassion (from the Latin *cum:* with; *passio:* suffer; "suffering with"). Because Jesus suffers with people he institutes mission to them. Mission is not motivated by Jesus' disgust for people because they are such sinners, nor even by an imperial sense that he has a right to people (a motive legitimate enough, rightly understood). Mission is motivated by the simpler fact of Jesus' compassion for lost people. Mission in Matthew's Gospel, therefore, is not first of all an enterprise by which missionaries go out and censorially shape the world up. Mission is first a task in which disciples go out and compassionately help people out by presenting them with their Shepherd.

When human sin is stressed inordinately as a source for mission, compassion is smothered rather than ignited. When Jesus looks out over the world it is the *helplessness* of people, their depression and suppression, that affects him most deeply. He sees people first as a *massa confusionis* before he sees them as a *massa perditionis* (though he *does* also see them as perishing, cf. 10:6). They appear to him exactly like sheep who have lost their shepherd and who are limping, matted and beat up, from one desperation to another. They need nothing so much as they need a good shepherd.

The two words describing the people—"harassed and helpless" (RSV, NEB)—mean literally "mangled and cast down" (Green, 117). "'Harassed'—Walking with difficulty. . . . 'Cast down'—A further step in misery" (Beng., 1:152).

By what are the people oppressed? By the deceitfulness of worldly life and by the excesses of a spiritual leadership that asks for more than it gives (see chapter 23 classically). In such a condition the main need people have is a good shepherd. Thus Christian disciples are to think first of all of the overwhelming need of people for *Jesus himself* in all his gracious helpfulness as he has been presented to us in chapters 5–9 of this Gospel. Here is a shepherd who does not first require his sheep to leap through hoops before they get pasture, but who on the slightest notice of need or danger is there (the Beatitudes, the healings). People need Jesus. That is principle one of mission. (Jesus' mission, quite simply, is based on need, Schn., 125.) And what people therefore need today above all is shepherds sent by this Shepherd, pastors from the Pastor, who will feed people with the grass of gospel—a grass that does not put to sleep or narcotize but that quickens and nourishes. People need Christian workers. That is principle two of mission.

"The trouble of flock, sheep, and crowds is the guilt of the pastors and the vice of the teachers" (Jero., 1:184). Cf. Ezek 34 for vivid OT commentary. The people's main problem is that they are terrified by their spiritual leaders *in God's name* and that they are given all sorts of scruples and prohibitions but not God's grace (Schl., *Das,* 151).

To say that people primarily need the Shepherd and his shepherds is to say that people need evangelical (i.e., grace-, Christ-, and faith-centered) and expositional (i.e., biblically and church-historically based) *preaching and teaching* as the source of their energies. Only this grass is green, only this nutrition feeds people messianically, gives rich pasture, gives *Jesus* in all his fullness—in both his prophetic toughness (e.g., Matt 5–7) and his pastoral tenderness (e.g., Matt 8–9).

People desperately need the compassionate Jesus through the pasture of *expository* teaching—teaching that points the finger also at *us,* teaching that proceeds regularly through whole paragraphs, pericopes, and units of Holy Scripture and that will not skip hard or uncongenial passages, that will not subjectively pick and choose texts for Sunday sermons, and that follows church lectionaries or biblical books. They need the expository teaching that disregards or demotes most "special Sundays" (the Protestant form of Saints' Days) and diverting, thematic months and weeks, and that will see as its only theme, no matter what the Sunday, the gospel of Jesus. Such teaching sees integral units of Scripture as its only text for presenting the imperial gospel theme. On this ground—the ground of the heart of Christ in the Word of God—mission can grow; all other ground is sinking sand. Only on this ground are we permitted a view of the Whole Christ with his whole heart, and only this Whole Christ moves us into the whole world in wholesome mission.

"Harassed and helpless." Religion harasses; much *Christian* religion oppresses; but at least Christian religion (which uses its Bible at all) has the built-in corrective of Jesus. The world religions have Jesus only in very mangled forms, and these religions are often grandiose programs of self-salvation (Hendrik Kraemer; Karl Barth versus Hans Küng). The world drama of liberation and development is frustratingly impeded by religious taboo and requirement: from Roman Catholic strictures on family planning in the Philippines to Hindu strictures on cows in India and Quranic strictures on women in the world of Islam. Religion uninformed by the grace of Jesus needs to be taken off people's backs.

People are also badly oppressed by the new secular religions—the ideologies. They, too, are filled with historical "laws," with "class requirements," and with precious little grace. These new religions enflame their devotees with hatred for oppressors; but they cannot supply shepherds—they lack heart. These mighty contemporary faiths need the Whole Christ with his prophetic power, hurt-heart, and real-presence in disciples. The secular religions, though they march under the banner of the people, simply decimate people in the end. (The western Holocaust, the eastern Gulag, the southern Kampuchea and South Africa, and an economically and militarily colonialized Third World everywhere we look are only the most conspicuous recent examples of ideological mayhem in our century.) The harassment and oppression of the contemporary peoples is largely religious (or ideological, which is the same thing); relief can come in deep forms only from better religion, for people cannot live without the dimension of depth—religion or ideology. The best religion is the Christ of God, a shepherd of the peoples who keeps his promises, who is able both to excite liberating passions and to tame enslaving ones, the Whole Christ. The Gospel of Matthew presents him.

B. The Prayer of Disciples (9:37–38)

"Then Jesus said [literally, "says," now!] to his disciples, 'The harvest is huge, but there are hardly any workers; so pray the Lord of the harvest to thrust workers into his harvest.'"

We can be encouraged by Jesus' realism: the task is overwhelming. The numbers of people who do not have the Shepherd are immense; the numbers who work for this Shepherd are minuscule. The task looks hopeless, and Jesus admits as much with his contrasts of "huge" and "hardly any." But statistics and quantities are not ultimate realities. The only reality worth taking with ultimate seriousness is the Living God. Jesus refers us to this God, unapologetically, in prayer. The source of mission from the human side is prayer meetings as from the divine side it is the compassion of Christ. Christian mission in Acts was born, humanly speaking, in prayer meetings (Acts 1:14; 4:24–31; and 13:1–3, for example). Christian mission in Matthew, too, is now broached for the first time formally; and, significantly, it is conceived as an enterprise of prayer.

We do not make ourselves or others into workers; we pray the Lord to do this. Jesus is not recorded saying, "The harvest is huge, the laborers are few; therefore *go* as workers into the harvest." Rather, in the face of the immense need, and of the paucity of recruits, the disciples are referred to the Lord of the harvest in prayer and to *his* recruiting. This means that mission is principally a matter of prayer and prayer meetings, which is another way of saying that mission, too, belongs to the sovereignty of God (cf. Bornkamm, "End," 18).

It is in Matthew's interest that the church learn that mission is a divine matter, that mission is *missio Dei*, and that the closest we can get to the proper allocation of resources and to the recruitment of personnel is prayer. Attempts to augment mission that bypass prayer and that depend largely on reorganization or pleas for more generous stewardship come across as shrill and are doomed to frustration.

Many conservative-evangelical churches pray. This simple fact is an important part of the answer to the question "Why conservative churches grow?" Where there is prayer there is mission. Where there is little prayer there is little mission. The fact that nonconservative churches are less apt to hold prayer meetings than they are small-group or committee meetings is a symptom of malaise. A creeping death sweeps over the mission of many churches in our time because, quite simply, prayer meetings have ceased. And beneath the death of prayer, at a deeper level, lies the death of a real belief that only Jesus Christ literally saves people. Faith in Christ as *Savior* has perceptibly declined in some of our churches. But faith is the mother of prayer, and prayer the mother of mission. Thus the theology of prayer that is Matthew 8–9 precedes the theology of mission that is Matthew 10.

On the realistic basis of the apparent statistical hopelessness of Christian mission ever winning the great majority of the people of the world, Jaroslav Pelikan, in his *Jesus Through the Centuries: His Place in the History of Culture* (New Haven: Yale Univ. Press, 1985), 228–33, argues for Christian tolerance and for the recognition of God's revelation everywhere rather than for Christian missionary aggressiveness and the exclusive Christ. But Jesus in our passage looks out at an overwhelmingly hopeless world, even statistically, and tells his disciples to pray for Christian workers. Look what happened in the first century alone.

"Workers" (*ergatas*) is the simple, unpretentious, even somewhat unappealing name given in this story to missionaries, evangelists, and disciplers. Jesus does not tell us that the need is for leadership or for experts, or even for particularly fiery types; the need is simply for workers. And their work is not even described as sowing (an image used elsewhere for mission), but as working on *an already present harvest.* The picture presented to our imagination is of a work practically finished, a work done mainly by the Lord himself, in which we have the relatively simple and uncomplicated task of entering in to gather work already done. The impression is of a need not for highly skilled spiritual entrepreneurs who will *develop* a mission or even execute it, but for simple, obedient workers who will gather an already ripe harvest.

Cf. Klostermann, 85, on this subject. Chrysostom, 32:4:212, was as impressed by the *easiness* as by the necessity of Jesus' mission mandate here—that Jesus sends us out not to sow but to reap, not to a planting but to a harvesting. Cf. Jn 4:35–38!

These pictures of mission—of harvest rather than sowing, of simple workers rather than of initiating planters—are particularly appropriate to the current mission situation. We have entered an era in mission when it seems poignantly clear that sometimes the worst thing the Western (or Northern) churches can continue to do for the Southern or Third World churches is to send experts or specialists. The fruit of the work of such experts is often self-doubt and inhibition in the receiving churches, no matter how great the expertise. Churches inundated by overseas experts are churches crushed in personhood.

What are needed in mission today are the simplest (and noblest) workers— evangelists and pastors—not leaders or specialists. The latter, when they come from beyond national boundaries, frequently but unintentionally wreak havoc in the self-respect of the receiving churches, which are given the sometimes un- conscious impression by the very presence of leaders and specialists that they themselves lack the leadership and specialization necessary for the successful prosecution of mission.

Is there any significance in the fact that Jesus asks us to pray that the Lord will literally "thrust out" (*ekbalē*) workers? ("The forcible expression springing from the sense of pressing want," Meyer in Beng., 1:153.) Jesus does not say "find" or "recruit" workers. The idea is this: there *are* Christian workers already there in this first, and in every subsequent Christian community, and they need to have a fire lit under them to thrust them out of their comforts into the world of need.

What is the specific work of the workers? In context it is bringing people into discipled faith in Jesus, as the immediately preceding chapters have described discipleship (Matt 5–7) and faith (8–9). There are other kinds of Christian work— for example, teaching, administration, social, or medical work. But as everyone who works in these positions knows, or should know, these tasks are auxiliary to the principal mission task of harvesting, or, in language that Matthew develops, discipling, disciple-making. As prayer is the simple *base* of mission, so discipling is the simple *goal* of mission.

"Whenever we see a lack of good pastors, we must lift up our eyes to Him, to bring us the remedy" (Cal., 1:278). "If only there were enough preachers" (McN., 130). "When disciples make the lack of workers a cause for prayer they already perform an important part of their service" (Schl., *Das*, 152).

C. The Gifts of Ministry (10:1)

"And when Jesus had summoned his twelve disciples he gave them authority over unclean spirits so that they could cast them out and heal every disease and every sickness." The third source of mission is gifts of ministry. Jesus is going to send his twelve out on a model mission. Through Jesus' teaching in this inaugural mission Matthew will teach us the basic principles of all Christian work right here in the heart of his Gospel.

The twelve represent by their very number the seriousness of Jesus' intention to summon the whole Israel of all twelve tribes. ("The number twelve indicated the coming restoration of the Church. . . . the birth of a new people. . . . a new Israel," Cal., 1:289f. Cf. Schl., *Das*, 153; Davies, 59.) In Mark and Luke at this point the twelve are simply called "the twelve," but Matthew distinctively defines their nature with the noun, "the twelve *disciples.*" At their first appearance Matthew wants us to see the twelve not as a ruling hierarchy, as a kind of sacrosanct Christian administration, but as twelve *disciples,* as twelve persons entirely absorbed in the life-filling task of following Jesus. (Contrast in this respect the well-intentioned but misleading third chapter of Vatican II's *Dogmatic Constitution on the Church,* "The Hierarchical Structure of the Church. . . ," where the "sacred power" of the twelve and their successors strikes Protestant ears as problematic.) And as if to deepen his christocentric impression Matthew calls them "*his* twelve disciples," for they belong to Jesus; they are, as it were, Jesus' property and his responsibility.

"He *gave* them." There are few doctrines more encouraging than the doctrine of gifts. Paul develops the doctrine richly, especially in 1 Corinthians 12–14 (cf. also Rom 12 and Eph 4). Matthew only touches the doctrine of gifts slightly here. But the permanent truth of the doctrine is this: Jesus does not call us to mission without equipping us for it (see Matt 28:18–20; Luke 24:49; John 20:21–22; and Acts 1:8, for exactly this point).

The twelve disciples were given the authority, specifically, to exorcise and to heal. Three matters call for notice here: (1) The separation of exorcism and healing indicates that not all sickness was traced to demonic sources; there were sicknesses that were traced to demonic causes, and there were other sicknesses, perhaps including at times even mental, emotional, and nervous sicknesses, that were not in any direct relationship with the demonic (cf. Kl., 85; McK., 80). (2) In the Great Commission at the end of the Gospel, this exorcising-healing authority was *not* explicitly given to the disciples (and therefore by implication not given to the subsequent church). Rather, quite emphatically there, "all authority in heaven and earth is given to *me*" (28:18), exclusively to Jesus. Thus at the end of the Gospel the disciples are commissioned simply to do three things: (a) disciple, (b) baptize, and (c) teach. Conspicuous and surprising by its absence in the Great Commission is the authority to exorcise or heal. There are still gifts of healing in the church. But Matthew's Great Commission focuses on discipling, baptizing, and teaching, that is, on Word and sacrament. And this leads us, in turn, to the third consideration. (3) Matthew uses the exact words for the disciples' mission of healing here which, a few moments before, he had used to describe Jesus' own peripatetic ministry of healing: "heal every disease and every sickness" (cf. 9:35b). Matthew wants us to see that *Jesus'* healing ministry, laid out for us in an impressive series in chapters 8 and 9, has now become the *disciples'* healing ministry in chapter 10. The disciples are to become—though Matthew never uses the expression—"the body of Christ." They are to carry out in their mission what Jesus carried out in his: exorcism, healing, and later, as we will see, teaching.

The power of the name of Jesus Christ over the evil spirits was one of the most convincing evangelical facts in the mission of the patristic church. Many Christians today believe that the name of Jesus is still laden with power. But, and this is the important fact for us, exorcising power and the miraculously healing experiences that accompany all Christian confidence are gifts of Jesus ("he *gave* them"). We can only operate with the gifts that Jesus clearly, explicitly, and unambiguously *gave* us. It is not fair for charismatic Christians to tell us that Jesus has also given *us* these same apostolic gifts and that we simply do not appropriate or appreciate them, even when we have *not* been told explicitly by Jesus that we have been given them. (And notice, *all* the disciples here appear to have been given the gift of healing; contrast 1 Cor 12:30.)

According to the Great Commission at the end of Matthew, Word gets unrivaled presidency in the church, and the sacraments (which are acted Word) get vice-presidency. But there can be no extended exposure to this Word (and its physical form as sacrament) without discovering that it is a Word of unusual concern for people's *bodies*. Jesus did not give the lepers tracts or the blind sermons: he gave them cleansing and sight. Similarly, when contemporary disciples are confronted by raw physical need they are to do everything responsible to meet that need. We are not ordinarily armed today with authority to cleanse lepers or to heal the blind—this must be clearly stressed against the Pentecostals, charismatics, and others who would make us think we are. Yet no reader of the Gospel can doubt for a moment that we are armed with the Christian responsibility to do what we can, and to invoke the Lord who can do all things, to bring every possible help to people in desperate, subhuman needs. This is another way of saying that the healing stories of the Gospels do mandate us to solidarity with the sick and to warfare against their afflictions, without always having the apostles' gift of direct authority from Jesus to heal particular cases. We do have the privilege of direct authority from Jesus to care, to help, and to pray for healing (or for special strength to bear the sickness, 2 Cor 12). The entire Call of Mercy that is the fifth chapter of Matthew is a call for just such care. The fact that today disciples are not all given the authority to heal should keep Christians humble; that fact that we are all given the responsibility to seek some form of healing and to care should keep Christians praying. ("The gift of healing that Christ bestowed on the apostles was not an inheritance for them to hand down to their descendants, but a seal of the preaching of the gospel for that occasion," Cal., 2:1. The Reformers did not betray the gospel by this restriction; they were simply honest.)

D. The Fellowship of the Church (10:2–4)

Our final missionary resource is the apostolic fellowship of the church. "And these are the names of the twelve apostles: first, Simon, who was nicknamed Peter [Rocky] and Andrew his brother; and James the son of Zebedee and John his brother; Philip and Bartholomew; Thomas and Matthew the tax collector; James the son of Alphaeus and Thaddeus; Simon the Zealot and Judas Iscariot, the man who betrayed him" (10:2–4).

Matthew calls the twelve "disciples" (his favorite title) the "apostles" only in this text. We will notice that Matthew has a definite antihierarchical bias, or understood Jesus to have (see especially Matt 20:20–28; 23:8–12). Titles that would enhance the sense of official position in the church were usually avoided by this evangelist. But here faithful Matthew records what he found in his tradition and calls the twelve disciples the "twelve apostles" (meaning the "Sent Ones," "Authorized Ones," Str.-B., 1:530; "Ambassadors," McN., 131).

Matthew's Jesus wanted his first disciples to have a sense of their significance and mission authority, not as officials but as representatives of another, not as masters but as another's ministers. As Jesus will later say to the whole church, "you have only one Master," "and you are all brothers" (23:8, 10). One senses in a largely Catholic missionary environment in the Philippines (and in the episcopally governed Methodist and United Church of Christ in the Philippines) that the clergy's single most galling fact and persistent problem is the officiousness of bishops.

Simon Peter is given an emphatic first place by Matthew (though the other two evangelists also *place* Peter first, only Matthew writes the underlining word "first"). This "first" and Matthew's later well-known gift of a certain primacy to Peter (16:13–19) stand in tension with Matthew's documented antihierarchicalism. But it should be remembered that throughout the Gospel of Matthew, Peter is as often first in folly as in leadership, as often the Gospel court jester as he is the disciples' spokesman. There is leadership in the church, but it is kept in its place by the Gospel.

"He was . . . first *among* the apostles, not placed *over* the apostles; *in* the apostolic office, not beyond it" (Beng., 1:155; Vatican II's *Dogmatic Constitution on the Church* moved decisively in this evangelical direction by the introduction of collegiality). In chapters 10, 11, and 15 of Acts, Peter is obliged to defend himself before other leaders; and as is better known, Paul feels free to criticize and correct Peter's deviant theological behavior in Galatia (Galatians 2). Peter was not a pope in the medieval or even modern sense. His primacy in Matthew, too, is a primacy of representativeness: he represents better than any other disciple the heights of faith and the depths of denial that are the lot of all disciples. Peter *is* first—in faith and in failure; he is named, within a few verses of one chapter, both Rock and Satan (16:18–23), a foundation of the church and a troubling shaker of the foundations, a hope and a peril. We should put rigidly hierarchical presuppositions to one side when we think of Peter's place in Matthew's church.

The two sets of brothers (Peter and Andrew, James and John), whose call we saw in chapter 4, come first. And though Matthew (unlike Luke) does not give us a record of Jesus sending the disciple-apostles out two by two, the fact that he here groups them two by two suggests as much (McN., 130; discussion in Beng., 1:154f; Green, 107f). Twoness protects the church from personality cult and serves constantly to remind us that we need one another. There is a power in two, moreover, that is not ordinarily present in one. (Cf. Eccl 4:9–12, and the witness of the Christian couple or family, for example.) But Matthew does not make a great deal of this twoness and so neither should we.

We have the story of the calls of only five of these twelve (the two sets of brothers in chapter 4 and Matthew in chapter 9). The fact that seven other calls are left unrecorded illustrates the selectivity of the Gospel tradition and its editing.

Only in Matthew is the seventh disciple-apostle called Matthew "the tax collector" in order, apparently, to remind us that this is the Matthew whose call we followed in chapter 9. The tradition of the late second-century church attributed the writing of this Gospel to this former quisling, as if to say: "See what God makes of us!" A *comprador*-collaborator, the most despicable of men, is transformed into the church's principal canonical evangelist by this tradition, and into one of the twelve disciples by the author of this Gospel. The presence of the four women in the geneology (1 A), of the idolator-magi at the Christmas party (2/A), and of the three outcasts at the head of the miracle stories (8/A), all lend support to the length of Jesus' reach in Matthew's Gospel.

The words "Matthew the tax collector" teach the church that mission is exercised by sinners transformed by grace, not by saints without problems, by debtors not creditors, by people not angels. "Good and upright is the Lord; therefore he instructs *sinners* in the way. He leads the *humble* in what is right" (Ps 25:8–9 RSV).

"The other evangelists put Matthew first and Thomas second in the conjunction of names, nor do they mention Matthew's former office as publican, lest in reminding us of his former way of life they might seem to be degrading the evangelist. . . . But Matthew places himself *after* Thomas and calls *himself* publican that 'where sin abounded, there superabounded grace'" (Jero. 1:186). "He does not call Peter, Andrew, etc. 'the fishermen'; but he does call himself 'the publican'" (Beng., 1:155).

At the next to the last position in Matthew's and Mark's lists is "Simon, a member of the Zealot party" (10:4 NEB). The Zealot party was the revolutionary anti-Roman-imperialism movement in Israel. A Zealot was as far removed from a tax collector as a contemporary Marxist guerrilla is from a John Birch conservative. That the two would now find themselves in Jesus' special society suggests the power of Jesus. He is able to take both collaborating and revolutionary mentalities, both *comprador*-bourgeoise and guerrilla-patriots and, by uniting them to himself, to unite them to each other.

Just as Jesus tamed the wild men in the tombs in the eighth chapter, so he can tame the economic and political passions that make people reactionary or radical in every age. The church today is instructed by the juxtaposition of collaborator and freedom fighter to believe that Jesus is still able, by his Word and presence, to overcome the most insuperable social, political, economic, psychic, and class barriers and to form churches.

For descriptions of the Zealots see TDNT, 2:884–88; lēstēs, TDNT, 4:257–62; Schl., *Das,* 153; Barc., 1:359.

"And Judas Iscariot, the man who betrayed him" (v 4). The presence of an outright traitor in the original twelve perpetually reminds the church of the mortal insecurity of each member. If one whom Jesus called fell, what should we expect of those whom we call? There is a sense in which the Gospel of Matthew teaches a doctrine of "eternal insecurity." I do not mean to contradict the important Reformation teaching of assurance; I do mean to contradict the careless modern evangelical interpretation of this doctrine which often teaches that no matter what a person who has once believed later does, he or she will be saved.

One of the twelve whom Jesus Christ *called* is Judas Iscariot. This ominous final person in the list of twelve teaches us at least this: to be called (and to respond to the call) is not yet to be in (cf. 22:11–14). The Christian life is a *life,* and it is a dangerous life ("Snatch us from the evil one," we cry at the end of the prayer Jesus gave us), and Judas "who betrayed him" should stand as a warning to every disciple that we have not yet reached the goal (cf. Matt 13:20–21; Acts 8:13, 20–24; Schl., *Das*, 154).

Matthew's list of twelve teaches the church that Jesus does his work of mission through a community of very different individuals. The list teaches us that we need each other like we need Christ, prayer, and spiritual gifts. Christian mission is a community enterprise in which we all need one another's very unique gifts (1 Cor 12; Rom 12; Eph 4; 1 Pet 4).

The sources of mission, then, are the heart of the living Christ, the prayers of Christ's disciples, and the gifts and fellowship of Christ's church. In contact with the living Christ, especially in worship services, in prayer to the Father, especially in prayer meetings, and in the exercise of our various gifts of ministry, especially in fellowship groups but not least in committees and services in church and world, we are able to be missionary and evangelistic. Without trinitarian contact with Christ in his Word, the Father in prayer, and each other's Spiritual gifts in fellowship, we are powerless in mission. We need Christ; we need prayer; we need each other When we have all three, we are missionary

II. MISSION INSTRUCTIONS (10:5–39)

Introduced to mission sources, we are now ready for the specific mission instructions of the sermon. They fall into three parts: (1) travel instructions (vv 5–15); (2) trouble instructions (vv 16–25); and (3) trust instructions (vv 26–39). The sermon's center of gravity lies in the second and third sections—the trouble and trust instructions—where Matthew presents us with Jesus' deepest evangelistic and missionary principles. (But the economic simplicity of the travel instructions is still relevant, too.)

A. Travel Instructions (10:5–15)

*"It was these twelve whom Jesus sent out [*apesteilen, *which we can render "apostled," "missioned," or "commissioned"] with these instructions: 'Don't go off to gentile country, and don't go into any Samaritan town. Just keep going to the lost sheep of the house of Israel. And as you go, be heralding this message: "Here comes the kingdom of heaven!" Be healing the sick, raising the dead, cleansing lepers, exorcising demons.*

"'You got freely, give freely. Don't ever try to get gold, silver, or copper for your wallets, or a pack for your trip, or a second shirt, or sandals, or a walking stick. After all, the worker deserves his food.

"'And whenever you get to a town or village find out who is worthy there; and stay there till you leave. When you go into the house give it your greeting ["Peace be with you."] And if it is a worthy house your peace will come right over it; but if it is not worthy your peace will turn right around and come back to you. And when someone won't welcome you or even listen to your words, just step outside that house or town and shake its dust from your feet. Amen, I tell you, it will go better in the day of judgment for the land of Sodom and Gomorrah than it will for that town.'"

"This 'mission charge' [esp. 10:9–15] is found in the synoptic gospels in no fewer than four versions. This makes the mission of the disciples during Jesus' ministry 'one of the best attested facts of the gospel' (Manson), and suggests that the instructions from it were carefully preserved and acted upon" (Green, 109), cf. Mark 6:8–11; Luke 9:2–5; 10:4–12.

The travel instructions break down into two subsections: general (vv 5–10) and then particular (vv 11–15). Matthew wants the church to follow certain general missionary principles in quite particular ways; he felt that Jesus made these principles clear when he gave his disciples their first Israel mission.

10:5–6 The instructions apply to the *twelve* in special particular because Matthew places the words "these twelve" at the head of the sentence for emphasis. Matthew stresses this restriction because we immediately learn that the disciples' field in *this* mission is not gentile or Samaritan but exclusively Jewish: "the lost sheep of the house of Israel" (v 6). Since readers know that this Gospel ends with Jesus giving a Great Commission to disciple *all nations*, it is important to know that this exclusively Jewish mission was given to the twelve for *then* and for *them* and not for *ever* and for *us* in every particular but only in the deep principles.

"We are not to believe that a regular or fixed rule is prescribed for all ministers of the Word" here (Cal., 1:289), rather these *travel* instructions (in 10:5–15) "apply only to that first mission" (Cal., 1:296); contra Beare, 252, who believes Matthew intended an exclusively Jewish mission for his church.

By this present restriction Matthew wants the church, the world, and especially the old people of God to know that Israel was given the first chance. Jesus came for Israel. And Jesus sent his missionaries to Israel first of all. Jesus really loves the old people of God. He was not only a Jew himself; he came for the Jews first. Jesus believed God's economy of salvation was, as he read his Old Testament, for "the Jews first"—and first not just chronologically but first always. It is important to the witness of Matthew's Gospel that this Jewish-first-chance be given full coverage. Jesus did not skip the Jews and head straight for the more receptive gentiles. ("The Jewish Chance" would make a good subtitle for especially chapters 21 and 22 of this Gospel.) There will be a time for a gentile mission, but that time will never cancel, but will always include the mission to the lost sheep of the house of Israel.

"This text is not contrary to the command that follows, 'Go, teach all nations, baptizing them in the name of the Father, Son, and Holy Spirit' [28:19], because our text [Matt 10] was said before the resurrection, the other text [Matt 28] after the resurrection. It was necessary to announce the coming of Christ first to the Jews lest they have a good excuse, saying, 'We rejected the Lord because He sent His apostles to the gentiles and the Samaritans'" (Jero., 1:188). But G. Barth, 100 n. 4, shows that Matthew nowhere makes a distinction between 'before resurrection' and 'after resurrection' time. Therefore, the most fruitful solution to a difficult text is this: in mission, Israel *always* has precedence. Thus in our text (vv 5–6) and in 15:24 we can see the evangelist Matthew's ties to his own people; "in spite of rejection and persecution the Gospel belongs to them first of all" (G. Barth). Trilling, 102, also disputes the exclusively chronological schema "first the Jews, then the gentiles" in Matthew.

10:6 "But just keep going to the lost sheep of the house of Israel." The present tense verb *poreuesthe* stresses a *continuing* mission to Israel. The phrase "house of Israel" is either partitive, "the lost sheep *in* the house of Israel," or epexegetical and inclusive, "the lost sheep who *are* the house of Israel." (Stendahl, 782, prefers the former; Hill, 185, and Gundry, 185, the latter.) Both meanings are possible. Jesus is sent to *all* Israel, and in Israel especially to the lost sheep *in* the house of Israel, that is, to the despised *am ha 'arez*, "the people of the land," the riff-raff, the middlebrows and lowbrows in Israel, the spiritual Philistines, the Babbitts, the common people, the nobodies who were practically everybody in Israel. With a few exceptions (Pharisees, Bible teachers, lay leaders) most everyone in Israel was spiritually petite-bourgeoise and despised for lack of commitment, for the frivolous character of their lives, and for the emptiness of their pleasures. It was to these reputedly spiritual ciphers, to the devastated sheep in the house of Israel that Jesus sent his first missionaries.

The perfect participle *apolōlota* does not mean "lost" (AV, RV, RSV) "in the sense of 'strayed,' but [it means lost in the sense of] 'perished'" (McN., 134). "Go to the destroyed house of Israel." Jesus thought of the larger part of Israel as so sunk in natural passions that their only real religion was how to make God serve their natural happiness (Schl., *Der*, 329). Jesus saw people in a more perilous and endangered state than we are accustomed to see people. We scoff at the older missionaries who went out to "save the lost" and "rescue the perishing." Yet it may be only this vision that really germinates mission, sustains it, and is true to Jesus' vision of the world. We have "lost" something. (See Matt 2 for a comparably grim anthropology.)

One may question Jesus' strategy—"to the *lost* sheep of . . . Israel." He does not single out leaders as some evangelistic and missionary groups do. Jesus' explicit missionary target is not the *leading* sheep in the house of Israel. One finds oneself back in the atmosphere of the Beatitudes. Jesus seems to have had a peculiar interest in the least interesting people: the poor-spirited, the heartbroken, and the powerless (to recall only the first three Beatitudes). Jesus had some kind of feeling for people for whom most others have traditionally had the least. (Jesus would have liked Greyhound Bus Stations.) We read often in the biographies of great men and women that they "did not suffer fools gladly" and that they had little patience for the dull-witted, the slow, the unimpressive. Yet it is one of the most authentic marks of Jesus in the Gospels that unimpressive people impressed him.

This fact is convicting to all who work in mission. For in the missionary enterprise it is not long before missionaries discover that, as everywhere else, the big problem is not extraordinary difficulties but ordinary people. It is this ordinariness that drives some Christian workers out of mission altogether; it is to this ordinariness that Jesus calls his disciples again and again. Jesus never tires of warning his workers to "watch out lest you despise one of the *least* of these little people" (18:10 and, similarly, often); it is the little people who make up the stuff of most Christian mission, in the West as well as the East. (One is reminded of Paul's admonition—which Paul may have gotten from the stories or Spirit of Jesus—"Do not be haughty, but go about with humble folk," Rom 12:16 NEB.)

This incidentally is another reason why it is often strategically unwise to send experts or specialists into mission rather than (to use Jesus' word, 9:38) simple "workers," because experts, by definition highly trained, are usually the most easily discouraged. Unless they are equipped with unusual Christian grace, ungracious personal conflicts constantly arise. To mix "experts" with exploited peoples is to mix fire with dry powder and is not recommended.

10:7 "The first consideration with one sent of God must be to know precisely where to go, where not to go" (Stier in Beng., 1:156). With the first missionary venue clearly impressed—Israel, especially its lost sheep, *not* now the gentile or Samaritan worlds—Jesus can proceed to give the twelve their message and ministry. The message is the heralding of the inbreaking kingdom: "Here comes the kingdom of heaven!" There is something exhilarating about *telling* people when we speak that the kingdom is happening as we speak. We have heard this message of the inbreaking kingdom twice before: when the public ministries of both John the Baptist and Jesus were introduced (3:2; 4:17). Now we hear it when the public ministry of the disciples is introduced. And here too, fact telling, announcement, and assurance are the principal idioms of the Christian preaching of the kingdom.

Commentators have noticed that Jesus does *not* here give his disciples the message that John the Baptist and Jesus both gave: "Repent!" "Come back!" Is this omission due to Jesus' pity for Israel? (So, e.g., Gundry, 185, following Bornkamm, "End," 18 n. 1.) But the New Testament message of repentance and return is full of pity and joy. Strecker, 195 n. 6, believes that the preaching of Jesus' "eschatological demand" (i.e., Jesus' tough teaching, as in the Sermon on the Mount) is itself the message of repentance that delivers saving help to people.

It is difficult to know what sense the message, "Here comes the kingdom of heaven," all by itself, would make to hearers. We should therefore assume that the apostles explained the kingdom message with the help of the teachings, miracles, and controversies of Jesus as we have them classically in Matthew 4–9.

10:8a However, the accent in this mission, as we noticed earlier in the conferral of gifts (10:1), falls decidedly on healing. "Be healing the sick, raising the dead, cleansing lepers, exorcising demons" (v 8a). These words summarize Jesus' just-completed healing ministry almost perfectly. Only Matthew has these words. He seems thus to say, "The disciples will carry on Jesus' own ministry. 'As the Father sent Him, so now Jesus sends them'" (cf. John 20:21). Israel gets Jesus incognito in the disciples, particularly the healing Jesus.

Raising dead people is no mean trick. Did the disciple-apostles actually do this? The Book of Acts reports that they did (9:36–43; cf. 20:9–10) and that they were able to perform other miracles such as Jesus had performed (3; 5:12–16; cf. 8:6–14). These first missionaries were equipped with gifts of healing in order to pave a highway for faith in Jesus as the Messiah. I have been told by the Wycliffe Bible Translators (the Summer Institute of Linguistics) at Nasuli, Philippines, that they have the impression that healings often occur when they first approach tribes. Might missionary insertion be divinely accompanied with healings? I am not sure, but I believe that Jesus intended for his first disciples on their first mission to be equipped with almost the entire panoply of his healing gifts.

Jerome, 1:190: "Lest no one trust the promises of the kingdom of heaven given by these rustics who have no attractiveness of speech, who are uneducated and illiterate, He gives them power [to heal various diseases] . . . in order that the greatness of the promises might be guaranteed by the greatness of the signs."

Chrysostom, 32:11:218–19, eloquently concludes his sermon on Matthew 10:1–15 by applying the apostolic miracles to his fourth-century hearers' lives in this way: "But if thou wouldest work miracles also, be rid of transgressions, and thou hast quite accomplished it. Yea, for sin is a great demon, beloved; and if thou exterminate this, thou hast wrought a greater thing than they do who drive out ten thousand demons." Then Chrysostom points out how Paul preferred virtue to miracles in 1 Corinthians 12:31 where he asks us to covet earnestly the best gifts and then says he will show us a more excellent way. "And when [Paul] was to declare this [more excellent] 'way,' he spoke not of raising the dead, not of cleansing lepers, not of any such thing; but in the place of all these he set charity. . . . For if thou change from inhumanity to almsgiving, thou hast stretched forth the hand that was withered. If thou withdraw from theatres and go to the church, thou hast cured the lame foot. If thou draw back thine eyes from an harlot, and from beauty not thine own, thou hast opened them when they were blind. If instead of satanical songs, thou hast learned spiritual psalms, being dumb, thou hast spoken. These are the greatest miracles, these the wonderful signs."

10:8b–10 The next two sentences treat economic matters. The disciples are warned not to use their ministry for commercial ends. "You got freely, give freely" (v 8b). It didn't cost any money for the disciples to get Jesus' help; it should not cost believing Israel any money to get his disciples' help (McN., 134; Schw. 239). When one has spiritual power one is always tempted to use this power for other than just spiritual ends. Both preaching and healing can become commercial ventures; they are inauthentic the moment they do. Healers who charge are counterfeit; preachers who make profit from their preaching (and not just a living) may be shrewd business persons but they are not true Christians. The work of the gospel is to be free of and unburdened with the onus of commerce.

Disciples are not to use their powers to make money—even for missions. This "you got freely, give freely" principle is serious, and only where mission is clearly marked by this principle is mission either credible or Christian. (That part of the "Electronic Church" that spends inordinate time and energy raising money for its ministries is indicted by this principle.)

"Don't ever try to get gold, silver, or copper for your wallets, or a pack for your trip, or a second shirt, or sandals, or a walking stick" (vv 9–10a). It is well-known that spiritual benefits awaken the deepest gratitude. This was true in Israel where rabbis were often paid with large gifts for their services (Schl., *Der,* 331f); it is true today where thankfulness to Christian teachers is sometimes expressed by substantial gifts. The apostles are warned not to make such gratitude even slightly a goal of mission. Disciples cannot always help it if they awaken gratitude; but they can seek to avoid commercial or financial entanglements; they can even say "no thank you," though one must be very sensitive to the culture when one does this. This much is clear: Jesus is not happy when mission is colored green, when dollar signs appear too prominently in the graphics of the mission, when there is too much money around, where clothes are too in evidence and the furnishings too impressive. The aorist imperative verb used here by Matthew means don't *ever* try to "get" (*ktēsesthe*) these things, the same word used of Simon Magus's attempt to "get" the Holy Spirit in Acts 8:20. Matthew's Jesus does not say don't *take* money or these other things (as Mark and Luke heard), but he clearly says we should not try to *acquire* money or things beyond necessities by means of our ministries.

Chrysostom, 32:7:214f, who read, spoke, and wrote Greek, saw the "acquire" force of *ktasthai,* and Jesus' reasons for it: to put disciples above suspicion, to free them from material care, and to teach them his power. "Thus they were taught apostolic contentment" (Beng., 1:156–57). They are to avoid the appearance of well-heeled tourists or business people (Allen, 102–03). McNeile, 135, finds this text is "not a prohibition against accepting payments for acts of ministry" but that it means "'Do not procure' . . . as a *provision before* starting" (emphasis mine; also Hill, 186).

This "no provision before" is clearly Mark's and Luke's meaning; Matthew's meaning, however, in the opinion of most interpreters, is that disciples ought not to seek to procure—get, win, or acquire (more than is necessary for life, 10:10c)—even *by* or *during* their ministry (especially Schl., *Der,* 331–32; also Allen, 102–03; Grund., 290; Gundry, 186, writes, "Thus the prohibitions against taking money *for* the itinerant ministry [in Mark and Luke] become [in Matthew] prohibitions against acquisition *from* the itinerant ministry.").

The intention of Matthew's report is to keep mission from economic *motives,* while the intention of Mark's and Luke's is to keep mission from sumptuous economic *accouterments.* This is the one message in all three evangelists: mission should be economically simple and unostentatious. Expensive mission is a contradiction in terms; a well-to-do missionary is an offense to the gospel. But many missionaries soon find themselves among the *nouveau riche* in the little international colonies into which or near which they are often settled. At first this suddenly wealthy situation bothers missionaries; in due time one's conscience adjusts—mental health perhaps requires it. But mission health forbids it; mission is ill served by opulent missionaries.

One is inclined to think that the Western missionary era should have ended soon after a beachhead had been established in the receiving countries and that the present era of missionary experts should have been briefer. National churches could have immediately taken over the responsibility of mission after the pioneer evangelists had done their work. Roland Allen's *Missionary Methods: St. Paul's or Ours?* (1912) made an impressive early case for just such an approach. "Simple mission" is the meaning of the ninth and tenth verses of this chapter. All subsequent missionaries are asked to rub their consciences along these two verses.

10:10c "After all, the worker deserves his food." (Luke has "wage" for "food"; they mean the same thing: the worker earns his way.) The disciple should receive a living by her or his work; the disciple is a worker and needs to eat to work.

The Christian worker is presented here as a person deserving a responsible income; the Christian worker is not to be a beggar or mendicant (Schl., *Das,* 157). The missionary or evangelist is not to be a Christian *arhat* seeking alms for ministry. The economic base that Jesus lays for mission is a base of right, not mercy; of work, not alms. This clear fact must elicit financial responsibility in the churches. While Christian workers are to be unmaterialistic (vv 8–10), Christian people are to be materially supportive (Barc., 1:366–68). The Epistles are full of admonitions in this direction (see just 1 Thess 5:12f; 1 Tim 5:17f; in the OT see, e.g., 2 Chr 31:4).

Work, wage, worthy—these finally are the key and uncomplex terms of Jesus' economic doctrine of mission. Where mission has lost touch with these fundamental economic motives it has internally sickened, however smartly it may have been able to live externally—and most missionary houses and the services that come with them are very comfortable, as most missionaries will admit.

Jesus is not inculcating a strict asceticism here; he is simply making practical the workers' faith in God's providence (McNeile, 136, who refers to this text's influence on St. Francis). Gundry, 186, summarizes the matter well. There have been ingenious attempts to reconcile Matthew 10:10's forbidding a staff and Mark 6:8's commanding it. Bengel, 1:157, correctly saw that Matthew's acquire-verb removed most difficulties in this seeming contradiction; Augustine's mystical interpretation (*Harm.*, 2:30:71:75) has the problems of mystical interpretation (e.g., not acquiring two coats, he says, means not being duplicitous, etc.).

10:11 So now in the body of the sermon we have traversed two major fields: the spiritual nature of the mission (to the lost of Israel; preaching and especially healing) and the physical or economic nature of the mission (simple and unacquisitive, on a work-wage basis). We come next to surprisingly elaborate practical instructions on how to come in and go out of a town or house. First the missionaries are to do a little research (*exetasate;* only in Matthew) to find out just who in town is worthy—translate for "worthy," a term Matthew loves, the word "receptive." (Worthiness, in Matthew's lexicon, is receptivity to the gospel and its messengers and has little to do with other abstract principles of worth or value; cf. McK., 80).

When the apostles found a receptive-worthy house they were to stay there and only there until they left town. This means that mission is to have a certain stability in town, a base, a place of reference, a headquarters, and that workers are not to move their residence around town. "Stay there till you leave" (v 11c). One is surprised by the rather sober nature of Jesus' missionary methods economically and now tactically; there is a normalcy (work for a wage) and a stability (make your base in one house for as long as you are in town) to Jesus' mission that we do not ordinarily associate with mission. One might think that a little moving around might move the gospel around, too; why should one family get all the blessings? Yet it is better to stay in one place and avoid misunderstanding than to move from place to place and almost predictably create comparisons. Simplicity (economically) and stability (tactically) seem to be the name of the on-site missionary method so far, and neither is a particularly exotic missionary principle.

10:12–13a More attention is then given to the actual greeting than some find necessary. But for an Oriental a greeting is more than a greeting: *Shalom aleichem,* "Peace be with you," was actually a religious blessing and Shalom was a name for Yahweh. (Many cultural greetings have a divine name tucked away in them—this was originally a safety measure intended to ward off the unknown spirits of strangers.) A house receptive to the disciples' greeting is promised the *getting* of the disciples' words: "Your peace will come right over it" (10:13a). In a small but seminal sense, the apostles' regular greeting is invested with gospel power, and those who welcome the messengers have already experienced the birth of peace.

As we will see especially at the end of the sermon, Jesus is building up the self-confidence and self-consciousness of his apostle-disciples; whoever warmly receives *them* actually receives *him* and all his benefits (10:40; Schl., *Der,* 333). Apostles, disciples, missionaries, evangelists, and Christian workers are supposed to know that when they are graciously taken in, these receptive "worthies" are receiving the very peace and grace of Christ himself. This happy fact gives excitement to the social life of Christian workers. They are bearers of invisible but potent blessings, and all who are decent to them are halfway there, spiritually, because in receiving Christian workers kindly people are receiving the Christian workers' Christ and his peace (Schw., 239).

10:13b–15 "But if [the house] is not worthy [receptive], your peace will turn right around and come back to you. And when someone won't welcome you or even listen to your words, just step outside that house or town and shake its dust from your feet. Amen, I tell you, it will go better in the day of judgment for the land of Sodom and Gomorrah than it will for that town."

This is a long section comparatively, which we might entitle "How to Leave Unreceptive Places." Jesus will not predict that his disciples' mission will be a Blitzkrieg, a triumphal procession; there will be unreceptive persons and hostile places. But disciples must not think that unreceptive situations mean failure in their mission or in divine providence. Jesus *predicts* such rejecting situations (and see the coming "trouble instructions," too) and now even arms disciples beforehand with the right equipment for meeting them—the art of "dust shaking."

Jews who traveled in foreign territories were taught a kind of "spiritual customs duty": to shake the pagan dust thoroughly from their clothes and sandals before reentering Palestine, lest they bring back into the holy land anything unclean. Pagan cities and countries were believed to be liberally sprinkled with the unclean (Str.-B., 1:571; with qualifications, Beare, 243f). Thus when disciples are told to shake off even the dust of the houses and cities of *the old people of God* who proved unreceptive, they were taught that *even in Israel* those who were unreceptive to the gospel were spiritually pagan. (Stendahl, 783, makes the important observation that the dust-shaking rite was to be used with towns and houses, not individuals.)

One reason for this curious rite was the fortification of the consciousness of disciples. Disciples are tempted to be discouraged when they encounter resistance. ("Isn't the *Lord* in this?") But the dust-shaking ritual constantly reminds them, like a little sacrament, that "Jesus predicted this; the losers are these unreceptive people, not we; the Lord is not frustrated." While this rite strengthened self-consciousness, it also made a sobering impression on sensitive spectators. The disciples' gesture here is a foretaste of their later authority to loose and to bind, Matthew 18:15–20 (Bengel's German Bible, in Beng., 1:157).

Finally, by his unfavorable comparison of unreceptive places with Sodom and Gomorrah, Jesus warns that in the last judgment unreceptivity to the gospel is a sin more culpable than the gross sins of those cities. Unreceptivity to the gospel, Jesus says, is the capital offense, the crowning sin, and its seriousness cannot be overestimated. When the apostolic message is proclaimed a kind of mini-last judgment is in progress and people determine their own final destinies by their receptivity to the message. (John's Gospel makes this point repeatedly.) The unattentive and rejecting fall deeper than Sodom; the attentive and believing receive divine Shalom. Jesus fills Christian workers with the consciousness that they represent issues of moment, that they are persons of destiny. "You are the salt of the earth; you are the light of the world." This self-consciousness is not antithetical to Christian humility; it is not humble to disbelieve the importance of the gospel or the role disciples have been assigned in its service. True humility is believing the Lord.

Cf. Cal., 1:295, for good exposition. Sodom's sin is sometimes understood only sexually. But see Ezekiel 16:49, in a context where God, like Jesus here, warns Israel of sins as serious as sexual immorality: "Behold, this was the guilt of your sister Sodom: she and her daughters had pride, surfeit of food, and prosperous ease, but did not aid the poor and needy." America?

This set of instructions on entering and leaving worthy places is less protocol or spiritual Miss Manners than it is consciousness-raising. The communication of a sense of importance to disciples, of a conviction of significance, seems to be one of the major purposes of Jesus' entire discipling ministry: from the "I shall make you fishers of people" at their call, through their ordination to be the salt and light of the whole world and now their Shalom/Sodom significance, to, finally, the world-wide ministry given them at the end of the Gospel, disciples are important people. There is a doctrine of "significance by faith" in the gospel of Jesus Christ that comes close to being the heart of Jesus' ministry to disciples.

B. Trouble Instructions (10:16–25)

Following the somewhat more external travel instructions in the first third of the sermon, Jesus in the next two-thirds gives us a little disquisition on the nature of Christian missionary-discipleship itself. Matthew has collected every saying of Jesus related to missionary-discipleship he could find, and he has put them here all together in a semisystematic way in order to instruct the church in Jesus' mission-ary and discipling mind. ("Missionary" and "disciple" are simply, and respectively, words for the outward and inward sides of the same reality: the Christian.)

Two threads can be discerned in the tapestry of the next two sections: trouble and trust. (1) Trouble, suffering, problems, "static"—these are to discipleship what water is to fish, discipleship's environment. Trouble is the *habitat* of Christian work. (2) Trust, decision, commitment, standing up for Christ in front of other people, abandonment of one's own life to Christ's cause—these are the inward realities of discipleship. Trust is the *habit* of Christian work.

Calvin, 1:297, already saw the composite nature of this section: "Of course, it may be that Matthew put together into this one passage speeches spoken at different times." Barclay, 1:372, also speaks of Matthew's "love of orderly arrangement" and so his collecting here "the things which Jesus said on various occasions about persecution." Chrysostom, 33:1:219, gives the main reasons for Jesus' trouble instructions at all: "Having made them feel confident . . . , having . . . cast out their anxiety [in the supportive travel instructions of vv 5–15] . . . He speaks in what follows of the evils that were to befall them" in order (1) to encourage them with His foreknowledge of trouble, (2) lest any suspect "that through weakness of their Master came these evils upon them," and so that (3) the persecuted would not be surprised. Cf. Dan 7:21–22a: "As I looked, this horn made war with the saints, and *prevailed* over them, until the Ancient of Days came, . . ." Strecker, 41, believes that from v 17 to the end of the sermon Matthew's Jesus is no longer just talking about the mission of the disciples but about the whole church's destiny of suffering. True, the remainder of the sermon is about the entire Christian church; but the entire church is engaged in mission. See Bornkamm, "End," 18, 29–30, for thorough discussion.

10:16 *"Look, I am sending you out like sheep in the midst of wolves; so be wise as snakes and gentle as doves."* This is the motto of missionary-discipleship. If missionary-disciples made coats of arms, they could make theirs with four panels and four animals on them—a sheep, a wolf, a snake, and a dove—to symbolize the complex nature of Jesus' call to mission. In a message in which Jesus treats us with such respect and summons our red blood we may be disappointed to be first called "sheep." Sheep are not the most impressive creatures in the animal kingdom. Yet the challenge of discipleship is precisely the challenge to give up the world's standards of heroism—the Beatitudes have already taught this.

Yet Jesus does not say that we are to "become" sheep, but, more fundamentally, that when we go into the world in his obedience we are in fact going out *"as"* sheep—in the midst of wolves. This vulnerability is due to the nonviolent nature of Jesus' work, as we learned it from the Sermon on the Mount. We are not primarily fighters, we are not allowed to be haters, and we cannot even use the arsenal of invective that revolutionary movements find indispensable for motivation; thus in these ways disciples, factually, *are* sheep. It is the nature of sheep to be pushed around; that is why sheep need shepherds. Thus "sheep" means that disciples and the missionary movements they enter are not to see themselves as conquering armies or victorious crusades. Disciples are to have a sense of importance, but not these kinds. Jesus' cross was not an exception to the rule; it is the rule. Outwardly, physical-political power will usually conquer disciples, they will not usually conquer it. Disciples will lose the battles and win the war.

"Let us then be ashamed, who do the contrary, who set like wolves upon our enemies. For so long as we are sheep, we conquer. . . . But if we become wolves, we are worsted, for the help of our Shepherd departs from us: for He feeds not wolves, but sheep" (Chrys., 33:1:220). "There was then at that time a herd of wolves, and but few sheep. [But] when the many wolves killed the few sheep, the wolves were changed and became sheep" (Aug., *Serm.*, 14(64):1:305).

Just as sheep are not flattering depictions of disciples, neither are wolves flattering to the world. At the beginning of the sermon, Jesus likened the world to lost sheep (9:36); now images are switched and it is disciples who are sheep and the world wolf. Which *is* the world: battered sheep (9:36) or threatening wolves (10:16)? The doctrine of man with which we have become acquainted in the Gospel ever since chapter 2 (magi/Herod) suggests that we are both. People are so complex; we need as much help as battered sheep, and in this sense we awaken feelings of compassion and mission. At the same time, human instability fosters insatiable greed and aggression. Thus what one moment are harmless sheep are the next moment snarling wolves. The human being, as Pascal rediscovered, is both Madonna and beast, angel and demon, godlike and carnivorous. The world is in the paradoxical double situation of needing mission like sheep and of resisting mission like wolves. The world despises what it needs, resists its cure, fights its ground of being. This schizophrenic sheep-wolf nature adds to the poignancy of the human tragedy of life and to the urgency of the divine comedy of mission.

See the proverbs: *Homo homini lupus,* "Man is a wolf to man." Montaigne: "Man unto man is either a God or a Wolfe." ODEP s.v. Wolf. Jerome, 1:196, correctly sees that by wolves Jesus has mainly the leaders of the old people of God in mind; also Gundry, 191: "Thus a certain solidarity exists between the persecuted missionaries and the harried people [cf. 9:36]; both suffer from the same source"—namely, from the religious leaders. The context, however, shows that Jesus thought of persecution from secular leaders, too.

Jesus' emphatic "Look, *I* am sending you" (*idou egō apostellō hymas*) means that his mission of sheep to wolves is not a mistake; it is the way the true God, in contrast to all false gods, works in history; it is the way of intended, accepted vulnerability.

Disciples must not be tempted to look for the guerrillas' more "effective" love with the seemingly more realistic revolutionary methods of Marx and Lenin. Guns have recently been put into countless disciples' hands in the name of a more effective love for the masses. But armed sheep are a contradiction in terms and a denial of Christ. (Contrast Mendoza and Fr. Gabriel in the movie *The Mission,* two kinds of liberation theology.) We either trust Jesus' way of weakness or we leave it entirely. Jesus is the one who determined to send us out into the seemingly hopeless mission of sheep converting wolves, of the nonviolent overcoming the violent ("He knows that fierceness is not quenched by fierceness, but by gentleness," Chrys., 33:3:221).

What power is the gospel against pagan communisms or capitalisms, Jesus' nonviolent ethic against all the imperialisms, Jesus' social ethic against contemporary Third World feudalisms? To ask the question is immediately to know the answer: Quite a bit! Let us then simply accept our weakness in an outwardly more powerful world and appreciate the fact that this weakness is not due to Jesus' miscalculations but to his deliberate plan. (Paul learned this: "*When* I am weak, *then* I am strong," 2 Cor 12:10c, not "once . . . , but now.")

The emphatic *egō,* "*I,*" at the head of the sentence, shows that Jesus *planned* this weakness for his disciples in mission. Bengel, 1:158, calls Jesus' authoritative I-sentence "a safe conduct."

"So be wise as snakes and gentle as doves" (v 16b). Jesus is full of animal pictures! His portrait of sheep amid wolves was to impress upon disciple-missionaries that they are vulnerable; his portrait of snakes is to teach them not to be stupidly vulnerable. The canniness of snakes is proverbial. Disciples are not asked to imitate everything in snakes: their stealth or poisonous attacks, for example; only their intelligence: "Be *wise* as snakes." This means, translated, that disciples should not go looking for wolves, seeking trouble, flaunting weakness. Unintelligent mission is not what Jesus seeks when he sends us out as sheep. If we are to be sheep among wolves—and this *is* Jesus' intention—then we should at least be smart sheep, sheep who use our heads, sheep who don't overestimate the benevolence of wolves or the beauty of the surroundings. The final wisdom of serpents is simply the prudent realization that they *are* amid wolves.

But lest the snake imagery encourage a Christian guile or a too prudent cleverness, Jesus paints in doves to complete his mural: "and gentle as doves." And so Jesus' last animal word is like his first: doves are in the bird-world what sheep are in the world of beasts—peaceful, harmless, nonviolent, simple. The animals on the seals of great states are almost invariably impressive creatures: lions, eagles, bears, and other fearful looking beasts. The main animals on the seal of mission are quite different: sheep and doves. These animals portray the qualitatively other character of Jesus' approach to life, an approach that is as civil as that of others is martial.

Christians are to be little pockets of civilization in a mad world, little cadres of moral culture in a world crazy with false notions of strength. Christians are to be the true nonconformists in a world where almost all others want to be tigers and eagles; to be people who frankly recognize that, not only in the world's view but also in Jesus', their lifestyle is not outwardly powerful, their tactics are simple to the point of being simplistic, and their hopes of changing the real power structures seem statistically remote.

Bengel, 1:158, gives David's relation to Saul as an example of one who was at the same time both wise as a serpent and gentle as a dove. Stier (in Beng., 1:158) adds, "But to see the wonderful union [of wisdom and gentleness] perfected, look at Him who requires and can give it!" Excellent discussion in Schl., *Der*, 336–38; Schl., *Das*, 159–60.

Equipped then with a realistic picture of our historical situation—sheep among wolves—and with a memo of the spiritual equipment necessary for our transit there—the good sense of serpents and the good spirit of doves—Jesus proceeds to fill in the missionary details of sheeplike existence in a wolf world.

10:17-20 *"Be wary of people! Because they will get you arrested and take you to court, beat you up in their meeting places, and confront you with governors and kings, all because of me, so that you can bear witness to them and to the nations. And when they arrest you do not worry about how or what you will speak; because in the hour you need it you will be given what to say. You see, it is not you talking but the Spirit of your Father who is talking in you."*

10:17a It is part of the sense of serpents to be wary of people. Serpents don't expect exemplary treatment. Similarly, disciples should not assume that people are basically wonderful and would not even think of doing them wrong. Disciples are called to love their neighbor and even their enemy, but they are warned here not to let their love be apotheosized into awe. A sanguine opinion of the human race is not required of disciples; it is now forbidden. "Beware of Greeks, even when bearing gifts." The missionary message is not *l'humanité*. Disciples are not to preach "the goodness of man"; they are to bear faithful witness to the Son of God and his teaching. And one of his teachings gives this earthy advice to "be wary of people." The Maoist counsel to "trust the people" will strike disciples as naive. Love does involve a certain trust, for love includes respect, and the deepest respect we pay to another is to trust him or her.

Disciples are not to have a cynical suspicion of everyone—that would violate both the sheep and dove character of discipleship. But disciples are not asked, either, to have a boundless confidence in people, to believe with Mencius that "heaven speaks as my people speak," or with Roman wisdom that *vox populi vox Dei.* The people are not God; only God is God, and so only God is to be feared, worshiped, and in this sense, trusted. "Be wary [not worshipful] of people," therefore, is an important part of Jesus' missionary counsel.

10:17-18 Jesus gives reasons for this wariness. People are going to give the disciples a hard time: arrests, beatings, and confrontations are going to be their lot. But all of this will turn out for good. These arrests, beatings, and confrontations ("ABCs," mnemonically) will give disciples a chance to stand up for Jesus, take abuse with poise, and to say a good word for him. The curious fact about Jesus' mission, as reported in this text, is that Jesus sees mission mainly as something we *back* into, via arrests, beatings, and confrontations, rather than as something we run into in conquests, conversions, and revivals. It is as though Jesus expects saving mission to occur more through the bad things that happen to us than through the good. (It is curious that Jesus does not place great evangelistic rallies anywhere on his canvas of mission.) Mission goes forward mainly by going backward, gives its witness in the process of giving up its ghost. The history of the mission of the earliest church confirms this impression. (See, classically, Tertullian's *Apology.*)

10:19 The keenest desire of disciples in these circumstances is to do the right thing by their Lord. Jesus acknowledges that the disciples' concern to do right under persecution could paralyze them. Hence he supplies a tranquilizer at this point: "Do not worry about how or what you will speak; because in the hour you need it you will be given what to say" (v 19). Thus the first responsibility of disciples in danger is to relax and believe, now if ever, in the reality of God. "Be it your only care not to care" (Beng., 1:159).

The sense of Matt 10:19 is caught well at 2 Tim 4:16–18: "At my first defense no one took my part; . . . but the Lord stood by me and gave me strength to proclaim the word fully, that all the Gentiles might hear it" (RSV).

"You see, it is not *you* talking but the Spirit of your Father who is talking in [*en*] you" (v 20). (Grundmann, 293, argues against the instrumental understanding of the *en* here: the Spirit speaks *to* disciples, consciously, not *through* them, rapturously. Disciples intelligently articulate what the Spirit says *to* and *in* them. The New Testament Spirit does not evacuate mental responsibility.) There is a nice doctrine of Word and Spirit here: the Spirit talks when disciples bear witness; the two go together. ("The Spirit does not speak without words," Beng., 1:159.) The Dove-Spirit does not so much talk immediately to governors, kings, and nations from heaven as she does *mediately* through the words of disciples. Where true disciples speak in critical situations, the Spirit speaks.

It is interesting that in Matthew's Gospel the Holy Spirit is hardly referred to at all in the life of disciples outside contexts of crisis: of initiation (3:11, 16; 28:19) or of violent confrontation (here, v 20). It is as though Matthew is not comfortable with a *too* spiritualized conception of Christian discipleship; it is as though Matthew wants disciples to take responsibility for their lives in obedience to Christ, as though he wishes to see the major focus of the disciples' life be the historical, teaching Messiah, the Lord Jesus, and not an invisible Spirit. (While Luke and John end their Gospels with Jesus' promise of the Spirit, compare Matthew's Jesus' last words: "Look! *I* [stressed, *egō*] am with you always. . . .") But at one point the invisible Spirit is welcomingly recalled by all four evangelists—in times of trouble and needed testimony (Mark 13:11; Luke 12:12; Matt 10:20; and John 14:26; 15:26 in their contexts). The special mission of the Holy Spirit is the defense of Jesus' case in critical situations (Schl., *Der*, 340; see this happening throughout the Book of Acts, e.g., Acts 4, especially vv 7–8, 31).

The explanatory verse then proceeds, twice, in the *present* tense to describe the disciples' speech in this way: "You see, it is not you talking but the Spirit of your Father who is talking in you" (v 20). This present tense verse describes a really present time fact—present in every age to every new hearer of biblical texts—the fact, namely, that when the apostles speak (as we hear them speaking through their witnesses in the New Testament) the Spirit speaks. Apostolic speech (that is, the preached New Testament) is Spirit speech. The word of the Spirit is the witness of the gospel. Jesus "advanc[es] the apostles into the dignity of [Old Testament] prophets" (Chrys., 33:4:222).

10:21–22 *"And a brother will hand over his brother to death and a father his child, and children will rise up against their parents and have them put to death. And you will be hated by absolutely everybody because of my name. But the person who has stuck to the end will be saved."*

The plot thickens. We have moved from civil and religious arrests to family troubles. And the most painful form of family trouble is betrayal. (Even in the fourth century, Jerome, 1:198, could write, "We see this [family betrayal] happen often in persecutions; there is no fidelity among persons of different faiths.") But why does Jesus put such unrelieved stress on the bad news in a message intended to thrill disciples with mission? Why is there so little prediction of success, of souls won, of lives changed, of cities transformed, and instead so much of suffering, arrest, trial, beatings, and now, of betrayals? Isn't this an overly negative picture of mission? The history of the mission of the church indicates that it is not.

Christian workers—and not only in the earliest centuries—have had a hard time in the world. It has always been dangerous to be a missionary (for medical reasons, often, in the nineteenth century; for political reasons, often, in the twentieth century). Matthew's Jesus does not wish to spare his church a full assessment of the pain of mission. Christian workers may be unusually significant persons (vv 12–15), but this does not mean that, seen from outside, they will be unusually successful ones (vv 16–25). Significance and success are not synonymous and may at times be antithetical—the cross is proof. The more deeply mission is described in Jesus' trouble instructions the more dire the missionary situation becomes, until the instructions cascade into two final statements: "And you will be hated by absolutely everybody because of my name. But the person who sticks to the end will be saved" (v 22).

The circles of hostility around disciples have progressively narrowed, from political and religious hostility to domestic turmoil until now, finally, a noose is tightly placed around the neck with the news that absolutely *everybody (pantōn)* will hate disciples because of his name. How do we put two sets of fact together: the apostles go out and, mainly, *heal* all diseases (10:8), and the upshot of their mission activity is that they will be universally *hated* (v 22)? Why will service be met with hatred? We are in the presence of "the mystery of iniquity." The same set of questions can be asked of the career of Jesus of Nazareth, and with more right. For all other Christian mission is infected, more or less, with paternalism, maternalism, imperialism, and all the other isms and sicknesses of things done by zealous human beings. Jesus' own personal mission seems devoid of these features. Yet he ended his life deeply hated, too.

Barclay, 1:374–78, has vivid illustrations of how Christianity was hated in the ancient world, especially in two areas—its adverse influence on certain businesses (cf. Acts 19:24–27) and its unsettling egalitarianism with slaves. Cf. also Pelikan's appreciations, *Jesus Through the Centuries*, 222–30.

I cannot say that today in the West I have a sense of the Christian community's being universally hated. To be a Christian in the West today seems more often a means of social establishment than of disestablishment. In the description of Matthew's Jesus, however, to be a missionary-disciple involves sinking deeper and deeper into a net of contempt. Is it possible that the presence or absence of social esteem provides a fair abacus for knowing the presence or absence of discipleship? The question is important to ask. If our commitment to Jesus were as real as this chapter describes commitment, might we find ourselves more often outside rather than inside our present circles of respect? The exact character of true commitment is the special subject of the final paragraphs of the chapter still ahead of us.

10:22a "You will be hated by absolutely everybody because of my name." This is one of the handful of sayings in the Gospel handed on to us almost verbatim by all the evangelists (Matt 24:9; Mark 13:13; Luke 21:12; adapted in John 15:18–19). It seems to be one of the most certain of the statements of Jesus. The Lord who called us to the universal love of even our enemies—another of the assured *ipsissimma verba* of Jesus—now predicts as our destiny, just as assuredly, universal human hatred. The two do not seem to jibe, and yet here they are. We must allow ourselves to be astonished that true discipleship will not mean greater popularity. Our minds are so infected by the success syndrome we can hardly believe that if Christ is true, and that if discipleship to Christ is the true way to live, that the result of discipleship will be a fouling of relationships. Something seems wrong here; life according to the truth should lead to fullness of life and to some kind of prosperity and success, should it not? And yet: "You will be hated by absolutely everybody because of my name." What does this mean?

Schniewind, 130, has suggested that "hated . . . because of my name" means that the hatred is due to Christians' insistence upon the exclusiveness of Jesus Christ as the one and only Savior ("because of my *name*"), an insistence that notoriously rankles. Is Jesus the *only* way? Has not God given us Saviors and liberators from time to time who, while not ranking *with* Christ, can stand modestly beside him, or at least just beneath him? When disciples say a firm no, and press for a clear decision for the exclusive messiahship of Jesus, the not infrequent response will be a contempt for what is called the arrogance of those claiming this exclusive allegiance. (For true disciples, the mottoes "God *and* country" or "God *and* the party," when the second member is apotheosized, are already intolerable idolatries.) Few things are as contested in contemporary Christian mission as the *exclusive* right of Jesus to messianic enthusiasm. There are, it is said, many other ways of salvation, or several other necessities, beyond Jesus, for the winning or preservation of full human liberty, and to make Jesus into the *only* way is sheer hubris.

McKenzie, 81, reminds us that Roman writers accused the earliest Christians of *odium generis humani*, "hatred of the human race"; but Matthew's Jesus inverts the relation: it is disciples whom the human race hates.

Others have suggested that the source of the world's hatred for Christians will be the Christians' commitment to Jesus' *cause*, namely, human liberation (Gutiérrez, Küng). Here it is proposed that if Christians cared as much as their Lord for the poor they would inevitably be drawn into the great social concerns of our time; and the moment they began even slightly rocking the boat, even slightly agitating for change, even slightly threatening the pocketbooks of the comfortable and the interests of the powerful, they would be in trouble. The world's hatred will be due to Christians' fidelity to Jesus' teaching rather than, somewhat abstractly (it is said), to his person. I think the truth of social responsibility affirmed by contemporary social Christians must be accepted by all Christians with conscience. But the radical significance of Jesus' social mission must be affirmed *without denying*, as too much liberation Christianity seems to do, the exclusive significance of Jesus' person. Spiritual-Christians who are insufficiently social (and in their idolatry of country, insufficiently spiritual, really) and social-Christians who are insufficiently Christ-centered, form the main face off in contemporary Christianity.

10:22b "But the person who has stuck [*hypomeinas*] to the end will be saved." With typical moderation, it is the steadfast person, not the spectacular one, to whom Matthew's Jesus promises salvation. It is not persons who overwhelm in successful mission to whom the palm is given; the person who sticks wins. (The sudden singular—"person"—in this paragraph of plurals also underlines the minority position of true disciples.) In Matthew's Gospel, constancy under pressure is the mark of the disciple. The little word "sticks" (or literally, "has stuck [it out]") should glisten and gleam before the eyes of Christians and beckon to fidelity.

10:23 *"And when they persecute you in one city, run to the next. Because, amen, I tell you, you will not finish visiting the towns of Israel before the Son of Man returns."*

The second half of this verse is one of the most difficult statements in the New Testament. Albert Schweitzer and other "consistent-eschatological" theologians used this and parallel texts for the thesis of Jesus' expectation of an imminent end to history and his subsequent disappointment (Schweitzer, *Quest*, 357–63; contrast Kümmel, 149f).

The main options for understanding this half-verse are these: (1) Jesus expected this particular mission to be the last; the Son of Man would return before the disciples' completed mission to every town in Israel. This seems the simplest and most straightforward interpretation. But to state it is immediately to see its problems. Did the historical Jesus expect *only* a Jewish mission and not a gentile one at all? Did Matthew understand the text in this sense and yet, nevertheless, still expand his Gospel until it issues in the Great Commission to all nations at the end of his Gospel? It is possible that the answer to these questions is yes and that we learn the honesty of Matthew in preserving contradictory or awkward texts handed down to him by those who remembered Jesus' words. (Cf. Kümmel, 63; Beare, 245; and in particular Green, 111, who believes this verse and 10:5–6 represent a conservative Jewish-Christian wing in Matthew's church who heard Jesus limit mission to Jews only and who frowned on gentile mission.)

(2) Might the coming of the Son of Man occur in a way that is not apocalyptic, say, in the resurrection, or at Pentecost, or in early mission outreach, or in the judgment of the Fall of Jerusalem in A.D. 70, or even in personal spiritual interventions? These less obvious and therefore less satisfying interpretations, all of which have able exponents, save the text from its present embarrassing form, agree in some ways with the Gospel of John's eschatology, but are all more or less won at the price of a spiritualization of the text's simplest meaning.

The most satisfying explanation of this type is represented, e.g., by Davies, 197, who sees the Great Commission of the risen Christ at the end of Matthew's Gospel (28:16–20) as "the scene of a proleptic parousia or more precisely the description of the enthronement of the Son of Man [Dan 7:14, LXX], in which he sends forth envoys to summon the nations to obedience." Similarly, Grund., 294–95. The least satisfactory explanation is represented, e.g., in the usually sober Calvin, 1:302: "Christ is said to 'come' when He brings relief in time of desperation." (Similarly Origen and Chrysostom, along the lines of John 14:23, in McN., 143.) Gundry, 194–95, believes Matthew has this verse in order to guarantee continuance of a Christian mission to Israel—always. Matthew 21:43, therefore, should not be interpreted as the end of a Christian Jewish mission, according to Gundry.

I prefer to dangle between both unsatisfactory solutions—and both are unsatisfactory—and believe we are in the presence of a confusing text. Clear at least in the first half of this verse is the responsibility of hounded workers to flee persecution. This is part of the sheep's serpent-wisdom. While they are to be *stickers* in sober Christian discipleship, they are not to be foolish. Moral constancy does not mean geographical inflexibility. One can stick to the gospel and still leave hostile situations. "Bravado is not martyrdom" (Barc., 1:378–79). Thus the twelve are called to be morally fixed and geographically fluid, strategically solid and tactically liquid. Finding this balance will be part of the art of mission and a continuing subject of discussion in Christian missionary communities.

10:24–25 *"A disciple is not above the teacher nor is a servant above his lord. It is enough if the disciple can be like his teacher and the servant like his lord. If people called the head of the house 'Beelzebul,' how much more so his domestic servants."*

"He who keeps this saying in his heart will never complain of suffering" (Quesnel in Beng., 1:160).

"He suffered under Pontius Pilate." The Apostles' Creed wisely subsumed the whole of Jesus' earthly ministry between birth and passion under the single verb "suffered." Therefore, the words "a disciple is not above the teacher" are strangely comforting. Disciples need to be reminded that trouble, persecution, and betrayal were the experiences of their *Lord.* To know this is instantly to receive courage in one's own troubles. And since disciples are not above their Lord, but definitely beneath him, *we* have every right to expect bad seasons in ministry, too. Jesus was called satanic ("Beelzebul"), fanatic, dangerously liberal, heretical, and every other disqualifying name in the spiritual lexicon; this will fortify disciples amid similar abuse.

One gets the impression that one goal of Christian ethic in Matthew's Gospel is to encourage disciples when their work meets resistance. Jesus' earlier successful mission descended precipitously downhill into execution; disciples should not expect better.

The fact that this was *Jesus'* experience, the *Lord's,* should teach disciples that success, as the world (and many in religion) count it, should be no criterion whatever for discipleship. Success, in the deepest sense, in the Christian sense, is ability to be like Jesus. Verses 24 and 25 are postponed commentary on the words, "the person who sticks to the end will be saved," and they instruct disciples that Jesus stuck to a very bitter end, and only in the resurrection was he delivered.

The major heroism advocated in this Gospel is the heroism of "staying-under" (the literal meaning of the word translated "stuck": *hypomeinas—hypo,* under; *meinas,* stay). To "stay under" is to stay down low in obedience to Jesus' commands. It is the special concern of the section we next enter to spell out in detail *the way* disciples stay under and stick.

C. Trust Instructions (10:26–39)

10:26–31 *"So do not ever be afraid of these people; because there is nothing covered up that will not be uncovered, or hidden that will not be known. What I am telling you in the dark you must repeat in broad daylight; and what you hear whispered you must shout from the housetops. And stop being afraid of those who kill the body but who do not have the power to kill the soul. Fear instead the One who has the power to destroy the soul as well as the body in hell. Aren't sparrows selling two for a penny at the market? And not one of them will fall to the ground without your Father. And you? Even the hairs on your head have all been counted. So stop being afraid; you are worth more than many sparrows."*

Jesus' initial advice now in this trust section of his address is not to be troubled in the midst of trouble. We should be prepared for trouble but not frightened by it. And the way Jesus secures this fearlessness is by teaching the special kind of Father disciples have. Jesus teaches what theology calls the providence of God (cf. Conz., 55).

10:26–27 The meaning of the "nothing [is] covered up that will not be uncovered" text (v 26) is at first difficult to decipher. In Luke 12:2 it is a warning against hypocrisy, but in connection with Matthew 10:27, which Matthew forms in such a way as to emphasize what *"I am telling you,"* we understand Matthew's two verses together to say: "Don't you be afraid to teach the whole of my teaching—let there be no covering up of difficult subjects."

Thus the majority of interpreters: Chrys., 34:2:227f; Jero., 1:200; Cal., 1:304–05; Allen, 108; Schw., 246; Stend., 783; McK., 81; Green, 112; Beare, 247; Gund., 196. In a secondary sense, the text can also be consoling, meaning, "the truth will out," "your unjust persecutors will see justice" (Chrys., 34:1:227; Jero., 1:200; Schn., 132; Davies, 459).

Jesus' final words in this Gospel, comparably, are "teaching them to keep *everything* [*panta hosa*] I have commanded you; and look, I am with you always, even to the end of history" (28:20). Jesus' words to his apostles are history's major treasure, and both here in the Sermon on Mission and at the end of the Gospel in the missionary commission, the apostles are urged to broadcast Jesus' total Word into the field of the whole world, not tiptoeing around in fear of people, not temporizing, but speaking out, expositing, interpreting, and proclaiming Jesus' complete teaching.

It is fear that makes preachers pick and choose their texts rather than to allow their texts to pick and choose them; that is, it is fear that makes them topical rather than expository or lectional. It is the task of apostolic discipleship—of apostolic succession—to teach Jesus' whole Word and nothing but that Word, and that Word in all its depth and width. We do not have to search for sermon sources; our single sermon and teaching source is the Word of God, which here again we are commanded to proclaim fearlessly and completely. What Jesus has even "whispered in the ear," that is, taught privately, disciples are to shout from the housetops (Str.-B., 1:579–80; Gund., 196); what Jesus has said to the apostles "in the dark," that is, even the hard sayings, disciples are to give themselves so to understanding that they can say that Word "in the light," that is, in contemporary interpretation and application.

There is no word in the world like the Word of Jesus. Disciples are to appreciate this and to give themselves to the thrilling task of understanding and explaining Jesus' entire teaching.

The Reformed branch of the catholic church, returning to the practice of early Christian centuries, commends a *lectio continua* —a preaching of whole books, in order, so that the people of God have an ordered instruction in God's Word. One happy way that this is being restored to the church in our time is by way of the *lectio selecta* —the lectionary preaching of the Word of God, particularly during the church (half-) year from Advent (December) to Pentecost (late May, early June), combined with an exposition of whole books in course (*lectio continua*) from June through November. See the helpful discussion by Horace T. Allen, Jr., "Understanding the Lectionary," in his *A Handbook for the Lectionary* (Philadelphia: The Geneva Press, 1980), 36–41.

The fear of people, the unbecoming solicitude for saying what people would like to hear, the craven concern for a relevance at any price, the too timid fear of offending, will lead many Christian teachers to look elsewhere than to Jesus' clear Word for their messages. This Word will seem to some preachers, under the impress of a supposed world-come-of-age and of modern concerns, to be a Word that is largely passé and naive. And so the teaching of the church will either be topics like peace of mind and power in life (in spiritual churches) or humanization and liberation (in social churches)—topics legitimate enough in themselves— rather than Jesus' own words, and almost exclusively his words, and their church-critical, world-critical views of peace, power, humanization, and liberation.

Apostolic succession is present where passion for the catholic exposition of the gospel is present. "Don't be afraid of people: tell them *everything* I told you—that is your mission." This is what Jesus is saying in these two verses.

10:28 In this verse we are commanded not to fear those who can only kill the body, but to fear him who can kill both body and soul in hell. A somewhat Greek idea may be at work in the separation of body and soul (though see Gundry, 197, on *Hebrew* separation of body and soul as at Isa 10:18; 38:10, 12, 17), but this does not alter the point: people can hurt us only temporarily; the Father can sentence us permanently. The disciple will transfer fears from people to God, from what people will do to what the Father will do. The one who fears the Father is liberated from fear of people—no little liberation. The tender-minded message that the Father of Jesus Christ is not to be feared but only loved is a pious fraud. "The fear of the Lord is the chief part of wisdom, and those who live by it grow in understanding" (Ps 111:10 NEB, mg.).

Fear God or fear everything! "He who does not fear God, fears everything save Him: 1 Pet 3:14–15" (Beng., 1:161). "Let us fear therefore, that we may not fear" (Aug., *Serm.*,

15(65):1:306). It is *God* who is to be feared in this text; we are never told to fear Satan in Scripture (McN., 145; Gund., 197). Augustine, *Serm.*, 15(65):7:308, gives the best sense of Matthew 10:28 in its context: "Fear not then, O Martyr, the sword of thy executioner; fear only thine own tongue, lest thou do execution upon thine own self, and slay, not thy body, but thy soul."

We live in a time in which "the people" have been nearly deified. The people are celebrated everywhere. "The People's Republic of China," "The New People's Army," and yesterday one could read in the paper of a person who kidnapped "for the sake of the people." In the West, polls indicate the importance of the opinion of the people, and Western democracies honor the rule of the people. Yet important as people are, they are not God, and they are not to be made disciples' final criterion. Only God is God. Jesus liberates his people from the lordship of people. And the way he does this is by substituting a more worthy fear: the fear of the God who can destroy us entirely (*apolesai*, the word used here, means "to destroy" once for all). The picture is a little gruesome, but Jesus does not shy away from hard pictures.

A person can be destroyed, and this destruction can be willed by God. ("I . . . kill, and I give life," Deut 32:33.) From John the Baptist's Fire Sermon in chapter 3 to Jesus' Sermon on Mission here in chapter 10, the reality of a judgment in which chaff gets burned and in which hell is hot is put before the conscience of *disciples.* Only a serious fear of God and of what God is capable of doing, independent of our notions of what God *should* do, will carry a disciple through a world in which people are so imposing. The fear of the Lord *is* the beginning of wisdom.

10:29 And yet the biblical fear of the Lord is not a servile fear. It is a fear qualified by the character of the one feared, a filial fear. This is made clear by Jesus' next word about sparrows and his use of the word "Father." Sparrows sell two for a penny in the market and yet, Jesus reminds us, not a single one of them will ever fall dead to the ground without a prior decision of the Father that this happen ("without your Father's leave," NEB; "without your Father's consent," TEV).

I like the simplicity of the Greek phrase, retained in the RSV: "without your Father," as though the Father not only determines the bird's fall but accompanies it.

The divine government is not so taken up with international problems that it has no time for birds. Views of God that say God hasn't time for little things are not characterized by the largeness of their God. The death of a sparrow is no more troublesome to the Father than the death of empires—so large is the God to whom Jesus commends disciples.

10:30–31 Jesus then makes the human connection: "And you? [emphasized in the text]. Even the hairs on your head have all been counted. So stop being afraid; *you* are worth more than many sparrows" (vv 30–31). The Father whose eye is on the sparrow, a little bird, is the Father who has an intimate inventory of the number of hairs on each of our heads—very insignificant data. Yet apparently this number is significant to the Father, which is another way of saying that God is engrossed with his people. As Schlatter puts it (*Der*, 165), no fist is going to hit a disciple's face without the Father's approval; and every fist that does hit it has been providentially permitted. Jesus' Word is not a protection from martyrdom; it is assurance that we, like sparrows, will not suffer anything, even death, "without the Father" (McN., 146; Gund., 198).

"The bird falls through cold, hunger, or storm, not in spite of, but with the knowledge of the Father. The inexorable, and apparently cruel, laws of nature are not outside the loving care of God" (McN., 146).

It is interesting that Jesus has inserted his treatment of the doctrine of providence into the middle of a Sermon on Mission. For it is those who do his work of mission who most need this doctrine. They need to know that the Father who lets them get in trouble, who lets them get arrested, and who, in a word, *backs* disciples into a mission filled with trouble and persecution, is not, contrary to all appearances, a weak God.

The great Old Testament source of the doctrine of providence is the story of the patriarch Joseph, Genesis 37–50. John Calvin's doctrine of providence is one of the most exciting parts of his theology, *Institutes of the Christian Religion,* Book 1, chapters 16–17. I am not acquainted with an outstanding modern treatment.

10:32–33 *"So every person who stands up for me in front of other people, I will stand up for that person in front of my Father who is in the heavens; and every person who denies me in front of other people, I will deny that person in front of my Father who is in the heavens."*

Here, suddenly, Jesus himself appears: "Every person who stands up for *me* . . . , *I* will stand up for," etc. Why did Matthew put these words here? In the preceding paragraph Matthew had reshaped the words of the Q source to read "what *I* say *to you* in the dark," etc., giving a christological twist to a providential paragraph. For it is not just general fear from which Jesus is delivering us; it is the particular fear of standing up for Jesus in tough situations. More often than we realize we are called upon in even little situations every day to stand up for Jesus in front of other people. Jesus here promises that when we do he will reciprocate in a grand way. He will stand up for us before the Father now and at the final judgment at the last day.

Standing up for Jesus (literally, "confessing" him) combines both faith in and love for God, the old contestants for justification in the sixteenth-century controversy between Protestants (faith) and Catholics (love). Matthew's "confessing" Jesus may help us to synthesize the best of Paul-John and the best of Matthew-James, the concerns of Luther and the concerns of St. Thomas. Each of us, in a particular vocation, has opportunity either to deny Jesus or to stand up for him by making moral decisions in accordance with his Word. (In relation to sex, men and women confess Jesus as much by what they do as by what they say.) Almost every human encounter gives the opportunity, either ethically or evangelistically (and the two are often profoundly intertwined, as the Sermon on the Mount teaches), to stand up for Jesus, to confess him, to bear witness to him.

Our stand before the Father is determined by our stand for or against Jesus and his words in the presence of other people. Theologically, we have moved from the doctrine of providence in vv 28–31 to the doctrine of justification or judgment here in these two verses. We will be justified before the Father (justification is the language of Paul) by our standing up for (Paul would say, faith in) Jesus in front of other people. We will be condemned before the Father by our denial of (Paul and John would say unbelief in) Jesus in the presence of other people. "Standing up for" is a good modern definition of faith.

It is strange that Matthew has put justification-judgment language in the middle of a missionary sermon (not to outsiders but) to apostle-disciples. Even apostles need to know that their justification depends upon the reality of their living relation to Jesus.

Calvin, 1:309, comments on the urgency of this text even for members of the family of God—for *Christians:* "If a man runs away or keeps silence, is he not, by frustrating the work of the Son of God, taking himself out of the family of God?"

10:34–39 *"Don't ever think I came to bring peace to the earth; I didn't come to bring peace, but a sword. I mean, I came to divide a man from his father, and a daughter from her mother, and a bride from her mother-in-law; and a person's worst enemies will be members of one's own family. So whoever loves a father or a mother more than me is not worthy of me, and whoever loves a son or a daughter more than me is not worthy of me. And whoever does not accept one's cross and follow me is not worthy of me. The person who has made his life secure will lose it, and the person who has thrown her life away for my sake will find it."*

10:34 So central is trouble to the Christian mission that Jesus now says his *purpose* in coming is division. We are so accustomed to the angelic greeting at Christmas, "and *peace* on earth to men with whom He is well-pleased" (Luke 2:14) and with similar biblical remarks that it comes as a shock to be told that peace is not Jesus' purpose but that division is. This is a hard sentence. How is it meant?

What Jesus wants is confidence (faith) in himself as God's representative, and understanding (love) for the neighbor. The consequence of confidence and understanding *is* peace for the individual. But peace in Scripture—*shalom*—is mainly a social word, a word meaning "welfare," "social and spiritual well-being"; it is not mainly an individual, inward, or psychological reality. Jesus will bind people to himself in faith at center and move them out constantly into life in love at the edges, but the historic consequences of the acts of faith and love have always been as much *division* as reconciliation. A few will believe the truth of Christ, but most will oppose it. Jesus is aware of this demographic fact and therefore says, boldly, that it is his *purpose* to bring this opposition, this trouble, this conflict. He so prefers loyal discipleship and mission, with their inevitable divisiveness, to all social accommodations and false peace that he is willing to say that he came *in order* to divide.

"The *effects* produced by the preaching [namely, divisions] are given as the *purpose* for which Christ came. This is in accord with a Semitic way of speaking . . . about God," cf. Amos 3:6 (Beare, 249). But theology (specifically, the sovereignty of God) is at work here, not just Semitic idiom.

We are again in the presence of the realism of Jesus. Jesus is not expansive about the possibilities of Christian mission; he knows that his mission is a rugged minority movement, a tough, divisive affair, and he prefers to make this clear rather than give false hopes. "The gate is wide and the way pleasant that leads to destruction, and many people [a majority] go this route; but the gate is narrow and the way is tough that leads to real life and very few people [a minority] find this way" (7:13–14). The effect of this little minority movement as it moves aggressively into the massive majority culture is bound to be friction. Jesus does not want his disciples to expect great victories and then, when persecution, hostility, and rejection are their actual experience, to feel betrayed. "This is the way it goes," Jesus assures them; indeed, "this is the way I *plan* it to go."

"He fashioned His discourse accordingly; lest any one should say it was by flattery He persuaded them, and by concealing the hardships" (Chrys., 35:1:232). Nevertheless, what Jesus says *is* offensive, as Calvin, 1:310, clearly saw: "Since the Prophets always promise that under the reign of Christ there will be peace and tranquil times, what else would the disciples have hoped for, but that everything would at once be pacified, wherever they should travel?"

Therefore, when things get rough and even go down in mission we are not to believe that this necessarily means Christ and his church have failed, that either he in his sovereignty or we in our dedication have been lacking (though we will need to practice a close self-criticism). Somehow failure is the way Jesus goes around succeeding; somehow the cross leads, inconsequently, to the resurrection; somehow all this trouble and division lead to some peace, reconciliation, and success now and then. Why the Lord works this way and not in more auspicious ways is beyond our ken. It is sufficient to know that it is his sovereign *purpose* to work this strange backward way.

10:35–36 The kind of rough times, the kind of (literally) "sword" that Jesus came to bring is then particularly spelled out as family divisions. "I mean, I came to divide a man from his father, . . . and a person's worst enemies will be members of one's own family" (vv 35–36).

The sword of decision for Jesus goes right down the middle of families. Jesus will not always make families happier by a family member's Christian decision. "Decision is division." The moment someone in the family decides seriously to be a disciple the trouble starts. The father won't like it or the mother-in-law or the son, or someone else close. (It is interesting that here as often elsewhere in Matthew [contrast Luke 18:29], Jesus is not interested in suggesting any breach between husband and wife. The marriage relation is too precious to be threatened with division; it is not Jesus' purpose in any way to bring a sword here, though one sometimes comes.) When apparently unavoidable family religious arguments begin, disciples may recall these words of their Lord—"he told me so"—and take heart. Otherwise disciples will be inclined to think "this trouble cannot be the will of God."

Disciples, of course, must always be on the alert for their own fanaticism. The whole Gospel has taught us this. But the simple, fundamental decision to follow Jesus as a disciple is not fanatical; it is the supremely rational act.

It is not celibacy, but evangelical decision to prefer Christ to parents or children that is the main sacrifice that the Jesus of the Gospels calls disciples to make in relation to family. (Grundmann, 300, in fact, sees the sword of Jesus' text to be the generation gap, the younger versus the older generation, and vice versa.)

Jesus came to cause the trouble of a serious decision for himself, a decision that must, in the nature of the case, be a decision against the absoluteness of the family, or of the family name, or even of family honor. (Cf. Arthur Miller's play, "All My Sons.") In the Orient especially, where the family is so honored, the revolutionary character of this Word of Jesus is felt with force. The family and its happiness are simply not the last word and are certainly not the main purpose of Jesus' work; indeed, the family and its happiness will be the disciples' major obstacle to giving crown rights to their King. "A person's worst enemies will be members of one's own family."

Nothing *human* is more beautiful than a close family. Many Christian families know that they owe their cohesiveness and quality to the presence and grace of Jesus Christ at the center of their homes. It is not sub-Christian to love the family. But precisely because Jesus is now touching final human realities we are made aware that "Jesus shines brighter, Jesus shines purer, than all the angels heaven can boast." In the final analysis, for the sake of the family, Jesus is greater than the family. Only when for his sake we are willing to lose our family will we find it—and for many this analogy is not inapt, for "life" is, for them, their family. For this high reason, Jesus proceeds to put himself in competition with the best thing on earth.

"Each home has its unbelievers and its believers, and therefore a good war is sent [to each home] to break a bad peace. . . . Priority [*ordo*] in all love is important. Love, after God, your father; love your mother, love your children. But if it becomes necessary to balance the one against the other . . . , then *odium in suos pietas in Deum est* (hatred for one's own is piety toward God)" (Jero., 1:206, 208).

The truth of 1 Timothy 5:8 must always be weighed in the balance here: "If anyone does not provide for his relatives, and especially for his own family, he has disowned the faith and is worse than an unbeliever" (RSV). This conviction is corroborated by Jesus' defense of the family against religious subterfuge in Matthew 15:1–6. The Christian must go the narrow way between family idolatry and family neglect. Calvin's interpretation of a parallel Gospel passage (Luke 14:33: "So, then, whoever . . . renounces not all he has cannot be my disciple"), 1:314, is representative of Reformation caution against fanaticism in the area of the family: "It would be a ridiculous proceeding to insist exactly on the literal sense, as if no-one could be a disciple of Christ who did not throw all he possessed into the sea, divorced his wife and said farewell to his children. This sort of fiction has led many stupid men into Monasticism, wishing to come nearer Christ by forfeiting their humanity. The truest way to renounce all one's possessions is to be ready at any instant to abandon everything."

The background of Jesus' words has recently been helpfully illumined by Beare, 249: "When the son or daughter of a devout family became a Christian while the father and mother did not (or vice versa), it caused the bitterest hostility within the family. This came about in Gentile families perhaps even more acutely than in Jewish; for all the members of the family had a part to play in the domestic cult which was carried on every day, as well as in the ceremonies of the public cults. A son or a daughter converted to Christianity could not so much as pour a libation to the household gods, or walk in procession to the temple, or to Eleusis, say. Such an attitude could not fail to infuriate the parents. It could also happen that the children would rebel when the parents were converted. For many, this alienation would be harder to bear than the danger of arrest, or flogging, or death."

10:37 "So whoever loves a father or a mother more than me is not worthy of me." "More than *me* . . . is not worthy of *me.*" Jesus' self-consciousness in this sermon and Gospel is distracting. Who does he think he is? He comes crashing into history, and then into our lives, and takes over, preempting our most instinctive loyalties, presuming on our deepest affections, usurping our natural ties, and asking (and so claiming) to be the most important person in our lives. We would not tolerate this presumption in most. Somehow it is appropriate in Jesus. We sense that his claim brings us to our real home, reintegrates us with the true Father, restores us to the primal family.

10:38 "And whoever does not accept one's cross and follow me is not worthy of me." In this context, accepting one's cross must mean accepting one's family trouble and social pressure. Elsewhere, in other contexts, this same cross Word will have other meanings, all of them troublesome—a cross is not a parasol. But it is also important to see that a cross is a gift, it is called here something a person "accepts" (*lambanei*). A cross is not something one goes out to get (contra John Howard Yoder's influential radical discipleship interpretation in *The Politics of Jesus*, 45, 97, 132f); a cross is something that is given to one to accept (see Küng's good discussion, 570–80). Crosses are givens, they are events; they are not here or ever our creations. Whoever therefore does not receive the cross of his or her family division as an assignment from the Lord and walk with it behind Jesus is not worthy of him. As McNeile, 147, has pointed out, Jesus is speaking from personal experience—his own family once thought him crazy (Mark 3:21, 31; cf. Matt 12:49–50). "A disciple is not above his lord." It is good for disciples to be weighed down by crosses—it keeps them near their Lord and on the ground.

The major interpretation of Jesus' call to accept one's cross is the decision to be prepared not only for death, but for violent death (Chrys., 35:3:233; Allen, 111; McN., 148; Gund., 200). This interpretation is as relevant to Christian workers and missionaries in the ideologically inflamed present as it ever was in the past. But the context of this particular reference to the cross (it is slightly different in each usage) suggests family divisions more than political hostility.

It is important that the words "and follow me" are added to "accept one's cross" because it is precisely Christ-following that *enables* cross-carrying. Who would be willing to have family and world against them if they did not have Jesus for and ahead of them? The privilege of being invited into Jesus' school, the dignity of having been personally invited to take part in his world-mission, the worthwhileness of being at history's central task—discipleship and disciple-making—these surpassing values more than compensate for the loss of that value which, before, most gripped us—the life of the family. Following Jesus means more than even sitting around the fireplace.

10:39 "The person who has made his life secure will lose it, and the person who has thrown her life away for my sake will find it." There are persons whose passion is to "make it." To work in the best situation, to live in the best neighborhood, to have only the best things in the house—this is "finding" or "making" one's life or one's security. Jesus promises this search one thing—destruction. Life was not

meant to be lived like this; it is too selfish. Yuppiedom self-destructs. Thus preaching that is devoted mainly to helping people "make it," helping them find themselves, giving them spiritual and psychological tips on how to be a success, how to
have peace of mind, how to love oneself, how to be a transformed person, and the
rest, is often rank betrayal. It is teaching people to concentrate on the very
matters Jesus wants them to forget.

Christian ethics and life (and so, then, Christian preaching and teaching), we
have learned in this sermon, are to be drawn only from what Jesus tells his apostles,
only what he whispers to them, only what he says in the dark to them—in a word,
only from the New Testament apostolic Word—it is not to be drawn from secular
persuasions about peace or prosperity. We are simply not supposed to be in the
business of encouraging people to find their lives; it is exactly this self-searching,
this "everlasting gazing at one's own navel," that Jesus wants us to be finished with.

Jesus often contrasts eternal life and this life. Our time needs the corrective of an
evangelical other-worldliness in order to be braver and more decisive in this life. Schlatter's comment on Jesus' words here, *Das*, 168–69, is perceptive, as often: "For those
who forget God it will become their chief concern to make something of their lives and
make it their whole business to make their lives rich with pleasure. . . . But precisely
those who [in this way] have won life, have thrown it away." Gundry, 201, believes those
who "find" their lives in this passage are "professing disciples who have actually re-
trieved their lives by recanting or keeping quiet during persecution."

"The person who has thrown her life away for my sake will find it." The verb I
translated "thrown away," usually rendered "loses" or "lost," is closest to the meaning "destroys." And the destroying is not a present participle "destroys/destroy-
ing"; it is an aorist, a past tense "destroy*ed*, and reads, literally, "and he who *has*
destroy*ed*." This construction paints a picture of a definite decision in time: a
decisive move, a definitive turn of the screw, a decision to live in a way that will
have no relation to success or the ladder up. *Such* self-destruction is the opposite of
suicide: it is the way to life's making sense.

It is well known even humanly that the world's happier persons are not those
trying to make themselves happy; the happy are usually those caught up in a cause
and who one day notice—they're happy! The cause of causes is discipleship. The
life-decision to go the way of serious discipleship, which can appear to a family as
socially-professionally self-destroying, is the road to a life that makes sense.

The important middle words in this line should be noted: "for my sake." There
is a self-denial whose sake is covertly or overtly to find oneself. The only self-
denial to which Jesus adds his promise is that which is "for my sake." The sake of
Jesus has been spelled out by the Gospel to this point. Jesus' "sake" is the Sermon
on the Mount and the Ten Miracles—these are the things he is about. And we give
ourselves to these by giving ourselves, decisively, in a great life-decision (the force
of the verb "destroyed") to Jesus himself and to the hurting world.

And so the Sermon on Mission has moved from the sources of mission (Jesus'
compassion, praying disciples, spiritual gifts, and church fellowship) through
Jesus' travel instructions (travel light), to his trouble instructions (be ready for the
worst), to, finally, his trust instructions (stand up for Jesus). Jesus seeks, beyond
the fear of people and above the love of family—two of the primal emotions—to

bind us to himself. He saves this best part for last. Mission will be rough. But that's all right: we have fellowship with the Lord Jesus Christ.

III. HOSPITALITY AWARDS (10:40–42; 11:1)

"Whoever welcomes you welcomes me, and whoever welcomes me welcomes the One who sent me. The person who welcomes a prophet, convinced that the other is a prophet, will receive a prophet's reward; and the person who welcomes a righteous person, convinced that the other is a righteous person, will receive a righteous person's reward. And whoever gives a glass of cold water to even one of the least significant of these, convinced that the other is a disciple, amen, I tell you, that person is going to get such a great reward!" (10:40–42).*

The Sermon on Mission ends by promising awards to people hospitable to Christian workers. Some Christians do not feel strong in Christian work; but if they can be warmly hospitable to those who are, in the Lord's eyes they are as valuable as these Christian workers themselves. For "even the prophet must get his breakfast" (Barc., 1:399).

This is a classic text in honor of the Christian ministry. Calvin, 2:217–18, says here: "It is therefore a notable commendation of the outward ministry when Christ declares that any honour and reverence paid to the preaching of men (granting it be faithful preaching), God acknowledged as paid to Himself. . . . the preeminent worship of God, the sacrifice of a sweet odour, is to hear Him speaking by the mouth of men and to submit ourselves to his Word as it is brought by men no less than if He himself had come down from heaven or had revealed His purpose by an angel. . . . Here Christ splendidly extols the dignity of pastors who exercise their ministry sincerely and faithfully." Jesus' respect for his ministers finds echoes as early in the New Testament as 1 Thessalonians 5:12–13 and as late as 1 Timothy 5:17–18. In the early church cf. especially the letters of Ignatius of Antioch, a near contemporary of Matthew and probably from the same city.

10:40 "Whoever welcomes you welcomes me, and whoever welcomes me welcomes the One who sent me." Matthew's text should be interpreted, first, in its strictest sense: it applies first of all to the twelve apostle-disciples themselves. To receive these *apostles* is to receive the Christ, and to receive him is to receive God. This was the original meaning of the words and Matthew's original sense in handing them on. The apostles' living mission was the very mission of God.

This narrow meaning has then still wider ramifications: the apostles' *witness*, the church has always believed, is contained in the documents of the New Testament. Therefore, to receive the apostles today means to receive their message delivered yesterday; most simply it means to receive the New Testament gospel—and by doing so we receive the Lord himself. In other words, to be hospitable to apostolic Scripture, to give it wide berth in our lives, to come to its exposition in the congregation eagerly, to hear it gladly, to obey it seriously, and to allow it to judge our lives and guide our decisions, is to be in communion with the living Lord who first sent the apostles in mission. Whoever gives a hospitable hearing to the New Testament message is, by that very fact, giving hospitality to the Lord and the One who sent him. The apostolic mission goes on in the reception of the New Testament's message.

Both Roman and non-Roman churches have always believed that the purpose of apostolic succession is the *message,* the pure doctrine, and the teaching of the apostles (Küng, 489). The *manner* of apostolic succession has always been taken seriously for the sake, principally, of the *matter* of apostolic succession, who is the authentic Jesus Christ handed on to us by his apostles in the New Testament's message. The ordinary ministry exists to protect the extraordinary message. The message is really everything. The Reformation came to believe that when the message is jeopardized by the ministry to which it was entrusted, then deep and searching reforms are in order; the ministry, as then understood, had to be altered for the sake of the preeminent message. In the Reformation tradition we believe that apostolic succession in this evangelical sense continues down into our time wherever the pure New Testament message is heard hospitably. We are simply the latest links in a venerable chain of missioners extending from the missionary God himself down to the person who, most recently, explained the New Testament to us. This is inner apostolic succession. And so in a singular way the New Testament is honored in this paragraph.

"As far as the idea of a living [apostolic] succession is concerned everything depends on the *antecessor* being regarded as alive and having free power over against the *successor.* But if, as here, the *antecessor* has long since died, this [succession] can happen only if his proclamation has been fixed in writing and if it is acknowledged that he still has life and free power over the Church to-day in this written word of his. On the written nature of the Canon, on its character as *scriptura sacra,* hangs his autonomy and independence, and consequently his free power over against the Church and the living nature of the succession" (Karl Barth, *Church Dogmatics,* I/1, 4:2:104). Irenaeus, especially, teaches the church to be open to an apostolic succession of *persons.* Reformation and Neo-Reformation witness requests us only to ask what the persons *teach.* High church and low can meet.

But the passage has a personal sense, too. Indeed, the first reference of the text, as we saw, concerned the receiving of persons—the twelve themselves. Thus this text must always be viewed at least personally. The persons who received the living apostles with the hospitality of faith became, in fact, members of the apostolic church who, in turn, passed on the apostolic message to still other hospitable persons, and so on, in a great chain of witnesses that extends down to us. Therefore, whoever receives a Christian worker hospitably today receives Jesus and the Father, too, just as at the first hospitable apostolic reception.

McNeile, 149, believes that our text "attaches itself to the thought of [10:]11–14, 'he that receives you into his house.'" Green, 113, sees our text as the flip side of [10:] 24–25 ("a disciple is not above his lord") where "the disciple is to expect the same [hard] treatment as the Lord received; here [in our text, on the other hand] service to [the disciple] is reckoned as service to the Lord." Jerome, 1:208, 210, exults: "Beautiful arrangement! He sends them out to preach, he teaches them not to be afraid of dangers, he subjects affections to religion; above, he took away gold, he snatched money from their wallets. The hard life of evangelists! Whence, then, their support, whence the necessities of life? He tempers the rigor of the commands with the hope of promises: He says, 'Who receives you, receives me, and whoever receives me receives him who sent me,' so that every believer may realize that in receiving the apostles he or she is receiving Christ." Vatican II teaches that *bishops* are the apostles' successors.

People outside the church who make Christian friends, receive them warmly, and deepen their friendship with them, may not fully realize what they are doing; and Christian friends may not be fully aware of what they are doing either, but this text promises that the warm reception of Christians is at least en route to the warm reception of the Christians' Lord. In other words, a great deal of unrealized evangelism is going on in simple friendship. Thus this paragraph dignifies all disciples' social life. Wherever there is a befriended Christian there is the possibility of the reception of the living Christ and so of God.

10:41–42 Matthew's Jesus gives a more careful definition to the hospitality he has in mind when he specifically introduces the words (literally) "receives a prophet *in the name of a prophet* . . . receives a righteous person *in the name of a righteous person* . . . receives one of these least significant persons *in the name of a disciple.* . . ." These little "in the name ofs" qualify the hospitality given; it is not simply general, casual, completely unconscious hospitality that is meant here (this will be one of the meanings in chapter 25 when even the *unconscious* good deed to "one of the least of these my brethren" is done to the Lord). This "in-the-name-of" hospitality means hospitality given because one person believes another person to be a speaker for God (a prophet), or a special man or woman of God (a righteous person), or, at least, a simple disciple of the true God. In other words, it is not just general hospitality that is in view here. (Cf. Cal., 1:315; Beng., 1:163; Kl., 93; Gund., 202.) A hospitality as specific as financial support or physical assistance is, of course, included in Jesus' meaning.

But when this has been said, we are still more in contact with the stuff of daily social life than we realize. Some people are particularly sensitive to Christians because they believe Christians are somehow representatives of God. There may be a certain amount of superstition in this sensitivity. But Jesus puts the best face on it.

This happy fact has beneficent ramifications. First, it teaches Christians to be more encouraged about the impact of their evangelism, an impact they too often discount. In the light of this text, the simple fact that people sometimes like Christians and reach out to them should tell them they are actually reaching out for, are touching, and are being touched by the Lord who deigns to represent himself *in* disciples. Second, this text teaches us to be a little more sympathetic to the many churchless pagans who, simply by virtue of their befriending Christian individuals, are not so far outside the church as we or they may think. As long as they are in touch with their Christian friends, they are somehow in touch with the Lord. It is still of course the disciples' intention to bring as many friends as they can into the *living room* of the Father's family, which is the organized fellowship of the (unapologetically) institutional church. But even in the backyard or on the lawn they are somehow on the Father's property, and we should be taught by this text to be grateful for small blessings. The text is not designed to make us less evangelistic, less churchly, less interested in seeing friends who are in the backyard being brought into the living room. But it does teach us that the reach of disciples' evangelism is wider than disciples themselves usually realize.

One is reminded of the marvelous mission text in John's Gospel where a disciple asks our very question: "Lord, how is it that you will manifest yourself to us [disciples], and not to [the rest of] the world?" And Jesus answers, "If a man loves me, he will keep my word, and my Father will love him, and we will come to him and make our home with him" (John 14:22–23). Jesus' answer in John to our question of "Why us and not the rest of the world?" is, "I will reach the rest of the world through my Word-keeping disciples." Jesus' method of world mission is good disciples, in whom he and his Father take up residence, and through whom Father and Son give revelation to others.

The full reception of a Christian worker "in the name of" a Christian worker, *because one is* a Christian worker bears, finally, an ecclesiastical sense. We have looked at (1) the apostolic or New Testament sense and at (2) the contemporary personal sense in which this paragraph on "apostolic succession" can be understood. But our understanding would be clearly incomplete if we left out (3) the churchly sense. The apostles' witness in the New Testament and Christian workers today are finally received, and their Christ and his Father are appropriately welcomed, when people join the church that treasures the apostolic witness and succession. I know that people are in church in a sense whenever they are with Christians; we are fully aware, as is said usually too glibly, that "the church is not a building." Nevertheless, when this is said, most people *do* hear the Word of God and receive the sacraments in a building set up for these purposes somewhere or other, and thus in this sense the church is rarely other than a group of people meeting round their Lord in buildings and between four walls. Therefore, this text is finally and fully understood when it is read to mean: People who receive Christian people, that is, who join them at the place of their deepest reference and reverence—around the preached and sacramental Word, in the church—are people who receive Christ and the Father. People who find their way into churches and so accept other Christian people are people who, by accepting them, by joining their fellowship through baptism and feasting with them in Lord's Suppers, join the Spirit, the Christ, and the Father whom Christians confess as God.

If these verses are not understood finally as ecclesiastical verses, they are not understood at all. We can read our New Testament in privacy, we can be friends in the backyard cordially, but until we sit down together seriously in the *living* room—in the fellowship of the church—we have not yet really received either Christian workers or their Lord. A Christianity that remains unchurched is not real Christianity; an evangelism that does not tend churchward as toward magnetic north is not the evangelism envisioned by the New Testament.

There is wise counsel on apostolic and episcopal succession in the important contemporary ecumenical consensus, *Baptism, Eucharist, and Ministry*, 34–55.

Christian workers are to know that the central meetings in history are not finally the great political and economic conferences where the world's leaders assemble; they are all those little places in the world where people extend hospitality to Christians—*there* the really big issues are being joined. Jesus said the words recorded in this paragraph in order to give Christian workers a sense of their worth (Kl., 93; Schl., *Der,* 351; Schl., *Das,* 170; Lohm., 182). Nothing less than a sense of destiny is Jesus' final gift to his disciples in his Sermon on Mission.

A few concluding technical remarks will bring the message of this paragraph into its sharpest focus. As astonishing as the equation is that accepting Christians equals accepting Christ—which is certainly a major meaning of this text—equally astonishing is the fact that Jesus believes that accepting *him* equals accepting the one who sent him, that is, *God.* We must not allow the simple way that Jesus says this to escape our surprise. Jesus actually believes that when people accept him they accept God. The straight line Jesus draws between himself and his Father, this uncomplicated access, the fact that having Jesus means having God is, as we all know, at the heart of the gospel. But we should never allow this heart to cease beating inside us. *God* has made himself not only comprehensible, plausible, and credible; God has made himself *available* in this Jew. That is, on its face, almost *in*credible, *im*plausible, *in*comprehensible, and yet all Christians know that it is true and that it is this equation, this joining, this fact that makes God and life comprehensible.

McNeile, 149, believes Jesus' claim to come from God in v 40 rivals the highest christological claims in John 12:44, 48–49; 13:30; 20:21. Cf. also the "I came" texts of Matthew 5:17; 9:13; 10:34–35; 20:28. Bengel, 1:162–63, points out helpfully that Jesus does not say receiving disciples "is *as if* [one] received me"; rather, the receiver "receives me." We may extend this observation to Jesus' relation to God: receiving Jesus is not as if receiving God; it is receiving God.

In the light of this christological fact the ecclesiastical sense of the paragraph becomes even more moving: in receiving us ordinaries, people are receiving God! Such is the union of Jesus with his apostolic church, that it is really true: accepting Christians is accepting Christ, and accepting Christ is accepting God. Simple as these equations are, they are not commonplace.

God is the original "apostle." This is the next technical remark required by our text. "The one who *sent* [*aposteilanta*] me," Jesus calls God. This is one of Jesus' few other names for God besides "Father" in this Gospel. "He who sent Jesus" is one of the names, and main meanings, of the God of the universe. The biblical God is missionary, itinerant, sending, going places, in motion, with plans, purposes, strategies, and tactics. God is not the motionless, changeless One of Greek thought *for* whom we do mission; God is the Hebrews' moving, flexible, living God who *does* mission and by whom, therefore, we too are able to do mission. Mission is not so much done for this God as by this God; God is as much the means of mission as the goal, as much the energy as the final resting point.

Original apostolic succession, then, begins with the Father, enters history classically in the Son, and continues ecclesiastically in history until the end in disciples who are churchmen and churchwomen true to the apostolic tradition and the historic Nicene faith. Wherever the latest warm welcome has been given to a disciple because he or she is felt to be spiritually important, the latest link in a grand chain of apostolic succession has been forged.

"There is a kind of identity between the Matthean Christian and his Lord which is not unlike the understanding of Christians as being 'in Christ' which we find in Paul (Matt 10:40; 18:5; 15:31–32; 25:30, 46)" (Davies, 97–98, 459). The Jewish *Shaliach* ("he that is sent by a man is as the man himself") is discussed by Rengstorff, TDNT, 1:400–03; Held, 252 n. 3; Grund., 302. Gundry, 201–02, believes that Jesus is encouraging disciples to harbor those who are fleeing persecution for the sake of Christ. Sanctuary!

"Prophet" in our text is best understood as a person who speaks God's Word; "a righteous person" is a serious Christian; and "disciple," coupled, as it is, with "one of these least," means "simple Christian," one of the "ordinary church members" (cf. Gund., 203). ("Though he may be doing no such great work, he is a man, inhabiting the same world with thee, beholding the same sun," Chrys., 35:5:235.) Thus we come up with the following paraphrase of the final two verses of our chapter: "Whoever receives a person who speaks God's Word with a sense that this is, indeed, a person who speaks God's Word, will receive the reward of a person who speaks God's Word; and whoever welcomes a serious Christian with a specific sense that this person is, indeed, a serious Christian, will receive a serious Christian's reward. And whoever gives a glass of cold water to even one of the most insignificant of these persons simply because this person is a disciple, amen, I tel˙ you, the reward of that hospitable person will be very special" (vv 41–42).

Both Jerome, 1:212, and Chrysostom, 35:4:234, remark that Jesus spoke of giving even a cup of cold water "lest anyone should allege poverty." They mean, Jesus does not want our lack of affluence to be an excuse for thinking we cannot do much to help the Christian enterprise. The simplest help is noticed by the heavenly Father.

In summary, the simple Christian who can do no more for the Christian mission than be hospitable to its workers will be encouraged to know that this simple hospitality to Christian workers is fully equivalent, in God's eyes, to being one of these Christian workers oneself. The Christian mission is a blessing-bringing thing, and those who carry it and those who give hospitality to its carriers should know that the Father watches rewardingly. God cares for this mission more than for any other program in history. The Christian world mission is God's craft, God's enterprise in history, and all those who work to advance God's mission, directly or indirectly, with sermons or cups of cold water, with medicine or bread, with home visitations or financial assistance, are in line for the most substantial rewards. Jesus wants all disciples to know this. Not a single disciple is left out of the mission: some "do" it, and others support its doers—all receive the same great reward. Jesus wants *every* disciple to feel a part of mission and to feel in line for divine appreciation. (For further discussion of the rewards see Cal., 1:315; Grund., 302; Green, 113.)

11:1 *"And when Jesus finished instructing his twelve disciples, he left that place to teach and preach in their cities."*

This sentence concludes the Sermon on Mission. It is an interesting sentence for a number of reasons: (1) it calls the sermon "instructions" (*diatassōn*); (2) the twelve are again called "his twelve disciples" not apostles; and (3) the results of the disciples' mission are not reported.

Each of these points deserves brief attention. First, disciples need teaching (*didachē*), as in the Sermon on the Mount, in order to know how to *be* disciples. Then they need instructions (*diatagē*) in order to know how to *do* discipling. The Sermon on the Mount makes us disciples; the Sermon on Mission makes us disciplers. First a course in ethics, then a course in evangelism.

Second, Matthew prefers here to call even these original twelve men "disciples" rather than, as only once in his Gospel, "apostles." Matthew does not seem to like official names or official-sounding titles. When he has his choice of words he calls even these august pillars of the church "disciples," a name no different than ours. They are not lords of the manor; they are, like the rest of us, disciples of the one Lord. They are not primarily rulers, but subjects; they are not primarily even leaders, but like the rest of us, they are disciples, students, or apprentices "of the *one* Leader, the Christ," "the *one* Teacher, and *all* the rest of you are brothers" (23:8–10).

Third, not a word is lost telling us about the twelve's missionary experiences, for the Gospel is primarily a story of Jesus' Word and deeds and only then (and only where necessary) the story of the churches', the disciples', or anyone else's words and deeds (cf. Schl., *Der*, 355). The focus of the Gospel is Jesus himself. There will always be the tug in Christian preaching and teaching to talk about our own experience—and a modest amount of this is not only wholesome, it sometimes makes what we say credible and interesting. But on the whole, disciples will have to be alert that stories of our experience do not eclipse the exposition and glory of the Words and experiences of Jesus himself, which are our reason for standing up to talk at all. Stories of our experiences can, if we are not careful, subtly center on ourselves, no matter how often we assure ourselves and our hearers that we are telling these for his sake or theirs. Personal experience is like salt: a little is tasteful, a lot is noxious.

The Doctrine of Means in the Reformation Tradition

The exciting doctrinal fact about chapter 10 is that it teaches Jesus' *means* of mission: the ministry of disciples. "He who receives you receives me." The way God's salvation in Christ gets out into the world is through Christian workers bringing Christ's Word and sacraments. I find it intriguing that right after the high christology of chaps 5–9 this chapter on mission appears. Matthew 10 fits Matthew 5–9 like Christ's body fits his soul, like the church fits the Lord. Matthew 5–9 teaches us Christ's Word and Work; Matthew 10 teaches us how this Word and Work get out.

Immediately after the famous fourth chapter on justification in the earliest formal Protestant Confession of Faith comes the chapter in Reformation confessional literature that addresses Christian workers most appealingly because it tells how saving faith gets *to* people—a very important matter.

> "To obtain such [saving] faith God instituted the office of the ministry, that is, provided the Gospel and the sacraments. Through these, as through means, he gives the Holy Spirit, who works faith, when and where he pleases in those who hear the Gospel. And the Gospel teaches that we have a gracious God, not by our own merits but by the merit of Christ, when we believe this.
>
> "Condemned are the Anabaptists and others who teach that the Holy Spirit comes to us through our own preparations, thoughts, and works without the external word of the Gospel" (*Augsburg Confession* [1530], art. 5).

The key fact to see here is that the Holy Spirit who works saving faith comes to us through *outward* means: through people who minister the gospel Word and sacraments. Those who teach that the Holy Spirit, justification, and faith come to us "through our own preparations, thoughts, and works without the *external* word of the Gospel" are specifically condemned. This doctrine defends the gospel from all teaching of mystic routes to saving grace and faith, all arcane, invisible, internal, or inward paths to salvation. God's salvation comes to us through the mundane, outward, human, earthy way of ministering disciples, of people who faithfully pass on to us the gospel Word and its sacraments.

The Holy Spirit and saving faith do not come to us immediately (meaning, literally, without means), but mediately through the Mediator and his media of the believing and teaching church. This truth makes marvelously historical our understanding of God's great plan of salvation; it demystifies and clarifies God's ways. It honors the teaching of Holy Scripture about Israel and the church, about the ministry that God deigns to use, the ministry of earthly men and women. (Cf., again, the great second-century Irenaeus.)

The kind of teaching Reformation theology *combats* is illustrated by an ad for the Unity Church in Spokane in 1980 that had these words: "Set Yourself Free . . . 'Truth is within ourselves; it takes no rise from outward things, what e're [*sic*] you may believe. There is an inmost center in us all, where truth abides in fullness . . . and, to know, rather consists in opening out a way whence the imprisoned splendor may escape, than in effecting entry for a light supposed to be without.'—Robert Browning." Quite the contrary! "Truth takes . . . rise from *outward* things," namely, from the historical Christ, ministered through historical human beings. Even Browning is trying to minister his inward truth through his outward words just cited.

Humans simply do not come by truth without having truth ministered to them through words and senses. Hence the all-importance of the earthly ministry of Jesus of Nazareth in the years 1–30 of our era, and of Jesus' disciples in the fellowship of his church ever since. "To obtain . . . faith God instituted the office of the ministry." And this ministry is not just understood clerically; it is the ministry of "the Gospel and the sacraments." Meant is the ministry of the oral, preached, taught, spoken gospel, and of water, bread, and wine. "Through *these,* as through *means,* he gives the Holy Spirit, who works faith, when and where he pleases."

In Paul's splendid words, "Faith comes by *hearing,* and hearing by *the preaching of Christ*" (Rom 10:17). Faith is inward, of course, but it is worked *in* us by an *outward* fact: faithful people preaching Christ. This is made crystal clear by Paul's exciting chain of cause-and-effect:

[1] Everyone who calls on the name of the Lord shall be saved.
[2] But how shall they call on someone they don't believe?
[3] And how will they believe in someone they haven't heard of?
[4] And how will they hear without someone preaching?
[5] And how will they preach unless they're sent? As it is written, "How beautiful are the feet of those who evangelize Good News!" . . .
[6] Thus this faith comes by hearing; and this hearing comes through the preaching of Christ (Rom 10:13–17).

God does his work historically. It is easy to say, "Everyone who calls on his name shall be saved." But between this great truth and actual faith there is a beautiful chain of divine sending, faithful preaching, and receptive hearing. The Reformation rightly reveled in this historical and divine truth.

In "Against the Heavenly Prophets" (a title of a book on this very subject, 1524), Luther wrote these important words: "The outward things [of Word and sacrament] should and must go first. . . . Therefore God has determined that He will not give any person the inward things [of the Holy Spirit and faith] without the means of these outward things." (Cf. LW 40:146 for a fresh translation of this important message.)

For other resources cf. *Augsburg Confession*, art. 13; Lu., *Smalcald Articles*, part III, art. 8:3–5, 9–10; Cal., *Inst.*, IV. i; *Heidelberg Catechism*, QQ 21, 65; *Second Helvetic Confession*, chap 1:4–7; chap 18:144; *Westminster Confession of Faith*, chap 14; *Confession of 1967*, 49.

The truly exciting fact about the doctrine of means has been clearly expressed in Matthew 10:40: "Whoever welcomes you welcomes me, and whoever welcomes me welcomes the One who sent me." Paul's remark serves as a kind of commentary on Jesus' word (and note that Paul is not speaking of a written Word read, but of a spoken Word *heard*): "And we thank God constantly for this, that when you received the word of God which you *heard* from us, you accepted it not as the word of men but as what it really is, the word of God, which is at work in you believers" (1 Thess 2:13).

The biblical doctrine of means dignifies the work of disciples incomparably.

"As regards the giving of the growth, the planter and waterer are nothing, but as regards planting and watering they are not nothing, seeing that the supreme work of the Spirit in the Church of God is to teach and to exhort" (Luther, *Bondage of the Will*, 286). "The words I have spoken to you bring God's life-giving Spirit" (John 6:63 TEV). See also Calvin's magisterial treatment of the ministry in *Inst.*, IV.i–iii and viii.

Chapters Eleven and Twelve
The Six Portraits
The Doctrine of the Person of Christ

In the final two chapters of *The Christbook* we are presented with a portfolio of photographs of the *person* of Christ. Having heard Jesus' Word, seen his works, and learned his mission we are now prepared to investigate the final mystery of his person. Who is this one who teaches and acts this way? Chapters 11 and 12 answer this question.

It is particularly in the organization of these two chapters that I have made Matthew more systematic than he really is. Matthew 11 and 12 are a potpourri of discourse and controversy. Matthew 11:2–19, for example, includes a long speech on John the Baptist (and his relation to the Christ), almost forming a third great sermon in the first half of the Gospel, "the Sermon on John." And Matthew 12 is a collection of three controversy stories, comparable to the three controversy stories of Matthew 9 (vv 1–13).

But it seems to me that the organizing principle of these two mixed genre chapters, Matthew 11–12, is discernible in the question that introduces them: "Are *you* [*su ei*, emphasized] the One who is coming or should we be waiting for someone else?" (11:3). (On "the One who is coming," or "the Coming One" as a messianic designation, cf. Ps 118:26; Dan 7:13; Matt 3:11.) Who *are* you? is the question that echoes down the corridors of Matthew 11–12. John the Baptist who introduced Jesus in Matthew 3 (and who then disappeared) surfaces again in the eleventh chapter to reintroduce Jesus, this time less positively. In chapter 3 the Baptist introduced Jesus with fiery exclamations; now in chapter 11 he comes to Jesus with doubt-filled interrogation. Is Jesus the Christ? Who is Jesus? These *person* questions, in my opinion, dominate the next two chapters enough to make the theme of both chapters the person of Christ. As chapters 5–7 gave us the Word of Christ, 8–9 his works, and 10 his mission, so now 11–12 give us his person.

There are three major paragraphs in chapter 11: the first long paragraph revolves around John the Baptist and teaches, all in all, that John is the forerunner of the Christ—and that Jesus is this Christ; the second, shorter paragraph, historically called "Woes to the Unrepentant Cities," presents Jesus in his office as Judge; and in the final paragraph Jesus invites the heavy-laden to himself and stands there primarily as Savior. Thus chapter 11 teaches that Jesus is the promised Messiah from the past, the coming Judge of the future, and the gracious Savior in the present.

The ancient fish symbol of the Christ fits this chapter's theme almost perfectly. IXTHYS in Greek means "fish"; the word also supplies the first letters of the Greek words Iēsous Xristos THeou Yios Sōtēr, literally, "Jesus Christ, of God the Son, Savior." And in chapter 11 Jesus is exactly each of these in turn—first he is the long-promised *Christ* (IX-); then he is the coming *Son of God* who judges the world (-THY-); and finally and supremely he is the *Savior* of the needy (-S). While there is judgment in the small central paragraph, chapter 11's main theme is Jesus' salvation of needy folk.

In Matthew 12, on the other hand, those especially addressed are the Pharisees (vv 2–3, 24–25, 38–39) in three straight controversy stories—controversies about the Sabbath, the Spirit, and signs—and thus the ambience in the twelfth chapter is especially judgment. As Matthew 11 contains three paragraphs presenting Jesus as mainly the saving Christ, so Matthew 12 finds Jesus embroiled in three controversies presenting Jesus in his mainly critical offices of Sabbath-Lord, Spirit-King, and Significant-Kinsman.

Jesus Christ is both Fish and Fire; he is there for needy folk with the food of salvation, and there for false believers with the fire of judgment. Jesus—Savior (chapter 11) and Judge (chapter 12)—is himself the unifying theme of the chapters.

John the Baptist first introduced us to Jesus' two great offices as Savior and as Judge when he promised that the Coming One "will baptize you with the Holy Spirit [of salvation] and with the fire [of judgment]" (3:11). Some Christians and churches overstress Christ as personal Savior, to the hurt of the gospel's full-bodied presentation of the justice-seeking Christ. Pastors and persons in rebellion against legalistic fundamentalisms and bland traditionalisms often flee their rigid pasts and cling to a relational Christ, a highly subjective Jesus, a psychological Christ who only accepts people as they are, without any repentance, and with hardly any judgment in his blood; and as a result the gospel is seriously diluted.

Other Christians and churches so stress Christ as Judge that they miss his real purpose in coming. Reacting against sentimental Christianity they become mainly scolders and harsh. Chapters 11 and 12 together give us the healthy wholeness of Jesus Christ in such a way that the church is guarded from interpreting Scripture's Christ one-sidedly. As Jesus' Sermon on the Mount and Ten Miracles together gave us a full Jesus who both taught and touched, so now the Fish and Fire Christs of Matthew 11 and 12 together give us the one great Christ of salvation and judgment.

In my design, chaps 11 and 12 conclude *The Christbook* by teaching the doctrine of the *person* of Christ. But there is a good case for seeing chaps 11 and 12 (first adumbrated in chap 10 and then expounded in chap 13) as dominated by the theme of *opposition* to Jesus (Bonn., 160; Green, iii; Kingsb., *Struc.*, 18, 20; Gund., 203–04). My outline in Matt 11–12 serves systematic theological purposes. But even Green, 114, calls chap 11 "Jesus' Witness to Himself," and Schweizer, 255, sees Jesus' person as the point of at least the opening paragraph of Matt 11:2–6. It is in fact against the background of doubt, opposition, and rejection—all of which are prominent in these two chapters—that Jesus' person most sharply emerges and that we see exactly who he is.

Chapter Eleven
The Fish Christ
The Doctrine of Christ the Savior

I. CHRIST JESUS (11:2–19)

"When John heard in prison about the works of the Christ, he sent word by his disciples and asked Jesus, 'Are you the Coming One or should we be looking for someone else?' And Jesus answered and said to them, 'Go tell John the things you are hearing and seeing: the blind see again and the lame are walking; lepers are cleansed and the deaf hear; the dead are being raised and the little people are being encouraged; and—blessed is the person who is not offended by me'" (11:2–6).

11:2–3 In introducing John the Baptist here, Matthew interestingly calls the just preceding materials of the Gospel "the works of the Christ." Between chapters 5 and 10 we have in fact seen Jesus' works as the Christ: helping people deeply himself (in the Sermon on the Mount and the Ten Miracles), and then most recently enabling his *disciples* to do his works of helping people deeply (in the Sermon on Mission). John heard about these works, and he wondered if they really were the works of *the Christ*, at least of the Christ whom he had preached as the Coming One in the third chapter of this Gospel.

Why was John in doubt? Because John's Coming One in chapter 3, we recall, was mainly a figure of power, a bringer mainly of judgment, a carrier (to use his favorite word) mainly of "fire," with an ax in one hand to chop down the unfruitful tree and a shovel in the other hand to sift out the chaff in his granary (3:10–12). There is good reason to wonder if the Jesus *since* chapter 3 fit John's descriptions.

For immediately after John's sermon, Jesus comes (like a sinner) to *be* baptized—and in water! John even tried to dissuade Jesus from being baptized (3:13–15). In John's eyes, Jesus was from the beginning a little baffling, a little strange; less messianic than John had expected and less cataclysmic than John had preached.

In the chapter that follows the baptism, in the temptations, Jesus rejects rather than accepts the ways of ministry offered by Satan (and even well-meaningly predicted by John): sensational, spectacular, and speedy ministries (4:1–11). In the Three Services (4:12–25), Jesus called his first disciples with power—but just a few were called (four are recorded), they were not persons of great influence or eloquence, they were simply fishermen, and their task seemed less to be setting the world on fire by destroying evil (John's main picture) than it was, more prosaically, "catching people" into salvation (Jesus' main picture).

In the Sermon on the Mount Jesus taught "with authority," but what he taught seemed more calculated to put axes in the hands of his opponents than in the hands of his disciples: disciples were specifically forbidden avenging attacks on evil, were specifically promised persecution and tough times, and when his talk did come to treat of great and powerful deeds (7:22), as we saw, Jesus less encouraged

than warned. The whole Sermon on the Mount calls to simple deeds and to obediences such as biblical piety, temperamental patience, sexual purity, moral poise,
and spiritual gentleness (5:17–48). Are these the mighty deeds of the Coming One
prophesied in the Old Testament and preached by John?

In the Ten Miracles Jesus comes closer to messianic type. But if we take a second
look, none of the miracles occurs in Jerusalem, the strategic city in a program
calculated to affect all Israel. All the miracles happen in the backwoods of Galilee,
way out in the provinces—"in northern Idaho." Messianic programs usually aim
for capital cities and strategic groups. Jesus' miracles miss both sites. Most of his
miracles occurred with individuals; they were not yet social miracles. And yet
everyone knows that individualism is a weakness, not a strength, in any movement
aiming at historical or mass change.

Furthermore, Jesus has not yet attacked any of the reigning political or economic powers; in his miracles he has simply picked up the pieces left by evil forces.
Today, Jesus' work would be derisively called "an ambulance ministry," picking up
the crushed victims of evil structures but failing to combat those evil structures
themselves. Jesus will fight these structures—especially Pharisaism—but in his
own way. Meanwhile he drives his ambulance around the province. Everyone
indoctrinated into radical action knows that ambulance ministries are counter-
revolutionary. Jesus heals a leper: why doesn't he go to the root of Palestine's skin
problems—its economic injustices, institutionalized in the big cities? Similar questions could be asked of almost every one of Jesus' miracles.

In a word, Jesus is out in the provinces healing sick, insignificant little individuals here and there, but not doing anything to change the basic structural problems
in Israel's life. The Pharisees still control popular religious life; the Sadducees still
control the temple; the whole rotten religio-ideological system seems thoroughly
unthreatened by Jesus' do-goodism in the hills. What is more, John (the propagan-
dist of The New Order) is in prison, and Herod (the embodiment of the oppressive
Establishment) is still on the throne and about to have John's head. What kind of a
Messiah is this who works so individualistically, so piecemeal? What is needed is
not a ministry of palliatives, but a strategic, effective, community program that
does things systemically, attacks problems at their roots, challenges the structures
at their core.

Cf. especially, Schlatter, *Das,* 171–72; *Der,* 359–60, for profound analyses of John's
question. John's being in prison adds poignancy to John's question, especially when the
Messiah he promised was a Messiah who would *free* prisoners (Isa 61:1; Luke 4:18; cf.
Bonn., 161; Hill, 198; Gund., 204). Incidentally, that John could send his disciples with
his own message from prison indicates lamentably that "ancient prisons were often less
inhumane than modern ones; one could stay in contact with the exterior world" (Bonn.,
160; cf. Acts 5:21, 23; 16:26; Phil 1:7–17).

I have gone into detail in order to show that John the Baptist's searching question, which introduces the next two chapters, is not merely rhetorical; it is the
question to ask for a right assessment of Jesus. Origen, Chrysostom, Jerome, and
Augustine in the early church, and Calvin and Bengel in the Reformation
churches, did not enjoy seeing a hero of the faith like John the Baptist asking a
doubting question, and so they suggested that John only asked the question for the

sake of John's *disciples,* to lead them to John's own unshaken faith in Jesus, for saints do not doubt. But saints do doubt, Matthew here tells us, and doubt for good reasons, as a survey of chapters 3 to 10 has shown us. Let John's question stand, then, grateful that John asked it for us: "Are *you* [emphasized in the text] the Coming One or should we be looking for someone else?" (Cf. Origen in McN., 151–52; Chrys., 36:1–2:239; Jero., 1:214–18; Aug., *Serm* 16(66):3–4:310; Cal., 2:2–3; Beng., 1:164.)

"The Coming One" is an almost technical term for "the Messiah." John the Baptist had promised that *"the one who is coming* after me is stronger than I" (3:11; cf. John 1:15, 27; 6:14). In Malachi the people had wearied the Lord by asking, "Where is the God of justice?" And they had been told in no uncertain terms "Look, I am sending my messenger, who will clear a path before me. Suddenly the Lord whom you seek *will come* to his temple" (Mal 2:17—3:1). And in Isaiah the poor and anxious were promised, "Behold, your God *will come* with vengeance, with the vengeance of God. He *will come* to save you. Then the eyes of the blind shall be opened," etc. (Isa 35:4–5). The Old Testament is replete with references to the coming of God, or his prophet, or his Messiah, in judgment and blessing. John had believed that this Coming One would be accompanied by a larger measure of judgment, vengeance, and retribution than John had been able to notice so far in the activity of Jesus.

John's difficulty with Jesus, then, is Israel's problem with Jesus to this day: Jesus does not seem sufficiently messianic. And this same difficulty is also offensive today to some liberation Christians. Jesus does not make a good guerrilla. He seems to promise more oppression, not liberation from it. This is hard to take. John's question, then, is the question of us all: "Are you really the promised Liberator or should we be looking for someone else?" (Gundry, 205, shows how the Greek word used for "someone else," *heteron,* actually means "should we expect *a different kind* of Coming One?" Cf. also TDNT, 2:702.)

One form that a subtle "looking for somebody else" can take in our time, a form with which I am acquainted in the progressive wing of the Roman Catholic Church in the Philippines, goes roughly like this: "Jesus brought us eternal salvation, but he did not intend to give us a program for national liberation. He expected the near end of history and was not in the business of giving political solutions. But history has continued and has not come to an end. The Christian is therefore free to adopt those scientific tools and methods that will most serve his people's social, political, and economic liberation at any given time and place. Marxism-Leninism-Mao-Tse-tung-Thought provides the concrete, scientific means to answer the temporal, not eternal, questions of oppressed peoples. Thus the conscientious Christian in our time will look to Jesus Christ for his eternal liberation and to contemporary Marxism for his temporal liberation." The organization, "Christians for National Liberation" in the Philippines, therefore, looked for a twofold salvation—a spiritual one from Jesus Christ, for that is what he came to give, and a temporal one from (as it was then called) MLMTT (Marxism-Leninism-Mao-Tse-tung-Thought).

But this double vision will not work; no one can look for two messiahs, for one will always eclipse the other, and in our experience in the Philippines the one eclipsed was Jesus. Jesus is either the fully competent, Absolute Liberator, or he is nothing at all. (See *The Heidelberg Catechism,* questions 29–30, cited below, p. 442.)

Here the fork in the road appears, and the Christian must go one of two ways; one cannot go both. John's question still lives. Who is this Jesus? Is he "The Comer," or as

Germa . .ranslations often have it, "The Future," *(der Zukünftige),* or is Marx or Mao or the American Way of Life or the Movement or the Poor or something or someone else the rea vave of the future?

All the questions that can be asked of Jesus can be asked, *mutatis mutandi,* of Jesus' church *Jesus'* provincialism, individualism, and seemingly counter-revolutionary methods car be excused, for, after all, he was a man of his time. But can the *church* come off as well? For often the church's provincialism and individualism have come as much from her lov of the present order and her own privileges in it as they have from love of her Lord. And yet the church is not always hated by socially concerned Christians because of the church's sin; one has the feeling that she is as often hated for her unimpressiveness, her piecemeal ministries, and her slowness; she is scorned for just helping (as it is thoughtlessly said) "little old ladies," instead of overthrowing dictators.

The church has the double disadvantage of suffering not only for her sins, which are many, but also for her obediences. And this latter suffering, when it is inflicted by other Christians, is cruel. Contemporary hatred for the church is often disguised hatred for Christ. The reasons Jesus was nailed to wood are often the reasons the church is left in the lurch. A too glorified view of what "messiah" means, a triumphalist vision of what "Jesus Christ is doing in the world today," will lead many Christians, through questions very much like John the Baptist's, into false movements of liberation where Jesus is finally denied.

11:4 Jesus' answer was to tell John's disciples to return to John with a report of "the things you are hearing and seeing" (v 4): "hearing" represents the Sermon on the Mount (5–7) and "seeing," the subsequent Ten Miracles (8–9). It is exposure to Jesus' words and works that makes faith.

Schlatter *(Das,* 173) has a beautiful comment on this dominical reply: "Seeing what Jesus does and hearing what he says is the only way that leads to faith. Another means by which we could make ourselves or others into believers simply does not exist." John the Baptist needs faith that Jesus is the Christ. The way to bring him to this faith is simply to tell him Jesus' words and deeds. Our churches need faith, we need faith, and many of our friends need faith. The way to this faith is hearing what Jesus says and seeing what he does.

The strength of Rudolf Bultmann's approach to the New Testament, beyond his clean historical work, is his theological conviction that *Jesus speaks* (present tense) *today* in the proclamation of what the biblical authors wrote about Jesus' words and deeds yesterday. Speaking of Mark's Gospel, e.g., Bultmann wrote (and note his "all"), "The foundational presupposition [is] that in all the sayings of Jesus which were reported, *he speaks* [notice the present tense] who, as the proclamation makes known his works and [passes] on his sayings, was [himself] actually present for the church" (my emphasis, 348).

Practically speaking, Jesus' answer to John means that the way for the dynamite of faith to be planted in and under our congregations and families is simply a more frequent and faithful exposure to the words and works of Jesus. An expository, evangelical teaching ministry is the way to faith. Other techniques for church growth or renewal, for picking up the discouraged like John, or for guiding the eager like Peter, may be of help, but the gift of faith comes only from Jesus' Word. ("Faith comes from hearing, and hearing comes from the preaching of Christ," Rom 10:17.) The Reformation knew that the Word gives birth to faith: "To obtain this faith God instituted the ministry, that is, he provided the Gospel and the sacraments, by which, as through means, he gives the Holy Spirit, who works faith, when and where he pleases, in those who hear the Gospel" (*The Augsburg Confession* [1530], art. 5).

Jesus' good Semitic confidence in the bodily senses—"hearing and seeing"—as a dependable means to a knowledge of reality can be fruitfully contrasted with Plato's distrust of the physical: "Surely the soul can best reflect when it is free of all distractions such as hearing or sight or pain or pleasure of any kind—that is, when it ignores the body and becomes as far as possible independent, avoiding all physical contacts and associations as much as it can, in its search for reality" (*Phaedo*, 65c; cf. 6a, 83a).

11:5 What are the "things you are hearing and seeing"? Jesus explains, and in so doing he summarizes his ministry as it has been spread out for us between chapters 5 and 10: "The blind see again and the lame are walking; lepers are cleansed and the deaf hear; the dead are being raised and the little people are being encouraged" (v 5). Jesus does not say that he is quoting Scripture, but John will hear these words of Jesus and recall the words of Isaiah: "See, your God comes . . . he comes to save you. Then shall blind men's eyes be opened, and the ears of the deaf unstopped. Then shall the lame man leap like a deer, and the tongue of the dumb shout aloud" (Isa 35:4–6; cf. Isa 29:18–19; 61:1). In a kind of code, familiar to those steeped in Scripture, Jesus is telling John: "This is it, John; the messianic time has broken into our time as you can see from the things I have been able to do. John, I *am* the one who is coming" (cf. McN., 152).

It has interested commentators that Jesus puts at the end of his list as the apparent climax what most of us would think is the least impressive of the things he did: "And the little people are being encouraged" (literally, "the poor are evangelized," v 5c). Standing next to "the dead are being raised," this evangelization of the poor comes as anticlimax. Surely talking to the poor cannot compare with raising the dead? But Jesus, or at least Matthew, feels that this talking was Jesus' main deed. The encouraging Word, the Good News he gave the poor, the down, the grief-stricken, the little people, Jesus counts among his best work. (A good example of how Jesus preached good news to the poor is the invitation at the end of this very chapter, "Come to me," vv 28–30, Olshausen in Beng., 1:171.)

One gets the impression with the phrase "the poor are being evangelized" that Matthew's Jesus intends to summarize the Sermon on the Mount, which begins "Blessed are the poor in spirit." The Sermon on the Mount is meant to be an encouraging message to little people; Matthew's Jesus thought that the Sermon *was* Good News and that even raising the dead did not rival renewing the living. The Sermon on the Mount is the *Magna Carta* of the little people, it is common men and women's best news because it tells them how they are regarded and how to live—and why. It raises from the dead in its own way: it raises the little into big, broad, and humane life, the common into an uncommon life, the insignificant into a life with new meaning.

Giving life to the dead is something; but giving the living a way to live is something, too.

11:6 Yet for the end of his sermon to John, Jesus saves these words, tailor-made for John himself (and through John, for all of us who are tempted to wonder if Jesus is It): "And—blessed is the person who is not offended by me" (v 6). These are kind words. Jesus does not shame John by saying something like, "And blessed is the person who never doubts if I am the Messiah"—words of that kind would have hurt John because doubt was exactly John's experience. Nor does Jesus here bless those who in discouraging situations glow with vital faith. All such triumphal words would have been the worst possible pastoral counseling for John in his state. Instead Jesus pitches his tune low, puts the blessing at a level John can reach, and promises, in so many words, "And God bless you, John, if you do not throw the whole thing over because I am different."

Bacon, 288, translates Matt 11:6: "Also, Blessed is he who is not repelled by anything in me." The blessing comes on people who are not offended by the way Jesus decided to minister among us (Grund., 306; good discussion in Schl., *Das*, 174–75). The TEV translation of Matt 11:6 is unfortunate here (often the TEV translations are apt): "How happy are those who have no doubts about me!" How would John like that?! Better is this translation "And blessed is he who shall not be made to stumble in *Me*" (Allen, 114), or "And blessed is he who does not take offense [stumble into sin] at me" (Gund., 207). Bonnard, 161–62, believes that John's knowledge of both John's and Jesus' imminent *deaths* is the stumblingblock par excellence: Isn't death the cancellation of the truth of Jesus? But for Matthew's Jesus, Bonnard concludes, death *underlines* the truth; "without [his death] these signs [of the Messiah, vv 4–5] would be nothing but satanic triumphs (cf. 4:1–11)."

The word used here, *skandalisthē*, from which we get our "scandalized," means, literally "trip," and then "fall down." Jesus' human, common, defeated, and sometimes seemingly defeatist way *is* hard to accept (cf. 13:57; 26:31f). But if John and the rest of us can learn that Jesus' way may in the long run be the more effective and relevant way, that the world's successist way of looking at life may have a fatal flaw, that Jesus' roundabout way of being Messiah and doing messianic things may be God's way and, in the long haul, the most effective and humane way of doing salvation and liberation, then all will be well.

We do Jesus no honor when we allow him to be only the heavenly Messiah but give the earth's messianic tasks to contemporary movements. For even in *this world*, Jesus is the Christ. "The American Dream" is not to be the disciples' first loyalty or main export. Jesus is. For Jesus, and he alone, is the Christ, the Messiah, which means in our time's most engaging term, the Liberator.

We now enter a section that we might call "Johnology." Here Matthew has gathered most of the major John material he has assembled (outside the summary of John's ministry in chapter 3, and the report of John's crisis and beheading, which he tells independently in chapter 14). And yet this is not just a Johannine grab bag; it serves a special purpose. For while Jesus is talking about John, Matthew is teaching christology. While Jesus is talking about John, Matthew is talking about Jesus. Notice:

11:7-15 *"As John's disciples were leaving, Jesus began to talk to the people about John. 'What did you go out into the desert to look at? A reed being blown around by the wind?! Well, what did you go out to see? A man all dressed up in fine clothes?! Look, people in fine clothes are in the houses of kings. What did you go out to see, then? Was it a prophet? Yes indeed, I tell you, and much more than a prophet. This man is the very person about whom Scripture has it in writing: "Look! I am sending out my messenger in* *front of your face, and he will prepare your way before you." Amen, I tell you, no woman has ever given birth to a greater man than John the Baptist. And yet the least significant person in the kingdom of heaven is greater than he. But from the days of John the Baptist till now the kingdom of heaven suffers violence, and violent people are trying to wipe it out. For all the prophets and the law prophesied till John. And if you are willing to accept it, John is Elijah, the one who is about to come. Let the person who has ears really listen.'"*

11:7–10 As John's disciples were leaving with Jesus' little sermon *to* John, Jesus preaches a sermon *about* John. Here we are in the presence of good "talking behind the back." ("The world praises to the face, censures behind the back. Divine truth, the opposite," Beng., 1:164–65.) In his rough, popular manner, Jesus seems to chide the crowd: "What did you go out into the desert to look at? Some weak thing like a reed tossed around by the wind?" A weather vane, a "trendie" (Schw., 260, 265)? John was no reed, he was a redwood, and the wind did not blow him around; if anything, he blew the wind around. (It is kind of Jesus to suggest that John is *not* a reed blowing in the wind because, having just doubted Jesus, John could have been described that way. Jesus defends people; he does not take their most recent behavior as typical.) "Did you go out to see a fashion show, then?" (Jesus may be indirectly scolding the people here because they came to John as though looking at a new coat, and then left without changing, without obedience; thus Schl., *Das*, 176.) John was not really the latest thing in men's clothing. Finally Jesus asks, "'Did you go out to see a prophet? Yes, indeed, I tell you, and much more than a prophet. This man is the very person about whom Scripture has it in writing: "Look! I am sending out my messenger in front of your face, and he will prepare your way before you"'" (vv 9–10).

John is more than a prophet; he was prophes*ied*. He is more than a bearer of prophecy; he is a specifically mentioned *object* of prophecy (Kl., 97). He is more than a bringer of the Word of God; he is someone whom the Word of God itself predicted. Prophets are something, but prophesied prophets are something else. So John is the prophet who was promised as the advance-man for the Messiah. John is nothing less than God's next-to-last-man.

And thus we see what Matthew is driving at in this section: if someone is the next-to-last-man, the question naturally arises, "Who is the last man?" If John is the messenger "in front of *your* face," then who is the "you" in "your"; *whose* face is coming? If John is not only a prophet but more than a prophet, what does this make Jesus? Matthew intends for us to ask these questions.

An interesting transformation has come to the Malachi text in Christians' hands. In both the revered Hebrew and old Greek texts, Malachi 3:1 read like this: "Look, I [the Lord] am sending my messenger, and he will prepare *a* way before *my* face." In both Matthew and Luke (and therefore, presumably, in what is called Q, the old source from which both evangelists drew) this sacred text has been expanded and altered to read (and I will underline the expansion and alterations): "Look, I am sending my messenger before *your face*, who will prepare *your way* before *you*" (cf. Luke 7:27). Where the Malachi text had said just once, "*my* face," referring in context to "the Lord," the evangelists' text has the second person singular—three times—"*your* face," "*your* way," "*you*." God is replaced three times by some "you." This "you," as Matthew and every reader know, is Jesus—standing now in God's place. Matthew intends this substitution. He is building up to something.

If John is more-than-a-prophet, then Jesus is more than a more-than-a-prophet. Jesus, Matthew will have us believe, stands in the place of God. The God who was going to send his messenger before *his own* face, has now sent his messenger before *Jesus'* face. Did God change his mind, then, and send someone else? Or is it possible that nothing has changed and that the one he sent just might be, somehow, in some way, no one less than God's own self—indeed, "God-with-us"? Ever since the first chapter's "Emmanuel," Matthew intended for us to think God when we encountered Jesus. The threefold change in personal pronouns (from "my" to "you[r]") suggests ultimate ideas about Jesus. Matthew will not say it directly; in fact few New Testament writers felt comfortable saying Jesus is God directly; but they all lead the church eventually, indirectly, gently, evangelically to the later Johannine (John 1:1, 18; 20:28) and still later definitive Nicene confidence that Jesus is no one less than the very Lord God in visitation with us.

Bonnard, 163, believes that Matthew's altered Malachi citation means "the coming of Jesus is as important as the coming of God himself." I prefer to say that Matthew means the coming of Jesus *is* the coming of God himself. Schlatter, *Der,* 363, even hears God talking to the preexistent Christ in the evangelists' altered version of Malachi. The evangelist Mark made the same christological alterations with the Malachi (and Isaiah) citation in his Gospel (Mark 1:2–3). Lest these Christian modifications of the Old Testament texts disturb readers, Nineham, 60, makes this pertinent comment: "In the Old Testament it was God himself for whom the forerunner was to prepare, and certain small changes have been introduced into the texts to make the quotations refer to Christ. This should not be taken as a sign of dishonesty or intention to deceive. Neither Christians nor Jews approached the Old Testament along the lines of modern historical or critical study; both agreed that such passages as these referred to God's eschatological intervention, and if in the event, as Christians believed, God had chosen to intervene in the person of his Messiah, then it was right to rephrase the prophecy so as to put its precise application beyond doubt."

The careful reader will have noticed an even earlier allusion in this chapter to an OT text where God becomes Jesus. At verse 5 where "the blind see," etc., Jesus was paraphrasing an Isaian text that read, exactly:

> "See, your *God* comes with vengeance,
> with dread retribution he comes to save you.
> *Then* shall blind men's eyes be opened,
> and the ears of the deaf unstopped.
> Then shall the lame man leap like a deer,
> and the tongue of the dumb shout aloud" (Isa 35:4–5).

Matthew saw Jesus' deity in Jesus' doing what Isaiah predicted God would do (Gund., 206; cf. Schn., 139–41).

The coming of God and the coming of the Messiah were closely related in the mind of Israel. Matthew causes this relation to remain—and to crystallize—in the utterly human Jesus who is at the same time the divine Messiah. So many Old Testament God-texts become New Testament Jesus-texts that the church has always felt she read the person of Jesus most faithfully when she gave him no next-to-last or penultimate predicates, but final and ultimate ones. ("It is a most conclusive proof of the divinity of Christ, that much is said of Christ in the New Testament which is simply repeated from the Old Testament, and is there attributed exclusively to God," Beng., 1:166. Bengel refers, e.g., to John 12:41; Acts 2:33; Rom 9:33; 14:11; 1 Cor 1:31; 10:9; Eph 4:8; Heb 1:6, 8, 10, 11; Rev 1:9, 17.)

11:11 "Amen, I tell you, no woman has ever given birth to a greater man than John the Baptist. And yet the least significant person in the kingdom of heaven is greater than he." Once again we are led to Matthew's argument, called the argument *a fortiori,* from the lesser to the greater: If John is the greatest man ever born, what does this make Jesus? Or to stay even closer to our text, if John is the greatest man ever born, and if the most insignificant person in the kingdom of heaven is still greater than John, what does this make the bringer of the kingdom, Jesus himself? Matthew, I am convinced, believes that we simply cannot think too highly of Jesus. Jesus is talking about John; Matthew is talking about Jesus; we are talking about God.

But this verse gives not only a high christology; it contains a high ecclesiology as well. Who is "the least significant person in the kingdom of heaven"? (Some interpreters believe that Jesus is cryptically referring to himself; though the idea is attractive, I doubt it.) John towers over all pre-Christian history as, in Jesus' opinion, antiquity's greatest man. And yet now something *totaliter aliter,* something qualitatively different, has entered history with the coming of the kingdom of heaven. Even the littlest person in this completely new world stands higher than tall John. A difference of kind and not only of degree has entered history. The kingdom of heaven is the invasion of a new world into this old one: people in it are qualitatively different. (This verse also shows the striking distance, in the view of Matthew's Jesus, between the Old Testament and the New; Neander in Beng., 1:167.) Certainly the most retiring, most simple, most insignificant little member of newborn Christendom is not charismatically greater than John the Baptist, or professionally greater, or, even personally greater. Nevertheless, Jesus dares to say that the kingdom's littlest person is greater than even ancient history's greatest man.

The self-confidence of Jesus in making statements like this about the kingdom he brings should astonish us. We have to ask: Who does Jesus think he is? I do not think Jesus is intentionally or subtly boasting. Some people know how to talk about others in such a way that it reflects impressively on themselves. We do not catch this subtlety in Jesus. He is praising John first, then those of the kingdom; he has not intentionally or cleverly praised himself. Yet readers cannot help wondering who this praiser is. Certainly one conclusion is this: he is a man with a remarkable self-confidence. Jesus seemed—self-confidently but unselfcenteredly—to believe he was ultimate. In fact it is Jesus' combination of a clear impression of his ultimacy with his equally clear teaching of the necessarily low way he is to go that creates the mystery of his person. John's question "Are *you?*" is prompted by this mystery of Jesus' high claims and low way; the constant christological question in the life of the church is prompted by this mystery: the high Messiah in this low way? The Lord on a cross? He thinks he is somebody, but he goes the way of a nobody—how do these two fit? They somehow do, and by the Spirit's alchemy in the human heart the mixture of these two creates belief in Jesus as God's Son and our Savior. Only

God could think of this way of coming. Jesus' majesty and modesty together, somehow, spell his deity.

11:12 The text just studied ("The least significant person in the kingdom of heaven is greater than John") can be called a "majesty text" because it expresses Jesus' high self-consciousness. But the text immediately following it has to be called a "modesty text" because it presents Jesus' curiously juxtaposed conviction that the kingdom *suffers.* "But from the days of John the Baptist till now the kingdom of heaven suffers violence, and violent people are trying to wipe it out" (v 12).

What is a kingdom-suffering text doing next to a kingdom-as-qualitatively-other-world text? When a divine world enters a human world, doesn't this mean divine conquest? If the kingdom is the new world, exalting even the littlest people over the old world's greatest people, then what is it doing being practically wiped out by this world's worst people—the violent? Verses 11 and 12 do not seem to fit. Verse 11: the kingdom is the new world; verse 12: the kingdom is the violated world. And yet this fundamental puzzle, raised here about the kingdom, raised earlier by John about the Messiah, will be raised later again by Peter about the to-be-crucified Christ ("Oh no, Lord, this will never happen to you," 16:22), and will probably continue to be raised for as long as the church is confronted with this puzzling Messiah and his *suffering* way of working in the world. How can he be so supremely confident about himself, as we see him throughout the present section, and yet so seemingly pessimistic about the success of his kingdom in the world?

Verse 12 is a famous crux of interpretation. Does Jesus say, as most versions put it, that "from John till now the kingdom of heaven *suffers* violence" (making the verb passive)? Or does Jesus say that "the kingdom of heaven moves forward violently" (as the same verb, *biazetai,* can mean in the middle voice)?

The phrase that follows heightens the impression of *suffered* violence: "and violent people are trying to wipe it out" (v 12c). The kingdom of heaven in this verse is a victim (outwardly at least), not a victor. This view of the kingdom in chapter 11 squares with Jesus' view of mission in chapter 10. John's present location (prison) and imminent end (by beheading) are exhibits A and B in evidence of this suffering interpretation. Jesus' own career will seal the evidence.

The difficulty in our text stems from the ambiguity of the Greek word *biazetai* used here, which can be either in the middle voice ("exercises violence") or the passive ("suffers violence"). The context, therefore, must determine the correct translation. Advocates of the middle voice interpretation include Luke 16:16; Chrys., 37:4:245–46; Jero., 1:222; Cal., 2:7 ("aspiring after Him with burning affection and, so to say, breaking through by a vehement effort"); McN., 155; Schn., 144; Stend., 784; McK., 82; Grund., 307–09. Advocates of the passive voice interpretation are Allen, 116; Schl., *Das,* 178; Barc., 2:8; Kingsb., *Struc.,* 142 (who writes that the violent ones who attack the kingdom are "the devil and all the false Christians," "by leading 'sons of the Kingdom' astray and causing them to lose their faith," 142 n. 48); Hill, 200–01; Streck., 168; Schw., 262; Gund., 210–11; Beare, 258. The context supports this latter interpretation of a kingdom that suffers violence.

And so this qualitatively new world enters our old world, elevates even its littlest members into history's highest stratum, and then the kingdom proceeds to plunge into a grand canyon of suffered violence. To enter the kingdom is to enter high society—and the abyss; to become almost superhuman and to be treated as almost subhuman; ecstasy and agony; high life and low life; the sublime and the ridiculous. This new world begets new people and it gives them power—the power to endure. This new world creates new men and women and enables them to fish other men and women—and to be violated by them.

Schlatter (*Der*, 368–69) has suggested that the violence spoken of in this text is violence "from above," an established violence, specifically the violence of the hedonism of the time, represented grossly in Herod's circle (see 14 A in *The Churchbook* for a glimpse of this hedonism), and pervasively in the free-thought influence widely accepted by the Sadducean party in Jesus' time. It was from these fashionable revolutionaries, these thoroughly cultured persons, that the greatest violence was done to both John and Jesus. John lost his head to sensualists, not the Zealots; Jesus was crucified by the establishment, not revolutionaries. The really subtle violence suffered by the kingdom "from the days of John the Baptist till now" was, and is, the violence mounted by culture-conformists, not anticonformists. Secularism more than zealotry fights the kingdom.

When contemporary Christians hear this they learn to assess a subtler violence in their own environment: the violence of secular culture. Liberal culture with its Gucci shoes is a finally more dangerous foe of the kingdom than liberationist counterculture with its guerrilla boots. Liberal thought fights the kingdom more violently than Marxist thought, for its fight is not straightforward and frank but subtle and often comes donned in religious or humanist clothing. The free thinkers are the real enemies of the gospel of the kingdom; the religion of culture, the value-system that thoroughly penetrates television from comedy to crime, the sensualism, secularism, and sensationalism of popular culture—these do more real violence to Jesus than do the counterculture rebels (who, however, can be quite easily assimilated into secular culture's macho values).

11:13 "For all the prophets and the law prophesied till John." This is a curious verse and means that Old Testament prophecies had a limit: the time of John, the messianic time. After that, the new world of the kingdom took over and the Messiah's Word became the new prophecy. This is another way of saying that the old prophecy in law and prophets pointed to Jesus and found complete fulfillment in him; then he came and took over the old office of law and prophets.

This view of Scripture reminds us of the events of the transfiguration (Matt 17 A). There, Moses (representing the law) and Elijah (representing the prophets) talk with Jesus. But when the Voice from heaven has explained to the bewildered disciples that "*This* [singular—Jesus] is my priceless Son; listen to *him* [again singular]," then Moses and Elijah (the law and the prophets) disappear and the disciples look up and "see Jesus only." The meaning, there as here, is this: Jesus has taken over. The Old Testament's Messiah-pointing ministry continues, of course, until the end of the age. But the Old Testament's Messiah has now *come* with his kingdom and Word, and he has total sovereignty over the old. The law and prophets had their task in prophesying *till* the kingdom age inaugurated by John and Jesus. As long as law and prophets are read as pointing to the Messiah they still exercise authority in the people of God. But the law and prophets have *no* office beyond pointing to the Messiah. This leads to an important corollary.

One of the most misleading movements in our time is the prophecy movement that reads the Old Testament Scriptures as a kind of code by which to decipher contemporary events and predict future ones. The law and the prophets are not read with an exclusive christocentricity, they are read as predicting the Common Market, the Israel-Arab conflicts, and the wars of Russia and America. Instead of being read as pointers to the Word, the law and prophets are read as pointers to the world and to all kinds of words, political, social, and economical. The Old Testament is made a crystal ball instead of a Christ-pointer. *But the law and the prophets do their work of prophecy only "till John."* When they are read as pointing only to the time inaugurated by John—the messianic time—they are read legitimately. But Old Testament prophecy that goes around, over, and even through, but still past John and Jesus into modern events, is not prophecy any more in the evangelical sense, it is voodoo. The Old Testament is not about the late great planet earth; it is about the Messiah. This is the apostolic conviction, seen in the verse before us, and no honor is done either to Scripture's prophecy or to Jesus' work by turning the Old Testament into a cabalism giving keys to current events.

In popular prophecy teaching dishonor is done to Jesus and to the complete centrality and sufficiency of Jesus' work by a refocusing of our attention on past political predictions and future political fulfillments. Christians, however, are to be occupied with obedience to the words of Jesus, not with puzzling ancient predictions about still more puzzling future events. This is certainly Matthew's intention in this purposely limiting verse: "*All* [only Matthew uses this word, and he has put it at the very front of the sentence for emphasis] the prophets and the law prophesied *till* John." We may conclude that any Old Testament prophet or law-giver who is used to prophesy *beyond* John's Messiah, giving other than christocentric information, is illegitimate, subevangelical, and antiapostolic, however spiritual the language may appear.

We know that modern prophetic movements *seek* to honor Jesus Christ by showing the relevance of Scripture to current problems. But this relevance is not rightly sought by attaching Old Testament words to modern events; the only legitimate Old Testament attachment, in the Christian conviction, is Jesus the Messiah. Jesus the Messiah is relevant to modern events in a way that has little to do with what prophetic Christians call prophecy, and much to do with what the church calls discipleship and evangelism. We are to preach Jesus as our prophecy and Jesus as the meaning of past, present, and future, and discipleship to Jesus as the way to live in the present and to walk into the future. We are not to send Christians running to their newspapers to decipher political and economic fulfillments of texts from Ezekiel and Daniel. The day of Old Testament predictions has been over ever since John baptized Jesus. When people use the Old Testament, from an overzealous attempt to show its authority, to point believers into exotic particulars in the twentieth century rather than to Jesus—come and coming—they lose the Old Testament's real Point.

It was rabbinic conviction in the days of Jesus that "the prophets have prophesied only till the days of the Messiah" (Str.-B, 1:602). The best New Testament cross reference to Matt 11:13 is Paul's 2 Cor 1:20: "For *all* the promises of God find their Yes in him," that is, in Christ. (The Greek *hosai*, at the front of Paul's sentence for emphasis, translated "all" here, literally means "whatever there are"; there is no "the" in this Greek sentence, and thus we can render 2 Cor 1:20, "Whatever promises of God there are, they all find their Yes in Christ." Christ is the point, and the whole point, of the divine promises.)

"Expect therefore nothing further, neither wait for anyone else" (Chrys., 37:4:245). Jesus' words do not mean that after John there are no more prophets—see Agabus and the daughters of Philip in Acts, and Paul's list of gifts in 1 Cor 12–14; Jesus' words mean "that whatever *[quicquid]* the law and the prophets prophesied in those writings that we read [in the Old Testament] have been fulfilled by the Lord" (Jero., 1:222, and "until John" means "until the time of Christ," *ibid*.).

For rabbis, Scripture was essentially instructional Torah; for the early Christians, Scripture was essentially prophecy of Christ and the church (Hare, 15). For Matthew, the whole Old Testament (law and prophets) has prophetic structure and so remains the church's perpetually Christ-preaching book (Frankemölle, 299, 299 n. 110, 387). Trilling, 173, 178, says that in Matthew's view, Old Testament Scripture as a prophecy-book has ended, but that Scripture as a normative law-book continues. But if OT Scripture is still preached (as it should be) in a Christ-centered way, which in Matthew's conviction is its intended way, then OT Scripture has not ended as a prophecy-book either. When the OT is used to prophesy anything other than the Christ who came and who comes again, however, it is abused. (Cf., e.g., Gutiérrez, *Theol. of Lib.*, 161: The biblical Promise is "not exhausted by these [OT] promises nor by their [NT] fulfillment." But they are.) The other great christocentric-Scripture texts are Luke 24:25–27, 44–49 and John 5:39f.

11:14 "And if you are willing to accept it, John [the Baptist] is Elijah, the one who is about to come [just before the Messiah]." In every orthodox Jewish home at Passover one empty chair is left for Elijah, the anticipated predecessor of the Messiah. And at one point in the ritual at the table a son goes to the front door to look for Elijah and returns announcing that he has not yet come. All this is based on the final words of the final book in our Old Testament, Malachi 4:5–6 (NEB): "Look, I will send you the prophet Elijah before the great and terrible day of the Lord comes. He will reconcile fathers to sons and sons to fathers, lest I come and put the land under a ban to destroy it." Therefore orthodox Jews still look forward to the return of Elijah. One of the impediments to Israel's faith in Jesus as the Messiah was the fact that they had not yet been visited by Elijah (see the conversation in Matt 17:10–13).

Elijah had been one of the few Old Testament personalities whose death was not recorded (Enoch is the most famous other). We recall that Elijah had gone off to heaven in a chariot (2 Kgs 2:11). Consequently, folk belief was filled with stories of Elijah's "comings." Evidence of this widespread view appears in the passion story itself where Jesus cries, "Eli, Eli, lama sabachthani," and is interpreted by his hearers as calling for Elijah (27:47–49).

Jesus now addresses this folk belief and says, "*if you are willing* to accept it, John is Elijah, the one who is about to come." This is a revealing remark. Jesus does not force belief in his John-Elijah equation. It is not a part of required orthodoxy to make John the Baptist the equivalent of the returning Elijah (indeed, contrast John 1:21 where the Baptist *denies* that he is Elijah!; and cf. Beare, 261). Jesus does not require a *sacrificium intellectus* and say, "you had better believe that John is Elijah," or even, "if you are childlike enough you will believe that John is Elijah." Instead he makes a gracious and latitudinarian remark: "if you are willing to accept it, John is Elijah." Not everybody will either be willing or able to believe, really, that John is, somehow, the promised Elijah—to them John will simply be John, an independent and quite adequate predecessor of Jesus the Messiah, without the need of importing old expectations. Most others will find no difficulty in believing that "somehow"

John is what Malachi means, in office—the promised Elijah, predecessor of the Messiah. And a final type will believe without any difficulty at all that John literally is Elijah, without any questions asked, simply because the Bible says so or because Jesus says so. All three answers pass. No one is forced. "Let every one be fully convinced in his own mind" (Rom 14:5 RSV).

Thus Jesus' "if you are willing to accept it" tells us something of the way Jesus read his Bible. He was an open, free reader. His unparalleled reverence for Holy Scripture (see e.g., 4:1–11 and 5:17–20) led him to this freedom and nonrigidity. His evangelists all caught his spirit, and so we have the remarkable documents we call the Gospels with their diversity and yet unity in the presentation and interpretation of Scripture and Jesus. All four Gospels have quite different slants, lenses, and convictions about exactly who Jesus is and what he does. They do not differ in the ultimate convictions—in basic doctrine it would be fair to say that they come together in chorus. But the chorus or quartet has its bass (Matthew), its tenor (John), its baritone (Mark), and its alto (Luke). They all sing the same *song* with slightly (or, in John, with very) different, but finally quite complementary *parts*. The difference in parts is due to the freedom of interpretation that Jesus gave his disciples, as illustrated strikingly both in the Gospels and in the text before us. In a number of places, as here, disciples are free to make of an event what they are able or willing to make of it. Jesus will not require of us a literalness that breaks our conscience. Thus this verse's service in the church is its teaching Jesus' occasional (and perhaps even thematic) freedom in biblical interpretation. Jesus himself was biblically conservative at most points; he will not require this conservatism, however, of everyone at every point. "If you are willing to accept it, John is Elijah."

Cf. Schl., *Der*, 371. Jesus does not mean that John is the reincarnation of Elijah; rather, as in Luke 1:17, John came *in the spirit and power* of Elijah, had the same austerity in life and rigor in principles, lived like Elijah in the desert, wore his kind of leather girdle, and he convicted Herod and Herodias as Elijah had convicted Ahab and Jezebel (Jero., 1:222–24; cf. Calvin, 1:138: Malachi does not mean Elijah *himself* but "a simple comparison to this effect"; Bengel, 1:168: the absence of the Greek definite article before Elijah's name, antonomasia, shows that John is not literally Elijah, but is like him in office). Matthew simply means that "as through Jesus' activity the Christ came, so also through the Baptist's activity Elijah came" (Schl.).

11:15 "Let the person who has ears really listen." This is Jesus' famous code sentence in the parables (see 13:9, 43; Mark 4:9, 23; Luke 8:8, etc.). It means: "Be alert!" It also means, "listen carefully." And it implies that the mere possession of ears does not yet mean the possession of the priceless gift of hearing. Hearing requires not only unimpeded access to sound; of even more importance it requires the use of the head and the insertion of the will into what is heard.

This sentence on right hearing applies to this entire section on Jesus and John that has just preceded. And in this context Matthew means, "If John is everything I have just reported that Jesus said he is—prophet, more than prophet, preparer of the way of the Lord, greatest man born prior to the kingdom, terminus of all prophecy, and even (for those able to accept it) Elijah—what does this make Jesus?" Jesus has not been talking directly about himself in this section; but the person who hears more than sounds in words will come to the conclusion that Jesus must be the Coming One, the inaugurator of the kingdom, the Messiah after Elijah. That is real listening. Real hearing, which is more than auditing, which is listening, leads persons to the conviction that Jesus is ultimate—in a word, to faith in him as God with us.

11:16–19 *"To what shall I compare people today? They are like children sitting in the marketplace and shouting to their playmates, 'We played wedding music to you and you wouldn't dance; we played funeral music and you wouldn't cry.' You see, John came neither eating nor drinking [like others] and people are saying, 'He is a fanatic.' The Son of Man came eating and drinking [like others], and people say, 'Look at this greedy fellow, this drunkard; he is a friend of collaborators and immoral people.' Well, God's wisdom has been vindicated by its works."*

Jesus' long John-sermon comes to an end with this altar call to repentance. The people of Israel had been a deeply privileged people the last few months. In their midst they had had no less than the greatest man of antiquity (John the Baptist) *and* the Messiah himself. Had any other generation in history been as blessed? But while many had been baptized when they heard John (3:5–6), and quite a few had been impressed when they heard Jesus (4:23–25; 7:28–29), the overall result of the ministries of both (we learn now from this and future texts) had been more passing interest than permanent change, more fascination than faith. This text is the first so far in Matthew to tell us explicitly that the ministries of John and Jesus had not been entirely successful (cf. McK., 82). Until now the general impression has been that John and Jesus went over well. We saw large numbers of people around both John and Jesus in their previous appearances. But apparently most people in these crowds were merely excited or curious—nothing much came of their attendance at the meetings.

"People today" (literally "this generation," an important expression in Jesus' vocabulary, cf. TDNT, 1:660–61) remind Jesus of pouting children sitting on the curbstone complaining that their playmates will not play the games *they* want to play; so they will not play with them. The meaning, in the context before us, is that people will not play John's and Jesus' game because John and Jesus will not play theirs. People are not willing to play the kingdom's game because the bringers of the kingdom, classically John and Jesus, do not meet their expectations (John is too ascetic, Jesus too free).

There is another interpretation of this parable (e.g., in Beng., 1:168) that I find attractive. In this interpretation, those sitting on the curbstone are John and Jesus who call to people today saying, "We played wedding music and you would not dance" (this is Jesus' gospel ministry), "we played funeral music and you would not cry" (this is John's ministry of the law). In neither case did the people like the games being played by their new playmates. Neither the inviting, winning wedding music of Jesus with his grace notes and good news, nor the solemn, serious, foreboding music of John with his grave notes and bad news, really, finally, lastingly appealed to people today. For John's music came on too loud and Jesus' too soft—in both cases people kept playing their old game of unchanged life.

This disinterest affected John and Jesus—in John's case it led to genuine doubt of Jesus; in Jesus' case it led to the present lament and, in a moment, to a very severe warning of judgment. Both John and Jesus had reason to be discouraged with people and with their unwillingness to give a final commitment to the game that John and Jesus wished to start with their ministries of law and gospel, of repentance and faith, of funeral and wedding, of death to sin and life to God.

11:18 Jesus then explains his parable: "You see, John came neither eating nor drinking [like others], and people are saying 'He is a fanatic' [literally, "he has a demon"]." John was altogether too alarmist for popular consumption; he had "a thing" (they called it "a demon") about wrath, fire, and judgment—he was a hellfire preacher with the faults of all hellfire preachers: too little sense of humor, too little polish, too little balance. So he was not taken too seriously.

11:19a "The Son of Man came eating and drinking [like others], and people say, 'Look at this greedy fellow, this drunkard; he is a friend of collaborators and immoral people.'" Jesus' way was too social, too normal, too everyday, too natural for the taste of the decision-makers in Israel. Jesus did not seem spiritual enough, different enough, separated enough. He did not even seem to fast regularly (9:14–15); he apparently made few scruples about what he ate or drank—he came, as they said critically, "eating and drinking." But worst of all, he seemed to lack either the discrimination or the moral resolve to separate himself from Israel's inferior elements—the comprador bourgeoisie who made money off Israel's colonial occupation, and the lowlife and secularists who demoralized Israel. Apparently Jesus could be seen often enough in the company of these two groups to make him open to these criticisms.

Calvin, 2:11, is good on the difference between John's and Jesus' social life: "This is a passage which they should note who place the height of perfection in outward austerity of life and define the angelic life as abstemiousness or self-mortification in fasting. By this rule, John is better than the Son of God."

11:19b "But by their fruits you shall know them" (7:16, 20). And this is Jesus' own conclusion: "Well, God's wisdom has been vindicated by its works" (v 19b). "Wisdom," here, means "God's plan," "God's providence," "God's way," or perhaps most simply of all, "God's Christ," Jesus himself. The first commentary our text received is recorded in Luke and in several of the Greek manuscripts in Matthew: "And wisdom has already been justified by its *children.*" The "children," this gloss says, are the "works." I doubt that the works meant by Matthew's Jesus are Jesus' miracles (Gund., 213). The new *people* that wisdom created through the law of John and the gospel of Jesus were the justification for God's going the way of John and Jesus.

The first large unit in chapter 11, the John sermon, teaches us that John is God's next-to-last man, and Jesus is God's last; that John is the promised Elijah (however interpreted) and Jesus the promised Coming One. Thus Matthew 11 A points us toward the past and the Hebrew Bible, and tells us how to read them: as grand preparations for the Christ. The first truth we learn in this chapter is in christology that *Jesus* is the Christ.

II. JUDGE JESUS (11:20–24)

"Then Jesus began to scold the cities where he had done most of his miracles because they had not changed their lives. 'Woe to you, Chorazin! and woe to you, Bethsaida! Because if

*the miracles that happened in your midst had happened in Tyre and Sidon they would
have been in sackcloth and ashes a long time ago; they would have changed their lives. But
I tell you, it will go better for Tyre and Sidon in the day of judgment than it will for you.*

*"'And you Capernaum, do you think that you are going to be "lifted up to heaven"? You
are going to be "cast down to hell"! Because if the miracles that happened in you had
happened in Sodom, that city would be still standing today. But I tell you, it will go better
for Sodom in the day of judgment than it will for you.'"*

Until now Jesus has not been much of a judgment preacher. On the whole, Jesus
has preached a message of good news and lived a ministry of mercy. We have seen
him heal people, but we have not seen him "judge," confront, or convict many
people yet. Until now, judgment has been mainly a matter for John the Baptist.
But so that we may know that Jesus did not just tiptoe through Galilee, Matthew
gives us another portrait of Jesus in his eleventh chapter gallery.

Jesus is not only the lowly Messiah wandering around a distant province doing
public health, he is the future judge of the world. Though Jesus does not call
himself judge in this text nor use any of the titles of the future world judge here
(such as Son of Man), Jesus claims to know not only what will happen in judgment
to Jewish cities (Capernaum, Bethsaida, and Chorazin), but to pagan cities as well
(Tyre, Sidon, and Sodom). Jesus talks as if he knows what will happen to people in
the coming great world judgment. In that sense, we catch a glimpse of Jesus as
judge.

It is important that we see just where and how Jesus preached judgment. Interestingly, we have no record of his preaching judgment to pagans. Jesus' words of
severe warning and his frequent references to hell are all reserved for the privileged, for the old and new people of God, for the people who thought they were
in. It is well known that Matthew's Jesus, the preacher of the Sermon on the Mount
and the personification of mercy, preached more about the seriousness of judgment and hell than any other New Testament figure except John the Baptist. But it
is equally important to see *to whom* he preached this message: not, as we might have
thought, to those outside, but to those *inside;* not to those needing conversion (as
we think of conversion), but to those who thought they already had it (or its
equivalent, the experience of the miraculous).

It is the religious of Israel, the disciples of Jesus, and the spiritually privileged of
Galilee who got the message of judgment from Jesus. Judgment is a message for
spiritual people—and ever since Matthew's Gospel it is a message for Christians—
for Christians who smile and wink when they hear what Jesus says; for comfortable
Christians—in a word, for unreal Christians. (And who of us is not in some way
unreal?)

The people of Bethsaida, Chorazin, and Capernaum had experienced Jesus and
had seen his power. But merely having *had* Jesus, his presence, even his grace
in their midst, is not salvation; it is *having,* not having *had;* it is changing now in
response to that presence now, it is reacting to grace. The Christian world should
feel itself seriously confronted by this judgment addressed *to the places where Jesus
had done most of his miracles.* Jesus Christ *has* been present in his church and Word
in Christendom, and there he has done most of his miracles. But that, finally, is not
the point. The point is: Have we changed? Are we changing? Capernaum had
almost made a town motto of Isaiah 14:13: "lifted to heaven," perhaps from

a sense of civic pride in having had Jesus' ministry based in their town (Schw., 267). "Lifted up to heaven" sounded then something like America's "In God We Trust" sounds now (a little too much like a boast). But Jesus is not interested in the sponsoring of his presence; he is interested in response to his presence, he is interested in *repentance* (changed life, vv 20–21).

Christian countries are in special trouble on judgment day, not because Jesus has not really been in their communities but because he has. Jesus' presence, without change, can lead to a damnation deeper than Sodom's. That is the message of our text. Sodom will have a better day in court than Capernaum, though Capernaum was Jesus' mission base and Sodom was a byword for perversion; Capernaum had more opportunities than Sodom; Capernaum experienced Jesus' kindness but would not let that kindness come to term in changed life. Every member of a church has Jesus, for Jesus is present in his Word, fellowship, and sacraments. But Jesus does not *have* every member of his church; he has only those who, under the impact of his miraculous grace, are actually changing. ("Every hearer of the New Testament is either much more blessed [11:11] or much more wretched than they of old time" [11:20–24], Beng., 1:169.)

If the first observation that needs to be made about Jesus' judgment message is that it is addressed to those who have had the privilege of Jesus' miraculous grace and not (as is often supposed) to the raw pagan world, the second observation that needs to be made, already intimated, is that the message of judgment is addressed to a particular group *within* the community of those blessed by Jesus' presence: the unrepentant. Jesus' judgment Word is for those who have had Jesus' miraculous presence but for whom this presence has not meant enough to cause honest change of life. Jesus the judge is for the (1) Christian (2) unrepentant.

This needs to be stressed because the message of Judge Jesus is *not* ordinarily or unreflectively for the contrite, the brokenhearted, the repentant, or the seriously sorry. What the needy and contrite need—and what they fully get in the next story—is the grace and help of Jesus. The last thing brokenhearted Christians need or receive from Jesus is scolding—their own consciences do enough of that. The occupational hazard of pulpits is scolding. Pastors, thinking themselves little Amoses, can be driven into the error of berating the congregation Sunday after Sunday, thinking thereby that they are faithful preachers of the gospel or, at least, of the gospel's message of judgment. But the unrelieved message of judgment— scolding—only depresses sensitive Christians; by itself, judgment is no final help at all. Therefore it needs to be stressed that Jesus is Judge Jesus only for those who in his presence have not made the decision to change.

The old saying that preaching is "to afflict the comfortable and to comfort the afflicted" is exactly the meaning, and in that order, of the Judge Jesus and the Savior Jesus stories that conclude Matthew 11. In these two stories Jesus is preached as judge only to the unrepentant, as savior only to the heavy-laden. The art of the Christian pastor and teacher is to distinguish who's who, or to preach Scripture's whole counsel so fully that the Spirit will make the distinctions and applications. To scold the repentant and to comfort the unrepentant is perverse. The good pastor will so faithfully minister the whole counsel of God, law and gospel, that the unrepentant will be convicted and the repentant comforted. In old Reformation theology this discernment was called distinguishing law from gospel; in the old translation of the Bible it was called "rightly dividing the word of truth" (2 Tim 2:15 AV). The fact is that most of us are a mix of both repentance and unrepentance, a part of every Christian heart is unserious. Therefore we *all* need both law and gospel, judgment and grace, 11:20–24 and 11:25–30, in right doses at the right times. God blesses pastors and teachers who give their people "their food in season" (24:45–46).

To minister the law when the gospel is needed, *or* to minister the gospel when the law is needed, is to fall under the indictment of the prophet who said "you have disheartened the righteous falsely, although I have not disheartened him, and you have encouraged the wicked, that he should not turn from his wicked way to save his life" (Ezek 13:22 RSV). Theology calls ministering the gospel of God's forgiveness, without a concomitant ministry of the law of God's commands and warnings, antinomianism ("anti-law-ism"), a false teaching that greatly concerned Luther, e.g., in his exposition of the great chapter on judgment in Genesis 19: "The antinomians, those modern prophets, maintain that people must be dealt with gently and must not be frightened by examples of God's wrath. But Paul states the opposite in 2 Tim 3:16–17. He says there that Scripture is also 'profitable for reproof and correction, that the man of God may be complete, equipped for every good work.' [Cf. also 1 Cor 10:6]. . . . No matter how righteous we may be, [the law and wrath of God] should be proclaimed in the church frequently, lest we fall into the madness of the antinomians, who remove the Law from the church, as if everybody in the church were actually a saint and there were no need for such examples of God's wrath. The world, of course, is fond of such teachers, as in the Book of Jeremiah the people say: 'Speak the things that please us.' But . . . sins should be denounced, and God's wrath should be exhibited for the sake of the unbelievers who are in the church, yes, also for the sake of the believers, lest they yield to sin, which still adheres to them, and to their natural weakness" (*Lectures on Genesis* [1537–1539], *LW* 3:239, 269). Much preaching in our time is antinomian.

We can be grateful that the evangelist Matthew repeatedly supplies us with both judge and savior stories as here, side by side. When we come to them we should preach each faithfully. We should seize upon the presence of a judge story as divine direction to preach judgment (though not without gospel for the sorry), and upon the presence of a savior story to preach salvation (though not without judgment for the indifferent)—and preach both *to the people of God!* Expository preaching gives pastor and teacher the opportunity to be faithful to the real meaning of consecutive texts. Soft preachers uncomfortable with warning can learn to warn by being expositors; rough preachers unaccustomed to comforting can learn to comfort by hearing Scripture's passages of comfort. What is basically needed for the health of our churches is receiving the whole Christ through the preaching of the whole Word (together with the regular administration of sacraments). The desideratum is evangelical expository preaching. In this way pastor and teacher learn to say both law and gospel, to administer both judgment and grace, to present Jesus Christ in his wholeness—as judge of the smug and savior of the sorry. Judge Jesus is not the first Word—either of this chapter or of most faithful preaching—Christ Jesus is. Nor is Judge Jesus intended to be the last Word of this chapter or of faithful preaching—Savior Jesus is. But Judge Jesus *is* the constant middle Word of faithful preaching, as he is in this model christological chapter. (Cf. also the middle line of judgment in the genealogy that opens the Gospel, 1:7–11.)

11:20 "Then Jesus began to scold the cities where he had done most of his miracles because they had not changed their lives." The word for miracles used here is *dynameis*—"dynamics." The miracle-working Jesus, by definition, is dynamic. Those privileged to be in dynamic Christian churches or groups are persons not only of privilege but of fearful responsibility. For to have the presence of Christ's dynamics and yet not to change one's way of living is to make oneself more subject to the grim judgments of God than even Sodom will be. ("The activity of Jesus . . . commits a person who witnesses it to a responsibility infinitely greater than does ignorance of God and moral depravity," Bonn., 166.)

The word "repentance" was not used in the miracle chapters of Matthew 8 and 9; those chapters were almost entirely taken up with presenting the goodness of Jesus. But if the miracles of grace and faith do not work repentance there is judgment. The purpose of Jesus' dynamic is changed lives: this is the special theme of Matthew's moral Gospel. Lives unchanged by the work of Jesus the helper are lives summoned before the bar of Jesus the judge. Miracles are in order to repentance; dynamics are for the sake of change. Where these ends are not worked by these means it is time for the introduction of God's middle Word of judgment (cf. Schl., *Der*, 377).

The Word of judgment is, in its way, no less gracious than many words of grace. To warn a child of the dangers of going too near the river, for example, is no less gracious than to pull the child out of the river: both the warning and the rescue save the child. ("Those whom I love, I reprove and chasten; so be zealous and repent," Rev 3:19.) Pastors are not being more loving when they avoid all reference to judgment. It is part of the grace of God that God warns us.

Augustine, *Serm.*, 27 (77):3:343, refers here to the good prophet who said "I will wound and I will heal" (Deut 32:39) and adds that God "gives pain, it is true; but he only gives pain, that he may bring the patient on to health." Conzelmann, 78, puts what is involved here interestingly: "Through the destruction of security *(securitas)* the idea of judgment makes possible the certainty *(certitudo)* of hope."

11:21–22 Tyre and Sidon were notorious pagan coastal cities northwest of Israel to which, as far as we know, Jesus never got (in 15:21 he is only in the neighborhood). But Jesus here warns the cities to which he *had* gotten and in which he had done most of his dynamics that on judgment day it would go worse for cities he had visited than it would for those unvisited. There is an instructive doctrine of both mission and judgment here. Some Christian towns are going to be worse off at judgment than some pagan towns; some Christian people are going to receive more baleful judgments than some pagan people because, among other things, Jesus knows what cities and people in them would have done if they had been reached. "If the miracles that happened in your midst had happened in Tyre and Sidon, they would have been in sackcloth and ashes a long time ago" (v. 21).

This is an encouraging Word for those concerned about the unreached; it is a sobering Word for the reached. According to our text will Jesus judge the world at the last day not only on the basis of what they have done but on the basis of what they would have done? Is it on such a basis that Jesus can later say "many who are first shall be last and many who are last shall be first" (19:30; 20:16)? We simply cannot make *final* judgments about the unreached, and we must even be cautious about making final judgments about the reached. Faith in Jesus saves with certainty; unfaith in Jesus, where his dynamics have not been present, may not damn with certainty, for men and women may be judged, like Tyre and Sidon, on the basis of what they would have done if those dynamics had been present. But unfaith in Jesus where his dynamics have been present, an unfaith proved by failure to change one's life under the impact of grace, does bring judgment.

"If you say, 'Behold, we did not know this,' does not he who weighs the heart perceive it? Does not he who keeps watch over your soul know it, and will he not requite man according to his work?" (Prov 24:12 RSV). "Shall not the Judge of all the earth do right?" (Gen 18:25 RSV).

Tyre and Sidon—great pagan cities of Jesus' time; Peking and Delhi or Tokyo and Cairo or any other of the great contemporary non-Christian cities that, comparatively, have not seen as much of Jesus' dynamism as New York and Manila or as London and Rome—those pagan cities are compared favorably with the "Christian" cities of Capernaum, Bethsaida, and Chorazin. The lesson is that Christian cities, especially, need the message of judgment.

11:23–24 Capernaum's case was especially grim: it was Jesus' mission base and adult hometown (4:13). Here Jesus had done most of his major miracles. The city may even have subtly advertised the fact, not least, for commercial reasons: "The City Lifted to Heaven: Home of Jesus Wonder-Worker." Jesus refers to this self-consciousness—"Capernaum, do you think that you are going to be 'lifted up to heaven'? You are going to be 'cast down to hell!'"

It is not the mere presence of Jesus' dynamic that saves, it is an honest response to it. That is Matthew's Gospel. *Many* Christians, Jesus has already taught us, are going to say on judgment day, "Lord, Lord, did we not preach, exorcize, and do miracles, and all of these in your name?" But, Jesus warned, in effect, "you are going to hell" (7:22–23). Jesus has taught us that the unrepentant are not merely the many secular careless; they are also the spiritual elite, the small groups of dynamic Christians who are zealous in changing everybody's lives but their own, in winning whole nations to Christ but in the process losing their own souls (cf. the exposition of 4:8–10 and 16:26). The superspiritual come under as severe attack as the subspiritual in Jesus' teaching, for both neglected the basic rule: repent, change, take Jesus seriously for your *own* life.

Capernaum stands for all self-conscious Christianity, for all Christianity smug in its possession of Jesus, in its being the center of Jesus' work. One thinks almost automatically of the super-Christian movements of our time that come sweeping into countries and cities with big claims, big plans, big purposes—all for Christ—and who consistently look down on all the dog-eared, inefficient, ungrowing work of most struggling churches and Christians. Armed with growth techniques, with steps to victorious Christian living and baptism in the Spirit, with strategies for church expansion and personal power, these Christians and movements fairly burst with the consciousness of being, by the grace of God, "lifted up to heaven" (higher life). Jesus is not always impressed. It is going to go better in the judgment day for notorious pagans than for self-satisfied saints.

The sum of the matter is this: *Christians* should take Jesus seriously. When they do, they escape judgment; when they do not, they invite it. And all those places outside the mission reach of the clear dynamic of Jesus are to be sought out eagerly, for there is no salvation outside repentant faith in Christ. But what mission cannot reach may be left to Christ's secret work in the Spirit and his fair judgment at the last day. Meanwhile the call is for all *Christians* to respond to Jesus' dynamic with—repentance.

"None of the men who have seen my glory and my signs which I wrought in Egypt and in the wilderness, and yet have put me to the proof these ten times and have not hearkened to my voice, shall see the land which I swore to give to their fathers" (Num 14:22–23 RSV). Matthew heard Jesus preach judgment more than Mark or Luke. G. Barth, 58–59, gives us the following interesting statistics on word-usage in Matthew/Mark/Luke: *krisis* (judgment)—12/0/4; *hēmera kriseōs* (day of judgment)—4/0/0; "into the outer darkness"—3/0/0; "there, there will be wailing and gnashing of teeth"—6/0/1.

III. SAVIOR JESUS (11:25–30)

"At that very period Jesus responded and said, 'Thank you, Father, Lord of heaven and earth, for hiding these things from the wise and learned and for revealing them to little people; yes, Father, for this was your sovereign plan.

"'Absolutely everything has been handed over to me by my Father; and no one really knows the Son except the Father, and no one really knows the Father except the Son and the one to whom the Son chooses to reveal him.

"'Come here to me all of you who are working hard and carrying too much, and I will refresh you. Here, take my yoke upon you, and learn from me, because I am gentle and simple at heart, and you will experience refreshing deep down in your lives. You see, my yoke is easy and my burden is light.'"

Having warned the care-less of judgment, Jesus now invites the care-full to rest. For Jesus is essentially savior. "Jesus" *means* "savior" (1:21). Jesus warns of judgment *for the sake of* salvation. He has not really come to judge but to save. Judgment is Jesus' middle Word but he does not intend for it to be his last Word—unless stubborn hearts insist. Jesus uses his Word of judgment to draw us to his Word of salvation, his law to drive us to his gospel.

The Savior Jesus section is divided into three subsections: (1) *A Thanksgiving* to the Father for his way of revelation (to the lowly, vv 25–26); (2) *A Claim* about the content of revelation (the exclusivity of the Son, v 27); and (3) *An Invitation* to those encountered by revelation (to receive renewal, vv 28–30).

A. Jesus' Thanksgiving (11:25–26)

11:25 "At that very period Jesus . . . said, 'Thank you, Father. . . .'" At a period when Jesus could have been most discouraged, when he had to preach judgment to the unresponsive, when he had to characterize people as childish and had to acknowledge that he was not getting the kind of response—even from John the Baptist, the hardiest of all believers—that one expected a Messiah to get, Jesus gave thanks. "Thank you, Father, Lord of heaven and earth, for hiding these things from the wise and learned and for revealing them to little people." (McNeile, 161, believes "Jesus was thankful, not that the ["wise"] were ignorant, but that the ["little people"] knew.") The world's response is a source of pain to Jesus ("woe," v 21); the Father's sovereignty is a source of encouragement to him ("thank you," v 25). Somehow and somewhere, behind and above a discouraging world, stands a poised Father, completely in control and utterly unfrustrated. By looking to this Father Jesus can feel grateful that events have fallen out as they have; to believe that human beings are the final arbiters of history is inevitably to become a whiner rather than a thanker, because human irresponsibility is an embittering reality.

The church needs this look to the sovereignty of God if she is to have poise in her ministry. An excessive attention to an unresponsive world, and an insufficient appreciation of the happy fact of God's sovereignty, will drive Christians into the slough of despond. Humanism without theism is cynical; theism without humanism is cruel.

Who are the "wise and learned," and who are the "little people"? By the "wise," Jesus "means . . . wisdom . . . which they seemed to have through natural shrewdness. Wherefore neither did He say, 'thou hast revealed it to fools'" (Chrys., 38:1:251). According to Augustine, *Serm.*, 17(67):8:312, the wise and learned are simply the proud; the little people ("babes") are simply the humble. McNeile, 161–62, with other commentators, sees the wise and learned against the background of Isa 29:14 (and its echo in 1 Cor 1:19–21), and the meaning of little people, in the light of Pss. 19:7; 119:130, as the simple or open-minded.

Bonnard, 167–68, believes the wise and learned represent the religious elite, "the educated, the specialists, the authorities in religious matters," while the little people *(les petits, le petit peuple)* are the poor or the poor in spirit of the Beatitudes, "the 'sinners' of the countryside for whom the Pharisees have nothing but scorn." Bonnard, 168, citing Dupont-Sommer, points out that Qumran gave its deepest spiritual truths and mysteries only to "'those who had attained the desired degree of intelligence and wisdom.'" Unfortunately, Origen frequently speaks this offputting way. Similarly the stoic house-philosophers of Augustus (Kl., 102). Calvin, 2:21: "We always seek what is brilliant; and nothing seems more incongruous than that the heavenly Kingdom of the Son of God, its glory so magnificently extolled by the prophets, should consist of the offscourings and refuse of the people. And yet it is of God's wonderful purpose, that with the whole world in His hands, He prefers to choose His people from the humble masses [rather] than from the leaders who might adorn Christ's name with their excellence."

11:26 "Yes, Father, for this was your sovereign plan." The Father's plan, celebrated repeatedly in the Old Testament, is that "this is [the person] to whom I will look, [the one] that is humble and contrite in spirit, and trembles at my word" (Isa 66:2 RSV), and "thus says the high and lofty One, who inhabits eternity, whose name is Holy: 'I dwell in the high and holy place, and also with [the one] who is of a contrite and humble spirit, to revive the spirit of the humble, and to revive the heart of the contrite'" (Isa 57:15 RSV). The theme of both Testaments, the plan of the Great God, is to have spiritual fellowship with little people: "God opposes the proud, but gives grace to the humble" (Prov 3:34 LXX; 1 Pet 5:5; Jas 4:6); "Everyone who exalts himself shall be humbled and everyone who humbles himself shall be exalted" (Job 22:29; Prov 19:23; Ezek 21:26; Matt 5:3–6; 23:12; Luke 14:11; 18:14). This plan goes contrary to the expectation of elitist reason. To such reason it is the wise, the refined, the *rich* in spirit who deserve revelation. But by a divine paradox, the high and holy One is closer to the low and little ones than he is to the high and mighty, simply because (apparently) the little people need him more.

Here Matthew and Paul meet: "For since, in the wisdom of God, the world did not know God through wisdom, it pleased [*eudokēsen*, the same word used here at v 26] God through the folly of what we preach to save those who believe" (1 Cor 1:21 RSV). The words of Matthew's Jesus, "You have hidden these things from the wise *(sophōn)* and learned *(sunetōn)*" is echoed almost exactly by Paul's Corinthian quotation from Isaiah: "For it is written, 'I will destroy the wisdom of the wise *(sophian tōn sophōn)*, and the cleverness of the clever *(sunesin tou sunetōn)* I will thwart'" (1 Cor 1:19).

Thus both the Old Testament prophets and the New Testament apostles agree in God's great plan: to bless the little people. We have found this plan everywhere in Matthew's Gospel: from the genealogy's aliens through the Beatitudes' poor and the miracles' outcasts to our present text. "No one is so great that God needs him; none so little that God cannot reach him" (Schlatter).

The plan of God—it is the gospel itself—is to bless the poor in spirit, the mourning, the meek, the hungry for righteousness, the childlike, the little. The genuinely little people may not always be visible to the human eye, and may not always be exactly the people we think are little. Paul was little spiritually but he comes on awfully strong in his letters. Jesus was little pedagogically (11:29), but we have heard his thunder. Luther was little before God but not always before men. And some of God's little people around us today may not always strike us as exactly little in self-consciousness. Littleness, like faith, is often something only God can see, and we should be cautious in forming a Little Who's Who.

But while we cannot, by our own natural powers, make ourselves genuinely little or humble—we can only pray that we will be so made—we are served notice by the text before us, in case we feel especially sophisticated spiritually *(sophoi)*, intellectual, or theologically astute *(sunetoi)*: Look out! For exactly those with such self-consciousness are denied revelation. "Those who think they have God by the toe have the devil by the fist." The plan, then, is this: Those who feel their sin, are sorry for it, and come asking for help—these find in Jesus' Father open arms. Those who feel their spiritual brilliance, and are sorry for those who fall so far beneath them, who bask in self-importance—these find in Jesus' Father a back. "Yes, Father, for this was your sovereign plan."

Bonnard, 167, believes that the hiding and revealing of the sovereign God is the covering theme for chaps 11–13, and the key to understanding these three chapters. "It is not man, nor Jesus, but God who is the subject of [this hiding and revealing]; 11:26 . . . underline[s] this again strongly; the unbelief and faith that Jesus meets are not accidents nor are they the positive or negative results of [Jesus'] very personal efforts; the authority and the good pleasure of God govern his whole activity; that is the sense of [11:26]." Calvin, 2:22–23, stresses the sovereignty of God at work in these two verses of Jesus' thanksgiving—Jesus is thanking God for his sovereign grace, not believers for their voluntary humility, and "the Lord lays down for us the rule that we must regard as right whatever is pleasing to God." In the Augustinian-Reformation tradition, humility is not an attitude that earns God's grace; it is a gift of that grace. McNeile, 164, cites Johannes Weiss's opinion about how Jesus came to say what is recorded in vv 25–26, just reviewed, but McNeile dismisses Weiss's explanation as too subjective. I like what Weiss says: "'He [Jesus] had thought that his call to the Messiahship involved the huge burden of winning the whole nation; and yet the mass of them, especially the Scribes, remained so dull and unimpressionable! Was He the chosen of God after all? But the doubts melted away at this supreme moment. He realized that the secret of His Person was meant only for a few . . . , to whom it was especially revealed. And freed from the greater burden, He now understood that His work was to bring this revelation to the few.'" While Weiss's hypothesis may be too schematized and somewhat romantic ("His doubts melted away at this supreme moment"), I like Weiss's taking Jesus' humanity seriously ("he learned obedience through what he suffered," Heb 5:8). This interpretation tallies, too, with the human experience of Christian workers.

B. Jesus' Claim (11:27)

After his surprising thanksgiving—a kind of thanksgiving for failure—Jesus proceeds to unfold the content of revelation. He has, as it were, touched the *motives* of revelation in his thanksgiving; he will now describe the *meat* of revelation in his affirmation.

"Absolutely everything has been handed over to me by my Father; and no one really knows *(epiginōskei)* the Son except the Father, and no one really knows *(epiginōskei)* the Father except the Son and the one to whom the Son chooses to reveal him" (v 27).

At the heart of the revelation of truth is this simple fact: Everything of God has been placed in and revealed through Jesus the Son. The key to divine revelation is Jesus. I am reminded of Luther's advice in the first chapter of his Lectures on Galatians, to the effect: "Stop speculating about the Godhead and climbing into heaven to see who or what or how God is; hold on to this man Jesus, he is the only God we've got!" (See *LW* 26:28–29, on Gal 1:3.) In the light of Matthew's present text and of a multiplication of such texts elsewhere, especially in the literature of John, the church believes that we have all there is to have of God in Jesus and nowhere else. "Absolutely everything" *(panta,* "everything," placed at the head of the sentence, gives the word "everything" an absolute flavor) was handed over by the Father to his Son. Luther argues logically that, since in Isa 42:8 the Lord says "my glory I give to no other," it must follow that "to whomever He *does* give this glory [as here], that person must also be true God" (W², 7:833). As a master craftsman gives his son all the arts of his craft and his complete confidence and shop, so similarly God the Father has eternally given to his Son his full confidence and "shop," and all of this came to light in the history of Jesus of Nazareth. The eternally good relationship of the Father and the Son had a chance once in the middle of human history to be seen under klieg lights. The Son became the man Jesus and, ever since, history has been flooded with the knowledge of God. This knowledge is found nowhere else. No one else is the Father's natural Son; only "the" Son really knows the Father. All the rest of us who have come to know the Father have come to know him only through Jesus the Son; we are adopted sons and daughters; unlike the Son, we are children of God by grace not by nature, by election not by constitution.

According to Numbers 12:6–8, the OT prophets knew the Lord God through visions and dreams, while Moses knew this Lord mouth to mouth. But Jesus knows the Father heart to heart, our Matthew text tells us. "For," in Jerome's words (1:232) against the Arians, "it is one thing to know through equality of nature [as the Son knows the Father], and quite another thing to know through the dignity of revelation [as all others come to know Father and Son]" (cf. Chrys., 38:2:252 to the same effect). Jerome also shows, on the same page, that the "absolutely everything" the Father gives over to the Son does not mean a surrender of the Father's sovereignty; it means the gift of mediation, of exclusive mediation, to the Son as the one authorized way to the Father.

Bultmann, 358, considers vv 27–30 to be one of the several texts where Matthew "raises the stature of Jesus into the divine by using the appropriate expressions."

And "no one really knows the *Son* except the Father." Later on in this Gospel, when Peter comes to know who Jesus really is and confesses, "You are the Christ the Son of the living God" (16:16), Jesus immediately tells Peter the source of this most important knowledge: "You are a blessed person, Simon, Son of Jonah, because flesh and blood has not revealed this to you, but my *Father* who is in heaven" (16:17). Whenever a person comes finally like Peter to know who Jesus is—his ultimacy ("the Christ") and his divinity ("the Son of the living God") it is always and only because of Jesus' electing Father. "Flesh and blood," that is, our own human resources, do not deliver this precious cargo. When Jesus finally makes sense, when he is finally understood, the source of this knowledge is exclusively grace not works, the divine will not the human. ("To you [disciples] it has *been given [dedotai*, perfect passive] to know . . . ," 13:11.)

John the evangelist's great encomium comes to mind at this point. Speaking of those who have *become* children of God by receiving Jesus Christ and believing in his name, John immediately adds, "who were born [again] not of [hereditary] bloods [*sic*] nor by human will power nor by the will of any man, but *by God [alone]*" (John 1:13). Understanding Jesus Christ the Son—that is, *under*-standing him, submitting to him, receiving his claim, believing him—is gift. (Cf., classically, *The Scots Confession*, 1560, chap 12.)

As little as a human son has a part in effecting his physical birth, so little does a spiritual son have a part in effecting his spiritual birth: all birth is gift, and all spiritual birth is virgin birth. "For by grace you have been saved through faith; and this [grace, salvation, faith] is not your own doing, it is the *gift* of God" (Eph 2:8–9).

All the apostles felt it important to stress the awesome gift-character of knowing Jesus Christ lest humans take credit for what is not theirs—their becoming children of God. "What have you gotten that you have not received; and if you have received it, why do you boast as if you had not received it?" asks Paul (1 Cor 4:7) in one of Augustine's favorite texts against the Pelagians. If Peter confesses Jesus Christ rightly, if anyone receives Jesus Christ responsibly, it is a gift not of flesh and blood but of the heavenly Father.

This is not to suggest that the Father does not use human means to bring his Son to birth. He used the Blessed Virgin. He used his apostle-disciples: "He who receives *you* [apostle-disciples] receives me, and he who receives me receives him who sent me" (10:40). The Father also uses free human faith. But faith, too, as we have seen, is a gift. The knowledge of God comes *through* and *to* flesh and blood but not *from* it. Flesh and blood is the conduit and receptacle, not the spring. The words, "no one really knows the Son except the Father" and "flesh and blood has not revealed this to you" do not mean that the Father does not use human flesh and blood *means* to make the Son known; the words mean that these means are only means—their power, their "meaning-*full*-ness," their impact, is from the Father. (Cf. Cal., *Inst.*, IV. i and viii.)

Jesus' definition of revelation comes to its climax with the very exclusive (and for this reason perennially offensive) word: "and no one really knows the Father except the Son and the one to whom the Son chooses to reveal him" (v 27c). The only person who really knows God is Jesus Christ the Son. All other persons knowing God come to know God through the sovereign decision of this Son: "and the one to whom *the Son* chooses to reveal him." No one else knows God, *really* knows God. This is the offense of the cross, the scandal of particularity, the affront to all other religions, the wound to all human spiritual sensitivity and intellectual power; the Christian church must simply carry this offense around with her as part of the cross if she wishes to be faithful to the revelation given her by the Son.

The church has learned from Jesus to believe that the world and its religions have a general knowledge of God—a knowledge that God exists, for example. But mixed with this general "knowledge that" is a great deal of error and superstition. (Cf. especially the theological work of the Dutch missiologist Hendrik Kraemer.) Only the Son of God—Jesus Christ himself—really knows *who* God is—the Father. This is the singular claim of the text before us, unique in a way in the synoptic tradition (with Luke 10:22), pervasive in the Gospel of John (cf. John 3:35; 5:20; 7:29; 10:15; 13:3; 17:25). Only the Son *really* knows the Father. (The *epi*-intensifier placed before the verb to know, *ginōskei*, in our verse, makes "*really* know" the best translation.)

Luke 10:22 has the simple *ginōskei*, "knows," then adds, perfectly, "*who*" [*tis*]. Only the Son and his subjects know *who* the Father is.

This "no one but the Son *really* knows," or "knows *who* the Father is," makes sense, when one thinks about it in the light of John's Gospel. If Jesus alone is the only-begotten Son of God, Son by nature and in eternity, it figures that he alone really knows the Father. The shocking fact here in Matthew's Gospel is that Jesus claims to be this Son and to *have* this knowledge. But by now any serious reader of the Gospel will not find this claim difficult. Jesus does seem to be a man "uniquely near-stationed to God"; he does indeed seem to carry a kind of authority in his teaching (the Sermon on the Mount illustrates this), does indeed seem to give things that we ordinarily expect only deity to deliver (forgiveness of sins and raising the dead, for example). Finally, Christians find themselves compelled by the sheer outward power of Jesus' historical person and by the inward power of his Holy Spirit, to assent to Jesus' Lordship, to his complete deity, to his exclusive knowledge of the Father. It is not hard for a Christian to believe that only Jesus really knows the Father.

It *is* hard, however, for unbelievers, or even for some Christians, to believe that the only other persons who really understand the Father are those "to whom the Son chooses to reveal him." Does this mean that only Christians really know God? The Christian must come close to saying this. Of course the believer will have to permit God to have his own past, contemporary, and future Jobs and Namaans—pagans who are drawn to the true knowledge of God outside the company of God's explicitly called people (and cf. the encouragement of the immediately preceding paragraph, vv 10–24). But Christians will feel equally obliged to confess to all who ask them that they believe even the knowledge of God the Father *outside* the church is communicated through the Son who is the exclusive revealer of the Father. The classic Christian conviction is this: There is no knowledge anywhere of God the Father that is not mediated through God the Son and that is not brought into the individual heart through God the Holy Spirit. If God is the God revealed in Scripture, Christians feel they must say these things. "No one really knows the Father except the Son and the one to whom the Son chooses to reveal him."

Christians must also allow the Son, if he chooses, to reveal his Father to those outside Christendom. "There are many sheep outside the flock, and many wolves within" (Augustine). God is God and God is free, and while *we* are bound to God's revelation in Jesus Christ, God is not bound to *us*. God may reveal himself to whomever he chooses. But we still believe, instructed by this text, that only the Son makes the Father known anywhere.

When this has been said, the church would exhibit a false modesty if she should *deny* that, or be unsure if, all who believe and join her Christian fellowship have been given a true knowledge of God the Father. We believe that we have not been given to know any other place than the church where Jesus Christ reveals the Father. We say that God *can* reveal himself outside the church, and we leave that revelation exclusively to God's sovereign pleasure. But we confess that God *has* revealed himself to the human race classically and sufficiently, fully and savingly in the gospel of Jesus Christ, i.e., in the community of persons who hear that gospel—in the church.

A Reformation church that is truly catholic will confess no less readily than a Roman church that is truly catholic that as far as humans are given to know, "outside the church there is no salvation," *extra ecclesiam nulla salus.* Jesus Christ is exclusively present, as far as the church knows, in the gospel of Jesus Christ that is preached exclusively, as far as revelation allows us to know, in the church of Jesus Christ. Calvin's biblical rule in this connection was, "The secret things belong unto God; but the things that are revealed belong unto us and unto our children" (Deut 29:29).

The non-Christian world and many contemporary Christians find this claim unbearably arrogant. Catholic Christians, however, will have to say that to claim anything else is unbearably ingrate. The Father, at immense cost, gave *himself* to the world in the incarnation, death, and resurrection of Jesus Christ. To say that apart from this self-giving of God, God can still be known at other places and in other ways is to flaunt God's "One Great Hour of Sharing." We have not been authorized to say that there is salvation anywhere else than in faith in Jesus Christ, God's self-gift. We have not been empowered to preach to persons in the world that as long as they are sincere, that for as long as Hindus will be sincere Hindus, Buddhists sincere Buddhists, secularists sincere searchers, or atheists sincere servants of people, they will be saved. All of these salvations by sincerity bypass the one truly sincere thing that Christians believe has happened in history: the life, death, and resurrection of Jesus. *This* act of sincerity, we believe, got God; indeed, in this act of sincerity God gave himself to be gotten. And through the preaching of this *divine* sincerity we believe the Spirit prompts people everywhere to place their trust in the Father through the revelation of the Son and so to be saved. We know of no other way. (Contrast the more generous Vatican II texts, *Dogmatic Constitution on the Church,* 16, and *Pastoral Constitution on the Church in the Modern World,* 22 and below.)

We leave to God his secrets; we preach Christ. The catholic church will never tolerate "any other God" before the face of the one and only God she has been given to know.

This confession is "the offense of the cross," "the scandal," the unbearable hubris of true Christianity, and it cannot be shunned by any who are called to take their cross and follow Jesus. But when this has been firmly said, and it must be firmly said in the face of many modern denials even in Christendom, one must in fairness add that a great deal depends on *how* Christians assert the exclusiveness of Jesus Christ.

When indispensable Christian confession is given in such a way that the *confessor* seems to say in the confession that "there is no other religion quite like Christianity" or "no other persons quite like us Christians," or even, too smugly, "no other Savior like *our* Christ," a great deal of harm is done to the confession of Christ. When members of other religions are insulted, when members of other faiths are told that they are inferior to Christians, and their religion inferior to Christianity, that *they* are ignorant or of little account, then faithful witness to the One Savior has not been given.

Disciples must learn—and the Holy Spirit is able to teach disciples how—to honor Jesus Christ without dishonoring others. The God of Jesus Christ must be glorified, and this exclusive focusing of glory will of course involve, at least implicitly, the removing of glory from other gods, other saviors, and other ideologies, but it need not involve the explicit shaming of the adherents of other gods, saviors, and ideologies. It is a delicate matter, this bearing faithful witness to Christ without bearing faithless witness to other people. It calls for unusual tact to be bold for Christ without being base to others.

There will probably never be such a thing as a completely inoffensive witness to the exclusiveness of Jesus Christ. Jesus' career is evidence enough of this; his self-witness was not liked, and he got what the devout felt he deserved for making it. And disciples are not above their Lord. We must preach a crucified Christ as God's only way of salvation—ridiculous to the intellectually sophisticated and offensive to those with spiritual sensitivities—but to those called to believe this crucified Christ, Jesus is indeed the wisest thing God ever did, the most powerful reality we have ever experienced (1 Cor 1). But *how* this is said—not just *that* this is said—determines the authenticity of the witness.

"Absolutely everything has been handed over [*paredothē,* aorist passive] to me. . . ." When did this "handing over" occur? Allen, 122–23, makes a case for a pretemporal act and so for the preexistence of the Son. Allen also sees the problem with a preexistence interpretation: "Whether the words as originally uttered [by Jesus] involved consciousness of pre-existence is, no doubt, open to question. But it is difficult not to suppose that the editor of this Gospel interpreted them in this sense," and Allen then refers, serially, to the supernatural virgin birth (1:18–25), the infancy narrative's "out of Egypt I called my son" (2:15), the Father's direct voice of sonship at Jesus' baptism, the devil's specific contesting of this sonship in the temptations (4:3, 6), and Jesus' mysterious "I came" (5:17; 10:34). On these bases, Allen believes v 27 is best understood as referring to a preexistent Son and "since the Son was pre-existent with God it follows that no one knows the Son (i.e., knows fully) except the Father; and the reverse is equally true."

Albright-Mann's arguments for preexistence on the basis of this text, 145–46, strike me as weak. Stendahl, 784, argues against preexistence. For recent pro-preexistence interpretation of this text see Conz., 47; and Gund., 217–18. When Beare, 267, on the contrary, writes that "the entire passage should be regarded as a later construction of Christological speculation, not as an utterance of Jesus himself," he seems to me to overlook the good textual grounds for considering this an authentic saying of Jesus (e.g., the rare absolute use here of "the Son" as in Matt 24:36; Mark 13:32; Luke 10:22, the two former as unecclesiastical admissions of ignorance—cf. Allen, 123, and Gund., 218). Furthermore, in theological exegesis even the fact that a saying of Jesus *is* a later construction of the church does not argue against the saying's being the way that God wants us to hear Jesus. For, first, there is probably not one saying of Jesus in the New Testament that is "untouched by human hands," unedited by the church, and in these senses "late." Second, the fact that a saying of Jesus has become a text of Scripture is enough for the church to take the text with seriousness (a seriousness that involves by definition the use of the historical-critical method). Thus when a commentator tells us that a text is not a saying of Jesus but is a later church construction, I often doubt the commentator's "not . . . but" inference, because every saying of Jesus, and all divine revelation for that matter, comes to us wrapped in the always later convictions and constructions of Israel and the church.

C. Jesus' Invitation (11:28–30)

"'Come here to me all of you who are working hard and carrying too much, and I will refresh you. Here, take my yoke upon you, and learn from me, because I am gentle and simple at heart, and you will experience refreshing deep down in your lives. You see, my yoke is easy and my burden is light.'"

11:28 Of immediate interest is the fact that Jesus does not say come to *God*" and receive these promises. Instead, quite in keeping with the line that has been developed in this chapter and throughout the Gospel, he presents *himself* as the fully authorized representative of God. (Contrast Socrates, *Phaedo*, 91b: "If you will take my advice, you will think very little of Socrates and much more of the truth." For the New Testament, Jesus *is* the truth.) Without any mitigating self-consciousness or explanations, Jesus invites all troubled persons to *himself:* "Come here to *me* all of you who are working hard. . . ." In Jesus, God gets a face. Jesus invites us to *himself,* and we feel quite naturally that we are invited to God. The naturalness of this—that Jesus so easily makes us think God when he speaks of himself—can only be explained, finally, by the Nicene-Chalcedonian confessions that Jesus is God, *Deus verus.* By the time one has worked even this far into the Gospel it is not hard to believe that the church's creedal faith in the true deity and true humanity of Jesus Christ is a right faith.

Only a certain kind of person is invited by Jesus to himself—just as in the previous paragraph only a certain kind of person was rebuked by Jesus. Jesus invites those who are having a hard time of it, those for whom life is a "working hard" and who feel overwhelmed.

Bonnard, 169, translates the invitation: "Come to me all you who are fatigued and overwhelmed"; Barclay, 2:15: "Come to me, all you who are exhausted and weighted down beneath your burdens." Luther exclaims (W^2, 7), "Ah, what a strange invitation this is!" (834), for in it Jesus is saying, in effect, "my kingdom is a hospital for invalids" (837). *All* people experiencing hard times are explicitly invited by Jesus: "Come here to me, all *(pantes)* of you who . . . ," and Calvin, 2:25, comments, "the particle 'all' is to be noted . . . lest anyone should shut the door on himself by a perverted doubt."

The needy are those to whom Jesus has consistently addressed himself and for whom he is persistently there. ("The Lord upholds all who are *falling,* and raises up all *who are bowed down,*" Ps 145:14.) Jesus' invitation goes out to all those for whom religion has become a grind, for whom being good is laborious, to those, in a word, from whom the juice has gone out of life and all that is left is the rind. Jesus' heart goes out to such people. They are serious but discouraged; they want to be good and to please God and to help people but they feel quite selfish, quite "un-up" to the task, quite inadequate, and, finally, failures. ("Failure makes us fit to receive His grace," comments Calvin, 2:25.) Burdened with this sense of guilt and inadequacy, bowed down, tired out, Jesus appears and promises not only refreshment, but also equipment for carrying future burdens and duties.

11:29 "Here, take my yoke upon you. . . ." A yoke is a work-instrument. Thus when Jesus offers a yoke he offers what at first we might think tired workers least need. They need a mattress or a vacation, not a yoke. But Jesus realizes that the most restful gift he can give the tired is a new way to carry life, a new way of bearing responsibilities. For in the final analysis, realism sees that life simply is a succession of burdens; we cannot get away from them; thus instead of offering escape, Jesus offers equipment (cf. Schl., *Das,* 186; *Der* 386).

Jesus means that obedience to his teaching (which *is* the taking of his yoke) as that teaching is given us, for example, in his Sermon on the Mount—will develop in us a peace and a balance, a "way" of carrying life that will give more rest than we now find ourselves able to experience. To keep Jesus' commands by faith, as the teaching of Jesus everywhere beckons us to do, is to breathe with new freedom, live with new quality, and so—in Jesus' Word—to find oneself "refreshed."

The twelve step programs have discovered the relevance of Jesus' teaching for human health. In his fine essay on the law, Gutbrod, *nomos,* TDNT, 4:1060–1062, shows how Matt 11:28–30 both negates *and* affirms the OT law of God, for (1) in v 28 "Jesus pronounces these words precisely to those who are so burdened under the law that they no longer have any *anapausis* [rest]" (1060); and yet Jesus not only *lifts* the burden of the law, (2) in v 29 he *imposes* his own yoke (1062).

In Matthew's Gospel, Jesus is both the end of the law (as in Paul, Rom 10:4) *and* Jesus is our new commander. "The one yoke . . . gives place to another; *independent* and *gods* we can never be" (Stier in Beng., 1:172). Luther clearly saw this twofoldness—the free justification of the "come to me" and the costly cross of the "take my yoke"—and Luther believed that the bearing of the yoke was "the reason why people do not run to Christ" (W[2], 7:837–38).

Nor is Calvin afraid of ruining the grace of Jesus' "come" by the rigor of Jesus' "yoke": "When Christ has promised peaceful joy to those labouring wretchedly in their consciences, He tells them that He is the Deliverer *on condition* that they take His yoke upon them" (2:26, emphasis added). Davies, xvi, makes vv 28–30 the motto of his book and his frontispiece, to which he adds these words: "Matt 11:28–30: The quintessence of the Matthean interpretation of Christianity as Gospel and Law."

But while a yoke is a work-instrument and is best equated in context with Jesus' teachings, particularly with the Sermon on the Mount, the phrase that immediately follows the yoking is a phrase that brings us into an even more personal relation with Jesus: "Take my yoke upon you, *and learn from me.* . . ." It is important to notice that Jesus says "learn *from (ap')* me" not just "learn *about (peri)* me." This phrase does not mean that Jesus speaks to us mystically apart from his Word. It means that with the second phrase, "learn from me," Jesus is repeating his first phrase, "take my yoke," and adding a more personal sense to it. "Take my yoke" means "take Jesus' Word," and "learn from me" means "take Jesus' person" as he is present *in* his Word.

Perhaps a paraphrase can make the meaning more graphic: "Take my Sermon on the Mount upon you and let *me* speak to you through it" is the sense, or "Take my Word upon you and let me be your personal teacher through it." The personal "learn from me" existentializes Jesus' instrumental "take my yoke." For we are not just to take on a cold, memorized Word every morning as we set out to work; we are to commune with a living person through his Word.

"Learn from me" means that Jesus wants to be our personal Teacher, our living Tutor. After all, he *has* risen from the dead, he is alive; and he now offers to speak to us personally through his presence in his Word. Every time we listen to Christian exposition of the Word and attend to it with reverence we are receiving instruction from Jesus himself; every time we hear or read Scripture with piety we are sitting at Jesus' feet. The Lord's Supper is the most personal learning of all, for here Jesus even physically touches us.

Even more precisely, a yoke is not a sitting instrument; it is a walking instrument. Jesus does not say, "Take my chair and learn from me," he says, "Take my yoke and learn from me," which means that as we seek to *live* in simple obedience to Jesus we learn from Jesus. Jesus is an *itinerant* teacher and teaches best in movement. Other teachers prefer stationary listeners; Jesus prefers to teach en route, on the way, in the life-process. This action emphasis is quite Matthean.

Then Jesus appeals even more personally: "because I am gentle and simple at heart." We are told that rabbis and biblical teachers in Jesus' time were characterized by great strictness, discipline, and high purpose (rather like Professor Kingsfield in "The Paper Chase"). Schlatter says that the scribes were perfectionists (*Der*, 387–88). Allen, 124, says that the Pharisees' conception of religion made them disdainful of unlearned and common people. But Jesus does not describe his teaching office in austere terms; he presents himself as gentle and simple, as almost the exact opposite of his contemporary teachers. A teacher's manner is nine-tenths the teacher's impact. Jesus believes that his manner is a reason why studying with him brings refreshment. His gentlemanliness means that he will be patient with slow students, and thoughtful in correction; his simplicity at heart means that his relationship with the Father, a relationship characterized by warm mutual knowledge, will enable him to bend to the lowly who join his school. Jesus believes that persons who study with him will find that as they study his Word and seek to put it into practice they will find Jesus' gentlemanliness and simplicity relaxing and refreshing them. By contrast, Jesus rebukes the Bible teachers of his time because "they bind heavy burdens, hard to bear, and lay them on men's shoulders; but they themselves will not [even] move them with their finger" (23:4 RSV). Jesus' commands, however, are accompanied with Jesus' help.

Thus in the four clauses of Jesus' invitation we have something of a summary of the four ways Jesus has been presented to us so far in this Gospel: "Come here to me" (as I came to you, Matt 1–4), "take my yoke" (in the Sermon on the Mount, 5–7), "and learn from me" (through my grace by faith, as in the Ten Miracles and mission, 8–10) "because I am really gentle and simple at heart" (the person of the Six Portraits of chapters 11 and 12).

And to this "taking Jesus Christ seriously" (as we can summarize the combined lessons of the entire Gospel till now), Jesus now attaches a simple promise, "and you will experience refreshing deep down in your lives" (v 29c). Paul says this when he writes, "The just person shall *live* [really *live*] by faith" (Rom 1:17). Faith in Christ makes *alive*. After a while, as we have listened to Jesus and sought to obey his teachings in life, we find that his lessons are a better way to live, his gentleness is relaxing us, and his simplicity is refreshing us. We find that deep down in our lives—in our *psyches* (the actual word used here)—we feel refreshed and renewed. There are finally no techniques for the renewal of Christians or congregations; there is simply taking Jesus seriously in his Word. The refreshment, renewal, and quickening that Jesus promises here may indeed be, as Calvin, 2:26, believes, nothing else than "the free forgiveness of sins which alone gives us peace."

11:30 "You see, my yoke is easy and my burden is light." How can Jesus in one place describe the way that leads to life as narrow and hard (7:14) and yet here call his yoke easy and light? Is the Sermon on the Mount both hard *and* easy? And are the duties that Jesus has imposed so far in this Gospel really light? The solution to this paradox, or even contradiction, must certainly be the reality of the risen Christ himself. It is he who, alive, makes the Sermon on the Mount a delight for believers and who makes his tough commands, somehow (frequently by experiencing the bitterness of *not* keeping them) light. The yoke of *not* living Jesus' hard way is harder living, really (thus Chrys., 38:3:252–53, too). For Christians everywhere and at all times finally have to confess that being a Christian is, indeed, a good way to live—and this in spite of the toughness of Jesus' commands. "His commandments are not burdensome" (1 John 5:3).

Since love of *any* subject makes all things connected with it finally easy ("Love makes all [things] . . . easy," as Augustine, *Serm.*, 20(70):1–3:317, shows with several human examples), love of the Lord, too, makes living for him finally easy. "He who has love in his breast has spurs in his sides." Christ is he whom to serve is to reign, *Christus cui servire est regnare* (McN., 167). "Make me a captive, Lord, and then I shall be free."

All high experiences are *both* difficult and delightful. The Christian experience is in this case similar. In a sense, it is precisely the difficulty of Jesus' Sermon on the Mount that makes Christian discipleship invigorating; and it is the personal presence of Jesus himself that takes the burdensomeness out of the rigor. The simple secret of the church is nothing else than the living Lord Jesus Christ, whose companionship we experience by faith in the Word in his community.

"And he said, 'My presence will go with you, and I will give you rest'" (Exod 33:14 RSV).

"He makes me lie down in green pastures, He leads me beside the waters of rest; He restores my soul" (Ps 23:2–3, Hebrew).

"For I will satisfy the weary soul, and every languishing soul I will replenish" (Jer 31:25 RSV).

"I myself will be the shepherd of my sheep, and I will make them lie down, says the Lord God. I will seek the lost, and I will bring back the strayed, and I will bind up the crippled, and I will strengthen the weak" (Ezek 34:15–16 RSV).

*   *   *

In the eleventh chapter we have walked through the first wing of Matthew's gallery of six portraits. In Jesus' long "Sermon on John" (vv 1–19) we saw Jesus as Christ; in Jesus' "Woes to Impenitent Cities" in the middle of the chapter (vv 20–24) we saw Jesus as Judge; and in the final portrait (vv 25–30), Jesus offered himself as Savior. To be more precise, we may say that in this chapter Jesus has been present to doubters and the wavering as the long-promised Christ, to the impenitent and self-sufficient as the coming Judge, and to the overwhelmed and weary as the present Savior. Jesus is the divinely given answer to the great questions of, respectively, the past, the future, and the present—as Messiah, Judge, and Savior.

*   *   *

The *Solus Christus* and the *Extra Ecclesiam Nulla Salus* Teachings of Reformation Confessional Theology

Reformation theology revels in the all-sufficiency of Jesus Christ, the doctrine of "Christ Alone" *(solus Christus)*. In the Lutheran Confessions this doctrine is most prominent in the controversy with the Roman cult of saints, but it is also "the first and chief article" of Luther's personal faith, *The Smalcald Articles,* Part II, art. 1. Christ alone is also the principal doctrine everywhere in the Reformed, Calvinist tradition.

The direct corollary of faith in Christ alone is the conviction that, in history and as far as we can know, Christ is found in the church alone: that "outside the church there is no salvation," *extra ecclesiam nulla salus.* I will document these two teachings in order.

A. *Solus Christus* (Christ Alone)

The whole purpose of Matthew 11, as we have seen, is to propose Jesus as Savior. Nowhere have I seen the full meaning of Jesus as Savior in all his biblical exclusivity more beautifully spelled out than in two consecutive questions in *The Heidelberg Catechism* (1563).

"Question 29. Why is the Son of God called JESUS, which means SAVIOR?

"Answer. Because he saves us from our sins, and because salvation is to be sought or found *in no other.*

"Question 30. Do those who seek their salvation and well-being from saints, by their own efforts, or by other means really believe in the *only [einigen]* Savior Jesus?

"Answer. No. Rather, by such actions they deny Jesus, the *only* Savior and Redeemer, even though they boast of belonging to him. It therefore follows that either Jesus is not a *perfect* Savior, or those who receive this Savior with true faith must possess in him *all* that is necessary for their salvation" (emphasis added).

The *Second Helvetic Confession* (1566) teaches the same truth with a comparable emphasis in chapter 11, entitled "Of Jesus Christ, True God and Man, the Only Savior of the World."

The *Theological Declaration of Barmen* (1934) was written specifically to prevent the compromising of the *solus Christus* with national, social, or political enthusiasms. The first and third theses of *Barmen* say *solus Christus:*

"1. 'I am the way, and the truth, and the life; *no* one comes to the Father, but by *me*' (John 14:6). 'Truly, truly, I say to you, he who does not enter by *the* [singular = the single] door but climbs in by *another way*, that man is a thief and a robber. . . . I am the door' . . . (John 10:1, 9).

"Jesus Christ, as he is attested for us in Holy Scripture, is the *one* Word of God which we have to hear and which we have to trust and obey in life and in death. . . .

"3. . . . We reject the *false doctrine* [that] the Church [could be] permitted to abandon the form *[Gestalt]* of its message and order to its own pleasure or to changes in prevailing ideological *[weltanschauliche]* and political convictions" (emphases added).

B. *Extra Ecclesiam Nulla Salus* (Outside the Church No Salvation)

Luther's view of the ministry of the church is notoriously high. In the *Large Catechism* (1529), Luther explains the third article of the Creed—"I believe in the Holy Spirit, the holy Christian church," etc.—in this way, in part: "In other words, [the Holy Spirit]*first* leads us into his holy community, placing us upon the bosom of the *church*, where he preaches to us and brings us to Christ. . . .

". . . where Christ is not preached there is no Holy Spirit to create, call, and gather the Christian church, and *outside it [the church] no one can come to the Lord Christ.* . . .

"But *outside the Christian church* (that is, where the Gospel is not) *there is no forgiveness*, and hence no holiness. . .

"All this, then, is the office and work of the Holy Spirit, to begin and daily to increase holiness on earth through these *two means, the Christian church and the forgiveness of sins.* Then, when we pass from this life, he will instantly perfect our holiness and will eternally preserve us in it by means of the last two parts of the [third] article [that is, the resurrection of the body and the life everlasting]. . . .

"This, then, is the article [of the Creed] which must always remain in force. Creation is past and redemption is accomplished, but the Holy Spirit carries on his work unceasingly until the last day. For this purpose he has appointed *a community on earth*, through which he speaks and does all his work."

Calvin also has a high doctrine of the church, especially preserved in the moving first chapter of the fourth book of his *Institutes* (1559–60) on "The True Church with which as Mother of All the Godly We Must Keep Unity," a chapter that can be read profitably and frequently by church teachers. A few excerpts will illustrate Calvin's churchmanship: for those to whom God is Father the church is mother (section 1) and thus "no hope of future inheritance remains to us unless we have been united with all other members [of Christ's body the church] under Christ, our head" (2); "so powerful is participation in the church that it keeps us in the society of God" (3); "our weakness does not allow us to be dismissed from her school until we have been pupils all our lives. Furthermore, away from her bosom one cannot hope for any forgiveness of sins or any salvation" (4); "the Lord esteems the communion of his church so highly that he accounts as a traitor and apostate from Christianity anyone who arrogantly leaves any Christian society, provided it cherishes the true ministry of Word and sacraments" (10).

In his *Geneva Catechism* (1541, emphasis added), Calvin summarized his high doctrine of the church in his discussion of the third article of the Creed ("I believe in the Holy Spirit," etc.) in this way: "104. Why [is] . . . this article [about "forgiveness of sins"] *after* the Church? [Answer:] "Because no man obtains pardon for his sins without being previously incorporated into the people of God, persevering in unity and communion with the Body of Christ in such a way as to be a true member of the Church."

The *Scots Confession* (1560) continues the Reformation high ecclesiology in chapter 16 on "The Kirk." The *extra ecclesiam* teaching in the middle of the chapter is particularly interesting. "As we believe in *one* God, Father, Son, and Holy Ghost, so we firmly believe that from the beginning there has been, now is, and to the end of the world shall be, *one Kirk*, that is to say, *one* company and multitude of men chosen by God, who rightly worship and embrace him by true faith in Christ Jesus, who is the *only Head* of the Kirk, even as it is the body and spouse of Christ Jesus. This Kirk is *catholic, that is, universal*, because it contains the chosen of all ages, of all realms, nations, and tongues. . . . *Out of this Kirk there is neither life nor eternal felicity.* Therefore we utterly abhor the blasphemy of those who hold that men who live according to equity and justice shall be saved, no matter what religion they profess. For since there is neither life nor salvation without Christ Jesus; so shall none have part therein but those whom the Father has given unto his Son Christ Jesus, and those who in time come to him, avow his doctrine, and believe in him" (emphases added).

The *Second Helvetic Confession* (1566) puts the doctrine just as emphatically but, with a judiciousness typical of this confession, it adds an important qualification. "OUTSIDE THE CHURCH OF GOD THERE IS NO SALVATION. But we esteem fellowship with the true Church of Christ so highly that we deny that those can live before God who do not stand in fellowship with the true Church of God, but separate themselves from it. For as there was no salvation outside Noah's ark when the world perished in the flood; so we believe that *there is no certain salvation outside Christ*, who offers himself to be enjoyed by the elect *in the Church;* and hence we teach that those who wish to live ought not to be separated from the true Church of Christ.

"THE TRUE CHURCH IS NOT BOUND TO ITS SIGNS. Nevertheless, by the signs [of the true Church] mentioned above, we do not so narrowly restrict the Church as to teach that all those are outside the Church who either do not participate in the sacraments, at least not willingly and through contempt, but rather, being forced by necessity, unwillingly abstain from them or are deprived of them; or in whom faith sometimes fails, though it is not entirely extinguished and does not wholly cease; or in whom imperfections and errors due to weakness are found. For *we know that God had some friends in the world outside the commonwealth of Israel"* [emphases added, chap 17].

The *Pastoral Constitution on the Church in the Modern World (Gaudium et Spes)* (1965), the Second Vatican Council's final constitution, put the matter in a provocative way in two striking sentences, and I will emphasize critical words: "All this [about the way of salvation through Christ] holds true not only for Christians, but for *all* men of good will in whose hearts grace works in an unseen way. For, since Christ died *for* all men, and since the ultimate vocation of man is in fact one, and divine, we ought to believe that the Holy Spirit in a manner known only to God offers *to* every man the possibility of being associated *[consoscientur]* with this paschal mystery" (22). The Council changed the final verb from the human active *se consoscient* to the divine passive *consoscientur*—i.e., from persons actively "associating *themselves*" with salvation to, instead, *God's* enabling a "*being* associated" with salvation—thus making it clear that the only real agent of salvation is God and that the paschal mystery of salvation can only "be received" (cf. Ratzinger, *Commentary on the Documents of Vatican II*, 5:162). The editors of Abbott's *The Documents of Vatican II* comment on the above two sentences of the constitution in this way: "This statement ratifies traditional interpretations of the well-known dictum: '*Extra Ecclesiam nulla salus*'" (222 n.67). *Gaudium et Spes*, 22 is an improvement on the semi-Pelagian *Lumen Gentium*, 16.

But the peril of even this more careful formulation is that the secret work of the Spirit will be used unevangelically to relativize the historic work of Christ, as we saw liberation theology doing above (pp 156–59), and then the mission of the Spirit, which is precisely to glorify Christ, suffers harm. It is wisest to proceed without too much emphasis on, or positive proclamation of, the secret work of the Spirit, which is little of our business and even less of our knowledge for, again, "the secret things belong to the Lord our God; but the things that are *revealed* belong to us and to our children for ever" (Deut 29:29 RSV).

Chapter Twelve
The Fire Christ
The Doctrine of Christ the Judge

IN CHAPTER 11 WE SAW MAINLY the compassionate Christ as Messiah, Judge, and Savior. In chapter 12 we are introduced to the controversial Christ as Lord, King, and Kinsman. First the Low Christ, then the High; first the compassionate Christ, then the controversial; first the Fish, then the Fire.

Three controversies dominate and determine the twelfth chapter: (1) the introductory Sabbath Controversy, covering almost half the chapter (vv 1–21); (2) the Spirit Controversy, occupying the large central section of the chapter (vv 22–37); and (3) the Sign Controversy, concluding the chapter (vv 38–50). In this chapter Jesus is at war. He is almost entirely the Baptizer with Fire.

All commentators see controversy as the activity and Pharisees as the audience uniting the stories of chap 12 (cf. Schn., 155; Allen, xvii, 125; Bult., 40 nn. 1–2, 147, 356; Schw., 275). Mark's first great controversy discourse (with five particular controversy stories) covers the large and programmatic section of Mark 2:1—3:6. Matthew took the first three Mark controversies (about forgiveness, fellowship, and fasting) and placed them in Matthew 9, inserted two chaps in between (chap 10's Sermon on Mission and chap 11's Sermon on John with additions), and then put together three more Markan controversy stories (on Sabbath, spirits, and signs) to form our present twelfth chap. There are thus two great controversy chaps in the first half of Matthew's Gospel— chaps 9 and 12—as there are two main controversy chaps in the last half—22 (the chap of questions) and 23 (The Sermon of Woes). In a sense, the entire Gospel is one long controversy between God's Son and false religious leadership.

Technically, there are eight pericopes (or paragraphs) in this chap (Bonn., 171): the first three can be subsumed under the Sabbath Controversy (cf., e.g., Gund.,   220); the middle two make up the two parts of the long Spirit Controversy (thus most commentaries); and the last three can be grouped together as parts of the Sign Controversy. There is artificiality in this grouping, but teaching considerations compensate.

I. THE SABBATH-LORD: THE SABBATH CONTROVERSY (12:1–21)

A. The First Incident: Picking Grain (12:1–8)

"At that time Jesus walked on the Sabbath through the grainfields; and his disciples were hungry and began picking ears of grain and eating them. The Separate saw this and said to Jesus, 'Look, your disciples are doing what it is not biblical to do on the Sabbath.' And he said to them, 'Haven't you read what David did when he and his companions were hungry? How he went right into the house of God and ate the very Bread of the Presence, which it was not right for David or his companions to eat? Only priests had this right. Or haven't you read in the law that on the Sabbath the priests in the temple defile the Sabbath [by working on it] and

yet they are guiltless? But I tell you, more than the temple is here! And if you only knew what the verse means that says "I want mercy and not sacrifice" you would not have condemned the innocent. For the Son of Man is Lord of the Sabbath.'"

The opening story of this chapter presents Jesus to us in his grandeur. With a sovereign freedom Jesus exalts himself above all those realities that the people of God held dearest: the Sabbath day, the sanctuary temple, and the Scripture law. Jesus says for the first time those mysterious words, to be heard three times in this chapter, "More . . . is here," or "a greater is here," referring indirectly in each case to the majesty of his person (or what is the same thing, referring to the mystery of the kingdom present in his ministry).

12:1–2 Actually, in Matthew's rendering it is not Jesus himself who is challenged for eating grain on the Sabbath day; it is *the hungry disciples* who are accused ("his disciples . . . began picking"; "look, your *disciples* are doing . . . ," vv 1–2). The Separate accost Jesus because Jesus is the disciples' Master and thus responsible for their conduct. Did Jesus sit loose to Scripture, was he indifferent to its reverent application? The Scripture at its highest place—in the Ten Commandments—said clearly "but on the Sabbath Day you shall not do *any* work." Yet here the disciples are doing on the Sabbath what laborers did the other six days, picking grain. So for the sake of the community's morals and even more deeply for the sake of the honor of God as revealed in Scripture, this careless practice must stop.

Freedom *from* the law is Paul's emphasis; freedom *within* the law is Matthew's emphasis, when the law is messianically interpreted by Jesus (cf., e.g., esp. Paul's Rom 3:31 and 10:4 on the one hand, and Matt 5:17–20 and 17:24–27 on the other). Strangely, tragically, a biblical seriousness anxious to *protect* the Bible's message can, as the Sabbath-controversies classically illustrate, *destroy* that message by a false zeal for Scripture. All of us who wish to take the Bible seriously should let ourselves be warned by Jesus' Sabbath controversies in Israel. I shall regularly call the Pharisees the "Separate," "Separatists," or the "Serious" in order in the first two cases to approximate the probable meaning of the word "Pharisees," and in order in the third case (the Serious) to indicate their nature more fairly than long usage of the word "Pharisee" has accustomed us to hearing.

Jesus counterattacks on his opponents' chosen ground—Scripture. The Separate have said that the disciples are doing something that "is not biblical" (or right) (*ouk exestin*) to do. But with three swift parries Jesus drives them back to their Bibles: "haven't you read?" (v 3), "haven't you read in the law?" (v 5), and "if you only knew what that verse means . . . 'I want mercy . . .'" (v 7). Their strong suit was Bible knowledge. But in quick succession Jesus pulls a Davidic example out of the historical books (1 Sam 21:1–6), a priestly example out of the law (Num 28:9–10), and a prophetic saying out of the prophets (Hos 6:6), to show the people of God that they have more freedom under Scripture than their teachers gave them.

12:3–4 The first example is taken from the life of a central figure of the old revelation, David himself, the great type of the Messiah. When David and his men were hungry they had had the audacity to go right into the holy place, take the holy Bread of the Presence, and eat it. And the Old Testament text does not berate them for their act (1 Sam 21:1–6). The meaning of the ancient text seems to be that in extreme situations people are permitted to take even the holiest of things and use them. At certain times there is, in fact, "a God-pleasing trespassing of the commandment" (Schl., *Der,* 394). Yet the Serious would certainly have countered, "It was a life and death necessity for David and his men to eat, but your disciples are not even in a remotely similar situation; they are in no danger of starvation. And besides, David is David—who are you?! And finally, what do any of your arguments have to do with *Sabbath* observance?"

Can a man say one moment, "Whoever loosens up even one of the least of these commands,   . . will be called 'Least' in the kingdom of heaven" (5:19) and then the next moment proceed to relax one of the Ten Commandments himself? More to the point, what has David's act *in extremis* to do with the disciples' on a stroll? But the David story is used only as a parry, as an interesting example of David's freedom under the law, from the law. Jesus will drive home his point more deeply by his second illustration. (The example of David, because it was not found in one of the five books of the law, and because its force was inferential rather than prescriptive, was called *haggada,* a less weighty form of argument than *halacha*— prescriptive law—which now follows.)

12:5 "Or haven't you read in the law that on the Sabbath the priests in the temple defile the Sabbath [by working on it] and yet they are guiltless?" The earlier David example had not directly touched the Sabbath or sacred day question; it had really touched only the sacred food question, and so had been, as we saw, preliminary, haggadic, and inconclusive. But both the law (*halacha,* cf. Lev 24:8–9) and experience told even the obdurate in Israel that *priests* could work on the Sabbath and not be guilty. (Indeed, priestly duties were doubled on the Sabbath, Num 28:9, cf. Swete, 49.) If one wanted to press the fourth commandment, as the Separate seemed often to do, it says "you shalt not do *any* work" on the Sabbath. Yet Israel knows that priests who work on the Sabbath are clean. Jesus shares Israel's conviction that priests can work on the holy day and, in this sense, "profane" it because the *place* where they work—the temple—overcomes the *act* of their work, and so cancels guilt. (The fundamental text in the rabbinic tradition was Mishnah Shabbath 132b: "Temple-service suppresses Sabbath-observance," cf. Str.-B., 1:620ff; Kl., 105.)

12:6 Jesus is getting closer and closer to his main point. And it is this, "But I tell you, more than the temple is here!" Finally, Jesus' arguments hold together: if place covers act, if temple sanctifies Sabbath, then it follows that a *greater* than the temple can, with even more right, cover, sanctify, and validate Sabbath work. Jesus claims to be that greater one. Now we see why Jesus could use his David example with impunity. David certainly did not consider himself greater than the temple. But Jesus considers himself to be. Therefore, if *David* had freedom in holy things, "great David's greater Son" has more freedom. And therefore, finally, the disciples of this greater-than-temple-and-David can do whatever this greater one permits them to do.

For this hierarchical argument, a rabbinical method called "the light and the heavy," see Beng., 1:173; Allen, 127f; Gund., 223–24. Jesus, as Bengel noticed, does not say "*I* am greater than the temple"—he is "lowly in heart" (11:29); nor, as Bornkamm and Gundry point out, does Jesus say that he is greater than the law—indeed (cf. Davies, 456–57) Jesus appeals *to* the law. But the majestically indirect "more than the temple is here" indicates to believers that Jesus has taken the place of both temple and Torah. He is their Lord. This claim, when perceived, leads both to Jesus' crucifixion and to his rule in the hearts of God's people. "Matthew turns the [Sabbath] dispute into a Messianic affirmation" (McK., 84). The real theme of each controversy story is the *person* of Christ.

12:7 "And if you only knew what the verse means that says 'I want mercy and not sacrifice' you would not have condemned the innocent." For a third time Jesus takes the Bible out of the Bible believers' hands and thrusts it home. It is as though Jesus were saying, "The *point* of the law is not the scrupulous self-sacrifice you derive from it; it is the wide-hearted humanity the prophets make of it. 'I desire mercy and not sacrifice' means I desire heart not will, human sympathy not superhuman disciplines, personalism not perfectionism."

Bonnard, 171, translates, "It is mercy that I want and not religious exercises" (*et non les pratiques religieuses*). The Greek word translated "sacrifice" in our English versions, *thusia*, "is figurative of obedience to the letter of the law at any cost," McN., 169. G. Barth, 82–83, believes that the meaning of Hos 6:6 in Jesus' teaching ("mercy, not sacrifice") is that the God of the Bible is primarily the kind one rather than primarily the one making demands. It is Strecker's merit to have shown, however, that demand cannot be moved from the center of Matthew's Gospel without violence. To be sure, Matthew's Gospel gives us a Jesus in whom kindness everywhere envelops demand. The commands of the Sermon on the Mount, for example, are preceded by Jesus' kind Beatitudes, and they are followed by his gracious Lord's Prayer. When demand is surrounded by kindness, the church teaches Jesus' narrow way appropriately: "Come here to me all you who are working hard" (kindness), "take my yoke upon you" (demand), "and learn from me, for I am gentle" (kindness) (vv 28–30). This is the evangelical model. (Cf. 28:18–20 for another prominent example of the demand within kindnesses structure.)

In the evangelicalism with which I am familiar the emphasis on discipline has at times gotten out of hand. Such emphasis is sometimes placed on the disciplines of devotions, Bible study, prayer, fellowship, and witnessing or personal evangelism, that these good obediences begin to obscure simpler ones such as honest conversation with another person (without the attempt to bring the conversation to Christ), openness to the opinion of others, time for perhaps unstrategic persons (such as parents and family), fidelity to the (sometimes unimpressive) local and institutional church, readiness to be of simple help to people around, concern for social justice in the several communities to which we are responsible, and the like. People are eclipsed by disciplines in some forms of disciplined Christianity.

This paragraph has been Jesus' interpretation of the Sabbath commandment. It has been the equivalent of a "but I say unto you" antithesis (cf. chapter 5). The Sabbath commandment is really kept when its inner meaning is kept. Jesus Christ, and no longer the law—or more precisely in Matthew's spirit, Jesus' mercy-interpretation of the law—must "dominate," be *Dominus,* Lord, in the lives of the people of God.

Even if the final saying of the paragraph, "the Son of Man is Lord of the Sabbath" (v 8) is a creation of the early Christian community rather than a word of the historical Jesus—thus, e.g., Colpe, TDNT, 8:452—believers are not daunted because believers, by definition, *believe* that the risen Lord Jesus inspired the early church to interpret the real meaning of Jesus' historical words. Even a saying that careful scholarship shows convincingly to be "inauthentic," or a church construction rather than an actual utterance of the historical Jesus—and there are many such—turns out sometimes to be the most illuminating saying in the text. The largest example of this is the Gospel of John— almost every saying in it is from, or is decisively shaped by the Johannine church under the risen Lord—and yet for many, John's Gospel is the most illuminating book in the Bible.

The short meaning of the first story in the Sabbath Controversy is that Jesus is Lord.

*   *   *

The Reformation Interpretation of the Sabbath

The Reformers had a remarkable freedom in their understanding of the Sabbath. They refused to see the Old Testament Sabbath law carried over into the New Testament. Here they were simply being faithful to the spirit of Jesus' Sabbath controversy. Two texts of the apostle Paul, moreover, severely criticized any slavish observance of certain days or seasons as more holy than others. "How can you turn back again to the weak and beggarly elemental spirits, whose slaves you want to be once more? *You observe days, and months, and seasons, and years!* I am afraid I have labored over you in vain" (Gal 4:9–11 RSV). "Therefore let no one pass judgment on you in questions of food and drink or with regard to a festival or a new moon *or a sabbath.* These are only a shadow of what is to come; but the substance belongs to Christ" (Col 2:16–17 RSV; cf. also Rom 14:5).

The official Lutheran understanding of the matter is put beautifully in *The Augsburg Confession* (1530).

"The Scriptures, not the church, abrogated the Sabbath, for after the revelation of the Gospel all ceremonies of the Mosaic law can be omitted. [Nevertheless, for the sake of order and worship, Sunday as the Lord's Day was substituted by the church for the Saturday Sabbath] . . . and it seems that the church was the more pleased to do this for the additional reason that men would have an example of Christian liberty and would know that the keeping neither of the Sabbath nor of any other day is necessary" (art. 28:59–60, Latin version).

Luther's *Small Catechism* (1529) has the whole Sabbath commandment revolve entirely around hearing the preached Word, not around work or rest. Thus the Sabbath commandment, in one clear sentence, means that "we should fear and love God, and so we should not despise his *Word* and the *preaching* of the same, but deem it holy and gladly hear and learn it."

Calvin has a clear understanding of the priorities, too. He discussed the Sabbath commandment at length in the first edition of his later monumental *Institutes*—the 1536 *Institution of the Christian Religion* (1:13, with my emphases).

"There is absolutely no doubt that this [Sabbath commandment] was a foreshadowing, and enjoined upon the Jews during the era of ceremonies, in order to represent to them under outward observance the spiritual worship of God. Therefore at the coming of

Christ, who is the light of snadows and the truth of the figures, it was *abolished*, like the remaining shadows of the Mosaic Law, as Paul clearly testifies (Gal 4:8–11; Col 2:16–17)."

But, Calvin continues, the central truth of the Sabbath commandment is retained: we are to seek our rest in the Lord by a decisive repentance (1:13). And we Christians observe the Lord's Day now, but in a special and nonlegalistic way:

"[The Lord's Day] was *not* established for us to hallow it before all others, that is to count it more holy. For this is the prerogative of God alone, who has honored all days equally (Rom 14:5). But it was established for the church to gather for prayers and praises of God, for hearing the Word, for the use of the sacraments" (1:14).

At the same time, Calvin is eager to avoid what he calls "crass and carnal sabbatarian superstition" (1:14), and he refers to Isaiah for proof (Isa 1:13–15; 58:13).

The Reformed tradition that followed Calvin was less theologically free than Calvin (who honored the New Testament's liberty), but it was pedagogically faithful to the Reformer's practical intentions. "Question. What does God require in the fourth [i.e., Sabbath] commandment? Answer. First, that the ministry of the gospel and Christian education be maintained, and that I diligently attend church, especially on the Lord's day, to hear the Word of God, to participate in the holy Sacraments, to call publicly upon the Lord, and to give Christian service to those in need. Second, that I cease from my evil works all the days of my life, allow the Lord to work in me through his Spirit, and thus begin in this life the eternal Sabbath" (*Heidelberg Catechism*, [1563], Q. 103).

The Second Helvetic Confession (1566), 24:5:224–25, moves along the same lines: the Lord's Day exists for (1) church meetings and (2) for rest, but with an explicit disavowal of superstitious sabbatarian legalism.

But when we reach *The Westminster Confession of Faith* (1647), chap 21, a Protestant scholasticism has set in and, with all the good that is said, an unevangelical stringency has taken root. *The Westminster Shorter Catechism* (1647) summarizes the new, stricter position: "Question 60. How is the Sabbath to be sanctified? Answer. The Sabbath is to be sanctified by a holy resting all that day, even from such worldly employments and recreations as are lawful on other days; and spending the whole time in the public and private exercises of God's worship, except so much as is to be taken up in the works of necessity and mercy." *Chariots of Fire!*

B. The Second Incident: A Healing (12:9–14)

"And when Jesus left that place he came into their synagogue. And look, there was a man with a withered hand. And the Separate asked Jesus, 'Is it biblical to heal on the Sabbath?' They asked this question because they wanted to trap him. But Jesus said to them, 'What human being is there in your group who has just one sheep, sees it fall into a pit on the Sabbath day, and does not immediately grab it and pull it out? Thus a human being is worth a lot more than a sheep. So it is biblical on the Sabbath day to do the right thing.' Then Jesus said to the man, 'Stretch out your hand.' And the man stretched it out, and it became completely well just like his other hand. The Separate left and held a meeting against Jesus to find how they could destroy him."

This is the second straight Sabbath controversy story. In the first, Jesus defeated his enemies by piling Scripture on top of Scripture until the inhuman Bible-faith of the Separate was put in its place. In the present story Jesus argues from experience and common sense.

12:9–10 The opening question has the same key phrase that appeared in the center of the first incident in this chapter, "Is it biblical?" "Is it biblical on the Sabbath to heal?" Matthew tells us that this question was asked to trap Jesus. It was the conviction of the religious leadership that the Sabbath law forbidding work meant that only life-threatening sicknesses should be treated on the Sabbath day. The man's withered hand posed no such threat to life (Str.-B, 1:623).

An answer that would have protected Jesus' orthodoxy and revealed his piety would have been an answer like this: "I believe that it is biblical to treat serious cases on the Sabbath, but I believe that all other cases, out of reverence for God's Word, can wait twenty-four hours." Jesus, then, would have turned to the man with the withered hand and said something like this, "My heart goes out to you with your hand like that. But I love God and want to obey his clear command. And in order that you might know that I love you, too, let me invite you to come to my place immediately after sundown, when the Sabbath is over, and I will help you." This answer would have made Jesus more acceptable to the leadership of the old people of God.

Why did Jesus not give this answer? Apparently because Jesus did not like the casuistry that used Scripture as an even twenty-four hour cover for insensitivity to human need. ("He who takes a man's life is guilty of doing evil, but those who do not trouble to help the needy are little different from murderers," Cal., 2:32; cf. this same conviction in the Calvinist Scots Confession, chap 14.)

Jesus did not like the legerdemain by which a command intending the welfare of persons—Sabbath rest, a "holi-day" for workers, a command devoted to community renewal—could be turned into a command for religious showing-off, a day, really, for revealing distinctions in consecration. For Jesus, the supreme affront was that *God* was used as the pretext for this parading—as if the saving God who gave the Sabbath command wanted to be placed on hold, at least for twenty-four hours, while human beings hurt.

But scrupulosity was not the purpose of the divine labor law that is the Sabbath commandment. The purpose of the commandment was the refreshment of working people. The commandment goes to great pains to stipulate that not only masters and mistresses of the house were to rest on the Sabbath, but also "your manservant and your maidservant, your ox (!), . . . or any of your cattle" (Deut 5:12–15; cf. Exod 20:8–11). Even the animals are to have a day off, so inclusive, so mundane, is God's mercy. One divine purpose of the Sabbath command is clearly health. But now this command was being marshaled by the Serious for postponing health so that a stringent God could get all required attention. Jesus had not been able to read the command that way; he had seen a different God in its words. (Schniewind, 157, points out that in the Sermon on the Mount Jesus had authoritatively interpreted and set himself over the sixth, seventh, and eighth commandments of the Decalog—against murder, adultery, and theft; now Jesus shows himself Lord also of the fourth, Sabbath, commandment.)

12:11 This time, rather than use the Bible, Jesus used experience to attack his opponents' mistaken Bible obedience. He asked, if one of them with only one little sheep should find that sheep in a hole, even on the Sabbath day, wouldn't he immediately pull it out? Luke in his Gospel heard Jesus ask even more poignantly, "If any of you had a son . . . that happened to fall in a well . . . , would you not pull him out at once on the Sabbath itself?" (Luke 14:5 TEV). Jesus is asking his critics, in effect, "Would you shout down into the hole, 'Son, could you wait for just another thirteen or fourteen hours, when I'll be able to be of help to you in good conscience?'"

The answer to Jesus' pointed question, of course, is "No one would do that." Matthew's version of Jesus' reply pits a poor man's single animal against the false understanding of Sabbath rest, giving the question an economic dimension. The Serious, we are told elsewhere (Luke 16:14), valued property and money highly, probably inordinately. The problem was that their concern for property was often at the expense of concern for persons. Thus Jesus' rhetorical question forces them to admit that in this economic case they would "go to work" immediately, because the man's whole economy—his single sheep—was at stake. (Technically, on the Sabbath the rabbis permitted an animal only to be fed and assisted in the *animal's* work to free itself; it was wrong to work *oneself* to rescue it, Streck., 19; Schw., 280.)

12:12 Therefore, Jesus' final word to them has irony. "So it is biblical on the Sabbath day to do the right thing." God's purposes in giving the Sabbath command were for the good of human beings, to give them a rest, to contribute to their physical and spiritual health, to give people time to "be" and not just "do," and then to give them time for worship, which is the world's most wholesome reality. "*It is biblical* to do good on the Sabbath." The fact that the Serious have to be *told* this shows the pit into which *they* have fallen. The pursuit of one's own righteousness by the route of the law is shown in Matthew's Gospel to be as perverse as it is shown to be in Paul's "Gospel to the Romans" (see especially Rom 9 C and 10 A). Paul interpreted the problem of legalism more vertically and spiritually, Matthew's Jesus interpreted this fact more horizontally and socially.

If Jesus had been more diplomatic he may have reformed Judaism, but he would not have won the world. He would not have given us a gospel, a gospel that serves the depth intention of the law by freeing us from a slavish service to its surfaces.

12:13–14 So Jesus healed the man. The Separate went away furious. And they held a meeting. The shadows of the passion story begin to form. The agenda of the meeting was a simple one: how to destroy Jesus. When a person penetrates to the vitals of a movement, as Jesus had done with his people's religion of law, and shows its untenability, he threatens that movement intolerably. The threatener cannot be surprised, then, when his own existence is threatened. "The claim that Jesus' divine authority exceeded even the authority of Torah [as here] was bound to have this response" (Hare, 135–36). "They hate him who reproves in the gate, and they abhor him who speaks the truth" (Amos 5:10).

C. Prophetic Documentation: The Servant-Lord (12:15–21)

12:15–21 "*When Jesus knew [about this meeting to destroy him], he withdrew from that place. And many people followed him, and he healed them all. And he commanded them not to make him known. This all happened in order that the Word spoken through Isaiah the prophet might be fulfilled:*

'Look at my servant whom I have picked,
My priceless one, with whom I am deeply pleased.
I shall put my Spirit on him,
And he will proclaim justice to the peoples of the world.
He will not shout or scream;
No one will hear his voice out in the middle of the streets.
He will not snap off a broken reed,
Nor snuff out a smoldering wick,
Till he brings justice to victory;
And in his person the peoples of the world shall place their hopes
[Isa 42:1–4].'"

12:15–17 The immediate occasion of Matthew's use of this Isaiah quotation is to explain (1) Jesus' retreat, and (2) Jesus' commanding the people not to make him known. Both of these passive acts seemed curious for a Messiah. Messiahs do not ordinarily retreat, they advance; and Messiahs do not ordinarily seek to be hidden, they seek adherents. But Matthew wants to summarize the christology he has taught in his Gospel to this point, and for him Isaiah 42 seems the best way to do it (Lohm., 187). (The lengthy citation from Isa 42:1–4 here in vv 18–21 is the longest citation from the Old Testament in Matthew—a Gospel that abounds in Old Testament citations—and the length indicates the citation's strategic importance for Matthew at this point, Bonn., 178.)

12:18 First, Jesus is God's select servant (*pais*) or child (17:18; Lohm., 186–87; Grund., 325), his beloved, his hand-picked one, with whom God is deeply pleased and upon whom God places his Spirit. These words remind us of the opening passages of the Gospel where Jesus is presented to us as "the child" (*to paidon,* a diminutive of *pais*) nine times in chapter 2, and as the priceless Spirit-endowed one with whom the Father is deeply pleased in the baptism of chapter 3. "And [he] will proclaim justice" is exactly the program of the Sermon on the Mount. Jesus is the Torah teacher of the world (Davies, 136). Thus the first verse of Matthew's Isaiah citation (v 18) perfectly summarizes the first long section of Matthew's Gospel, chaps 1–7.

12:19 "He will not shout or scream; no one will hear his voice out in the middle of the streets." Here at the center of this quotation is Matthew's central point in this context. Jesus did not beard the hostile Separatists; he did not stay around "to show them" who is lord or to flaunt his divinely given powers. ("He will not wrangle" is Gundry's, 229, translation.) When confronted, as we saw in the two preceding Sabbath controversy stories, Jesus stood up and spoke out. But he does not loiter looking for trouble; he is not a fanatic. He is not the kind of person who seeks dramatic confrontations for the glory of God. Nor is he "a persistent solicitor" (Schl., *Der,* 402) or a spiritual Fuller Brush man. He prefers to do his work quietly and inconspicuously. This is the way *God's* Messiah works, in contrast to all false messiahs. (Compare Jesus' similar approach in the temptations of Matt 4 and the healings of Matt 8 and 9.) The Modest Messiah gripped Matthew, and he highlights him everywhere. He finds half of Jesus' appeal, half his divinity, in this way of Jesus.

12:20a "He will not snap off a broken reed, nor snuff out a smoldering wick."

This verse points to Jesus' *manner,* his *way* of being, just as his proclamation of justice had pointed to his *matter* and to his ministry of being. Jesus was a minister of justice (the Sermon on the Mount), but he was a gentle, sensitive minister of that justice (as the Beatitudes and the miracles show). The outcastes—lepers, gentiles, women, and the possessed—got his special attention (Matt 8), and in this sense, too, he did not snap off bruised reeds. These castoffs had been bruised enough. Jesus saw the world as battered sheep (9:36), and specifically invited all hurting, bent, broken people to himself (11:28). Jesus is the savior of failures and of little people (G. Barth, 127–28). "A broken reed, . . . a smoldering wick" is a person of low vigor and diminished vitality (Grund., 125)—Jesus helps exactly such persons most of all. "The Lord upholds all *who are falling,* and raises up all *who are bowed down*" (Ps 145:14).

Most revolutionary or messianic leaders have little time for the weak. The kind that are needed for all crusades—from the Sierra Madre and long marches on the Left to earnest soul winning on the Right—are the tough, the disciplined, the entirely committed. Bruised reeds do not make good cadres, and flickering flames are not good candidates for movements.

Jesus' quiet tactics have turned people away from John's day to ours. But maybe Jesus' way, beautifully outlined for us in this Isaiah quote, has more to suggest for revolution and reform than we credit. To be sure, its failure "to shout and scream," as revolutionaries and the Spirit-filled of all times are wont to do, its failure to work in the middle of the streets (as contemporary revolutionary and revivalist strategies both advise), and its strange penchant for working with bruised rather than with polished reeds, with flickering rather than with glowing flames, will often turn some people away from Jesus. "But blessed is the person who is not offended by me" (11:6).

12:20c "Till he brings justice to victory" ("till he puts forth justice successfully," Gund., 230). Jesus' method clear to the end will be the method of quiet revolution, the unlikely tactic of treating persons with great respect—the method of gentleness. There is nothing sensational or special about this method—but it has been determined ever since his baptism at least that this is the way Jesus will go, and Matthew now certifies this way as the *prophetic* way. Jesus is an unlikely candidate for Messiah or Liberator—except for God, Isaiah, and Matthew; for them he seems just right. And though Matthew's emphasis in the last two verses (following Isaiah) has been on what the Servant of the Lord will *not* do (stressed no less than four times), nevertheless, this Servant will never rest in his nonviolent zeal until he brings *justice* to earth. ("Justice" is the preferred translation for the Greek word *krisis* that Matthew's Isaiah uses twice in this citation, 12:18, 20: TDNT, 3:932–33; Bonn., 178; Davies, 131–37; Kingsb., 94–95—God's saving and judging justice; Gund., 229–30.) The Servant is quiet but not quietistic; nonviolent but not noninvolved; gentle but passionate for justice—a justice, we are promised, that he shall one day successfully bring to victory. There *shall* be justice on earth, and God's Servant Jesus will bring it.

12:21 "And in his person the peoples of the world shall place their hopes." "Name" in biblical parlance means "person" (Meier, *Vis.,* 86; Grund., 327; the Hebrew text had "his law" where Matthew put "his person"; Jesus is *our* law). The great, unnoticed, revolutionary figure of the peoples of the Third, Second, and First Worlds is Jesus. Many peoples of the world are finding that their real hope for a future of dignity resides in Jesus and his church. All over the world pockets of peoples gather round his Word and table and find their deepest nourishment and inspiration there. (Everywhere in the Bible, political hopes finally disappoint. "They shall be dismayed and confounded because of Ethiopia their hope and of Egypt their boast. And the inhabitants of this coastland will say in that day, 'Behold, *this* is what has happened to those in whom we hoped and to whom we fled for help to be delivered from the king of Assyria,'" Isa 20:5–6 RSV.)

In an admirable way this great Isaiah 42 quotation has covered almost the entire career of Jesus as Matthew has unfolded it for us so far in his Gospel—from the Servant-Child anointed with the Spirit at the beginning (1–4), through his proclamation of justice and his method of quiet in the middle (the Sermon on the Mount, the miracles, and the mission, respectively, 5–7, 8–9, and 10), to, now, the dignity, power, and hope of his person (11–12). Thus the Isaiah 42 text serves as a veritable table of contents to the material covered in Matthew's Gospel to this point.

Jesus is Lord: this has been the theme of the Sabbath controversy. It is impressive, therefore, that Matthew chooses to round off this section with a *Servant-Song*. For while Jesus is Lord of Sabbath, Sanctuary, and Scripture, he exercises his Lordship in a fresh way—as *Servant* of the Lord, as *Son* of Man, as the Quiet Savior. Jesus is *Servant*-Lord: the noun "Lord" tells us who Jesus is; the adjective "Servant" tells us how he is who he is.

II. THE SPIRIT-KING: THE SPIRIT CONTROVERSY (12:22–37)

In the middle passages of chapter 12, seen as a single unit by many commentators (e.g., Lohm., Schn., Stend., Bonn., Schw., Gund., *et al.*), we find Jesus in controversy with the Pharisees about the Spirit who is at work in him. This section is sometimes called "The Beelzebul Sermon" of Jesus. In the preceding Sabbath Controversy we saw Jesus challenging the contemporary religious interpretations of the major institutions in Israel: Sabbath, temple, and Scripture. In the present Spirit Controversy we see Jesus challenging the spirit-world and *invisible* institutions and theologies of his time. ("We are not contending against flesh and blood, but against the principalities, against the powers, against the world rulers of this present darkness," Eph 6:12 RSV.)

12:22–24 *"Then they brought him a demon-possessed man who was both blind and unable to speak. And Jesus healed him so that he was able to talk and see. And all the crowds were ecstatic [cf. Kl., 107] and started saying, 'Is it possible that this man could be the Son of David?' But the Separate, when they heard people saying this, replied, 'This fellow is able to cast out the demons because he is in league with Beelzebul the prince of demons.'"*

Matthew first gave us this scene at the end of the Ten Miracles (9:34) where he used the split vote of Israel to pose his own evangelistic question. Now Matthew has reinserted the same story into the heart of his person of Christ section in order this time to sharpen the question of Jesus' relation to the spirit world—a question of still fundamental importance, especially in the Third World.

"Is it possible that this man could be the Son of David?" the people ask (v 23).

(For this translation with its note of hope, cf. Grund., 308 n. 4a; Meier, *Vis.*, 86 n. 70; Gund., 231.) "The Son of David" was a royal title rooted in Nathan's prophecy to David that one of David's sons would be made a king *forever* (2 Sam 7), and the title had lately been invested with special messianic hopes (Ps Sol 17:21). Ever since David, but now acutely, Israel was looking for the appearance of this eternal Son of David, and now some in Israel are on the verge of believing that Jesus just may be he. (The "Son of David" title in this Gospel is seen usually in healing settings, interestingly, and is on the lips of common or miserable people most frequently.)

Throughout Matthew's Gospel it is important to see that a real distinction is drawn between the people and the people's religious leadership. In most of the Gospel it is not the Jewish people who bitterly oppose Jesus; it is their religious leadership. This is another way of saying that Matthew is not anti-Semitic; he is antifirst-century-Jewish-religious-leadership, a leadership that is not unique to Jews but that characterizes leaderships everywhere. It is religious leadership, not Jewish nationality, that is the foe in New Testament literature, and it is very important for subsequent readers—and leaders—to keep this in mind and conscience.

This indictment of religious leadership is not meant to encourage the cheap popular sport of antiestablishment or antiinstitutional querulousness. Christians are called to honor those in power—even the personally repugnant (1 Pet 2–3). When Paul railed against the high priest in Acts 23, he quickly recovered and cited the text that reprimands those who speak evil of their leadership (Acts 23:5; Exod 22:28).

Yet again and again the evangelist draws a clear line between the people—the "crowds"—and the people's spiritually serious leaders. The people were (superficially) attracted to Jesus, and were beginning (seriously) to open themselves to him and to his influence—which is to say (as we are about to see) that they were beginning to open themselves to the Holy Spirit who works in Jesus. The elite, the spiritually committed, the religious leadership of the time, stood between this work of the Spirit in Jesus and the work of the Spirit in the people by teaching the people that Jesus' spiritual impact was due to Beelzebul (v 24).

This, we may say already in anticipation, is the sin against the Holy Spirit about which Jesus warns so solemnly in a moment: to stand authoritatively between Jesus and people. For the Spirit works *through* Jesus *on* people. Wherever there is the effort to deflect people's confidence from Jesus as God's final manifestation ("Son of David"), then the sin against the Holy Spirit has been committed. (Surprisingly, in colleges and universities, this sin is approached not only by the much maligned social scientists of various types who are popularly known to enjoy this deflection, but by teachers of religion who believe that sophistication requires rejection of what is called the fundamentalist assertion of Jesus' ultimacy and exclusiveness.)

By attributing Jesus' exorcising to Beelzebul the leaders acknowledge that Jesus exorcises. They cannot deny that Jesus does miracles, but they can deny that he does them by all that is holy. This theology of spirits enabled the leaders to dismiss Jesus' work. Thus all who teach are put on guard against any theology or ideology, however impressive, that distracts people from confidence in Jesus as ultimate. Teaching that withdraws faith from Jesus is teaching that sins against the Spirit.

he does not attribute their exorcism to malign powers. Indeed, the logic of Jesus' remark is that the Pharisees did *not* exorcise by Beelzebul. This means, then, that some healings, exorcisms, and miracles take place without any evangelical significance at all. Jesus does not praise Pharisaic spiritual powers here. But on the other hand Jesus does not attack these powers either. He seems to take them for granted, just as one might take for granted the ability of native doctors, *herbolarios,* or Christian Science practitioners to do healing work with their compassion, herbs, roots, or powers of positive thinking.

Thus it would appear that there are at least three kinds of exorcism or miracle-working: (1) neutral or perhaps even neutral-positive, practiced by those like "the sons of the Serious"; (2) evangelical, practiced by Jesus and his servants; (3) and evil, practiced by charlatans or fanatics who may use the name of Jesus but who do not really honor him or do the will of his Father in heaven (cf. the miraculous and exorcising Lord-Lord-sayers of Matt 7:21–23 and the miracle-working false prophets of 24:24).

12:28 "But if it is through the Spirit of God that *I* am driving demons out, then the kingdom of God has overtaken you." This is the central verse in the story and it is the reason why I speak of the Spirit-*King* in this section. Where the Spirit works, the king and his dominion—this king-dom(inion)—comes. Jesus attributes his power of exorcism to the gift of the Holy Spirit, whom we saw coming over Jesus at baptism.

There are few references to the Holy Spirit in Matthew. We may say in summary that the Holy Spirit is the conceiving (Matt 1), enduing (Matt 3), defending (Matt 10), and exorcising (Matt 12) power of Jesus in the world. The Spirit's office is to help and to honor Jesus: first by bringing Jesus into the world, and then by defending his messianic (and necessarily modest) cause in the world.

It is interesting to notice that Jesus says here, "then the kingdom of God has overtaken *you* [plural]," speaking to the Serious! We might have expected him to say, "then the kingdom of God has overcome the person(s) I have healed." But one gets the impression that when Jesus by the Spirit works on a person, all those in the *community* who are in contact with that person are in some way also brought under the influence of the kingdom (cf. the logic of 11:20–24 and 12:43–45). The kingdom is a social word and reality, and when individual conversion or healing or help come *into* a community something also comes *over* a community, and this something is the kingdom of God.

This Spirit-kingdom Word of Jesus teaches us that wherever Jesus helps people the kingdom is present; that as one commentator put it, "in the unlikely Word of Jesus, God's new world is already present," that "the presence of Jesus Christ is the presence of the kingdom" (Schn., 159).

All commentators draw attention to the *presence* of the usually *future* kingdom of God in Matthew 12:28. Here the kingdom is not only near the community or on its way to it—it has even "arrived," it has "surprisingly overcome" (as the word can be translated, Schl., *Der,* 405; Bacon, 291) its environment. God's kingdom is as present as faith in his Son and it is as future as unmet need, and thus the kingdom is both present and future. As in 3:16 and 28:19, the Trinity is visible here in 12:28, too; Jero., 248; Gund., 235.

12:29 *"Or how can anybody get into the house of a strong man and take away his belongings if he does not first tie the strong man up? Then he can plunder his house."*

12:25-28 *"When Jesus knew their thoughts about him, this is what he said to them: 'Every kingdom that is divided against itself is on its way to ruin, and every city or house that is divided against itself will not long survive. And if Satan drives out Satan, then he is divided against himself; how, then, if this goes on, will his kingdom be able to last? And if I am driving out demons through Beelzebul, then how do your sons drive them out? For this reason, they themselves will be your critics at judgment day. But if it is through the Spirit of God that I am driving demons out, then the kingdom of God has overtaken you.'"*

12:25-26 Jesus challenges their spirit theology at its center: if Jesus is removing evil, then how can Jesus be doing this *through* evil without leading to evil's voluntary suicide? It is in the interest of demons to maim; how can they possibly undo their own work? How can they cooperate with anyone whose work is to ruin their work?

There are problems here. The early church Fathers and the Reformers, well-versed in the ways of the demonic, could see the guile of the devil precisely in his ability to hurt in order to heal, in order, in turn, *by this very healing,* to direct people's attention away from allegiance to Jesus. The apostles, too, saw that the devil could work "lying wonders" to lead astray, if possible, even the elect (cf. Matt 24:24; 2 Thess 2:9–10; Rev 13:13–14; Tert., *Apol.,* 22; Cal., 2:41). Thus the church has always been on guard against mistakenly crediting every healing and every miracle to God. For it seems that some power in the world, even when at times it appears beneficent, is sent by supernaturally evil rather than supernaturally benign forces. The church's test of the spirits is the increase or decrease of persons' focus on the historical Jesus, the human, earthly, gracious Lord so indelibly drawn for us in Matthew's portraiture and in the other Gospel accounts (cf. also 1 John 4 A, and 1 Cor 12 A's twin tests: the human *"Jesus* is Lord"). Where healers are genuinely seeking to engender confidence in the earthly Jesus, we may open ourselves to their influence; but where they seek to attract us, as is often the case in our experience, to a bizarre Jesus, to a "supernatural" Jesus of esoteric miracles, often for a price, and away from the simple, lowly, crucified Jesus of the Gospel accounts—beware!

12:27 The fact that exorcisms are not exclusive possibilities of the Messiah is underlined by Jesus' next question: "If I am driving out demons through Beelzebul, then how do your sons drive them out? For this reason, they themselves will be your critics at judgment day." Jesus clearly says that the Separate themselves were able to exorcise (cf. Acts 19:13; Kl., 109; Hill, 216 for documentation and discussion of Jewish exorcists). The lesson to draw is that exorcism or power in the spirit world is not something unique to the Christ and, therefore, cannot be used in the final analysis as a proof for the truth of exorcists' doctrine. Ability to work, or manipulate, in the spiritual world is at best neutral or amoral power, and it says nothing decisive about truth.

It is only one more fatal step from here to say, however, exactly what the Pharisees said about Jesus, "He does this through Beelzebul," and the text in its entirety seeks to guard us *against* saying this carelessly. (Church teachers must warn the people of God against false teachings; but our paragraph teaches us to be cautious in attacking as demonic those whom we believe are false teachers. We must say no to the false teachings and, usually, leave to God's judgment the false teachers. The "sons of the Serious" were able to exorcise, Jesus acknowledges, and

The last time we met a "strong man" was in John's preaching about Jesus (3:11), but Jesus has never used the name for himself. Here Jesus calls the devil a strong man. ("We ought not to be secure; our adversary is confirmed as 'strong' even by these words of his conqueror," Jero., 1:248; cf. Cal., 2:44.) But Jesus has already ("first") tied the strong man up and plundered his house. Jesus' victory over the devil happened in his temptations (4:11), in which his cross and resurrection were already germinally present (TDNT, 7:159). This victory over the devil, clearly present and worked out in Jesus' entire ministry, even (and especially) in the seeming defeat of the crucifixion, means two things for the thinking of believers: (1) the devil whom we encounter in our daily struggle is a *defeated* devil, and our faith in Jesus gives us a continuing victory over him; and (2) the world that does not know the Victor or his victory is in a prisoner-of-war situation. The world apart from faith in Christ is not only subjectively lost; it is in the tyrannical clutches of the strong man (Eph 2:1–3). This "world fact" means that Christians are engaged in a cosmic world war. Our comfort in this war is the knowledge that the decisive battle (the "Midway" of Jesus' battle in the middle of history) has already been won. Jesus himself built his message of the kingdom on the foundation of his victory over the devil in the temptations (see how 4:17 follows 4:1–11, Schl., *Der,* 407).

Christians learn from our present devil text to see the world in two ways: (1) as enemy country wherever faith in Christ has not yet occurred, and (2) as liberated country wherever Christ has given the obedience of faith. Distortions enter Christian teaching wherever either (1) the world's thralldom under the devil or (2) Christ's liberation of the world from the devil is absolutized undialectically—i.e., (1) a fatalism, defeatism, or negativism occurs where the devil is thought *too much of,* and (2) universalism (i.e., the teaching that all are saved) occurs along with a certain secularism and an unmissionary optimism whenever the devil is thought *too little of* (see Barth's theology as an example).

Caird, 154–55, illustrates the balance that should characterize the church's teaching of this and comparable texts on the devil, concluding, "the two kingdoms confront one another in a war that knows neither truce nor neutrality," and thus appropriately both in Matthew and Luke a "war" or "no neutrality" verse immediately follows this victory text (cf. Matt 12:29–30; Luke 11:21–23: "the person who is not with me is against me; and the person who does not gather with me, scatters from me," a text so important that both Matthew and Luke preserve it in identical terms).

The theology of universalism (that all are saved), widespread in contemporary mainline Christianity, breaks the connection that the Gospels establish between Jesus' victory (Matt 12:29; Luke 11:21–22) and Jesus' urgent call to evangelism (Matt 12:30; Luke 11:23). The missionary-apostle Paul, however, makes the necessary unbreakable connection between Christ's universal work *and therefore* Christ's universal mission: "[1] God was in Christ reconciling the world to himself, not counting their trespasses against them [= his universal work] *and* [2] entrusting to us the message of reconciliation" [= his universal mission] (2 Cor 5:19 RSV). What God has joined together (victory *and* mission), let no human being tear asunder.

Luther believed that the negative first half (Satan's captured world) of the dual truth we are discussing in this text (Satan's captured world *and* Christ's recapturing the world) was badly neglected by the humanist Christian thinking of late medieval scholastic theology and the sophisticated Erasmus, and that this neglect of Satan's malign rule in the world was the reason why theology at the time taught human free will: "What has become . . . of our belief that Satan is the prince of this world, who according to Christ (John 12:31; 14:30) and Paul (Eph 2:2; 6:12) reigns in the wills and minds of men who are his captive slaves? . . . For either the kingdom of Satan in man means nothing, and then Christ must be a liar, or else, if his kingdom is as Christ describes it, free choice must be nothing but a captive beast of burden for Satan, which can only be set free if the devil is first cast out by the finger of God" (Lu., *Bondage of the Will* [1525], 283–84).

Even much contemporary conservative evangelical theology espouses a free will doctrine that is hard to reconcile with the New Testament's doctrine of the devil (see the good discussion in Bloesch, *Essentials of Evangelical Theology*, 1:98–102, 112–13). But the dominant note to be struck in the exposition of our verse is surely hope, and this is the mark that the clearest OT cross reference (Isa 49:24–25 RSV) beautifully strikes: "Can the prey be taken from the mighty [the strong man!], or the captives of a tyrant be rescued? Surely, thus says the Lord: 'Even the captives of the mighty shall be taken, and the prey of the tyrant be rescued, for I will contend with those who contend with you, and I will save your children.'" This is encouraging for Christian parents.

Matthew's point in this context is to teach the church that Jesus is not in league with the devil; on the contrary, Jesus is the devil's major enemy, "thief," and plunderer. The mission of the *devil* in the world is the destruction of human beings in every possible respect and in particular the destruction of the cause and message of Jesus of Nazareth, humanity's Savior (cf. TDNT, 7:160). The mission of *Jesus* in the world is the salvaging of human beings in every respect and so the destruction of the work of the devil (cf. 1 John 3:8; Heb 2:14). Jesus and the devil are not allies in the same mission; they are sworn foes at cross purposes. Somehow, mysteriously, the devil is two things at once: (1) "tied up," to use the verb of our verse, and (2) tempting, as the rest of the New Testament teaches. The church must teach both truths (Foerster, *Satanas*, TDNT, 7:160).

Thus all who say that people who simply preach Jesus' gospel Word and who carry out Jesus' deeds of mercy in missionary history are counterrevolutionary, reactionary, or irrelevant, as the Left often says, or that such people are subversive, meddlesome do-gooders, or gospel-reductionists, as the Right often says, are in danger of committing the sin against the Holy Spirit. It is fashionable today for radicals to despise the simple teaching of Jesus' Word as escapist and to resist the simple ministering of Jesus' mercy as meliorist or reformist or, at the other pole, it is customary for conservatives to despise the teaching of Jesus' social Word as liberal and to condemn the attempt to follow Jesus in social obedience as communist. Let both sides be warned. And this warning is exactly what Jesus' next Word proffers.

12:30 *"The person who is not with me is against me, and the person who does not gather with me scatters from me."*

This word rings the death knell to neutralism toward Jesus. Those persons who hedge about devotion to Jesus (as "romanticism") or about the importance of a clear decision for him (as "fundamentalism"), those who question Jesus' exclusivity (as "fanaticism") and who disdain his gathering work of evangelism (as "proselytism" or "imperialism")—those persons are in trouble. They are not merely neutral or middle-of-the-road or broad-minded; they are "against me," they "scatter."

Jesus' exclusivity in this verse has often been felt to be in tension with his ecumenicity in Mark 9:40 where he says "whoever is not against us is for us" in defense of the strange exorcist. But the difference is in the pronouns—"me" and "us." In our exclusivity verse (and its identical twin in Luke 11:23) indifference or neutrality toward *Jesus* is actually hostility toward him. But in the ecumenicity verse of Mark 9:40 (and its close relative Luke 10:50) the servant of Jesus who is in another group than ours but who is not against *us,* is actually for us (cf. Chrys., 41:4:266). Our exclusivity must be in witness to *Christ,* not an exclusivity requiring, necessarily, membership in our branch of the church. These two sets of verses teach Christians to walk the narrow but exciting road of Christ-centeredness and church-openness, to be both deeply evangelical and broadly ecumenical. "Ecumenical openness (Mark 9:40) and the unambiguous [evangelical] demand for a clear confession of Jesus (Matt 12:30) are certainly compatible" (Schw., 287; cf. Davies, 458).

What is more, Jesus in this verse asks us not only to *side* decisively with him, but to *gather* with him, that is, to engage in his shepherd mission of gathering in a lost world—we call this evangelism or mission. Not to be actively engaged in gathering with him, Jesus warns, is to be in fact actively engaged in scattering from him. The sum of the matter is, in Calvin's comment on this text, "that there is no place for God's righteousness except among those who devote themselves earnestly to it" (similarly, Lu., *Bondage of the Will,* 275–76, 316). "You are neither cold nor hot. Would that you were cold or hot! So, because you are lukewarm, and neither cold nor hot, I will spew you out of my mouth" (Rev. 3:15–16 RSV).

It is easy enough in our time to be angry with a great deal that goes under the name of evangelism. Much media evangelism, I think one can fairly say, is caricature of the gospel. There is an arrogant evangelism, too, where preaching with authority is simply a covering name for teaching with demagoguery or for getting mad in public. But gold covered with dung is no less gold, and though evangelism is one of the least respected words in the contemporary vocabulary, *Jesus* is the evangel and no one deserves more honor.

12:31–32 *"So it is in this connection that I say to you: Every sin and blasphemy will be forgiven people, but the blasphemy against the Spirit will not be forgiven. And whoever says something against the Son of Man will be forgiven; but whoever speaks against the Holy Spirit will not be forgiven, either in this age or in the age to come."*

The spirit controversy began with the Separate pointing their finger at Jesus' spirit and condemning him; it concludes with Jesus pointing his finger at those who slander the Spirit and warning them. The tables are turned (Schl., *Der,* 408). From the defensive, Jesus has moved to the offensive. And though he is the suffering servant who "does not shout and scream" or "fight and brawl" (12:19), he can solemnly warn those who attack the Spirit of the dangers involved.

12:31 The first thing to be seen in this remarkable passage is that Jesus so clearly assumes that every other sin and blasphemy *will* or *can* be forgiven. This surprises us because we have become accustomed to the searing holiness and justice of God taught by Jesus elsewhere in the Gospel, particularly in the demand of repentance and in the commands of the Sermon on the Mount. Now we are suddenly told that "every sin and blasphemy will be forgiven people." It is only against the background of this breathtakingly wide forgiveness that Jesus' warning gets its gravity (Schw., TDNT, 6:397).

Of course this wide forgiveness is not to be interpreted to mean that everything

Jesus has previously taught about the seriousness of repentance from sin he now jettisons. To say this would be to render sterile the teaching ministry of Jesus. The meaning, certainly, is that *all* sin, with one exception, can be forgiven.

12:31b "But the blasphemy against the Spirit will not be forgiven." The precise identification of the blasphemy against the Spirit has vexed many. The proper pastoral approach has always been, "If you are worried that you have committed the sin against the Holy Spirit, you have not." For the spirit of the sin against the Spirit is an unworried adamancy. It is impenitence, the unwillingness to repent (Aug., *Serm.*, 21 [71], *passim;* Lu., *Bondage of the Will,* 116). It is not careless acts, it is a hardened state (McN., 179).

But what is the sin against the Spirit in our passage? In context, the substance of the sin against the Spirit is resistance to the mission of God at work in Jesus. Here, interestingly, the Holy Spirit is made unmistakenly personal: one can only *sin* against persons.

Not only do we have a clearly personal Spirit in this important text, we have another indication of the trinitarian God, as Schlatter, *Der,* 410, has seen: The Palestinian church for and from which Matthew wrote, "knew of two witnesses to God—the Son of Man and the Spirit—and the Spirit is the one who reveals what the Son is and gives." Over both the Son and the Spirit stands the sending God who works in both. "Therefore," Schlatter concludes, "the name in which the [earliest Christian] community worked was the trinitarian name." See this explicitly in Matthew's next to last verse, 28:19.

Mark's Jesus adds one more sentence to this passage, and it is clarifying: "*because* they were saying '*He* [Jesus] has an unclean spirit'" (Mark 3:30). In Mark, saying *Jesus* has an unclean spirit is the sin against the Holy Spirit. In context, in all three Gospels, the sin against the Spirit is not some arbitrary curse of deity or some foolish remark about either God or the Spirit per se, *it is trying to ruin Jesus in the eyes of others.*

The objection to this interpretation will be, "But this makes the unforgivable sin what Jesus said it was not—something said against the Son of Man" (v 32a). Yet, in reply, it is possible to say christologically inappropriate things about Jesus the lowly Son of Man and in this sense really but unintentionally to dishonor Jesus— and these can be forgiven. But *intentionally* to speak against the Holy Spirit powerfully at work then in Jesus and now in the church's message of Jesus, to question Jesus' motives or "spirit," *so that* others will not place their trust in him—this is quite another thing, this is quite another "spirit," and it will not be forgiven.

Sin against the Holy Spirit was the dangerous sin the Pharisees approached in their attributing Jesus' work to a malign spirit in order, in turn, to deflect the people of God from faith in Jesus as the Messiah, the Son of David (12:22–24). Jesus mercifully warned them of the danger of their teaching, but he did not yet accuse them of being guilty of the unpardonable sin. Indeed, in the paragraph that follows, Jesus calls his opponents sharply to repentance (vv 33–37). The church used Jesus' teaching on the sin against the Spirit as a warning to those who hear *her* message with hostility too, for in the church's message of Jesus the Holy Spirit actively works to make persons Christians (Colpe, TDNT 8:443). Defiant resistance to the wooing of the Spirit is in danger of becoming an unpardonable impenitence (Schw., *pneuma,* TDNT 6:397–98). In the final analysis, Jesus' teaching about the unpardonable sin is no different from all his warnings of judgment—rejection of Jesus invites damnation. But Jesus' teaching about the sin against the Holy Spirit is probably Jesus' most solemn warning of judgment. It "underlines what the biblical writings do not cease to report: that pardon is not a theory, automatically available, it is a sovereign act of the God who remains pardon's constant Lord" (Bonn., 182).

12:32b "But whoever speaks against the Holy Spirit will not be forgiven, *either in this age or in the age to come.*" This is one of the few "second chance" texts found in Scripture, so it should not be pressed. (This is a well-known principle of parable-interpretation: parables should not be made to walk on all fours; they have *one* central point and that, almost alone, is what the interpreter should discover and press home. But this principle can be made to apply to most speech: the key thing in speech is to get at what a person is trying mainly to say and not to force embellishments into center.) "Neither in this age nor in the age to come" implies that as there is a forgiveness in this age so there will be a forgiveness, too, in the coming age. (The coming age, as Calvin, 2:47, rightly remarks, is not an intermediate age—e.g., a purgatory—it is simply another way of saying the last day, the ultimate time.) But the main point of the "nor in the age to come" remark is to underline the seriousness—indeed, the fatality and finality—of dissuading people from faith *in our time, now.* The purpose of Jesus' remark is not, in the name of a putative second–chance, to dissuade people from the urgency of decision; it is to heighten the gravity of the sin of all such dissuasions from decision. Jesus means something by his remark, but this something must be controlled by the clear and central meaning of the context: "He who is not with me is against me, and he who does not gather with me scatters from me" (v 30).

The most sensitive comment I have read on the delicate question of the sin against the Holy Spirit is that of Vincent Taylor, 244, in a note in his master commentary on the Greek text of Mark's Gospel: "The truth of the saying must not be weakened or explained away, but it must always be estimated in the light of the major truth of the Gospel, namely that where there is true repentance, or even the possibility of repentance, sin can be and is forgiven by God. . . . [The sin against the Holy Spirit] is a perversion of spirit which, in defiance of moral values, elects to call light darkness. . . . Whether we admit the possibility of such 'a sin unto death' (1 John 5:16) will depend on whether we believe that there are final limits to which human self-assertion and self-worship can go, on our knowledge of life and history, and most of all on our recognition of the fact that the warning is that of Jesus. Of all religious teachers no one was less inclined than He to minimize possibilities of forgiveness and amendment and the boundless resources of divine grace."

12:33–37 *"Either make the tree good so that its fruit can be good, or make the tree bad so that its fruit can be bad; because you can tell the quality of a tree by the quality of its fruit. You pack of snakes: How can you possibly say what is right when what you are is so wrong? Speech is the overflow of the heart. The good person, from the overflow of a good reservoir in the heart, spills over with good things, and the bad person, out of the overflow of a bad reservoir within, spills over with bad things. But I say to you that every thoughtless word people say will have to be accounted for in the day of judgment; indeed, you will be set right with God by your words, and you will be put wrong with God by your words."*

12:33 The opening statement about the good tree and its fruit is a summons to conversion. It is as if Jesus were saying "Stop playing: either get converted ("make the tree good") or get out ("make the tree bad"). You need to be changed at t^he base of your life—you need to become a good tree" (cf. Gund., 239; Schw., 288).

12:34a "You pack of snakes: How can you possibly say what is right when what you are is so wrong?" "Snakes": John the Baptist had given the religious leadership the same unflattering name (3:7), and Jesus will again (23:33). It is hard to hear the words "pack of snakes" from a teacher who taught us to avoid calling anybody "idiot" or "liar" (5:22). One gets the impression here and in chapter 23 that Jesus places his hope of converting the Separate in the power and severity of his words; some people can be *shocked* out of unforgivable sin. Jesus is giving his opponents the treatment of prophetic roughness. It is a treatment that Jesus' followers should be exceptionally cautious in imitating.

12:34b–35 Jesus' picture of good people overflowing with good things and evil people overflowing with evil things says that good things in life do not spring primarily from calculations—"I shall be good," or from resolutions, "I *shall* be good"—but from *being*, from what Jesus here calls one's internal "treasure" or "reservoir." Doing comes from being, fruit from roots, speech from hearts. (In Matthew, however, in contrast to Paul, moral decision forms personal being—and destiny. Cf. Mohrlang.) Jesus is aiming deep, and he teaches here authoritatively that goodness is more spontaneous than it is pumped up, more overflow than willpower. Good people *are* good, and while they, too, try hard to be good, they do not have to try to get something they do not already have, by faith, within. The Reformation rediscovered this message of the gospel and so gave to love, a rather force-pumped thing in late medieval Catholicism, its rootage in faith, and thus gave good works their source in the divine gift.

In context, Jesus is telling the Pharisees why their speech borders on being the unforgivable sin against the Spirit. The reason is not insufficient prudence or flawed diplomacy; it is bad being. The Pharisees' slanderings of Jesus and his Spirit "are not accidents; they correspond to what the adversaries of Jesus 'are' (["*being* evil"], *ponēroi ontes*)" (Bonn., 183). Thoughtless, hurtful, careless speech of *all* kinds will be confronted at the judgment day, Jesus warns us here, but in context the speech that is especially dangerous is speech against Jesus (Stend., 785). It is almost a law that "that which is in the heart is also in the mouth" (in Bult., 84 n. 1). Therefore, "keep your heart with all vigilance; for from *it* flow the springs of life" (Prov 4:23 RSV). It has astonished commentators that Jesus so unsystematically assumes that there are "good people" in the (still non-Christian) world with good inner reservoirs (Kl., 110; Schn., 161. Cf. Jesus' equally astonishing assumption of universal sin, 7:11 "if you . . . being evil" [*ponēroi ontes*] the same words used here!). Jesus is so frequently conservative and evangelical (as at 7:11) that his almost as frequent liberal spirit should be appreciated when it appears (as here, v 35a).

12:36–37 "But I say to you that every thoughtless word people say will have to be accounted for in the day of judgment; indeed, you will be set right with God by your words, and you will be put wrong with God by your words." This controversy began with the Separate deterring people from faith by saying thoughtlessly (though it sounded rational) that Jesus' power came from evil sources. The controversy ends with Jesus warning the Separate and us against all thoughtless speech, especially religiously thoughtless speech. Jesus speaks of the danger of every thoughtless word, but in context the thoughtless words we are asked especially to avoid are words about Jesus himself. And the only way we can avoid these words is by a sound conversion in our innermost being.

Thus there is no place where careless speech is more dangerous than when it is spoken by leaders of the church. For in the church speech is made of God and of his Messiah Jesus. "The fairer the paper the fouler the blot." Careless words elsewhere are less fraught with eternal significance; but here, with reference to Jesus, careless words are damning words. Jesus gives this warning in order that all who speak about him in the future will be careful.

"You will be set right with God by your words, and you will be put wrong with God by your words" (v 37). Paul, too, could write that "the faith that leads to righteousness is in the heart, and the confession that leads to salvation is upon the lips" (Rom 10:10 NEB), making the same close connection between faith and speech. Matthew is telling us in another way, "Believe well of Jesus so that you may speak well of him, otherwise you are liable to say the most irresponsible things and so bring judgment on yourself."

Speech is a much larger part of our lives than we realize; it is the overflow of being; it is the main way we express what we "are"; it is the major fruit of our personhood; speech is the self *ex*-pressed ("pressed out"). Changing the way we talk can only be effectively done at the root in the innermost self. And this inner- most self—the heart—can only be right when it is rooted in a right relation with God, which is, evangelically expressed, the relation of discipleship to God's Son. "No human being can tame the tongue—[it is] a restless evil, full of deadly poison" (Jas 3:8). "Let us then understand, Dearly beloved, that if no man can tame the tongue, we must have recourse to God. . . . That the horse, and ox . . . and lion, and viper, may be tamed, man is sought for. Therefore let God be sought to [*sic*], that man may be tamed" (Aug., *Serm.*, 5 [55]:2:273).

III. THE SIGNIFICANT-KINSMAN: THE SIGN CONTROVERSY (12:38–50)

"Significant" comes from two Latin words meaning, literally, "sign-making" (*signum-facere*). In the third and final set of incidents in chapter 12, Jesus "makes signs" (in modern idiom we say "makes waves") in an encounter with the leaders (vv 38–45) and with his own family (vv 46–50). Jesus is himself the sign of God. The last controversy in chapter 12 is the controversy about a special sign. In this chapter's three controversies Jesus was first questioned about his relation to the Bible's law in the Sabbath Controversy, then he was questioned about his relation to evil spı s in the Spirit Controversy, and now he is questioned about his relation to God in the Sign Controversy. The stories go higher and higher in this chapter: from visible institutions through invisible powers to God.

12:38–42 *"Then some of the Bible teachers and Separate responded to what Jesus had just said by remarking, 'Teacher, we would like to see you produce a sign.' Jesus answered by saying, 'A perverse and marriage-breaking generation seeks passionately for a sign, and no sign will be given to it except the sign of Jonah the prophet. For just as "Jonah was in the belly of the whale for three days and three nights" so the Son of Man will be in the* *heart of the earth for three days and three nights. The people of Nineveh will be summoned at judgment day against this generation, and they will condemn it, because they changed their lives when they heard the preaching of Jonah; and look, more than Jonah is here. The Queen of the South will be summoned at judgment day against this generation, too, and she will condemn it, because she came from the end of the earth to listen to the wisdom of Solomon; and look, more than Solomon is here.'"*

12:38 A sign was a divine credential. It was proof or documentation that a person truly spoke for God. The difference between a sign and a miracle was that signs were believed to be delivered immediately from heaven, while miracles were done here on earth, mediately, through people and things. To put the matter graphically: a sign appeared in or from the sky; a miracle happened on earth. Furthermore, a sign ranked one level above a miracle as evidence of a person's authenticity because, while miracles could be done by all kinds of people, signs were given only to the divinely authorized.

So the Separate want something less ambiguous from Jesus than healings. They want Jesus to back up the several claims he has been making, implicitly and explicitly, by proving through a heaven-given sign that he really is who he says he is. The didactic connection with the preceding paragraph is this: Incensed or alarmed by Jesus' severe words against them in the Spirit Controversy, they now say, in effect, "If you want us not to speak ill of you, give us a sign that proves your messiahship" (Bonn., 183; cf. Gund., 242).

12:39 Jesus responds by saying that signs are not delivered on demand; they are not for show or sale to the most urgent bidder. In fact, in Jesus' words it is "a perverse and marriage-breaking generation that seeks passionately for a sign." It is not a good sign when people seek signs. Excessively *sensual* people love sensations; responsible evangelical people find Jesus sufficient. (It is customary for commentators to understand Jesus' word "adulterous" here symbolically, cf. Hos 1:2; Jero., 1:254; Grund., 333. I prefer the literal understanding: those unfaithful to covenants characteristically seek signs, cf. Schl., *Der*, 415; an "adulterous generation" is "a generation whose characteristic sin is immorality," Str-B., 1:641–42.) The more erratic and erotic persons are, the more they are taken in by the sensate, the remarkable, the impressive, and the less susceptible they are to the quiet, solid marks by which Divinity prefers to be documented.

12:40 There is one exception, one good sign: the sign of Jonah. "For just as 'Jonah was in the belly of the whale for three days and three nights' so the Son of Man will be in the heart of the earth for three days and three nights."

There are three main opinions in the commentaries and studies about the meaning of *the sign of Jonah:* (1) the sign is the *prophetic* Jesus: just as Jonah came from a foreign land to Nineveh and preached repentance, so the Son of Man came (or will come) to earth from heaven with judgment and salvation (thus, apparently, Luke 11:30; McN., 181–82; Bult., 118; cf. Green, 129; Stend., 785; Meier, *Vis.*, 87); (2) it is the crucifixion and *death* of Jesus: emphasized by Jonah's sojourn in the belly of the whale (Bonn., 184; Hill, 220); (3) the sign is the *resurrection* of Jesus (many commentators and cf. John 2:18–22). When numbers two and three—the death and resurrection of Jesus—are taken together we have the best parallel to the missionary career of Jonah, a career that includes number one's prophetic Jesus above (most clearly explained in Allen, 139). The death meaning of the Jonah saying, especially as it appears in Matthew is often neglected, and in this connection Bonnard, 184, makes a point: "The text is polemical; to those who request an extraordinary . . . sign, Jesus offers nothing but a 'counter-sign' of his near death." But Bonnard, I think, overstates his case—his "nothing but" is extreme, for every reader of the Jonah story knows not only of the awful swallowing of Jonah (and Bonnard is correct in saying that this is all Matthew speaks of), but knows of Jonah's miraculous deliverance as well. Thus death-and-resurrection—both, with neither neglected—gives the fullest understanding of Matthew's sign of Jonah (thus, similarly, Schw., 291; Meier, *Vis.*, 87; Marshall, 483–85; Gund., 244).

For those bothered by the mathematics of the text, "three days and three nights," the Hebrew method of reckoning a part for the whole, synecdoche, is usually recommended with Gen 40:13, 20; 2 Chron 10:5, 12; Hos 6:2 given as examples (e.g., Jero. 1:256; Alford in Beng., 1:180; Str.-B., 1:649). A Hebrew day *began* at sunset. Thus, Jesus was dead "for three days" on part of Friday, all of Saturday and part of Sunday (after Saturday's sunset). If one is eager for a perfect match between Jesus' prophecy and actual events in order to get the "three *nights*," an eagerness too close for comfort to the demand for a sign itself, one can refer to the night at noon (27:45), and to Friday and Saturday nights. But surely such harmonizing is unworthy.

Finally in this connection, we must admire *Mark's* understanding of Jesus' answer to the demand for a sign: "Amen, I say to you, *no* sign will be given to this generation" (Mark 8:11–12; the idiom that Mark uses to express this absolute no is very strong). In Mark's understanding of Jesus' reply, Jesus is himself the sufficient sign—Jesus' ministry all by itself is *signum-facere*, "significant," enough. Mark's interpretation is wonderfully evangelical, too. Mark and Matthew unite in one conviction: Jesus, whether in his ministry or in his passion-resurrection, is the one and only finally sufficient sign of God.

The resurrection of the crucified Jesus will be God's one great sensation, his single authorized sign, delivered once and for all and for all time—take it or leave it, reports Matthew. Jesus serves notice that God will not make signs (until the Second Coming) once he has made his main sign—the resurrection of the crucified Jesus. After Jesus' holy week, God is not in show business.

In conversation with others, the death-and-resurrection of Jesus is to be Christians' single documentation, their one claim of supernatural evidence, their one proof, their sensation. They are not to seek other special signs from heaven or from their own repertory. Visions, miracles, and other spiritual sensations are, after the resurrection of the crucified one, possible, equivocal, and inconclusive. The preaching and teaching of Jesus' passion week is to be God's perpetual sensation. God will do one impressive thing, not to please the sensationalists but to show the world his approval of his Son: he will raise him from the dead.

If the passion-resurrection of Jesus is to be the *only* sign given "this generation," then the zealous seeking of charismatic "signs and wonders" in spiritual churches or the political attention given to the reading of "the signs of the times" in social churches is put in question. Some, for example, read the signs of the times as telling us to downplay preaching and words since ours is a visual, image-conscious, pictorial generation; yet preaching the Word is the major responsibility of the church. Others read the signs of the times as teaching us to make revolution our major business because there are so many oppressed (and there are); yet if anything is clear in the gospel, it is Jesus' abhorrence of violence, even in the purest causes (his own defense, for example: 26:51–56). Still others (in spiritual churches) read the signs of the times as telling us to give up all political activity and social concern since, their prophecy conferences tell them, Christ is coming soon and so political-social activity is irrelevant or faithless; yet a major way we minister to Christ is feeding the hungry and helping the suffering (25:31–46), i.e., political and social activity.

Whenever the church has joined "this generation's" lust for signs, that is, has sought sensational events and movements in church or history as God's Word, she has been seriously drawn from center. The German Church Struggle in the 1930s is the main modern example of this aberration. Jesus in his Word, not signs in history—His-Story not history—is Christians' focus and agenda.

"Finding out what God is doing in history and joining him there" (Lehmann, Shaull, Cox) can be a call for a march into a wilderness of subjectivity and false causes. This call to find God in history is off center when it does not look for God in the one place in history he put himself to be surely found: in the proclamation of the history of Jesus, culminating in his death and resurrection and presented to us both in the church's means of grace (Acts 2:42) and in the world's poor (Matt 25:31–46).

This story of the only sign is supplemented by two stories in which Jesus calls persons to repentance and to listening—which are the same thing said two ways.

12:41–42 "The people of Nineveh will be summoned at judgment day against this generation, and they will condemn it, because they *changed their lives* when they heard the preaching of Jonah; and look, more than Jonah is here. The Queen of the South will be summoned at judgment day against this generation, too, and she will condemn it, because she came from the end of the earth to *listen* to the wisdom of Solomon; and look, more than Solomon is here."

The story of the sign of Jonah reminds us of the preaching of Jonah and of the subsequent repentance of Nineveh. "This generation" will be condemned by the pagans of Nineveh who, during Jonah's evangelistic campaign in their city, really changed their lives, turned themselves around, and got converted, while "this generation" (or, "people today," or "the modern world") with the many opportunities of exposure to Jesus and his story remains so unchanged. But "a greater than Jonah is here." We are warned by these words to realize that in Jesus we have been given a great deal—indeed, given everything God has to give—and that if we are wise, we will take him with a final seriousness. We will change our lives.

The Queen of the South will be summoned to testify against "the modern world" on judgment day, because she traveled a long distance to listen to King Solomon's wisdom when all the time we have had someone "greater than Solomon" here in Jesus and yet did not often give him a serious hearing. ("Solomon is wise, but here is Wisdom," Bengel.) Repentance and listening are synonyms in our text and in reality. One important way we repent is by deciding to listen with great care to God's Word, especially in its major living form, the Sunday sermon.

These pagans, these outsiders—the Assyrian Ninevites and the Ethiopian Queen—will be invited to the platform on judgment day, and many Christian peoples and persons will be shamed because these outsiders gave greater attention to Jonah and Solomon than we insiders gave to Jesus.

McNeile, 182, explains that the expression "to rise [or stand] up in judgment with" means in Aramaic "to accuse," and he cites Augustine to effect: "By comparison with these [foreign seekers], these [in the people of God] will be deservedly condemned. Cf. Cal., 2:59. In Jesus' Ethiopian Queen, notice the dignified place given a woman.

Three times in this chapter we have heard Jesus say "and more than such-and-such is here" (vv 6, 41, 42). He has claimed to be more than the temple (in the law), more than Jonah (in the prophets), and more than Solomon (in the poetic and wisdom literature), in other words, to be more than the entire revelation of Hebrew Scripture. Jesus has claimed in these remarks that he is The Revelation. Jesus is the final High Priest, greater than the temple; he is the final Prophet, greater than Jonah; and he is the final King, greater than Solomon. As God's final Prophet, Priest, and King he deserves humanity's final seriousness—the living faith of a changed and listening life.

Grundmann, 334 n. 12, cites Josephus, *Ant.*, 13:10:7, about the legendary Jewish hero John Hyrcanus whom "God honored . . . with the three highest honors: the Lordship [Kingship] of his people, the high-priestly honor, and the prophetic gift." In the history of the Western church, John Calvin was the first to develop Christ's three offices as prophet (in his teaching ministry), priest (in his sacrifice), and king (in his royal rule), *Inst.* II. xv. It is attractive to see these three offices present already in the three "more thans" of Matthew's twelfth chapter. Jesus' "more," finally, is the paradoxical more of less, as the "more than Jonah" especially shows, for "this 'more' presents itself in a humanity swallowed up in the death of the cross; to the infinite 'more' in dignity before God corresponds the 'less' in the eyes of men, and it is this that this generation will be unable to accept" (Bonn., 185).

Jesus concludes his confrontation with a warning of the very serious danger of failing to take him to heart. This warning is called "The Return of the Unclean Spirit."

12:43–45 *"But whenever an unclean spirit comes out of a person, it starts traveling through waterless places looking for rest, and it does not find it. Then it says, 'I will go back to my house that I left.' It comes back and finds the house empty, clean, and all fixed up. Then it goes out and gets seven other spirits, worse than itself, and they come in and make their permanent home there. The result is that the last days of this person are worse than the first. And that is exactly what is going to happen to this vicious present age."*

The presence of John and Jesus in Israel meant the exorcising of demons from, and thus the pitching of the kingdom tent over, large tracts of Israel (cf. 12:28). What would the towns where Jesus worked miracles *do* now? Would they take Jesus to heart, turn from their ways, believe in him, follow him, and do the will of his Father? Or would they merely bask in the excitement of his ministry, boast of his presence in their towns, be a little more religious perhaps, talk a little more about God and prayer, but actually make no serious decision to be disciples of Jesus? These are the questions raised by the story.

For when the demon went out (and we may say that this happened whenever Jesus came into people's lives and towns) there was an intermediate period, a period of opportunity, "the day of salvation," "a year of the Lord's favor," a period of grace. What would be done with this gift of time and opportunity? The story tells us that the unclean demon returned to find the house of these towns "empty, clean, and all fixed up" (TEV; "unoccupied, swept clean, and tidy," NEB). The key term is the first: "empty" or "unoccupied" (*scholazonta*, used only by Matthew).

The towns Jesus visited *had* swept themselves clean and had tidied themselves up as a result of Jesus' appearance. But tidying up, sweeping clean, externally fixing up are not Jesus' reasons for coming. In all of these religious but external activities the house itself remains unoccupied, vacant, and empty. The house is clean—and empty; the person is religious—and hollow; the community is outwardly moral—and inwardly purposeless. "Empty, clean, and all fixed up"—bourgeois life has never been better described.

Few realities are more vulnerable to demonic attack than good bourgeois life, precisely because this life is so empty, vacuous, and passionless. Since people do not live by bread alone but by their passions, great ideologies come sweeping in where houses have been swept out, and they fill people with the causes they need to live by. The old unclean spirit and seven isms come blowing into clean but empty communities and sweep them away. Let the suburbs be warned.

This warning of the return of the unclean spirits is commentary on Jesus' earlier important warning against neutralism: "the person who is not with me is against me, and the person who does not gather with me scatters from me" (v 30). Neutrality toward Jesus is an empty house; unemotional belief in Jesus is a merely swept, but unoccupied home; mere interest in Jesus, with no commitment to him, is a house in danger of haunting. Empty, neutral, externally Christianized people sooner or later find that their little passions—from civic clubs to sports, from politics to parlor games—are insufficiently filling. These activities become demonic when they start to fill the lives of their devotees, possessing them with curious passions and drives, making their lives empty and flat. For our own good, therefore, Jesus summons us to "fill the house," to join the church and take her worship services seriously, to appropriate and be filled by the Holy Spirit given to us in baptism, and to become Jesus' disciples in the world of our work. For our empty, swept, tidy house *will* be filled, sooner or later, by *something*, because houses are to be lived in. The question is not, Will I become "all involved" or not? It is, With *what* shall I become "all involved"? For life is a series of total involvements, whether we like it or not, and Jesus is trying to save us from demonic, obsessive, picayune, bourgeois involvements and to bring us into the little community of saints, the fellowship of disciples, the church and her mission.

But Jesus predicts that the end of this generation, the present age, will be worse than its beginning. Merely influenced by Jesus but, with rare exceptions, not really gathered by him or gathering for him; tidied up but not taken in by him, this Christian world will be virgin territory for an invasion of spirits. Jesus came and exorcized the old pagan spirit, but after a while that same paganism returned with seven spirits worse than itself and found the old house empty. The new paganism is more dangerous—and efficient—than the old. In a remarkable way, the story of the return of the unclean spirit is the story of Western civilization and of the Christendom of two world wars. The story serves as a perpetual warning to all Christians and says, "Be constantly filled with the Spirit" (the word "constantly" is the force of the present participle in Eph 5:18 and makes this verse perhaps the best one-verse commentary on the meaning of the Gospel story of the return of the unclean spirit).

The other great cross-reference to this story, so similar to it that it sounds like a paraphrase of it, is 2 Pet 2:20: "For if, after they have escaped the defilements of the world through the knowledge of our Lord and Savior Jesus Christ, they are again entangled in them and overpowered, the last state has become worse for them than the first." These texts teach the possibility of losing salvation, a teaching that is especially frequent in Matthew's form of the gospel. In danger are two groups: (1) believers among the *old* people of God who trust, without repentance, in Abraham's substitution (3:9), and (2) believers among the *new* people of God who are useless salt (5:13), spiritually or charismatically proud (7:21-23), without obedience to Jesus' words (7:24-27), who believe only during good times (13:21), who prove to be choked seed (13:22), rotten fish (13:47-50), unforgiving even though forgiven (18:21-35), wedding guests without wedding garments (22:11-14), servants of God who turn abusive (24:48-51), wedding guests without oiled lamps (25:1-13), stewards with unincreased talent (25:14-30) or with uncompassionate life (25:31-46); cf. Schl., *Der*, 420; Schn., 163-64. All these are "believers" who face judgment according to Matthew's Jesus.

Are sincere believers in Christ so threatened? Calvin insists that they are not, 2:52-53, "for believers, in whom God's Spirit dwells secure, are everywhere so garrisoned that no chink is left for Satan." But Calvin warns that even in believers there "is that emptiness which follows upon the neglect of divine grace. . . . We must not think the devil is overcome in one battle, when he has gone out of us once." On the other hand, "the unconquerable power of the Holy Spirit keeps [God's children] safe." Calvin, like the other Reformers, wants Christians to enjoy *certitudo,* but not *securitas*—Christian certainty but not a careless security. The prophets of Israel, Jesus, and the Reformers all resolutely rejected the official eschatologies of security in their times (Bonn., 186).

The story of the return of the unclean spirit, as we have seen, is Jesus' commentary on his earlier antineutralism statement, "The person who does not gather with me scatters from me" (v 30). The only responsible relation to Jesus is the relation of passionate commitment. For "the heart of man is a house which must have an occupant" (Caird, 155). The initial exorcism of the unclean spirits occurred when John and Jesus offered Israel repentance. "The devil is truly said to go out from the men to whom Christ offers Himself as Redeemer. . . . [Thus we see] what power lay in His very coming, and what it means to the evil spirits" (Cal., 2:51; cf. Allen, 140; Bacon, 211; Grund., 335; Green, 129). Originally, the demon-out period was the time of Israel's chance with (John and) Jesus; the demon-back-in period represented the danger to an entire generation if it rejected Jesus (Streck., 105-06). Ever since, the story of the return of the unclean spirit is addressed to all who accept Jesus only with a half-repentance, a semiseriousness, or a decreasing fervor. Who, then, dares to think that he or she is not also addressed by this text?

As chapter 11's christology ended with stories of judgment and grace (Judge Jesus and Savior Jesus), so now chapter 12, too, concludes not only with a story of *judgment* (the return of the unclean spirit) but with a story of *promise*—the following story of "Brother Jesus," the good kinsman (Schl., *Der*, 422; Schn., 158).

12:46-50 *"While Jesus was still talking to the crowds, look, his mother and brothers were standing outside trying to get him so that they could talk to him. Jesus responded to the person who told him this by saying, 'Who really is my mother and who are my brothers?' And he pointed toward his disciples and said, 'Look, my mother and my brothers! You see, whoever has done the will of my Father in heaven is my brother and sister and mother.'"*

It is instructive that Jesus' mother and brothers are described as "standing outside." Both words say indecision. They were not "sitting in a circle" at Jesus' feet as Mark tells us the disciples were arranged (Mark 3:34); they were "standing—outside." Standing (when Jesus is teaching) is the posture of distance, of half-heartedness, of reserve; it is a position from which one can readily walk away. It represents the very spirit of indecisiveness warned against in the preceding story.

The word "outside" says that Jesus' family was deliberately outside the orbit of Jesus' actual, "churchly," intimate teaching ministry. They are outsiders, near to, but not insiders, within. (This position is exactly the dangerous situation of emptiness warned of in the preceding story.) According to Mark's bolder account, Jesus' family even thought Jesus had lost his mind, and they had come to take him into their custody (cf. Mark 3:21, 31). Jesus' mother and brothers are the empty, clean, and all fixed up house of the prior story. They are Jesus' patrons, not his pupils; his sponsors, not his disciples. In their opinion, Jesus needs them more than they need Jesus. Perhaps Matthew is giving us a picture of people who feel that they own Jesus, that they are Jesus' "mother and brothers"—leaders in the community or even in the church, the trustees, the treasurers, the Sunday School teachers, and one or two of the elders, deacons, and officers of the several societies, of whom Jesus and his church (they think) are in real need.

It would have been easy for Jesus' mother and brothers to have felt proprietary rights to Jesus; they were members of the same family and were therefore responsible for him. This story warns us, then, of the peril of any paternal, maternal, or fraternal "standing outside" Jesus' innermost circle. The story invites us to come inside, to sit down, to be church *members,* inward members, sitting members, and to begin again to study at Jesus' feet. This story, with the last several in the chapter, calls us out of neutralism, out of cool distance, out of dignified standing, and most of all here particularly, out of paternalism and into partisanship, into warm contact, humble sitting, and inside discipleship at the feet of Jesus.

By pointing to his disciples and pronouncing them "my mother and my brothers," Jesus did his church a great honor. The disciples did not seem to be *doing* anything to deserve such an accolade; in fact, they were literally "sitting around." But the simple fact that they were *there,* sitting around Jesus' Word, that they did not mind looking or appearing committed in the eyes of all those who, in greater objectivity, "stood outside"—that already was a "doing the will of my Father in heaven." For the doing of this will begins with the hearing of the will to be done; giving love proceeds from a prior receiving it.

Being an attentive sitting disciple of Jesus' Word in the church is the presuppositional relation for doing the walking will of Jesus in the world. In the context of these two christological chapters it is not out of order to suggest that the "doing of the will of my Father" of which Jesus speaks here means, first of all, receiving Jesus' Word in his community with a will to doing it in ethically and socially just living in the world.

Biblical doing is *first of all* the obedience of believing—not last of all (*that* is the obedience of love that flows from believing) but first of all. The real doer of the will of God in Luke's beautiful story, for example, is first of all believing (sitting) Mary, not doing (working) Martha (Luke 10:39f); in that story it is primarily the person sitting responsively at Jesus' feet and not, surprisingly, the person moving in service all around Jesus' world who is doing the will of God. Out of the prior faith-doing of Mary's attentiveness to Jesus springs the deep and peaceful love-doing that comes to characterize Mary of Bethany. But out of the fervid works-doing of Martha issues mainly tense service and critical side-glances at those doing less, as well as all the other well-known accouterments of nervous Christian activism. The fundamental deed, the saving "work," is faith in Jesus. "*This* is the work of God," Jesus told those in John's Gospel who wanted to be doing the works of God, "to believe in him whom he has sent" (John 6:28–29).

This is another way of saying, theologically-spiritually, that faith precedes and enables love. It is to say that the fundamental doing of the will of God is to listen seriously to the Word of God telling us what to do and how to do it, and to assimilate the power of that Word in the liturgy or worship service by faith and so to be enabled to do it. The first form of Christian doing is to let God be the doer, to let Jesus say what to do in the world and to give the power to do it. In relation to God and his Son, vertically, it is more blessed to receive than to give; in relationship to God's world, horizontally, it is more blessed to give than to receive.

There is a broad consensus among commentators that the doing of the will of the Father spoken of by Jesus in this paragraph is faith. Calvin, 2:56, e.g., who refers helpfully to John 6:40, and Bultmann, 30, asserts that doing the will of God is being "an audience gathered around Jesus eager to learn from him" (cf. Schw., 295). While Matthew thematically stresses *praxis* and doing when referring to the will of God, nevertheless "here the text is less moral than christological: [it means] to attach oneself to Jesus" (Bonn., 187; cf. Stend., 785). But as Matthew's Gospel goes on to teach us more rigorously than any other form of the gospel in the New Testament, faith-attachment to Jesus, the serious listening to his Word, bears the fruit of *praxis* in good works and wide love. In particular, Matthew's Gospel consistently affirms that the will of God made known by Jesus' teachings can and must be *done,* joyously, concretely, and practically (Bonn., 188). The will of God is never an enigma in Jesus' teaching; it is made luminously clear in every reference to it by the words surrounding it; in this paragraph, for example, the will of God means sitting at Jesus' feet, listening to Jesus' Word. The problem with the will of God is not so much knowing it as doing it (Schl., *Der,* 423), but even this doing in Matthew (as contrasted with Paul; cf. Mohrlang, *passim*) is relatively unproblematic.

That Jesus' brothers here are best understood as Jesus' actual brothers (the Helvidian view vs. the Epiphanian and Hieronymian) is shown by Taylor, 247–49, and Bonnard, 187. That "sisters" are explicitly mentioned here by Jesus in equal billing with brothers is another indication of how often Jesus is "more than" anyone in the Judaism of his time in relation to women and more, too, than even Paul. Beare, 285 n. 1, who brought this point to my attention, cites Jean Héring's evangelical comment on Paul's subordination of women in 1 Corinthians 14:34–36: "Paul's imposition of ecclesial silence on women 'must be sought uniquely in the concern not to violate the rule of good behaviour generally accepted at the time. . . . In our contemporary civilization, where women, in enjoyment of all rights, do not shock anybody by taking the floor to speak in public, we are permitted to suppose that the restriction envisaged by the apostle has no longer any reason to be maintained.'" Happily, Jesus needs fewer such rescue operations than does Paul. "More than Paul is here."

It is noteworthy that Jesus points to his disciples and speaks of them generously as his mother, brothers, and sisters, but not as his father. Jesus has only one Father. This incident (which appears also in Mark and Luke) bears its own witness to the virgin birth of Jesus, or to put this in another and surer way, it bears witness to the entirely divine sonship of Christ. Jesus has many brothers, sisters, and mothers, this story says, but only one Father. One of this story's meanings is that Jesus is the unique Son of God. (Because of Mary's awkward presence in this story, the virgin birth doctrine is also put under considerable strain; cf. Tay., 246.)

Thus chapter 12 ends with Jesus claiming to be the human *brother* of the simple disciples and, at the same time (and more indirectly and mysteriously) to be the one divine *Son* of the Father. Jesus is both at once: lowly by intention, majestic in fact; servant of others by choice, Son of God by nature; low by will, high by person. Jesus can best be understood in the juxtaposition of these low and high christologies. They are Matthew's versions of "the two natures" doctrine, the christology of the later church. Jesus is utterly man, utterly God; Son of Mary and Son of God; the Nazarene and Emmanuel; little and big. And the full picture of Jesus is before us only when we have received both impressions of Jesus. Just as we see rightly and in perspective only when we see with both eyes, so we see Jesus the revelation of God rightly and in perspective only when we see him from both sides: from his little side, the side of his full humanity and lowliness, and from his big side, the side of his full deity and majesty.

The series of six portraits that Matthew has just passed before our eyes in these two chapters serves these two great christological ends. By the time we have studied these pictures of the manifold Jesus we feel that Jesus is as close to us as a kinsman and, at the same time, as above us as a lord or king.

The student of the Gospel realizes here in this culminating story that Jesus is pointing at him or her and saying, in effect, "By the simple fact that you are listening to this story seriously you are *sitting inside* with me, and I want you to know that *that* makes you my disciple, and if my disciple, then my brother, my sister, and my mother. You are home. You may not think that by reading or hearing these stories you are doing anything special. But if you are hearing them with faith, I want to point out to you, 'Look, you are my brother, my sister, my mother!'"

So this story is finally free mercy. We are made important by this story; we are made the brothers and sisters of Jesus the Son of God. We did not know that by just listening to Jesus we were doing much. But Jesus tells us that we are doing the main thing, the will of his Father.

Thus Matthew turns our attention in this final paragraph of chapter 12 (cf. Meier, *Vis.*, 88; Bonn., 186) from the contest and controversy that has marked much of chapter 11 and all of chapter 12's portraiture of Jesus amid his rejecting generation, and he prepares us for a more intensive study of Jesus' new family, the church, the theme of the last half of the Gospel. This paragraph, then, is the bridge between Matthew's Christbook (Matt 1–12) and his Churchbook (Matt 13–28).

Gospel Parallels in Mark and Luke, I

Since a commentary on Matthew's Gospel is, in many ways, also a commentary on practically all of Mark's Gospel and on a good part of Luke's as well, it can be helpful to have a chart of Gospel Parallels at hand. The interpreter working on a Mark or Luke passage may refer to the parallel columns below for interpretation in Matthew. (A further set of parallels to the last half of Matthew's Gospel will be found in the second volume, *The Churchbook.*)